50% OFF

Praxis Elementary Education: Multiple Subjects Prep Course!

By Mometrix

Dear Customer,

We consider it an honor and a privilege that you chose our Praxis Elementary Education: Multiple Subjects (5001) Practice Questions. As a way of showing our appreciation and to help us better serve you, we are offering **50% off our online Praxis 5001 Prep Course.** Many Praxis courses are needlessly expensive and don't deliver enough value. With our course, you get access to the best Praxis Elementary Education prep material, and **you only pay half price**.

We have structured our online course to perfectly complement your printed practice questions. The Praxis Elementary Education 5001 Prep Course contains **in-depth lessons** that cover all the most important topics, **300+ video reviews** that explain difficult concepts, over **800 online practice questions** to ensure you feel prepared, and more than **1,000 digital flashcards**, so you can study while you're on the go.

Online Praxis Elementary Education: Multiple Subjects (5001) Prep Course

Topics Covered:	Course Features:
<ul><li>Reading and Language Arts<ul><li>Literary analysis, grammar, and more</li></ul></li><li>Mathematics<ul><li>Algebra, trigonometry, and more</li></ul></li><li>Social Studies<ul><li>World history, government, and more</li></ul></li><li>Science<ul><li>Biology, chemistry, and more</li></ul></li></ul>	<ul><li>Praxis Elementary Education Study Guide<ul><li>Get content that complements our best-selling study guide.</li></ul></li><li>Full-Length Practice Tests and Flashcards<ul><li>With over 800 online practice questions and 1,000+ digital flashcards, you can test yourself again and again.</li></ul></li><li>Mobile Friendly<ul><li>If you need to study on the go, the course is easily accessible from your mobile device.</li></ul></li></ul>

To receive this discount, visit us at <u>mometrix.com/university/praxis5001/</u> and add the course to your cart. At the checkout page, enter the discount code: **50off5001**

If you have any questions or concerns, please contact us at <u>support@mometrix.com</u>.

SCAN HERE

FREE Study Skills Videos/DVD Offer

Dear Customer,

Thank you for your purchase from Mometrix! We consider it an honor and a privilege that you have purchased our product and we want to ensure your satisfaction.

As part of our ongoing effort to meet the needs of test takers, we have developed a set of Study Skills Videos that we would like to give you for <u>FREE</u>. These videos cover our *best practices* for getting ready for your exam, from how to use our study materials to how to best prepare for the day of the test.

All that we ask is that you email us with feedback that would describe your experience so far with our product. Good, bad, or indifferent, we want to know what you think!

To get your FREE Study Skills Videos, you can use the **QR code** below, or send us an **email** at <u>studyvideos@mometrix.com</u> with *FREE VIDEOS* in the subject line and the following information in the body of the email:

- The name of the product you purchased.
- Your product rating on a scale of 1-5, with 5 being the highest rating.
- Your feedback. It can be long, short, or anything in between. We just want to know your impressions and experience so far with our product. (Good feedback might include how our study material met your needs and ways we might be able to make it even better. You could highlight features that you found helpful or features that you think we should add.)

If you have any questions or concerns, please don't hesitate to contact me directly.

Thanks again!

Sincerely,

Jay Willis
Vice President
jay.willis@mometrix.com
1-800-673-8175

Praxis II

Elementary Education: Multiple Subjects (5001) Exam

SECRETS

Study Guide
Your Key to Exam Success

Copyright © 2023 by Mometrix Media LLC

All rights reserved. This product, or parts thereof, may not be reproduced, stored in a retrieval system, or transmitted in any form or by any means—electronic, mechanical, photocopy, recording, scanning, or other—except for brief quotations in critical reviews or articles, without the prior written permission of the publisher.

Written and edited by the Mometrix Teacher Certification Test Team

Printed in the United States of America

This paper meets the requirements of ANSI/NISO Z39.48-1992 (Permanence of Paper).

Mometrix offers volume discount pricing to institutions. For more information or a price quote, please contact our sales department at sales@mometrix.com or 888-248-1219.

Mometrix Media LLC is not affiliated with or endorsed by any official testing organization. All organizational and test names are trademarks of their respective owners.

Paperback
ISBN 13: 978-1-63094-814-6
ISBN 10: 1-63094-814-4

Ebook
ISBN 13: 978-1-5167-0277-0
ISBN 10: 1-5167-0277-8

Hardback
ISBN 13: 978-1-5167-0826-0
ISBN 10: 1-5167-0826-1

Dear Future Exam Success Story

First of all, **THANK YOU** for purchasing Mometrix study materials!

Second, congratulations! You are one of the few determined test-takers who are committed to doing whatever it takes to excel on your exam. **You have come to the right place.** We developed these study materials with one goal in mind: to deliver you the information you need in a format that's concise and easy to use.

In addition to optimizing your guide for the content of the test, we've outlined our recommended steps for breaking down the preparation process into small, attainable goals so you can make sure you stay on track.

We've also analyzed the entire test-taking process, identifying the most common pitfalls and showing how you can overcome them and be ready for any curveball the test throws you.

Standardized testing is one of the biggest obstacles on your road to success, which only increases the importance of doing well in the high-pressure, high-stakes environment of test day. Your results on this test could have a significant impact on your future, and this guide provides the information and practical advice to help you achieve your full potential on test day.

Your success is our success

We would love to hear from you! If you would like to share the story of your exam success or if you have any questions or comments in regard to our products, please contact us at **800-673-8175** or **support@mometrix.com**.

Thanks again for your business and we wish you continued success!

Sincerely,
The Mometrix Test Preparation Team

Need more help? Check out our flashcards at:
http://MometrixFlashcards.com/PraxisII

TABLE OF CONTENTS

Introduction

Thank you for purchasing this resource! You have made the choice to prepare yourself for a test that could have a huge impact on your future, and this guide is designed to help you be fully ready for test day. Obviously, it's important to have a solid understanding of the test material, but you also need to be prepared for the unique environment and stressors of the test, so that you can perform to the best of your abilities.

For this purpose, the first section that appears in this guide is the **Secret Keys**. We've devoted countless hours to meticulously researching what works and what doesn't, and we've boiled down our findings to the five most impactful steps you can take to improve your performance on the test. We start at the beginning with study planning and move through the preparation process, all the way to the testing strategies that will help you get the most out of what you know when you're finally sitting in front of the test.

We recommend that you start preparing for your test as far in advance as possible. However, if you've bought this guide as a last-minute study resource and only have a few days before your test, we recommend that you skip over the first two Secret Keys since they address a long-term study plan.

If you struggle with **test anxiety**, we strongly encourage you to check out our recommendations for how you can overcome it. Test anxiety is a formidable foe, but it can be beaten, and we want to make sure you have the tools you need to defeat it.

Copyright © Mometrix Media. You have been licensed one copy of this document for personal use only. Any other reproduction or redistribution is strictly prohibited. All rights reserved. This content is provided for test preparation purposes only and does not imply an endorsement by Mometrix of any particular political, scientific, or religious point of view.

Secret Key #1 – Plan Big, Study Small

There's a lot riding on your performance. If you want to ace this test, you're going to need to keep your skills sharp and the material fresh in your mind. You need a plan that lets you review everything you need to know while still fitting in your schedule. We'll break this strategy down into three categories.

Information Organization

Start with the information you already have: the official test outline. From this, you can make a complete list of all the concepts you need to cover before the test. Organize these concepts into groups that can be studied together, and create a list of any related vocabulary you need to learn so you can brush up on any difficult terms. You'll want to keep this vocabulary list handy once you actually start studying since you may need to add to it along the way.

Time Management

Once you have your set of study concepts, decide how to spread them out over the time you have left before the test. Break your study plan into small, clear goals so you have a manageable task for each day and know exactly what you're doing. Then just focus on one small step at a time. When you manage your time this way, you don't need to spend hours at a time studying. Studying a small block of content for a short period each day helps you retain information better and avoid stressing over how much you have left to do. You can relax knowing that you have a plan to cover everything in time. In order for this strategy to be effective though, you have to start studying early and stick to your schedule. Avoid the exhaustion and futility that comes from last-minute cramming!

Study Environment

The environment you study in has a big impact on your learning. Studying in a coffee shop, while probably more enjoyable, is not likely to be as fruitful as studying in a quiet room. It's important to keep distractions to a minimum. You're only planning to study for a short block of time, so make the most of it. Don't pause to check your phone or get up to find a snack. It's also important to **avoid multitasking**. Research has consistently shown that multitasking will make your studying dramatically less effective. Your study area should also be comfortable and well-lit so you don't have the distraction of straining your eyes or sitting on an uncomfortable chair.

The time of day you study is also important. You want to be rested and alert. Don't wait until just before bedtime. Study when you'll be most likely to comprehend and remember. Even better, if you know what time of day your test will be, set that time aside for study. That way your brain will be used to working on that subject at that specific time and you'll have a better chance of recalling information.

Finally, it can be helpful to team up with others who are studying for the same test. Your actual studying should be done in as isolated an environment as possible, but the work of organizing the information and setting up the study plan can be divided up. In between study sessions, you can discuss with your teammates the concepts that you're all studying and quiz each other on the details. Just be sure that your teammates are as serious about the test as you are. If you find that your study time is being replaced with social time, you might need to find a new team.

2

Copyright © Mometrix Media. You have been licensed one copy of this document for personal use only. Any other reproduction or redistribution is strictly prohibited. All rights reserved. This content is provided for test preparation purposes only and does not imply an endorsement by Mometrix of any particular political, scientific, or religious point of view.

Secret Key #2 – Make Your Studying Count

You're devoting a lot of time and effort to preparing for this test, so you want to be absolutely certain it will pay off. This means doing more than just reading the content and hoping you can remember it on test day. It's important to make every minute of study count. There are two main areas you can focus on to make your studying count.

Retention

It doesn't matter how much time you study if you can't remember the material. You need to make sure you are retaining the concepts. To check your retention of the information you're learning, try recalling it at later times with minimal prompting. Try carrying around flashcards and glance at one or two from time to time or ask a friend who's also studying for the test to quiz you.

To enhance your retention, look for ways to put the information into practice so that you can apply it rather than simply recalling it. If you're using the information in practical ways, it will be much easier to remember. Similarly, it helps to solidify a concept in your mind if you're not only reading it to yourself but also explaining it to someone else. Ask a friend to let you teach them about a concept you're a little shaky on (or speak aloud to an imaginary audience if necessary). As you try to summarize, define, give examples, and answer your friend's questions, you'll understand the concepts better and they will stay with you longer. Finally, step back for a big picture view and ask yourself how each piece of information fits with the whole subject. When you link the different concepts together and see them working together as a whole, it's easier to remember the individual components.

Finally, practice showing your work on any multi-step problems, even if you're just studying. Writing out each step you take to solve a problem will help solidify the process in your mind, and you'll be more likely to remember it during the test.

Modality

Modality simply refers to the means or method by which you study. Choosing a study modality that fits your own individual learning style is crucial. No two people learn best in exactly the same way, so it's important to know your strengths and use them to your advantage.

For example, if you learn best by visualization, focus on visualizing a concept in your mind and draw an image or a diagram. Try color-coding your notes, illustrating them, or creating symbols that will trigger your mind to recall a learned concept. If you learn best by hearing or discussing information, find a study partner who learns the same way or read aloud to yourself. Think about how to put the information in your own words. Imagine that you are giving a lecture on the topic and record yourself so you can listen to it later.

For any learning style, flashcards can be helpful. Organize the information so you can take advantage of spare moments to review. Underline key words or phrases. Use different colors for different categories. Mnemonic devices (such as creating a short list in which every item starts with the same letter) can also help with retention. Find what works best for you and use it to store the information in your mind most effectively and easily.

3

Copyright © Mometrix Media. You have been licensed one copy of this document for personal use only. Any other reproduction or redistribution is strictly prohibited. All rights reserved.
This content is provided for test preparation purposes only and does not imply an endorsement by Mometrix of any particular political, scientific, or religious point of view.

Secret Key #3 – Practice the Right Way

Your success on test day depends not only on how many hours you put into preparing, but also on whether you prepared the right way. It's good to check along the way to see if your studying is paying off. One of the most effective ways to do this is by taking practice tests to evaluate your progress. Practice tests are useful because they show exactly where you need to improve. Every time you take a practice test, pay special attention to these three groups of questions:

- The questions you got wrong
- The questions you had to guess on, even if you guessed right
- The questions you found difficult or slow to work through

This will show you exactly what your weak areas are, and where you need to devote more study time. Ask yourself why each of these questions gave you trouble. Was it because you didn't understand the material? Was it because you didn't remember the vocabulary? Do you need more repetitions on this type of question to build speed and confidence? Dig into those questions and figure out how you can strengthen your weak areas as you go back to review the material.

 Additionally, many practice tests have a section explaining the answer choices. It can be tempting to read the explanation and think that you now have a good understanding of the concept. However, an explanation likely only covers part of the question's broader context. Even if the explanation makes perfect sense, **go back and investigate** every concept related to the question until you're positive you have a thorough understanding.

As you go along, keep in mind that the practice test is just that: practice. Memorizing these questions and answers will not be very helpful on the actual test because it is unlikely to have any of the same exact questions. If you only know the right answers to the sample questions, you won't be prepared for the real thing. **Study the concepts** until you understand them fully, and then you'll be able to answer any question that shows up on the test.

It's important to wait on the practice tests until you're ready. If you take a test on your first day of study, you may be overwhelmed by the amount of material covered and how much you need to learn. Work up to it gradually.

On test day, you'll need to be prepared for answering questions, managing your time, and using the test-taking strategies you've learned. It's a lot to balance, like a mental marathon that will have a big impact on your future. Like training for a marathon, you'll need to start slowly and work your way up. When test day arrives, you'll be ready.

Start with the strategies you've read in the first two Secret Keys—plan your course and study in the way that works best for you. If you have time, consider using multiple study resources to get different approaches to the same concepts. It can be helpful to see difficult concepts from more than one angle. Then find a good source for practice tests. Many times, the test website will suggest potential study resources or provide sample tests.

Copyright © Mometrix Media. You have been licensed one copy of this document for personal use only. Any other reproduction or redistribution is strictly prohibited. All rights reserved. This content is provided for test preparation purposes only and does not imply an endorsement by Mometrix of any particular political, scientific, or religious point of view.

Practice Test Strategy

If you're able to find at least three practice tests, we recommend this strategy:

Untimed and Open-Book Practice

Take the first test with no time constraints and with your notes and study guide handy. Take your time and focus on applying the strategies you've learned.

Timed and Open-Book Practice

Take the second practice test open-book as well, but set a timer and practice pacing yourself to finish in time.

Timed and Closed-Book Practice

Take any other practice tests as if it were test day. Set a timer and put away your study materials. Sit at a table or desk in a quiet room, imagine yourself at the testing center, and answer questions as quickly and accurately as possible.

Keep repeating timed and closed-book tests on a regular basis until you run out of practice tests or it's time for the actual test. Your mind will be ready for the schedule and stress of test day, and you'll be able to focus on recalling the material you've learned.

Copyright © Mometrix Media. You have been licensed one copy of this document for personal use only. Any other reproduction or redistribution is strictly prohibited. All rights reserved. This content is provided for test preparation purposes only and does not imply an endorsement by Mometrix of any particular political, scientific, or religious point of view.

Secret Key #4 – Pace Yourself

Once you're fully prepared for the material on the test, your biggest challenge on test day will be managing your time. Just knowing that the clock is ticking can make you panic even if you have plenty of time left. Work on pacing yourself so you can build confidence against the time constraints of the exam. Pacing is a difficult skill to master, especially in a high-pressure environment, so **practice is vital**.

Set time expectations for your pace based on how much time is available. For example, if a section has 60 questions and the time limit is 30 minutes, you know you have to average 30 seconds or less per question in order to answer them all. Although 30 seconds is the hard limit, set 25 seconds per question as your goal, so you reserve extra time to spend on harder questions. When you budget extra time for the harder questions, you no longer have any reason to stress when those questions take longer to answer.

Don't let this time expectation distract you from working through the test at a calm, steady pace, but keep it in mind so you don't spend too much time on any one question. Recognize that taking extra time on one question you don't understand may keep you from answering two that you do understand later in the test. If your time limit for a question is up and you're still not sure of the answer, mark it and move on, and come back to it later if the time and the test format allow. If the testing format doesn't allow you to return to earlier questions, just make an educated guess; then put it out of your mind and move on.

On the easier questions, be careful not to rush. It may seem wise to hurry through them so you have more time for the challenging ones, but it's not worth missing one if you know the concept and just didn't take the time to read the question fully. Work efficiently but make sure you understand the question and have looked at all of the answer choices, since more than one may seem right at first.

Even if you're paying attention to the time, you may find yourself a little behind at some point. You should speed up to get back on track, but do so wisely. Don't panic; just take a few seconds less on each question until you're caught up. Don't guess without thinking, but do look through the answer choices and eliminate any you know are wrong. If you can get down to two choices, it is often worthwhile to guess from those. Once you've chosen an answer, move on and don't dwell on any that you skipped or had to hurry through. If a question was taking too long, chances are it was one of the harder ones, so you weren't as likely to get it right anyway.

On the other hand, if you find yourself getting ahead of schedule, it may be beneficial to slow down a little. The more quickly you work, the more likely you are to make a careless mistake that will affect your score. You've budgeted time for each question, so don't be afraid to spend that time. Practice an efficient but careful pace to get the most out of the time you have.

Copyright © Mometrix Media. You have been licensed one copy of this document for personal use only. Any other reproduction or redistribution is strictly prohibited. All rights reserved. This content is provided for test preparation purposes only and does not imply an endorsement by Mometrix of any particular political, scientific, or religious point of view.

Secret Key #5 – Have a Plan for Guessing

When you're taking the test, you may find yourself stuck on a question. Some of the answer choices seem better than others, but you don't see the one answer choice that is obviously correct. What do you do?

The scenario described above is very common, yet most test takers have not effectively prepared for it. Developing and practicing a plan for guessing may be one of the single most effective uses of your time as you get ready for the exam.

In developing your plan for guessing, there are three questions to address:

- When should you start the guessing process?
- How should you narrow down the choices?
- Which answer should you choose?

When to Start the Guessing Process

Unless your plan for guessing is to select C every time (which, despite its merits, is not what we recommend), you need to leave yourself enough time to apply your answer elimination strategies. Since you have a limited amount of time for each question, that means that if you're going to give yourself the best shot at guessing correctly, you have to decide quickly whether or not you will guess.

Of course, the best-case scenario is that you don't have to guess at all, so first, see if you can answer the question based on your knowledge of the subject and basic reasoning skills. Focus on the key words in the question and try to jog your memory of related topics. Give yourself a chance to bring the knowledge to mind, but once you realize that you don't have (or you can't access) the knowledge you need to answer the question, it's time to start the guessing process.

It's almost always better to start the guessing process too early than too late. It only takes a few seconds to remember something and answer the question from knowledge. Carefully eliminating wrong answer choices takes longer. Plus, going through the process of eliminating answer choices can actually help jog your memory.

Summary: Start the guessing process as soon as you decide that you can't answer the question based on your knowledge.

7

Copyright © Mometrix Media. You have been licensed one copy of this document for personal use only. Any other reproduction or redistribution is strictly prohibited. All rights reserved.
This content is provided for test preparation purposes only and does not imply an endorsement by Mometrix of any particular political, scientific, or religious point of view.

How to Narrow Down the Choices

The next chapter in this book (**Test-Taking Strategies**) includes a wide range of strategies for how to approach questions and how to look for answer choices to eliminate. You will definitely want to read those carefully, practice them, and figure out which ones work best for you. Here though, we're going to address a mindset rather than a particular strategy.

Your odds of guessing an answer correctly depend on how many options you are choosing from.

Number of options left	5	4	3	2	1
Odds of guessing correctly	20%	25%	33%	50%	100%

You can see from this chart just how valuable it is to be able to eliminate incorrect answers and make an educated guess, but there are two things that many test takers do that cause them to miss out on the benefits of guessing:

- Accidentally eliminating the correct answer
- Selecting an answer based on an impression

We'll look at the first one here, and the second one in the next section.

To avoid accidentally eliminating the correct answer, we recommend a thought exercise called **the $5 challenge**. In this challenge, you only eliminate an answer choice from contention if you are willing to bet $5 on it being wrong. Why $5? Five dollars is a small but not insignificant amount of money. It's an amount you could afford to lose but wouldn't want to throw away. And while losing

$5 once might not hurt too much, doing it twenty times will set you back $100. In the same way, each small decision you make—eliminating a choice here, guessing on a question there—won't by itself impact your score very much, but when you put them all together, they can make a big difference. By holding each answer choice elimination decision to a higher standard, you can reduce the risk of accidentally eliminating the correct answer.

The $5 challenge can also be applied in a positive sense: If you are willing to bet $5 that an answer choice *is* correct, go ahead and mark it as correct.

Summary: Only eliminate an answer choice if you are willing to bet $5 that it is wrong.

Copyright © Mometrix Media. You have been licensed one copy of this document for personal use only. Any other reproduction or redistribution is strictly prohibited. All rights reserved. This content is provided for test preparation purposes only and does not imply an endorsement by Mometrix of any particular political, scientific, or religious point of view.

Which Answer to Choose

You're taking the test. You've run into a hard question and decided you'll have to guess. You've eliminated all the answer choices you're willing to bet $5 on. Now you have to pick an answer. Why do we even need to talk about this? Why can't you just pick whichever one you feel like when the time comes?

The answer to these questions is that if you don't come into the test with a plan, you'll rely on your impression to select an answer choice, and if you do that, you risk falling into a trap. The test writers know that everyone who takes their test will be guessing on some of the questions, so they intentionally write wrong answer choices to seem plausible. You still have to pick an answer though, and if the wrong answer choices are designed to look right, how can you ever be sure that you're not falling for their trap? The best solution we've found to this dilemma is to take the decision out of your hands entirely. Here is the process we recommend:

Once you've eliminated any choices that you are confident (willing to bet $5) are wrong, select the first remaining choice as your answer.

Whether you choose to select the first remaining choice, the second, or the last, the important thing is that you use some preselected standard. Using this approach guarantees that you will not be enticed into selecting an answer choice that looks right, because you are not basing your decision on how the answer choices look.

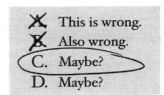

This is not meant to make you question your knowledge. Instead, it is to help you recognize the difference between your knowledge and your impressions. There's a huge difference between thinking an answer is right because of what you know, and thinking an answer is right because it looks or sounds like it should be right.

Summary: To ensure that your selection is appropriately random, make a predetermined selection from among all answer choices you have not eliminated.

9

Copyright © Mometrix Media. You have been licensed one copy of this document for personal use only. Any other reproduction or redistribution is strictly prohibited. All rights reserved.
This content is provided for test preparation purposes only and does not imply an endorsement by Mometrix of any particular political, scientific, or religious point of view.

Test-Taking Strategies

This section contains a list of test-taking strategies that you may find helpful as you work through the test. By taking what you know and applying logical thought, you can maximize your chances of answering any question correctly!

It is very important to realize that every question is different and every person is different: no single strategy will work on every question, and no single strategy will work for every person. That's why we've included all of them here, so you can try them out and determine which ones work best for different types of questions and which ones work best for you.

Question Strategies

⊘ READ CAREFULLY

Read the question and the answer choices carefully. Don't miss the question because you misread the terms. You have plenty of time to read each question thoroughly and make sure you understand what is being asked. Yet a happy medium must be attained, so don't waste too much time. You must read carefully and efficiently.

⊘ CONTEXTUAL CLUES

Look for contextual clues. If the question includes a word you are not familiar with, look at the immediate context for some indication of what the word might mean. Contextual clues can often give you all the information you need to decipher the meaning of an unfamiliar word. Even if you can't determine the meaning, you may be able to narrow down the possibilities enough to make a solid guess at the answer to the question.

⊘ PREFIXES

If you're having trouble with a word in the question or answer choices, try dissecting it. Take advantage of every clue that the word might include. Prefixes can be a huge help. Usually, they allow you to determine a basic meaning. *Pre-* means before, *post-* means after, *pro-* is positive, *de-* is negative. From prefixes, you can get an idea of the general meaning of the word and try to put it into context.

⊘ HEDGE WORDS

Watch out for critical hedge words, such as *likely, may, can, sometimes, often, almost, mostly, usually, generally, rarely,* and *sometimes.* Question writers insert these hedge phrases to cover every possibility. Often an answer choice will be wrong simply because it leaves no room for exception. Be on guard for answer choices that have definitive words such as *exactly* and *always.*

⊘ SWITCHBACK WORDS

Stay alert for *switchbacks.* These are the words and phrases frequently used to alert you to shifts in thought. The most common switchback words are *but, although,* and *however.* Others include *nevertheless, on the other hand, even though, while, in spite of, despite,* and *regardless of.* Switchback words are important to catch because they can change the direction of the question or an answer choice.

Copyright © Mometrix Media. You have been licensed one copy of this document for personal use only. Any other reproduction or redistribution is strictly prohibited. All rights reserved. This content is provided for test preparation purposes only and does not imply an endorsement by Mometrix of any particular political, scientific, or religious point of view.

⊘ FACE VALUE

When in doubt, use common sense. Accept the situation in the problem at face value. Don't read too much into it. These problems will not require you to make wild assumptions. If you have to go beyond creativity and warp time or space in order to have an answer choice fit the question, then you should move on and consider the other answer choices. These are normal problems rooted in reality. The applicable relationship or explanation may not be readily apparent, but it is there for you to figure out. Use your common sense to interpret anything that isn't clear.

Answer Choice Strategies

⊘ ANSWER SELECTION

The most thorough way to pick an answer choice is to identify and eliminate wrong answers until only one is left, then confirm it is the correct answer. Sometimes an answer choice may immediately seem right, but be careful. The test writers will usually put more than one reasonable answer choice on each question, so take a second to read all of them and make sure that the other choices are not equally obvious. As long as you have time left, it is better to read every answer choice than to pick the first one that looks right without checking the others.

⊘ ANSWER CHOICE FAMILIES

An answer choice family consists of two (in rare cases, three) answer choices that are very similar in construction and cannot all be true at the same time. If you see two answer choices that are direct opposites or parallels, one of them is usually the correct answer. For instance, if one answer choice says that quantity x increases and another either says that quantity x decreases (opposite) or says that quantity y increases (parallel), then those answer choices would fall into the same family. An answer choice that doesn't match the construction of the answer choice family is more likely to be incorrect. Most questions will not have answer choice families, but when they do appear, you should be prepared to recognize them.

⊘ ELIMINATE ANSWERS

Eliminate answer choices as soon as you realize they are wrong, but make sure you consider all possibilities. If you are eliminating answer choices and realize that the last one you are left with is also wrong, don't panic. Start over and consider each choice again. There may be something you missed the first time that you will realize on the second pass.

⊘ AVOID FACT TRAPS

Don't be distracted by an answer choice that is factually true but doesn't answer the question. You are looking for the choice that answers the question. Stay focused on what the question is asking for so you don't accidentally pick an answer that is true but incorrect. Always go back to the question and make sure the answer choice you've selected actually answers the question and is not merely a true statement.

⊘ EXTREME STATEMENTS

In general, you should avoid answers that put forth extreme actions as standard practice or proclaim controversial ideas as established fact. An answer choice that states the "process should be used in certain situations, if…" is much more likely to be correct than one that states the "process should be discontinued completely." The first is a calm rational statement and doesn't even make a definitive, uncompromising stance, using a hedge word *if* to provide wiggle room, whereas the second choice is far more extreme.

11

Copyright © Mometrix Media. You have been licensed one copy of this document for personal use only. Any other reproduction or redistribution is strictly prohibited. All rights reserved.
This content is provided for test preparation purposes only and does not imply an endorsement by Mometrix of any particular political, scientific, or religious point of view.

☑ Benchmark

As you read through the answer choices and you come across one that seems to answer the question well, mentally select that answer choice. This is not your final answer, but it's the one that will help you evaluate the other answer choices. The one that you selected is your benchmark or standard for judging each of the other answer choices. Every other answer choice must be compared to your benchmark. That choice is correct until proven otherwise by another answer choice beating it. If you find a better answer, then that one becomes your new benchmark. Once you've decided that no other choice answers the question as well as your benchmark, you have your final answer.

☑ Predict the Answer

Before you even start looking at the answer choices, it is often best to try to predict the answer. When you come up with the answer on your own, it is easier to avoid distractions and traps because you will know exactly what to look for. The right answer choice is unlikely to be word-for-word what you came up with, but it should be a close match. Even if you are confident that you have the right answer, you should still take the time to read each option before moving on.

General Strategies

☑ Tough Questions

If you are stumped on a problem or it appears too hard or too difficult, don't waste time. Move on! Remember though, if you can quickly check for obviously incorrect answer choices, your chances of guessing correctly are greatly improved. Before you completely give up, at least try to knock out a couple of possible answers. Eliminate what you can and then guess at the remaining answer choices before moving on.

☑ Check Your Work

Since you will probably not know every term listed and the answer to every question, it is important that you get credit for the ones that you do know. Don't miss any questions through careless mistakes. If at all possible, try to take a second to look back over your answer selection and make sure you've selected the correct answer choice and haven't made a costly careless mistake (such as marking an answer choice that you didn't mean to mark). This quick double check should more than pay for itself in caught mistakes for the time it costs.

☑ Pace Yourself

It's easy to be overwhelmed when you're looking at a page full of questions; your mind is confused and full of random thoughts, and the clock is ticking down faster than you would like. Calm down and maintain the pace that you have set for yourself. Especially as you get down to the last few minutes of the test, don't let the small numbers on the clock make you panic. As long as you are on track by monitoring your pace, you are guaranteed to have time for each question.

☑ Don't Rush

It is very easy to make errors when you are in a hurry. Maintaining a fast pace in answering questions is pointless if it makes you miss questions that you would have gotten right otherwise. Test writers like to include distracting information and wrong answers that seem right. Taking a little extra time to avoid careless mistakes can make all the difference in your test score. Find a pace that allows you to be confident in the answers that you select.

Copyright © Mometrix Media. You have been licensed one copy of this document for personal use only. Any other reproduction or redistribution is strictly prohibited. All rights reserved. This content is provided for test preparation purposes only and does not imply an endorsement by Mometrix of any particular political, scientific, or religious point of view.

⊘ Keep Moving

Panicking will not help you pass the test, so do your best to stay calm and keep moving. Taking deep breaths and going through the answer elimination steps you practiced can help to break through a stress barrier and keep your pace.

Final Notes

The combination of a solid foundation of content knowledge and the confidence that comes from practicing your plan for applying that knowledge is the key to maximizing your performance on test day. As your foundation of content knowledge is built up and strengthened, you'll find that the strategies included in this chapter become more and more effective in helping you quickly sift through the distractions and traps of the test to isolate the correct answer.

Now that you're preparing to move forward into the test content chapters of this book, be sure to keep your goal in mind. As you read, think about how you will be able to apply this information on the test. If you've already seen sample questions for the test and you have an idea of the question format and style, try to come up with questions of your own that you can answer based on what you're reading. This will give you valuable practice applying your knowledge in the same ways you can expect to on test day.

Good luck and good studying!

Copyright © Mometrix Media. You have been licensed one copy of this document for personal use only. Any other reproduction or redistribution is strictly prohibited. All rights reserved. This content is provided for test preparation purposes only and does not imply an endorsement by Mometrix of any particular political, scientific, or religious point of view.

Copyright © Mometrix Media. You have been licensed one copy of this document for personal use only. Any other reproduction or redistribution is strictly prohibited. All rights reserved.
This content is provided for test preparation purposes only and does not imply an endorsement by Mometrix of any particular political, scientific, or religious point of view.

Reading and Language Arts

Foundational Skills

LITERACY

Literacy is commonly understood as the **ability to read and write**. UNESCO, the United Nations Educational, Scientific, and Cultural Organization, has further defined literacy as the "ability to identify, understand, interpret, create, communicate, compute, and use printed and written materials associated with varying contexts." Under the UNESCO definition, understanding cultural, political, and historical contexts of communities falls under the definition of literacy. While **reading literacy** may be gauged simply by the ability to read a newspaper, **writing literacy** includes spelling, grammar, and sentence structure. To be literate in a foreign language, one would also need to be able to understand a language by listening and be able to speak the language. Some argue that visual representation and numeracy should be included in the requirements one must meet to be considered literate. **Computer literacy** refers to one's ability to utilize the basic functions of computers and other technologies. Subsets of reading literacy include phonological awareness, decoding, comprehension, and vocabulary.

PHONOLOGICAL AWARENESS

A subskill of literacy, phonological awareness is the ability to perceive sound structures in a spoken word, such as syllables and the individual phonemes within syllables. **Phonemes** are the sounds represented by the letters in the alphabet. The ability to separate, blend, and manipulate sounds is critical to developing reading and spelling skills. Phonological awareness is concerned with not only syllables, but also **onset sounds** (the initial sound in a word, such as /k/ in 'cat') and **rime** (the sounds that follow the onset in a word, such as /at/ in 'cat'). Phonological awareness is an auditory skill that does not necessarily involve print. It should be developed before the student has learned letter to sound correspondences. A student's phonological awareness is an indicator of future reading success.

> **Review Video: <u>Phonological and Phonemic Awareness, and Phonics</u>**
> Visit mometrix.com/academy and enter code: 197017
>
> **Review Video: <u>Components of Oral Language Development</u>**
> Visit mometrix.com/academy and enter code: 480589

COMMUNICATION DEVELOPMENT NORMALLY OCCURRING WITHIN A CHILD'S FIRST FIVE YEARS OF LIFE

Language and communication development depend strongly on the language a child develops within the first five years of life. During this time, three developmental periods are observed. At birth, the first period begins. This period is characterized by infant crying and gazing. Babies communicate their sensations and emotions through these behaviors, so they are expressive; however, they are not yet intentional. They indirectly indicate their needs through expressing how they feel, and when these needs are met, these communicative behaviors are reinforced. These expressions and reinforcement are the foundations for the later development of intentional communication. This becomes possible in the second developmental period, between 6 and 18 months. At this time, infants become able to coordinate their attention visually with other people relative to things and events, enabling purposeful communication with adults. During the third

15

Copyright © Mometrix Media. You have been licensed one copy of this document for personal use only. Any other reproduction or redistribution is strictly prohibited. All rights reserved.
This content is provided for test preparation purposes only and does not imply an endorsement by Mometrix of any particular political, scientific, or religious point of view.

developmental period, from 18 months on, children come to use language as their main way of communicating and learning. Preschoolers can carry on conversations, exercise self-control through language use, and conduct verbal negotiations.

MILESTONES OF NORMAL LANGUAGE DEVELOPMENT BY THE 2 YEARS OLD

By the time most children reach the age of 2 years, they have acquired a vocabulary of about 150 to 300 words. They can name various familiar objects found in their environments. They are able to use at least two prepositions in their speech (e.g., *in*, *on*, and/or *under*). Two-year-olds typically combine the words they know into short sentences. These sentences tend to be mostly noun-verb or verb-noun combinations (e.g., "Daddy work," "Watch this"). They may also include verb-preposition combinations (e.g., "Go out," "Come in"). By the age of 2 years, children use pronouns, such as *I*, *me*, and *you*. They typically can use at least two such pronouns correctly. A normally developing 2-year-old will respond to some commands, directions, or questions, such as "Show me your eyes" or "Where are your ears?"

SALIENT GENERAL ASPECTS OF HUMAN LANGUAGE ABILITIES FROM BEFORE BIRTH TO 5 YEARS OF AGE

Language and communication abilities are integral parts of human life that are central to learning, successful school performance, successful social interactions, and successful living. Human language ability begins before birth: the developing fetus can hear not only internal maternal sounds, but also the mother's voice, others' voices, and other sounds outside the womb. Humans have a natural sensitivity to human sounds and languages from before they are born until they are about 4½ years old. These years are critical for developing language and communication. Babies and young children are predisposed to greater sensitivity to human sounds than other sounds, orienting them toward the language spoken around them. Children absorb their environmental language completely, including vocal tones, syntax, usage, and emphasis. This linguistic absorption occurs very rapidly. Children's first 2½ years particularly involve amazing abilities to learn language, including grammatical expression.

6 MONTHS, 12 MONTHS, AND 18 MONTHS

Individual differences dictate a broad range of language development that is still normal. However, parents observing noticeably delayed language development in their children should consult professionals. Typically, babies respond to hearing their names by 6 months of age, turn their heads and eyes toward the sources of human voices they hear, and respond accordingly to friendly and angry tones of voice. By the age of 12 months, toddlers can usually understand and follow simple directions, especially when these are accompanied by physical and/or vocal cues. They can intentionally use one or more words with the correct meaning. By the age of 18 months, a normally developing child usually has acquired a vocabulary of roughly 5 to 20 words. Eighteen-month-old children use nouns in their speech most of the time. They are very likely to repeat certain words and/or phrases over and over. At this age, children typically are able to follow simple verbal commands without needing as many visual or auditory cues as at 12 months.

THREE YEARS

By the time they are 3 years old, most normally developing children have acquired vocabularies of between 900 and 1,000 words. Typically, they correctly use the pronouns *I*, *me*, and *you*. They use more verbs more frequently. They apply past tenses to some verbs and plurals to some nouns. 3-year-olds usually can use at least three prepositions; the most common are *in*, *on*, and *under*. The normally developing 3-year-old knows the major body parts and can name them. 3-year-olds typically use 3-word sentences with ease. Normally, parents should find approximately 75 to 100 percent of what a 3-year-old says to be intelligible, while strangers should find between 50 and 75

Copyright © Mometrix Media. You have been licensed one copy of this document for personal use only. Any other reproduction or redistribution is strictly prohibited. All rights reserved.
This content is provided for test preparation purposes only and does not imply an endorsement by Mometrix of any particular political, scientific, or religious point of view.

percent of a 3-year-old's speech intelligible. Children this age comprehend most simple questions about their activities and environments and can answer questions about what they should do when they are thirsty, hungry, sleepy, hot, or cold. They can tell about their experiences in ways that adults can generally follow. By the age of 3 years, children should also be able to tell others their name, age, and sex.

FOUR YEARS

When normally developing children are 4 years old, most know the names of animals familiar to them. They can use at least four prepositions in their speech (e.g., *in, on, under, to, from*, etc.). They can name familiar objects in pictures, and they know and can identify one color or more. Usually, they are able to repeat four-syllable words they hear. They verbalize as they engage in their activities, which Vygotsky dubbed "private speech." Private speech helps young children think through what they are doing, solve problems, make decisions, and reinforce the correct sequences in multistep activities. When presented with contrasting items, 4-year-olds can understand comparative concepts like bigger and smaller. At this age, they are able to comply with simple commands without the target stimuli being in their sight (e.g., "Put those clothes in the hamper" [upstairs]). Four-year-old children will also frequently repeat speech sounds, syllables, words, and phrases, similar to 18-month-olds' repetitions but at higher linguistic and developmental levels.

FIVE YEARS

Once most children have reached the age of 5 years, their speech has expanded from the emphasis of younger children on nouns, verbs, and a few prepositions, and is now characterized by many more descriptive words, including adjectives and adverbs. Five-year-olds understand common antonyms, such as big/little, heavy/light, long/short, and hot/cold. They can now repeat longer sentences they hear, up to about 9 words. When given three consecutive, uninterrupted commands, the typical 5-year-old can follow these without forgetting one or two. At age 5, most children have learned simple concepts of time like today, yesterday, and tomorrow; day, morning, afternoon, and night; and before, after, and later. Five-year-olds typically speak in relatively long sentences and normally should be incorporating some compound sentences (with more than one independent clause) and complex sentences (with one or more independent and dependent clauses). Five-year-old children's speech is also grammatically correct most of the time.

ACTIVITIES THAT TEACH PHONOLOGICAL AWARENESS

Classroom activities that teach phonological awareness include language play and exposure to a variety of sounds and the contexts of sounds. Activities that teach phonological awareness include:

- Clapping to the sounds of individual words, names, or all words in a sentence
- Practicing saying blended phonemes
- Singing songs that involve phoneme replacement (e.g., The Name Game)
- Reading poems, songs, and nursery rhymes out loud
- Reading patterned and predictable texts out loud
- Listening to environmental sounds or following verbal directions
- Playing games with rhyming chants or fingerplays
- Reading alliterative texts out loud
- Grouping objects by beginning sounds
- Reordering words in a well-known sentence or making silly phrases by deleting words from a well-known sentence (perhaps from a favorite storybook)

Copyright © Mometrix Media. You have been licensed one copy of this document for personal use only. Any other reproduction or redistribution is strictly prohibited. All rights reserved. This content is provided for test preparation purposes only and does not imply an endorsement by Mometrix of any particular political, scientific, or religious point of view.

TEACHING OF READING THROUGH PHONICS

Phonics is the process of learning to read by learning how spoken language is represented by letters. Students learn to read phonetically by sounding out the **phonemes** in words and then blending them together to produce the correct sounds in words. In other words, the student connects speech sounds with letters or groups of letters and blends the sounds together to determine the pronunciation of an unknown word. Phonics is a method commonly used to teach **decoding and reading**, but it has been challenged by other methods, such as the whole language approach. Despite the complexity of pronunciation and combined sounds in the English language, phonics is a highly effective way to teach reading. Being able to read or pronounce a word does not mean the student comprehends the meaning of the word, but context aids comprehension. When phonics is used as a foundation for decoding, children eventually learn to recognize words automatically and advance to decoding multisyllable words with practice.

ALPHABETIC PRINCIPLE AND ALPHABET WRITING SYSTEMS

The **alphabetic principle** refers to the use of letters and combinations of letters to represent speech sounds. The way letters are combined and pronounced is guided by a system of rules that establishes relationships between written and spoken words and their letter symbols. Alphabet writing systems are common around the world. Some are **phonological** in that each letter stands for an individual sound and words are spelled just as they sound. However, keep in mind that there are other writing systems as well, such as the Chinese **logographic** system and the Japanese **syllabic** system.

> **Review Video: Print Awareness and Alphabet Knowledge**
> Visit mometrix.com/academy and enter code: 541069

FACTS CHILDREN SHOULD KNOW ABOUT LETTERS

To be appropriately prepared to learn to read and write, a child should learn:

- That each letter is **distinct** in appearance
- What **direction and shape** must be used to write each letter
- That each letter has a **name**, which can be associated with the shape of a letter
- That there are **26** letters in the English alphabet, and letters are grouped in a certain order
- That letters represent **sounds of speech**
- That **words** are composed of letters and have meaning
- That one must be able to **correspond** letters and sounds to read

DEVELOPMENT OF LANGUAGE SKILLS

Children learn language through interacting with others, by experiencing language in daily and relevant context, and through understanding that speaking and listening are necessary for effective communication. Teachers can promote **language development** by intensifying the opportunities a child has to experience and understand language.

Teachers can assist language development by:

- Modeling enriched vocabulary and teaching new words
- Using questions and examples to extend a child's descriptive language skills
- Providing ample response time to encourage children to practice speech
- Asking for clarification to provide students with the opportunity to develop communication skills

Copyright © Mometrix Media. You have been licensed one copy of this document for personal use only. Any other reproduction or redistribution is strictly prohibited. All rights reserved. This content is provided for test preparation purposes only and does not imply an endorsement by Mometrix of any particular political, scientific, or religious point of view.

- Promoting conversations among children
- Providing feedback to let children know they have been heard and understood, and providing further explanation when needed

RELATIONSHIP BETWEEN ORAL AND WRITTEN LANGUAGE DEVELOPMENT

Oral and written language development occur simultaneously. The acquisition of skills in one area supports the acquisition of skills in the other. However, oral language is not a prerequisite to written language. An immature form of oral language development is babbling, and an immature form of written language development is scribbling. **Oral language development** does not occur naturally, but does occur in a social context. This means it is best to include children in conversations rather than simply talk at them. **Written language development** can occur without direct instruction. In fact, reading and writing do not necessarily need to be taught through formal lessons if the child is exposed to a print-rich environment. A teacher can assist a child's language development by building on what the child already knows, discussing relevant and meaningful events and experiences, teaching vocabulary and literacy skills, and providing opportunities to acquire more complex language.

PRINT-RICH ENVIRONMENT

A teacher can provide a **print-rich environment** in the classroom in a number of ways. These include:

- **Displaying** the following in the classroom:
  - Children's names in print or cursive
  - Children's written work
  - Newspapers and magazines
  - Instructional charts
  - Written schedules
  - Signs and labels
  - Printed songs, poems, and rhymes
- Using **graphic organizers** such as KWL charts or story road maps to:
  - Remind students about what was read and discussed
  - Expand on the lesson topic or theme
  - Show the relationships among books, ideas, and words
- Using **big books** to:
  - Point out features of print, such as specific letters and punctuation
  - Track print from left to right
  - Emphasize the concept of words and the fact that they are used to communicate

BENEFITS OF PRINT AND BOOK AWARENESS

Print and book awareness helps a child understand:

- That there is a **connection** between print and messages contained on signs, labels, and other print forms in the child's environment
- That reading and writing are ways to obtain information and communicate ideas
- That **print** written in English runs from left to right and from top to bottom
- That a book has **parts**, such as a title, a cover, a title page, and a table of contents
- That a book has an **author** and contains a **story**
- That **illustrations** can carry meaning

19

Copyright © Mometrix Media. You have been licensed one copy of this document for personal use only. Any other reproduction or redistribution is strictly prohibited. All rights reserved.
This content is provided for test preparation purposes only and does not imply an endorsement by Mometrix of any particular political, scientific, or religious point of view.

- That **letters and words** are different
- That **words and sentences** are separated by spaces and punctuation
- That different **text forms** are used for different functions
- That print represents **spoken language**
- How to **hold** a book

DECODING

Decoding is the method or strategy used to make sense of printed words and figure out how to correctly pronounce them. In order to **decode**, a student needs to know the relationships between letters and sounds, including letter patterns; that words are constructed from phonemes and phoneme blends; and that a printed word represents a word that can be spoken. This knowledge will help the student recognize familiar words and make informed guesses about the pronunciation of unfamiliar words. Decoding is not the same as comprehension. It does not require an understanding of the meaning of a word, only a knowledge of how to recognize and pronounce it. Decoding can also refer to the skills a student uses to determine the meaning of a **sentence**. These skills include applying knowledge of vocabulary, sentence structure, and context.

ROLE OF FLUENCY IN LITERACY DEVELOPMENT

Fluency is the goal of literacy development. It is the ability to read accurately and quickly. Evidence of fluency includes the ability to recognize words automatically and group words for comprehension. At this point, the student no longer needs to decode words except for complex, unfamiliar ones. He or she is able to move to the next level and understand the **meaning** of a text. The student should be able to self-check for comprehension and should feel comfortable expressing ideas in writing. Teachers can help students build fluency by continuing to provide:

- Reading experiences and discussions about text that gradually increase in level of difficulty
- Reading practice, both silently and out loud
- Word analysis practice
- Instruction on reading comprehension strategies
- Opportunities to express responses to readings through writing

> **Review Video: Fluency**
> Visit mometrix.com/academy and enter code: 531179

ROLE OF VOCABULARY IN LITERACY DEVELOPMENT

When students do not know the meaning of words in a text, their comprehension is limited. As a result, the text becomes boring or confusing. The larger a student's **vocabulary** is, the better their reading comprehension will be. A larger vocabulary is also associated with an enhanced ability to **communicate** in speech and writing. It is the teacher's role to help students develop a good working vocabulary. Students learn most of the words they use and understand by listening to the world around them (adults, other students, media, etc.) They also learn from their reading experiences, which include being read to and reading independently. Carefully designed activities can also stimulate vocabulary growth, and should emphasize useful words that students see frequently, important words necessary for understanding text, and difficult words and phrases, such as idioms or words with more than one meaning.

Copyright © Mometrix Media. You have been licensed one copy of this document for personal use only. Any other reproduction or redistribution is strictly prohibited. All rights reserved. This content is provided for test preparation purposes only and does not imply an endorsement by Mometrix of any particular political, scientific, or religious point of view.

Teaching Techniques Promoting Vocabulary Development

A student's **vocabulary** can be developed by:

- Calling upon a student's **prior knowledge** and making comparisons to that knowledge
- **Defining** a word and providing multiple examples of the use of the word in context
- Showing a student how to use **context clues** to discover the meaning of a word
- Providing instruction on **prefixes**, **roots**, and **suffixes** to help students break a word into its parts and decipher its meaning
- Showing students how to use a **dictionary and a thesaurus**
- Asking students to **practice** new vocabulary by using the words in their own writing
- Providing a **print-rich environment** with a word wall
- Studying a group of words related to a **single subject**, such as farm words, transportation words, etc. so that concept development is enhanced

Affixes, Prefixes, and Root Words

Affixes are syllables attached to the beginning or end of a word to make a derivative or inflectional form of a word. Both prefixes and suffixes are affixes. A **prefix** is a syllable that appears at the beginning of a word that creates a specific meaning in combination with the root or base word. For example, the prefix *mis* means wrong. When combined with the root word *spelling*, the word *misspelling* is created, which means wrong spelling. A **root word** is the base of a word to which affixes can be added. For example, the prefix *in-* or *pre-* can be added to the latin root word *vent* to create *invent* or *prevent*, respectively. The suffix *-er* can be added to the root word *manage* to create *manager*, which means one who manages. The suffix *-able*, meaning capable of, can be added to *manage* to create *managable*, which means capable of being managed.

Suffixes

A **suffix** is a syllable that appears at the end of a word that creates a specific meaning in combination with the root or base word. There are three types of suffixes:

- **Noun suffixes**—Noun suffixes can change a verb or adjective to a noun. They can denote the act of, state of, quality of, or result of something. For example, *-ment* added to *argue* becomes *argument*, which can be understood as the act the act of resulting state from arguing or the reasons given to prove an idea. Noun suffixes can also denote the doer, or one who acts. For example, *-eer* added to *auction* becomes *auctioneer*, meaning one who auctions. Other examples include *-hood*, *-ness*, *-tion*, *-ship*, and *-ism*.
- **Verb suffixes**—These change other words to verbs and denote to make or to perform the act of. For example, *-en* added to *soft* makes *soften*, which means to make soft. Other verb suffixes are *-ate* (perpetuate), *-fy* (dignify), and *-ize* (sterilize).
- **Adjectival suffixes**—These suffixes change other words to adjectives and include suffixes such as *-ful*, which means full of. When added to *care*, the word *careful* is formed, which means full of care. Other examples are *-ish* and *-less*.

Strategies to Improve Reading Comprehension

Teachers can model the strategies students can use on their own to better comprehend a text through a read-aloud. First, the teacher should do a walk-through of the story **illustrations** and ask, "What's happening here?" The teacher should then ask students to **predict** what the story will be about based on what they have seen. As the book is read, the teacher should ask open-ended questions such as, "Why do you think the character did this?" and "How do you think the character feels?" The teacher should also ask students if they can **relate** to the story or have background

21

Copyright © Mometrix Media. You have been licensed one copy of this document for personal use only. Any other reproduction or redistribution is strictly prohibited. All rights reserved.
This content is provided for test preparation purposes only and does not imply an endorsement by Mometrix of any particular political, scientific, or religious point of view.

knowledge of something similar. After the reading, the teacher should ask the students to **retell** the story in their own words to check for comprehension. Possible methods of retelling include performing a puppet show or summarizing the story to a partner.

> **Review Video: The Link Between Grammar Skills and Reading Comprehension**
> Visit mometrix.com/academy and enter code: 411287

ROLE OF PRIOR KNOWLEDGE IN DETERMINING APPROPRIATE LITERACY EDUCATION

Even preschool children have some literacy skills, and the extent and type of these skills have implications for instructional approaches. **Comprehension** results from relating two or more pieces of information. One piece comes from the text, and another piece might come from **prior knowledge** (something from a student's long-term memory). For a child, that prior knowledge comes from being read to at home; taking part in other literacy experiences, such as playing computer or word games; being exposed to a print-rich environment at home; and observing parents' reading habits. Children who have had **extensive literacy experience** are better prepared to further develop their literacy skills in school than children who have not been read to, have few books or magazines in their homes, are seldom exposed to high-level oral or written language activities, and seldom witness adults engaged in reading and writing. Children with a scant literacy background are at a disadvantage. The teacher must not make any assumptions about their prior knowledge, and should use intense, targeted instruction. Otherwise, the student may have trouble improving their reading comprehension.

CHAPTER QUIZ

1. Chinese uses which type of writing system?

   a. Alphabetic
   b. Syllabic
   c. Logographic
   d. Featural

2. Which of the following is an adjectival suffix?

   a. *-ish*
   b. *-eer*
   c. *-ize*
   d. *-fy*

3. Which of the following further defines literacy as the "ability to identify, understand, interpret, create, communicate, compute, and use printed and written materials associated with varying contexts"?

   a. W.H.O.
   b. N.A.E.D.U.
   c. U.N.E.S.C.O.
   d. D.O.E.

CHAPTER QUIZ ANSWER KEY

1. C: The alphabetic principle refers to the use of letters and combinations of letters to represent speech sounds. The way letters are combined and pronounced is guided by a system of rules that establishes relationships between written and spoken words and their letter symbols. Alphabet writing systems are common around the world. Some are phonological, meaning that each letter

Copyright © Mometrix Media. You have been licensed one copy of this document for personal use only. Any other reproduction or redistribution is strictly prohibited. All rights reserved. This content is provided for test preparation purposes only and does not imply an endorsement by Mometrix of any particular political, scientific, or religious point of view.

stands for an individual sound and words are spelled just as they sound. However, it is important to note that there are other writing systems as well, such as the Chinese logographic system and the Japanese syllabic system.

2. A: A suffix is a syllable that appears at the end of a word and creates a specific meaning in combination with the root or base word. There are three types of suffixes:

- Noun suffixes can change a verb or adjective to a noun. They can denote the act of, state of, quality of, or result of something. For example, *-ment* added to *argue* becomes *argument*, which can be understood as the resulting state from arguing or the reasons given to prove an idea. Noun suffixes can also denote the doer, or one who acts. For example, *-eer* added to *auction* becomes *auctioneer*, meaning one who auctions. Other examples include *-hood*, *-ness*, *-tion*, *-ship*, and *-ism*.
- Verb suffixes change other words to verbs and denote to make or to perform the act of. For example, *-en* added to *soft* makes *soften*, which means to make soft. Other verb suffixes are *-ate* (perpetuate), *-fy* (dignify), and *-ize* (sterilize).
- Adjectival suffixes change other words to adjectives and include suffixes such as *-ful*, which means full of. When added to *care*, the word *careful* is formed, which means full of care. Other examples are *-ish* and *-less*.

3. C: UNESCO, the United Nations Educational, Scientific, and Cultural Organization, has further defined literacy as the "ability to identify, understand, interpret, create, communicate, compute, and use printed and written materials associated with varying contexts." Under the UNESCO definition, understanding cultural, political, and historical contexts of communities falls under the definition of literacy.

THEORIES OF LANGUAGE DEVELOPMENT

Four theories of language development are:

- **Learning approach**—This theory assumes that language is first learned by imitating the speech of adults. It is then solidified in school through drills about the rules of language structures.
- **Linguistic approach**—Championed by Noam Chomsky in the 1950s, this theory proposes that the ability to use a language is innate. This is a biological approach rather than one based on cognition or social patterning.
- **Cognitive approach**—Developed in the 1970s and based on the work of Piaget, this theory states that children must develop appropriate cognitive skills before they can acquire language.
- **Sociocognitive approach**—In the 1970s, some researchers proposed that language development is a complex interaction of linguistic, social, and cognitive influences. This theory best explains the lack of language skills among children who are neglected, have uneducated parents, or live in poverty.

CLASSROOM PRACTICES BENEFITING SECOND LANGUAGE ACQUISITION

Since some students may have a limited understanding of English, a teacher should employ the following practices to promote second language acquisition:

- Make all instruction as **understandable** as possible and use simple and repeated terms.
- Relate instruction to the **cultures** of ESL children.
- Increase **interactive activities** and use gestures or nonverbal actions when modeling.

Copyright © Mometrix Media. You have been licensed one copy of this document for personal use only. Any other reproduction or redistribution is strictly prohibited. All rights reserved.
This content is provided for test preparation purposes only and does not imply an endorsement by Mometrix of any particular political, scientific, or religious point of view.

- Provide language and literacy development instruction in **all curriculum areas**.
- Establish **consistent routines** that help children connect words and events.
- Use a **schedule** so children know what will happen next and will not feel lost.
- Integrate ESL children into **group activities** with non-ESL children.
- Appoint bilingual students to act as **student translators**.
- Explain actions as activities happen so that a **word to action relationship** is established.
- Initiate opportunities for ESL children to **experiment** with and practice new language.
- Employ multisensory learning.

TEACHING STRATEGIES TO PROMOTE LISTENING SKILLS OF ESL STUDENTS

Listening is a critical skill when learning a new language. Students spend a great deal more time listening than they do speaking, and far less time reading and writing than speaking. One way to encourage ESL students to listen is to talk about topics that are of **interest** to the ESL learner. Otherwise, students may tune out the speaker because they don't want to put in that much effort to learn about a topic they find boring. Another way to encourage ESL students to listen is to talk about content or give examples that are **easy** to understand or are **related** to a topic that is familiar to ESL students. Culturally relevant materials will be more interesting to ESL students, will make them feel more comfortable, and will contain vocabulary that they may already be familiar with.

CONSIDERATIONS RELEVANT TO ESL STUDENTS RELATED TO LEARNING BY LISTENING

Listening is not a passive skill, but an **active** one. Therefore, a teacher needs to make the listening experience as rewarding as possible and provide as many auditory and visual clues as possible. Three ways that the teacher can make the listening experience rewarding for ESL students are:

- Avoid **colloquialisms** and **abbreviated or slang terms** that may be confusing to the ESL listener, unless there is enough time to define them and explain their use.
- Make the spoken English understandable by stopping to **clarify** points, **repeating** new or difficult words, and **defining** words that may not be known.
- Support the spoken word with as many **visuals** as possible. Pictures, diagrams, gestures, facial expressions, and body language can help the ESL learner correctly interpret the spoken language more easily and also leaves an image impression that helps them remember the words.

TOP-DOWN AND BOTTOM-UP PROCESSING

ESL students need to be given opportunities to practice both top-down and bottom-up processing. If they are old enough to understand these concepts, they should be made aware that these are two processes that affect their listening comprehension. In **top-down processing**, the listener refers to **background and global knowledge** to figure out the meaning of a message. For example, when asking an ESL student to perform a task, the steps of the task should be explained and accompanied by a review of the vocabulary terms the student already understands so that the student feels comfortable tackling new steps and new words. The teacher should also allow students to ask questions to verify comprehension. In **bottom-up processing**, the listener figures out the meaning of a message by using "**data**" obtained from what is said. This data includes sounds (stress, rhythm, and intonation), words, and grammatical relationships. All data can be used to make conclusions or interpretations. For example, the listener can develop bottom-up skills by learning how to detect differences in intonation between statements and questions.

Copyright © Mometrix Media. You have been licensed one copy of this document for personal use only. Any other reproduction or redistribution is strictly prohibited. All rights reserved. This content is provided for test preparation purposes only and does not imply an endorsement by Mometrix of any particular political, scientific, or religious point of view.

LISTENING LESSONS

All students, but especially ESL students, can be taught **listening** through specific training. During listening lessons, the teacher should guide students through three steps:

- **Pre-listening activity**—This establishes the purpose of the lesson and engages students' background knowledge. This activity should ask students to think about and discuss something they already know about the topic. Alternatively, the teacher can provide background information.
- **The listening activity**—This requires the listener to obtain information and then immediately do something with that information. For example, the teacher can review the schedule for the day or the week. In this example, students are being given information about a routine they already know, and need to be able to identify names, tasks, and times.
- **Post-listening activity**—This is an evaluation process that allows students to judge how well they did with the listening task. Other language skills can be included in the activity. For example, this activity could involve asking questions about who will do what according to the classroom schedule (Who is the lunch monitor today?) and could also involve asking students to produce whole sentence replies.

HELPING ESL STUDENTS UNDERSTAND SUBJECT MATTER

SPEAKING

To help ESL students better understand subject matter, the following teaching strategies using spoken English can be used:

- **Read aloud** from a textbook, and then ask ESL students to **verbally summarize** what was read. The teacher should assist by providing new words as needed to give students the opportunity to practice vocabulary and speaking skills. The teacher should then read the passage again to students to verify accuracy and details.
- The teacher could ask ESL students to explain why the subject matter is important to them and where they see it fitting into their lives. This verbalization gives them speaking practice and helps them relate to the subject.
- Whenever small group activities are being conducted, ESL students can be placed with **English-speaking students**. It is best to keep the groups to two or three students so that the ESL student will be motivated by the need to be involved. English-speaking students should be encouraged to include ESL students in the group work.

READING

There are supplemental printed materials that can be used to help ESL students understand subject matter. The following strategies can be used to help ESL students develop English reading skills.

- Make sure all ESL students have a **bilingual dictionary** to use. A thesaurus would also be helpful.
- Try to keep **content area books** written in the ESL students' native languages in the classroom. Students can use them side-by-side with English texts. Textbooks in other languages can be ordered from the school library or obtained from the classroom textbook publisher.
- If a student lacks confidence in his or her ability to read the textbook, the teacher can read a passage to the student and have him or her **verbally summarize** the passage. The teacher should take notes on what the student says and then read them back. These notes can be a substitute, short-form, in-their-own-words textbook that the student can understand.

Copyright © Mometrix Media. You have been licensed one copy of this document for personal use only. Any other reproduction or redistribution is strictly prohibited. All rights reserved. This content is provided for test preparation purposes only and does not imply an endorsement by Mometrix of any particular political, scientific, or religious point of view.

GENERAL TEACHING STRATEGIES TO HELP ESL STUDENTS

Some strategies can help students develop more than one important skill. They may involve a combination of speaking, listening, and viewing. Others are mainly classroom management aids. General teaching strategies for ESL students include:

- **Partner** English-speaking students with ESL students as study buddies and ask the English-speaking students to share notes.
- Encourage ESL students to ask **questions** whenever they don't understand something. They should be aware that they don't have to be able to interpret every word of text to understand the concept.
- Dictate **key sentences** related to the content area being taught and ask ESL students to write them down. This gives them practice in listening and writing, and also helps them identify what is important.
- **Alternate** difficult and easy tasks so that ESL students can experience academic success.
- Ask ESL students to **label** objects associated with content areas, such as maps, diagrams, parts of a leaf, or parts of a sentence. This gives students writing and reading experience and helps them remember key vocabulary.

CHAPTER QUIZ

1. Which theory of language development assumes that language is first learned by imitating the speech of adults?
- a. Linguistic approach
- b. Learning approach
- c. Cognitive approach
- d. Sociocognitive approach

CHAPTER QUIZ ANSWER KEY

1. B: Below are four theories of language development.

- Learning approach: This theory assumes that language is first learned by imitating the speech of adults. It is then solidified in school through drills about the rules of language structures.
- Linguistic approach: Championed by Noam Chomsky in the 1950s, this theory proposes that the ability to use language is innate. This is a biological approach rather than one based on cognition or social patterning.
- Cognitive approach: Developed in the 1970s and based on the work of Jean Piaget, this theory states that children must develop appropriate cognitive skills before they can acquire language.
- Socio-cognitive approach: In the 1970s, some researchers proposed that language development is a complex interaction of linguistic, social, and cognitive influences. This theory best explains the lack of language skills among children who are neglected, have uneducated parents, or live in poverty.

Literature and Informational Texts

COMMON FORMS OF PROSE FICTION
HISTORICAL, PICARESQUE, GOTHIC, AND PSYCHOLOGICAL FICTION

Historical fiction is set in particular historical periods, including prehistoric and mythological. Examples include Walter Scott's *Rob Roy* and *Ivanhoe*; Leo Tolstoy's *War and Peace;* Robert Graves'

Copyright © Mometrix Media. You have been licensed one copy of this document for personal use only. Any other reproduction or redistribution is strictly prohibited. All rights reserved. This content is provided for test preparation purposes only and does not imply an endorsement by Mometrix of any particular political, scientific, or religious point of view.

I, Claudius; Mary Renault's *The King Must Die* and *The Bull from the Sea* (an historical novel using Greek mythology); Virginia Woolf's *Orlando* and *Between the Acts;* and John Dos Passos's *U.S.A* trilogy. **Picaresque** novels recount episodic adventures of a rogue protagonist or *pícaro,* like Miguel de Cervantes' *Don Quixote* or Henry Fielding's *Tom Jones.* **Gothic** novels originated as a reaction against 18th-century Enlightenment rationalism, featuring horror, mystery, superstition, madness, supernatural elements, and revenge. Early examples include Horace Walpole's *Castle of Otranto,* Matthew Gregory Lewis' *Monk,* Mary Shelley's *Frankenstein,* and Bram Stoker's *Dracula.* In America, Edgar Allan Poe wrote many Gothic works. Contemporary novelist Anne Rice has penned many Gothic novels under the pseudonym A. N. Roquelaure. **Psychological** novels, originating in 17th-century France, explore characters' motivations. Examples include Abbé Prévost's *Manon Lescaut;* George Eliot's novels; Fyodor Dostoyevsky's *Crime and Punishment;* Tolstoy's *Anna Karenina;* Gustave Flaubert's *Madame Bovary;* and the novels of Henry James, James Joyce, and Vladimir Nabokov.

NOVELS OF MANNERS

Novels of manners are fictional stories that observe, explore, and analyze the social behaviors of a specific time and place. While deep psychological themes are more universal across different historical periods and countries, the manners of a particular society are shorter-lived and more varied; the **novel of manners** captures these societal details. Novels of manners can also be regarded as symbolically representing, in artistic form, certain established and secure social orders. Characteristics of novels of manners include descriptions of a society with defined behavioral codes; language that uses standardized, impersonal formulas; and inhibition of emotional expression, as contrasted with the strong emotions expressed in romantic or sentimental novels. Jane Austen's detailed descriptions of English society and characters struggling with the definitions and restrictions placed on them by society are excellent models of the novel of manners. In the 20th century, Evelyn Waugh's *Handful of Dust* is a novel of social manners, and his *Sword of Honour* trilogy contains novels of military manners. Another 20th-century example is *The Unbearable Bassington* by Saki (the pen name of writer H. H. Munro), focusing on Edwardian society.

WESTERN-WORLD SENTIMENTAL NOVELS

Sentimental love novels originated in the movement of Romanticism. Eighteenth-century examples of novels that emphasize the emotional aspect of love include Samuel Richardson's *Pamela* (1740) and Jean-Jacques Rousseau's *Nouvelle Héloïse* (1761). Also in the 18th century, Laurence Sterne's novel *Tristram Shandy* (1760-1767) is an example of a novel with elements of sentimentality. The Victorian era's rejection of emotionalism caused the term "sentimental" to have undesirable connotations. However, even non-sentimental novelists such as William Makepeace Thackeray and Charles Dickens incorporated sentimental elements in their writing. A 19th-century author of genuinely sentimental novels was Mrs. Henry Wood (e.g., *East Lynne,* 1861). In the 20th century, Erich Segal's sentimental novel *Love Story* (1970) was a popular bestseller.

EPISTOLARY NOVELS

Epistolary novels are told in the form of letters written by their characters rather than in typical narrative form. Samuel Richardson, the best-known author of epistolary novels like *Pamela* (1740) and *Clarissa* (1748), widely influenced early Romantic epistolary novels throughout Europe that freely expressed emotions. Richardson, a printer, published technical manuals on letter-writing for young gentlewomen; his epistolary novels were fictional extensions of those nonfictional instructional books. Nineteenth-century English author Wilkie Collins' *The Moonstone* (1868) was a mystery written in epistolary form. By the 20th century, the format of well-composed written letters came to be regarded as artificial and outmoded. A 20th-century evolution of letters was tape-recording transcripts, such as in French playwright Samuel Beckett's drama *Krapp's Last Tape.*

Copyright © Mometrix Media. You have been licensed one copy of this document for personal use only. Any other reproduction or redistribution is strictly prohibited. All rights reserved.
This content is provided for test preparation purposes only and does not imply an endorsement by Mometrix of any particular political, scientific, or religious point of view.

Though evoking modern alienation, Beckett still created a sense of fictional characters' direct communication without author intervention as Richardson had.

PASTORAL NOVELS

Pastoral novels lyrically idealize country life as idyllic and utopian, akin to the Garden of Eden. *Daphnis and Chloe*, written by Greek novelist Longus around the second or third century, influenced Elizabethan pastoral romances like Thomas Lodge's *Rosalynde* (1590), which inspired Shakespeare's *As You Like It*, and Philip Sidney's *Arcadia* (1590). Jacques-Henri Bernardin de St. Pierre's French work *Paul et Virginie* (1787) demonstrated the early Romantic view of the innocence and goodness of nature. Though the style lost popularity by the 20th century, pastoral elements can still be seen in novels like *The Rainbow* (1915) and *Lady Chatterley's Lover* (1928), both by D. H. Lawrence. Growing realism transformed pastoral writing into less ideal and more dystopian, distasteful and ironic depictions of country life in George Eliot's and Thomas Hardy's novels. Saul Bellow's novel *Herzog* (1964) may demonstrate how urban ills highlight an alternative pastoral ideal. The pastoral style is commonly thought to be overly idealized and outdated today, as seen in Stella Gibbons' pastoral satire, Cold Comfort Farm (1932).

BILDUNGSROMAN

Bildungsroman is German for "education novel." This term is also used in English to describe "apprenticeship" novels focusing on coming-of-age stories, including youth's struggles and searches for things such as identity, spiritual understanding, or the meaning in life. Johann Wolfgang von Goethe's *Wilhelm Meisters Lehrjahre* (1796) is credited as the origin of this genre. Two of Charles Dickens' novels, *David Copperfield* (1850) and *Great Expectations* (1861), also fit this form. H. G. Wells wrote *bildungsromans* about questing for apprenticeships to address the complications of modern life in *Joan and Peter* (1918) and from a Utopian perspective in *The Dream* (1924). School *bildungsromans* include Thomas Hughes' *Tom Brown's School Days* (1857) and Alain-Fournier's *Le Grand Meaulnes* (1913). Many Hermann Hesse novels, including *Demian, Steppenwolf, Siddhartha, Magister Ludi,* and *Beneath the Wheel* are *bildungsromans* about a struggling, searching youth. Samuel Butler's *The Way of All Flesh* (1903) and James Joyce's *A Portrait of the Artist as a Young Man* (1916) are two modern examples. Variations include J. D. Salinger's *The Catcher in the Rye* (1951), set both within and beyond school, and William Golding's *Lord of the Flies* (1955), a novel not set in a school but one that is a coming-of-age story nonetheless.

ROMAN À CLEF

Roman à clef, French for "novel with a key," refers to books that require a real-life frame of reference, or key, for full comprehension. In Geoffrey Chaucer's *Canterbury Tales,* the Nun's Priest's Tale contains details that confuse readers unaware of history about the Earl of Bolingbroke's involvement in an assassination plot. Other literary works fitting this form include John Dryden's political satirical poem "Absalom and Achitophel" (1681), Jonathan Swift's satire "A Tale of a Tub" (1704), and George Orwell's political allegory *Animal Farm* (1945), all of which cannot be understood completely without knowing their camouflaged historical contents. *Roman à clefs* disguise truths too dangerous for authors to state directly. Readers must know about the enemies of D. H. Lawrence and Aldous Huxley to appreciate their respective novels: *Aaron's Rod* (1922) and *Point Counter Point* (1928). Marcel Proust's *Remembrance of Things Past (À la recherché du temps perdu,* 1871-1922) is informed by his social context. James Joyce's *Finnegans Wake* is an enormous *roman à clef* containing multitudinous personal references.

> **Review Video: Major Forms of Prose**
> Visit mometrix.com/academy and enter code: 565543

Copyright © Mometrix Media. You have been licensed one copy of this document for personal use only. Any other reproduction or redistribution is strictly prohibited. All rights reserved. This content is provided for test preparation purposes only and does not imply an endorsement by Mometrix of any particular political, scientific, or religious point of view.

OTHER COMMON TYPES OF PROSE

- A **narrative** is any composition that tells a story. Narratives have characters, settings, and a structure. Narratives may be fiction or nonfiction stories and may follow a linear or nonlinear structure. The purpose of a narrative is generally to entertain, but nonfiction narratives can be informative, as well. Narratives also appear in a variety of structures and formats.

- **Biographies** are books written about another person's life. Biographies can be valuable historical resources. Though they provide a narrow view of the relevant time period and culture, their specificity can also provide a unique context for that period or culture. Biographies, especially those whose subject was a well-known and influential figure, can provide a more complete picture of the figure's life or contributions. Biographies can also serve as a source of inspiration or communicate a moral because of their focus on one person over an extended period of time.

- **Myths**, or stories from mythology, exist in most ancient cultures and continue to influence modern cultures. Mythology is so influential that it has even inspired numerous pieces of modern literature and media in popular culture. While popular culture most clearly references mythology from the Ancient Greek and Roman cultures, literature has been influenced by mythologies from around the entire world. Since mythology is so prevalent in ancient literature, it makes sense that universal themes and morals often appear in mythology and even drive some myths. This suggests connections between cultures through the stories they pass down.

- **Fables** are short, didactic stories that typically feature imaginary creatures or talking animals. The famous story "The Tortoise and the Hare" is a fable. Fables are still told and used today because of their universally understandable morals and characters, making them suitable for children's literature and media.

- **Fairy tales** are stories that involve fictional creatures or realistic characters with fantastical traits and abilities. Fairy tales often end happily and depict the victory of good over evil. The plots and characters in fairy tales are often far-fetched and whimsical.

- **Folk Tales** are stories that have withstood time and are usually popular in a particular region or culture. Folk tales often depict the clever success of a common person, though the story may, alternatively, end poorly for the protagonist. Folk tales are easily confused with fairytales because fairytales can be a type of folk tale.

- **Legends** are stories that typically focus on one character and highlight their victory over a particular enemy or obstacle. Legends often feature some facts or are inspired by true events, but are still understood to be either exaggerated or partially fictional. Heroes are often the protagonists of legends as they often save or protect others as they conquer enemies and obstacles.

- A **short story** is a fictional narrative that is shorter than a novel. However, there is not a definite page or word count that defines the short story category. Short stories tend to focus on one or few elements of a story in order to efficiently tell the story. Though they are often brief, short stories may still contain a moral or impact their readers.

> **Review Video: <u>Myths, Fables, Legends, and Fairy Tales</u>**
> Visit mometrix.com/academy and enter code: 347199

Copyright © Mometrix Media. You have been licensed one copy of this document for personal use only. Any other reproduction or redistribution is strictly prohibited. All rights reserved. This content is provided for test preparation purposes only and does not imply an endorsement by Mometrix of any particular political, scientific, or religious point of view.

COMMON GENRES IN PROSE

- The **mystery** genre includes stories with plots that follow a protagonist as they work to solve an unexplained situation, such as a murder, disappearance, or robbery. Protagonists of mysteries may be hired professionals or amateurs who solve the mystery despite their lack of experience and resources. Mysteries allow the reader to solve the case along with the protagonist, and often grant the reader an advantageous perspective, creating dramatic irony. The *Sherlock Holmes* novels by Sir Arthur Conan Doyle are examples of mystery novels.
- **Science fiction** is a genre that is based on the manipulation and exaggeration of real scientific discoveries and processes. These works are speculative and frequently depict a world where scientific discoveries and society have progressed beyond the point reached at the time of the work's creation. Works of science fiction often take place in a distant location or time, allowing for the dramatic advancements and conveniences they often depict. *Dune*, written by Frank Herbert, is an example of a science-fiction novel.
- The **fantasy** genre includes stories that feature imaginary creatures and supernatural abilities, but often take place in settings that resemble real places and cultures in history. Fantasy novels usually follow a gifted protagonist from humble beginnings as they embark on a quest, journey, or adventure and encounter mystical beings and personally challenging obstacles. Common themes in the fantasy genre include personal growth, good versus evil, and the value of the journey. J.R.R. Tolkien's *The Lord of the Rings* trilogy belongs to the fantasy genre.
- **Realistic fiction** describes fictional narratives that include events and characters that do not exist, but could appear in reality. Within the narrative, these characters and events may be depicted in real places. For example, Pip, the protagonist of Charles Dickens's *Great Expectations*, was not a real person, but the novel shows him living in London, England for much of his young adulthood. Realistic fiction contains no far-fetched or impossible elements and presents situations that can or do occur in real life. A contemporary example of realistic fiction is *Wonder* by R.J. Palacio.
- **Historical fiction** includes works that take place in the past and model their setting after real historical cultures, societies, and time periods. These works may include real historical figures and events, but they also may not. Works of historical fiction must be fully informed by the period and location they are set in, meaning both the major and minor details of the work must be historically compatible with the work's setting. Examples of historical fiction include Kathryn Stockett's *The Help* and Markus Zusak's *The Book Thief*.
- The phrase **literary nonfiction** describes nonfiction narratives that present true facts and events in a way that entertains readers and displays creativity. Literary nonfiction, also called creative nonfiction, may resemble fiction in its style and flow, but the truth of the events it describes sets it apart from fictional literature. Different types of books may be considered literary nonfiction, such as biographies, if they appear to employ creativity in their writing. An example of literary nonfiction is *The Immortal Life of Henrietta Lacks* by Rebecca Skloot.

REALISM AND SATIRE

REALISM

Realism is a literary form with the goal of representing reality as faithfully as possible. Its genesis in Western literature was a reaction against the sentimentality and extreme emotionalism of the works written during the Romantic literary movement, which championed feelings and emotional expression. Realists focused in great detail on immediacy of time and place, on specific actions of their characters, and the justifiable consequences of those actions. Some techniques of **realism**

Copyright © Mometrix Media. You have been licensed one copy of this document for personal use only. Any other reproduction or redistribution is strictly prohibited. All rights reserved. This content is provided for test preparation purposes only and does not imply an endorsement by Mometrix of any particular political, scientific, or religious point of view.

include writing in vernacular (conversational language), using specific dialects, and placing an emphasis on character rather than plot. Realistic literature also often addresses ethical issues. Historically, realistic works have often concentrated on the middle classes of the authors' societies. Realists eschew treatments that are too dramatic or sensationalistic as exaggerations of the reality that they strive to portray as closely as they are able. Influenced by his own bleak past, Fyodor Dostoevsky wrote several novels, such as *Crime and Punishment* (1866) that shunned romantic ideals and sought to portray a stark reality. Henry James was a prominent writer of realism in novels such as *Daisy Miller* (1879). Samuel Clemens (Mark Twain) skillfully represented the language and culture of lower-class Mississippi in his novel *The Adventures of Huckleberry Finn* (1885).

SATIRE

Satire uses sarcasm, irony, and humor as social criticism to lampoon human folly. Unlike realism, which intends to depict reality as it exists without exaggeration, **satire** often involves creating situations or ideas that deliberately exaggerate reality to appear ridiculous to illuminate flawed behaviors. Ancient Roman satirists included Horace and Juvenal. Alexander Pope's poem "The Rape of the Lock" satirized the values of fashionable members of the 18th-century upper-middle class, which Pope found shallow and trivial. The theft of a lock of hair from a young woman is blown out of proportion: the poem's characters regard it as seriously as they would a rape. Irishman Jonathan Swift satirized British society, politics, and religion in works like "A Modest Proposal" and *Gulliver's Travels*. In "A Modest Proposal," Swift used essay form and mock-serious tone, satirically "proposing" cannibalism of babies and children as a solution to poverty and overpopulation. He satirized petty political disputes in *Gulliver's Travels*.

CHAPTER QUIZ

1. Which novel is credited as the origin of the *bildungsroman*, or the "education novel" genre?

    a. *Don Quixote*
    b. *Herzog*
    c. *Steppenwolf*
    d. *Wilhelm Meisters Lehrjahre*

2. Which of the following is considered to be a *roman à clef*, or a "novel with a key"?

    a. H. G. Wells' *The Dream* (1924)
    b. Jacques-Henri Bernardin de St. Pierre's *Paul et Virginie* (1787)
    c. George Orwell's *Animal Farm* (1945)
    d. Jean-Jacques Rousseau's *Nouvelle Héloïse* (1761)

CHAPTER QUIZ ANSWER KEY

1. D: *Bildungsroman* is German for "education novel." This term is also used in English to describe so-called "apprenticeship" novels focusing on coming-of-age stories, including youth's struggles and searches for things such as identity, spiritual understanding, or the meaning in life. Johann Wolfgang von Goethe's *Wilhelm Meisters Lehrjahre* (1796) is credited as the origin of this genre. Two of Charles Dickens' novels, *David Copperfield* (1850) and *Great Expectations* (1861), also fit this form. H. G. Wells wrote *bildungsromans* about questing for apprenticeships to address the complications of modern life in *Joan and Peter* (1918) and from a Utopian perspective in *The Dream* (1924). School *bildungsromans* include Thomas Hughes' *Tom Brown's School Days* (1857) and Alain-Fournier's *Le Grand Meaulnes* (1913). Many Hermann Hesse novels, including *Demian, Steppenwolf, Siddhartha, Magister Ludi,* and *Beneath the Wheel* are *bildungsromans* about a struggling, searching

Copyright © Mometrix Media. You have been licensed one copy of this document for personal use only. Any other reproduction or redistribution is strictly prohibited. All rights reserved.
This content is provided for test preparation purposes only and does not imply an endorsement by Mometrix of any particular political, scientific, or religious point of view.

youth. Samuel Butler's *The Way of All Flesh* (1903) and James Joyce's *A Portrait of the Artist as a Young Man* (1916) are two modern examples. Variations include J. D. Salinger's *The Catcher in the Rye* (1951), set both within and beyond school; and William Golding's *Lord of the Flies* (1955), a novel not set in a school but one that is a coming-of-age story nonetheless.

2. C: *Roman à clef* is French for "novel with a key." It refers to books that require a real-life frame of reference, or key, for full comprehension. In Geoffrey Chaucer's *Canterbury Tales,* the Nun's Priest's Tale contains details that confuse readers unaware of history about the Earl of Bolingbroke's involvement in an assassination plot. Other literary works fitting this form include John Dryden's political satirical poem "Absalom and Achitophel" (1681), Jonathan Swift's satire "A Tale of a Tub" (1704), and George Orwell's political allegory *Animal Farm* (1945), all of which cannot be understood completely without knowing their camouflaged historical contents. *Roman à clefs* disguise truths too dangerous for authors to state directly.

POETRY TERMINOLOGY

Unlike prose, which traditionally (except in forms like stream of consciousness) consists of complete sentences connected into paragraphs, poetry is written in **verses**. These may form complete sentences, clauses, or phrases. Poetry may be written with or without rhyme. It can be metered, following a particular rhythmic pattern such as iambic, dactylic, spondaic, trochaic, or **anapestic**, or may be without regular meter. The terms **iamb** and **trochee**, among others, identify stressed and unstressed syllables in each verse. Meter is also described by the number of beats or stressed syllables per verse: **dimeter** (2), **trimeter** (3), **tetrameter** (4), **pentameter** (5), and so forth. Using the symbol ∪ to denote unstressed and / to denote stressed syllables, **iambic** = ∪/; **trochaic** = /∪; **spondaic** =//; **dactylic** =/∪∪; **anapestic** =∪∪/. **Rhyme schemes** identify which lines rhyme, such as ABAB, ABCA, AABA, and so on. Poetry with neither rhyme nor meter is called **free verse**. Poems may be in free verse, metered but unrhymed, rhymed but without meter, or using both rhyme and meter. In English, the most common meter is iambic pentameter. Unrhymed iambic pentameter is called **blank verse**.

> **Review Video: <u>Different Types of Rhyme</u>**
> Visit mometrix.com/academy and enter code: 999342
>
> **Review Video: <u>Evocative Words and Rhythm</u>**
> Visit mometrix.com/academy and enter code: 894610

MAJOR FORMS OF POETRY

From man's earliest days, he expressed himself with poetry. A large percentage of the surviving literature from ancient times is in **epic poetry**, utilized by Homer and other Greco-Roman poets. Epic poems typically recount heroic deeds and adventures, using stylized language and combining dramatic and lyrical conventions. **Epistolary poems**, poems that are written and read as letters, also developed in ancient times. In the fourteenth and fifteenth centuries, the **ballad** became a popular convention. Ballads often follow a rhyme scheme and meter and focus on subjects such as love, death, and religion. Many ballads tell stories, and several modern ballads are put to music. From these early conventions, numerous other poetic forms developed, such as **elegies**, **odes**, and **pastoral poems**. Elegies are mourning poems written in three parts: lament, praise of the deceased, and solace for loss. Odes evolved from songs to the typical poem of the Romantic time period, expressing strong feelings and contemplative thoughts. Pastoral poems idealize nature and country living. Poetry can also be used to make short, pithy statements. **Epigrams** (memorable rhymes with one or two lines) and **limericks** (two lines of iambic dimeter followed by two lines of iambic dimeter and another of iambic trimeter) are known for humor and wit.

Copyright © Mometrix Media. You have been licensed one copy of this document for personal use only. Any other reproduction or redistribution is strictly prohibited. All rights reserved. This content is provided for test preparation purposes only and does not imply an endorsement by Mometrix of any particular political, scientific, or religious point of view.

HAIKU

Haiku was originally a Japanese poetry form. In the 13th century, haiku was the opening phrase of renga, a 100-stanza oral poem. By the 16th century, haiku diverged into a separate short poem. When Western writers discovered haiku, the form became popular in English, as well as other languages. A haiku has 17 syllables, traditionally distributed across three lines as 5/7/5, with a pause after the first or second line. Haiku are syllabic and unrhymed. Haiku philosophy and technique are that brevity's compression forces writers to express images concisely, depict a moment in time, and evoke illumination and enlightenment. An example is 17th-century haiku master Matsuo Basho's classic: "An old silent pond… / A frog jumps into the pond, / splash! Silence again." Modern American poet Ezra Pound revealed the influence of haiku in his two-line poem "In a Station of the Metro." In this poem, line 1 has 12 syllables (combining the syllable count of the first two lines of a haiku) and line 2 has 7, but it still preserves haiku's philosophy and imagistic technique: "The apparition of these faces in the crowd; / Petals on a wet, black bough."

SONNETS

The sonnet traditionally has 14 lines of iambic pentameter, tightly organized around a theme. The Petrarchan sonnet, named for 14th-century Italian poet Petrarch, has an eight-line stanza, the octave, and a six-line stanza, the sestet. There is a change or turn, known as the volta, between the eighth and ninth verses, setting up the sestet's answer or summary. The rhyme scheme is ABBA/ABBA/CDECDE or CDCDCD. The English or Shakespearean sonnet has three quatrains and one couplet, with the rhyme scheme ABAB/CDCD/EFEF/GG. This format better suits English, which has fewer rhymes than Italian. The final couplet often contrasts sharply with the preceding quatrains, as in Shakespeare's sonnets—for example, Sonnet 130, "My mistress' eyes are nothing like the sun…And yet, by heaven, I think my love as rare / As any she belied with false compare." Variations on the sonnet form include Edmund Spenser's Spenserian sonnet in the 16th century, John Milton's Miltonic sonnet in the 17th century, and sonnet sequences. Sonnet sequences are seen in works such as John Donne's *La Corona* and Elizabeth Barrett Browning's *Sonnets from the Portuguese*.

> **Review Video: Structural Elements of Poetry**
> Visit mometrix.com/academy and enter code: 265216

CARPE DIEM TRADITION IN POETRY

Carpe diem is Latin for "seize the day." A long poetic tradition, it advocates making the most of time because it passes swiftly and life is short. It is found in multiple languages, including Latin, Torquato Tasso's Italian, Pierre de Ronsard's French, and Edmund Spenser's English, and is often used in seduction to argue for indulging in earthly pleasures. Roman poet Horace's Ode 1.11 tells a younger woman, Leuconoe, to enjoy the present, not worrying about inevitable aging. Two Renaissance Metaphysical Poets, Andrew Marvell and Robert Herrick, treated *carpe diem* more as a call to action. In "To His Coy Mistress," Marvell points out that time is fleeting, arguing for love, and concluding that because they cannot stop time, they may as well defy it, getting the most out of the short time they have. In "To the Virgins, to Make Much of Time," Herrick advises young women to take advantage of their good fortune in being young by getting married before they become too old to attract men and have babies.

"To His Coy Mistress" begins, "Had we but world enough, and time, / This coyness, lady, were no crime." Using imagery, Andrew Marvell describes leisure they could enjoy if time were unlimited. Arguing for seduction, he continues famously, "But at my back I always hear/Time's winged chariot hurrying near; / And yonder all before us lie / Deserts of vast eternity." He depicts time as turning beauty to death and decay. Contradictory images in "amorous birds of prey" and "tear our pleasures

Copyright © Mometrix Media. You have been licensed one copy of this document for personal use only. Any other reproduction or redistribution is strictly prohibited. All rights reserved. This content is provided for test preparation purposes only and does not imply an endorsement by Mometrix of any particular political, scientific, or religious point of view.

with rough strife / Through the iron gates of life" overshadow romance with impending death, linking present pleasure with mortality and spiritual values with moral considerations. Marvell's concluding couplet summarizes *carpe diem*: "Thus, though we cannot make our sun / Stand still, yet we will make him run." "To the Virgins, to Make Much of Time" begins with the famous "Gather ye rosebuds while ye may." Rather than seduction to live for the present, Robert Herrick's experienced persona advises young women's future planning: "Old time is still a-flying / And this same flower that smiles today, / Tomorrow will be dying."

EFFECT OF STRUCTURE ON MEANING IN POETRY

The way a poem is structured can affect its meaning. Different structural choices can change the way a reader understands a poem, so poets are careful to ensure that the form they use reflects the message they want to convey. The main structural elements in poetry include **lines** and **stanzas**. The number of lines within a stanza and the number of stanzas vary between different poems, but some poetic forms require a poem to have a certain number of lines and stanzas. Some of these forms also require each line to conform to a certain meter, or number and pattern of syllables. Many forms are associated with a certain topic or tone because of their meter. Poetic forms include sonnets, concrete poems, haiku, and villanelles. Another popular form of poetry is free verse, which is poetry that does not conform to a particular meter or rhyme scheme.

The arrangement of lines and stanzas determines the speed at which a poem is read. Long lines are generally read more quickly since the reader is often eager to reach the end of the line and does not have to stop to find the next word. Short lines cause the reader to briefly pause and look to the next line, so their reading is slowed. These effects often contribute to the meaning a reader gleans from a poem, so poets aim to make the line length compatible with the tone of their message.

For example, Edgar Allan Poe's poem "The Raven" is written with mostly long lines. The poem's speaker experiences troubling events and becomes paranoid throughout the poem, and he narrates his racing thoughts. Poe's use of long lines leads the reader to read each line quickly, allowing their reading experience to resemble the thoughts of the narrator:

> Deep into that darkness peering, long I stood there wondering, fearing,
> Doubting, dreaming dreams no mortal ever dared to dream before;
>   But the silence was unbroken, and the stillness gave no token,
>   And the only word there spoken was the whispered word, "Lenore?"
> This I whispered, and an echo murmured back the word, "Lenore!"—
>   Merely this and nothing more.

The poem's meter also contributes to its tone, but consider the same stanza written using shorter lines:

> Deep into that darkness peering,
> long I stood there wondering, fearing,
> Doubting, dreaming dreams no mortal
> ever dared to dream before;
>   But the silence was unbroken,
> and the stillness gave no token,
>   And the only word there spoken
> was the whispered word, "Lenore?"
> This I whispered, and an echo
> murmured back the word, "Lenore!"—
>   Merely this and nothing more.

Copyright © Mometrix Media. You have been licensed one copy of this document for personal use only. Any other reproduction or redistribution is strictly prohibited. All rights reserved. This content is provided for test preparation purposes only and does not imply an endorsement by Mometrix of any particular political, scientific, or religious point of view.

Breaking the lines apart creates longer pauses and a slower, more suspenseful experience for the reader. While the tone of the poem is dark and suspense is appropriate, the longer lines allow Poe to emphasize and show the narrator's emotions. The narrator's emotions are more important to the poem's meaning than the creation of suspense, making longer lines more suitable in this case.

CONCRETE POETRY

A less common form of poetry is concrete poetry, also called shape poetry. **Concrete poems** are arranged so the full poem takes a shape that is relevant to the poem's message. For example, a concrete poem about the beach may be arranged to look like a palm tree. This contributes to a poem's meaning by influencing which aspect of the poem or message that the reader focuses on. In the beach poem example, the image of the palm tree leads the reader to focus on the poem's setting and visual imagery. The reader may also look for or anticipate the mention of a palm tree in the poem. This technique allows the poet to direct the reader's attention and emphasize a certain element of their work.

FREE VERSE

Free verse is a very common form of poetry. Because **free verse** poetry does not always incorporate meter or rhyme, it relies more heavily on punctuation and structure to influence the reader's experience and create emphasis. Free verse poetry makes strategic use of the length and number of both lines and stanzas. While meter and rhyme direct the flow and tone of other types of poems, poets of free verse pieces use the characteristics of lines and stanzas to establish flow and tone, instead.

Free verse also uses punctuation in each line to create flow and tone. The punctuation in each line directs the reader to pause after certain words, allowing the poet to emphasize specific ideas or images to clearly communicate their message. Similar to the effects of line length, the presence of punctuation at the end of a line can create pauses that affect a reader's pace. **End-stopped** lines, or lines with a punctuation mark at the end, create a pause that can contribute to the poem's flow or create emphasis. **Enjambed** lines, or lines that do not end with a punctuation mark, carry a sentence to the next line and create an effect similar to long lines. The use of enjambment can speed up a poem's flow and reflect an idea within the poem or contribute to tone.

POETIC STRUCTURE TO ENHANCE MEANING

The opening stanza of Romantic English poet, artist and printmaker William Blake's famous poem "The Tyger" demonstrates how a poet can create tension by using line length and punctuation independently of one another: "Tyger! Tyger! burning bright / In the forests of the night, / What immortal hand or eye / Could frame thy fearful symmetry?" The first three lines of this stanza are **trochaic** (/ ͜), with "masculine" endings—that is, strongly stressed syllables at the ends of each of the lines. But Blake's punctuation contradicts this rhythmic regularity by not providing any divisions between the words "bright" and "In" or between "eye" and "Could." This irregular punctuation foreshadows how Blake disrupts the meter at the end of this first stanza by using a contrasting **dactyl** (/ ͜ ͜), with a "feminine" (unstressed) ending syllable in the last word, "symmetry." Thus, Blake uses structural contrasts to heighten the intrigue of his work.

In enjambment, one sentence or clause in a poem does not end at the end of its line or verse, but runs over into the next line or verse. Clause endings coinciding with line endings give readers a feeling of completion, but enjambment influences readers to hurry to the next line to finish and understand the sentence. In his blank-verse epic religious poem "Paradise Lost," John Milton wrote: "Anon out of the earth a fabric huge / Rose like an exhalation, with the sound / Of dulcet symphonies and voices sweet, / Built like a temple, where pilasters round / Were set, and Doric

Copyright © Mometrix Media. You have been licensed one copy of this document for personal use only. Any other reproduction or redistribution is strictly prohibited. All rights reserved. This content is provided for test preparation purposes only and does not imply an endorsement by Mometrix of any particular political, scientific, or religious point of view.

pillars overlaid / With golden architrave." Only the third line is end-stopped. Milton, describing the palace of Pandemonium bursting from Hell up through the ground, reinforced this idea through phrases and clauses bursting through the boundaries of the lines. A **caesura** is a pause in mid-verse. Milton's commas in the third and fourth lines signal caesuras. They interrupt flow, making the narration jerky to imply that Satan's glorious-seeming palace has a shaky and unsound foundation.

COUPLETS AND METER TO ENHANCE MEANING IN POETRY

When a poet uses a couplet—a stanza of two lines, rhymed or unrhymed—it can function as the answer to a question asked earlier in the poem, or the solution to a problem or riddle. Couplets can also enhance the establishment of a poem's mood, or clarify the development of a poem's theme. Another device to enhance thematic development is irony, which also communicates the poet's tone and draws the reader's attention to a point the poet is making. The use of meter gives a poem a rhythmic context, contributes to the poem's flow, makes it more appealing to the reader, can represent natural speech rhythms, and produces specific effects. For example, in "The Song of Hiawatha," Henry Wadsworth Longfellow uses trochaic (/ ◡) tetrameter (four beats per line) to evoke for readers the rhythms of Native American chanting: "*By* the *shores* of *Gitch*e *Gum*ee, / *By* the *shin*ing *Big*-Sea-*Wat*er / *Stood* the *wig*wam *of* No*kom*is." (Italicized syllables are stressed; non-italicized syllables are unstressed.)

REFLECTION OF CONTENT THROUGH STRUCTURE

Wallace Stevens' short yet profound poem "The Snow Man" is reductionist: the snow man is a figure without human biases or emotions. Stevens begins, "One must have a mind of winter," the criterion for realizing nature and life does not inherently possess subjective qualities; we only invest it with these. Things are not as we see them; they simply are. The entire poem is one long sentence of clauses connected by conjunctions and commas, and modified by relative clauses and phrases. The successive phrases lead readers continually to reconsider as they read. Stevens' construction of the poem mirrors the meaning he conveys. With a mind of winter, the snow man, Stevens concludes, "nothing himself, beholds nothing that is not there, and the nothing that is."

CONTRAST OF CONTENT AND STRUCTURE

Robert Frost's poem "Stopping by Woods on a Snowy Evening" (1923) is deceptively short and simple, with only four stanzas, each of only four lines, and short and simple words. Reinforcing this is Frost's use of regular rhyme and meter. The rhythm is iambic tetrameter throughout; the rhyme scheme is AABA in the first three stanzas and AAAA in the fourth. In an additional internal subtlety, B ending "here" in the first stanza is rhymed with A endings "queer," "near," and "year" of the second; B ending "lake" in the second is rhymed in A endings "shake," "mistake," and "flake" of the third. The final stanza's AAAA endings reinforce the ultimate darker theme. Though the first three stanzas seem to describe quietly watching snow fill the woods, the last stanza evokes the seductive pull of mysterious death: "The woods are lovely, dark and deep," countered by the obligations of living life: "But I have promises to keep, / And miles to go before I sleep, / And miles to go before I sleep." The last line's repetition strengthens Frost's message that despite death's temptation, life's course must precede it.

EFFECTS OF FIGURATIVE DEVICES ON MEANING IN POETRY

Through exaggeration, **hyperbole** communicates the strength of a poet's or persona's feelings and enhances the mood of the poem. **Imagery** appeals to the reader's senses, creating vivid mental pictures, evoking reader emotions and responses, and helping to develop themes. **Irony** also aids thematic development by drawing the reader's attention to the poet's point and communicating the poem's tone. Thematic development is additionally supported by the comparisons of **metaphors**

Copyright © Mometrix Media. You have been licensed one copy of this document for personal use only. Any other reproduction or redistribution is strictly prohibited. All rights reserved.
This content is provided for test preparation purposes only and does not imply an endorsement by Mometrix of any particular political, scientific, or religious point of view.

and **similes**, which emphasize similarities, enhance imagery, and affect readers' perceptions. The use of **mood** communicates the atmosphere of a poem, builds a sense of tension, and evokes the reader's emotions. **Onomatopoeia** appeals to the reader's auditory sense and enhances sound imagery even when the poem is visual (read silently) rather than auditory (read aloud). **Rhyme** connects and unites verses, gives the rhyming words emphasis, and makes poems more fluent. **Symbolism** communicates themes, develops imagery, evokes readers' emotions, and elicits a response from the reader.

> **Review Video: What is Sensory Language?**
> Visit mometrix.com/academy and enter code: 177314

REPETITION TO ENHANCE MEANING

A **villanelle** is a nineteen-line poem composed of five tercets and one quatrain. The defining characteristic is the repetition: two lines appear repeatedly throughout the poem. In Theodore Roethke's "The Waking," the two repeated lines are "I wake to sleep, and take my waking slow," and "I learn by going where I have to go." At first these sound paradoxical, but the meaning is gradually revealed through the poem. The repetition also fits with the theme of cycle: the paradoxes of waking to sleep, learning by going, and thinking by feeling represent a constant cycle through life. They also symbolize abandoning conscious rationalism to embrace spiritual vision. We wake from the vision to "Great Nature," and "take the lively air." "This shaking keeps me steady"—another paradox—juxtaposes and balances fear of mortality with ecstasy in embracing experience. The transcendent vision of all life's interrelationship demonstrates, "What falls away is always. And is near." Readers experience the poem holistically, like music, through Roethke's integration of theme, motion, and sound.

Sylvia Plath's villanelle "Mad Girl's Love Song" narrows the scope from universal to personal but keeps the theme of cycle. The two repeated lines, "I shut my eyes and all the world drops dead" and "(I think I made you up inside my head.)" reflect the existential viewpoint that nothing exists in any absolute reality outside of our own perceptions. In the first stanza, the middle line, "I lift my lids and all is born again," in its recreating the world, bridges between the repeated refrain statements—one of obliterating reality, the other of having constructed her lover's existence. Unlike other villanelles wherein key lines are subtly altered in their repetitions, Plath repeats these exactly each time. This reflects the young woman's love, constant throughout the poem as it neither fades nor progresses.

CHAPTER QUIZ

1. Unrhymed iambic pentameter is also known as which of the following?

    a. Anapestic verse
    b. Sonnet
    c. Free verse
    d. Blank verse

2. Which of the following refers to a mid-verse pause that interrupts flow?

    a. Caesura
    b. Exeunt
    c. Soliloquy
    d. Enjambment

Copyright © Mometrix Media. You have been licensed one copy of this document for personal use only. Any other reproduction or redistribution is strictly prohibited. All rights reserved. This content is provided for test preparation purposes only and does not imply an endorsement by Mometrix of any particular political, scientific, or religious point of view.

3. A villanelle is a nineteen-line poem that consists of which of the following?

    a. Four tercets and two quatrains
    b. Five tercets and one quatrain
    c. Four couplets and four tercets
    d. Five couplets and three tercets

CHAPTER QUIZ ANSWER KEY

1. D: Poems may be in free verse, metered but unrhymed, rhymed but without meter, or using both rhyme and meter. In English, the most common meter is iambic pentameter. Unrhymed iambic pentameter is called blank verse.

2. A: A caesura is a pause in mid-verse.

3. B: A villanelle is a 19-line poem composed of five tercets and one quatrain. The defining characteristic is the repetition: two lines appear repeatedly throughout the poem.

EARLY DEVELOPMENT

English **drama** originally developed from religious ritual. Early Christians established traditions of presenting pageants or mystery plays, traveling on wagons and carts through the streets to depict Biblical events. Medieval tradition assigned responsibility for performing specific plays to the different guilds. In Middle English, "mystery" referred to craft, or trade, and religious ritual and truth. Historically, mystery plays were to be reproduced exactly the same every time they were performed, like religious rituals. However, some performers introduced individual interpretations of roles and even improvised. Thus, drama was born. Narrative detail and nuanced acting were evident in mystery cycles by the Middle Ages. As individualized performance evolved, plays on other subjects also developed. Middle English mystery plays that still exist include the York Cycle, Coventry Cycle, Chester Mystery Plays, N-Town Plays, and Towneley/Wakefield Plays. In recent times, these plays began to draw interest again, and several modern actors, such as Dame Judi Dench, began their careers with mystery plays.

> **Review Video: Dramas**
> Visit mometrix.com/academy and enter code: 216060

DEFINING CHARACTERISTICS

In the Middle Ages, plays were commonly composed in **verse**. By the time of the Renaissance, Shakespeare and other dramatists wrote plays that mixed **prose**, **rhymed verse**, and **blank verse**. The traditions of costumes and masks were seen in ancient Greek drama, medieval mystery plays, and Renaissance drama. Conventions like **asides**, in which actors make comments directly to the audience unheard by other characters, and **soliloquies** were also common during Shakespeare's Elizabethan dramatic period. **Monologues** date back to ancient Greek drama. Elizabethan dialogue tended to use colloquial prose for lower-class characters' speech and stylized verse for upper-class characters. Another Elizabethan convention was the play-within-a-play, as in *Hamlet.* As drama moved toward realism, dialogue became less poetic and more conversational, as in most modern English-language plays. Contemporary drama, both onstage and onscreen, includes a convention of **breaking the fourth wall**, as actors directly face and address audiences.

COMEDY

Today, most people equate the idea of **comedy** with something funny, and of **tragedy** with something sad. However, the ancient Greeks defined these differently. Comedy needed not be humorous or amusing; it needed only a happy ending. The classical definition of comedy, as

Copyright © Mometrix Media. You have been licensed one copy of this document for personal use only. Any other reproduction or redistribution is strictly prohibited. All rights reserved.
This content is provided for test preparation purposes only and does not imply an endorsement by Mometrix of any particular political, scientific, or religious point of view.

included in Aristotle's works, is any work that tells the story of a sympathetic main character's rise in fortune. According to Aristotle, protagonists need not be heroic or exemplary, nor evil or worthless, but ordinary people of unremarkable morality. Comic figures who were sympathetic were usually of humble origins, proving their "natural nobility" through their actions as they were tested. Characters born into nobility were often satirized as self-important or pompous.

SHAKESPEAREAN COMEDY

William Shakespeare lived in England from 1564-1616. He was a poet and playwright of the Renaissance period in Western culture. He is generally considered the foremost dramatist in world literature and the greatest author to write in the English language. He wrote many poems, particularly sonnets, of which 154 survive today, and approximately 38 plays. Though his sonnets are greater in number and are very famous, he is best known for his plays, including comedies, tragedies, tragicomedies and historical plays. His play titles include: *All's Well That Ends Well, As You Like It, The Comedy of Errors, Love's Labour's Lost, Measure for Measure, The Merchant of Venice, The Merry Wives of Windsor, A Midsummer Night's Dream, Much Ado About Nothing, The Taming of the Shrew, The Tempest, Twelfth Night, The Two Gentlemen of Verona, The Winter's Tale, King John, Richard II, Henry IV, Henry V, Richard III, Romeo and Juliet, Coriolanus, Titus Andronicus, Julius Caesar, Macbeth, Hamlet, Troilus and Cressida, King Lear, Othello, Antony and Cleopatra,* and *Cymbeline.* Some scholars have suggested that Christopher Marlowe wrote several of Shakespeare's works. While most scholars reject this theory, Shakespeare did pay homage to Marlowe, alluding to several of his characters, themes, or verbiage, as well as borrowing themes from several of his plays (e.g., Marlowe's *Jew of Malta* influenced Shakespeare's *Merchant of Venice*).

When Shakespeare was writing, during the Elizabethan period of the Renaissance, Aristotle's version of comedies was popular. While some of Shakespeare's comedies were humorous and others were not, all had happy endings. *A Comedy of Errors* is a farce. Based and expanding on a Classical Roman comedy, it is lighthearted and includes slapstick humor and mistaken identity. *Much Ado About Nothing* is a romantic comedy. It incorporates some more serious themes, including social mores, perceived infidelity, marriage's duality as both trap and ideal, honor and its loss, public shame, and deception, but also much witty dialogue and a happy ending.

DRAMATIC COMEDY

Three types of dramas classified as comedy include the farce, the romantic comedy, and the satirical comedy.

FARCE

The **farce** is a zany, goofy type of comedy that includes pratfalls and other forms of slapstick humor. The characters in a farce tend to be ridiculous or fantastical in nature. The plot also tends to contain highly improbable events, featuring complications and twists that continue throughout, and incredible coincidences that would likely never occur in reality. Mistaken identity, deceptions, and disguises are common devices used in farcical comedies. Shakespeare's play *The Comedy of Errors,* with its cases of accidental mistaken identity and slapstick, is an example of farce. Contemporary examples of farce include the Marx Brothers' movies, the Three Stooges movies and TV episodes, and the *Pink Panther* movie series.

ROMANTIC COMEDY

Romantic comedies are probably the most popular of the types of comedy, in both live theater performances and movies. They include not only humor and a happy ending, but also love. In the typical plot of a **romantic comedy**, two people well suited to one another are either brought together for the first time, or reconciled after being separated. They are usually both sympathetic

Copyright © Mometrix Media. You have been licensed one copy of this document for personal use only. Any other reproduction or redistribution is strictly prohibited. All rights reserved. This content is provided for test preparation purposes only and does not imply an endorsement by Mometrix of any particular political, scientific, or religious point of view.

characters and seem destined to be together, yet they are separated by some intervening complication, such as ex-lovers, interfering parents or friends, or differences in social class. The happy ending is achieved through the lovers overcoming all these obstacles. William Shakespeare's *Much Ado About Nothing*, Walt Disney's version of *Cinderella* (1950), and Broadway musical *Guys and Dolls* (1955) are example of romantic comedies. Many live-action movies are also examples of romantic comedies, such as *The Princess Bride* (1987), *Sleepless in Seattle* (1993), *You've Got Mail* (1998), and *Forget Paris* (1995).

SATIRICAL COMEDY AND BLACK COMEDY

Satires generally mock and lampoon human foolishness and vices. **Satirical comedies** fit the classical definition of comedy by depicting a main character's rise in fortune, but they also fit the definition of satire by making that main character either a fool, morally corrupt, or cynical in attitude. All or most of the other characters in the satirical comedy display similar foibles. These include gullible types, such as cuckolded spouses and dupes, and deceptive types, such as tricksters, con artists, criminals, hypocrites, and fortune seekers, who prey on the gullible. Some classical examples of satirical comedies include *The Birds* by ancient Greek comedic playwright Aristophanes, and *Volpone* by 17th-century poet and playwright Ben Jonson, who made the comedy of humors popular. When satirical comedy is extended to extremes, it becomes **black comedy**, wherein the comedic occurrences are grotesque or terrible.

TRAGEDY

The opposite of comedy is tragedy, portraying a hero's fall in fortune. While by classical definitions, tragedies could be sad, Aristotle went further, requiring that they depict suffering and pain to cause "terror and pity" in audiences. Additionally, he decreed that tragic heroes be basically good, admirable, or noble, and that their downfalls result from personal action, choice, or error, not by bad luck or accident.

ARISTOTLE'S CRITERIA FOR TRAGEDY

In his *Poetics,* Aristotle defined five critical terms relative to tragedy:

- *Anagnorisis*: Meaning tragic insight or recognition, this is a moment of realization by a tragic hero or heroine that he or she has become enmeshed in a "web of fate."
- *Hamartia*: This is often called a "tragic flaw," but is better described as a tragic error. *Hamartia* is an archery term meaning a shot missing the bull's eye, used here as a metaphor for a mistake—often a simple one—which results in catastrophe.
- *Hubris*: While often called "pride," this is actually translated as "violent transgression," and signifies an arrogant overstepping of moral or cultural bounds—the sin of the tragic hero who over-presumes or over-aspires.
- *Nemesis*: translated as "retribution," this represents the cosmic punishment or payback that the tragic hero ultimately receives for committing hubristic acts.
- *Peripateia*: Literally "turning," this is a plot reversal consisting of a tragic hero's pivotal action, which changes his or her status from safe to endangered.

HEGEL'S THEORY OF TRAGEDY

Georg Wilhelm Friedrich Hegel (1770-1831) proposed a different theory of tragedy than Aristotle (384-322 BC), which was also very influential. Whereas Aristotle's criteria involved character and plot, Hegel defined tragedy as a dynamic conflict of opposite forces or rights. For example, if an individual believes in the moral philosophy of the conscientious objector (i.e., that fighting in wars is morally wrong) but is confronted with being drafted into military service, this conflict would fit Hegel's definition of a tragic plot premise. Hegel theorized that a tragedy must involve some

Copyright © Mometrix Media. You have been licensed one copy of this document for personal use only. Any other reproduction or redistribution is strictly prohibited. All rights reserved. This content is provided for test preparation purposes only and does not imply an endorsement by Mometrix of any particular political, scientific, or religious point of view.

circumstance in which two values, or two rights, are fatally at odds with one another and conflict directly. Hegel did not view this as good triumphing over evil, or evil winning out over good, but rather as one good fighting against another good unto death. He saw this conflict of two goods as truly tragic. In ancient Greek playwright Sophocles' tragedy *Antigone,* the main character experiences this tragic conflict between her public duties and her family and religious responsibilities.

REVENGE TRAGEDY

Along with Aristotelian definitions of comedy and tragedy, ancient Greece was the origin of the **revenge tragedy**. This genre became highly popular in Renaissance England, and is still popular today in contemporary movies. In a revenge tragedy, the protagonist has suffered a serious wrong, such as the murder of a family member. However, the wrongdoer has not been punished. In contemporary plots, this often occurs when some legal technicality has interfered with the miscreant's conviction and sentencing, or when authorities are unable to locate and apprehend the criminal. The protagonist then faces the conflict of suffering this injustice, or exacting his or her own justice by seeking revenge. Greek revenge tragedies include *Agamemnon* and *Medea.* Playwright Thomas Kyd's *The Spanish Tragedy* (1582-1592) is credited with beginning the Elizabethan genre of revenge tragedies. Shakespearean revenge tragedies include *Hamlet* (1599-1602) and *Titus Andronicus* (1588-1593). A Jacobean example is Thomas Middleton's *The Revenger's Tragedy* (1606, 1607).

HAMLET'S "TRAGIC FLAW"

Despite virtually limitless interpretations, one way to view Hamlet's tragic error generally is as indecision. He suffers the classic revenge tragedy's conflict of whether to suffer with his knowledge of his mother's and uncle's assassination of his father, or to exact his own revenge and justice against Claudius, who has assumed the throne after his crime went unknown and unpunished. Hamlet's famous soliloquy, "To be or not to be" reflects this dilemma. Hamlet muses "Whether 'tis nobler in the mind to suffer the slings and arrows of outrageous fortune, / Or to take arms against a sea of troubles, / And by opposing end them?" Hamlet both longs for and fears death, as "the dread of something after death ... makes us rather bear those ills we have / Than fly to others that we know not ... Thus, conscience does make cowards of us all." For most of the play, Hamlet struggles with his responsibility to avenge his father, who was killed by Hamlet's uncle, Claudius. So, Hamlet's tragic error at first might be considered a lack of action. But he then makes several attempts at revenge, each of which end in worse tragedy, until his efforts are ended by the final tragedy—Hamlet's own death.

CHAPTER QUIZ

1. How many critical terms relative to tragedy did Aristotle outline?

    a. Five
    b. Six
    c. Seven
    d. Eight

2. Who theorized that a tragedy must involve some circumstance in which two values, or two rights, are fatally at odds with one another and conflict directly?

    a. Aristophanes
    b. Hegel
    c. Shakespeare
    d. Marlowe

Copyright © Mometrix Media. You have been licensed one copy of this document for personal use only. Any other reproduction or redistribution is strictly prohibited. All rights reserved. This content is provided for test preparation purposes only and does not imply an endorsement by Mometrix of any particular political, scientific, or religious point of view.

Chapter Quiz Answer Key

1. A: In his *Poetics,* Aristotle defined five critical terms relative to tragedy.

- Anagnorisis: A tragic insight or recognition; a moment of realization by a tragic hero or heroine that he or she has become enmeshed in a "web of fate."
- Hamartia: Often called a "tragic flaw," but better described as a tragic error. *Hamartia* is an archery term meaning a shot missing the bull's eye, used here as a metaphor for a mistake—often a simple one—that results in catastrophe.
- Hubris: Often equated with pride, *hubris* in this context is actually translated as "violent transgression" and signifies an arrogant overstepping of moral or cultural bounds—the sin of the tragic hero who over-presumes or over-aspires.
- Nemesis: Translated as "retribution," this represents the cosmic punishment or payback that the tragic hero ultimately receives for committing hubristic acts.
- Peripateia: Literally "turning," this is a plot reversal consisting of a tragic hero's pivotal action, which changes his or her status from safe to endangered.

2. B: Georg Wilhelm Friedrich Hegel (1770-1831) proposed a different theory of tragedy than Aristotle (384-322 BC), which was also very influential. Whereas Aristotle's criteria involved character and plot, Hegel defined tragedy as a dynamic conflict of opposite forces or rights. For example, if an individual believes in the moral philosophy of the conscientious objector (i.e., that fighting in wars is morally wrong) but is confronted with being drafted into military service, this conflict would fit Hegel's definition of a tragic plot premise. Hegel theorized that a tragedy must involve some circumstance in which two values (or two rights) are fatally at odds with one another and conflict directly. Hegel did not view this as good triumphing over evil, or evil winning out over good, but rather as one good fighting against another good unto death. He saw this conflict of two goods as truly tragic. In ancient Greek playwright Sophocles' tragedy *Antigone,* the main character experiences this tragic conflict between her public duties and her family and religious responsibilities.

Text Features in Informational Texts

The **title of a text** gives readers some idea of its content. The **table of contents** is a list near the beginning of a text, showing the book's sections and chapters and their coinciding page numbers. This gives readers an overview of the whole text and helps them find specific chapters easily. An **appendix**, at the back of the book or document, includes important information that is not present in the main text. Also at the back, an **index** lists the book's important topics alphabetically with their page numbers to help readers find them easily. **Glossaries**, usually found at the backs of books, list technical terms alphabetically with their definitions to aid vocabulary learning and comprehension. Boldface print is used to emphasize certain words, often identifying words included in the text's glossary where readers can look up their definitions. **Headings** separate sections of text and show the topic of each. **Subheadings** divide subject headings into smaller, more specific categories to help readers organize information. **Footnotes**, at the bottom of the page, give readers more information, such as citations or links. **Bullet points** list items separately, making facts and ideas easier to see and understand. A **sidebar** is a box of information to one side of the main text giving additional information, often on a more focused or in-depth example of a topic.

Illustrations and **photographs** are pictures that visually emphasize important points in text. The captions below the illustrations explain what those images show. Charts and tables are visual forms of information that make something easier to understand quickly. Diagrams are drawings that show relationships or explain a process. Graphs visually show the relationships among multiple sets of information plotted along vertical and horizontal axes. Maps show geographical information

Copyright © Mometrix Media. You have been licensed one copy of this document for personal use only. Any other reproduction or redistribution is strictly prohibited. All rights reserved.
This content is provided for test preparation purposes only and does not imply an endorsement by Mometrix of any particular political, scientific, or religious point of view.

visually to help readers understand the relative locations of places covered in the text. Timelines are visual graphics that show historical events in chronological order to help readers see their sequence.

Review Video: Informative Text
Visit mometrix.com/academy and enter code: 924964

LANGUAGE USE
LITERAL AND FIGURATIVE LANGUAGE

As in fictional literature, informational text also uses both **literal language**, which means just what it says, and **figurative language**, which imparts more than literal meaning. For example, an informational text author might use a simile or direct comparison, such as writing that a racehorse "ran like the wind." Informational text authors also use metaphors or implied comparisons, such as "the cloud of the Great Depression." Imagery may also appear in informational texts to increase the reader's understanding of ideas and concepts discussed in the text.

EXPLICIT AND IMPLICIT INFORMATION

When informational text states something explicitly, the reader is told by the author exactly what is meant, which can include the author's interpretation or perspective of events. For example, a professor writes, "I have seen students go into an absolute panic just because they weren't able to complete the exam in the time they were allotted." This explicitly tells the reader that the students were afraid, and by using the words "just because," the writer indicates their fear was exaggerated out of proportion relative to what happened. However, another professor writes, "I have had students come to me, their faces drained of all color, saying 'We weren't able to finish the exam.'" This is an example of implicit meaning: the second writer did not state explicitly that the students were panicked. Instead, he wrote a description of their faces being "drained of all color." From this description, the reader can infer that the students were so frightened that their faces paled.

Review Video: Explicit and Implicit Information
Visit mometrix.com/academy and enter code: 735771

TECHNICAL LANGUAGE

Technical language is more impersonal than literary and vernacular language. Passive voice makes the tone impersonal. For example, instead of writing, "We found this a central component of protein metabolism," scientists write, "This was found a central component of protein metabolism." While science professors have traditionally instructed students to avoid active voice because it leads to first-person ("I" and "we") usage, science editors today find passive voice dull and weak. Many journal articles combine both. Tone in technical science writing should be detached, concise, and professional. While one may normally write, "This chemical has to be available for proteins to be digested," professionals write technically, "The presence of this chemical is required for the enzyme to break the covalent bonds of proteins." The use of technical language appeals to both technical and non-technical audiences by displaying the author or speaker's understanding of the subject and suggesting their credibility regarding the message they are communicating.

TECHNICAL MATERIAL FOR NON-TECHNICAL READERS

Writing about **technical subjects** for **non-technical readers** differs from writing for colleagues because authors place more importance on delivering a critical message than on imparting the maximum technical content possible. Technical authors also must assume that non-technical audiences do not have the expertise to comprehend extremely scientific or technical messages,

Copyright © Mometrix Media. You have been licensed one copy of this document for personal use only. Any other reproduction or redistribution is strictly prohibited. All rights reserved.
This content is provided for test preparation purposes only and does not imply an endorsement by Mometrix of any particular political, scientific, or religious point of view.

concepts, and terminology. They must resist the temptation to impress audiences with their scientific knowledge and expertise and remember that their primary purpose is to communicate a message that non-technical readers will understand, feel, and respond to. Non-technical and technical styles include similarities. Both should formally cite any references or other authors' work utilized in the text. Both must follow intellectual property and copyright regulations. This includes the author's protecting his or her own rights, or a public domain statement, as he or she chooses.

> **Review Video: Technical Passages**
> Visit mometrix.com/academy and enter code: 478923

NON-TECHNICAL AUDIENCES

Writers of technical or scientific material may need to write for many non-technical audiences. Some readers have no technical or scientific background, and those who do may not be in the same field as the authors. Government and corporate policymakers and budget managers need technical information they can understand for decision-making. Citizens affected by technology or science are a different audience. Non-governmental organizations can encompass many of the preceding groups. Elementary and secondary school programs also need non-technical language for presenting technical subject matter. Additionally, technical authors will need to use non-technical language when collecting consumer responses to surveys, presenting scientific or para-scientific material to the public, writing about the history of science, and writing about science and technology in developing countries.

USE OF EVERYDAY LANGUAGE

Authors of technical information sometimes must write using non-technical language that readers outside their disciplinary fields can comprehend. They should use not only non-technical terms, but also normal, everyday language to accommodate readers whose native language is different than the language the text is written in. For example, instead of writing that "eustatic changes like thermal expansion are causing hazardous conditions in the littoral zone," an author would do better to write that "a rising sea level is threatening the coast." When technical terms cannot be avoided, authors should also define or explain them using non-technical language. Although authors must cite references and acknowledge their use of others' work, they should avoid the kinds of references or citations that they would use in scientific journals—unless they reinforce author messages. They should not use endnotes, footnotes, or any other complicated referential techniques because non-technical journal publishers usually do not accept them. Including high-resolution illustrations, photos, maps, or satellite images and incorporating multimedia into digital publications will enhance non-technical writing about technical subjects. Technical authors may publish using non-technical language in e-journals, trade journals, specialty newsletters, and daily newspapers.

MAKING INFERENCES ABOUT INFORMATIONAL TEXT

With informational text, reader comprehension depends not only on recalling important statements and details, but also on reader inferences based on examples and details. Readers add information from the text to what they already know to draw inferences about the text. These inferences help the readers to fill in the information that the text does not explicitly state, enabling them to understand the text better. When reading a nonfictional autobiography or biography, for example, the most appropriate inferences might concern the events in the book, the actions of the subject of the autobiography or biography, and the message the author means to convey. When reading a nonfictional expository (informational) text, the reader would best draw inferences about problems and their solutions, and causes and their effects. When reading a nonfictional persuasive text, the reader will want to infer ideas supporting the author's message and intent.

Copyright © Mometrix Media. You have been licensed one copy of this document for personal use only. Any other reproduction or redistribution is strictly prohibited. All rights reserved. This content is provided for test preparation purposes only and does not imply an endorsement by Mometrix of any particular political, scientific, or religious point of view.

STRUCTURES OR ORGANIZATIONAL PATTERNS IN INFORMATIONAL TEXTS

Informational text can be **descriptive**, appealing to the five senses and answering the questions what, who, when, where, and why. Another method of structuring informational text is sequence and order. **Chronological** texts relate events in the sequence that they occurred, from start to finish, while how-to texts organize information into a series of instructions in the sequence in which the steps should be followed. **Comparison-contrast** structures of informational text describe various ideas to their readers by pointing out how things or ideas are similar and how they are different. **Cause and effect** structures of informational text describe events that occurred and identify the causes or reasons that those events occurred. **Problem and solution** structures of informational texts introduce and describe problems and offer one or more solutions for each problem described.

DETERMINING AN INFORMATIONAL AUTHOR'S PURPOSE

Informational authors' purposes are why they write texts. Readers must determine authors' motivations and goals. Readers gain greater insight into a text by considering the author's motivation. This develops critical reading skills. Readers perceive writing as a person's voice, not simply printed words. Uncovering author motivations and purposes empowers readers to know what to expect from the text, read for relevant details, evaluate authors and their work critically, and respond effectively to the motivations and persuasions of the text. The main idea of a text is what the reader is supposed to understand from reading it; the purpose of the text is why the author has written it and what the author wants readers to do with its information. Authors state some purposes clearly, while other purposes may be unstated but equally significant. When stated purposes contradict other parts of a text, the author may have a hidden agenda. Readers can better evaluate a text's effectiveness, whether they agree or disagree with it, and why they agree or disagree through identifying unstated author purposes.

IDENTIFYING AUTHOR'S POINT OF VIEW OR PURPOSE

In some informational texts, readers find it easy to identify the author's point of view and purpose, such as when the author explicitly states his or her position and reason for writing. But other texts are more difficult, either because of the content or because the authors give neutral or balanced viewpoints. This is particularly true in scientific texts, in which authors may state the purpose of their research in the report, but never state their point of view except by interpreting evidence or data.

To analyze text and identify point of view or purpose, readers should ask themselves the following four questions:

1. With what main point or idea does this author want to persuade readers to agree?
2. How does this author's word choice affect the way that readers consider this subject?
3. How do this author's choices of examples and facts affect the way that readers consider this subject?
4. What is it that this author wants to accomplish by writing this text?

Review Video: <u>Understanding the Author's Intent</u>
Visit mometrix.com/academy and enter code: 511819
Review Video: <u>Author's Position</u>
Visit mometrix.com/academy and enter code: 827954

Copyright © Mometrix Media. You have been licensed one copy of this document for personal use only. Any other reproduction or redistribution is strictly prohibited. All rights reserved. This content is provided for test preparation purposes only and does not imply an endorsement by Mometrix of any particular political, scientific, or religious point of view.

EVALUATING ARGUMENTS MADE BY INFORMATIONAL TEXT WRITERS

When evaluating an informational text, the first step is to identify the argument's conclusion. Then identify the author's premises that support the conclusion. Try to paraphrase premises for clarification and make the conclusion and premises fit. List all premises first, sequentially numbered, then finish with the conclusion. Identify any premises or assumptions not stated by the author but required for the stated premises to support the conclusion. Read word assumptions sympathetically, as the author might. Evaluate whether premises reasonably support the conclusion. For inductive reasoning, the reader should ask if the premises are true, if they support the conclusion, and if so, how strongly. For deductive reasoning, the reader should ask if the argument is valid or invalid. If all premises are true, then the argument is valid unless the conclusion can be false. If it can, then the argument is invalid. An invalid argument can be made valid through alterations such as the addition of needed premises.

USE OF RHETORIC IN INFORMATIONAL TEXTS

There are many ways authors can support their claims, arguments, beliefs, ideas, and reasons for writing in informational texts. For example, authors can appeal to readers' sense of **logic** by communicating their reasoning through a carefully sequenced series of logical steps to help "prove" the points made. Authors can appeal to readers' **emotions** by using descriptions and words that evoke feelings of sympathy, sadness, anger, righteous indignation, hope, happiness, or any other emotion to reinforce what they express and share with their audience. Authors may appeal to the **moral** or **ethical values** of readers by using words and descriptions that can convince readers that something is right or wrong. By relating personal anecdotes, authors can supply readers with more accessible, realistic examples of points they make, as well as appealing to their emotions. They can provide supporting evidence by reporting case studies. They can also illustrate their points by making analogies to which readers can better relate.

CHAPTER QUIZ

1. Which of the following is the first step in evaluating an informational text?
   a. Read word assumptions sympathetically
   b. List all premises sequentially
   c. Determine if the premises are true
   d. Identify the argument's conclusion

2. Which of the following is NOT considered a type of appeal for an author to use?
   a. Logic
   b. Ethics
   c. Emotions
   d. Imagination

CHAPTER QUIZ ANSWER KEY

1. D: When evaluating an informational text, the first step is to identify the argument's conclusion. After that comes identifying the author's premises that support the conclusion. The reader should try to paraphrase premises for clarification and make the conclusion and premises fit. List all premises first, sequentially numbered, then finish with the conclusion. Identify any premises or assumptions not stated by the author but required for the stated premises to support the conclusion. Read word assumptions sympathetically, as the author might. Evaluate whether premises reasonably support the conclusion. For inductive reasoning, the reader should ask if the premises are true, if they support the conclusion, and how strong that support is. For deductive reasoning, the reader should ask if the argument is valid or invalid. If all premises are true, then the

Copyright © Mometrix Media. You have been licensed one copy of this document for personal use only. Any other reproduction or redistribution is strictly prohibited. All rights reserved. This content is provided for test preparation purposes only and does not imply an endorsement by Mometrix of any particular political, scientific, or religious point of view.

argument is valid unless the conclusion can be false. If it can, then the argument is invalid. An invalid argument can be made valid through alterations such as the addition of needed premises.

2. D: There are many ways authors can support their claims, arguments, beliefs, ideas, and reasons for writing in informational texts. For example, authors can appeal to readers' sense of logic by communicating their reasoning through a carefully sequenced series of logical steps to support their positions. Authors can appeal to readers' emotions by using descriptions and words that evoke feelings of sympathy, sadness, anger, righteous indignation, hope, happiness, or any other emotion to reinforce what they express and share with their audience. Authors may appeal to the moral or ethical values of readers by using words and descriptions that can convince readers that something is right or wrong. By relating personal anecdotes, authors can appeal to readers' emotions and supply them with more accessible, realistic examples of points they make. They can provide supporting evidence by reporting case studies. They can also illustrate their points by making analogies to which readers can better relate.

PERSUASIVE TECHNIQUES

To **appeal using reason**, writers present logical arguments, such as using "If... then... because" statements. To **appeal to emotions**, authors may ask readers how they would feel about something or to put themselves in another's place, present their argument as one that will make the audience feel good, or tell readers how they should feel. To **appeal to character**, **morality**, or **ethics**, authors present their points to readers as the right or most moral choices. Authors cite expert opinions to show readers that someone very knowledgeable about the subject or viewpoint agrees with the author's claims. **Testimonials**, usually via anecdotes or quotations regarding the author's subject, help build the audience's trust in an author's message through positive support from ordinary people. **Bandwagon appeals** claim that everybody else agrees with the author's argument and persuade readers to conform and agree, also. Authors **appeal to greed** by presenting their choice as cheaper, free, or more valuable for less cost. They **appeal to laziness** by presenting their views as more convenient, easy, or relaxing. Authors also anticipate potential objections and argue against them before audiences think of them, thereby depicting those objections as weak.

Authors can use **comparisons** like analogies, similes, and metaphors to persuade audiences. For example, a writer might represent excessive expenses as "hemorrhaging" money, which the author's recommended solution will stop. Authors can use negative word connotations to make some choices unappealing to readers, and positive word connotations to make others more appealing. Using **humor** can relax readers and garner their agreement. However, writers must take care: ridiculing opponents can be a successful strategy for appealing to readers who already agree with the author, but can backfire by angering other readers. **Rhetorical questions** need no answer, but create effect that can force agreement, such as asking the question, "Wouldn't you rather be paid more than less?" **Generalizations** persuade readers by being impossible to disagree with. Writers can easily make generalizations that appear to support their viewpoints, like saying, "We all want peace, not war" regarding more specific political arguments. **Transfer** and **association** persuade by example: if advertisements show attractive actors enjoying their products, audiences imagine they will experience the same. **Repetition** can also sometimes effectively persuade audiences.

> **Review Video: Using Rhetorical Strategies for Persuasion**
> Visit mometrix.com/academy and enter code: 302658

Copyright © Mometrix Media. You have been licensed one copy of this document for personal use only. Any other reproduction or redistribution is strictly prohibited. All rights reserved. This content is provided for test preparation purposes only and does not imply an endorsement by Mometrix of any particular political, scientific, or religious point of view.

CLASSICAL AUTHOR APPEALS

In his *On Rhetoric,* ancient Greek philosopher Aristotle defined three basic types of appeal used in writing, which he called *pathos, ethos,* and *logos.* **Pathos** means suffering or experience and refers to appeals to the emotions (the English word *pathetic* comes from this root). Writing that is meant to entertain audiences, by making them either happy, as with comedy, or sad, as with tragedy, uses *pathos.* Aristotle's *Poetics* states that evoking the emotions of terror and pity is one of the criteria for writing tragedy. **Ethos** means character and connotes ideology (the English word *ethics* comes from this root). Writing that appeals to credibility, based on academic, professional, or personal merit, uses *ethos.* **Logos** means "I say" and refers to a plea, opinion, expectation, word or speech, account, opinion, or reason (the English word *logic* comes from this root.) Aristotle used it to mean persuasion that appeals to the audience through reasoning and logic to influence their opinions.

CRITICAL EVALUATION OF EFFECTIVENESS OF PERSUASIVE METHODS

First, readers should identify the author's **thesis**—what he or she argues for or against. They should consider the argument's content and the author's reason for presenting it. Does the author offer **solutions** to problems raised? If so, are they realistic? Note all central ideas and evidence supporting the author's thesis. Research any unfamiliar subjects or vocabulary. Readers should then outline or summarize the work in their own words. Identify which types of appeals the author uses. Readers should evaluate how well the author communicated meaning from the reader's perspective: Did they respond to emotional appeals with anger, concern, happiness, etc.? If so, why? Decide if the author's reasoning sufficed for changing the reader's mind. Determine whether the content and presentation were accurate, cohesive, and clear. Readers should also ask themselves whether they found the author believable or not, and why or why not.

EVALUATING AN ARGUMENT

Argumentative and persuasive passages take a stand on a debatable issue, seek to explore all sides of the issue, and find the best possible solution. Argumentative and persuasive passages should not be combative or abusive. The word *argument* may remind you of two or more people shouting at each other and walking away in anger. However, an argumentative or persuasive passage should be a calm and reasonable presentation of an author's ideas for others to consider. When an author writes reasonable arguments, his or her goal is not to win or have the last word. Instead, authors want to reveal current understanding of the question at hand and suggest a solution to a problem. The purpose of argument and persuasion in a free society is to reach the best solution.

EVIDENCE

The term **text evidence** refers to information that supports a main point or minor points and can help lead the reader to a conclusion about the text's credibility. Information used as text evidence is precise, descriptive, and factual. A main point is often followed by supporting details that provide evidence to back up a claim. For example, a passage may include the claim that winter occurs during opposite months in the Northern and Southern hemispheres. Text evidence for this claim may include examples of countries where winter occurs in opposite months. Stating that the tilt of the Earth as it rotates around the sun causes winter to occur at different times in separate hemispheres is another example of text evidence. Text evidence can come from common knowledge, but it is also valuable to include text evidence from credible, relevant outside sources.

> **Review Video: Textual Evidence**
> Visit mometrix.com/academy and enter code: 486236

Evidence that supports the thesis and additional arguments needs to be provided. Most arguments must be supported by facts or statistics. A fact is something that is known with certainty, has been

Copyright © Mometrix Media. You have been licensed one copy of this document for personal use only. Any other reproduction or redistribution is strictly prohibited. All rights reserved.
This content is provided for test preparation purposes only and does not imply an endorsement by Mometrix of any particular political, scientific, or religious point of view.

verified by several independent individuals, and can be proven to be true. In addition to facts, examples and illustrations can support an argument by adding an emotional component. With this component, you persuade readers in ways that facts and statistics cannot. The emotional component is effective when used alongside objective information that can be confirmed.

CREDIBILITY

The text used to support an argument can be the argument's downfall if the text is not credible. A text is **credible**, or believable, when its author is knowledgeable and objective, or unbiased. The author's motivations for writing the text play a critical role in determining the credibility of the text and must be evaluated when assessing that credibility. Reports written about the ozone layer by an environmental scientist and a hairdresser will have a different level of credibility.

> **Review Video: Author Credibility**
> Visit mometrix.com/academy and enter code: 827257

APPEAL TO EMOTION

Sometimes, authors will appeal to the reader's emotion in an attempt to persuade or to distract the reader from the weakness of the argument. For instance, the author may try to inspire the pity of the reader by delivering a heart-rending story. An author also might use the bandwagon approach, in which he suggests that his opinion is correct because it is held by the majority. Some authors resort to name-calling, in which insults and harsh words are delivered to the opponent in an attempt to distract. In advertising, a common appeal is the celebrity testimonial, in which a famous person endorses a product. Of course, the fact that a famous person likes something should not really mean anything to the reader. These and other emotional appeals are usually evidence of poor reasoning and a weak argument.

> **Review Video: Emotional Language in Literature**
> Visit mometrix.com/academy and enter code: 759390

COUNTER ARGUMENTS

When authors give both sides to the argument, they build trust with their readers. As a reader, you should start with an undecided or neutral position. If an author presents only his or her side to the argument, then they are not exhibiting credibility and are weakening their argument.

Building common ground with readers can be effective for persuading neutral, skeptical, or opposed readers. Sharing values with undecided readers can allow people to switch positions without giving up what they feel is important. People who may oppose a position need to feel that they can change their minds without betraying who they are as a person. This appeal to having an open mind can be a powerful tool in arguing a position without antagonizing other views. Objections can be countered on a point-by-point basis or in a summary paragraph. Be mindful of how an author points out flaws in counter arguments. If they are unfair to the other side of the argument, then you should lose trust with the author.

RHETORICAL DEVICES

- An **anecdote** is a brief story authors may relate to their argument, which can illustrate their points in a more real and relatable way.
- **Aphorisms** concisely state common beliefs and may rhyme. For example, Benjamin Franklin's "Early to bed and early to rise / Makes a man healthy, wealthy, and wise" is an aphorism.

Copyright © Mometrix Media. You have been licensed one copy of this document for personal use only. Any other reproduction or redistribution is strictly prohibited. All rights reserved. This content is provided for test preparation purposes only and does not imply an endorsement by Mometrix of any particular political, scientific, or religious point of view.

- **Allusions** refer to literary or historical figures to impart symbolism to a thing or person and to create reader resonance. In John Steinbeck's *Of Mice and Men,* protagonist George's last name is Milton. This alludes to John Milton, who wrote *Paradise Lost*, and symbolizes George's eventual loss of his dream.
- **Satire** exaggerates, ridicules, or pokes fun at human flaws or ideas, as in the works of Jonathan Swift and Mark Twain.
- A **parody** is a form of satire that imitates another work to ridicule its topic or style.
- A **paradox** is a statement that is true despite appearing contradictory.
- **Hyperbole** is overstatement using exaggerated language.
- An **oxymoron** combines seeming contradictions, such as "deafening silence."
- **Analogies** compare two things that share common elements.
- **Similes** (stated comparisons using the words *like* or *as*) and **metaphors** (stated comparisons that do not use *like* or *as*) are considered forms of analogy.
- When using logic to reason with audiences, **syllogism** refers either to deductive reasoning or a deceptive, very sophisticated, or subtle argument.
- **Deductive reasoning** moves from general to specific, **inductive reasoning** from specific to general.
- **Diction** is author word choice that establishes tone and effect.
- **Understatement** achieves effects like contrast or irony by downplaying or describing something more subtly than warranted.
- **Chiasmus** uses parallel clauses, the second reversing the order of the first. Examples include T. S. Eliot's "Has the Church failed mankind, or has mankind failed the Church?" and John F. Kennedy's "Ask not what your country can do for you; ask what you can do for your country."
- **Anaphora** regularly repeats a word or phrase at the beginnings of consecutive clauses or phrases to add emphasis to an idea. A classic example of anaphora was Winston Churchill's emphasis of determination: "[W]e shall fight on the beaches, we shall fight on the landing grounds, we shall fight in the fields and in the streets, we shall fight in the hills; we shall never surrender..."

CHAPTER QUIZ

1. Which of the following rhetorical devices exaggerates, ridicules, or pokes fun at human flaws or ideas?

   a. Allusions
   b. Satire
   c. Parody
   d. Hyperbole

2. An author arguing that his point is correct because everybody else already agrees with it is an example of which persuasive technique?

   a. Appeal to laziness
   b. Bandwagon appeal
   c. Testimonials
   d. Generalizations

Copyright © Mometrix Media. You have been licensed one copy of this document for personal use only. Any other reproduction or redistribution is strictly prohibited. All rights reserved.
This content is provided for test preparation purposes only and does not imply an endorsement by Mometrix of any particular political, scientific, or religious point of view.

CHAPTER QUIZ ANSWER KEY

1. B: Rhetorical devices:

- An anecdote is a brief story authors may relate to their argument, which can illustrate their points in a more real and relatable way.
- Aphorisms concisely state common beliefs and may rhyme. For example, Benjamin Franklin's "Early to bed and early to rise / Makes a man healthy, wealthy, and wise" is an aphorism.
- Allusions refer to literary or historical figures to impart symbolism to a thing or person and to create reader resonance. In John Steinbeck's *Of Mice and Men,* protagonist George's last name is Milton. This alludes to John Milton, who wrote *Paradise Lost*, and symbolizes George's eventual loss of his dream.
- Satire exaggerates, ridicules, or pokes fun at human flaws or ideas, as in the works of Jonathan Swift and Mark Twain.
- A parody is a form of satire that imitates another work to ridicule its topic or style.
- A paradox is a statement that is true despite appearing contradictory.
- Hyperbole is overstatement using exaggerated language.
- An oxymoron combines seeming contradictions, such as "deafening silence."
- Analogies compare two things that share common elements.
- Similes (stated comparisons using the words *like* or *as*) and metaphors (stated comparisons that do not use *like* or *as*) are considered forms of analogy.
- When using logic to reason with audiences, syllogism refers either to deductive reasoning or a deceptive, very sophisticated, or subtle argument.
- Deductive reasoning moves from general to specific, while inductive reasoning moves from specific to general.
- Diction is author word choice that establishes tone and effect.
- Understatement achieves effects like contrast or irony by downplaying or describing something more subtly than warranted.
- Chiasmus uses parallel clauses, with the second clause reversing the order of the first. Examples include T. S. Eliot's "Has the Church failed mankind, or has mankind failed the Church?" and John F. Kennedy's "Ask not what your country can do for you—ask what you can do for your country."
- Anaphora regularly repeats a word or phrase at the beginnings of consecutive clauses or phrases to add emphasis to an idea. A classic example of anaphora was Winston Churchill's emphasis of determination: "[W]e shall fight on the beaches, we shall fight on the landing grounds, we shall fight in the fields and in the streets, we shall fight in the hills; we shall never surrender..."

2. B: Bandwagon appeals claim that everybody else agrees with the author's argument and thus try to persuade readers to conform and agree as well.

AUTHOR'S ARGUMENT IN ARGUMENTATIVE WRITING

In argumentative writing, the argument is a belief, position, or opinion that the author wants to convince readers to believe as well. For the first step, readers should identify the **issue**. Some issues are controversial, meaning people disagree about them. Gun control, foreign policy, and the death penalty are all controversial issues. The next step is to determine the **author's position** on the issue. That position or viewpoint constitutes the author's argument. Readers should then identify the **author's assumptions**: things he or she accepts, believes, or takes for granted without needing proof. Inaccurate or illogical assumptions produce flawed arguments and can mislead readers.

Copyright © Mometrix Media. You have been licensed one copy of this document for personal use only. Any other reproduction or redistribution is strictly prohibited. All rights reserved. This content is provided for test preparation purposes only and does not imply an endorsement by Mometrix of any particular political, scientific, or religious point of view.

Readers should identify what kinds of **supporting evidence** the author offers, such as research results, personal observations or experiences, case studies, facts, examples, expert testimony and opinions, and comparisons. Readers should decide how relevant this support is to the argument.

> **Review Video: Argumentative Writing**
> Visit mometrix.com/academy and enter code: 561544

EVALUATING AN AUTHOR'S ARGUMENT

The first three reader steps to **evaluate an author's argument** are to identify the **author's assumptions**, identify the **supporting evidence**, and decide **whether the evidence is relevant**. For example, if an author is not an expert on a particular topic, then that author's personal experience or opinion might not be relevant. The fourth step is to assess the **author's objectivity**. For example, consider whether the author introduces clear, understandable supporting evidence and facts to support the argument. The fifth step is evaluating whether the author's **argument is complete**. When authors give sufficient support for their arguments and also anticipate and respond effectively to opposing arguments or objections to their points, their arguments are complete. However, some authors omit information that could detract from their arguments. If instead they stated this information and refuted it, it would strengthen their arguments. The sixth step in evaluating an author's argumentative writing is to assess whether the **argument is valid**. Providing clear, logical reasoning makes an author's argument valid. Readers should ask themselves whether the author's points follow a sequence that makes sense, and whether each point leads to the next. The seventh step is to determine whether the author's **argument is credible**, meaning that it is convincing and believable. Arguments that are not valid are not credible, so step seven depends on step six. Readers should be mindful of their own biases as they evaluate and should not expect authors to conclusively prove their arguments, but rather to provide effective support and reason.

EVALUATING AN AUTHOR'S METHOD OF APPEAL

To evaluate the effectiveness of an appeal, it is important to consider the author's purpose for writing. Any appeals an author uses in their argument must be relevant to the argument's goal. For example, a writer that argues for the reclassification of Pluto, but primarily uses appeals to emotion, will not have an effective argument. This writer should focus on using appeals to logic and support their argument with provable facts. While most arguments should include appeals to logic, emotion, and credibility, some arguments only call for one or two of these types of appeal. Evidence can support an appeal, but the evidence must be relevant to truly strengthen the appeal's effectiveness. If the writer arguing for Pluto's reclassification uses the reasons for Jupiter's classification as evidence, their argument would be weak. This information may seem relevant because it is related to the classification of planets. However, this classification is highly dependent on the size of the celestial object, and Jupiter is significantly bigger than Pluto. This use of evidence is illogical and does not support the appeal. Even when appropriate evidence and appeals are used, appeals and arguments lose their effectiveness when they create logical fallacies.

OPINIONS, FACTS, AND FALLACIES

Critical thinking skills are mastered through understanding various types of writing and the different purposes of authors can have for writing different passages. Every author writes for a purpose. When you understand their purpose and how they accomplish their goal, you will be able to analyze their writing and determine whether or not you agree with their conclusions.

Readers must always be aware of the difference between fact and opinion. A **fact** can be subjected to analysis and proven to be true. An **opinion**, on the other hand, is the author's personal thoughts

Copyright © Mometrix Media. You have been licensed one copy of this document for personal use only. Any other reproduction or redistribution is strictly prohibited. All rights reserved.
This content is provided for test preparation purposes only and does not imply an endorsement by Mometrix of any particular political, scientific, or religious point of view.

or feelings and may not be altered by research or evidence. If the author writes that the distance from New York City to Boston is about two hundred miles, then he or she is stating a fact. If the author writes that New York City is too crowded, then he or she is giving an opinion because there is no objective standard for overpopulation. Opinions are often supported by facts. For instance, an author might use a comparison between the population density of New York City and that of other major American cities as evidence of an overcrowded population. An opinion supported by facts tends to be more convincing. On the other hand, when authors support their opinions with other opinions, readers should employ critical thinking and approach the argument with skepticism.

> **Review Video: Fact or Opinion**
> Visit mometrix.com/academy and enter code: 870899

RELIABLE SOURCES

When you have an argumentative passage, you need to be sure that facts are presented to the reader from **reliable sources**. An opinion is what the author thinks about a given topic. An opinion is not common knowledge or proven by expert sources, instead the information is the personal beliefs and thoughts of the author. To distinguish between fact and opinion, a reader needs to consider the type of source that is presenting information, the information that backs-up a claim, and the author's motivation to have a certain point-of-view on a given topic. For example, if a panel of scientists has conducted multiple studies on the effectiveness of taking a certain vitamin, then the results are more likely to be factual than those of a company that is selling a vitamin and simply claims that taking the vitamin can produce positive effects. The company is motivated to sell their product, and the scientists are using the scientific method to prove a theory. Remember, if you find sentences that contain phrases such as "I think...", then the statement is an opinion.

BIASES

In their attempts to persuade, writers often make mistakes in their thought processes and writing choices. These processes and choices are important to understand so you can make an informed decision about the author's credibility. Every author has a point of view, but authors demonstrate a **bias** when they ignore reasonable counterarguments or distort opposing viewpoints. A bias is evident whenever the author's claims are presented in a way that is unfair or inaccurate. Bias can be intentional or unintentional, but readers should be skeptical of the author's argument in either case. Remember that a biased author may still be correct. However, the author will be correct in spite of, not because of, his or her bias.

A **stereotype** is a bias applied specifically to a group of people or a place. Stereotyping is considered to be particularly abhorrent because it promotes negative, misleading generalizations about people. Readers should be very cautious of authors who use stereotypes in their writing. These faulty assumptions typically reveal the author's ignorance and lack of curiosity.

> **Review Video: Bias and Stereotype**
> Visit mometrix.com/academy and enter code: 644829

CHAPTER QUIZ

1. Which of the following is NOT one of the first three steps of evaluating an author's argument?

    a. Identify the author's assumptions
    b. Identify the supporting evidence
    c. Evaluate if the author's argument is complete
    d. Decide if the supporting evidence is relevant

Copyright © Mometrix Media. You have been licensed one copy of this document for personal use only. Any other reproduction or redistribution is strictly prohibited. All rights reserved. This content is provided for test preparation purposes only and does not imply an endorsement by Mometrix of any particular political, scientific, or religious point of view.

CHAPTER QUIZ ANSWER KEY

1. C: The first three reader steps to evaluate an author's argument are to identify the author's assumptions, identify the supporting evidence, and decide whether the evidence is relevant. For example, if an author is not an expert on a particular topic, then that author's personal experience or opinion might not be relevant. The fourth step is to assess the author's objectivity. For example, consider whether the author introduces clear, understandable supporting evidence and facts to support the argument. The fifth step is evaluating whether the author's argument is complete. When authors give sufficient support for their arguments and also anticipate and respond effectively to opposing arguments or objections to their points, their arguments are complete. However, some authors omit information that could detract from their arguments. If instead they stated this information and refuted it, it would likely strengthen their arguments. The sixth step in evaluating an author's argumentative writing is to assess whether the argument is valid. Providing clear, logical reasoning makes an author's argument valid. Readers should ask themselves whether the author's points follow a sequence that makes sense, and whether each point leads to the next. The seventh step is to determine whether the author's argument is credible, meaning that it is convincing and believable. Arguments that are not valid are not credible, so step seven depends on step six. Readers should be mindful of their own biases as they evaluate and should not expect authors to conclusively prove their arguments, but rather to provide effective support and reason.

LITERARY TERMINOLOGY

- In works of prose such as novels, a group of connected sentences covering one main topic is termed a **paragraph**.
- In works of poetry, a group of verses similarly connected is called a **stanza**.
- In drama, when early works used verse, these were also divided into stanzas or **couplets**.
- Drama evolved to use predominantly prose. Overall, whether prose or verse, the conversation in a play is called **dialogue**.
- Large sections of dialogue spoken by one actor are called **soliloquies** or **monologues**.
- Dialogue that informs audiences but is unheard by other characters is called an **aside**.
- Novels and plays share certain common elements, such as:
  - **Characters** - the people in the story.
  - **Plot** - the action of the story.
  - **Climax** - when action or dramatic tension reaches its highest point.
  - **Denouement** - the resolution following the climax.
- Sections dividing novels are called **chapters**, while sections of plays are called **acts**.
- Subsections of plays' acts are called **scenes**. Novel chapters usually do not have subsections. However, some novels do include groups of chapters that form different sections.

LITERARY ANALYSIS

The best literary analysis shows special insight into at least one important aspect of a text. When analyzing literary texts, it can be difficult to find a starting place. Many texts can be analyzed several different ways, often leaving an overwhelming number of options for writers to consider. However, narrowing the focus to a particular element of literature can be helpful when preparing to analyze a text. Symbolism, themes, and motifs are common starting points for literary analysis. These three methods of analysis can lead to a holistic analysis of a text, since they involve elements that are often distributed throughout the text. However, not all texts feature these elements in a way that facilitates a strong analysis, if they are present at all. It is also common to focus on character or plot development for analysis. These elements are compatible with theme, symbolism, and allusion. Setting and imagery, figurative language, and any external contexts can also contribute to analysis

Copyright © Mometrix Media. You have been licensed one copy of this document for personal use only. Any other reproduction or redistribution is strictly prohibited. All rights reserved. This content is provided for test preparation purposes only and does not imply an endorsement by Mometrix of any particular political, scientific, or religious point of view.

or complement one of these other elements. The application of a critical, or literary, theory to a text can also provide a thorough and strong analysis.

SETTING AND TIME FRAME

A literary text has both a setting and time frame. A **setting** is the place in which the story as a whole is set. The **time frame** is the period in which the story is set. This may refer to the historical period the story takes place in or if the story takes place over a single day. Both setting and time frame are relevant to a text's meaning because they help the reader place the story in time and space. An author uses setting and time frame to anchor a text, create a mood, and enhance its meaning. This helps a reader understand why a character acts the way he does, or why certain events in the story are important. The setting impacts the **plot** and character **motivations**, while the time frame helps place the story in **chronological context**.

EXAMPLE

Read the following excerpt from The Adventures of Huckleberry Finn by Mark Twain and analyze the relevance of setting to the text's meaning:

> We said there warn't no home like a raft, after all. Other places do seem so cramped up and smothery, but a raft don't. You feel mighty free and easy and comfortable on a raft.

This excerpt from *The Adventures of Huckleberry Finn* by Mark Twain reveals information about the **setting** of the book. By understanding that the main character, Huckleberry Finn, lives on a raft, the reader can place the story on a river, in this case, the Mississippi River in the South before the Civil War. The information about the setting also gives the reader clues about the **character** of Huck Finn: he clearly values independence and freedom, and he likes the outdoors. The information about the setting in the quote helps the reader to better understand the rest of the text.

THEME

The **theme** of a passage is what the reader learns from the text or the passage. It is the lesson or **moral** contained in the passage. It also is a unifying idea that is used throughout the text; it can take the form of a common setting, idea, symbol, design, or recurring event. A passage can have two or more themes that convey its overall idea. The theme or themes of a passage are often based on **universal themes**. They can frequently be expressed using well-known sayings about life, society, or human nature, such as "Hard work pays off" or "Good triumphs over evil." Themes are not usually stated **explicitly**. The reader must figure them out by carefully reading the passage. Themes are often the reason why passages are written; they give a passage unity and meaning. Themes are created through **plot development**. The events of a story help shape the themes of a passage.

EXAMPLE

Explain why "Take care of what you care about" accurately describes the theme of the following excerpt.

> Luca collected baseball cards, but he wasn't very careful with them. He left them around the house. His dog liked to chew. One day, Luca and his friend Bart were looking at his collection. Then they went outside. When Luca got home, he saw his dog chewing on his cards. They were ruined.

This excerpt tells the story of a boy who is careless with his baseball cards and leaves them lying around. His dog ends up chewing them and ruining them. The lesson is that if you care about something, you need to take care of it. This is the theme, or point, of the story. Some stories have

Copyright © Mometrix Media. You have been licensed one copy of this document for personal use only. Any other reproduction or redistribution is strictly prohibited. All rights reserved.
This content is provided for test preparation purposes only and does not imply an endorsement by Mometrix of any particular political, scientific, or religious point of view.

more than one theme, but this is not really true of this excerpt. The reader needs to figure out the theme based on what happens in the story. Sometimes, as in the case of fables, the theme is stated directly in the text. However, this is not usually the case.

> **Review Video: Themes in Literature**
> Visit mometrix.com/academy and enter code: 732074

PLOT AND STORY STRUCTURE

The **plot** includes the events that happen in a story and the order in which they are told to the reader. There are several types of plot structures, as stories can be told in many ways. The most common plot structure is the chronological plot, which presents the events to the reader in the same order they occur for the characters in the story. Chronological plots usually have five main parts, the **exposition**, **rising action**, the **climax**, **falling action**, and the **resolution**. This type of plot structure guides the reader through the story's events as the characters experience them and is the easiest structure to understand and identify. While this is the most common plot structure, many stories are nonlinear, which means the plot does not sequence events in the same order the characters experience them. Such stories might include elements like flashbacks that cause the story to be nonlinear.

> **Review Video: How to Make a Story Map**
> Visit mometrix.com/academy and enter code: 261719

EXPOSITION

The **exposition** is at the beginning of the story and generally takes place before the rising action begins. The purpose of the exposition is to give the reader context for the story, which the author may do by introducing one or more characters, describing the setting or world, or explaining the events leading up to the point where the story begins. The exposition may still include events that contribute to the plot, but the **rising action** and main conflict of the story are not part of the exposition. Some narratives skip the exposition and begin the story with the beginning of the rising action, which causes the reader to learn the context as the story intensifies.

CONFLICT

A **conflict** is a problem to be solved. Literary plots typically include one conflict or more. Characters' attempts to resolve conflicts drive the narrative's forward movement. **Conflict resolution** is often the protagonist's primary occupation. Physical conflicts like exploring, wars, and escapes tend to make plots most suspenseful and exciting. Emotional, mental, or moral conflicts tend to make stories more personally gratifying or rewarding for many audiences. Conflicts can be external or internal. A major type of internal conflict is some inner personal battle, or **man versus self**. Major types of external conflicts include **man versus nature**, **man versus man**, and **man versus society**. Readers can identify conflicts in literary plots by identifying the protagonist and antagonist and asking why they conflict, what events develop the conflict, where the climax occurs, and how they identify with the characters.

Read the following paragraph and discuss the type of conflict present:

> Timothy was shocked out of sleep by the appearance of a bear just outside his tent. After panicking for a moment, he remembered some advice he had read in preparation for this trip: he should make noise so the bear would not be startled. As Timothy started to hum and sing, the bear wandered away.

56

Copyright © Mometrix Media. You have been licensed one copy of this document for personal use only. Any other reproduction or redistribution is strictly prohibited. All rights reserved.
This content is provided for test preparation purposes only and does not imply an endorsement by Mometrix of any particular political, scientific, or religious point of view.

There are three main types of conflict in literature: **man versus man**, **man versus nature**, and **man versus self**. This paragraph is an example of man versus nature. Timothy is in conflict with the bear. Even though no physical conflict like an attack exists, Timothy is pitted against the bear. Timothy uses his knowledge to "defeat" the bear and keep himself safe. The solution to the conflict is that Timothy makes noise, the bear wanders away, and Timothy is safe.

> **Review Video: Conflict**
> Visit mometrix.com/academy and enter code: 559550
>
> **Review Video: Determining Relationships in a Story**
> Visit mometrix.com/academy and enter code: 929925

RISING ACTION

The **rising action** is the part of the story where conflict **intensifies**. The rising action begins with an event that prompts the main conflict of the story. This may also be called the **inciting incident**. The main conflict generally occurs between the protagonist and an antagonist, but this is not the only type of conflict that may occur in a narrative. After this event, the protagonist works to resolve the main conflict by preparing for an altercation, pursuing a goal, fleeing an antagonist, or doing some other action that will end the conflict. The rising action is composed of several additional events that increase the story's tension. Most often, other developments will occur alongside the growth of the main conflict, such as character development or the development of minor conflicts. The rising action ends with the **climax**, which is the point of highest tension in the story.

CLIMAX

The **climax** is the event in the narrative that marks the height of the story's conflict or tension. The event that takes place at the story's climax will end the rising action and bring about the results of the main conflict. If the conflict was between a good protagonist and an evil antagonist, the climax may be a final battle between the two characters. If the conflict is an adventurer looking for heavily guarded treasure, the climax may be the adventurer's encounter with the final obstacle that protects the treasure. The climax may be made of multiple scenes, but can usually be summarized as one event. Once the conflict and climax are complete, the **falling action** begins.

FALLING ACTION

The **falling action** shows what happens in the story between the climax and the resolution. The falling action often composes a much smaller portion of the story than the rising action does. While the climax includes the end of the main conflict, the falling action may show the results of any minor conflicts in the story. For example, if the protagonist encountered a troll on the way to find some treasure, and the troll demanded the protagonist share the treasure after retrieving it, the falling action would include the protagonist returning to share the treasure with the troll. Similarly, any unexplained major events are usually made clear during the falling action. Once all significant elements of the story are resolved or addressed, the story's resolution will occur. The **resolution** is the end of the story, which shows the final result of the plot's events and shows what life is like for the main characters once they are no longer experiencing the story's conflicts.

RESOLUTION

The way the conflict is **resolved** depends on the type of conflict. The plot of any book starts with the lead up to the conflict, then the conflict itself, and finally the solution, or **resolution**, to the conflict. In **man versus man** conflicts, the conflict is often resolved by two parties coming to some sort of agreement or by one party triumphing over the other party. In **man versus nature** conflicts, the conflict is often resolved by man coming to some realization about some aspect of nature. In

Copyright © Mometrix Media. You have been licensed one copy of this document for personal use only. Any other reproduction or redistribution is strictly prohibited. All rights reserved.
This content is provided for test preparation purposes only and does not imply an endorsement by Mometrix of any particular political, scientific, or religious point of view.

man versus self conflicts, the conflict is often resolved by the character growing or coming to an understanding about part of himself.

SYNTAX AND WORD CHOICE

Authors use words and **syntax**, or sentence structure, to make their texts unique, convey their own writing style, and sometimes to make a point or emphasis. They know that word choice and syntax contribute to the reader's understanding of the text as well as to the tone and mood of a text.

> **Review Video: What is Syntax?**
> Visit mometrix.com/academy and enter code: 242280

ALLUSION

An allusion is an uncited but recognizable reference to something else. Authors use language to make allusions to places, events, artwork, and other books in order to make their own text richer. For example, an author may allude to a very important text in order to make his own text seem more important. Martin Luther King, Jr. started his "I Have a Dream" speech by saying "Five score years ago..." This is a clear allusion to President Abraham Lincoln's "Gettysburg Address" and served to remind people of the significance of the event. An author may allude to a place to ground his text or make a cultural reference to make readers feel included. There are many reasons that authors make allusions.

> **Review Video: Allusions**
> Visit mometrix.com/academy and enter code: 294065

COMIC RELIEF

Comic relief is the use of comedy by an author to break up a dramatic or tragic scene and infuse it with a bit of **lightheartedness**. In William Shakespeare's *Hamlet*, two gravediggers digging the grave for Ophelia share a joke while they work. The death and burial of Ophelia are tragic moments that directly follow each other. Shakespeare uses an instance of comedy to break up the tragedy and give his audience a bit of a break from the tragic drama. Authors sometimes use comic relief so that their work will be less depressing; other times they use it to create irony or contrast between the darkness of the situation and the lightness of the joke. Often, authors will use comedy to parallel what is happening in the tragic scenes.

> **Review Video: What is Comic Relief?**
> Visit mometrix.com/academy and enter code: 779604

MOOD AND TONE

Mood is a story's atmosphere, or the feelings the reader gets from reading it. The way authors set the mood in writing is comparable to the way filmmakers use music to set the mood in movies. Instead of music, though, writers judiciously select descriptive words to evoke certain **moods**. The mood of a work may convey joy, anger, bitterness, hope, gloom, fear, apprehension, or any other emotion the author wants the reader to feel. In addition to vocabulary choices, authors also use figurative expressions, particular sentence structures, and choices of diction that project and reinforce the moods they want to create. Whereas mood is the reader's emotions evoked by reading what is written, **tone** is the emotions and attitudes of the writer that she or he expresses in the writing. Authors use the same literary techniques to establish tone as they do to establish mood. An

Copyright © Mometrix Media. You have been licensed one copy of this document for personal use only. Any other reproduction or redistribution is strictly prohibited. All rights reserved.
This content is provided for test preparation purposes only and does not imply an endorsement by Mometrix of any particular political, scientific, or religious point of view.

author may use a humorous tone, an angry or sad tone, a sentimental or unsentimental tone, or something else entirely.

MOOD AND TONE IN THE GREAT GATSBY

To understand the difference between mood and tone, look at this excerpt from F. Scott Fitzgerald's *The Great Gatsby*. In this passage, Nick Caraway, the novel's narrator, is describing his affordable house, which sits in a neighborhood full of expensive mansions.

> "I lived at West Egg, the—well the less fashionable of the two, though this is a most superficial tag to express the bizarre and not a little sinister contrast between them. My house was at the very tip of the egg, only fifty yard from the Sound, and squeezed between two huge places that rented for twelve or fifteen thousand a season … My own house was an eyesore, but it was a small eyesore, and it had been overlooked, so I had a view of the water, a partial view of my neighbor's lawn, and the consoling proximity of millionaires—all for eighty dollars a month."

In this description, the mood created for the reader does not match the tone created through the narrator. The mood in this passage is one of dissatisfaction and inferiority. Nick compares his home to his neighbors', saying he lives in the "less fashionable" neighborhood and that his house is "overlooked," an "eyesore," and "squeezed between two huge" mansions. He also adds that his placement allows him the "consoling proximity of millionaires." A literal reading of these details leads the reader to have negative feelings toward Nick's house and his economic inferiority to his neighbors, creating the mood.

However, Fitzgerald also conveys an opposing attitude, or tone, through Nick's description. Nick calls the distinction between the neighborhoods "superficial," showing a suspicion of the value suggested by the neighborhoods' titles, properties, and residents. Nick also undermines his critique of his own home by calling it "a small eyesore" and claiming it has "been overlooked." However, he follows these statements with a description of his surroundings, claiming that he has "a view of the water" and can see some of his wealthy neighbor's property from his home, and a comparison between the properties' rent. While the mental image created for the reader depicts a small house shoved between looming mansions, the tone suggests that Nick enjoys these qualities about his home, or at least finds it charming. He acknowledges its shortcomings, but includes the benefits of his home's unassuming appearance.

> **Review Video: Style, Tone, and Mood**
> Visit mometrix.com/academy and enter code: 416961

CHARACTER DEVELOPMENT

When depicting characters or figures in a written text, authors generally use actions, dialogue, and descriptions as characterization techniques. Characterization can occur in both fiction and nonfiction and is used to show a character or figure's personality, demeanor, and thoughts. This helps create a more engaging experience for the reader by providing a more concrete picture of a character or figure's tendencies and features. Characterizations also gives authors the opportunity to integrate elements such as dialects, activities, attire, and attitudes into their writing.

To understand the meaning of a story, it is vital to understand the characters as the author describes them. We can look for contradictions in what a character thinks, says, and does. We can notice whether the author's observations about a character differ from what other characters in the story say about that character. A character may be dynamic, meaning they change significantly during the story, or static, meaning they remain the same from beginning to end. Characters may be

Copyright © Mometrix Media. You have been licensed one copy of this document for personal use only. Any other reproduction or redistribution is strictly prohibited. All rights reserved.
This content is provided for test preparation purposes only and does not imply an endorsement by Mometrix of any particular political, scientific, or religious point of view.

two-dimensional, not fully developed, or may be well developed with characteristics that stand out vividly. Characters may also symbolize universal properties. Additionally, readers can compare and contrast characters to analyze how each one developed.

A well-known example of character development can be found in Charles Dickens's *Great Expectations*. The novel's main character, Pip, is introduced as a young boy, and he is depicted as innocent, kind, and humble. However, as Pip grows up and is confronted with the social hierarchy of Victorian England, he becomes arrogant and rejects his loved ones in pursuit of his own social advancement. Once he achieves his social goals, he realizes the merits of his former lifestyle, and lives with the wisdom he gained in both environments and life stages. Dickens shows Pip's ever-changing character through his interactions with others and his inner thoughts, which evolve as his personal values and personality shift.

> **Review Video: <u>Character Changes</u>**
> Visit mometrix.com/academy and enter code: 408719

DIALOGUE

Effectively written dialogue serves at least one, but usually several, purposes. It advances the story and moves the plot, develops the characters, sheds light on the work's theme or meaning, and can, often subtly, account for the passage of time not otherwise indicated. It can alter the direction that the plot is taking, typically by introducing some new conflict or changing existing ones. **Dialogue** can establish a work's narrative voice and the characters' voices and set the tone of the story or of particular characters. When fictional characters display enlightenment or realization, dialogue can give readers an understanding of what those characters have discovered and how. Dialogue can illuminate the motivations and wishes of the story's characters. By using consistent thoughts and syntax, dialogue can support character development. Skillfully created, it can also represent real-life speech rhythms in written form. Via conflicts and ensuing action, dialogue also provides drama.

DIALOGUE IN FICTION

In fictional works, effectively written dialogue does more than just break up or interrupt sections of narrative. While **dialogue** may supply exposition for readers, it must nonetheless be believable. Dialogue should be dynamic, not static, and it should not resemble regular prose. Authors should not use dialogue to write clever similes or metaphors, or to inject their own opinions. Nor should they use dialogue at all when narrative would be better. Most importantly, dialogue should not slow the plot movement. Dialogue must seem natural, which means careful construction of phrases rather than actually duplicating natural speech, which does not necessarily translate well to the written word. Finally, all dialogue must be pertinent to the story, rather than just added conversation.

FORESHADOWING

Foreshadowing is a device authors use to give readers **hints** about events that will take place later in a story. Foreshadowing most often takes place through a character's dialogue or actions. Sometimes the character will know what is going to happen and will purposefully allude to future events. For example, consider a protagonist who is about to embark on a journey through the woods. Just before the protagonist begins the trip, another character says, "Be careful, you never know what could be out in those woods!" This alerts the reader that the woods may be dangerous and prompts the reader to expect something to attack the protagonist in the woods. This is an example of foreshadowing through warning. Alternatively, a character may unknowingly foreshadow later events. For example, consider a story where a brother and sister run through their house and knock over a vase and break it. The brother says, "Don't worry, we'll clean it up!

Copyright © Mometrix Media. You have been licensed one copy of this document for personal use only. Any other reproduction or redistribution is strictly prohibited. All rights reserved. This content is provided for test preparation purposes only and does not imply an endorsement by Mometrix of any particular political, scientific, or religious point of view.

Mom will never know!" However, the reader knows that their mother will most likely find out what they have done, so the reader expects the siblings to later get in trouble for running, breaking the vase, and hiding it from their mother.

SYMBOLISM

Symbolism describes an author's use of a **symbol**, an element of the story that **represents** something else. Symbols can impact stories in many ways, including deepening the meaning of a story or its elements, comparing a story to another work, or foreshadowing later events in a story. Symbols can be objects, characters, colors, numbers, or anything else the author establishes as a symbol. Symbols can be clearly established through direct comparison or repetition, but they can also be established subtly or gradually over a large portion of the story. Another form of symbolism is **allusion**, which is when something in a story is used to prompt the reader to think about another work. Many well-known works use **Biblical allusions**, which are allusions to events or details in the Bible that inform a work or an element within it.

POINT OF VIEW

Another element that impacts a text is the author's point of view. The **point of view** of a text is the perspective from which a passage is told. An author will always have a point of view about a story before he or she draws up a plot line. The author will know what events they want to take place, how they want the characters to interact, and how they want the story to resolve. An author will also have an opinion on the topic or series of events which is presented in the story that is based on their prior experience and beliefs.

The two main points of view that authors use, especially in a work of fiction, are first person and third person. If the narrator of the story is also the main character, or *protagonist*, the text is written in first-person point of view. In first person, the author writes from the perspective of *I*. Third-person point of view is probably the most common that authors use in their passages. Using third person, authors refer to each character by using *he* or *she*. In third-person omniscient, the narrator is not a character in the story and tells the story of all of the characters at the same time.

> **Review Video: Point of View**
> Visit mometrix.com/academy and enter code: 383336

FIRST-PERSON NARRATION

First-person narratives let narrators express inner feelings and thoughts, especially when the narrator is the protagonist as Lemuel Gulliver is in Jonathan Swift's *Gulliver's Travels*. The narrator may be a close friend of the protagonist, like Dr. Watson in Sir Arthur Conan Doyle's *Sherlock Holmes*. Or, the narrator can be less involved with the main characters and plot, like Nick Carraway in F. Scott Fitzgerald's *The Great Gatsby*. When a narrator reports others' narratives, she or he is a "**frame narrator**," like the nameless narrator of Joseph Conrad's *Heart of Darkness* or Mr. Lockwood in Emily Brontë's *Wuthering Heights*. **First-person plural** is unusual but can be effective. Isaac Asimov's *I, Robot*, William Faulkner's *A Rose for Emily*, Maxim Gorky's *Twenty-Six Men and a Girl*, and Jeffrey Eugenides' *The Virgin Suicides* all use first-person plural narration. Author Kurt Vonnegut is the first-person narrator in his semi-autobiographical novel *Timequake*. Also unusual, but effective, is a **first-person omniscient** (rather than the more common third-person omniscient) narrator, like Death in Markus Zusak's *The Book Thief* and the ghost in Alice Sebold's *The Lovely Bones*.

Copyright © Mometrix Media. You have been licensed one copy of this document for personal use only. Any other reproduction or redistribution is strictly prohibited. All rights reserved.
This content is provided for test preparation purposes only and does not imply an endorsement by Mometrix of any particular political, scientific, or religious point of view.

SECOND-PERSON NARRATION

While **second-person** address is very commonplace in popular song lyrics, it is the least used form of narrative voice in literary works. Popular serial books of the 1980s like *Fighting Fantasy* or *Choose Your Own Adventure* employed second-person narratives. In some cases, a narrative combines both second-person and first-person voices, using the pronouns *you* and *I*. This can draw readers into the story, and it can also enable the authors to compare directly "your" and "my" feelings, thoughts, and actions. When the narrator is also a character in the story, as in Edgar Allan Poe's short story "The Tell-Tale Heart" or Jay McInerney's novel *Bright Lights, Big City,* the narrative is better defined as first-person despite it also addressing "you."

THIRD-PERSON NARRATION

Narration in the third person is the most prevalent type, as it allows authors the most flexibility. It is so common that readers simply assume without needing to be informed that the narrator is not a character in the story, or involved in its events. **Third-person singular** is used more frequently than **third-person plural**, though some authors have also effectively used plural. However, both singular and plural are most often included in stories according to which characters are being described. The third-person narrator may be either objective or subjective, and either omniscient or limited. **Objective third-person** narration does not include what the characters described are thinking or feeling, while **subjective third-person** narration does. The **third-person omniscient** narrator knows everything about all characters, including their thoughts and emotions, and all related places, times, and events. However, the **third-person limited** narrator may know everything about a particular character, but is limited to that character. In other words, the narrator cannot speak about anything that character does not know.

ALTERNATING-PERSON NARRATION

Although authors more commonly write stories from one point of view, there are also instances wherein they alternate the narrative voice within the same book. For example, they may sometimes use an omniscient third-person narrator and a more intimate first-person narrator at other times. In J. K. Rowling's series of *Harry Potter* novels, she often writes in a third-person limited narrative, but sometimes changes to narration by characters other than the protagonist. George R. R. Martin's series *A Song of Ice and Fire* changes the point of view to coincide with divisions between chapters. The same technique is used by Erin Hunter (a pseudonym for several authors of the *Warriors, Seekers,* and *Survivors* book series). Authors using first-person narrative sometimes switch to third-person to describe significant action scenes, especially those where the narrator was absent or uninvolved, as Barbara Kingsolver does in her novel *The Poisonwood Bible.*

HISTORICAL AND SOCIAL CONTEXT

Fiction that is heavily influenced by a historical or social context cannot be comprehended as the author intended if the reader does not keep this context in mind. Many important elements of the text will be influenced by any context, including symbols, allusions, settings, and plot events. These contexts, as well as the identity of the work's author, can help to inform the reader about the author's concerns and intended meanings. For example, George Orwell published his novel *1984* in the year 1949, soon after the end of World War II. At that time, following the defeat of the Nazis, the Cold War began between the Western Allied nations and the Eastern Soviet Communists. People were therefore concerned about the conflict between the freedoms afforded by Western democracies versus the oppression represented by Communism. Orwell had also previously fought in the Spanish Civil War against a Spanish regime that he and his fellows viewed as oppressive. From this information, readers can infer that Orwell was concerned about oppression by totalitarian governments. This informs *1984*'s story of Winston Smith's rebellion against the

Copyright © Mometrix Media. You have been licensed one copy of this document for personal use only. Any other reproduction or redistribution is strictly prohibited. All rights reserved.
This content is provided for test preparation purposes only and does not imply an endorsement by Mometrix of any particular political, scientific, or religious point of view.

oppressive "Big Brother" government, of the fictional dictatorial state of Oceania, and his capture, torture, and ultimate conversion by that government. Some literary theories also seek to use historical and social contexts to reveal deeper meanings and implications in a text.

TEXTUAL EVIDENCE

No literary analysis is complete without textual evidence. Summaries, paraphrases, and quotes are all forms of textual evidence, but direct quotes from the text are the most effective form of evidence. The best textual evidence is relevant, accurate, and clearly supports the writer's claim. This can include pieces of descriptions, dialogue, or exposition that shows the applicability of the analysis to the text. Analysis that is average, or sufficient, shows an understanding of the text; contains supporting textual evidence that is relevant and accurate, if not strong; and shows a specific and clear response. Analysis that partially meets criteria also shows understanding, but the textual evidence is generalized, incomplete, only partly relevant or accurate, or connected only weakly. Inadequate analysis is vague, too general, or incorrect. It may give irrelevant or incomplete textual evidence, or may simply summarize the plot rather than analyzing the work. It is important to incorporate textual evidence from the work being analyzed and any supplemental materials and to provide appropriate attribution for these sources.

CHAPTER QUIZ

1. Which of the following is the least used form of narration used in literature?

    a. First-person
    b. Second-person
    c. Third-person limited
    d. Third-person omniscient

2. Which of the following lists the terms of chronological plots in order from first to last?

    a. Exposition, rising action, climax, falling action, resolution
    b. Rising action, exposition, falling action, climax, resolution
    c. Rising action, exposition, climax, falling action, resolution
    d. Resolution, exposition, climax, falling action, rising action

3. If a writer alludes to another piece of literature, that writer is doing which of the following?

    a. Admiring it
    b. Criticizing it
    c. Defending its conclusions
    d. Referencing it

CHAPTER QUIZ ANSWER KEY

1. B: While second-person address is very commonplace in popular song lyrics, it is the least used form of narrative voice in literary works. Popular serial books of the 1980s like *Fighting Fantasy* or *Choose Your Own Adventure* employed second-person narratives. In some cases, a narrative combines both second-person and first-person voices, using the pronouns *you* and *I*. This can draw readers into the story, and it can also enable the authors to compare directly "your" and "my" feelings, thoughts, and actions. When the narrator is also a character in the story, as in Edgar Allan Poe's short story "The Tell-Tale Heart" or Jay McInerney's novel *Bright Lights, Big City,* the narrative is better defined as first-person despite it also addressing "you."

2. A: The most common plot structure is the chronological plot, which presents the events to the reader in the same order they occur for the characters in the story. Chronological plots usually have

Copyright © Mometrix Media. You have been licensed one copy of this document for personal use only. Any other reproduction or redistribution is strictly prohibited. All rights reserved.
This content is provided for test preparation purposes only and does not imply an endorsement by Mometrix of any particular political, scientific, or religious point of view.

five main parts: the exposition, rising action, the climax, falling action, and the resolution. This type of plot structure guides the reader through the story's events as the characters experience them and is the easiest structure to understand and identify.

3. D: An allusion is an uncited but recognizable reference to something else. Authors use language to make allusions to places, events, artwork, and other books in order to make their own text richer. For example, an author may allude to a very important text in order to make his own text seem more important.

UNDERSTANDING A PASSAGE

One of the most important skills in reading comprehension is the identification of **topics** and **main ideas**. There is a subtle difference between these two features. The topic is the subject of a text (i.e., what the text is all about). The main idea, on the other hand, is the most important point being made by the author. The topic is usually expressed in a few words at the most while the main idea often needs a full sentence to be completely defined. As an example, a short passage might be written on the topic of penguins, and the main idea could be written as *Penguins are different from other birds in many ways*. In most nonfiction writing, the topic and the main idea will be **stated directly** and often appear in a sentence at the very beginning or end of the text. When being tested on an understanding of the author's topic, you may be able to skim the passage for the general idea by reading only the first sentence of each paragraph. A body paragraph's first sentence is often— but not always—the main **topic sentence** which gives you a summary of the content in the paragraph.

However, there are cases in which the reader must figure out an **unstated** topic or main idea. In these instances, you must read every sentence of the text and try to come up with an overarching idea that is supported by each of those sentences.

Note: The main idea should not be confused with the thesis statement. While the main idea gives a brief, general summary of a text, the thesis statement provides a **specific perspective** on an issue that the author supports with evidence.

Review Video: <u>Topics and Main Ideas</u>
Visit mometrix.com/academy and enter code: 407801

Supporting details are smaller pieces of evidence that provide backing for the main point. In order to show that a main idea is correct or valid, an author must add details that prove their point. All texts contain details, but they are only classified as supporting details when they serve to reinforce some larger point. Supporting details are most commonly found in informative and persuasive texts. In some cases, they will be clearly indicated with terms like *for example* or *for instance*, or they will be enumerated with terms like *first*, *second*, and *last*. However, you need to be prepared for texts that do not contain those indicators. As a reader, you should consider whether the author's supporting details really back up his or her main point. Details can be factual and correct, yet they may not be **relevant** to the author's point. Conversely, details can be relevant, but be ineffective because they are based on opinion or assertions that cannot be proven.

Review Video: <u>Supporting Details</u>
Visit mometrix.com/academy and enter code: 396297

An example of a main idea is: *Giraffes live in the Serengeti of Africa*. A supporting detail about giraffes could be: *A giraffe in this region benefits from a long neck by reaching twigs and leaves on tall*

Copyright © Mometrix Media. You have been licensed one copy of this document for personal use only. Any other reproduction or redistribution is strictly prohibited. All rights reserved.
This content is provided for test preparation purposes only and does not imply an endorsement by Mometrix of any particular political, scientific, or religious point of view.

trees. The main idea gives the general idea that the text is about giraffes. The supporting detail gives a specific fact about how the giraffes eat.

ORGANIZATION OF THE TEXT

The way a text is organized can help readers understand the author's intent and his or her conclusions. There are various ways to organize a text, and each one has a purpose and use. Usually, authors will organize information logically in a passage so the reader can follow and locate the information within the text. However, since not all passages are written with the same logical structure, you need to be familiar with several different types of passage structure.

> **Review Video: Organizational Methods to Structure Text**
> Visit mometrix.com/academy and enter code: 606263
>
> **Review Video: Sequence of Events in a Story**
> Visit mometrix.com/academy and enter code: 807512

CHRONOLOGICAL

When using **chronological** order, the author presents information in the order that it happened. For example, biographies are typically written in chronological order. The subject's birth and childhood are presented first, followed by their adult life, and lastly the events leading up to the person's death.

CAUSE AND EFFECT

One of the most common text structures is **cause and effect**. A **cause** is an act or event that makes something happen, and an **effect** is the thing that happens as a result of the cause. A cause-and-effect relationship is not always explicit, but there are some terms in English that signal causes, such as *since*, *because*, and *due to*. Furthermore, terms that signal effects include *consequently, therefore, this leads to*. As an example, consider the sentence *Because the sky was clear, Ron did not bring an umbrella.* The cause is the clear sky, and the effect is that Ron did not bring an umbrella. However, readers may find that sometimes the cause-and-effect relationship will not be clearly noted. For instance, the sentence *He was late and missed the meeting* does not contain any signaling words, but the sentence still contains a cause (he was late) and an effect (he missed the meeting).

> **Review Video: Cause and Effect**
> Visit mometrix.com/academy and enter code: 868099

MULTIPLE EFFECTS

Be aware of the possibility for a single cause to have **multiple effects.** (e.g., *Single cause*: Because you left your homework on the table, your dog engulfed the assignment. *Multiple effects*: As a result, you receive a failing grade, your parents do not allow you to go out with your friends, you miss out on the new movie, and one of your classmates spoils it for you before you have another chance to watch it).

MULTIPLE CAUSES

Also, there is the possibility for a single effect to have **multiple causes.** (e.g., *Single effect*: Alan has a fever. *Multiple causes*: An unexpected cold front came through the area, and Alan forgot to take his multi-vitamin to avoid getting sick.) Additionally, an effect can in turn be the cause of another effect, in what is known as a cause-and-effect chain. (e.g., As a result of her disdain for procrastination, Lynn prepared for her exam. This led to her passing her test with high marks. Hence, her resume was accepted and her application was approved.)

Copyright © Mometrix Media. You have been licensed one copy of this document for personal use only. Any other reproduction or redistribution is strictly prohibited. All rights reserved. This content is provided for test preparation purposes only and does not imply an endorsement by Mometrix of any particular political, scientific, or religious point of view.

CAUSE AND EFFECT IN PERSUASIVE ESSAYS

Persuasive essays, in which an author tries to make a convincing argument and change the minds of readers, usually include cause-and-effect relationships. However, these relationships should not always be taken at face value. Frequently, an author will assume a cause or take an effect for granted. To read a persuasive essay effectively, readers need to judge the cause-and-effect relationships that the author is presenting. For instance, imagine an author wrote the following: *The parking deck has been unprofitable because people would prefer to ride their bikes.* The relationship is clear: the cause is that people prefer to ride their bikes, and the effect is that the parking deck has been unprofitable. However, readers should consider whether this argument is conclusive. Perhaps there are other reasons for the failure of the parking deck: a down economy, excessive fees, etc. Too often, authors present causal relationships as if they are fact rather than opinion. Readers should be on the alert for these dubious claims.

PROBLEM-SOLUTION

Some nonfiction texts are organized to **present a problem** followed by a solution. For this type of text, the problem is often explained before the solution is offered. In some cases, as when the problem is well known, the solution may be introduced briefly at the beginning. Other passages may focus on the solution, and the problem will be referenced only occasionally. Some texts will outline multiple solutions to a problem, leaving readers to choose among them. If the author has an interest or an allegiance to one solution, he or she may fail to mention or describe accurately some of the other solutions. Readers should be careful of the author's agenda when reading a problem-solution text. Only by understanding the author's perspective and interests can one develop a proper judgment of the proposed solution.

COMPARE AND CONTRAST

Many texts follow the **compare-and-contrast** model in which the similarities and differences between two ideas or things are explored. Analysis of the similarities between ideas is called **comparison**. In an ideal comparison, the author places ideas or things in an equivalent structure, i.e., the author presents the ideas in the same way. If an author wants to show the similarities between cricket and baseball, then he or she may do so by summarizing the equipment and rules for each game. Be mindful of the similarities as they appear in the passage and take note of any differences that are mentioned. Often, these small differences will only reinforce the more general similarity.

> **Review Video: Compare and Contrast**
> Visit mometrix.com/academy and enter code: 798319

Thinking critically about ideas and conclusions can seem like a daunting task. One way to ease this task is to understand the basic elements of ideas and writing techniques. Looking at the ways different ideas relate to each other can be a good way for readers to begin their analysis. For instance, sometimes authors will write about two ideas that are in opposition to each other. Or, one author will provide his or her ideas on a topic, and another author may respond in opposition. The analysis of these opposing ideas is known as **contrast**. Contrast is often marred by the author's obvious partiality to one of the ideas. A discerning reader will be put off by an author who does not engage in a fair fight. In an analysis of opposing ideas, both ideas should be presented in clear and reasonable terms. If the author does prefer a side, you need to read carefully to determine the areas where the author shows or avoids this preference. In an analysis of opposing ideas, you should proceed through the passage by marking the major differences point by point with an eye that is looking for an explanation of each side's view. For instance, in an analysis of capitalism and communism, there is an importance in outlining each side's view on labor, markets, prices, personal

Copyright © Mometrix Media. You have been licensed one copy of this document for personal use only. Any other reproduction or redistribution is strictly prohibited. All rights reserved. This content is provided for test preparation purposes only and does not imply an endorsement by Mometrix of any particular political, scientific, or religious point of view.

responsibility, etc. Additionally, as you read through the passages, you should note whether the opposing views present each side in a similar manner.

SEQUENCE

Readers must be able to identify a text's **sequence**, or the order in which things happen. Often, when the sequence is very important to the author, the text is indicated with signal words like *first*, *then*, *next*, and *last*. However, a sequence can be merely implied and must be noted by the reader. Consider the sentence *He walked through the garden and gave water and fertilizer to the plants*. Clearly, the man did not walk through the garden before he collected water and fertilizer for the plants. So, the implied sequence is that he first collected water, then he collected fertilizer, next he walked through the garden, and last he gave water or fertilizer as necessary to the plants. Texts do not always proceed in an orderly sequence from first to last. Sometimes they begin at the end and start over at the beginning. As a reader, you can enhance your understanding of the passage by taking brief notes to clarify the sequence.

MAKING CONNECTIONS TO ENHANCE COMPREHENSION

Reading involves thinking. For good comprehension, readers make **text-to-self**, **text-to-text**, and **text-to-world connections**. Making connections helps readers understand text better and predict what might occur next based on what they already know, such as how characters in the story feel or what happened in another text. Text-to-self connections with the reader's life and experiences make literature more personally relevant and meaningful to readers. Readers can make connections before, during, and after reading—including whenever the text reminds them of something similar they have encountered in life or other texts. The genre, setting, characters, plot elements, literary structure and devices, and themes an author uses allow a reader to make connections to other works of literature or to people and events in their own lives. Venn diagrams and other graphic organizers help visualize connections. Readers can also make double-entry notes: key content, ideas, events, words, and quotations on one side, and the connections with these on the other.

SUMMARIZING LITERATURE TO SUPPORT COMPREHENSION

When reading literature, especially demanding works, **summarizing** helps readers identify important information and organize it in their minds. They can also identify themes, problems, and solutions, and can sequence the story. Readers can summarize before, during, and after they read. They should use their own words, as they do when describing a personal event or giving directions. Previewing a text's organization before reading by examining the book cover, table of contents, and illustrations also aids summarizing. Making notes of key words and ideas in a graphic organizer while reading can benefit readers in the same way. Graphic organizers are another useful method; readers skim the text to determine main ideas and then narrow the list with the aid of the organizer. Unimportant details should be omitted in summaries. Summaries can be organized using description, problem-solution, comparison-contrast, sequence, main ideas, or cause-and-effect.

> **Review Video: Summarizing Text**
> Visit mometrix.com/academy and enter code: 172903

PARAPHRASING

Paraphrasing is another method that the reader can use to aid in comprehension. When paraphrasing, one puts what they have read into their own words by rephrasing what the author has written, or one "translates" all of what the author shared into their own words by including as many details as they can.

Copyright © Mometrix Media. You have been licensed one copy of this document for personal use only. Any other reproduction or redistribution is strictly prohibited. All rights reserved. This content is provided for test preparation purposes only and does not imply an endorsement by Mometrix of any particular political, scientific, or religious point of view.

CHAPTER QUIZ

1. All of the following are used for good comprehension, EXCEPT:

    a. Text-to-self connections.
    b. Text-to-others connections.
    c. Text-to-text connections.
    d. Text-to-world connections.

2. All of the following are terms in English that signal causes, EXCEPT:

    a. Because.
    b. Due to.
    c. Since.
    d. Therefore.

CHAPTER QUIZ ANSWER KEY

1. B: Reading involves thinking. For good comprehension, readers make text-to-self, text-to-text, and text-to-world connections. Making connections helps readers understand text better and predict what might occur next based on what they already know, such as how characters in the story feel or what happened in another text. Text-to-self connections with the reader's life and experiences make literature more personally relevant and meaningful to readers. Readers can make connections before, during, and after reading—including whenever the text reminds them of something similar they have encountered in life or other texts. The genre, setting, characters, plot elements, themes, and literary structure and devices an author uses allow a reader to make connections to other works of literature or to people and events in their own lives. Venn diagrams and other graphic organizers help visualize connections. Readers can also make double-entry notes: key content, ideas, events, words, and quotations on one side, and the connections with these on the other.

2. D: One of the most common text structures is cause and effect. A cause is an act or event that makes something happen, and an effect is the thing that happens as a result of the cause. A cause-and-effect relationship is not always explicit, but there are some terms in English that signal causes, such as *since*, *because*, and *due to*. Furthermore, terms that signal effects include *consequently*, *therefore*, and *this leads to*. As an example, consider the sentence, "Because the sky was clear, Ron did not bring an umbrella." The cause is the clear sky, and the effect is that Ron did not bring an umbrella. However, readers may find that sometimes the cause-and-effect relationship will not be clearly noted. For instance, the sentence, "He was late and missed the meeting," does not contain any signaling words, but the sentence still contains a cause ("he was late") and an effect ("he missed the meeting").

MAKING PREDICTIONS

When we read literature, **making predictions** about what will happen in the writing reinforces our purpose for reading and prepares us mentally. A **prediction** is a guess about what will happen next. Readers constantly make predictions based on what they have read and what they already know. We can make predictions before we begin reading and during our reading. Consider the following sentence: *Staring at the computer screen in shock, Kim blindly reached over for the brimming glass of water on the shelf to her side.* The sentence suggests that Kim is distracted, and that she is not looking at the glass that she is going to pick up. So, a reader might predict that Kim is going to knock over the glass. Of course, not every prediction will be accurate: perhaps Kim will pick the glass up

Copyright © Mometrix Media. You have been licensed one copy of this document for personal use only. Any other reproduction or redistribution is strictly prohibited. All rights reserved. This content is provided for test preparation purposes only and does not imply an endorsement by Mometrix of any particular political, scientific, or religious point of view.

cleanly. Nevertheless, the author has certainly created the expectation that the water might be spilled.

As we read on, we can test the accuracy of our predictions, revise them in light of additional reading, and confirm or refute our predictions. Predictions are always subject to revision as the reader acquires more information. A reader can make predictions by observing the title and illustrations; noting the structure, characters, and subject; drawing on existing knowledge relative to the subject; and asking "why" and "who" questions. Connecting reading to what we already know enables us to learn new information and construct meaning. For example, before third-graders read a book about Johnny Appleseed, they may start a KWL chart—a list of what they *Know*, what they *Want* to know or learn, and what they have *Learned* after reading. Activating existing background knowledge and thinking about the text before reading improves comprehension.

> **Review Video: Predictive Reading**
> Visit mometrix.com/academy and enter code: 437248

Test-taking tip: To respond to questions requiring future predictions, your answers should be based on evidence of past or present behavior and events.

EVALUATING PREDICTIONS

When making predictions, readers should be able to explain how they developed their prediction. One way readers can defend their thought process is by citing textual evidence. Textual evidence to evaluate reader predictions about literature includes specific synopses of the work, paraphrases of the work or parts of it, and direct quotations from the work. These references to the text must support the prediction by indicating, clearly or unclearly, what will happen later in the story. A text may provide these indications through literary devices such as foreshadowing. Foreshadowing is anything in a text that gives the reader a hint about what is to come by emphasizing the likelihood of an event or development. Foreshadowing can occur through descriptions, exposition, and dialogue. Foreshadowing in dialogue usually occurs when a character gives a warning or expresses a strong feeling that a certain event will occur. Foreshadowing can also occur through irony. However, unlike other forms of foreshadowing, the events that seem the most likely are the opposite of what actually happens. Instances of foreshadowing and irony can be summarized, paraphrased, or quoted to defend a reader's prediction.

> **Review Video: Textual Evidence for Predictions**
> Visit mometrix.com/academy and enter code: 261070

DRAWING CONCLUSIONS FROM INFERENCES

Inferences about literary text are logical conclusions that readers make based on their observations and previous knowledge. An inference is based on both what is found in a passage or a story and what is known from personal experience. For instance, a story may say that a character is frightened and can hear howling in the distance. Based on both what is in the text and personal knowledge, it is a logical conclusion that the character is frightened because he hears the sound of wolves. A good inference is supported by the information in a passage.

IMPLICIT AND EXPLICIT INFORMATION

By inferring, readers construct meanings from text that are personally relevant. By combining their own schemas or concepts and their background information pertinent to the text with what they read, readers interpret it according to both what the author has conveyed and their own unique perspectives. Inferences are different from **explicit information**, which is clearly stated in a

Copyright © Mometrix Media. You have been licensed one copy of this document for personal use only. Any other reproduction or redistribution is strictly prohibited. All rights reserved.
This content is provided for test preparation purposes only and does not imply an endorsement by Mometrix of any particular political, scientific, or religious point of view.

passage. Authors do not always explicitly spell out every meaning in what they write; many meanings are implicit. Through inference, readers can comprehend implied meanings in the text, and also derive personal significance from it, making the text meaningful and memorable to them. Inference is a natural process in everyday life. When readers infer, they can draw conclusions about what the author is saying, predict what may reasonably follow, amend these predictions as they continue to read, interpret the import of themes, and analyze the characters' feelings and motivations through their actions.

EXAMPLE OF DRAWING CONCLUSIONS FROM INFERENCES

Read the excerpt and decide why Jana finally relaxed.

> Jana loved her job, but the work was very demanding. She had trouble relaxing. She called a friend, but she still thought about work. She ordered a pizza, but eating it did not help. Then, her kitten jumped on her lap and began to purr. Jana leaned back and began to hum a little tune. She felt better.

You can draw the conclusion that Jana relaxed because her kitten jumped on her lap. The kitten purred, and Jana leaned back and hummed a tune. Then she felt better. The excerpt does not explicitly say that this is the reason why she was able to relax. The text leaves the matter unclear, but the reader can infer or make a "best guess" that this is the reason she is relaxing. This is a logical conclusion based on the information in the passage. It is the best conclusion a reader can make based on the information he or she has read. Inferences are based on the information in a passage, but they are not directly stated in the passage.

Test-taking tip: While being tested on your ability to make correct inferences, you must look for **contextual clues**. An answer can be true, but not the best or most correct answer. The contextual clues will help you find the answer that is the **best answer** out of the given choices. Be careful in your reading to understand the context in which a phrase is stated. When asked for the implied meaning of a statement made in the passage, you should immediately locate the statement and read the **context** in which the statement was made. Also, look for an answer choice that has a similar phrase to the statement in question.

> **Review Video: Inference**
> Visit mometrix.com/academy and enter code: 379203
>
> **Review Video: How to Support a Conclusion**
> Visit mometrix.com/academy and enter code: 281653

CHAPTER QUIZ

1. Which of the following describes logical conclusions that readers make based on their observations and previous knowledge?

   a. Imperatives
   b. Interrogatives
   c. Inferences
   d. Predictions

CHAPTER QUIZ ANSWER KEY

1. C: Inferences about literary text are logical conclusions that readers make based on their observations and previous knowledge. An inference is based on both what is found in a passage or a story and what is known from personal experience. For instance, a story may say that a character is

Copyright © Mometrix Media. You have been licensed one copy of this document for personal use only. Any other reproduction or redistribution is strictly prohibited. All rights reserved.
This content is provided for test preparation purposes only and does not imply an endorsement by Mometrix of any particular political, scientific, or religious point of view.

frightened and can hear howling in the distance. Based on both what is in the text and personal knowledge, it is a logical conclusion that the character is frightened because they hear the sound of wolves. A good inference is supported by the information in a passage.

PURPOSES FOR WRITING

In order to be an effective reader, one must pay attention to the author's **position** and **purpose**. Even those texts that seem objective and impartial, like textbooks, have a position and bias. Readers need to take these positions into account when considering the author's message. When an author uses emotional language or clearly favors one side of an argument, his or her position is clear. However, the author's position may be evident not only in what he or she writes, but also in what he or she doesn't write. In a normal setting, a reader would want to review some other texts on the same topic in order to develop a view of the author's position. If this was not possible, then you would want to at least acquire some background about the author. However, since you are in the middle of an exam and the only source of information is the text, you should look for language and argumentation that seems to indicate a particular stance on the subject.

> **Review Video: Author's Position**
> Visit mometrix.com/academy and enter code: 827954

Usually, identifying the author's **purpose** is easier than identifying his or her position. In most cases, the author has no interest in hiding his or her purpose. A text that is meant to entertain, for instance, should be written to please the reader. Most narratives, or stories, are written to entertain, though they may also inform or persuade. Informative texts are easy to identify, while the most difficult purpose of a text to identify is persuasion because the author has an interest in making this purpose hard to detect. When a reader discovers that the author is trying to persuade, he or she should be skeptical of the argument. For this reason, persuasive texts often try to establish an entertaining tone and hope to amuse the reader into agreement. On the other hand, an informative tone may be implemented to create an appearance of authority and objectivity.

An author's purpose is evident often in the organization of the text (e.g., section headings in bold font points to an informative text). However, you may not have such organization available to you in your exam. Instead, if the author makes his or her main idea clear from the beginning, then the likely purpose of the text is to inform. If the author begins by making a claim and provides various arguments to support that claim, then the purpose is probably to persuade. If the author tells a story or wants to gain the reader's attention more than to push a particular point or deliver information, then his or her purpose is most likely to entertain. As a reader, you must judge authors on how well they accomplish their purpose. In other words, you need to consider the type of passage (e.g., technical, persuasive, etc.) that the author has written and if the author has followed the requirements of the passage type.

MAKING LOGICAL CONCLUSIONS ABOUT A PASSAGE

A reader should always be drawing conclusions from the text. Sometimes conclusions are **implied** from written information, and other times the information is **stated directly** within the passage. One should always aim to draw conclusions from information stated within a passage, rather than to draw them from mere implications. At times an author may provide some information and then describe a counterargument. Readers should be alert for direct statements that are subsequently rejected or weakened by the author. Furthermore, you should always read through the entire passage before drawing conclusions. Many readers are trained to expect the author's conclusions at either the beginning or the end of the passage, but many texts do not adhere to this format.

Copyright © Mometrix Media. You have been licensed one copy of this document for personal use only. Any other reproduction or redistribution is strictly prohibited. All rights reserved.
This content is provided for test preparation purposes only and does not imply an endorsement by Mometrix of any particular political, scientific, or religious point of view.

Drawing conclusions from information implied within a passage requires confidence on the part of the reader. **Implications** are things that the author does not state directly, but readers can assume based on what the author does say. Consider the following passage: *I stepped outside and opened my umbrella. By the time I got to work, the cuffs of my pants were soaked.* The author never states that it is raining, but this fact is clearly implied. Conclusions based on implication must be well supported by the text. In order to draw a solid conclusion, readers should have **multiple pieces of evidence**. If readers have only one piece, they must be assured that there is no other possible explanation than their conclusion. A good reader will be able to draw many conclusions from information implied by the text, which will be a great help on the exam.

DRAWING CONCLUSIONS

A common type of inference that a reader has to make is **drawing a conclusion**. The reader makes this conclusion based on the information provided within a text. Certain facts are included to help a reader come to a specific conclusion. For example, a story may open with a man trudging through the snow on a cold winter day, dragging a sled behind him. The reader can logically **infer** from the setting of the story that the man is wearing heavy winter clothes in order to stay warm. Information is implied based on the setting of a story, which is why **setting** is an important element of the text. If the same man in the example was trudging down a beach on a hot summer day, dragging a surf board behind him, the reader would assume that the man is not wearing heavy clothes. The reader makes inferences based on their own experiences and the information presented to them in the story.

Test-taking tip: When asked to identify a conclusion that may be drawn, look for critical "hedge" phrases, such as *likely*, *may*, *can*, and *will often*, among many others. When you are being tested on this knowledge, remember the question that writers insert into these hedge phrases to cover every possibility. Often an answer will be wrong simply because there is no room for exception. Extreme positive or negative answers (such as always or never) are usually not correct. When answering these questions, the reader **should not** use any outside knowledge that is not gathered directly or reasonably inferred from the passage. Correct answers can be derived straight from the passage.

EXAMPLE

Read the following sentence from *Little Women* by Louisa May Alcott and draw a conclusion based upon the information presented:

> *You know the reason Mother proposed not having any presents this Christmas was because it is going to be a hard winter for everyone; and she thinks we ought not to spend money for pleasure, when our men are suffering so in the army.*

Based on the information in the sentence, the reader can conclude, or **infer**, that the men are away at war while the women are still at home. The pronoun *our* gives a clue to the reader that the character is speaking about men she knows. In addition, the reader can assume that the character is speaking to a brother or sister, since the term "Mother" is used by the character while speaking to another person. The reader can also come to the conclusion that the characters celebrate Christmas, since it is mentioned in the **context** of the sentence. In the sentence, the mother is presented as an unselfish character who is opinionated and thinks about the wellbeing of other people.

Copyright © Mometrix Media. You have been licensed one copy of this document for personal use only. Any other reproduction or redistribution is strictly prohibited. All rights reserved.
This content is provided for test preparation purposes only and does not imply an endorsement by Mometrix of any particular political, scientific, or religious point of view.

COMPARING TWO STORIES

When presented with two different stories, there will be **similarities** and **differences** between the two. A reader needs to make a list, or other graphic organizer, of the points presented in each story. Once the reader has written down the main point and supporting points for each story, the two sets of ideas can be compared. The reader can then present each idea and show how it is the same or different in the other story. This is called **comparing and contrasting ideas**.

The reader can compare ideas by stating, for example: "In Story 1, the author believes that humankind will one day land on Mars, whereas in Story 2, the author believes that Mars is too far away for humans to ever step foot on." Note that the two viewpoints are different in each story that the reader is comparing. A reader may state that: "Both stories discussed the likelihood of humankind landing on Mars." This statement shows how the viewpoint presented in both stories is based on the same topic, rather than how each viewpoint is different. The reader will complete a comparison of two stories with a conclusion.

> **Review Video: Comparing Two Stories**
> Visit mometrix.com/academy and enter code: 833765

OUTLINING A PASSAGE

As an aid to drawing conclusions, **outlining** the information contained in the passage should be a familiar skill to readers. An effective outline will reveal the structure of the passage and will lead to solid conclusions. An effective outline will have a title that refers to the basic subject of the text, though the title does not need to restate the main idea. In most outlines, the main idea will be the first major section. Each major idea in the passage will be established as the head of a category. For instance, the most common outline format calls for the main ideas of the passage to be indicated with Roman numerals. In an effective outline of this kind, each of the main ideas will be represented by a Roman numeral and none of the Roman numerals will designate minor details or secondary ideas. Moreover, all supporting ideas and details should be placed in the appropriate place on the outline. An outline does not need to include every detail listed in the text, but it should feature all of those that are central to the argument or message. Each of these details should be listed under the corresponding main idea.

> **Review Video: Outlining**
> Visit mometrix.com/academy and enter code: 584445

USING GRAPHIC ORGANIZERS

Ideas from a text can also be organized using **graphic organizers**. A graphic organizer is a way to simplify information and take key points from the text. A graphic organizer such as a timeline may have an event listed for a corresponding date on the timeline, while an outline may have an event listed under a key point that occurs in the text. Each reader needs to create the type of graphic organizer that works the best for him or her in terms of being able to recall information from a story. Examples include a spider-map, which takes a main idea from the story and places it in a bubble with supporting points branching off the main idea. An outline is useful for diagramming the main and supporting points of the entire story, and a Venn diagram compares and contrasts characteristics of two or more ideas.

> **Review Video: Graphic Organizers**
> Visit mometrix.com/academy and enter code: 665513

Copyright © Mometrix Media. You have been licensed one copy of this document for personal use only. Any other reproduction or redistribution is strictly prohibited. All rights reserved.
This content is provided for test preparation purposes only and does not imply an endorsement by Mometrix of any particular political, scientific, or religious point of view.

SUMMARIZING

A helpful tool is the ability to **summarize** the information that you have read in a paragraph or passage format. This process is similar to creating an effective outline. First, a summary should accurately define the main idea of the passage, though the summary does not need to explain this main idea in exhaustive detail. The summary should continue by laying out the most important supporting details or arguments from the passage. All of the significant supporting details should be included, and none of the details included should be irrelevant or insignificant. Also, the summary should accurately report all of these details. Too often, the desire for brevity in a summary leads to the sacrifice of clarity or accuracy. Summaries are often difficult to read because they omit all of the graceful language, digressions, and asides that distinguish great writing. However, an effective summary should communicate the same overall message as the original text.

EVALUATING A PASSAGE

It is important to understand the logical conclusion of the ideas presented in an informational text. **Identifying a logical conclusion** can help you determine whether you agree with the writer or not. Coming to this conclusion is much like making an inference: the approach requires you to combine the information given by the text with what you already know and make a logical conclusion. If the author intended for the reader to draw a certain conclusion, then you can expect the author's argumentation and detail to be leading in that direction.

One way to approach the task of drawing conclusions is to make brief **notes** of all the points made by the author. When the notes are arranged on paper, they may clarify the logical conclusion. Another way to approach conclusions is to consider whether the reasoning of the author raises any pertinent questions. Sometimes you will be able to draw several conclusions from a passage. On occasion these will be conclusions that were never imagined by the author. Therefore, be aware that these conclusions must be **supported directly by the text**.

EVALUATION OF SUMMARIES

A summary of a literary passage is a condensation in the reader's own words of the passage's main points. Several guidelines can be used in evaluating a summary. The summary should be complete yet concise. It should be accurate, balanced, fair, neutral, and objective, excluding the reader's own opinions or reactions. It should reflect in similar proportion how much each point summarized was covered in the original passage. Summary writers should include tags of attribution, like "Macaulay argues that" to reference the original author whose ideas are represented in the summary. Summary writers should not overuse quotations; they should only quote central concepts or phrases they cannot precisely convey in words other than those of the original author. Another aspect of evaluating a summary is considering whether it can stand alone as a coherent, unified composition. In addition, evaluation of a summary should include whether its writer has cited the original source of the passage they have summarized so that readers can find it.

CHAPTER QUIZ

1. Which of the following is most important when drawing conclusions from a text?
- a. The conclusions make sense to others.
- b. The conclusions are supported directly by the text.
- c. The conclusions agree with previous convictions.
- d. The conclusions align with the author's purpose for writing the text.

Copyright © Mometrix Media. You have been licensed one copy of this document for personal use only. Any other reproduction or redistribution is strictly prohibited. All rights reserved.
This content is provided for test preparation purposes only and does not imply an endorsement by Mometrix of any particular political, scientific, or religious point of view.

2. All of the following are true about summaries, EXCEPT:
   a. They should focus on the main point of the text rather than proportional to how much each point was covered in the passage.
   b. They should be accurate, balanced, fair, neutral, and objective.
   c. They should be complete and concise.
   d. They should only quote central concepts or phrases that cannot be precisely conveyed in words other than those of the original author.

CHAPTER QUIZ ANSWER KEY

1. B: It is important to understand the logical conclusion of the ideas presented in an informational text. Identifying a logical conclusion can help readers determine whether they agree with the writer or not. Coming to this conclusion is much like making an inference: the approach requires readers to combine the information given by the text with what they already know and make a logical conclusion. If the author intended for the reader to draw a certain conclusion, then readers can expect the author's argumentation and detail to be leading in that direction. Sometimes a reader will be able to draw several conclusions from a passage. On occasion these will be conclusions that were never imagined by the author. Therefore, be aware that these conclusions must be supported directly by the text.

2. A: A summary of a literary passage is a condensation in the reader's own words of the passage's main points. Several guidelines can be used in evaluating a summary. The summary should be complete yet concise. It should be accurate, balanced, fair, neutral, and objective, excluding the reader's own opinions or reactions. It should reflect in similar proportion how much each point summarized was covered in the original passage. Summary writers should include tags of attribution, like "Macaulay argues that" to reference the original author whose ideas are represented in the summary. Summary writers should not overuse quotations, but only quote central concepts or phrases they cannot precisely convey in words other than those of the original author. Another aspect of evaluating a summary is considering whether it can stand alone as a coherent, unified composition. In addition, evaluation of a summary should include whether its writer has cited the original source of the passage they have summarized so that readers can find it.

DIVERSITY AND SITUATIONAL NATURE OF LANGUAGE

Language is a diverse tool that allows people to communicate. However, language is often impacted and molded by the culture that uses it. This can make it difficult to learn and use a new language, since not all native speakers of the language will use it or interpret it the same way. For example, English is spoken all over America, but Americans in various regions of the country speak using different **dialects**. Other differences in speech include **accents** and **rhythm of speech**. Language is also manipulated by situations. Some terms and phrases have multiple meanings. A word's meaning often depends on the **context** in which the word or phrase is used, meaning that non-native speakers must learn to interpret situations to understand messages.

FACTORS OF LANGUAGE AND COMMUNICATION

INFLUENCES ON LANGUAGE

While dialect and diction are heavily influenced by an individual's culture and the location and history of the place they live, other personal factors can also impact language. A person's ethnicity, religious beliefs or background, and gender can influence the way they use and understand language. **Ethnicity** impacts language by incorporating a group's communication norms into an individual's speech and behavior. These norms may affect a speaker's tone, volume, or pace. These factors may lead others outside of that group to misinterpret the speaker's message, depending on

Copyright © Mometrix Media. You have been licensed one copy of this document for personal use only. Any other reproduction or redistribution is strictly prohibited. All rights reserved.
This content is provided for test preparation purposes only and does not imply an endorsement by Mometrix of any particular political, scientific, or religious point of view.

their understanding of how those factors are used in speech. A person's **religious beliefs** can also affect their use of language. Religious beliefs and practices may lead an individual to abstain from using certain terms and may change the context in which a speaker uses specific words, or change their understanding of the word's usage. Additionally, a person may use language differently depending on their gender. **Gender's** influence on communication varies by region and industry. A region or industry's treatment of gender roles often impacts language use among its members. This can lead members of one gender group to be more assertive or submissive or to use different terms and phrases.

CULTURE AND COMMUNICATION

Individuals from different countries and cultures communicate differently. Not only do many people speak different languages, but they also speak using different inflections, volumes, tones, and dialects. These factors can have a significant impact on communication, even if the communicators speak the same language. In different cultures, certain behaviors are associated with different meanings and implications. When communicators from different cultures have a conversation, these expectations and associations may lead to misunderstanding. For example, Americans are considered to be louder and more demonstrative than people from other countries. Someone from a country where people speak more quietly who is not aware of this characterization may perceive an American's volume or large gestures as an indication of anger, when in reality, the American speaker is calm. The American may similarly perceive the other person as sad or shy due to their quiet voice, when the speaker is actually happy and comfortable in the conversation. Awareness of these factors and effects promotes respect for others and helps speakers understand the reasons for differences in communication, rather than allowing these differences to create division or conflict.

LANGUAGE VS. DIALECT

Languages are distinct and structured forms of verbal communication. Languages have cohesive sets of rules and words that are shared between the majority of that language's users. The main identifier of a language is that members of one language group are incapable of communicating fluently with members of another language group. New languages are formed as different dialects grow further apart until the members of each dialect can no longer innately communicate with each other.

Dialects are subsets of languages that do not violate the rules of the language as a whole, but which vary from other dialects in vocabulary usage, grammar forms, pronunciation, and spelling. Two major groupings of dialects are American and British English. Most American English and British English speakers can communicate with relative ease with one another, though the pronunciation, vocabulary (torch vs. flashlight; trunk vs. boot), spelling (meter vs. metre; color vs. colour), and grammar (in American English, collective nouns are always considered singular, but can be singular or plural in British English).

DEVELOPMENT OF DIALECTS OVER TIME

Dialects are formed primarily through the influences of location and time, but can be the result of other elements of **social stratification** as well (economic, ethnic, religious, etc.). As one group of a language's speakers is separated from another, in British and American English speakers for example, the language develops in isolated locations at the same time, resulting in distinct dialects. Language changes continuously over time as new words and phrases are adopted and others are phased out. Eventually, these small changes result culminate into enough grammar and vocabulary changes that the speakers of the distinct dialects cannot easily communicate with one another. The dialects can then be recognized as distinct languages.

Copyright © Mometrix Media. You have been licensed one copy of this document for personal use only. Any other reproduction or redistribution is strictly prohibited. All rights reserved. This content is provided for test preparation purposes only and does not imply an endorsement by Mometrix of any particular political, scientific, or religious point of view.

USE OF DIALECT IN MEDIA

Literary authors often use dialect when writing dialogue to illustrate the social and geographical backgrounds of specific characters, which supports character development. For example, in *The Adventures of Huckleberry Finn* (1885), Mark Twain's novel is written in the dialect of a young, uneducated, white, Southern character, opening with this sentence: "You don't know about me without you have read a book by the name of The Adventures of Tom Sawyer, but that ain't no matter." Twain uses a different and exaggerated dialect to represent the speech of the African-American slave Jim: "We's safe, Huck, we's safe! Jump up and crack yo' heels. Dat's de good ole Cairo at las', I jis knows it."

In *To Kill a Mockingbird,* author Harper Lee used dialect in the characters' dialogue to portray an uneducated boy in the American South: "Reckon I have. Almost died the first year I come to school and et them pecans—folks say he pizened 'em." Lee also uses many Southern regional expressions, such as "right stove up," "What in the sam holy hill?", "sit a spell," "fess" (meaning "confess"), "jim-dandy," and "hush your fussing." These contribute to Lee's characterization of the people she describes, who live in a small town in Alabama circa the 1930s. In *Wuthering Heights* (1847), Emily Bronte reproduces Britain's 18th–19th-century Yorkshire dialect in the speech of servant Joseph: "Running after t'lads, as usuald!... If I war yah, maister, I'd just slam t'boards i' their faces all on 'em, gentle and simple! Never a day ut yah're off, but yon cat o' Linton comes sneaking hither; and Miss Nelly, shoo's a fine lass!"

DIALECT VS. DICTION

When written as characters' dialogue in literary works, dialect represents the particular pronunciation, grammar, and figurative expressions used by certain groups of people based on their geographic region, social class, and cultural background. For example, when a character says, "There's gold up in them thar hills," the author is using dialect to add to the characterization of that individual. Diction is more related to individual characters than to groups of people. The way in which a specific character speaks, including his or her choice of words, manner of expressing himself or herself, and use of grammar all represent individual types of diction. For example, two characters in the same novel might describe the same action or event using different diction: One says "I'm heading uptown for the evening," and the other says "I'm going out for a night on the town." These convey the same literal meaning, but due to their variations in diction, the speakers are expressing themselves in slightly different ways.

> **Review Video: Dialogue, Paradox, and Dialect**
> Visit mometrix.com/academy and enter code: 684341

INFLUENCES ON REGIONAL DIALECT

Linguistic researchers have identified regional variations in vocabulary choices, which have evolved because of differences in local climates and how they influence human behaviors. For example, in the Southern United States, the Linguistic Atlas of the Gulf States (LAGS) Project by Dr. Lee Pederson of Emory University discovered and documented that people living in the northern or Upland section of the Piedmont plateau region call the fungal infection commonly known as athlete's foot "toe itch," but people living in the southern or Lowland section call it "ground itch." The explanation for this difference is that in the north, temperatures are cooler and people wear shoes accordingly, so they associate the itching with the feet in their description, but in the south, temperatures are hotter and people often went barefoot, so they associated the itching with the ground that presumably transmitted the infection.

Copyright © Mometrix Media. You have been licensed one copy of this document for personal use only. Any other reproduction or redistribution is strictly prohibited. All rights reserved. This content is provided for test preparation purposes only and does not imply an endorsement by Mometrix of any particular political, scientific, or religious point of view.

USING DIALECT IN WRITING

Dialect is most appropriate for informal or creative writing. Using dialectal writing when communicating casually or informally, such as in a text message or a quick email to a peer, is acceptable. However, in academic and professional contexts, writing using indications of dialect is inappropriate and often unacceptable. If the audience includes individuals who have a higher rank than the author, or authority over the author, it is best not to write in a way that suggests a dialect.

CHAPTER QUIZ

1. Dialect can be used in all of the following situations, EXCEPT:

    a.   Creative writing.
    b.   Text messages.
    c.   Emails to peers.
    d.   Professional contexts.

CHAPTER QUIZ ANSWER KEY

1. D: Dialect is most appropriate for informal or creative writing. Using dialectal writing when communicating casually or informally, such as in a text message or a quick email to a peer, is acceptable. However, in academic and professional contexts, writing using indications of dialect is inappropriate and often unacceptable. If the audience includes individuals who have a higher rank than the author, or authority over the author, then it is best not to write in a way that suggests a dialect.

AMERICAN LITERARY PERIODS

DARK ROMANTICS

In American literature, a group of late Romantic writers are recognized as **Dark Romantics**. These authors' works may be associated with both the Romantic and Gothic movements. These works emphasize nature and emotion, aligning them with Romanticism, and include dark themes and tones, aligning them with Gothic literature. However, these works do not all feature the historically inspired characteristics of Gothic literature, and their morals or outcomes more closely resemble those of Romantic literature. The Dark Romantics include writers such as Edgar Allan Poe, Nathaniel Hawthorne, Emily Dickinson, and Herman Melville.

TRANSCENDENTALISM

Transcendentalism was a smaller movement that occurred alongside the American Romantic movement. The **transcendentalists** shared the Romantic emphasis on emotion and also focused heavily on how a person experiences life through their senses. They extended these sentiments to suggest that through embracing one's senses, an individual could transcend, or experience a state of being above physical humanity. They also extended the Romantic emphasis on subjectivity through their praise of self-sufficiency, as exemplified through Ralph Waldo Emerson's *Self-Reliance*. Emerson was a prominent transcendentalist. His writings included an essay titled *Nature*, which explains a progression from the use of the senses to the achievement of transcendence. Transcendentalist literature includes several essays that discuss the value of the senses and emotions or the process of transcendence. Transcendentalists also wrote poetry that includes the frequent use of imagery, metaphors, and references to nature. These elements reflect the ideas of transcendentalism and create a resemblance to the alleged experience of transcendence. Ralph Waldo Emerson, Henry David Thoreau, and Walt Whitman were all prominent writers in this movement.

Copyright © Mometrix Media. You have been licensed one copy of this document for personal use only. Any other reproduction or redistribution is strictly prohibited. All rights reserved.
This content is provided for test preparation purposes only and does not imply an endorsement by Mometrix of any particular political, scientific, or religious point of view.

COLONIAL AMERICA

The **colonial era** in America was influenced by immigration from England to what is now New England. These immigrants were mainly Puritans who centered their society in New England on their religious beliefs, allowing those beliefs to inform all aspects of their lives. This is apparent in the literature of the time, as much of it includes essays and sermons that discuss religion or the way the Puritans believed one should live and conduct themselves. Colonial literature also includes many poems, and these works also discuss or reference religious ideas and themes. There was not much fiction written in Colonial America, as most of the literature was written to inform or persuade.

ROMANTIC PERIOD

The **American Romantic** movement is also known as the American Renaissance. This movement yielded several notable American writers and works that began characterizing American literature and differentiating it from British literature. This literature, written after the American Revolutionary War and until the end of the Civil War, praised individualism and featured an expression of national pride and patriotism. The transcendentalists' extreme ideas about self-sufficiency and subjectivity reiterated this individualism, and their recommendations about society and its structure furthered the separation of American literature from British literature. While this period shaped the definition of American literature, it is criticized for featuring a narrow view of American politics and social issues at the time, as well as promoting a small group of similar writers.

> **Review Video: Authors in the Romantic Period**
> Visit mometrix.com/academy and enter code: 752719

HARLEM RENAISSANCE

The **Harlem Renaissance** took place in America during the 1920s and 1930s. The changing economy and opportunities led African Americans in the south to seek new lifestyles in other parts of America at the beginning of the 20th century. Many moved to Harlem, a small area in New York City. This group of African Americans yielded highly influential scholarly and artistic works, including poetry, fiction, music, and plays. The Harlem Renaissance marked an opportunity for these intellectuals and artists, who were largely ignored in the aftermath of the Civil War, to use their talents and express themselves through their works. While artists often featured personal expression in their works, the Harlem Renaissance was unique in its volume of culturally expressive works. This cultural expression and the movement's main ideas also contributed to the Civil Rights movement by promoting a spirit of unity among African Americans. The Harlem Renaissance eventually ended in the wake of the stock market crash in 1929. As the Great Depression began, financial support for the arts dwindled, making it difficult for many artists to succeed financially. Some members of the Harlem Renaissance who influenced American literature include Langston Hughes, Zora Neale Hurston, and Paul Robeson.

BRITISH LITERARY PERIODS
NEOCLASSICAL

The **British Neoclassical** period began in the middle of the 17th century and ended in the late 18th century. The latter part of the movement also took place alongside the Enlightenment, a period of scientific discovery and study that influenced many Western cultures. The Enlightenment's concern with intellectual pursuits and improvement increased discussions of introspection, or an individual's analysis of their own behavior, thoughts, and self. These ideas also affected society in England, as they contributed to a general attitude of complacency and a desire to ignore the past.

Copyright © Mometrix Media. You have been licensed one copy of this document for personal use only. Any other reproduction or redistribution is strictly prohibited. All rights reserved. This content is provided for test preparation purposes only and does not imply an endorsement by Mometrix of any particular political, scientific, or religious point of view.

The period saw a slightly increased acceptance of female writers, as their works were viewed as a method of self-reflection and improvement. The changes in British society allowed several new forms of literature to gain popularity and acceptance, usually for their introspective qualities. Essays, diaries, and letters all displayed the author's thoughts and experience, aligning them with the culture's values. Novels also gained popularity, as many were fictional diaries or epistolary novels. Journalism flourished during the Neoclassical period, leading to the creation of the newspaper. Literary criticism also gained popularity, though it was used to criticize an author and their style rather than examine or analyze the content of the work.

VICTORIAN

The **Victorian Era** in England was influenced by a variety of events and ideas, many of which were influenced by the Victorians' economy. The Industrial Revolution in England changed the circumstances of work for the Victorians. The changing industries and lack of labor laws led to several problems and a wide division between Victorian social classes. These factors inspired and saturated much of Victorian literature. Many novels' plots and characters were heavily influenced by social and economic issues, and many poems referenced and criticized specific events that occurred during this period.

While the structure of Victorian society was a major influence on literature, there were other popular topics that appeared in literature. Topics like evolution, psychology, and colonization frequently appeared in Victorian literature, reflecting the concerns and interests of the Victorian culture. The Victorian society was also characterized by a strict moral code that supported the view of women as homemakers and criticized the idea of female writers. Not only did this affect the portrayal of women in literature, but it also led some female novelists, such as the Bronte sisters, to write under a pseudonym and present their works as having been written by a man. Victorian literature also popularized forms of literature, including the novel and the dramatic monologue, a poetic form developed by Robert Browning. Victorian writers include Charles Dickens, Oscar Wilde, Elizabeth Barrett Browning, Emily Bronte, Matthew Arnold, and Thomas Hardy.

WORLD LITERARY CHARACTERISTICS AND PERIODS

While many other nations shared literary movements with America and England, there are numerous literary movements that are unique to other countries and cultures. Some of these literary movements can be understood as variations of movements like Romanticism or modernism, since they occurred at similar times and feature similar elements, but the political and cultural events of each country shaped their version of each movement. Most regions also have some type of mythology, and while different mythologies have similar characters and events, each region's mythology is unique and significant to the region's literature. Another common feature of world literature is colonialism. Many nations are former colonies of European countries, and the effects of colonization are present in modern literature from countries worldwide, making it a key feature of many regions' body of literature.

AFRICAN LITERATURE

Literature from some cultures was not recorded until the 19th century, causing any movements and trends to be informed by ideas told aloud. This is true of African literature, where stories and ideas were spoken and passed down through the generations. Early African poetry was often metaphorical, structured or written to form a paradox, and included a riddle or puzzling statement. Proverbs and didactic tales were also told frequently, reflecting the dominant religions in a given region and time period. These poems and stories also reflect the variety of languages spoken in Africa and the shifts in each language's usage. Early African literature, once people began writing it down, included stories and proverbs that had been passed down, translations of religious texts, and

Copyright © Mometrix Media. You have been licensed one copy of this document for personal use only. Any other reproduction or redistribution is strictly prohibited. All rights reserved. This content is provided for test preparation purposes only and does not imply an endorsement by Mometrix of any particular political, scientific, or religious point of view.

descriptions of the way of life in different African cultures or groups. These cultures and the events specific to each of them produce a unique body of literature that places emphasis on certain topics and ideas. For example, much of the modern literature written in South Africa discusses politics and issues of race, since the country's history is characterized by events and movements that revolved around these topics.

ASIAN LITERATURE

Asian literature features writings from several different countries and languages and has spanned many centuries. Many popular forms of writing have come from Asia, such as the haiku. A couple of significant literary movements include The Hungry Generation in South Asia and the Misty Poets in China. The Hungry Generation is a literary movement involving literature written in the Bengali language, spoken mainly in West Bengal and Bangladesh. The literature is characterized by unique and innovative writing, which impacted the use of figurative language in the region. The Hungry Generation also discussed cultural issues, particularly colonization in the region, and many participants were arrested for their work. The Misty Poets in China were characterized by their expressive use of abstractions. Their name, Misty Poets, comes from their writings, which were difficult to interpret due to their use of abstract language and ambiguity. This movement was partly inspired by the Misty Poets' distaste for literary realism, though its influence is detectable within their poetry. Many of the Misty Poets were punished for their poetry, since the poetry of this movement was also politically critical.

LATIN AMERICAN LITERATURE

Latin American literature has several literary movements, many of which occurred near the same time as American and British literary movements and share ideas and trends with their English counterparts. Despite these similarities, each of these movements is distinguishable as its own movement with unique impacts of Latin American literature. By the 17th century, written language was in use in Mexico, and Latin American literary trends and figures had been recognized. During the 18th century, Latin American literature featured a variety of ideas and themes within each form of literature. By the 19th century, literary themes were more unified throughout popular Latin American literature. In the early 19th century, Latin American literature embraced the Romantic movement as it came to an end in England and the United States. Several Latin American countries were also fighting for independence during this time, amplifying the Romantic idea of national pride and identity.

In the wake of the Romantic movement, Latin American literature introduced the unique *Modernismo* movement, which yielded a large volume of poetry and is characterized by the use of whimsical imagery and discussions of spiritual ideas. Following *Modernismo* was the *Vanguardia* movement, which was created to introduce diversity within Latin American literature after modernism permeated the literature of the time. *Vanguardia* involved writers taking risks in their writing and breaking the mold from typical Latin American literature. In the 20th century, *Estridentismo* followed the *Vanguardia* movement, marrying the *Vanguardia* movement with the European Avant-Garde movement. Other 20th century movements functioned similarly by adapting literary movements from other regions to suit the themes and trends in Latin American literature, reflect Latin American cultures, and set their literature apart from other cultures.

Copyright © Mometrix Media. You have been licensed one copy of this document for personal use only. Any other reproduction or redistribution is strictly prohibited. All rights reserved. This content is provided for test preparation purposes only and does not imply an endorsement by Mometrix of any particular political, scientific, or religious point of view.

CHAPTER QUIZ

1. Which of the following writers is NOT considered a Dark Romantic?

    a. Edgar Allan Poe
    b. Emily Dickinson
    c. Herman Melville
    d. Ralph Waldo Emerson

2. Langston Hughes, Zora Neale Hurston, and Paul Robeson were members of which literary movement?

    a. British Neoclassical period
    b. American Romantic movement
    c. Harlem Renaissance
    d. Hungry Generation

CHAPTER QUIZ ANSWER KEY

1. D: In American literature, a group of late Romantic writers are recognized as Dark Romantics. These authors' works may be associated with both the Romantic and Gothic movements. These works emphasize nature and emotion, aligning them with Romanticism—and include dark themes and tones, aligning them with Gothic literature. However, these works do not all feature the historically inspired characteristics of Gothic literature, and their morals or outcomes more closely resemble those of Romantic literature. The Dark Romantics include writers such as Edgar Allan Poe, Nathaniel Hawthorne, Emily Dickinson, and Herman Melville.

2. C: The Harlem Renaissance took place in America during the 1920s and 1930s. The changing economy and opportunities led African Americans in the south to seek new lifestyles in other parts of America at the beginning of the 20th century. Many moved to Harlem, a small area in New York City. This group of African Americans yielded highly influential scholarly and artistic works, including poetry, fiction, music, and plays. The Harlem Renaissance marked an opportunity for these intellectuals and artists, who were largely ignored in the aftermath of the Civil War, to use their talents and express themselves through their works. While artists often featured personal expression in their works, the Harlem Renaissance was unique in its volume of culturally expressive works. This cultural expression and the movement's main ideas also contributed to the Civil Rights movement by promoting a spirit of unity among African Americans. The Harlem Renaissance eventually ended in the wake of the stock market crash in 1929. As the Great Depression began, financial support for the arts dwindled, making it difficult for many artists to succeed financially. Some members of the Harlem Renaissance who influenced American literature include Langston Hughes, Zora Neale Hurston, and Paul Robeson.

OLD ENGLISH

The English language developed over a long period of time through interactions between different groups in Europe, including the Romans, the Germans, and the Celtics. The Anglo-Saxons, a group that left what is now Germany and settled in England, further established the English language by using what is now called **Old English**. While Old English laid foundations for modern English, its usage fundamentally differs from the way English is used today. For example, Old English relied on inflections to create meaning, placing little importance on the order of the words in the sentence. Its use of verbs and tenses also differs from modern English grammar. The Anglo-Saxons also used kennings, or compound words that functioned as figurative language.

Old English, as a language influenced by several cultures, had dialects from its inception. Differences in usage also came from the division between secular and religious cultures. This

Copyright © Mometrix Media. You have been licensed one copy of this document for personal use only. Any other reproduction or redistribution is strictly prohibited. All rights reserved. This content is provided for test preparation purposes only and does not imply an endorsement by Mometrix of any particular political, scientific, or religious point of view.

division heavily influenced Old English literature, as most of the literature from the time is categorized according to the set of beliefs it reflects. Most of the influential literature of the time includes riddles, poems, or translations of religious texts. Surviving Old English poetry mainly discusses real heroes and battles or provides a narrative about a fictional hero. Many of these fictional poems are considered *lays*, or *lais*, which are narrative poems that are structured using couplets of lines containing eight syllables each. The translations were often of passages from the Christian Bible, adaptations of Biblical passages, or copies of Christian hymns. Old English persisted until the 12th century, where it was eventually replaced with Middle English. Influential literature from this period includes *Beowulf*, "The Wanderer," "The Wife's Lament," and "The Seafarer."

MIDDLE ENGLISH

Old English was replaced by **Middle English**, which was used from the 12th century to the 16th century. Old English was not governed by a consistent set of grammatical rules until the Norse people, their language, and its structure influenced the integration of grammar into English, leading to Middle English. Middle English relied less on inflections than Old English, instead creating variations by using affixes and synonyms. The development of grammar was further facilitated by the printing press, which made it easier for writers to comply with grammar rules since the printing of identical copies reduced variation between texts.

Old English's evolution into Middle English can be narrowed down to three stages: Early, Central, and Late Middle English. Early Middle English, though it showed a change in the language, maintained the writing style of Old English. Central Middle English is characterized by the development of dialects within written communication, which is partly due to scribes who translated texts or parts of texts using terms from their own dialect, rather than the source. Late Middle English includes numerous developments that created the foundation for Modern English. *The Canterbury Tales*, "Sir Gawain and the Green Knight," and "Le Morte d'Arthur" are all Middle English texts that are still read and studied today.

THE RENAISSANCE

The **Renaissance** swept through Europe and lasted for multiple centuries, bringing many developments in culture, the arts, education, and philosophy. The Renaissance in England did not begin until the late 15th century. Though ideas and cultures of the past, especially those of the ancient Greeks and Romans, inspired the Renaissance, the period saw innumerable developments in the English language and literature. The Renaissance was characterized by a focus on the humanities, allowing the arts, including literature, to flourish. At the time, drama was possibly the most popular form of literature, as the popularity of plays and theatrical performances greatly increased. Much of Renaissance literature is still studied today, maintaining its influence on Western literature. Poetry was also popular, and the period saw the development of new forms of poetry, such as the sonnet. Sonnets are often recognized according to one of four styles, each of which was popularized by a Renaissance writer. Lyrical poetry, which discusses emotions and is often written using first-person point of view, was also popular during the Renaissance.

In addition to new forms and literary trends, the Renaissance period also impacted English literature by facilitating discussion over the translation of the Bible. Education at the time often included instruction in Greek and Latin, allowing those with an education to read ancient texts in their original language. However, this instruction did not reach the majority of the public. The Protestant Reformation encouraged discussions about translating the Bible to make it accessible to more people. This suggestion was challenged by those who doubted the ability of the English language to fully reflect the original text. Eventually, the Bible was translated to English, and William Tyndale's partial translation became especially influential for later translations and the

Copyright © Mometrix Media. You have been licensed one copy of this document for personal use only. Any other reproduction or redistribution is strictly prohibited. All rights reserved.
This content is provided for test preparation purposes only and does not imply an endorsement by Mometrix of any particular political, scientific, or religious point of view.

continuing development of the English language. Influential writers of the English Renaissance include William Shakespeare, John Donne, John Milton, Edmund Spenser, and Christopher Marlowe.

GOTHIC

The Gothic literary movement, beginning in the 18th century and persisting through the 19th century, took inspiration from the architecture and cultures of the Late Middle Ages in Europe. The Late Middle Ages saw the popularity of Gothic architecture, most prominently in places of worship. These structures inspired many of the settings in **Gothic literature**, as a large volume of Gothic literature takes place in an impressive location, such as a castle or ornate mansion. Gothic works also are often set in the past, long before the time the story was written. This aligns with prominent themes in Gothic literature, as several pieces are informed by an event that occurred before the story begins or a character who died before the plot's first event.

Another common characteristic of Gothic literature is its eerie, dark, suspenseful tone. Authors of Gothic literature often created this tone by setting their works in secluded and strange locations and incorporating intense, unsettling, or even supernatural events and scenarios into the plot. This tone is also created through the theme of death or mortality that often appears in Gothic literature. These characteristics support the aim of many Gothic writers to create fiction that evokes a certain emotion from the reader or shapes their reading experience. Well-known authors of Gothic literature include Horace Walpole, Ann Radcliffe, Edgar Allan Poe, and Nathaniel Hawthorne. While the Gothic literary movement took place in the 18th and 19th centuries, many works have been published in more recent centuries that have several characteristics of Gothic literature and may be included within the overall Gothic genre.

NATURALISM

Naturalism was an active literary movement in the late 19th century, taking place alongside movements such as realism and modernism. **Naturalism**, like realism, rejected the emotional focus and sentimentality of Romanticism and provided a type of social commentary. However, the naturalist movement stretched the ideas of realism, promoting literature that authentically depicts the life of the common man and criticizing the influence of morality on such literature. Naturalist literature often includes characters who belong to a lower class and experience circumstances beyond their own control and takes place in urban settings. Prominent themes in naturalist literature include nature as an apathetic force, the influence of heredity, and life as something to be endured and survived. One of the most influential naturalist writers is French writer Emile Zola. Influential American Naturalists include Stephen Crane, Hamlin Garland, and Theodore Dreiser.

MODERNISM

The Modernist literary movement was largely influenced by industrialization, which heavily impacted both the Unites States and England, primarily in the 19th century. **Modernism** in literature was characterized by an attempt to turn away from the norms and traditions of literature and use new techniques and methods. Modernist literature was often written in first person and used literary devices and techniques to reveal problems within society. For the American modernists, these societal changes came from industrialization and the first World War, which effected the general view of human nature and reliability. In England, there were additional factors contributing to this shift. Modernism began during Queen Victoria's reign, which defined the period known as the Victorian Era. The Victorian society was characterized by a strict moral code that permeated England's society at the time. This moral code was incompatible with the Modernist's desire to turn away from tradition, but the changes that accompanied Victoria's death in 1901 enabled the Modernist movement to grow in England. American Modernist writers include Ezra

Copyright © Mometrix Media. You have been licensed one copy of this document for personal use only. Any other reproduction or redistribution is strictly prohibited. All rights reserved. This content is provided for test preparation purposes only and does not imply an endorsement by Mometrix of any particular political, scientific, or religious point of view.

Pound, William Carlos Williams, and Gertrude Stein. British Modernist writers include Matthew Arnold, William Butler Yeats, T. S. Eliot, and Joseph Conrad.

POSTMODERNISM

Postmodernism grew out of Modernism's reliance on science and universal assertions, but emphasized the individual's subjective perception of reality, as it is often more authentic to an individual's experience than a universally applied statement. Postmodernism asserts that since each person creates their own version of reality, fully and accurately defining reality is futile and impossible. Due to this skepticism, postmodern writers use many concrete details, rather than abstract details, because they can be objectively observed and are not left up to the individual. The postmodernist literary movement began around the 1960s. The literary movement included a variety of new genres and techniques, reflecting the postmodernist idea that things like art cannot be truly defined or simplified. Notable American writers of the postmodernist movement include Kurt Vonnegut, John Barth, and Thomas Pynchon. British postmodernist writers include John Fowles and Julian Barnes.

CHAPTER QUIZ

1. Which of the following writers is included in the postmodernist movement?

    a.   Kurt Vonnegut
    b.   T. S. Eliot
    c.   Joseph Conrad
    d.   Stephen Crane

CHAPTER QUIZ ANSWER KEY

1. A: Postmodernism grew out of Modernism's reliance on science and universal assertions, but emphasized the individual's subjective perception of reality because it is often more authentic to an individual's experience than a universally applied statement. Postmodernism asserts that, because each person creates their own version of reality, fully and accurately defining reality is futile and impossible. Due to this skepticism, postmodern writers use many concrete details because, unlike abstract details, they can be objectively observed and are not left up to the individual. The postmodernist literary movement began around the 1960s. The literary movement included a variety of new genres and techniques, reflecting the postmodernist idea that things like art cannot be truly defined or simplified. Notable American writers of the postmodernist movement include Kurt Vonnegut, John Barth, and Thomas Pynchon. British postmodernist writers include John Fowles and Julian Barnes.

SPEECHES

Speeches are written to be delivered in spoken language in public, to various groups of people, at formal or informal events. Some generic types include welcome speeches, thank-you speeches, keynote addresses, position papers, commemorative and dedication speeches, and farewell speeches. Speeches are commonly written in present tense and usually begin with an introduction greeting the audience. At official functions, specific audience members are named ("Chairperson [name]," "Principal [name], teachers, and students," etc.) and when audiences include a distinguished guest, he or she is often named as well. Then the speaker introduces him or herself by name, position, and department or organization as applicable. After the greeting, the speaker then introduces the topic and states the purpose of the speech. The body of the speech follows, similarly to the body of an essay, stating its main points, an explanation of each point, and supporting

Copyright © Mometrix Media. You have been licensed one copy of this document for personal use only. Any other reproduction or redistribution is strictly prohibited. All rights reserved.
This content is provided for test preparation purposes only and does not imply an endorsement by Mometrix of any particular political, scientific, or religious point of view.

evidence. Finally, in the conclusion, the speaker states his or her hope for accomplishing the speech's purpose and thanks the audience for attending and listening to the speech.

CLEARLY WRITTEN PROSE AND SPEECHES

To achieve **clarity**, a writer or speaker must first define his or her purpose carefully. The speech should be organized logically, so that sentences make sense and follow each other in an understandable order. Sentences must also be constructed well, with carefully chosen words and structure. Organizing a speech in advance using an outline provides the writer or speaker with a blueprint, directing and focusing the composition to meet its intended purpose. Organized speeches enable audiences to comprehend and retain the presented information more easily. Humans naturally seek to impose order on the world by seeking patterns. Hence, when ideas in a speech are well-organized and adhere to a consistent pattern, the speaker communicates better with listeners and is more convincing. Speechwriters can use chronological patterns to organize events, sequential patterns to organize processes by their steps, and spatial patterns to help audiences visualize geographical locations and movements or physical scenarios. Also, comparison-contrast patterns give audiences insight about similarities and differences between and among topics, especially when listeners are more familiar with one than the other.

EVALUATING SPEECHES FOR CONCISE INFORMATION

To convince or persuade listeners or reinforce a message, speeches must be succinct. Audiences can become confused by excessive anecdotes and details. If a speaker takes three minutes or more to get to the point, audience members' attention will start to fade and will only worsen when details deviate from the main subject. When answering a question, the asker and speaker may even forget the original question if the speaker takes too long. Speakers should practice not only rehearsing written speeches, but also developing skill for spontaneous question-and-answer sessions after speeches. Speakers should differentiate necessary from simply interesting information because audiences can become overwhelmed by too much information. Speakers should know what points they wish to make. They should not be afraid to pause before responding to questions, which indicates thoughtfulness and control rather than lack of knowledge. Restating questions increases comprehension and appropriate responses, and allows time to form answers mentally.

ORGANIZATIONAL PATTERNS FOR SPEECHES

A speechwriter who uses an **advantages-disadvantages** pattern of organization presents the audience with the pros and cons of a topic. This aids writers in discussing two sides of an issue objectively without an argumentative position, enabling listeners to weigh both aspects. When a speechwriter uses a **cause-and-effect** pattern, it can help to persuade audiences to agree with an action or solution by showing significant relationships between factors. Writers may separate an outline into two main "cause" and "effect" sections or into separate sections for each cause, including the effect for each. Persuasive writing also benefits from **problem-solution** patterns: by establishing the existence of a problem, writers induce audiences to realize a need for change. By supplying a solution and supporting its superiority above other solutions, the writer convinces audiences of the value of that solution. When none of these patterns—or **chronological**, **sequential**, **spatial**, or **comparison-contrast** patterns—applies, speechwriters often use topical patterns. These organize information by various subtopics and types within the main topic or category.

EFFECTIVE SPEECH DELIVERY

Speakers should deliver speeches in a natural, conversational manner rather than being rigidly formal or theatrical. Effective delivery is also supported by confidence. Speakers should be direct, building audience rapport through personal connection and vivid imagery. Speakers should be

Copyright © Mometrix Media. You have been licensed one copy of this document for personal use only. Any other reproduction or redistribution is strictly prohibited. All rights reserved. This content is provided for test preparation purposes only and does not imply an endorsement by Mometrix of any particular political, scientific, or religious point of view.

mindful of the occasion, subject, and audience of their speeches and take care to use appropriate language. Good speakers learn vocal control, including volume, speed, pitch, use of pauses, tonal variety, correct pronunciation, and clear articulation. They can express enthusiasm and emphasize important points with their voices. Nonverbal behaviors, such as eye contact, facial expressions, gestures, good posture, and body movements clarify communication, stress important ideas, and influence perceptions that the speaker is trustworthy, competent, and credible. Nonverbal communications should seem as spontaneous and natural as vocal or verbal ones. Speakers should know their speeches well and practice frequently, taking care to avoid nervous or irrelevant movements such as tapping or pacing.

CHAPTER QUIZ

1. Speeches should be delivered in which manner?
   a. Flat and formal
   b. Natural and conversational
   c. Loud and theatrical
   d. Stoic and academic

CHAPTER QUIZ ANSWER KEY

1. B: Speakers should deliver speeches in a natural, conversational manner rather than being rigidly formal or theatrical. Effective delivery is also supported by confidence. Speakers should be direct, building audience rapport through personal connection and vivid imagery. Speakers should be mindful of the occasion, subject, and audience of their speeches and take care to use appropriate language. Good speakers learn vocal control, including volume, speed, pitch, use of pauses, tonal variety, correct pronunciation, and clear articulation. They can express enthusiasm and emphasize important points with their voices. Nonverbal behaviors, such as eye contact, facial expressions, gestures, good posture, and body movements clarify communication, stress important ideas, and influence perceptions that the speaker is trustworthy, competent, and credible. Nonverbal communications should seem as spontaneous and natural as vocal or verbal ones. Speakers should know their speeches well and practice frequently, taking care to avoid nervous or irrelevant movements such as tapping or pacing.

MEDIA AND FORMAT CHOICES

Effective communication depends on choosing the correct method. Media and format choices are influenced by the target audience, the budget, and the needs of the audience.

INSTRUCTIONAL VIDEOS

Instructional videos have potential for excellent two-way communication because questions and feedback can be built in. Videos can be targeted to particular audiences, and they can be paused for discussion or replayed to reinforce concepts. Viewers can see processes, including "before," "during," and "after" phases. Videos are accessible because most communities have at least one DVD player or computer. Moreover, video players and computers are continually becoming less expensive to buy and use. Disadvantages include the necessity of editing software and equipment in some cases, as well as the need for support from other print materials. There is also danger of overuse, if other media or methods are more appropriate, and higher up-front costs. Producers of instructional videos must account for the costs of script development and hiring local performers as needed.

DVDS AND CDS

Interactive DVDs and CDs, such as games, give viewers the opportunity to actively participate as they learn information. Additionally, videos are considered to be a professional method of sharing

Copyright © Mometrix Media. You have been licensed one copy of this document for personal use only. Any other reproduction or redistribution is strictly prohibited. All rights reserved. This content is provided for test preparation purposes only and does not imply an endorsement by Mometrix of any particular political, scientific, or religious point of view.

information. Compared to many other media formats, discs are comparatively inexpensive to make and are easy to transport due to their small size and weight. They are more resistant to damage and aging than older videotape technology, making them more durable. Some disadvantages include needing access to technology to play what is stored on the disc and access to certain software programs to add new content to a disc, especially if the producer wants to include video animation or audio commentary. Producers must also consider expenses concerning paid staff and production and labeling expenses. Content that would appear on DVDs and CDs can alternatively be shared through streaming services or digital files stored on a computer or other compatible device.

TELEVISION AND RADIO

Both television and radio are forms of mass media that reach many people. TV has the broadest reach and can market to the general public or be customized for target audiences, while radio only tends to reach specific target audiences. TV has the advantage of video plus audio, while radio broadcasts only feature audio. However, access to television programs is more expensive than access to radio broadcasts. A shared disadvantage is that TV and radio audiences can only interact directly during call-in programs. Additionally, programming times may be inconvenient, but tape, digital sound, and digital video recording (DVR) can remedy this. Many streaming services also provide access to these programs. Both television and radio are useful for communicating simple slogans and messages, and both can generate awareness, interest, and excitement.

NEWSPAPERS

Except for the occasional community columns, news releases, and letters to the editor, newspaper pages and features afford little opportunity for audience input or participation. However, they do reach and appeal to the general public. Cost is an advantage: hiring a PR writer and paying for a news advertisement costs much less than a radio or TV spot. Additionally, newspaper features are high-status, and audiences can reread and review them as often as they like. However, newspaper ads may have difficulty affecting the reader as deeply without audio or video, and they require a literate audience. Their publication is also subject to editors' whims and biases. Newspaper pieces combining advertising and editorial content—"advertorials"—provide inclusion of paid material, but are viewed as medium-status and cost more.

WEBSITES, BLOGS, MOBILE PHONES, AND TEXT MESSAGING

Computer literacy is required for online material, but participation potential is high via websites, e-networking, and blogging. Mobile phones and text messaging are used for enormous direct, public, two-way and one-on-one communication, with timely information and reminders. Web media need a literate public and can be tailored for specific audiences. They afford global information, are accessible by increasingly technology-literate populations, and are high-status. Web media disadvantages include the necessity of computers and people to design, manage, and supply content, as well as to provide technical support. Mobile and text media are globally popular, but appeal especially to certain demographics like teens and young adults. They are increasingly available, especially in rural regions, and are decreasing in cost. Mobile and text media disadvantages include required brevity in texts and provider messaging charges. Links to related websites and pages within existing sites are also advantages of digital media.

PUBLIC PRESENTATIONS AND SLIDESHOWS

Public presentations have great potential for audience participation and can directly target various audiences. They can encourage the establishment of partnerships and groups, stimulate local ownership of issues and projects, and make information public. A drawback to public presentations is that they are limited to nights, weekends, or whenever audiences are available and do not always attract the intended audience.

Copyright © Mometrix Media. You have been licensed one copy of this document for personal use only. Any other reproduction or redistribution is strictly prohibited. All rights reserved.
This content is provided for test preparation purposes only and does not imply an endorsement by Mometrix of any particular political, scientific, or religious point of view.

Another method of presentation is to use **slideshows**. These presentations are best for sophisticated audiences like professionals, civil servants, and service organizations. Well-designed slideshows are good for stimulating audience interest, selling ideas, and marketing products. Also, they are accessible online as well as in-person so they can reach a broader audience. Slideshow disadvantages include the necessity of projectors and other equipment. They are also limited to communicating more general points, outlines, and summaries rather than conveying a multitude of information in more detail.

POSTERS AND BROCHURES

Both **posters** and **brochures** can target audiences of the general public and more specific public sectors. Posters are better for communicating simple slogans and messages, while brochures can include more detail and are better for printing instructional information. Both can be inexpensive to produce, especially if printed only as needed and in-house. Posters can often be printed in-house without using outside printing companies. However, it is difficult to get feedback on both posters and brochures—unless they have been broadly tested, or if their publication is accompanied by workshops and other participatory events. A disadvantage of using posters is that they are designed to draw attention and communicate quickly, as they are mostly viewed in passing. This means that their messages must be simple and communicate efficiently. A disadvantage of using brochures is that they can only be distributed to a specific, limited group or area. Posters and brochures are also only understood when audiences are literate in both written language and visual elements.

FLYERS AND FACT SHEETS

Flyers and fact sheets have one-way communication potential because readers cannot give feedback. Their target audiences are general. Some advantages of using this form of media include flexibility: people can distribute them at meetings or events, put them on car windshields in parking lots, leave them in stores or on bulletin boards at community agencies and schools, hand them out from booths and other displays, or mail them. When printed in black and white, they can be very inexpensive. They afford recipients the convenience of being able to review them at their leisure. Organizations and individuals can produce flyers and fact sheets in-house, or even at home with desktop publishing software. Disadvantages include their limitation to single facts or tips and specific information on specified topics.

EVALUATING MEDIA INFORMATION SOURCES

With the wealth of media in different formats available today, users are more likely to take media at face value. However, to understand the content of media, consumers must **critically evaluate each source**.

Users should ask themselves the following questions about media sources:

- Who is delivering this message and why?
- What methods do a media source's publishers employ to gain and maintain users' attention?
- Which points of view is the media source representing?
- What are the various ways this message could be interpreted?
- What information is missing from the message?
- Is the source scholarly, i.e., peer-reviewed?
- Does it include author names and their credentials as they relate to the topic?
- Who publishes it and why?
- Who is the target audience?
- Is the language technically specific or non-technical?

Copyright © Mometrix Media. You have been licensed one copy of this document for personal use only. Any other reproduction or redistribution is strictly prohibited. All rights reserved. This content is provided for test preparation purposes only and does not imply an endorsement by Mometrix of any particular political, scientific, or religious point of view.

- Are sources cited, research claims documented, conclusions based on furnished evidence, and references provided?
- Is the publication current?

OTHER CONSIDERATIONS FOR THE VALIDITY OF SOURCES

For books, consider whether information is **up-to-date** and whether **historical perspectives** apply. Content is more likely to be **scholarly** if publishers are universities, government, or professional organizations. Book reviews can also provide useful information. For articles, identify the author, publisher, frequency of the periodical's publication, and what kind of advertising, if any, is included. Looking for book reviews also informs users. For articles, look for biographical author information, publisher name, frequency of the periodical's publication, and whether advertising is included and, if so, whether it is for certain occupations or disciplines. For web pages, check their domain names, identify publishers or sponsors, look for the author or publisher's contact information, check dates of most recent page updates, be alert to biases, and verify the validity of the information on the webpage. The quality and accuracy of web pages located through search engines rather than library databases varies widely and requires careful user inspection. Web page recommendations from reliable sources like university faculties can help indicate quality and accuracy. Citations of websites by credible or scholarly sources also show reliability. Authors' names, relevant credentials, affiliations, and contact information support their authority. Site functionality, such as ease of navigation, ability to search, site maps, and indexes, is also a criterion to consider.

PERSUASIVE MEDIA

Advertising, public relations, and advocacy media all use **persuasion**. Advertisers use persuasion to sell goods and services. The public relations field uses persuasion to give good impressions of companies, governments, or organizations. Advocacy groups use persuasion to garner support or votes. Persuasion can come through commercials, public service announcements, speeches, websites, and newsletters, among other channels. Activists, lobbyists, government officials, and politicians use political rhetoric involving persuasive techniques. Basic techniques include using celebrity spokespersons, whom consumers admire or aspire to resemble, or conversely, "everyday people" (albeit often portrayed by actors) with whom consumers identify. Using expert testimonials lends credibility. Explicit claims of content, effectiveness, quality, and reliability—which often cannot be proven or disproven—are used to persuade. While news and advocacy messages mostly eschew humor for credibility's sake (except in political satire), advertising often persuades via humor, which gets consumer attention and associates its pleasure with advertised products and services. Qualifiers and other misleading terms, sometimes called "Weasel words," are often combined with exaggerated claims. Intensifiers, such as hyperboles, superlatives, repetitions, and sentimental appeals are also persuasive.

INTERMEDIATE TECHNIQUES

Dangerous propagandist Adolf Hitler said people suspect little lies more than big ones; hence the "Big Lie" is a persuasion method that cannot be identified without consumers' keen critical thinking. A related method is **charisma**, which can induce people to believe messages they would otherwise reject. **Euphemisms** substitute abstract, vague, or bland terms in place of more graphic, clear, and unpleasant ones. For example, the terms "layoffs" and "firing" are replaced by "downsizing," and "torture" is replaced with "intensive interrogation techniques." **Extrapolation** bases sweeping conclusions on small amounts of minor information to appeal to what consumers wish or hope. Flattery appeals to consumer self-esteem needs, such as L'Oréal's "You're worth it." Flattery is sometimes accomplished through contrast, like ads showing others' mistakes to make consumers feel superior and smarter. "Glittering generalities" refer to claims based on concepts

90

Copyright © Mometrix Media. You have been licensed one copy of this document for personal use only. Any other reproduction or redistribution is strictly prohibited. All rights reserved.
This content is provided for test preparation purposes only and does not imply an endorsement by Mometrix of any particular political, scientific, or religious point of view.

such as beauty, love, health, democracy, freedom, and science. Persuaders use this tactic to gain consumer acceptance without consumers questioning what they mean. The opposite is name-calling to persuade consumers to reject someone or something.

American citizens love new ideas and technology. Persuaders exploit this by emphasizing the **newness** of products, services, and candidates. Conversely, they also use **nostalgia** to evoke consumers' happy memories, which they often remember more than unhappy ones. Citing "scientific evidence" is an intermediate version of the basic technique of expert testimonials. Consumers may accept this as proof, but some advertisers, politicians, and other persuaders may present inaccurate or misleading "evidence." Another intermediate technique is the "simple solution." Although the natures of people and life are complex, when consumers feel overwhelmed by complexity, persuaders exploit this by offering policies, products, or services they claim will solve complicated problems by simple means. Persuaders also use symbols, images, words, and names we associate with more general, emotional concepts like lifestyle, country, family, religion, and gender. While symbols have power, their significance also varies across individuals. For example, some consumers regard the Hummer SUV as a prestigious status symbol, while others regard it as environmentally harmful and irresponsible.

ADVANCED TECHNIQUES

Ad hominem, Latin for "against the man" attacks the person behind an idea rather than criticizing the idea itself. It operates by association: if a person is considered immoral or uneducated, then his or her ideas must be bad as well. **"Stacking the deck"** misleads by presenting only selected information that supports one position. **Apophasis**, or a false denial, allows the speaker or writer to indirectly bring attention to a flaw in an opponent's credibility. For example, a politician saying, "I won't mention my opponent's tax evasion issues" manages to mention them while seeming less accusatory. Persuaders may also use **majority belief**, making statements such as "Four out of five dentists recommend this brand" or "[insert number] people can't be wrong." In an intensified version, persuaders exploit group dynamics at rallies, speeches, and other live-audience events where people are vulnerable to surrounding crowd influences. **Scapegoating**, blaming one person or group for complex problems, is a form of the intermediate "simple solution" technique, a practice common in politics. **Timing** also persuades, like advertising flowers and candy in the weeks preceding Valentine's Day, ad campaigns preceding new technology rollouts, and politician speeches following big news events.

VISUAL MEDIA

Some images have the power to communicate more information than an entire paragraph. Images can contain several elements and be interpreted different ways, making them an effective vessel for abstract and emotionally appealing ideas. Humans are also able to understand images before they fully acquire language, meaning that images can reach more people than language can at any time. Images are also more quickly comprehended than text, making them a highly efficient method of communication. People can remember or memorize images more easily than text, also. Historically, images have been used for propaganda and subliminal messaging. Images are also used by different companies as an effective technique to entice customers to buy their products. Though images do not always contain text, they can still convey explicit and implicit meanings. An image's explicit meaning would be the most recognizable shape or concept in the image. The implicit meaning may be obscured within the image through the use of negative space, background images, or out-of-focus shapes.

Copyright © Mometrix Media. You have been licensed one copy of this document for personal use only. Any other reproduction or redistribution is strictly prohibited. All rights reserved. This content is provided for test preparation purposes only and does not imply an endorsement by Mometrix of any particular political, scientific, or religious point of view.

INTERPRETING AND EVALUATING PERSUASIVE MEDIA

Most messages can be interpreted in different ways. They can be interpreted explicitly, where the literal meaning of the words in the message creates the meaning of the message, and no context is considered. Alternatively, other contexts can be considered alongside the explicit meaning of the message. These create alternative, not clearly stated meanings called **implicit meanings**. Politics, current events, regional norms, and even emotions are examples of contexts that can add implicit meanings to a message. These implicit meanings can change the effect a message has on its recipient. Many products have slogans with both implicit and explicit meanings. These implicit meanings must be considered to fully interpret a message.

Messages come in different forms, and each form has a unique way of communicating both explicit and implicit meanings. Images can come with captions that communicate a message, but some images carry subliminal messages. This means that their implicit meaning is received by the viewer, but the viewer is not aware of it. The term **propaganda** describes messages that advocate for a specific opinion or way of thinking. Most propaganda is politically driven and has been used during historical periods, most notably World War II. Unlike messages with hidden or veiled implicit meanings, most propaganda aggressively communicates its entire meaning and is difficult to misinterpret. Documentaries are another prominent form of communication. Documentaries are informational videos that focus on a specific figure, subject, phenomenon, or time period. While documentaries are primarily fact based and contain excerpts from interviews and testimonials, documentaries feature a limited view of their subject and sometimes attempt to persuade viewers to take action or embrace their central message. While some documentaries communicate this clearly, some hide an implicit meaning through the way they present each piece of information.

CHAPTER QUIZ

1. An *ad hominem* argument does which of the following?
   a. Misleads by presenting only selected information that supports one position
   b. Blames one group or person for complex problems
   c. Attacks the person behind an idea rather than refuting the idea itself
   d. Indirectly brings attention to a flaw in an opponent's credibility

2. An apophasis argument does which of the following?
   a. Misleads by presenting only selected information that supports one position
   b. Blames one group or person for complex problems
   c. Attacks the person behind an idea rather than refuting the idea itself
   d. Indirectly brings attention to a flaw in an opponent's credibility

CHAPTER QUIZ ANSWER KEY

1. C: *Ad hominem*, Latin for "against the man," attacks the person behind an idea rather than criticizing the idea itself. It operates by association: if a person is considered immoral or uneducated, then his or her ideas must be similarly flawed or meritless.

2. D: Apophasis, or a false denial, allows the speaker or writer to indirectly bring attention to a flaw in an opponent's credibility. For example, a politician saying, "I won't mention my opponent's tax evasion issues" manages to mention them while seeming less accusatory.

Copyright © Mometrix Media. You have been licensed one copy of this document for personal use only. Any other reproduction or redistribution is strictly prohibited. All rights reserved. This content is provided for test preparation purposes only and does not imply an endorsement by Mometrix of any particular political, scientific, or religious point of view.

Writing

BRAINSTORMING

Brainstorming is a technique that is used to find a creative approach to a subject. This can be accomplished by simple **free-association** with a topic. For example, with paper and pen, write every thought that you have about the topic in a word or phrase. This is done without critical thinking. You should put everything that comes to your mind about the topic on your scratch paper. Then, you need to read the list over a few times. Next, look for patterns, repetitions, and clusters of ideas. This allows a variety of fresh ideas to come as you think about the topic.

FREE WRITING

Free writing is a more structured form of brainstorming. The method involves taking a limited amount of time (e.g., 2 to 3 minutes) to write everything that comes to mind about the topic in complete sentences. When time expires, review everything that has been written down. Many of your sentences may make little or no sense, but the insights and observations that can come from free writing make this method a valuable approach. Usually, free writing results in a fuller expression of ideas than brainstorming because thoughts and associations are written in complete sentences. However, both techniques can be used to complement each other.

PLANNING

Planning is the process of organizing a piece of writing before composing a draft. Planning can include creating an outline or a graphic organizer, such as a Venn diagram, a spider-map, or a flowchart. These methods should help the writer identify their topic, main ideas, and the general organization of the composition. Preliminary research can also take place during this stage. Planning helps writers organize all of their ideas and decide if they have enough material to begin their first draft. However, writers should remember that the decisions they make during this step will likely change later in the process, so their plan does not have to be perfect.

DRAFTING

Writers may then use their plan, outline, or graphic organizer to compose their first draft. They may write subsequent drafts to improve their writing. Writing multiple drafts can help writers consider different ways to communicate their ideas and address errors that may be difficult to correct without rewriting a section or the whole composition. Most writers will vary in how many drafts they choose to write, as there is no "right" number of drafts. Writing drafts also takes away the pressure to write perfectly on the first try, as writers can improve with each draft they write.

REVISING, EDITING, AND PROOFREADING

Once a writer completes a draft, they can move on to the revising, editing, and proofreading steps to improve their draft. These steps begin with making broad changes that may apply to large sections of a composition and then making small, specific corrections. **Revising** is the first and broadest of these steps. Revising involves ensuring that the composition addresses an appropriate audience, includes all necessary material, maintains focus throughout, and is organized logically. Revising may occur after the first draft to ensure that the following drafts improve upon errors from the first draft. Some revision should occur between each draft to avoid repeating these errors. The **editing** phase of writing is narrower than the revising phase. Editing a composition should include steps such as improving transitions between paragraphs, ensuring each paragraph is on topic, and improving the flow of the text. The editing phase may also include correcting grammatical errors that cannot be fixed without significantly altering the text. **Proofreading** involves fixing misspelled words, typos, other grammatical errors, and any remaining surface-level flaws in the composition.

Copyright © Mometrix Media. You have been licensed one copy of this document for personal use only. Any other reproduction or redistribution is strictly prohibited. All rights reserved.
This content is provided for test preparation purposes only and does not imply an endorsement by Mometrix of any particular political, scientific, or religious point of view.

RECURSIVE WRITING PROCESS

However you approach writing, you may find comfort in knowing that the revision process can occur in any order. The **recursive writing process** is not as difficult as the phrase may make it seem. Simply put, the recursive writing process means that you may need to revisit steps after completing other steps. It also implies that the steps are not required to take place in any certain order. Indeed, you may find that planning, drafting, and revising can all take place at about the same time. The writing process involves moving back and forth between planning, drafting, and revising, followed by more planning, more drafting, and more revising until the writing is satisfactory.

> **Review Video: Recursive Writing Process**
> Visit mometrix.com/academy and enter code: 951611

TECHNOLOGY IN THE WRITING PROCESS

Modern technology has yielded several tools that can be used to make the writing process more convenient and organized. Word processors and online tools, such as databases and plagiarism detectors, allow much of the writing process to be completed in one place, using one device.

TECHNOLOGY FOR PLANNING AND DRAFTING

For the planning and drafting stages of the writing process, word processors are a helpful tool. These programs also feature formatting tools, allowing users to create their own planning tools or create digital outlines that can be easily converted into sentences, paragraphs, or an entire essay draft. Online databases and references also complement the planning process by providing convenient access to information and sources for research. Word processors also allow users to keep up with their work and update it more easily than if they wrote their work by hand. Online word processors often allow users to collaborate, making group assignments more convenient. These programs also allow users to include illustrations or other supplemental media in their compositions.

TECHNOLOGY FOR REVISING, EDITING, AND PROOFREADING

Word processors also benefit the revising, editing, and proofreading stages of the writing process. Most of these programs indicate errors in spelling and grammar, allowing users to catch minor errors and correct them quickly. There are also websites designed to help writers by analyzing text for deeper errors, such as poor sentence structure, inappropriate complexity, lack of sentence variety, and style issues. These websites can help users fix errors they may not know to look for or may have simply missed. As writers finish these steps, they may benefit from checking their work for any plagiarism. There are several websites and programs that compare text to other documents and publications across the internet and detect any similarities within the text. These websites show the source of the similar information, so users know whether or not they referenced the source and unintentionally plagiarized its contents.

TECHNOLOGY FOR PUBLISHING

Technology also makes managing written work more convenient. Digitally storing documents keeps everything in one place and is easy to reference. Digital storage also makes sharing work easier, as documents can be attached to an email or stored online. This also allows writers to publish their work easily, as they can electronically submit it to other publications or freely post it to a personal blog, profile, or website.

Copyright © Mometrix Media. You have been licensed one copy of this document for personal use only. Any other reproduction or redistribution is strictly prohibited. All rights reserved. This content is provided for test preparation purposes only and does not imply an endorsement by Mometrix of any particular political, scientific, or religious point of view.

CHAPTER QUIZ

1. Which of the following is a more structured form of brainstorming?

a. Free writing
b. Planning
c. Drafting
d. Proofreading

CHAPTER QUIZ ANSWER KEY

1. A: Free writing is a more structured form of brainstorming. The method involves taking a limited amount of time (e.g., two to three minutes) to write everything that comes to mind about the topic in complete sentences. When time expires, review everything that has been written down. Many of the sentences may make little or no sense, but the insights and observations that can come from free writing make this method a valuable approach. Usually, free writing results in a fuller expression of ideas than brainstorming because thoughts and associations are written in complete sentences. However, both techniques can be used to complement each other.

MAIN IDEAS, SUPPORTING DETAILS, AND OUTLINING A TOPIC

A writer often begins the first paragraph of a paper by stating the **main idea** or point, also known as the **topic sentence**. The rest of the paragraph supplies particular details that develop and support the main point. One way to visualize the relationship between the main point and supporting information is by considering a table: the tabletop is the main point, and each of the table's legs is a supporting detail or group of details. Both professional authors and students can benefit from planning their writing by first making an outline of the topic. Outlines facilitate quick identification of the main point and supporting details without having to wade through the additional language that will exist in the fully developed essay, article, or paper. Outlining can also help readers to analyze a piece of existing writing for the same reason. The outline first summarizes the main idea in one sentence. Then, below that, it summarizes the supporting details in a numbered list. Writing the paper then consists of filling in the outline with detail, writing a paragraph for each supporting point, and adding an introduction and conclusion.

INTRODUCTION

The purpose of the introduction is to capture the reader's attention and announce the essay's main idea. Normally, the introduction contains 50-80 words, or 3-5 sentences. An introduction can begin with an interesting quote, a question, or a strong opinion—something that will **engage** the reader's interest and prompt them to keep reading. If you are writing your essay to a specific prompt, your introduction should include a **restatement or summarization** of the prompt so that the reader will have some context for your essay. Finally, your introduction should briefly state your **thesis or main idea**: the primary thing you hope to communicate to the reader through your essay. Don't try to include all of the details and nuances of your thesis, or all of your reasons for it, in the introduction. That's what the rest of the essay is for!

> **Review Video: Introduction**
> Visit mometrix.com/academy and enter code: 961328

THESIS STATEMENT

The thesis is the main idea of the essay. A temporary thesis, or working thesis, should be established early in the writing process because it will serve to keep the writer focused as ideas develop. This temporary thesis is subject to change as you continue to write.

Copyright © Mometrix Media. You have been licensed one copy of this document for personal use only. Any other reproduction or redistribution is strictly prohibited. All rights reserved.
This content is provided for test preparation purposes only and does not imply an endorsement by Mometrix of any particular political, scientific, or religious point of view.

The temporary thesis has two parts: a **topic** (i.e., the focus of your essay based on the prompt) and a **comment**. The comment makes an important point about the topic. A temporary thesis should be interesting and specific. Also, you need to limit the topic to a manageable scope. These three questions are useful tools to measure the effectiveness of any temporary thesis:

- Does the focus of my essay have enough interest to hold an audience?
- Is the focus of my essay specific enough to generate interest?
- Is the focus of my essay manageable for the time limit? Too broad? Too narrow?

The thesis should be a generalization rather than a fact because the thesis prepares readers for facts and details that support the thesis. The process of bringing the thesis into sharp focus may help in outlining major sections of the work. Once the thesis and introduction are complete, you can address the body of the work.

> **Review Video: Thesis Statements**
> Visit mometrix.com/academy and enter code: 691033

SUPPORTING THE THESIS

Throughout your essay, the thesis should be **explained clearly and supported** adequately by additional arguments. The thesis sentence needs to contain a clear statement of the purpose of your essay and a comment about the thesis. With the thesis statement, you have an opportunity to state what is noteworthy of this particular treatment of the prompt. Each sentence and paragraph should build on and support the thesis.

When you respond to the prompt, use parts of the passage to support your argument or defend your position. Using supporting evidence from the passage strengths your argument because readers can see your attention to the entire passage and your response to the details and facts within the passage. You can use facts, details, statistics, and direct quotations from the passage to uphold your position. Be sure to point out which information comes from the original passage and base your argument around that evidence.

BODY

In an essay's introduction, the writer establishes the thesis and may indicate how the rest of the piece will be structured. In the body of the piece, the writer **elaborates** upon, **illustrates**, and **explains** the **thesis statement**. How writers arrange supporting details and their choices of paragraph types are development techniques. Writers may give examples of the concept introduced in the thesis statement. If the subject includes a cause-and-effect relationship, the author may explain its causality. A writer will explain or analyze the main idea of the piece throughout the body, often by presenting arguments for the veracity or credibility of the thesis statement. Writers may use development to define or clarify ambiguous terms. Paragraphs within the body may be organized using natural sequences, like space and time. Writers may employ **inductive reasoning**, using multiple details to establish a generalization or causal relationship, or **deductive reasoning**, proving a generalized hypothesis or proposition through a specific example or case.

> **Review Video: Drafting Body Paragraphs**
> Visit mometrix.com/academy and enter code: 724590

PARAGRAPHS

After the introduction of a passage, a series of body paragraphs will carry a message through to the conclusion. Each paragraph should be **unified around a main point**. Normally, a good topic

Copyright © Mometrix Media. You have been licensed one copy of this document for personal use only. Any other reproduction or redistribution is strictly prohibited. All rights reserved. This content is provided for test preparation purposes only and does not imply an endorsement by Mometrix of any particular political, scientific, or religious point of view.

sentence summarizes the paragraph's main point. A topic sentence is a general sentence that gives an introduction to the paragraph.

The sentences that follow support the topic sentence. However, though it is usually the first sentence, the topic sentence can come as the final sentence to the paragraph if the earlier sentences give a clear explanation of the paragraph's topic. This allows the topic sentence to function as a concluding sentence. Overall, the paragraphs need to stay true to the main point. This means that any unnecessary sentences that do not advance the main point should be removed.

The main point of a paragraph requires adequate development (i.e., a substantial paragraph that covers the main point). A paragraph of two or three sentences does not cover a main point. This is especially true when the main point of the paragraph gives strong support to the argument of the thesis. An occasional short paragraph is fine as a transitional device. However, a well-developed argument will have paragraphs with more than a few sentences.

METHODS OF DEVELOPING PARAGRAPHS

Common methods of adding substance to paragraphs include examples, illustrations, analogies, and cause and effect.

- **Examples** are supporting details to the main idea of a paragraph or a passage. When authors write about something that their audience may not understand, they can provide an example to show their point. When authors write about something that is not easily accepted, they can give examples to prove their point.
- **Illustrations** are extended examples that require several sentences. Well-selected illustrations can be a great way for authors to develop a point that may not be familiar to their audience.
- **Analogies** make comparisons between items that appear to have nothing in common. Analogies are employed by writers to provoke fresh thoughts about a subject. These comparisons may be used to explain the unfamiliar, to clarify an abstract point, or to argue a point. Although analogies are effective literary devices, they should be used carefully in arguments. Two things may be alike in some respects but completely different in others.
- **Cause and effect** is an excellent device to explain the connection between an action or situation and a particular result. One way that authors can use cause and effect is to state the effect in the topic sentence of a paragraph and add the causes in the body of the paragraph. This method can give an author's paragraphs structure, which always strengthens writing.

TYPES OF PARAGRAPHS

A **paragraph of narration** tells a story or a part of a story. Normally, the sentences are arranged in chronological order (i.e., the order that the events happened). However, flashbacks (i.e., an anecdote from an earlier time) can be included.

A **descriptive paragraph** makes a verbal portrait of a person, place, or thing. When specific details are used that appeal to one or more of the senses (i.e., sight, sound, smell, taste, and touch), authors give readers a sense of being present in the moment.

A **process paragraph** is related to time order (i.e., First, you open the bottle. Second, you pour the liquid, etc.). Usually, this describes a process or teaches readers how to perform a process.

Comparing two things draws attention to their similarities and indicates a number of differences. When authors contrast, they focus only on differences. Both comparing and contrasting may be

97

Copyright © Mometrix Media. You have been licensed one copy of this document for personal use only. Any other reproduction or redistribution is strictly prohibited. All rights reserved. This content is provided for test preparation purposes only and does not imply an endorsement by Mometrix of any particular political, scientific, or religious point of view.

done point-by-point, noting both the similarities and differences of each point, or in sequential paragraphs, where you discuss all the similarities and then all the differences, or vice versa.

Breaking Text into Paragraphs

For most forms of writing, you will need to use multiple paragraphs. As such, determining when to start a new paragraph is very important. Reasons for starting a new paragraph include:

- To mark off the introduction and concluding paragraphs
- To signal a shift to a new idea or topic
- To indicate an important shift in time or place
- To explain a point in additional detail
- To highlight a comparison, contrast, or cause and effect relationship

Paragraph Length

Most readers find that their comfort level for a paragraph is between 100 and 200 words. Shorter paragraphs cause too much starting and stopping and give a choppy effect. Paragraphs that are too long often test the attention span of readers. Two notable exceptions to this rule exist. In scientific or scholarly papers, longer paragraphs suggest seriousness and depth. In journalistic writing, constraints are placed on paragraph size by the narrow columns in a newspaper format.

The first and last paragraphs of a text will usually be the introduction and conclusion. These special-purpose paragraphs are likely to be shorter than paragraphs in the body of the work. Paragraphs in the body of the essay follow the subject's outline (e.g., one paragraph per point in short essays and a group of paragraphs per point in longer works). Some ideas require more development than others, so it is good for a writer to remain flexible. A paragraph of excessive length may be divided, and shorter ones may be combined.

Coherent Paragraphs

A smooth flow of sentences and paragraphs without gaps, shifts, or bumps will lead to paragraph **coherence**. Ties between old and new information can be smoothed using several methods:

- **Linking ideas clearly**, from the topic sentence to the body of the paragraph, is essential for a smooth transition. The topic sentence states the main point, and this should be followed by specific details, examples, and illustrations that support the topic sentence. The support may be direct or indirect. In **indirect support**, the illustrations and examples may support a sentence that in turn supports the topic directly.
- The **repetition of key words** adds coherence to a paragraph. To avoid dull language, variations of the key words may be used.
- **Parallel structures** are often used within sentences to emphasize the similarity of ideas and connect sentences giving similar information.
- Maintaining a **consistent verb tense** throughout the paragraph helps. Shifting tenses affects the smooth flow of words and can disrupt the coherence of the paragraph.

> **Review Video: How to Write a Good Paragraph**
> Visit mometrix.com/academy and enter code: 682127

Sequence Words and Phrases

When a paragraph opens with the topic sentence, the second sentence may begin with a phrase like *first of all*, introducing the first supporting detail or example. The writer may introduce the second supporting item with words or phrases like *also*, *in addition*, and *besides*. The writer might

Copyright © Mometrix Media. You have been licensed one copy of this document for personal use only. Any other reproduction or redistribution is strictly prohibited. All rights reserved.
This content is provided for test preparation purposes only and does not imply an endorsement by Mometrix of any particular political, scientific, or religious point of view.

introduce succeeding pieces of support with wording like, *another thing, moreover, furthermore,* or *not only that, but.* The writer may introduce the last piece of support with *lastly, finally,* or *last but not least.* Writers get off the point by presenting off-target items not supporting the main point. For example, a main point *my dog is not smart* is supported by the statement, *he's six years old and still doesn't answer to his name.* But *he cries when I leave for school* is not supportive, as it does not indicate lack of intelligence. Writers stay on point by presenting only supportive statements that are directly relevant to and illustrative of their main point.

Review Video: <u>Sequence</u>
Visit mometrix.com/academy and enter code: 489027

TRANSITIONS

Transitions between sentences and paragraphs guide readers from idea to idea and indicate relationships between sentences and paragraphs. Writers should be judicious in their use of transitions, inserting them sparingly. They should also be selected to fit the author's purpose—transitions can indicate time, comparison, and conclusion, among other purposes. Tone is also important to consider when using transitional phrases, varying the tone for different audiences. For example, in a scholarly essay, *in summary* would be preferable to the more informal *in short.*

When working with transitional words and phrases, writers usually find a natural flow that indicates when a transition is needed. In reading a draft of the text, it should become apparent where the flow is disrupted. At this point, the writer can add transitional elements during the revision process. Revising can also afford an opportunity to delete transitional devices that seem heavy handed or unnecessary.

Review Video: <u>Transitions in Writing</u>
Visit mometrix.com/academy and enter code: 233246

Copyright © Mometrix Media. You have been licensed one copy of this document for personal use only. Any other reproduction or redistribution is strictly prohibited. All rights reserved.
This content is provided for test preparation purposes only and does not imply an endorsement by Mometrix of any particular political, scientific, or religious point of view.

Types of Transitional Words

Time	Afterward, immediately, earlier, meanwhile, recently, lately, now, since, soon, when, then, until, before, etc.
Sequence	too, first, second, further, moreover, also, again, and, next, still, besides, finally
Comparison	similarly, in the same way, likewise, also, again, once more
Contrasting	but, although, despite, however, instead, nevertheless, on the one hand... on the other hand, regardless, yet, in contrast.
Cause and Effect	because, consequently, thus, therefore, then, to this end, since, so, as a result, if... then, accordingly
Examples	for example, for instance, such as, to illustrate, indeed, in fact, specifically
Place	near, far, here, there, to the left/right, next to, above, below, beyond, opposite, beside
Concession	granted that, naturally, of course, it may appear, although it is true that
Repetition, Summary, or Conclusion	as mentioned earlier, as noted, in other words, in short, on the whole, to summarize, therefore, as a result, to conclude, in conclusion
Addition	and, also, furthermore, moreover
Generalization	in broad terms, broadly speaking, in general

Review Video: Transitional Words and Phrases
Visit mometrix.com/academy and enter code: 197796

Review Video: What are Transition Words?
Visit mometrix.com/academy and enter code: 707563

Review Video: How to Effectively Connect Sentences
Visit mometrix.com/academy and enter code: 948325

Conclusion

Two important principles to consider when writing a conclusion are strength and closure. A strong conclusion gives the reader a sense that the author's main points are meaningful and important, and that the supporting facts and arguments are convincing, solid, and well developed. When a conclusion achieves closure, it gives the impression that the writer has stated all necessary information and points and completed the work, rather than simply stopping after a specified length. Some things to avoid when writing concluding paragraphs include:

- Introducing a completely new idea
- Beginning with obvious or unoriginal phrases like "In conclusion" or "To summarize"
- Apologizing for one's opinions or writing
- Repeating the thesis word for word rather than rephrasing it
- Believing that the conclusion must always summarize the piece

Review Video: Drafting Conclusions
Visit mometrix.com/academy and enter code: 209408

Copyright © Mometrix Media. You have been licensed one copy of this document for personal use only. Any other reproduction or redistribution is strictly prohibited. All rights reserved. This content is provided for test preparation purposes only and does not imply an endorsement by Mometrix of any particular political, scientific, or religious point of view.

CHAPTER QUIZ

1. Which of the following is considered the main idea of an essay?

   a. Topic
   b. Body
   c. Theme
   d. Thesis

2. Which of the following are supporting details to the main idea of a paragraph or a passage?

   a. Analogies
   b. Examples
   c. Cause and effect
   d. Transitions

3. Which of the following is NOT a transitional word or phrase in the concession category?

   a. Granted that
   b. Naturally
   c. Broadly speaking
   d. It may appear

CHAPTER QUIZ ANSWER KEY

1. D: The thesis is the main idea of an essay. A temporary thesis, or working thesis, should be established early in the writing process because it will serve to keep the writer focused as ideas develop. This temporary thesis is subject to change as writing continues. The thesis should be a generalization rather than a fact because the thesis prepares readers for facts and details that support the thesis. The process of bringing the thesis into sharp focus may help in outlining major sections of the work. Once the thesis and introduction are complete, the body of the work can be addressed.

2. B: Examples are supporting details to the main idea of a paragraph or a passage. When authors write about something that their audience may not understand or that is not easily accepted, they can provide an example to show their point.

Copyright © Mometrix Media. You have been licensed one copy of this document for personal use only. Any other reproduction or redistribution is strictly prohibited. All rights reserved. This content is provided for test preparation purposes only and does not imply an endorsement by Mometrix of any particular political, scientific, or religious point of view.

3. C: Types of transitional words

Time	Afterward, immediately, earlier, meanwhile, recently, lately, now, since, soon, when, then, until, before, etc.
Sequence	Too, first, second, further, moreover, also, again, and, next, still, besides, finally
Comparison	Similarly, in the same way, likewise, also, again, once more
Contrasting	But, although, despite, however, instead, nevertheless, on the one hand... on the other hand, regardless, yet, in contrast.
Cause and effect	Because, consequently, thus, therefore, then, to this end, since, so, as a result, if... then, accordingly
Examples	For example, for instance, such as, to illustrate, indeed, in fact, specifically
Place	Near, far, here, there, to the left/right, next to, above, below, beyond, opposite, beside
Concession	Granted that, naturally, of course, it may appear, although it is true that
Repetition, summary, or conclusion	As mentioned earlier, as noted, in other words, in short, on the whole, to summarize, therefore, as a result, to conclude, in conclusion
Addition	And, also, furthermore, moreover
Generalization	In broad terms, broadly speaking, in general

WRITING STYLE AND LINGUISTIC FORM

Linguistic form encodes the literal meanings of words and sentences. It comes from the phonological, morphological, syntactic, and semantic parts of a language. **Writing style** consists of different ways of encoding the meaning and indicating figurative and stylistic meanings. An author's writing style can also be referred to as his or her **voice**.

Writers' stylistic choices accomplish three basic effects on their audiences:

- They **communicate meanings** beyond linguistically dictated meanings,
- They communicate the **author's attitude**, such as persuasive or argumentative effects accomplished through style, and
- They communicate or **express feelings**.

Within style, component areas include:

- Narrative structure
- Viewpoint
- Focus
- Sound patterns
- Meter and rhythm
- Lexical and syntactic repetition and parallelism
- Writing genre
- Representational, realistic, and mimetic effects
- Representation of thought and speech
- Meta-representation (representing representation)
- Irony

102

Copyright © Mometrix Media. You have been licensed one copy of this document for personal use only. Any other reproduction or redistribution is strictly prohibited. All rights reserved. This content is provided for test preparation purposes only and does not imply an endorsement by Mometrix of any particular political, scientific, or religious point of view.

- Metaphor and other indirect meanings
- Representation and use of historical and dialectal variations
- Gender-specific and other group-specific speech styles, both real and fictitious
- Analysis of the processes for inferring meaning from writing

LEVEL OF FORMALITY

The relationship between writer and reader is important in choosing a **level of formality** as most writing requires some degree of formality. **Formal writing** is for addressing a superior in a school or work environment. Business letters, textbooks, and newspapers use a moderate to high level of formality. **Informal writing** is appropriate for private letters, personal emails, and business correspondence between close associates.

For your exam, you will want to be aware of informal and formal writing. One way that this can be accomplished is to watch for shifts in point of view in the essay. For example, unless writers are using a personal example, they will rarely refer to themselves (e.g., "*I* think that *my* point is very clear.") to avoid being informal when they need to be formal.

Also, be mindful of an author who addresses his or her audience **directly** in their writing (e.g., "Readers, *like you*, will understand this argument.") as this can be a sign of informal writing. Good writers understand the need to be consistent with their level of formality. Shifts in levels of formality or point of view can confuse readers and cause them to discount the message.

CLICHÉS

Clichés are phrases that have been **overused** to the point that the phrase has no importance or has lost the original meaning. These phrases have no originality and add very little to a passage. Therefore, most writers will avoid the use of clichés. Another option is to make changes to a cliché so that it is not predictable and empty of meaning.

Examples:

> When life gives you lemons, make lemonade.

> Every cloud has a silver lining.

JARGON

Jargon is **specialized vocabulary** that is used among members of a certain trade or profession. Since jargon is understood by only a small audience, writers will use jargon in passages that will only be read by a specialized audience. For example, medical jargon should be used in a medical journal but not in a New York Times article. Jargon includes exaggerated language that tries to impress rather than inform. Sentences filled with jargon are not precise and are difficult to understand.

Examples:

> "He is going to *toenail* these frames for us." (Toenail is construction jargon for nailing at an angle.)

> "They brought in a *kip* of material today." (Kip refers to 1000 pounds in architecture and engineering.)

Copyright © Mometrix Media. You have been licensed one copy of this document for personal use only. Any other reproduction or redistribution is strictly prohibited. All rights reserved.
This content is provided for test preparation purposes only and does not imply an endorsement by Mometrix of any particular political, scientific, or religious point of view.

SLANG

Slang is an **informal** and sometimes private language that is understood by some individuals. Slang terms have some usefulness, but they can have a small audience. So, most formal writing will not include this kind of language.

Examples:

"Yes, the event was a blast!" (In this sentence, *blast* means that the event was a great experience.)

"That attempt was an epic fail." (By *epic fail*, the speaker means that his or her attempt was not a success.)

COLLOQUIALISM

A colloquialism is a word or phrase that is found in informal writing. Unlike slang, **colloquial language** will be familiar to a greater range of people. However, colloquialisms are still considered inappropriate for formal writing. Colloquial language can include some slang, but these are limited to contractions for the most part.

Examples:

"Can *y'all* come back another time?" (Y'all is a contraction of "you all.")

"Will you stop him from building this *castle in the air*?" (A "castle in the air" is an improbable or unlikely event.)

ACADEMIC LANGUAGE

In educational settings, students are often expected to use academic language in their schoolwork. Academic language is also commonly found in dissertations and theses, texts published by academic journals, and other forms of academic research. Academic language conventions may vary between fields, but general academic language is free of slang, regional terminology, and noticeable grammatical errors. Specific terms may also be used in academic language, and it is important to understand their proper usage. A writer's command of academic language impacts their ability to communicate in an academic or professional context. While it is acceptable to use colloquialisms, slang, improper grammar, or other forms of informal speech in social settings or at home, it is inappropriate to practice non-academic language in academic contexts.

TONE

Tone may be defined as the writer's **attitude** toward the topic, and to the audience. This attitude is reflected in the language used in the writing. The tone of a work should be **appropriate to the topic** and to the intended audience. While it may be fine to use slang or jargon in some pieces, other texts should not contain such terms. Tone can range from humorous to serious and any level in between. It may be more or less formal, depending on the purpose of the writing and its intended audience. All these nuances in tone can flavor the entire writing and should be kept in mind as the work evolves.

WORD SELECTION

A writer's choice of words is a signature of their style. Careful thought about the use of words can improve a piece of writing. A passage can be an exciting piece to read when attention is given to the use of vivid or specific nouns rather than general ones.

Copyright © Mometrix Media. You have been licensed one copy of this document for personal use only. Any other reproduction or redistribution is strictly prohibited. All rights reserved. This content is provided for test preparation purposes only and does not imply an endorsement by Mometrix of any particular political, scientific, or religious point of view.

Example:

>General: His kindness will never be forgotten.

>Specific: His thoughtful gifts and bear hugs will never be forgotten.

Attention should also be given to the kind of verbs that are used in sentences. Active verbs (e.g., run, swim) are about an action. Whenever possible, an **active verb should replace a linking verb** to provide clear examples for arguments and to strengthen a passage overall. When using an active verb, one should be sure that the verb is used in the active voice instead of the passive voice. Verbs are in the active voice when the subject is the one doing the action. A verb is in the passive voice when the subject is the recipient of an action.

Example:

>Passive: The winners were called to the stage by the judges.

>Active: The judges called the winners to the stage.

CONCISENESS

Conciseness is writing that communicates a message in the fewest words possible. Writing concisely is valuable because short, uncluttered messages allow the reader to understand the author's message more easily and efficiently. Planning is important in writing concise messages. If you have in mind what you need to write beforehand, it will be easier to make a message short and to the point. Do not state the obvious.

Revising is also important. After the message is written, make sure you have effective, pithy sentences that efficiently get your point across. When reviewing the information, imagine a conversation taking place, and concise writing will likely result.

APPROPRIATE KINDS OF WRITING FOR DIFFERENT TASKS, PURPOSES, AND AUDIENCES

When preparing to write a composition, consider the audience and purpose to choose the best type of writing. Three common types of writing are persuasive, expository, and narrative. **Persuasive**, or argumentative writing, is used to convince the audience to take action or agree with the author's claims. **Expository** writing is meant to inform the audience of the author's observations or research on a topic. **Narrative** writing is used to tell the audience a story and often allows more room for creativity. While task, purpose, and audience inform a writer's mode of writing, these factors also impact elements such as tone, vocabulary, and formality.

For example, students who are writing to persuade their parents to grant them some additional privilege, such as permission for a more independent activity, should use more sophisticated vocabulary and diction that sounds more mature and serious to appeal to the parental audience. However, students who are writing for younger children should use simpler vocabulary and sentence structure, as well as choose words that are more vivid and entertaining. They should treat their topics more lightly, and include humor when appropriate. Students who are writing for their classmates may use language that is more informal, as well as age-appropriate.

> **Review Video: <u>Writing Purpose and Audience</u>**
> Visit mometrix.com/academy and enter code: 146627

105

Copyright © Mometrix Media. You have been licensed one copy of this document for personal use only. Any other reproduction or redistribution is strictly prohibited. All rights reserved.
This content is provided for test preparation purposes only and does not imply an endorsement by Mometrix of any particular political, scientific, or religious point of view.

CHAPTER QUIZ

1. Which of the following would NOT be considered formal writing?

    a. Private letters
    b. Business letters
    c. Textbooks
    d. Newspapers

2. Which of the following sentences contains a verb in the passive voice?

    a. The judges called the winners to the stage for their awards.
    b. Each applicant must fill out all of the forms required.
    c. He raced through the copse of trees with the grace of a deer.
    d. I was told that there would be food available at the party.

CHAPTER QUIZ ANSWER KEY

1. A: The relationship between writer and reader is important in choosing a level of formality because most writing requires some degree of formality. Formal writing is for addressing a superior in a school or work environment. Business letters, textbooks, and newspapers use a moderate to high level of formality. Informal writing is appropriate for private letters, personal emails, and business correspondence between close associates.

2. D: Attention should also be given to the kind of verbs that are used in sentences. Active verbs (e.g., run, swim) are about an action. Whenever possible, an active verb should replace a linking verb to provide clear examples for arguments and to strengthen a passage overall. When using an active verb, one should be sure that the verb is used in the active voice instead of the passive voice. Verbs are in the active voice when the subject is the one doing the action. A verb is in the passive voice when the subject is the recipient of an action.

ESSAYS

Essays usually focus on one topic, subject, or goal. There are several types of essays, including informative, persuasive, and narrative. An essay's structure and level of formality depend on the type of essay and its goal. While narrative essays typically do not include outside sources, other types of essays often require some research and the integration of primary and secondary sources.

The basic format of an essay typically has three major parts: the introduction, the body, and the conclusion. The body is further divided into the writer's main points. Short and simple essays may have three main points, while essays covering broader ranges and going into more depth can have almost any number of main points, depending on length.

An essay's introduction should answer three questions:

1. What is the **subject** of the essay?

   If a student writes an essay about a book, the answer would include the title and author of the book and any additional information needed—such as the subject or argument of the book.

2. How does the essay **address** the subject?

   To answer this, the writer identifies the essay's organization by briefly summarizing main points and the evidence supporting them.

3. What will the essay **prove**?

106

Copyright © Mometrix Media. You have been licensed one copy of this document for personal use only. Any other reproduction or redistribution is strictly prohibited. All rights reserved.
This content is provided for test preparation purposes only and does not imply an endorsement by Mometrix of any particular political, scientific, or religious point of view.

This is the thesis statement, usually the opening paragraph's last sentence, clearly stating the writer's message.

The body elaborates on all the main points related to the thesis, introducing one main point at a time, and includes supporting evidence with each main point. Each body paragraph should state the point in a topic sentence, which is usually the first sentence in the paragraph. The paragraph should then explain the point's meaning, support it with quotations or other evidence, and then explain how this point and the evidence are related to the thesis. The writer should then repeat this procedure in a new paragraph for each additional main point.

The conclusion reiterates the content of the introduction, including the thesis, to remind the reader of the essay's main argument or subject. The essay writer may also summarize the highlights of the argument or description contained in the body of the essay, following the same sequence originally used in the body. For example, a conclusion might look like: Point 1 + Point 2 + Point 3 = Thesis, or Point 1 → Point 2 → Point 3 → Thesis Proof. Good organization makes essays easier for writers to compose and provides a guide for readers to follow. Well-organized essays hold attention better and are more likely to get readers to accept their theses as valid.

INFORMATIVE VS. PERSUASIVE WRITING

Informative writing, also called explanatory or expository writing, begins with the basis that something is true or factual, while **persuasive** writing strives to prove something that may or may not be true or factual. Whereas argumentative text is written to **persuade** readers to agree with the author's position, informative text merely **provides information and insight** to readers. Informative writing concentrates on **informing** readers about why or how something is as it is. This can include offering new information, explaining how a process works, and developing a concept for readers. To accomplish these objectives, the essay may name and distinguish various things within a category, provide definitions, provide details about the parts of something, explain a particular function or behavior, and give readers explanations for why a fact, object, event, or process exists or occurs.

NARRATIVE WRITING

Put simply, **narrative** writing tells a story. The most common examples of literary narratives are novels. Non-fictional biographies, autobiographies, memoirs, and histories are also narratives. Narratives should tell stories in such a way that the readers learn something or gain insight or understanding. Students can write more interesting narratives by describing events or experiences that were meaningful to them. Narratives should start with the story's actions or events, rather than long descriptions or introductions. Students should ensure that there is a point to each story by describing what they learned from the experience they narrate. To write an effective description, students should include sensory details, asking themselves what they saw, heard, felt or touched, smelled, and tasted during the experiences they describe. In narrative writing, the details should be **concrete** rather than **abstract**. Using concrete details enables readers to imagine everything that the writer describes.

> **Review Video: Narratives**
> Visit mometrix.com/academy and enter code: 280100

SENSORY DETAILS

Students need to use vivid descriptions when writing descriptive essays. Narratives should also include descriptions of characters, things, and events. Students should remember to describe not only the visual detail of what someone or something looks like, but details from other senses, as

Copyright © Mometrix Media. You have been licensed one copy of this document for personal use only. Any other reproduction or redistribution is strictly prohibited. All rights reserved. This content is provided for test preparation purposes only and does not imply an endorsement by Mometrix of any particular political, scientific, or religious point of view.

well. For example, they can contrast the feeling of a sea breeze to that of a mountain breeze, describe how they think something inedible would taste, and compare sounds they hear in the same location at different times of day and night. Readers have trouble visualizing images or imagining sensory impressions and feelings from abstract descriptions, so concrete descriptions make these more real.

CONCRETE VS. ABSTRACT DESCRIPTIONS IN NARRATIVE

Concrete language provides information that readers can grasp and may empathize with, while **abstract language**, which is more general, can leave readers feeling disconnected, empty, or even confused. "It was a lovely day" is abstract, but "The sun shone brightly, the sky was blue, the air felt warm, and a gentle breeze wafted across my skin" is concrete. "Ms. Couch was a good teacher" uses abstract language, giving only a general idea of the writer's opinion. But "Ms. Couch is excellent at helping us take our ideas and turn them into good essays and stories" uses concrete language, giving more specific examples of what makes Ms. Couch a good teacher. "I like writing poems but not essays" gives readers a general idea that the student prefers one genre over another, but not why. But when reading, "I like writing short poems with rhythm and rhyme, but I hate writing five-page essays that go on and on about the same ideas," readers understand that the student prefers the brevity, rhyme, and meter of short poetry over the length and redundancy of longer prose.

AUTOBIOGRAPHICAL NARRATIVES

Autobiographical narratives are narratives written by an author about an event or period in their life. Autobiographical narratives are written from one person's perspective, in first person, and often include the author's thoughts and feelings alongside their description of the event or period. Structure, style, or theme varies between different autobiographical narratives, since each narrative is personal and specific to its author and his or her experience.

REFLECTIVE ESSAY

A less common type of essay is the reflective essay. **Reflective essays** allow the author to reflect, or think back, on an experience and analyze what they recall. They should consider what they learned from the experience, what they could have done differently, what would have helped them during the experience, or anything else that they have realized from looking back on the experience. Reflection essays incorporate both objective reflection on one's own actions and subjective explanation of thoughts and feelings. These essays can be written for a number of experiences in a formal or informal context.

JOURNALS AND DIARIES

A **journal** is a personal account of events, experiences, feelings, and thoughts. Many people write journals to express their feelings and thoughts or to help them process experiences they have had. Since journals are **private documents** not meant to be shared with others, writers may not be concerned with grammar, spelling, or other mechanics. However, authors may write journals that they expect or hope to publish someday; in this case, they not only express their thoughts and feelings and process their experiences, but they also attend to their craft in writing them. Some authors compose journals to record a particular time period or a series of related events, such as a cancer diagnosis, treatment, surviving the disease, and how these experiences have changed or affected them. Other experiences someone might include in a journal are recovering from addiction, journeys of spiritual exploration and discovery, time spent in another country, or anything else someone wants to personally document. Journaling can also be therapeutic, as some people use journals to work through feelings of grief over loss or to wrestle with big decisions.

Copyright © Mometrix Media. You have been licensed one copy of this document for personal use only. Any other reproduction or redistribution is strictly prohibited. All rights reserved. This content is provided for test preparation purposes only and does not imply an endorsement by Mometrix of any particular political, scientific, or religious point of view.

EXAMPLES OF DIARIES IN LITERATURE

The Diary of a Young Girl by Dutch Jew Anne Frank (1947) contains her life-affirming, nonfictional diary entries from 1942-1944 while her family hid in an attic from World War II's genocidal Nazis. *Go Ask Alice* (1971) by Beatrice Sparks is a cautionary, fictional novel in the form of diary entries by Alice, an unhappy, rebellious teen who takes LSD, runs away from home and lives with hippies, and eventually returns home. Frank's writing reveals an intelligent, sensitive, insightful girl, raised by intellectual European parents—a girl who believes in the goodness of human nature despite surrounding atrocities. Alice, influenced by early 1970s counterculture, becomes less optimistic. However, similarities can be found between them: Frank dies in a Nazi concentration camp while the fictitious Alice dies from a drug overdose. Both young women are also unable to escape their surroundings. Additionally, adolescent searches for personal identity are evident in both books.

> **Review Video: Journals, Diaries, Letters, and Blogs**
> Visit mometrix.com/academy and enter code: 432845

LETTERS

Letters are messages written to other people. In addition to letters written between individuals, some writers compose letters to the editors of newspapers, magazines, and other publications, while some write "Open Letters" to be published and read by the general public. Open letters, while intended for everyone to read, may also identify a group of people or a single person whom the letter directly addresses. In everyday use, the most-used forms are business letters and personal or friendly letters. Both kinds share common elements: business or personal letterhead stationery; the writer's return address at the top; the addressee's address next; a salutation, such as "Dear [name]" or some similar opening greeting, followed by a colon in business letters or a comma in personal letters; the body of the letter, with paragraphs as indicated; and a closing, like "Sincerely/Cordially/Best regards/etc." or "Love," in intimate personal letters.

EARLY LETTERS

The Greek word for "letter" is *epistolē*, which became the English word "epistle." The earliest letters were called epistles, including the New Testament's epistles from the apostles to the Christians. In ancient Egypt, the writing curriculum in scribal schools included the epistolary genre. Epistolary novels frame a story in the form of letters. Examples of noteworthy epistolary novels include:

- *Pamela* (1740), by 18th-century English novelist Samuel Richardson
- *Shamela* (1741), Henry Fielding's satire of *Pamela* that mocked epistolary writing.
- *Lettres persanes* (1721) by French author Montesquieu
- *The Sorrows of Young Werther* (1774) by German author Johann Wolfgang von Goethe
- *The History of Emily Montague* (1769), the first Canadian novel, by Frances Brooke
- *Dracula* (1897) by Bram Stoker
- *Frankenstein* (1818) by Mary Shelley
- *The Color Purple* (1982) by Alice Walker

BLOGS

The word "blog" is derived from "weblog" and refers to writing done exclusively on the internet. Readers of reputable newspapers expect quality content and layouts that enable easy reading. These expectations also apply to blogs. For example, readers can easily move visually from line to line when columns are narrow, while overly wide columns cause readers to lose their places. Blogs must also be posted with layouts enabling online readers to follow them easily. However, because the way people read on computer, tablet, and smartphone screens differs from how they read print

Copyright © Mometrix Media. You have been licensed one copy of this document for personal use only. Any other reproduction or redistribution is strictly prohibited. All rights reserved. This content is provided for test preparation purposes only and does not imply an endorsement by Mometrix of any particular political, scientific, or religious point of view.

on paper, formatting and writing blog content is more complex than writing newspaper articles. Two major principles are the bases for blog-writing rules: The first is while readers of print articles skim to estimate their length, online they must scroll down to scan; therefore, blog layouts need more subheadings, graphics, and other indications of what information follows. The second is onscreen reading can be harder on the eyes than reading printed paper, so legibility is crucial in blogs.

RULES AND RATIONALES FOR WRITING BLOGS

1. Format all posts for smooth page layout and easy scanning.
2. Column width should not be too wide, as larger lines of text can be difficult to read
3. Headings and subheadings separate text visually, enable scanning or skimming, and encourage continued reading.
4. Bullet-pointed or numbered lists enable quick information location and scanning.
5. Punctuation is critical, so beginners should use shorter sentences until confident in their knowledge of punctuation rules.
6. Blog paragraphs should be far shorter—two to six sentences each—than paragraphs written on paper to enable "chunking" because reading onscreen is more difficult.
7. Sans-serif fonts are usually clearer than serif fonts, and larger font sizes are better.
8. Highlight important material and draw attention with **boldface**, but avoid overuse. Avoid hard-to-read *italics* and ALL CAPITALS.
9. Include enough blank spaces: overly busy blogs tire eyes and brains. Images not only break up text but also emphasize and enhance text and can attract initial reader attention.
10. Use background colors judiciously to avoid distracting the eye or making it difficult to read.
11. Be consistent throughout posts, since people read them in different orders.
12. Tell a story with a beginning, middle, and end.

SPECIALIZED MODES OF WRITING

EDITORIALS

Editorials are articles in newspapers, magazines, and other serial publications. Editorials express an opinion or belief belonging to the majority of the publication's leadership. This opinion or belief generally refers to a specific issue, topic, or event. These articles are authored by a member, or a small number of members, of the publication's leadership and are often written to affect their readers, such as persuading them to adopt a stance or take a particular action.

RESUMES

Resumes are brief, but formal, documents that outline an individual's experience in a certain area. Resumes are most often used for job applications. Such resumes will list the applicant's work experience, certification, and achievements or qualifications related to the position. Resumes should only include the most pertinent information. They should also use strategic formatting to highlight the applicant's most impressive experiences and achievements, to ensure the document can be read quickly and easily, and to eliminate both visual clutter and excessive negative space.

REPORTS

Reports summarize the results of research, new methodology, or other developments in an academic or professional context. Reports often include details about methodology and outside influences and factors. However, a report should focus primarily on the results of the research or development. Reports are objective and deliver information efficiently, sacrificing style for clear and effective communication.

Copyright © Mometrix Media. You have been licensed one copy of this document for personal use only. Any other reproduction or redistribution is strictly prohibited. All rights reserved. This content is provided for test preparation purposes only and does not imply an endorsement by Mometrix of any particular political, scientific, or religious point of view.

MEMORANDA

A memorandum, also called a memo, is a formal method of communication used in professional settings. Memoranda are printed documents that include a heading listing the sender and their job title, the recipient and their job title, the date, and a specific subject line. Memoranda often include an introductory section explaining the reason and context for the memorandum. Next, a memorandum includes a section with details relevant to the topic. Finally, the memorandum will conclude with a paragraph that politely and clearly defines the sender's expectations of the recipient.

CHAPTER QUIZ

1. The Greek word *epistolē* means:

    a. Pistol.
    b. Epistaxis.
    c. Essay.
    d. Letter.

2. What are the two major principles used to create an orderly blog?

    a. The content must be interesting with various fonts and color combinations, and it should take less than 10 minutes to read in its entirety.
    b. Blog layouts need more subheadings, graphics, and other indications of what information follows, and the content must be interesting with various fonts and color combinations.
    c. Legibility is crucial because onscreen reading is hard on the eyes, and it should take less than 10 minutes to read in its entirety.
    d. Blog layouts need more subheadings, graphics, and other indications of what information follows, and legibility is crucial because onscreen reading is hard on the eyes.

CHAPTER QUIZ ANSWER KEY

1. D: The Greek word for "letter" is *epistolē*, which became the English word "epistle." The earliest letters were called epistles, including the New Testament's epistles from the apostles to the Christians. In ancient Egypt, the writing curriculum in scribal schools included the epistolary genre. Epistolary novels frame a story in the form of letters.

2. D: There are two major principles that form the basis for blog-writing rules. The first is that while readers of print can skim articles to estimate their length, they must scroll down to scan something published online, meaning that blog layouts need more subheadings, graphics, and other indications of what information follows. The second principle is that onscreen reading can be harder on the eyes than reading printed paper, so legibility is crucial in blogs.

Language

THE EIGHT PARTS OF SPEECH

NOUNS

When you talk about a person, place, thing, or idea, you are talking about a **noun**. The two main types of nouns are **common** and **proper** nouns. Also, nouns can be abstract (i.e., general) or concrete (i.e., specific).

Copyright © Mometrix Media. You have been licensed one copy of this document for personal use only. Any other reproduction or redistribution is strictly prohibited. All rights reserved.
This content is provided for test preparation purposes only and does not imply an endorsement by Mometrix of any particular political, scientific, or religious point of view.

COMMON NOUNS

Common nouns are generic names for people, places, and things. Common nouns are not usually capitalized.

Examples of common nouns:

People: boy, girl, worker, manager

Places: school, bank, library, home

Things: dog, cat, truck, car

> **Review Video: What is a Noun?**
> Visit mometrix.com/academy and enter code: 344028

PROPER NOUNS

Proper nouns name specific people, places, or things. All proper nouns are capitalized.

Examples of proper nouns:

People: Abraham Lincoln, George Washington, Martin Luther King, Jr.

Places: Los Angeles, California; New York; Asia

Things: Statue of Liberty, Earth, Lincoln Memorial

Note: When referring to the planet that we live on, capitalize *Earth*. When referring to the dirt, rocks, or land, lowercase *earth*.

GENERAL AND SPECIFIC NOUNS

General nouns are the names of conditions or ideas. **Specific nouns** name people, places, and things that are understood by using your senses.

General nouns:

Condition: beauty, strength

Idea: truth, peace

Specific nouns:

People: baby, friend, father

Places: town, park, city hall

Things: rainbow, cough, apple, silk, gasoline

COLLECTIVE NOUNS

Collective nouns are the names for a group of people, places, or things that may act as a whole. The following are examples of collective nouns: *class, company, dozen, group, herd, team,* and *public*. Collective nouns usually require an article, which denotes the noun as being a single unit. For instance, a choir is a group of singers. Even though there are many singers in a choir, the word choir is grammatically treated as a single unit. If we refer to the members of the group, and not the group itself, it is no longer a collective noun.

Copyright © Mometrix Media. You have been licensed one copy of this document for personal use only. Any other reproduction or redistribution is strictly prohibited. All rights reserved.
This content is provided for test preparation purposes only and does not imply an endorsement by Mometrix of any particular political, scientific, or religious point of view.

Incorrect: The *choir are* going to compete nationally this year.

Correct: The *choir is* going to compete nationally this year.

Incorrect: The *members* of the choir *is* competing nationally this year.

Correct: The *members* of the choir *are* competing nationally this year.

PRONOUNS

Pronouns are words that are used to stand in for nouns. A pronoun may be classified as personal, intensive, relative, interrogative, demonstrative, indefinite, and reciprocal.

Personal: *Nominative* is the case for nouns and pronouns that are the subject of a sentence. *Objective* is the case for nouns and pronouns that are an object in a sentence. *Possessive* is the case for nouns and pronouns that show possession or ownership.

Singular

	Nominative	Objective	Possessive
First Person	I	me	my, mine
Second Person	you	you	your, yours
Third Person	he, she, it	him, her, it	his, her, hers, its

Plural

	Nominative	Objective	Possessive
First Person	we	us	our, ours
Second Person	you	you	your, yours
Third Person	they	them	their, theirs

Intensive: I myself, you yourself, he himself, she herself, the (thing) itself, we ourselves, you yourselves, they themselves

Relative: which, who, whom, whose

Interrogative: what, which, who, whom, whose

Demonstrative: this, that, these, those

Indefinite: all, any, each, everyone, either/neither, one, some, several

Reciprocal: each other, one another

> **Review Video: Nouns and Pronouns**
> Visit mometrix.com/academy and enter code: 312073

VERBS

If you want to write a sentence, then you need a verb. Without a verb, you have no sentence. The verb of a sentence indicates action or being. In other words, the verb shows something's action or state of being or the action that has been done to something.

Copyright © Mometrix Media. You have been licensed one copy of this document for personal use only. Any other reproduction or redistribution is strictly prohibited. All rights reserved. This content is provided for test preparation purposes only and does not imply an endorsement by Mometrix of any particular political, scientific, or religious point of view.

TRANSITIVE AND INTRANSITIVE VERBS

A **transitive verb** is a verb whose action (e.g., drive, run, jump) indicates a receiver (e.g., car, dog, kangaroo). **Intransitive verbs** do not indicate a receiver of an action. In other words, the action of the verb does not point to a subject or object.

>   **Transitive**: He plays the piano. | The piano was played by him.

>   **Intransitive**: He plays. | John plays well.

A dictionary will tell you whether a verb is transitive or intransitive. Some verbs can be transitive and intransitive.

ACTION VERBS AND LINKING VERBS

Action verbs show what the subject is doing. In other words, an action verb shows action. Unlike most types of words, a single action verb, in the right context, can be an entire sentence. **Linking verbs** link the subject of a sentence to a noun or pronoun, or they link a subject with an adjective. You always need a verb if you want a complete sentence. However, linking verbs on their own cannot be a complete sentence.

Common linking verbs include *appear, be, become, feel, grow, look, seem, smell, sound,* and *taste.* However, any verb that shows a condition and connects to a noun, pronoun, or adjective that describes the subject of a sentence is a linking verb.

Action: He sings. | Run! | Go! | I talk with him every day. | She reads.

Linking:

>   Incorrect: I am.

>   Correct: I am John. | The roses smell lovely. | I feel tired.

Note: Some verbs are followed by words that look like prepositions, but they are a part of the verb and a part of the verb's meaning. These are known as phrasal verbs, and examples include *call off, look up,* and *drop off.*

> **Review Video: Action Verbs and Linking Verbs**
> Visit mometrix.com/academy and enter code: 743142

VOICE

Transitive verbs come in active or passive **voice**. If something does an action or is acted upon, then you will know whether a verb is active or passive. When the subject of the sentence is doing the action, the verb is in **active voice**. When the subject is acted upon, the verb is in **passive voice**.

>   **Active**: Jon drew the picture. (The subject *Jon* is doing the action of *drawing a picture.*)

>   **Passive**: The picture is drawn by Jon. (The subject *picture* is receiving the action from Jon.)

VERB TENSES

A verb **tense** shows the different form of a verb to point to the time of an action. The present and past tense are indicated by the verb's form. An action in the present, *I talk,* can change form for the

Copyright © Mometrix Media. You have been licensed one copy of this document for personal use only. Any other reproduction or redistribution is strictly prohibited. All rights reserved.
This content is provided for test preparation purposes only and does not imply an endorsement by Mometrix of any particular political, scientific, or religious point of view.

past: *I talked*. However, for the other tenses, an auxiliary (i.e., helping) verb is needed to show the change in form. These helping verbs include *am, are, is | have, has, had | was, were, will* (or *shall*).

Present: I talk	Present perfect: I have talked
Past: I talked	Past perfect: I had talked
Future: I will talk	Future perfect: I will have talked

Present: The action happens at the current time.

Example: He *walks* to the store every morning.

To show that something is happening right now, use the progressive present tense: I *am walking*.

Past: The action happened in the past.

Example: He *walked* to the store an hour ago.

Future: The action is going to happen later.

Example: I *will walk* to the store tomorrow.

Present perfect: The action started in the past and continues into the present or took place previously at an unspecified time.

Example: I *have walked* to the store three times today.

Past perfect: The second action happened in the past. The first action came before the second.

Example: Before I walked to the store (Action 2), I *had walked* to the library (Action 1).

Future perfect: An action that uses the past and the future. In other words, the action is complete before a future moment.

Example: When she comes for the supplies (future moment), I *will have walked* to the store (action completed before the future moment).

> **Review Video: <u>Present Perfect, Past Perfect, and Future Perfect Verb Tenses</u>**
> Visit mometrix.com/academy and enter code: 269472

CONJUGATING VERBS

When you need to change the form of a verb, you are **conjugating** a verb. The key forms of a verb are singular, present tense (dream); singular, past tense (dreamed); and the past participle (have dreamed). Note: the past participle needs a helping verb to make a verb tense. For example, I *have dreamed* of this day. The following tables demonstrate some of the different ways to conjugate a verb:

Copyright © Mometrix Media. You have been licensed one copy of this document for personal use only. Any other reproduction or redistribution is strictly prohibited. All rights reserved. This content is provided for test preparation purposes only and does not imply an endorsement by Mometrix of any particular political, scientific, or religious point of view.

Singular

Tense	First Person	Second Person	Third Person
Present	I dream	You dream	He, she, it dreams
Past	I dreamed	You dreamed	He, she, it dreamed
Past Participle	I have dreamed	You have dreamed	He, she, it has dreamed

Plural

Tense	First Person	Second Person	Third Person
Present	We dream	You dream	They dream
Past	We dreamed	You dreamed	They dreamed
Past Participle	We have dreamed	You have dreamed	They have dreamed

MOOD

There are three **moods** in English: the indicative, the imperative, and the subjunctive.

The **indicative mood** is used for facts, opinions, and questions.

> Fact: You can do this.

> Opinion: I think that you can do this.

> Question: Do you know that you can do this?

The **imperative** is used for orders or requests.

> Order: You are going to do this!

> Request: Will you do this for me?

The **subjunctive mood** is for wishes and statements that go against fact.

> Wish: I wish that I were famous.

> Statement against fact: If I were you, I would do this. (This goes against fact because I am not you. You have the chance to do this, and I do not have the chance.)

ADJECTIVES

An **adjective** is a word that is used to modify a noun or pronoun. An adjective answers a question: *Which one? What kind?* or *How many?* Usually, adjectives come before the words that they modify, but they may also come after a linking verb.

> Which one? The *third* suit is my favorite.

> What kind? This suit is *navy blue*.

> How many? I am going to buy *four* pairs of socks to match the suit.

Review Video: Descriptive Text
Visit mometrix.com/academy and enter code: 174903

116

Copyright © Mometrix Media. You have been licensed one copy of this document for personal use only. Any other reproduction or redistribution is strictly prohibited. All rights reserved.
This content is provided for test preparation purposes only and does not imply an endorsement by Mometrix of any particular political, scientific, or religious point of view.

ARTICLES

Articles are adjectives that are used to distinguish nouns as definite or indefinite. **Definite** nouns are preceded by the article *the* and indicate a specific person, place, thing, or idea. **Indefinite** nouns are preceded by *a* or *an* and do not indicate a specific person, place, thing, or idea. *A*, *an*, and *the* are the only articles. Note: *An* comes before words that start with a vowel sound. For example, "Are you going to get an **u**mbrella?"

> **Definite**: I lost *the* bottle that belongs to me.

> **Indefinite**: Does anyone have *a* bottle to share?

> **Review Video: <u>Function of Articles</u>**
> Visit mometrix.com/academy and enter code: 449383

COMPARISON WITH ADJECTIVES

Some adjectives are relative and other adjectives are absolute. Adjectives that are **relative** can show the comparison between things. **Absolute** adjectives can also show comparison, but they do so in a different way. Let's say that you are reading two books. You think that one book is perfect, and the other book is not exactly perfect. It is not possible for one book to be more perfect than the other. Either you think that the book is perfect, or you think that the book is imperfect. In this case, perfect and imperfect are absolute adjectives.

Relative adjectives will show the different **degrees** of something or someone to something else or someone else. The three degrees of adjectives include positive, comparative, and superlative.

The **positive** degree is the normal form of an adjective.

> Example: This work is *difficult*. | She is *smart*.

The **comparative** degree compares one person or thing to another person or thing.

> Example: This work is *more difficult* than your work. | She is *smarter* than me.

The **superlative** degree compares more than two people or things.

> Example: This is the *most difficult* work of my life. | She is the *smartest* lady in school.

> **Review Video: <u>What is an Adjective?</u>**
> Visit mometrix.com/academy and enter code: 470154

ADVERBS

An **adverb** is a word that is used to **modify** a verb, adjective, or another adverb. Usually, adverbs answer one of these questions: *When? Where? How?* and *Why?* The negatives *not* and *never* are considered adverbs. Adverbs that modify adjectives or other adverbs **strengthen** or **weaken** the words that they modify.

Examples:

> He walks *quickly* through the crowd.

> The water flows *smoothly* on the rocks.

Copyright © Mometrix Media. You have been licensed one copy of this document for personal use only. Any other reproduction or redistribution is strictly prohibited. All rights reserved.
This content is provided for test preparation purposes only and does not imply an endorsement by Mometrix of any particular political, scientific, or religious point of view.

Note: Adverbs are usually indicated by the morpheme *-ly*, which has been added to the root word. For instance, *quick* can be made into an adverb by adding *-ly* to construct *quickly*. Some words that end in *-ly* do not follow this rule and can behave as other parts of speech. Examples of adjectives ending in *-ly* include: *early, friendly, holy, lonely, silly*, and *ugly*. To know if a word that ends in *-ly* is an adjective or adverb, check your dictionary. Also, while many adverbs end in *-ly*, you need to remember that not all adverbs end in *-ly*.

Examples:

He is *never* angry.

You are *too* irresponsible to travel alone.

> **Review Video: What is an Adverb?**
> Visit mometrix.com/academy and enter code: 713951
>
> **Review Video: Adverbs that Modify Adjectives**
> Visit mometrix.com/academy and enter code: 122570

COMPARISON WITH ADVERBS

The rules for comparing adverbs are the same as the rules for adjectives.

The **positive** degree is the standard form of an adverb.

Example: He arrives *soon*. | She speaks *softly* to her friends.

The **comparative** degree compares one person or thing to another person or thing.

Example: He arrives *sooner* than Sarah. | She speaks *more softly* than him.

The **superlative** degree compares more than two people or things.

Example: He arrives *soonest* of the group. | She speaks the *most softly* of any of her friends.

PREPOSITIONS

A **preposition** is a word placed before a noun or pronoun that shows the relationship between an object and another word in the sentence.

Common prepositions:

about	before	during	on	under
after	beneath	for	over	until
against	between	from	past	up
among	beyond	in	through	with
around	by	of	to	within
at	down	off	toward	without

Copyright © Mometrix Media. You have been licensed one copy of this document for personal use only. Any other reproduction or redistribution is strictly prohibited. All rights reserved. This content is provided for test preparation purposes only and does not imply an endorsement by Mometrix of any particular political, scientific, or religious point of view.

Examples:

> The napkin is *in* the drawer.
>
> The Earth rotates *around* the Sun.
>
> The needle is *beneath* the haystack.
>
> Can you find "me" *among* the words?

Review Video: Prepositions
Visit mometrix.com/academy and enter code: 946763

CONJUNCTIONS

Conjunctions join words, phrases, or clauses and they show the connection between the joined pieces. **Coordinating conjunctions** connect equal parts of sentences. **Correlative conjunctions** show the connection between pairs. **Subordinating conjunctions** join subordinate (i.e., dependent) clauses with independent clauses.

COORDINATING CONJUNCTIONS

The **coordinating conjunctions** include: *and, but, yet, or, nor, for,* and *so*

Examples:

> The rock was small, *but* it was heavy.
>
> She drove in the night, *and* he drove in the day.

CORRELATIVE CONJUNCTIONS

The **correlative conjunctions** are: *either...or | neither...nor | not only...but also*

Examples:

> *Either* you are coming *or* you are staying.
>
> He *not only* ran three miles *but also* swam 200 yards.

Review Video: Coordinating and Correlative Conjunctions
Visit mometrix.com/academy and enter code: 390329

Review Video: Adverb Equal Comparisons
Visit mometrix.com/academy and enter code: 231291

SUBORDINATING CONJUNCTIONS

Common **subordinating conjunctions** include:

after	since	whenever
although	so that	where
because	unless	wherever
before	until	whether
in order that	when	while

Copyright © Mometrix Media. You have been licensed one copy of this document for personal use only. Any other reproduction or redistribution is strictly prohibited. All rights reserved.
This content is provided for test preparation purposes only and does not imply an endorsement by Mometrix of any particular political, scientific, or religious point of view.

Examples:

> I am hungry *because* I did not eat breakfast.

> He went home *when* everyone left.

> **Review Video: <u>Subordinating Conjunctions</u>**
> Visit mometrix.com/academy and enter code: 958913

INTERJECTIONS

Interjections are words of exclamation (i.e., audible expression of great feeling) that are used alone or as a part of a sentence. Often, they are used at the beginning of a sentence for an introduction. Sometimes, they can be used in the middle of a sentence to show a change in thought or attitude.

> Common Interjections: Hey! | Oh, | Ouch! | Please! | Wow!

CHAPTER QUIZ

1. Which of the following is NOT considered a type of mood?

   a. Indicative
   b. Imperative
   c. Subjunctive
   d. Conjunctive

2. How many different degrees of relative adjectives are there?

   a. Two
   b. Three
   c. Four
   d. Five

3. In general, adverbs may modify all of the following, EXCEPT:

   a. Another adverb.
   b. Adjectives.
   c. Proper nouns.
   d. Verbs.

CHAPTER QUIZ ANSWER KEY

1. D: There are three moods in English: the indicative, the imperative, and the subjunctive.

2. B: Relative adjectives will show the different degrees of something or someone to something else or someone else. The three degrees of adjectives include positive, comparative, and superlative.

3. C: An adverb is a word that is used to modify a verb, adjective, or another adverb. Usually, adverbs answer one of the questions: *When? Where? How?* and *Why?* The negatives *not* and *never* are considered adverbs. Adverbs that modify adjectives or other adverbs strengthen or weaken the words that they modify.

SUBJECTS AND PREDICATES

SUBJECTS

The **subject** of a sentence names who or what the sentence is about. The subject may be directly stated in a sentence, or the subject may be the implied *you*. The **complete subject** includes the

Copyright © Mometrix Media. You have been licensed one copy of this document for personal use only. Any other reproduction or redistribution is strictly prohibited. All rights reserved.
This content is provided for test preparation purposes only and does not imply an endorsement by Mometrix of any particular political, scientific, or religious point of view.

simple subject and all of its modifiers. To find the complete subject, ask *Who* or *What* and insert the verb to complete the question. The answer, including any modifiers (adjectives, prepositional phrases, etc.), is the complete subject. To find the **simple subject**, remove all of the modifiers in the complete subject. Being able to locate the subject of a sentence helps with many problems, such as those involving sentence fragments and subject-verb agreement.

Examples:

simple
subject

The small, red car is the one that he wants for Christmas.

complete
subject

simple
subject

The young artist is coming over for dinner.

complete
subject

> **Review Video: Subjects in English**
> Visit mometrix.com/academy and enter code: 444771

In **imperative** sentences, the verb's subject is understood (e.g., [You] Run to the store), but is not actually present in the sentence. Normally, the subject comes before the verb. However, the subject comes after the verb in sentences that begin with *There are* or *There was*.

Direct:

John knows the way to the park.	Who knows the way to the park?	John
The cookies need ten more minutes.	What needs ten minutes?	The cookies
By five o'clock, Bill will need to leave.	Who needs to leave?	Bill
There are five letters on the table for him.	What is on the table?	Five letters
There were coffee and doughnuts in the house.	What was in the house?	Coffee and doughnuts

Implied:

| Go to the post office for me. | Who is going to the post office? | You |
| Come and sit with me, please? | Who needs to come and sit? | You |

PREDICATES

In a sentence, you always have a predicate and a subject. The subject tells what the sentence is about, and the **predicate** explains or describes the subject.

Think about the sentence *He sings*. In this sentence, we have a subject (He) and a predicate (sings). This is all that is needed for a sentence to be complete. Most sentences contain more information, but if this is all the information that you are given, then you have a complete sentence.

Copyright © Mometrix Media. You have been licensed one copy of this document for personal use only. Any other reproduction or redistribution is strictly prohibited. All rights reserved. This content is provided for test preparation purposes only and does not imply an endorsement by Mometrix of any particular political, scientific, or religious point of view.

Now, let's look at another sentence: *John and Jane sing on Tuesday nights at the dance hall.*

<u>subject</u>   <u>predicate</u>
John and Jane   sing on Tuesday nights at the dance hall.

SUBJECT-VERB AGREEMENT

Verbs **agree** with their subjects in number. In other words, singular subjects need singular verbs. Plural subjects need plural verbs. **Singular** is for **one** person, place, or thing. **Plural** is for **more than one** person, place, or thing. Subjects and verbs must also share the same point of view, as in first, second, or third person. The present tense ending *-s* is used on a verb if its subject is third person singular; otherwise, the verb's ending is not modified.

> **Review Video: Subject-Verb Agreement**
> Visit mometrix.com/academy and enter code: 479190

NUMBER AGREEMENT EXAMPLES:

singular singular
subject verb
Single Subject and Verb: Dan   calls   home.

Dan is one person. So, the singular verb *calls* is needed.

plural plural
subject verb
Plural Subject and Verb: Dan and Bob   call   home.

More than one person needs the plural verb *call*.

PERSON AGREEMENT EXAMPLES:

First Person: I *am* walking.

Second Person: You *are* walking.

Third Person: He *is* walking.

COMPLICATIONS WITH SUBJECT-VERB AGREEMENT
WORDS BETWEEN SUBJECT AND VERB

Words that come between the simple subject and the verb have no bearing on subject-verb agreement.

Examples:

singular   singular
subject   verb
The joy of my life returns home tonight.

The phrase *of my life* does not influence the verb *returns*.

singular   singular
subject   verb
The question that still remains unanswered is "Who are you?"

Don't let the phrase "*that still remains*..." trouble you. The subject *question* goes with *is*.

Copyright © Mometrix Media. You have been licensed one copy of this document for personal use only. Any other reproduction or redistribution is strictly prohibited. All rights reserved.
This content is provided for test preparation purposes only and does not imply an endorsement by Mometrix of any particular political, scientific, or religious point of view.

COMPOUND SUBJECTS

A compound subject is formed when two or more nouns joined by *and*, *or*, or *nor* jointly act as the subject of the sentence.

JOINED BY AND

When a compound subject is joined by *and*, it is treated as a plural subject and requires a plural verb.

Examples:

You and Jon **are** invited to come to my house.
(plural subject) (plural verb)

The pencil and paper **belong** to me.
(plural subject) (plural verb)

JOINED BY OR/NOR

For a compound subject joined by *or* or *nor*, the verb must agree in number with the part of the subject that is closest to the verb (italicized in the examples below).

Examples:

Today or tomorrow **is** the day.
(subject) (verb)

Stan or Phil **wants** to read the book.
(subject) (verb)

Neither the pen nor the book **is** on the desk.
(subject) (verb)

Either the blanket or pillows **arrive** this afternoon.
(subject) (verb)

INDEFINITE PRONOUNS AS SUBJECT

An indefinite pronoun is a pronoun that does not refer to a specific noun. Different indefinite pronouns may only function as a singular noun, only function as a plural noun, or change depending on how they are used.

ALWAYS SINGULAR

Pronouns such as *each*, *either*, *everybody*, *anybody*, *somebody*, and *nobody* are always singular.

Examples:

Each of the runners **has** a different bib number.
(singular subject) (singular verb)

Is either of you ready for the game?
(singular verb) (singular subject)

Copyright © Mometrix Media. You have been licensed one copy of this document for personal use only. Any other reproduction or redistribution is strictly prohibited. All rights reserved.
This content is provided for test preparation purposes only and does not imply an endorsement by Mometrix of any particular political, scientific, or religious point of view.

Note: The words *each* and *either* can also be used as adjectives (e.g., *each* person is unique). When one of these adjectives modifies the subject of a sentence, it is always a singular subject.

singular subject · singular verb

Everybody grows a day older every day.

singular subject · singular verb

Anybody is welcome to bring a tent.

ALWAYS PLURAL

Pronouns such as *both*, *several*, and *many* are always plural.

Examples:

plural subject · plural verb

Both of the siblings were too tired to argue.

plural subject · plural verb

Many have tried, but none have succeeded.

DEPEND ON CONTEXT

Pronouns such as *some*, *any*, *all*, *none*, *more*, and *most* can be either singular or plural depending on what they are representing in the context of the sentence.

Examples:

singular subject · singular verb

All of my dog's food was still there in his bowl.

plural subject · plural verb

By the end of the night, all of my guests were already excited about coming to my next party.

OTHER CASES INVOLVING PLURAL OR IRREGULAR FORM

Some nouns are **singular in meaning but plural in form**: news, mathematics, physics, and economics.

The *news is* coming on now.

Mathematics is my favorite class.

Some nouns are plural in form and meaning, and have **no singular equivalent**: scissors and pants.

Do these *pants come* with a shirt?

The *scissors are* for my project.

Copyright © Mometrix Media. You have been licensed one copy of this document for personal use only. Any other reproduction or redistribution is strictly prohibited. All rights reserved.
This content is provided for test preparation purposes only and does not imply an endorsement by Mometrix of any particular political, scientific, or religious point of view.

Mathematical operations are **irregular** in their construction, but are normally considered to be **singular in meaning**.

> *One plus one is* two.

> *Three times three is* nine.

Note: Look to your **dictionary** for help when you aren't sure whether a noun with a plural form has a singular or plural meaning.

COMPLEMENTS

A complement is a noun, pronoun, or adjective that is used to give more information about the subject or verb in the sentence.

DIRECT OBJECTS

A direct object is a noun or pronoun that takes or receives the **action** of a verb. (Remember: a complete sentence does not need a direct object, so not all sentences will have them. A sentence needs only a subject and a verb.) When you are looking for a direct object, find the verb and ask *who* or *what*.

Examples:

> I took *the blanket*.

> Jane read *books*.

INDIRECT OBJECTS

An indirect object is a word or group of words that show how an action had an **influence** on someone or something. If there is an indirect object in a sentence, then you always have a direct object in the sentence. When you are looking for the indirect object, find the verb and ask *to/for whom or what*.

Examples:

We taught the old dog a new trick. (indirect object: the old dog; direct object: a new trick)

I gave them a math lesson. (indirect object: them; direct object: a math lesson)

> **Review Video: Direct and Indirect Objects**
> Visit mometrix.com/academy and enter code: 817385

PREDICATE NOMINATIVES AND PREDICATE ADJECTIVES

As we looked at previously, verbs may be classified as either action verbs or linking verbs. A linking verb is so named because it links the subject to words in the predicate that describe or define the subject. These words are called predicate nominatives (if nouns or pronouns) or predicate adjectives (if adjectives).

Copyright © Mometrix Media. You have been licensed one copy of this document for personal use only. Any other reproduction or redistribution is strictly prohibited. All rights reserved. This content is provided for test preparation purposes only and does not imply an endorsement by Mometrix of any particular political, scientific, or religious point of view.

Examples:

subject — predicate nominative

My father is a lawyer.

subject — predicate adjective

Your mother is patient.

PRONOUN USAGE

The **antecedent** is the noun that has been replaced by a pronoun. A pronoun and its antecedent **agree** when they have the same number (singular or plural) and gender (male, female, or neutral).

Examples:

antecedent — pronoun

Singular agreement: John came into town, and he played for us.

antecedent — pronoun

Plural agreement: John and Rick came into town, and they played for us.

To determine which is the correct pronoun to use in a compound subject or object, try each pronoun **alone** in place of the compound in the sentence. Your knowledge of pronouns will tell you which one is correct.

Example:

Bob and (I, me) will be going.

Test: (1) *I will be going* or (2) *Me will be going*. The second choice cannot be correct because *me* cannot be used as the subject of a sentence. Instead, *me* is used as an object.

Answer: Bob and I will be going.

When a pronoun is used with a noun immediately following (as in "we boys"), try the sentence **without the added noun**.

Example:

(We/Us) boys played football last year.

Test: (1) *We played football last year* or (2) *Us played football last year*. Again, the second choice cannot be correct because *us* cannot be used as a subject of a sentence. Instead, *us* is used as an object.

Answer: We boys played football last year.

| Review Video: **Pronoun Usage** |
| Visit mometrix.com/academy and enter code: 666500 |
| Review Video: **What is Pronoun-Antecedent Agreement?** |
| Visit mometrix.com/academy and enter code: 919704 |

Copyright © Mometrix Media. You have been licensed one copy of this document for personal use only. Any other reproduction or redistribution is strictly prohibited. All rights reserved. This content is provided for test preparation purposes only and does not imply an endorsement by Mometrix of any particular political, scientific, or religious point of view.

A pronoun should point clearly to the **antecedent**. Here is how a pronoun reference can be unhelpful if it is puzzling or not directly stated.

                antecedent   pronoun

Unhelpful: Ron and Jim went to the store, and he bought soda.

Who bought soda? Ron or Jim?

              antecedent   pronoun

Helpful: Jim went to the store, and he bought soda.

The sentence is clear. Jim bought the soda.

Some pronouns change their form by their placement in a sentence. A pronoun that is a **subject** in a sentence comes in the **subjective case**. Pronouns that serve as **objects** appear in the **objective case**. Finally, the pronouns that are used as **possessives** appear in the **possessive case**.

Examples:

    Subjective case: *He* is coming to the show.

    The pronoun *He* is the subject of the sentence.

    Objective case: Josh drove *him* to the airport.

    The pronoun *him* is the object of the sentence.

    Possessive case: The flowers are *mine*.

    The pronoun *mine* shows ownership of the flowers.

The word *who* is a subjective-case pronoun that can be used as a **subject**. The word *whom* is an objective-case pronoun that can be used as an **object**. The words *who* and *whom* are common in subordinate clauses or in questions.

Examples:

                subject   verb

    He knows who wants to come.

                     object   verb

    He knows the man whom we want at the party.

CLAUSES

A clause is a group of words that contains both a subject and a predicate (verb). There are two types of clauses: independent and dependent. An **independent clause** contains a complete thought, while a **dependent (or subordinate) clause** does not. A dependent clause includes a subject and a verb, and may also contain objects or complements, but it cannot stand as a complete thought without being joined to an independent clause. Dependent clauses function within sentences as adjectives, adverbs, or nouns.

Copyright © Mometrix Media. You have been licensed one copy of this document for personal use only. Any other reproduction or redistribution is strictly prohibited. All rights reserved.
This content is provided for test preparation purposes only and does not imply an endorsement by Mometrix of any particular political, scientific, or religious point of view.

Example:

independent   dependent
clause   clause

I am running   because I want to stay in shape.

The clause *I am running* is an independent clause: it has a subject and a verb, and it gives a complete thought. The clause *because I want to stay in shape* is a dependent clause: it has a subject and a verb, but it does not express a complete thought. It adds detail to the independent clause to which it is attached.

> **Review Video: What is a Clause?**
> Visit mometrix.com/academy and enter code: 940170
>
> **Review Video: Independent and Dependent Clauses**
> Visit mometrix.com/academy and enter code: 556903

TYPES OF DEPENDENT CLAUSES

ADJECTIVE CLAUSES

An **adjective clause** is a dependent clause that modifies a noun or a pronoun. Adjective clauses begin with a relative pronoun (*who, whose, whom, which,* and *that*) or a relative adverb (*where, when,* and *why*).

Also, adjective clauses come after the noun that the clause needs to explain or rename. This is done to have a clear connection to the independent clause.

Examples:

independent   adjective
clause   clause

I learned the reason   why I won the award.

independent   adjective
clause   clause

This is the place   where I started my first job.

An adjective clause can be an essential or nonessential clause. An essential clause is very important to the sentence. **Essential clauses** explain or define a person or thing. **Nonessential clauses** give more information about a person or thing but are not necessary to define them. Nonessential clauses are set off with commas while essential clauses are not.

Examples:

essential
clause

A person who works hard at first can often rest later in life.

nonessential
clause

Neil Armstrong, who walked on the moon, is my hero.

> **Review Video: Adjective Clauses and Phrases**
> Visit mometrix.com/academy and enter code: 520888

Copyright © Mometrix Media. You have been licensed one copy of this document for personal use only. Any other reproduction or redistribution is strictly prohibited. All rights reserved.
This content is provided for test preparation purposes only and does not imply an endorsement by Mometrix of any particular political, scientific, or religious point of view.

ADVERB CLAUSES

An **adverb clause** is a dependent clause that modifies a verb, adjective, or adverb. In sentences with multiple dependent clauses, adverb clauses are usually placed immediately before or after the independent clause. An adverb clause is introduced with words such as *after, although, as, before, because, if, since, so, unless, when, where*, and *while*.

Examples:

$$\overbrace{\text{When you walked outside,}}^{\text{adverb clause}} \text{ I called the manager.}$$

$$\text{I will go with you } \overbrace{\text{unless you want to stay.}}^{\text{adverb clause}}$$

NOUN CLAUSES

A **noun clause** is a dependent clause that can be used as a subject, object, or complement. Noun clauses begin with words such as *how, that, what, whether, which, who,* and *why*. These words can also come with an adjective clause. Unless the noun clause is being used as the subject of the sentence, it should come after the verb of the independent clause.

Examples:

$$\text{The real mystery is } \overbrace{\text{how you avoided serious injury.}}^{\text{noun clause}}$$

$$\overbrace{\text{What you learn from each other}}^{\text{noun clause}} \text{ depends on your honesty with others.}$$

SUBORDINATION

When two related ideas are not of equal importance, the ideal way to combine them is to make the more important idea an independent clause and the less important idea a dependent or subordinate clause. This is called **subordination**.

Example:

Separate ideas: The team had a perfect regular season. The team lost the championship.

Subordinated: Despite having a perfect regular season, *the team lost the championship.*

PHRASES

A phrase is a group of words that functions as a single part of speech, usually a noun, adjective, or adverb. A **phrase** is not a complete thought, but it adds detail or explanation to a sentence, or renames something within the sentence.

PREPOSITIONAL PHRASES

One of the most common types of phrases is the prepositional phrase. A **prepositional phrase** begins with a preposition and ends with a noun or pronoun that is the object of the preposition. Normally, the prepositional phrase functions as an **adjective** or an **adverb** within the sentence.

129

Copyright © Mometrix Media. You have been licensed one copy of this document for personal use only. Any other reproduction or redistribution is strictly prohibited. All rights reserved.
This content is provided for test preparation purposes only and does not imply an endorsement by Mometrix of any particular political, scientific, or religious point of view.

Examples:

prepositional
phrase
The picnic is on the blanket.

prepositional
phrase
I am sick with a fever today.

prepositional
phrase
Among the many flowers, John found a four-leaf clover.

VERBAL PHRASES

A **verbal** is a word or phrase that is formed from a verb but does not function as a verb. Depending on its particular form, it may be used as a noun, adjective, or adverb. A verbal does **not** replace a verb in a sentence.

Examples:

verb
Correct: Walk a mile daily.

This is a complete sentence with the implied subject *you*.

verbal
Incorrect: To walk a mile.

This is not a sentence since there is no functional verb.

There are three types of verbal: **participles**, **gerunds**, and **infinitives**. Each type of verbal has a corresponding **phrase** that consists of the verbal itself along with any complements or modifiers.

PARTICIPLES

A **participle** is a type of verbal that always functions as an adjective. The present participle always ends with *-ing*. Past participles end with *-d, -ed, -n,* or *-t.*

present   past
verb   participle   participle
Examples: dance | dancing | danced

Participial phrases most often come right before or right after the noun or pronoun that they modify.

Copyright © Mometrix Media. You have been licensed one copy of this document for personal use only. Any other reproduction or redistribution is strictly prohibited. All rights reserved.
This content is provided for test preparation purposes only and does not imply an endorsement by Mometrix of any particular political, scientific, or religious point of view.

Examples:

participial
phrase

Shipwrecked on an island, the boys started to fish for food.

participial
phrase

Having been seated for five hours, we got out of the car to stretch our legs.

participial
phrase

Praised for their work, the group accepted the first-place trophy.

GERUNDS

A **gerund** is a type of verbal that always functions as a **noun**. Like present participles, gerunds always end with -*ing*, but they can be easily distinguished from one another by the part of speech they represent (participles always function as adjectives). Since a gerund or gerund phrase always functions as a noun, it can be used as the subject of a sentence, the predicate nominative, or the object of a verb or preposition.

Examples:

gerund

We want to be known for teaching the poor.
object of preposition

gerund

Coaching this team is the best job of my life.
subject

gerund

We like practicing our songs in the basement.
object of verb

INFINITIVES

An **infinitive** is a type of verbal that can function as a noun, an adjective, or an adverb. An infinitive is made of the word *to* and the basic form of the verb. As with all other types of verbal phrases, an infinitive phrase includes the verbal itself and all of its complements or modifiers.

131

Copyright © Mometrix Media. You have been licensed one copy of this document for personal use only. Any other reproduction or redistribution is strictly prohibited. All rights reserved.
This content is provided for test preparation purposes only and does not imply an endorsement by Mometrix of any particular political, scientific, or religious point of view.

Examples:

infinitive
To join the team is my goal in life.
noun

infinitive
The animals have enough food to eat for the night.
adjective

infinitive
People lift weights to exercise their muscles.
adverb

> **Review Video: Gerunds, Infinitives, and Participles**
> Visit mometrix.com/academy and enter code: 634263

APPOSITIVE PHRASES

An **appositive** is a word or phrase that is used to explain or rename nouns or pronouns. Noun phrases, gerund phrases, and infinitive phrases can all be used as appositives.

Examples:

appositive
Terriers, hunters at heart, have been dressed up to look like lap dogs.

The noun phrase *hunters at heart* renames the noun *terriers*.

appositive
His plan, to save and invest his money, was proven as a safe approach.

The infinitive phrase explains what the plan is.

Appositive phrases can be **essential** or **nonessential**. An appositive phrase is essential if the person, place, or thing being described or renamed is too general for its meaning to be understood without the appositive.

Examples:

essential
Two of America's Founding Fathers, George Washington and Thomas Jefferson, served as presidents.

nonessential
George Washington and Thomas Jefferson, two Founding Fathers, served as presidents.

ABSOLUTE PHRASES

An absolute phrase is a phrase that consists of **a noun followed by a participle**. An absolute phrase provides **context** to what is being described in the sentence, but it does not modify or explain any particular word; it is essentially independent.

Copyright © Mometrix Media. You have been licensed one copy of this document for personal use only. Any other reproduction or redistribution is strictly prohibited. All rights reserved.
This content is provided for test preparation purposes only and does not imply an endorsement by Mometrix of any particular political, scientific, or religious point of view.

Examples:

noun participle

The alarm ringing, he pushed the snooze button.

absolute phrase

noun participle

The music paused, she continued to dance through the crowd.

absolute phrase

PARALLELISM

When multiple items or ideas are presented in a sentence in series, such as in a list, the items or ideas must be stated in grammatically equivalent ways. In other words, if one idea is stated in gerund form, the second cannot be stated in infinitive form. For example, to write, *I enjoy reading and to study* would be incorrect. An infinitive and a gerund are not equivalent. Instead, you should write *I enjoy reading and studying*. In lists of more than two, all items must be parallel.

Example:

Incorrect: He stopped at the office, grocery store, and the pharmacy before heading home.

The first and third items in the list of places include the article *the*, so the second item needs it as well.

Correct: He stopped at the office, *the* grocery store, and the pharmacy before heading home.

Example:

Incorrect: While vacationing in Europe, she went biking, skiing, and climbed mountains.

The first and second items in the list are gerunds, so the third item must be as well.

Correct: While vacationing in Europe, she went biking, skiing, and *mountain climbing*.

> **Review Video: Parallel Sentence Construction**
> Visit mometrix.com/academy and enter code: 831988

SENTENCE PURPOSE

There are four types of sentences: declarative, imperative, interrogative, and exclamatory.

A **declarative** sentence states a fact and ends with a period.

The football game starts at seven o'clock.

An **imperative** sentence tells someone to do something and generally ends with a period. An urgent command might end with an exclamation point instead.

Don't forget to buy your ticket.

An **interrogative** sentence asks a question and ends with a question mark.

Are you going to the game on Friday?

Copyright © Mometrix Media. You have been licensed one copy of this document for personal use only. Any other reproduction or redistribution is strictly prohibited. All rights reserved. This content is provided for test preparation purposes only and does not imply an endorsement by Mometrix of any particular political, scientific, or religious point of view.

An **exclamatory** sentence shows strong emotion and ends with an exclamation point.

I can't believe we won the game!

Review Video: Functions of a Sentence
Visit mometrix.com/academy and enter code: 475974

SENTENCE STRUCTURE

Sentences are classified by structure based on the type and number of clauses present. The four classifications of sentence structure are the following:

Simple: A simple sentence has one independent clause with no dependent clauses. A simple sentence may have **compound elements** (i.e., compound subject or verb).

Examples:

single subject · single verb
Judy watered the lawn.

compound subject · single verb
Judy and Alan watered the lawn.

single subject · compound verb · compound verb
Judy watered the lawn and pulled weeds.

compound subject · compound verb · compound verb
Judy and Alan watered the lawn and pulled weeds.

Compound: A compound sentence has two or more independent clauses with no dependent clauses. Usually, the independent clauses are joined with a comma and a coordinating conjunction or with a semicolon.

Examples:

independent clause · independent clause
The time has come, and we are ready.

independent clause · independent clause
I woke up at dawn; the sun was just coming up.

Complex: A complex sentence has one independent clause and at least one dependent clause.

Examples:

dependent clause · independent clause
Although he had the flu, Harry went to work.

independent clause · dependent clause
Marcia got married, after she finished college.

Copyright © Mometrix Media. You have been licensed one copy of this document for personal use only. Any other reproduction or redistribution is strictly prohibited. All rights reserved.
This content is provided for test preparation purposes only and does not imply an endorsement by Mometrix of any particular political, scientific, or religious point of view.

Compound-Complex: A compound-complex sentence has at least two independent clauses and at least one dependent clause.

Examples:

independent clause — John is my friend | dependent clause — who went to India, | independent clause — and he brought back souvenirs.

independent clause — You may not realize this, | independent clause — but we heard the music | dependent clause — that you played last night.

> **Review Video: Sentence Structure**
> Visit mometrix.com/academy and enter code: 700478

Sentence variety is important to consider when writing an essay or speech. A variety of sentence lengths and types creates rhythm, makes a passage more engaging, and gives writers an opportunity to demonstrate their writing style. Writing that uses the same length or type of sentence without variation can be boring or difficult to read. To evaluate a passage for effective sentence variety, it is helpful to note whether the passage contains diverse sentence structures and lengths. It is also important to pay attention to the way each sentence starts and avoid beginning with the same words or phrases.

SENTENCE FRAGMENTS

Recall that a group of words must contain at least one **independent clause** in order to be considered a sentence. If it doesn't contain even one independent clause, it is called a **sentence fragment**.

The appropriate process for **repairing** a sentence fragment depends on what type of fragment it is. If the fragment is a dependent clause, it can sometimes be as simple as removing a subordinating word (e.g., when, because, if) from the beginning of the fragment. Alternatively, a dependent clause can be incorporated into a closely related neighboring sentence. If the fragment is missing some required part, like a subject or a verb, the fix might be as simple as adding the missing part.

Examples:

Fragment: Because he wanted to sail the Mediterranean.

Removed subordinating word: He wanted to sail the Mediterranean.

Combined with another sentence: Because he wanted to sail the Mediterranean, he booked a Greek island cruise.

RUN-ON SENTENCES

Run-on sentences consist of multiple independent clauses that have not been joined together properly. Run-on sentences can be corrected in several different ways:

Join clauses properly: This can be done with a comma and coordinating conjunction, with a semicolon, or with a colon or dash if the second clause is explaining something in the first.

Copyright © Mometrix Media. You have been licensed one copy of this document for personal use only. Any other reproduction or redistribution is strictly prohibited. All rights reserved. This content is provided for test preparation purposes only and does not imply an endorsement by Mometrix of any particular political, scientific, or religious point of view.

Example:

> **Incorrect**: I went on the trip, we visited lots of castles.

> **Corrected**: I went on the trip, and we visited lots of castles.

Split into separate sentences: This correction is most effective when the independent clauses are very long or when they are not closely related.

Example:

> **Incorrect**: The drive to New York takes ten hours, my uncle lives in Boston.

> **Corrected**: The drive to New York takes ten hours. My uncle lives in Boston.

Make one clause dependent: This is the easiest way to make the sentence correct and more interesting at the same time. It's often as simple as adding a subordinating word between the two clauses or before the first clause.

Example:

> **Incorrect**: I finally made it to the store and I bought some eggs.

> **Corrected**: When I finally made it to the store, I bought some eggs.

Reduce to one clause with a compound verb: If both clauses have the same subject, remove the subject from the second clause, and you now have just one clause with a compound verb.

Example:

> **Incorrect**: The drive to New York takes ten hours, it makes me very tired.

> **Corrected**: The drive to New York takes ten hours and makes me very tired.

Note: While these are the simplest ways to correct a run-on sentence, often the best way is to completely reorganize the thoughts in the sentence and rewrite it.

> **Review Video: <u>Fragments and Run-on Sentences</u>**
> Visit mometrix.com/academy and enter code: 541989

Copyright © Mometrix Media. You have been licensed one copy of this document for personal use only. Any other reproduction or redistribution is strictly prohibited. All rights reserved.
This content is provided for test preparation purposes only and does not imply an endorsement by Mometrix of any particular political, scientific, or religious point of view.

DANGLING AND MISPLACED MODIFIERS
DANGLING MODIFIERS

A dangling modifier is a dependent clause or verbal phrase that does not have a clear logical connection to a word in the sentence.

Example:

dangling
modifier

Incorrect: Reading each magazine article, the stories caught my attention.

The word *stories* cannot be modified by *Reading each magazine article*. People can read, but stories cannot read. Therefore, the subject of the sentence must be a person.

dependent
clause

Corrected: Reading each magazine article, I was entertained by the stories.

Example:

dangling
modifier

Incorrect: Ever since childhood, my grandparents have visited me for Christmas.

The speaker in this sentence can't have been visited by her grandparents when *they* were children, since she wouldn't have been born yet. Either the modifier should be clarified or the sentence should be rearranged to specify whose childhood is being referenced.

dependent
clause

Clarified: Ever since I was a child, my grandparents have visited for Christmas.

dependent
clause

Rearranged: I have enjoyed my grandparents visiting for Christmas, ever since childhood.

MISPLACED MODIFIERS

Because modifiers are grammatically versatile, they can be put in many different places within the structure of a sentence. The danger of this versatility is that a modifier can accidentally be placed where it is modifying the wrong word or where it is not clear which word it is modifying.

Example:

modifier

Incorrect: She read the book to a crowd that was filled with beautiful pictures.

The book was filled with beautiful pictures, not the crowd.

modifier

Corrected: She read the book that was filled with beautiful pictures to a crowd.

137

Copyright © Mometrix Media. You have been licensed one copy of this document for personal use only. Any other reproduction or redistribution is strictly prohibited. All rights reserved. This content is provided for test preparation purposes only and does not imply an endorsement by Mometrix of any particular political, scientific, or religious point of view.

Example:

Ambiguous: Derek saw a bus nearly hit a man $\overbrace{\text{on his way to work.}}^{\text{modifier}}$

Was Derek on his way to work or was the other man?

Derek: $\overbrace{\text{On his way to work,}}^{\text{modifier}}$ Derek saw a bus nearly hit a man.

The other man: Derek saw a bus nearly hit a man $\overbrace{\text{who was on his way to work.}}^{\text{modifier}}$

SPLIT INFINITIVES

A split infinitive occurs when a modifying word comes between the word *to* and the verb that pairs with *to*.

Example: To *clearly* explain vs. *To explain* clearly | To *softly* sing vs. *To sing* softly

Though considered improper by some, split infinitives may provide better clarity and simplicity in some cases than the alternatives. As such, avoiding them should not be considered a universal rule.

DOUBLE NEGATIVES

Standard English allows **two negatives** only when a **positive** meaning is intended. For example, *The team was not displeased with their performance*. Double negatives to emphasize negation are not used in standard English.

Negative modifiers (e.g., never, no, and not) should not be paired with other negative modifiers or negative words (e.g., none, nobody, nothing, or neither). The modifiers *hardly, barely*, and *scarcely* are also considered negatives in standard English, so they should not be used with other negatives.

CHAPTER QUIZ

1. Which of the following is an imperative statement?
a. John knows the way to the park.
b. There are five letters on the table for him.
c. Go to the post office for me.
d. The cookies need to cook for a few more minutes.

2. Which of the following is NOT a word used to combine nouns to make a compound subject?
a. Or
b. Nor
c. And
d. Also

3. Which of the following is always singular?
a. Each
b. Both
c. Several
d. Many

Copyright © Mometrix Media. You have been licensed one copy of this document for personal use only. Any other reproduction or redistribution is strictly prohibited. All rights reserved.
This content is provided for test preparation purposes only and does not imply an endorsement by Mometrix of any particular political, scientific, or religious point of view.

4. Identify the indirect object of the following sentence: "We taught the old dog a new trick."

  a.   We
  b.   Taught
  c.   The old dog
  d.   A new trick

5. Identify the infinitive of the following sentence: "The animals have enough food to eat for the night."

  a.   The animals
  b.   Have enough food
  c.   To eat
  d.   For the night

6. How many types of sentences are there?

  a.   Three
  b.   Four
  c.   Five
  d.   Six

7. Which of the following sentences correctly expresses the idea of parallelism?

  a.   He stopped at the office, grocery store, and the pharmacy before heading home.
  b.   While vacationing in Europe, she went biking, skiing, and climbed mountains.
  c.   The crowd jumped and cheered, roared and hollered, and whistled as the game concluded.
  d.   The flurry of blows left him staggered, discombobulated, and overwhelmed before falling.

8. Identify the phrase, "The music paused," in the following sample sentence:

"The music paused, she continued to dance through the crowd."

  a.   Subordinate phrase
  b.   Essential appositive
  c.   Nonessential appositive
  d.   Absolute phrase

CHAPTER QUIZ ANSWER KEY

1. C: In an imperative sentence, the verb's subject is understood without actually appearing or being named in the sentence itself. For example, in the imperative sentence, "Run to the store," the subject is the person being told to run.

2. D: A compound subject is formed when two or more nouns joined by *and*, *or*, or *nor* jointly act as the subject of the sentence.

3. A: Pronouns such as *each*, *either*, *everybody*, *anybody*, *somebody*, and *nobody* are always singular.

4. C: An indirect object is a word or group of words that show how an action had an influence on someone or something. If there is an indirect object in a sentence, then there will always be a direct

Copyright © Mometrix Media. You have been licensed one copy of this document for personal use only. Any other reproduction or redistribution is strictly prohibited. All rights reserved.
This content is provided for test preparation purposes only and does not imply an endorsement by Mometrix of any particular political, scientific, or religious point of view.

object in the sentence. When looking for the indirect object, find the verb and ask *to*, *for whom*, or *what*.

indirect
object   direct
object

We taught the old dog a new trick.

5. C: An infinitive is a type of verbal that can function as a noun, an adjective, or an adverb. An infinitive is made of the word *to* and the basic form of the verb. As with all other types of verbal phrases, an infinitive phrase includes the verbal itself and all of its complements or modifiers.

infinitive

The animals have enough food to eat for the night.

adjective

6. B: There are four types of sentences: declarative, imperative, interrogative, and exclamatory.

7. D: When multiple items or ideas are presented in a sentence in series, such as in a list, the items or ideas must be stated in grammatically equivalent ways. In other words, if one idea is stated in gerund form, the second cannot be stated in infinitive form. For example, writing "I enjoy *reading* and *to study*" would be incorrect. An infinitive and a gerund are not equivalent. Instead, the sentence should be, "I enjoy *reading* and *studying*." In lists of more than two, all items must be parallel.

Example:

Incorrect: He stopped at the office, grocery store, and the pharmacy before heading home.

(The first and third items in the list of places include the article *the*, so the second item needs it as well.)

Correct: He stopped at the office, *the* grocery store, and the pharmacy before heading home.

8. D: An absolute phrase is a phrase that consists of a noun followed by a participle. An absolute phrase provides context to what is being described in the sentence, but it does not modify or explain any particular word; it is essentially independent.

noun   participle

The music paused, she continued to dance through the crowd.

absolute
phrase

END PUNCTUATION
PERIODS

Use a period to end all sentences except direct questions and exclamations. Periods are also used for abbreviations.

Examples: 3 p.m. | 2 a.m. | Mr. Jones | Mrs. Stevens | Dr. Smith | Bill, Jr. | Pennsylvania Ave.

Note: An abbreviation is a shortened form of a word or phrase.

Copyright © Mometrix Media. You have been licensed one copy of this document for personal use only. Any other reproduction or redistribution is strictly prohibited. All rights reserved. This content is provided for test preparation purposes only and does not imply an endorsement by Mometrix of any particular political, scientific, or religious point of view.

QUESTION MARKS

Question marks should be used following a **direct question**. A polite request can be followed by a period instead of a question mark.

Direct Question: What is for lunch today? | How are you? | Why is that the answer?

Polite Requests: Can you please send me the item tomorrow. | Will you please walk with me on the track.

Review Video: **Question Marks**
Visit mometrix.com/academy and enter code: 118471

EXCLAMATION MARKS

Exclamation marks are used after a word group or sentence that shows much feeling or has special importance. Exclamation marks should not be overused. They are saved for proper **exclamatory interjections**.

Example: We're going to the finals! | You have a beautiful car! | "That's crazy!" she yelled.

Review Video: **Exclamation Points**
Visit mometrix.com/academy and enter code: 199367

COMMAS

The comma is a punctuation mark that can help you understand connections in a sentence. Not every sentence needs a comma. However, if a sentence needs a comma, you need to put it in the right place. A comma in the wrong place (or an absent comma) will make a sentence's meaning unclear. These are some of the rules for commas:

Use Case	Example
Before a **coordinating conjunction** joining independent clauses	Bob caught three fish, and I caught two fish.
After an **introductory phrase**	After the final out, we went to a restaurant to celebrate.
After an **adverbial clause**	Studying the stars, I was awed by the beauty of the sky.
Between **items in a series**	I will bring the turkey, the pie, and the coffee.
For **interjections**	Wow, you know how to play this game.
After *yes* and *no* responses	No, I cannot come tomorrow.
Separate **nonessential modifiers**	John Frank, who coaches the team, was promoted today.
Separate **nonessential appositives**	Thomas Edison, an American inventor, was born in Ohio.
Separate **nouns of direct address**	You, John, are my only hope in this moment.
Separate **interrogative tags**	This is the last time, correct?
Separate **contrasts**	You are my friend, not my enemy.
Writing **dates**	July 4, 1776, is an important date to remember.
Writing **addresses**	He is meeting me at 456 Delaware Avenue, Washington, D.C., tomorrow morning.
Writing **geographical names**	Paris, France, is my favorite city.
Writing **titles**	John Smith, PhD, will be visiting your class today.
Separate **expressions like *he said***	"You can start," she said, "with an apology."

Copyright © Mometrix Media. You have been licensed one copy of this document for personal use only. Any other reproduction or redistribution is strictly prohibited. All rights reserved.
This content is provided for test preparation purposes only and does not imply an endorsement by Mometrix of any particular political, scientific, or religious point of view.

Also, you can use a comma **between coordinate adjectives** not joined with *and*. However, not all adjectives are coordinate (i.e., equal or parallel).

Incorrect: The kind, brown dog followed me home.

Correct: The kind, loyal dog followed me home.

There are two simple ways to know if your adjectives are coordinate. One, you can join the adjectives with *and*: *The kind and loyal dog*. Two, you can change the order of the adjectives: *The loyal, kind dog*.

> **Review Video: When to Use a Comma**
> Visit mometrix.com/academy and enter code: 786797

SEMICOLONS

The semicolon is used to connect major sentence pieces of equal value. Some rules for semicolons include:

Use Case	Example
Between closely connected independent clauses **not connected with a coordinating conjunction**	You are right; we should go with your plan.
Between independent clauses **linked with a transitional word**	I think that we can agree on this; however, I am not sure about my friends.
Between items in a **series that has internal punctuation**	I have visited New York, New York; Augusta, Maine; and Baltimore, Maryland.

> **Review Video: How to Use Semicolons**
> Visit mometrix.com/academy and enter code: 370605

COLONS

The colon is used to call attention to the words that follow it. A colon must come after a **complete independent clause**. The rules for colons are as follows:

Use Case	Example
After an independent clause to **make a list**	I want to learn many languages: Spanish, German, and Italian.
For **explanations**	There is one thing that stands out on your resume: responsibility.
To give a **quote**	He started with an idea: "We are able to do more than we imagine."
After the **greeting in a formal letter**	To Whom It May Concern:
Show **hours and minutes**	It is 3:14 p.m.
Separate a **title and subtitle**	The essay is titled "America: A Short Introduction to a Modern Country."

> **Review Video: Colons**
> Visit mometrix.com/academy and enter code: 868673

Copyright © Mometrix Media. You have been licensed one copy of this document for personal use only. Any other reproduction or redistribution is strictly prohibited. All rights reserved. This content is provided for test preparation purposes only and does not imply an endorsement by Mometrix of any particular political, scientific, or religious point of view.

PARENTHESES

Parentheses are used for additional information. Also, they can be used to put labels for letters or numbers in a series. Parentheses should be not be used very often. If they are overused, parentheses can be a distraction instead of a help.

Examples:

> **Extra Information**: The rattlesnake (see Image 2) is a dangerous snake of North and South America.

> **Series**: Include in the email (1) your name, (2) your address, and (3) your question for the author.

> **Review Video: Parentheses**
> Visit mometrix.com/academy and enter code: 947743

QUOTATION MARKS

Use quotation marks to close off **direct quotations** of a person's spoken or written words. Do not use quotation marks around indirect quotations. An indirect quotation gives someone's message without using the person's exact words. Use **single quotation marks** to close off a quotation inside a quotation.

> **Direct Quote**: Nancy said, "I am waiting for Henry to arrive."

> **Indirect Quote**: Henry said that he is going to be late to the meeting.

> **Quote inside a Quote**: The teacher asked, "Has everyone read 'The Gift of the Magi'?"

Quotation marks should be used around the titles of **short works**: newspaper and magazine articles, poems, short stories, songs, television episodes, radio programs, and subdivisions of books or websites.

Examples:

> "Rip Van Winkle" (short story by Washington Irving)

> "O Captain! My Captain!" (poem by Walt Whitman)

Although it is not standard usage, quotation marks are sometimes used to highlight **irony** or the use of words to mean something other than their dictionary definition. This type of usage should be employed sparingly, if at all.

Examples:

The boss warned Frank that he was walking on "thin ice."	Frank is not walking on real ice. Instead, he is being warned to avoid mistakes.
The teacher thanked the young man for his "honesty."	The quotation marks around *honesty* show that the teacher does not believe the young man's explanation.

> **Review Video: Quotation Marks**
> Visit mometrix.com/academy and enter code: 884918

Copyright © Mometrix Media. You have been licensed one copy of this document for personal use only. Any other reproduction or redistribution is strictly prohibited. All rights reserved. This content is provided for test preparation purposes only and does not imply an endorsement by Mometrix of any particular political, scientific, or religious point of view.

Periods and commas are put **inside** quotation marks. Colons and semicolons are put **outside** the quotation marks. Question marks and exclamation points are placed inside quotation marks when they are part of a quote. When the question or exclamation mark goes with the whole sentence, the mark is left outside of the quotation marks.

Examples:

Period and comma	We read "The Gift of the Magi," "The Skylight Room," and "The Cactus."
Semicolon	They watched "The Nutcracker"; then, they went home.
Exclamation mark that is a part of a quote	The crowd cheered, "Victory!"
Question mark that goes with the whole sentence	Is your favorite short story "The Tell-Tale Heart"?

APOSTROPHES

An apostrophe is used to show **possession** or the **deletion of letters in contractions**. An apostrophe is not needed with the possessive pronouns *his, hers, its, ours, theirs, whose*, and *yours*.

Singular Nouns: David's car | a book's theme | my brother's board game

Plural Nouns that end with *-s*: the scissors' handle | boys' basketball

Plural Nouns that end without *-s*: Men's department | the people's adventure

> **Review Video: When to Use an Apostrophe**
> Visit mometrix.com/academy and enter code: 213068
>
> **Review Video: Punctuation Errors in Possessive Pronouns**
> Visit mometrix.com/academy and enter code: 221438

HYPHENS

Hyphens are used to **separate compound words**. Use hyphens in the following cases:

Use Case	Example
Compound numbers from 21 to 99 when written out in words	This team needs twenty-five points to win the game.
Written-out fractions that are used as adjectives	The recipe says that we need a three-fourths cup of butter.
Compound adjectives that come before a noun	The well-fed dog took a nap.
Unusual compound words that would be hard to read or easily confused with other words	This is the best anti-itch cream on the market.

Note: This is not a complete set of the rules for hyphens. A dictionary is the best tool for knowing if a compound word needs a hyphen.

> **Review Video: Hyphens**
> Visit mometrix.com/academy and enter code: 981632

Copyright © Mometrix Media. You have been licensed one copy of this document for personal use only. Any other reproduction or redistribution is strictly prohibited. All rights reserved. This content is provided for test preparation purposes only and does not imply an endorsement by Mometrix of any particular political, scientific, or religious point of view.

DASHES

Dashes are used to show a **break** or a **change in thought** in a sentence or to act as parentheses in a sentence. When typing, use two hyphens to make a dash. Do not put a space before or after the dash. The following are the functions of dashes:

Use Case	Example
Set off parenthetical statements or an **appositive with internal punctuation**	The three trees—oak, pine, and magnolia—are coming on a truck tomorrow.
Show a **break or change in tone or thought**	The first question—how silly of me—does not have a correct answer.

ELLIPSIS MARKS

The ellipsis mark has **three** periods (…) to show when **words have been removed** from a quotation. If a **full sentence or more** is removed from a quoted passage, you need to use **four** periods to show the removed text and the end punctuation mark. The ellipsis mark should not be used at the beginning of a quotation. The ellipsis mark should also not be used at the end of a quotation unless some words have been deleted from the end of the final sentence.

Example:

"Then he picked up the groceries…paid for them…later he went home."

BRACKETS

There are two main reasons to use brackets:

Use Case	Example
Placing **parentheses inside of parentheses**	The hero of this story, Paul Revere (a silversmith and industrialist [see Ch. 4]), rode through towns of Massachusetts to warn of advancing British troops.
Adding **clarification or detail to a quotation** that is not part of the quotation	The father explained, "My children are planning to attend my alma mater [State University]."

> **Review Video: Brackets**
> Visit mometrix.com/academy and enter code: 727546

CHAPTER QUIZ

1. Which of the following correctly implements the use of parentheses?
   a. The rattlesnake (see Image 2) is a dangerous snake of North and South America.
   b. The rattlesnake see (Image 2) is a dangerous snake of North and South America.
   c. The rattlesnake see Image (2) is a dangerous snake of North and South America.
   d. The rattlesnake (see Image) (2) is a dangerous snake of North and South America.

2. Which of the following correctly describes the placement of punctuation in reference to quotations?
   a. Periods and commas are put outside quotation marks; colons and semicolons go inside.
   b. Periods and colons are put outside quotation marks; commas and semicolons go inside.
   c. Periods and commas are put inside quotation marks; colons and semicolons go outside.
   d. Periods and colons are put inside quotation marks; commas and semicolons go outside.

Copyright © Mometrix Media. You have been licensed one copy of this document for personal use only. Any other reproduction or redistribution is strictly prohibited. All rights reserved. This content is provided for test preparation purposes only and does not imply an endorsement by Mometrix of any particular political, scientific, or religious point of view.

3. Which of the following correctly implements the use of commas?

    a. He is meeting me at, 456 Delaware Avenue, Washington, D.C., tomorrow morning.
    b. He is meeting me at 456 Delaware Avenue, Washington, D.C., tomorrow morning.
    c. He is meeting me at 456 Delaware Avenue Washington, D.C. tomorrow morning.
    d. He is meeting me at 456 Delaware Avenue, Washington, D.C. tomorrow morning.

CHAPTER QUIZ ANSWER KEY

1. A: Parentheses are used for additional information. Also, they can be used to put labels for letters or numbers in a series. Parentheses should be not be used very often because their overuse can become a distraction.

2. C: Periods and commas are put inside quotation marks, while colons and semicolons are put outside quotation marks. Question marks and exclamation points are placed inside quotation marks when they are part of a quote. When the question mark or exclamation point is not part of a quoted section but instead part of an entire sentence, then it is left outside of the quotation marks.

3. B: These are some of the rules for commas:

Use Case	Example
Before a **coordinating conjunction** joining independent clauses	Bob caught three fish, and I caught two fish.
After an **introductory phrase**	After the final out, we went to a restaurant to celebrate.
After an **adverbial clause**	Studying the stars, I was awed by the beauty of the sky.
Between **items in a series**	I will bring the turkey, the pie, and the coffee.
For **interjections**	Wow, you know how to play this game.
After *yes* and *no* responses	No, I cannot come tomorrow.
Separate **nonessential modifiers**	John Frank, who coaches the team, was promoted today.
Separate **nonessential appositives**	Thomas Edison, an American inventor, was born in Ohio.
Separate **nouns of direct address**	You, John, are my only hope in this moment.
Separate **interrogative tags**	This is the last time, correct?
Separate **contrasts**	You are my friend, not my enemy.
Writing **dates**	July 4, 1776, is an important date to remember.
Writing **addresses**	He is meeting me at 456 Delaware Avenue, Washington, D.C., tomorrow morning.
Writing **geographical names**	Paris, France, is my favorite city.
Writing **titles**	John Smith, PhD, will be visiting your class today.
Separate **expressions like "he said"**	"You can start," she said, "with an apology."

Copyright © Mometrix Media. You have been licensed one copy of this document for personal use only. Any other reproduction or redistribution is strictly prohibited. All rights reserved. This content is provided for test preparation purposes only and does not imply an endorsement by Mometrix of any particular political, scientific, or religious point of view.

WORD CONFUSION
WHICH, THAT, AND WHO

The words *which*, *that*, and *who* can act as **relative pronouns** to help clarify or describe a noun.

Which is used for things only.

> Example: Andrew's car, *which is old and rusty*, broke down last week.

That is used for people or things. *That* is usually informal when used to describe people.

> Example: Is this the only book *that Louis L'Amour wrote?*

> Example: Is Louis L'Amour the author *that wrote Western novels?*

Who is used for people or for animals that have an identity or personality.

> Example: Mozart was the composer *who wrote those operas.*

> Example: John's dog, *who is called Max,* is large and fierce.

HOMOPHONES

Homophones are words that sound alike (or similar) but have different **spellings** and **definitions**. A homophone is a type of **homonym**, which is a pair or group of words that are pronounced or spelled the same, but do not mean the same thing.

TO, TOO, AND TWO

To can be an adverb or a preposition for showing direction, purpose, and relationship. See your dictionary for the many other ways to use *to* in a sentence.

> Examples: I went to the store. | I want to go with you.

Too is an adverb that means *also, as well, very,* or *in excess.*

> Examples: I can walk a mile too. | You have eaten too much.

Two is a number.

> Example: You have two minutes left.

THERE, THEIR, AND THEY'RE

There can be an adjective, adverb, or pronoun. Often, *there* is used to show a place or to start a sentence.

> Examples: I went there yesterday. | There is something in his pocket.

Their is a pronoun that is used to show ownership.

> Examples: He is their father. | This is their fourth apology this week.

They're is a contraction of *they are.*

> Example: Did you know that they're in town?

Copyright © Mometrix Media. You have been licensed one copy of this document for personal use only. Any other reproduction or redistribution is strictly prohibited. All rights reserved.
This content is provided for test preparation purposes only and does not imply an endorsement by Mometrix of any particular political, scientific, or religious point of view.

KNEW AND NEW

Knew is the past tense of *know*.

>Example: I knew the answer.

New is an adjective that means something is current, has not been used, or is modern.

>Example: This is my new phone.

THEN AND THAN

Then is an adverb that indicates sequence or order:

>Example: I'm going to run to the library and then come home.

Than is special-purpose word used only for comparisons:

>Example: Susie likes chips more than candy.

ITS AND IT'S

Its is a pronoun that shows ownership.

>Example: The guitar is in its case.

It's is a contraction of *it is*.

>Example: It's an honor and a privilege to meet you.

Note: The *h* in honor is silent, so *honor* starts with the vowel sound *o*, which must have the article *an*.

YOUR AND YOU'RE

Your is a pronoun that shows ownership.

>Example: This is your moment to shine.

You're is a contraction of *you are*.

>Example: Yes, you're correct.

SAW AND SEEN

Saw is the past-tense form of *see*.

>Example: I saw a turtle on my walk this morning.

Seen is the past participle of *see*.

>Example: I have seen this movie before.

AFFECT AND EFFECT

There are two main reasons that *affect* and *effect* are so often confused: 1) both words can be used as either a noun or a verb, and 2) unlike most homophones, their usage and meanings are closely related to each other. Here is a quick rundown of the four usage options:

Copyright © Mometrix Media. You have been licensed one copy of this document for personal use only. Any other reproduction or redistribution is strictly prohibited. All rights reserved.
This content is provided for test preparation purposes only and does not imply an endorsement by Mometrix of any particular political, scientific, or religious point of view.

Affect (n): feeling, emotion, or mood that is displayed

Example: The patient had a flat *affect*. (i.e., his face showed little or no emotion)

Affect (v): to alter, to change, to influence

Example: The sunshine *affects* the plant's growth.

Effect (n): a result, a consequence

Example: What *effect* will this weather have on our schedule?

Effect (v): to bring about, to cause to be

Example: These new rules will *effect* order in the office.

The noun form of *affect* is rarely used outside of technical medical descriptions, so if a noun form is needed on the test, you can safely select *effect*. The verb form of *effect* is not as rare as the noun form of *affect*, but it's still not all that likely to show up on your test. If you need a verb and you can't decide which to use based on the definitions, choosing *affect* is your best bet.

HOMOGRAPHS

Homographs are words that share the same spelling, but have different meanings and sometimes different pronunciations. To figure out which meaning is being used, you should be looking for context clues. The context clues give hints to the meaning of the word. For example, the word *spot* has many meanings. It can mean "a place" or "a stain or blot." In the sentence "After my lunch, I saw a spot on my shirt," the word *spot* means "a stain or blot." The context clues of "After my lunch" and "on my shirt" guide you to this decision. A homograph is another type of homonym.

BANK

(noun): an establishment where money is held for savings or lending

(verb): to collect or pile up

CONTENT

(noun): the topics that will be addressed within a book

(adjective): pleased or satisfied

(verb): to make someone pleased or satisfied

FINE

(noun): an amount of money that acts a penalty for an offense

(adjective): very small or thin

(adverb): in an acceptable way

(verb): to make someone pay money as a punishment

INCENSE

(noun): a material that is burned in religious settings and makes a pleasant aroma

(verb): to frustrate or anger

Copyright © Mometrix Media. You have been licensed one copy of this document for personal use only. Any other reproduction or redistribution is strictly prohibited. All rights reserved. This content is provided for test preparation purposes only and does not imply an endorsement by Mometrix of any particular political, scientific, or religious point of view.

LEAD

(noun): the first or highest position

(noun): a heavy metallic element

(verb): to direct a person or group of followers

(adjective): containing lead

OBJECT

(noun): a lifeless item that can be held and observed

(verb): to disagree

PRODUCE

(noun): fruits and vegetables

(verb): to make or create something

REFUSE

(noun): garbage or debris that has been thrown away

(verb): to not allow

SUBJECT

(noun): an area of study

(verb): to force or subdue

TEAR

(noun): a fluid secreted by the eyes

(verb): to separate or pull apart

CHAPTER QUIZ

1. Which of the following correctly implements the word "affect"?
   a. These new rules will affect order in the office.
   b. What affect will this weather have on our schedule?
   c. The patient had a flat affect during her examination.
   d. His narcissism had a detrimental affect on everyone around him.

2. "Affect" and "effect" would be considered which of the following?
   a. Homographs
   b. Synonyms
   c. Antonyms
   d. Homophones

CHAPTER QUIZ ANSWER KEY

1. C: There are two main reasons that *affect* and *effect* are so often confused: 1) both words can be used as either a noun or a verb; and 2) unlike most homophones, their usage and meanings are closely related to each other. Here is a quick rundown of the four usage options:

Copyright © Mometrix Media. You have been licensed one copy of this document for personal use only. Any other reproduction or redistribution is strictly prohibited. All rights reserved.
This content is provided for test preparation purposes only and does not imply an endorsement by Mometrix of any particular political, scientific, or religious point of view.

Affect (n): feeling, emotion, or mood that is displayed

> Example: The patient had a flat *affect* (i.e., his face showed little or no emotion).

Affect (v): to alter, to change, to influence

> Example: The sunshine *affects* the plant's growth.

Effect (n): a result, a consequence

> Example: What *effect* will this weather have on our schedule?

Effect (v): to bring about, to cause to be

> Example: These new rules will *effect* order in the office.

The noun form of *affect* is rarely used outside of technical medical descriptions, so if a noun form is needed on the test, *effect* is a safe selection. The verb form of *effect* is not as rare as the noun form of *affect*, but it's still not likely to show up on a test. If a verb is needed and the definitions aren't enough of an indicator for which one to use, choosing *affect* is the safest option.

2. D: Homophones are words that sound alike (or similar) but have different spellings and definitions. A homophone is a type of homonym, which is a pair or group of words that are pronounced or spelled the same, but do not mean the same thing.

Synonyms and Antonyms

When you understand how words relate to each other, you will discover more in a passage. This is explained by understanding **synonyms** (e.g., words that mean the same thing) and **antonyms** (e.g., words that mean the opposite of one another). As an example, *dry* and *arid* are synonyms, and *dry* and *wet* are antonyms.

There are many pairs of words in English that can be considered synonyms, despite having slightly different definitions. For instance, the words *friendly* and *collegial* can both be used to describe a warm interpersonal relationship, and one would be correct to call them synonyms. However, *collegial* (kin to *colleague*) is often used in reference to professional or academic relationships, and *friendly* has no such connotation.

If the difference between the two words is too great, then they should not be called synonyms. *Hot* and *warm* are not synonyms because their meanings are too distinct. A good way to determine whether two words are synonyms is to substitute one word for the other word and verify that the meaning of the sentence has not changed. Substituting *warm* for *hot* in a sentence would convey a different meaning. Although warm and hot may seem close in meaning, warm generally means that the temperature is moderate, and hot generally means that the temperature is excessively high.

Antonyms are words with opposite meanings. *Light* and *dark*, *up* and *down*, *right* and *left*, *good* and *bad*: these are all sets of antonyms. Be careful to distinguish between antonyms and pairs of words that are simply different. *Black* and *gray*, for instance, are not antonyms because gray is not the opposite of black. *Black* and *white*, on the other hand, are antonyms.

Not every word has an antonym. For instance, many nouns do not. What would be the antonym of *chair*? During your exam, the questions related to antonyms are more likely to concern adjectives. You will recall that adjectives are words that describe a noun. Some common adjectives include

151

Copyright © Mometrix Media. You have been licensed one copy of this document for personal use only. Any other reproduction or redistribution is strictly prohibited. All rights reserved.
This content is provided for test preparation purposes only and does not imply an endorsement by Mometrix of any particular political, scientific, or religious point of view.

purple, *fast*, *skinny*, and *sweet*. From those four adjectives, *purple* is the item that lacks a group of obvious antonyms.

> **Review Video: What Are Synonyms and Antonyms?**
> Visit mometrix.com/academy and enter code: 105612

AFFIXES

Affixes in the English language are morphemes that are added to words to create related but different words. Derivational affixes form new words based on and related to the original words. For example, the affix *–ness* added to the end of the adjective *happy* forms the noun *happiness*. Inflectional affixes form different grammatical versions of words. For example, the plural affix *–s* changes the singular noun *book* to the plural noun *books*, and the past tense affix *–ed* changes the present tense verb *look* to the past tense *looked.* Prefixes are affixes placed in front of words. For example, *heat* means to make hot; *preheat* means to heat in advance. Suffixes are affixes placed at the ends of words. The *happiness* example above contains the suffix *–ness.* Circumfixes add parts both before and after words, such as how *light* becomes *enlighten* with the prefix *en-* and the suffix *–en.* Interfixes create compound words via central affixes: *speed* and *meter* become *speedometer* via the interfix *–o–*.

> **Review Video: Affixes**
> Visit mometrix.com/academy and enter code: 782422

WORD ROOTS, PREFIXES, AND SUFFIXES TO HELP DETERMINE MEANINGS OF WORDS

Many English words were formed from combining multiple sources. For example, the Latin *habēre* means "to have," and the prefixes *in-* and *im-* mean a lack or prevention of something, as in *insufficient* and *imperfect*. Latin combined *in-* with *habēre* to form *inhibēre,* whose past participle was *inhibitus.* This is the origin of the English word *inhibit,* meaning to prevent from having. Hence by knowing the meanings of both the prefix and the root, one can decipher the word meaning. In Greek, the root *enkephalo-* refers to the brain. Many medical terms are based on this root, such as encephalitis and hydrocephalus. Understanding the prefix and suffix meanings (*-itis* means inflammation; *hydro-* means water) allows a person to deduce that encephalitis refers to brain inflammation and hydrocephalus refers to water (or other fluid) in the brain.

> **Review Video: Determining Word Meanings**
> Visit mometrix.com/academy and enter code: 894894
>
> **Review Video: Root Words in English**
> Visit mometrix.com/academy and enter code: 896380

PREFIXES

While knowing prefix meanings helps ESL and beginning readers learn new words, other readers take for granted the meanings of known words. However, prefix knowledge will also benefit them for determining meanings or definitions of unfamiliar words. For example, native English speakers and readers familiar with recipes know what *preheat* means. Knowing that *pre-* means in advance can also inform them that *presume* means to assume in advance, that *prejudice* means advance judgment, and that this understanding can be applied to many other words beginning with *pre-*. Knowing that the prefix *dis-* indicates opposition informs the meanings of words like *disbar,*

Copyright © Mometrix Media. You have been licensed one copy of this document for personal use only. Any other reproduction or redistribution is strictly prohibited. All rights reserved. This content is provided for test preparation purposes only and does not imply an endorsement by Mometrix of any particular political, scientific, or religious point of view.

disagree, disestablish, and many more. Knowing *dys-* means bad, impaired, abnormal, or difficult informs *dyslogistic, dysfunctional, dysphagia,* and *dysplasia.*

SUFFIXES

In English, certain suffixes generally indicate both that a word is a noun, and that the noun represents a state of being or quality. For example, *-ness* is commonly used to change an adjective into its noun form, as with *happy* and *happiness, nice* and *niceness,* and so on. The suffix *–tion* is commonly used to transform a verb into its noun form, as with *converse* and *conversation or move* and *motion.* Thus, if readers are unfamiliar with the second form of a word, knowing the meaning of the transforming suffix can help them determine meaning.

PREFIXES FOR NUMBERS

Prefix	Definition	Examples
bi-	two	bisect, biennial
mono-	one, single	monogamy, monologue
poly-	many	polymorphous, polygamous
semi-	half, partly	semicircle, semicolon
uni-	one	uniform, unity

Copyright © Mometrix Media. You have been licensed one copy of this document for personal use only. Any other reproduction or redistribution is strictly prohibited. All rights reserved.
This content is provided for test preparation purposes only and does not imply an endorsement by Mometrix of any particular political, scientific, or religious point of view.

Prefixes for Time, Direction, and Space

Prefix	Definition	Examples
a-	in, on, of, up, to	abed, afoot
ab-	from, away, off	abdicate, abjure
ad-	to, toward	advance, adventure
ante-	before, previous	antecedent, antedate
anti-	against, opposing	antipathy, antidote
cata-	down, away, thoroughly	catastrophe, cataclysm
circum-	around	circumspect, circumference
com-	with, together, very	commotion, complicate
contra-	against, opposing	contradict, contravene
de-	from	depart
dia-	through, across, apart	diameter, diagnose
dis-	away, off, down, not	dissent, disappear
epi-	upon	epilogue
ex-	out	extract, excerpt
hypo-	under, beneath	hypodermic, hypothesis
inter-	among, between	intercede, interrupt
intra-	within	intramural, intrastate
ob-	against, opposing	objection
per-	through	perceive, permit
peri-	around	periscope, perimeter
post-	after, following	postpone, postscript
pre-	before, previous	prevent, preclude
pro-	forward, in place of	propel, pronoun
retro-	back, backward	retrospect, retrograde
sub-	under, beneath	subjugate, substitute
super-	above, extra	supersede, supernumerary
trans-	across, beyond, over	transact, transport
ultra-	beyond, excessively	ultramodern, ultrasonic

Negative Prefixes

Prefix	Definition	Examples
a-	without, lacking	atheist, agnostic
in-	not, opposing	incapable, ineligible
non-	not	nonentity, nonsense
un-	not, reverse of	unhappy, unlock

154

Copyright © Mometrix Media. You have been licensed one copy of this document for personal use only. Any other reproduction or redistribution is strictly prohibited. All rights reserved. This content is provided for test preparation purposes only and does not imply an endorsement by Mometrix of any particular political, scientific, or religious point of view.

EXTRA PREFIXES

Prefix	Definition	Examples
for-	away, off, from	forget, forswear
fore-	previous	foretell, forefathers
homo-	same, equal	homogenized, homonym
hyper-	excessive, over	hypercritical, hypertension
in-	in, into	intrude, invade
mal-	bad, poorly, not	malfunction, malpractice
mis-	bad, poorly, not	misspell, misfire
neo-	new	Neolithic, neoconservative
omni-	all, everywhere	omniscient, omnivore
ortho-	right, straight	orthogonal, orthodox
over-	above	overbearing, oversight
pan-	all, entire	panorama, pandemonium
para-	beside, beyond	parallel, paradox
re-	backward, again	revoke, recur
sym-	with, together	sympathy, symphony

Below is a list of common suffixes and their meanings:

ADJECTIVE SUFFIXES

Suffix	Definition	Examples
-able (-ible)	capable of being	toler*able*, ed*ible*
-esque	in the style of, like	picturesque, grotesque
-ful	filled with, marked by	thankful, zestful
-ific	make, cause	terrific, beatific
-ish	suggesting, like	churlish, childish
-less	lacking, without	hopeless, countless
-ous	marked by, given to	religious, riotous

Copyright © Mometrix Media. You have been licensed one copy of this document for personal use only. Any other reproduction or redistribution is strictly prohibited. All rights reserved.
This content is provided for test preparation purposes only and does not imply an endorsement by Mometrix of any particular political, scientific, or religious point of view.

NOUN SUFFIXES

Suffix	Definition	Examples
-acy	state, condition	accuracy, privacy
-ance	act, condition, fact	acceptance, vigilance
-ard	one that does excessively	drunkard, sluggard
-ation	action, state, result	occupation, starvation
-dom	state, rank, condition	serfdom, wisdom
-er (-or)	office, action	teacher, elevator, honor
-ess	feminine	waitress, duchess
-hood	state, condition	manhood, statehood
-ion	action, result, state	union, fusion
-ism	act, manner, doctrine	barbarism, socialism
-ist	worker, follower	monopolist, socialist
-ity (-ty)	state, quality, condition	acidity, civility, twenty
-ment	result, action	Refreshment
-ness	quality, state	greatness, tallness
-ship	position	internship, statesmanship
-sion (-tion)	state, result	revision, expedition
-th	act, state, quality	warmth, width
-tude	quality, state, result	magnitude, fortitude

VERB SUFFIXES

Suffix	Definition	Examples
-ate	having, showing	separate, desolate
-en	cause to be, become	deepen, strengthen
-fy	make, cause to have	glorify, fortify
-ize	cause to be, treat with	sterilize, mechanize

DENOTATIVE VS. CONNOTATIVE MEANING

The **denotative** meaning of a word is the literal meaning. The **connotative** meaning goes beyond the denotative meaning to include the emotional reaction that a word may invoke. The connotative meaning often takes the denotative meaning a step further due to associations the reader makes with the denotative meaning. Readers can differentiate between the denotative and connotative meanings by first recognizing how authors use each meaning. Most non-fiction, for example, is fact-based and authors do not use flowery, figurative language. The reader can assume that the writer is using the denotative meaning of words. In fiction, the author may use the connotative meaning. Readers can determine whether the author is using the denotative or connotative meaning of a word by implementing context clues.

> **Review Video: Connotation and Denotation**
> Visit mometrix.com/academy and enter code: 310092

NUANCES OF WORD MEANING RELATIVE TO CONNOTATION, DENOTATION, DICTION, AND USAGE

A word's denotation is simply its objective dictionary definition. However, its connotation refers to the subjective associations, often emotional, that specific words evoke in listeners and readers. Two or more words can have the same dictionary meaning, but very different connotations. Writers use diction (word choice) to convey various nuances of thought and emotion by selecting synonyms for other words that best communicate the associations they want to trigger for readers. For example,

156

Copyright © Mometrix Media. You have been licensed one copy of this document for personal use only. Any other reproduction or redistribution is strictly prohibited. All rights reserved. This content is provided for test preparation purposes only and does not imply an endorsement by Mometrix of any particular political, scientific, or religious point of view.

a car engine is naturally greasy; in this sense, "greasy" is a neutral term. But when a person's smile, appearance, or clothing is described as "greasy," it has a negative connotation. Some words have even gained additional or different meanings over time. For example, *awful* used to be used to describe things that evoked a sense of awe. When *awful* is separated into its root word, awe, and suffix, -ful, it can be understood to mean "full of awe." However, the word is now commonly used to describe things that evoke repulsion, terror, or another intense, negative reaction.

> **Review Video: Word Usage in Sentences**
> Visit mometrix.com/academy and enter code: 197863

CONTEXT CLUES

Readers of all levels will encounter words that they have either never seen or have encountered only on a limited basis. The best way to define a word in **context** is to look for nearby words that can assist in revealing the meaning of the word. For instance, unfamiliar nouns are often accompanied by examples that provide a definition. Consider the following sentence: *Dave arrived at the party in hilarious garb: a leopard-print shirt, buckskin trousers, and bright green sneakers.* If a reader was unfamiliar with the meaning of garb, he or she could read the examples (i.e., a leopard-print shirt, buckskin trousers, and high heels) and quickly determine that the word means *clothing*. Examples will not always be this obvious. Consider this sentence: *Parsley, lemon, and flowers were just a few of the items he used as garnishes.* Here, the word *garnishes* is exemplified by parsley, lemon, and flowers. Readers who have eaten in a variety of restaurants will probably be able to identify a garnish as something used to decorate a plate.

> **Review Video: Context Clues**
> Visit mometrix.com/academy and enter code: 613660

USING CONTRAST IN CONTEXT CLUES

In addition to looking at the context of a passage, readers can use contrast to define an unfamiliar word in context. In many sentences, the author will not describe the unfamiliar word directly; instead, he or she will describe the opposite of the unfamiliar word. Thus, you are provided with some information that will bring you closer to defining the word. Consider the following example: *Despite his intelligence, Hector's low brow and bad posture made him look obtuse.* The author writes that Hector's appearance does not convey intelligence. Therefore, *obtuse* must mean unintelligent. Here is another example: *Despite the horrible weather, we were beatific about our trip to Alaska.* The word *despite* indicates that the speaker's feelings were at odds with the weather. Since the weather is described as *horrible*, then *beatific* must mean something positive.

SUBSTITUTION TO FIND MEANING

In some cases, there will be very few contextual clues to help a reader define the meaning of an unfamiliar word. When this happens, one strategy that readers may employ is **substitution**. A good reader will brainstorm some possible synonyms for the given word, and he or she will substitute these words into the sentence. If the sentence and the surrounding passage continue to make sense, then the substitution has revealed at least some information about the unfamiliar word. Consider the sentence: *Frank's admonition rang in her ears as she climbed the mountain.* A reader unfamiliar with *admonition* might come up with some substitutions like *vow*, *promise*, *advice*, *complaint*, or *compliment*. All of these words make general sense of the sentence, though their meanings are diverse. However, this process has suggested that an admonition is some sort of message. The substitution strategy is rarely able to pinpoint a precise definition, but this process can be effective as a last resort.

Copyright © Mometrix Media. You have been licensed one copy of this document for personal use only. Any other reproduction or redistribution is strictly prohibited. All rights reserved.
This content is provided for test preparation purposes only and does not imply an endorsement by Mometrix of any particular political, scientific, or religious point of view.

Occasionally, you will be able to define an unfamiliar word by looking at the descriptive words in the context. Consider the following sentence: *Fred dragged the recalcitrant boy kicking and screaming up the stairs.* The words *dragged*, *kicking*, and *screaming* all suggest that the boy does not want to go up the stairs. The reader may assume that *recalcitrant* means something like unwilling or protesting. In this example, an unfamiliar adjective was identified.

Additionally, using description to define an unfamiliar noun is a common practice compared to unfamiliar adjectives, as in this sentence: *Don's wrinkled frown and constantly shaking fist identified him as a curmudgeon of the first order.* Don is described as having a *wrinkled frown and constantly shaking fist*, suggesting that a *curmudgeon* must be a grumpy person. Contrasts do not always provide detailed information about the unfamiliar word, but they at least give the reader some clues.

Words with Multiple Meanings

When a word has more than one meaning, readers can have difficulty determining how the word is being used in a given sentence. For instance, the verb *cleave*, can mean either *join* or *separate*. When readers come upon this word, they will have to select the definition that makes the most sense. Consider the following sentence: *Hermione's knife cleaved the bread cleanly.* Since a knife cannot join bread together, the word must indicate separation. A slightly more difficult example would be the sentence: *The birds cleaved to one another as they flew from the oak tree.* Immediately, the presence of the words *to one another* should suggest that in this sentence *cleave* is being used to mean *join*. Discovering the intent of a word with multiple meanings requires the same tricks as defining an unknown word: look for contextual clues and evaluate the substituted words.

Context Clues to Help Determine Meanings of Words

If readers simply bypass unknown words, they can reach unclear conclusions about what they read. However, looking for the definition of every unfamiliar word in the dictionary can slow their reading progress. Moreover, the dictionary may list multiple definitions for a word, so readers must search the word's context for meaning. Hence context is important to new vocabulary regardless of reader methods. Four types of context clues are examples, definitions, descriptive words, and opposites. Authors may use a certain word, and then follow it with several different examples of what it describes. Sometimes authors actually supply a definition of a word they use, which is especially true in informational and technical texts. Authors may use descriptive words that elaborate upon a vocabulary word they just used. Authors may also use opposites with negation that help define meaning.

Examples and Definitions

An author may use a word and then give examples that illustrate its meaning. Consider this text: "Teachers who do not know how to use sign language can help students who are deaf or hard of hearing understand certain instructions by using gestures instead, like pointing their fingers to indicate which direction to look or go; holding up a hand, palm outward, to indicate stopping; holding the hands flat, palms up, curling a finger toward oneself in a beckoning motion to indicate 'come here'; or curling all fingers toward oneself repeatedly to indicate 'come on', 'more', or 'continue.'" The author of this text has used the word "gestures" and then followed it with examples, so a reader unfamiliar with the word could deduce from the examples that "gestures" means "hand motions." Readers can find examples by looking for signal words "for example," "for instance," "like," "such as," and "e.g."

While readers sometimes have to look for definitions of unfamiliar words in a dictionary or do some work to determine a word's meaning from its surrounding context, at other times an author

Copyright © Mometrix Media. You have been licensed one copy of this document for personal use only. Any other reproduction or redistribution is strictly prohibited. All rights reserved. This content is provided for test preparation purposes only and does not imply an endorsement by Mometrix of any particular political, scientific, or religious point of view.

may make it easier for readers by defining certain words. For example, an author may write, "The company did not have sufficient capital, that is, available money, to continue operations." The author defined "capital" as "available money," and heralded the definition with the phrase "that is." Another way that authors supply word definitions is with appositives. Rather than being introduced by a signal phrase like "that is," "namely," or "meaning," an appositive comes after the vocabulary word it defines and is enclosed within two commas. For example, an author may write, "The Indians introduced the Pilgrims to pemmican, cakes they made of lean meat dried and mixed with fat, which proved greatly beneficial to keep settlers from starving while trapping." In this example, the appositive phrase following "pemmican" and preceding "which" defines the word "pemmican."

DESCRIPTIONS

When readers encounter a word they do not recognize in a text, the author may expand on that word to illustrate it better. While the author may do this to make the prose more picturesque and vivid, the reader can also take advantage of this description to provide context clues to the meaning of the unfamiliar word. For example, an author may write, "The man sitting next to me on the airplane was obese. His shirt stretched across his vast expanse of flesh, strained almost to bursting." The descriptive second sentence elaborates on and helps to define the previous sentence's word "obese" to mean extremely fat. A reader unfamiliar with the word "repugnant" can decipher its meaning through an author's accompanying description: "The way the child grimaced and shuddered as he swallowed the medicine showed that its taste was particularly repugnant."

OPPOSITES

Text authors sometimes introduce a contrasting or opposing idea before or after a concept they present. They may do this to emphasize or heighten the idea they present by contrasting it with something that is the reverse. However, readers can also use these context clues to understand familiar words. For example, an author may write, "Our conversation was not cheery. We sat and talked very solemnly about his experience and a number of similar events." The reader who is not familiar with the word "solemnly" can deduce by the author's preceding use of "not cheery" that "solemn" means the opposite of cheery or happy, so it must mean serious or sad. Or if someone writes, "Don't condemn his entire project because you couldn't find anything good to say about it," readers unfamiliar with "condemn" can understand from the sentence structure that it means the opposite of saying anything good, so it must mean reject, dismiss, or disapprove. "Entire" adds another context clue, meaning total or complete rejection.

SYNTAX TO DETERMINE PART OF SPEECH AND MEANINGS OF WORDS

Syntax refers to sentence structure and word order. Suppose that a reader encounters an unfamiliar word when reading a text. To illustrate, consider an invented word like "splunch." If this word is used in a sentence like "Please splunch that ball to me," the reader can assume from syntactic context that "splunch" is a verb. We would not use a noun, adjective, adverb, or preposition with the object "that ball," and the prepositional phrase "to me" further indicates "splunch" represents an action. However, in the sentence, "Please hand that splunch to me," the reader can assume that "splunch" is a noun. Demonstrative adjectives like "that" modify nouns. Also, we hand someone some*thing*—a thing being a noun; we do not hand someone a verb, adjective, or adverb. Some sentences contain further clues. For example, from the sentence, "The princess wore the glittering splunch on her head," the reader can deduce that it is a crown, tiara, or something similar from the syntactic context, without knowing the word.

SYNTAX TO INDICATE DIFFERENT MEANINGS OF SIMILAR SENTENCES

The syntax, or structure, of a sentence affords grammatical cues that aid readers in comprehending the meanings of words, phrases, and sentences in the texts that they read. Seemingly minor

159

Copyright © Mometrix Media. You have been licensed one copy of this document for personal use only. Any other reproduction or redistribution is strictly prohibited. All rights reserved. This content is provided for test preparation purposes only and does not imply an endorsement by Mometrix of any particular political, scientific, or religious point of view.

differences in how the words or phrases in a sentence are ordered can make major differences in meaning. For example, two sentences can use exactly the same words but have different meanings based on the word order:

- "The man with a broken arm sat in a chair."
- "The man sat in a chair with a broken arm."

While both sentences indicate that a man sat in a chair, differing syntax indicates whether the man's or chair's arm was broken.

DETERMINING MEANING OF PHRASES AND PARAGRAPHS

Like unknown words, the meanings of phrases, paragraphs, and entire works can also be difficult to discern. Each of these can be better understood with added context. However, for larger groups of words, more context is needed. Unclear phrases are similar to unclear words, and the same methods can be used to understand their meaning. However, it is also important to consider how the individual words in the phrase work together. Paragraphs are a bit more complicated. Just as words must be compared to other words in a sentence, paragraphs must be compared to other paragraphs in a composition or a section.

DETERMINING MEANING IN VARIOUS TYPES OF COMPOSITIONS

To understand the meaning of an entire composition, the type of composition must be considered. **Expository writing** is generally organized so that each paragraph focuses on explaining one idea, or part of an idea, and its relevance. **Persuasive writing** uses paragraphs for different purposes to organize the parts of the argument. **Unclear paragraphs** must be read in the context of the paragraphs around them for their meaning to be fully understood. The meaning of full texts can also be unclear at times. The purpose of composition is also important for understanding the meaning of a text. To quickly understand the broad meaning of a text, look to the introductory and concluding paragraphs. Fictional texts are different. Some fictional works have implicit meanings, but some do not. The target audience must be considered for understanding texts that do have an implicit meaning, as most children's fiction will clearly state any lessons or morals. For other fiction, the application of literary theories and criticism may be helpful for understanding the text.

ADDITIONAL RESOURCES FOR DETERMINING WORD MEANING AND USAGE

While these strategies are useful for determining the meaning of unknown words and phrases, sometimes additional resources are needed to properly use the terms in different contexts. Some words have multiple definitions, and some words are inappropriate in particular contexts or modes of writing. The following tools are helpful for understanding all meanings and proper uses for words and phrases.

- **Dictionaries** provide the meaning of a multitude of words in a language. Many dictionaries include additional information about each word, such as its etymology, its synonyms, or variations of the word.
- **Glossaries** are similar to dictionaries, as they provide the meanings of a variety of terms. However, while dictionaries typically feature an extensive list of words and comprise an entire publication, glossaries are often included at the end of a text and only include terms and definitions that are relevant to the text they follow.

Copyright © Mometrix Media. You have been licensed one copy of this document for personal use only. Any other reproduction or redistribution is strictly prohibited. All rights reserved.
This content is provided for test preparation purposes only and does not imply an endorsement by Mometrix of any particular political, scientific, or religious point of view.

- **Spell Checkers** are used to detect spelling errors in typed text. Some spell checkers may also detect the misuse of plural or singular nouns, verb tenses, or capitalization. While spell checkers are a helpful tool, they are not always reliable or attuned to the author's intent, so it is important to review the spell checker's suggestions before accepting them.
- **Style Manuals** are guidelines on the preferred punctuation, format, and grammar usage according to different fields or organizations. For example, the Associated Press Stylebook is a style guide often used for media writing. The guidelines within a style guide are not always applicable across different contexts and usages, as the guidelines often cover grammatical or formatting situations that are not objectively correct or incorrect.

CHAPTER QUIZ

1. Which of the following affixes refers to the *-o-* in "speedometer"?

a. Prefix
b. Suffix
c. Interfix
d. Circumfix

2. Adding the suffix *-ness* to a word typically does which of the following?

a. Changes a verb to a noun
b. Changes a verb to an adjective
c. Changes an adjective to a noun
d. Changes a noun to a verb

3. Which of the following is NOT considered a common adjective suffix?

a. *-acy*
b. *-able*
c. *-ish*
d. *-less*

4. Which of the following defines the noun suffix *-ation*?

a. Act, condition, fact
b. Action, state, result
c. Quality, state, result
d. State, rank, condition

CHAPTER QUIZ ANSWER KEY

1. C: Prefixes are affixes placed in front of words. For example, *heat* means to make hot, while *preheat* means to heat in advance. Suffixes are affixes placed at the ends of words. The *happiness* example above contains the suffix *-ness.* Circumfixes add parts both before and after words, such as how *light* becomes *enlighten* with the prefix *en-* and the suffix *-en.* Interfixes create compound words via central affixes: *speed* and *meter* become *speedometer* via the interfix *-o-.*

2. C: In English, certain suffixes generally indicate both that a word is a noun, and that the noun represents a state of being or quality. For example, *-ness* is commonly used to change an adjective into its noun form, as with *happy* and *happiness, kind* and *kindness,* and so on.

Copyright © Mometrix Media. You have been licensed one copy of this document for personal use only. Any other reproduction or redistribution is strictly prohibited. All rights reserved. This content is provided for test preparation purposes only and does not imply an endorsement by Mometrix of any particular political, scientific, or religious point of view.

3. A: Adjective suffixes:

Suffix	Definition	Examples
-able (-ible)	capable of being	tolerable, edible
-esque	in the style of, like	picturesque, grotesque
-ful	filled with, marked by	thankful, zestful
-ific	make, cause	terrific, beatific
-ish	suggesting, like	churlish, childish
-less	lacking, without	hopeless, countless
-ous	marked by, given to	religious, riotous

4. B: Noun suffixes:

Suffix	Definition	Examples
-acy	state, condition	accuracy, privacy
-ance	act, condition, fact	acceptance, vigilance
-ard	one that does excessively	drunkard, sluggard
-ation	action, state, result	occupation, starvation
-dom	state, rank, condition	serfdom, wisdom
-er (-or)	office, action	teacher, elevator, honor
-ess	feminine	waitress, duchess
-hood	state, condition	manhood, statehood
-ion	action, result, state	union, fusion
-ism	act, manner, doctrine	barbarism, socialism
-ist	worker, follower	monopolist, socialist
-ity (-ty)	state, quality, condition	acidity, civility, twenty
-ment	result, action	refreshment
-ness	quality, state	greatness, tallness
-ship	position	internship, statesmanship
-sion (-tion)	state, result	revision, expedition
-th	act, state, quality	warmth, width
-tude	quality, state, result	magnitude, fortitude

LITERAL AND FIGURATIVE MEANING

When language is used **literally**, the words mean exactly what they say and nothing more. When language is used **figuratively**, the words mean something beyond their literal meaning. For example, "The weeping willow tree has long, trailing branches and leaves" is a literal description. But "The weeping willow tree looks as if it is bending over and crying" is a figurative description—specifically, a **simile** or stated comparison. Another figurative language form is **metaphor**, or an implied comparison. A good example is the metaphor of a city, state, or city-state as a ship, and its governance as sailing that ship. Ancient Greek lyrical poet Alcaeus is credited with first using this metaphor, and ancient Greek tragedian Aeschylus then used it in *Seven Against Thebes,* and then Plato used it in the *Republic.*

FIGURES OF SPEECH

A **figure of speech** is a verbal expression whose meaning is figurative rather than literal. For example, the phrase "butterflies in the stomach" does not refer to actual butterflies in a person's

Copyright © Mometrix Media. You have been licensed one copy of this document for personal use only. Any other reproduction or redistribution is strictly prohibited. All rights reserved.
This content is provided for test preparation purposes only and does not imply an endorsement by Mometrix of any particular political, scientific, or religious point of view.

stomach. It is a metaphor representing the fluttery feelings experienced when a person is nervous or excited—or when one "falls in love," which does not mean physically falling. "Hitting a sales target" does not mean physically hitting a target with arrows as in archery; it is a metaphor for meeting a sales quota. "Climbing the ladder of success" metaphorically likens advancing in one's career to ascending ladder rungs. Similes, such as "light as a feather" (meaning very light, not a feather's actual weight), and hyperbole, like "I'm starving/freezing/roasting," are also figures of speech. Figures of speech are often used and crafted for emphasis, freshness of expression, or clarity.

> **Review Video: Figures of Speech**
> Visit mometrix.com/academy and enter code: 111295

FIGURATIVE LANGUAGE

Figurative language extends past the literal meanings of words. It offers readers new insight into the people, things, events, and subjects covered in a work of literature. Figurative language also enables readers to feel they are sharing the authors' experiences. It can stimulate the reader's senses, make comparisons that readers find intriguing or even startling, and enable readers to view the world in different ways. When looking for figurative language, it is important to consider the context of the sentence or situation. Phrases that appear out of place or make little sense when read literally are likely instances of figurative language. Once figurative language has been recognized, context is also important to determining the type of figurative language being used and its function. For example, when a comparison is being made, a metaphor or simile is likely being used. This means the comparison may emphasize or create irony through the things being compared. Seven specific types of figurative language include: alliteration, onomatopoeia, personification, imagery, similes, metaphors, and hyperbole.

> **Review Video: Figurative Language**
> Visit mometrix.com/academy and enter code: 584902

ALLITERATION AND ONOMATOPOEIA

Alliteration describes a series of words beginning with the same sounds. **Onomatopoeia** uses words imitating the sounds of things they name or describe. For example, in his poem "Come Down, O Maid," Alfred Tennyson writes of "The moan of doves in immemorial elms, / And murmuring of innumerable bees." The word "moan" sounds like some sounds doves make, "murmuring" represents the sounds of bees buzzing. Onomatopoeia also includes words that are simply meant to represent sounds, such as "meow," "kaboom," and "whoosh."

> **Review Video: Alliterations Are All Around**
> Visit mometrix.com/academy and enter code: 462837

PERSONIFICATION

Another type of figurative language is **personification**. This is describing a non-human thing, like an animal or an object, as if it were human. The general intent of personification is to describe things in a manner that will be comprehensible to readers. When an author states that a tree *groans* in the wind, he or she does not mean that the tree is emitting a low, pained sound from a mouth. Instead, the author means that the tree is making a noise similar to a human groan. Of course, this personification establishes a tone of sadness or suffering. A different tone would be established if the author said that the tree was *swaying* or *dancing*. Alfred Tennyson's poem "The Eagle" uses all of these types of figurative language: "He clasps the crag with crooked hands." Tennyson used

Copyright © Mometrix Media. You have been licensed one copy of this document for personal use only. Any other reproduction or redistribution is strictly prohibited. All rights reserved. This content is provided for test preparation purposes only and does not imply an endorsement by Mometrix of any particular political, scientific, or religious point of view.

alliteration, repeating /k/ and /kr/ sounds. These hard-sounding consonants reinforce the imagery, giving visual and tactile impressions of the eagle.

Review Video: <u>Personification</u>
Visit mometrix.com/academy and enter code: 260066

SIMILES AND METAPHORS

Similes are stated comparisons using "like" or "as." Similes can be used to stimulate readers' imaginations and appeal to their senses. Because a simile includes *like* or *as,* the device creates more space between the description and the thing being described than a metaphor does. If an author says that *a house was like a shoebox,* then the tone is different than the author saying that the house *was* a shoebox. Authors will choose between a metaphor and a simile depending on their intended tone.

Similes also help compare fictional characters to well-known objects or experiences, so the reader can better relate to them. William Wordsworth's poem about "Daffodils" begins, "I wandered lonely as a cloud." This simile compares his loneliness to that of a cloud. It is also personification, giving a cloud the human quality loneliness. In his novel *Lord Jim* (1900), Joseph Conrad writes in Chapter 33, "I would have given anything for the power to soothe her frail soul, tormenting itself in its invincible ignorance like a small bird beating about the cruel wires of a cage." Conrad uses the word "like" to compare the girl's soul to a small bird. His description of the bird beating at the cage shows the similar helplessness of the girl's soul to gain freedom.

Review Video: <u>Similes</u>
Visit mometrix.com/academy and enter code: 642949

A **metaphor** is a type of figurative language in which the writer equates something with another thing that is not particularly similar, instead of using *like* or *as*. For instance, *the bird was an arrow arcing through the sky*. In this sentence, the arrow is serving as a metaphor for the bird. The point of a metaphor is to encourage the reader to consider the item being described in a *different way*. Let's continue with this metaphor for a flying bird. You are asked to envision the bird's flight as being similar to the arc of an arrow. So, you imagine the flight to be swift and bending. Metaphors are a way for the author to describe an item *without being direct and obvious*. This literary device is a lyrical and suggestive way of providing information. Note that the reference for a metaphor will not always be mentioned explicitly by the author. Consider the following description of a forest in winter: *Swaying skeletons reached for the sky and groaned as the wind blew through them*. In this example, the author is using *skeletons* as a metaphor for leafless trees. This metaphor creates a spooky tone while inspiring the reader's imagination.

LITERARY EXAMPLES OF METAPHOR

A **metaphor** is an implied comparison, i.e., it compares something to something else without using "like", "as", or other comparative words. For example, in "The Tyger" (1794), William Blake writes, "Tyger Tyger, burning bright, / In the forests of the night." Blake compares the tiger to a flame not by saying it is like a fire, but by simply describing it as "burning." Henry Wadsworth Longfellow's poem "O Ship of State" (1850) uses an extended metaphor by referring consistently throughout the entire poem to the state, union, or republic as a seagoing vessel, referring to its keel, mast, sail, rope, anchors, and to its braving waves, rocks, gale, tempest, and "false lights on the shore." Within the extended metaphor, Wordsworth uses a specific metaphor: "the anchors of thy hope!"

Copyright © Mometrix Media. You have been licensed one copy of this document for personal use only. Any other reproduction or redistribution is strictly prohibited. All rights reserved. This content is provided for test preparation purposes only and does not imply an endorsement by Mometrix of any particular political, scientific, or religious point of view.

TED HUGHES' ANIMAL METAPHORS

Ted Hughes frequently used animal metaphors in his poetry. In "The Thought Fox," a model of concise, structured beauty, Hughes characterizes the poet's creative process with succinct, striking imagery of an idea entering his head like a wild fox. Repeating "loneliness" in the first two stanzas emphasizes the poet's lonely work: "Something else is alive / Beside the clock's loneliness." He treats an idea's arrival as separate from himself. Three stanzas detail in vivid images a fox's approach from the outside winter forest at starless midnight—its nose, "Cold, delicately" touching twigs and leaves; "neat" paw prints in snow; "bold" body; brilliant green eyes; and self-contained, focused progress—"Till, with a sudden sharp hot stink of fox," he metaphorically depicts poetic inspiration as the fox's physical entry into "the dark hole of the head." Hughes ends by summarizing his vision of a poet as an interior, passive idea recipient, with the outside world unchanged: "The window is starless still; the clock ticks, / The page is printed."

> **Review Video: Metaphors in Writing**
> Visit mometrix.com/academy and enter code: 133295

HYPERBOLE

Hyperbole is excessive exaggeration used for humor or emphasis rather than for literal meaning. For example, in *To Kill a Mockingbird*, Harper Lee wrote, "People moved slowly then. There was no hurry, for there was nowhere to go, nothing to buy and no money to buy it with, nothing to see outside the boundaries of Maycomb County." This was not literally true; Lee exaggerates the scarcity of these things for emphasis. In "Old Times on the Mississippi," Mark Twain wrote, "I... could have hung my hat on my eyes, they stuck out so far." This is not literal, but makes his description vivid and funny. In his poem "As I Walked Out One Evening", W. H. Auden wrote, "I'll love you, dear, I'll love you / Till China and Africa meet, / And the river jumps over the mountain / And the salmon sing in the street." He used things not literally possible to emphasize the duration of his love.

> **Review Video: Hyperbole and Understatement**
> Visit mometrix.com/academy and enter code: 308470

LITERARY IRONY

In literature, irony demonstrates the opposite of what is said or done. The three types of irony are **verbal irony**, **situational irony**, and **dramatic irony**. Verbal irony uses words opposite to the meaning. Sarcasm may use verbal irony. One common example is describing something that is confusing as "clear as mud." For example, in his 1986 movie *Hannah and Her Sisters,* author, director, and actor Woody Allen says to his character's date, "I had a great evening; it was like the Nuremburg Trials." Notice these employ similes. In situational irony, what happens contrasts with what was expected. O. Henry's short story *The Gift of the Magi* uses situational irony: a husband and wife each sacrifice their most prized possession to buy each other a Christmas present. The irony is that she sells her long hair to buy him a watch fob, while he sells his heirloom pocket-watch to buy her the jeweled combs for her hair she had long wanted; in the end, neither of them can use their gifts. In dramatic irony, narrative informs audiences of more than its characters know. For example, in *Romeo and Juliet,* the audience is made aware that Juliet is only asleep, while Romeo believes her to be dead, which then leads to Romeo's death.

> **Review Video: What is the Definition of Irony?**
> Visit mometrix.com/academy and enter code: 374204

Copyright © Mometrix Media. You have been licensed one copy of this document for personal use only. Any other reproduction or redistribution is strictly prohibited. All rights reserved.
This content is provided for test preparation purposes only and does not imply an endorsement by Mometrix of any particular political, scientific, or religious point of view.

IDIOMS

Idioms create comparisons, and often take the form of similes or metaphors. Idioms are always phrases and are understood to have a meaning that is different from its individual words' literal meaning. For example, "break a leg" is a common idiom that is used to wish someone luck or tell them to perform well. Literally, the phrase "break a leg" means to injure a person's leg, but the phrase takes on a different meaning when used as an idiom. Another example is "call it a day," which means to temporarily stop working on a task, or find a stopping point, rather than literally referring to something as "a day." Many idioms are associated with a region or group. For example, an idiom commonly used in the American South is "'til the cows come home." This phrase is often used to indicate that something will take or may last for a very long time, but not that it will literally last until the cows return to where they reside.

CHAPTER QUIZ

1. Who is credited with first using the metaphor of a city, state, or city-state as a ship?

 a. Theseus
 b. Aeschylus
 c. Alcaeus
 d. Plato

2. How many forms of irony are there?

 a. Two
 b. Three
 c. Four
 d. Five

CHAPTER QUIZ ANSWER KEY

1. C: Another figurative language form is metaphor, or an implied comparison. A good example is the metaphor of a city, state, or city-state as a ship, and its governance as sailing that ship. Ancient Greek lyrical poet Alcaeus is credited with first using this metaphor, followed by ancient Greek tragedian Aeschylus using it in *Seven Against Thebes,* and then Plato using it in the *Republic.*

2. B: In literature, irony demonstrates the opposite of what is said or done. The three types of irony are verbal irony, situational irony, and dramatic irony. Verbal irony uses words opposite to the meaning. Sarcasm may use verbal irony. One common example is describing something that is confusing as "clear as mud." In his 1986 movie *Hannah and Her Sisters,* author, director, and actor Woody Allen says to his character's date, "I had a great evening; it was like the Nuremburg Trials." Notice these employ similes. In situational irony, what happens contrasts with what was expected. O. Henry's short story *The Gift of the Magi* uses situational irony: a husband and wife each sacrifice their most prized possession to buy each other a Christmas present. The irony is that she sells her long hair to buy him a watch fob, while he sells his heirloom pocket-watch to buy her the jeweled combs for her hair she had long wanted; in the end, neither of them can use their gifts. In dramatic irony, narrative informs audiences of more than its characters know. For example, in *Romeo and Juliet,* the audience is made aware that Juliet is only asleep, while Romeo believes her to be dead, which then leads to Romeo's death.

Copyright © Mometrix Media. You have been licensed one copy of this document for personal use only. Any other reproduction or redistribution is strictly prohibited. All rights reserved.
This content is provided for test preparation purposes only and does not imply an endorsement by Mometrix of any particular political, scientific, or religious point of view.

Mathematics

Numbers and Operations

CLASSIFICATIONS OF NUMBERS

Numbers are the basic building blocks of mathematics. Specific features of numbers are identified by the following terms:

Integer – any positive or negative whole number, including zero. Integers do not include fractions $\left(\frac{1}{3}\right)$, decimals (0.56), or mixed numbers $\left(7\frac{3}{4}\right)$.

Prime number – any whole number greater than 1 that has only two factors, itself and 1; that is, a number that can be divided evenly only by 1 and itself.

Composite number – any whole number greater than 1 that has more than two different factors; in other words, any whole number that is not a prime number. For example: The composite number 8 has the factors of 1, 2, 4, and 8.

Even number – any integer that can be divided by 2 without leaving a remainder. For example: 2, 4, 6, 8, and so on.

Odd number – any integer that cannot be divided evenly by 2. For example: 3, 5, 7, 9, and so on.

Decimal number – any number that uses a decimal point to show the part of the number that is less than one. Example: 1.234.

Decimal point – a symbol used to separate the ones place from the tenths place in decimals or dollars from cents in currency.

Decimal place – the position of a number to the right of the decimal point. In the decimal 0.123, the 1 is in the first place to the right of the decimal point, indicating tenths; the 2 is in the second place, indicating hundredths; and the 3 is in the third place, indicating thousandths.

The **decimal**, or base 10, system is a number system that uses ten different digits (0, 1, 2, 3, 4, 5, 6, 7, 8, 9). An example of a number system that uses something other than ten digits is the **binary**, or base 2, number system, used by computers, which uses only the numbers 0 and 1. It is thought that the decimal system originated because people had only their 10 fingers for counting.

Rational numbers include all integers, decimals, and fractions. Any terminating or repeating decimal number is a rational number.

Irrational numbers cannot be written as fractions or decimals because the number of decimal places is infinite and there is no recurring pattern of digits within the number. For example, pi (π) begins with 3.141592 and continues without terminating or repeating, so pi is an irrational number.

Copyright © Mometrix Media. You have been licensed one copy of this document for personal use only. Any other reproduction or redistribution is strictly prohibited. All rights reserved. This content is provided for test preparation purposes only and does not imply an endorsement by Mometrix of any particular political, scientific, or religious point of view.

Real numbers are the set of all rational and irrational numbers.

> **Review Video: Classification of Numbers**
> Visit mometrix.com/academy and enter code: 461071
>
> **Review Video: Prime and Composite Numbers**
> Visit mometrix.com/academy and enter code: 565581

NUMBERS IN WORD FORM AND PLACE VALUE

When writing numbers out in word form or translating word form to numbers, it is essential to understand how a place value system works. In the decimal or base-10 system, each digit of a number represents how many of the corresponding place value—a specific factor of 10—are contained in the number being represented. To make reading numbers easier, every three digits to the left of the decimal place is preceded by a comma. The following table demonstrates some of the place values:

Power of 10	10^3	10^2	10^1	10^0	10^{-1}	10^{-2}	10^{-3}
Value	1,000	100	10	1	0.1	0.01	0.001
Place	thousands	hundreds	tens	ones	tenths	hundredths	thousandths

For example, consider the number 4,546.09, which can be separated into each place value like this:

4: thousands
5: hundreds
4: tens
6: ones
0: tenths
9: hundredths

This number in word form would be *four thousand five hundred forty-six and nine hundredths.*

> **Review Video: Place Value**
> Visit mometrix.com/academy and enter code: 205433

RATIONAL NUMBERS

The term **rational** means that the number can be expressed as a ratio or fraction. That is, a number, r, is rational if and only if it can be represented by a fraction $\frac{a}{b}$ where a and b are integers and b does not equal 0. The set of rational numbers includes integers and decimals. If there is no finite way to represent a value with a fraction of integers, then the number is **irrational**. Common examples of irrational numbers include: $\sqrt{5}$, $\left(1 + \sqrt{2}\right)$, and π.

> **Review Video: Rational and Irrational Numbers**
> Visit mometrix.com/academy and enter code: 280645

THE NUMBER LINE

A number line is a graph to see the distance between numbers. Basically, this graph shows the relationship between numbers. So a number line may have a point for zero and may show negative

Copyright © Mometrix Media. You have been licensed one copy of this document for personal use only. Any other reproduction or redistribution is strictly prohibited. All rights reserved.
This content is provided for test preparation purposes only and does not imply an endorsement by Mometrix of any particular political, scientific, or religious point of view.

numbers on the left side of the line. Any positive numbers are placed on the right side of the line. For example, consider the points labeled on the following number line:

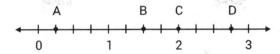

We can use the dashed lines on the number line to identify each point. Each dashed line between two whole numbers is $\frac{1}{4}$. The line halfway between two numbers is $\frac{1}{2}$.

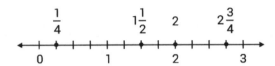

Review Video: The Number Line
Visit mometrix.com/academy and enter code: 816439

ABSOLUTE VALUE

A precursor to working with negative numbers is understanding what **absolute values** are. A number's absolute value is simply the distance away from zero a number is on the number line. The absolute value of a number is always positive and is written $|x|$. For example, the absolute value of 3, written as $|3|$, is 3 because the distance between 0 and 3 on a number line is three units. Likewise, the absolute value of –3, written as $|-3|$, is 3 because the distance between 0 and –3 on a number line is three units. So $|3| = |-3|$.

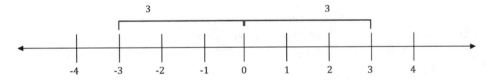

Review Video: Absolute Value
Visit mometrix.com/academy and enter code: 314669

OPERATIONS

An **operation** is simply a mathematical process that takes some value(s) as input(s) and produces an output. Elementary operations are often written in the following form: *value operation value*. For instance, in the expression $1 + 2$ the values are 1 and 2 and the operation is addition. Performing the operation gives the output of 3. In this way we can say that $1 + 2$ and 3 are equal, or $1 + 2 = 3$.

ADDITION

Addition increases the value of one quantity by the value of another quantity (both called **addends**). Example: $2 + 4 = 6$ or $8 + 9 = 17$. The result is called the **sum**. With addition, the order does not matter, $4 + 2 = 2 + 4$.

Copyright © Mometrix Media. You have been licensed one copy of this document for personal use only. Any other reproduction or redistribution is strictly prohibited. All rights reserved.
This content is provided for test preparation purposes only and does not imply an endorsement by Mometrix of any particular political, scientific, or religious point of view.

When adding signed numbers, if the signs are the same simply add the absolute values of the addends and apply the original sign to the sum. For example, $(+4) + (+8) = +12$ and $(-4) + (-8) = -12$. When the original signs are different, take the absolute values of the addends and subtract the smaller value from the larger value, then apply the original sign of the larger value to the difference. Example: $(+4) + (-8) = -4$ and $(-4) + (+8) = +4$.

SUBTRACTION

Subtraction is the opposite operation to addition; it decreases the value of one quantity (the **minuend**) by the value of another quantity (the **subtrahend**). For example, $6 - 4 = 2$ or $17 - 8 = 9$. The result is called the **difference**. Note that with subtraction, the order does matter, $6 - 4 \neq 4 - 6$.

For subtracting signed numbers, change the sign of the subtrahend and then follow the same rules used for addition. Example: $(+4) - (+8) = (+4) + (-8) = -4$

MULTIPLICATION

Multiplication can be thought of as repeated addition. One number (the **multiplier**) indicates how many times to add the other number (the **multiplicand**) to itself. Example: $3 \times 2 = 2 + 2 + 2 = 6$. With multiplication, the order does not matter, $2 \times 3 = 3 \times 2$ or $3 + 3 = 2 + 2 + 2$, either way the result (the **product**) is the same.

If the signs are the same, the product is positive when multiplying signed numbers. Example: $(+4) \times (+8) = +32$ and $(-4) \times (-8) = +32$. If the signs are opposite, the product is negative. Example: $(+4) \times (-8) = -32$ and $(-4) \times (+8) = -32$. When more than two factors are multiplied together, the sign of the product is determined by how many negative factors are present. If there are an odd number of negative factors then the product is negative, whereas an even number of negative factors indicates a positive product. Example: $(+4) \times (-8) \times (-2) = +64$ and $(-4) \times (-8) \times (-2) = -64$.

DIVISION

Division is the opposite operation to multiplication; one number (the **divisor**) tells us how many parts to divide the other number (the **dividend**) into. The result of division is called the **quotient**. Example: $20 \div 4 = 5$. If 20 is split into 4 equal parts, each part is 5. With division, the order of the numbers does matter, $20 \div 4 \neq 4 \div 20$.

The rules for dividing signed numbers are similar to multiplying signed numbers. If the dividend and divisor have the same sign, the quotient is positive. If the dividend and divisor have opposite signs, the quotient is negative. Example: $(-4) \div (+8) = -0.5$.

> **Review Video: Mathematical Operations**
> Visit mometrix.com/academy and enter code: 208095

PARENTHESES

Parentheses are used to designate which operations should be done first when there are multiple operations. Example: $4 - (2 + 1) = 1$; the parentheses tell us that we must add 2 and 1, and then subtract the sum from 4, rather than subtracting 2 from 4 and then adding 1 (this would give us an answer of 3).

> **Review Video: Mathematical Parentheses**
> Visit mometrix.com/academy and enter code: 978600

Copyright © Mometrix Media. You have been licensed one copy of this document for personal use only. Any other reproduction or redistribution is strictly prohibited. All rights reserved. This content is provided for test preparation purposes only and does not imply an endorsement by Mometrix of any particular political, scientific, or religious point of view.

EXPONENTS

An **exponent** is a superscript number placed next to another number at the top right. It indicates how many times the base number is to be multiplied by itself. Exponents provide a shorthand way to write what would be a longer mathematical expression, Example: $2^4 = 2 \times 2 \times 2 \times 2$. A number with an exponent of 2 is said to be "squared," while a number with an exponent of 3 is said to be "cubed." The value of a number raised to an exponent is called its power. So 8^4 is read as "8 to the 4th power," or "8 raised to the power of 4."

> **Review Video: Introduction to Exponents**
> Visit mometrix.com/academy and enter code: 600998

ROOTS

A **root**, such as a square root, is another way of writing a fractional exponent. Instead of using a superscript, roots use the radical symbol ($\sqrt{}$) to indicate the operation. A radical will have a number underneath the bar, and may sometimes have a number in the upper left: $\sqrt[n]{a}$, read as "the nth root of a." The relationship between radical notation and exponent notation can be described by this equation:

$$\sqrt[n]{a} = a^{\frac{1}{n}}$$

The two special cases of $n = 2$ and $n = 3$ are called square roots and cube roots. If there is no number to the upper left, the radical is understood to be a square root ($n = 2$). Nearly all of the roots you encounter will be square roots. A square root is the same as a number raised to the one-half power. When we say that a is the square root of b ($a = \sqrt{b}$), we mean that a multiplied by itself equals b: ($a \times a = b$).

A **perfect square** is a number that has an integer for its square root. There are 10 perfect squares from 1 to 100: 1, 4, 9, 16, 25, 36, 49, 64, 81, 100 (the squares of integers 1 through 10).

> **Review Video: Roots**
> Visit mometrix.com/academy and enter code: 795655
>
> **Review Video: Square Root and Perfect Squares**
> Visit mometrix.com/academy and enter code: 648063

WORD PROBLEMS AND MATHEMATICAL SYMBOLS

When working on word problems, you must be able to translate verbal expressions or "math words" into math symbols. This chart contains several "math words" and their appropriate symbols:

Phrase	Symbol
equal, is, was, will be, has, costs, gets to, is the same as, becomes	$=$
times, of, multiplied by, product of, twice, doubles, halves, triples	$\times$
divided by, per, ratio of/to, out of	$\div$
plus, added to, sum, combined, and, more than, totals of	$+$
subtracted from, less than, decreased by, minus, difference between	$-$
what, how much, original value, how many, a number, a variable	$x, n,$ etc.

EXAMPLES OF TRANSLATED MATHEMATICAL PHRASES

- The phrase four more than twice a number can be written algebraically as $2x + 4$.

Copyright © Mometrix Media. You have been licensed one copy of this document for personal use only. Any other reproduction or redistribution is strictly prohibited. All rights reserved.
This content is provided for test preparation purposes only and does not imply an endorsement by Mometrix of any particular political, scientific, or religious point of view.

- The phrase half a number decreased by six can be written algebraically as $\frac{1}{2}x - 6$.
- The phrase the sum of a number and the product of five and that number can be written algebraically as $x + 5x$.
- You may see a test question that says, "Olivia is constructing a bookcase from seven boards. Two of them are for vertical supports and five are for shelves. The height of the bookcase is twice the width of the bookcase. If the seven boards total 36 feet in length, what will be the height of Olivia's bookcase?" You would need to make a sketch and then create the equation to determine the width of the shelves. The height can be represented as double the width. (If x represents the width of the shelves in feet, then the height of the bookcase is $2x$. Since the seven boards total 36 feet, $2x + 2x + x + x + x + x + x = 36$ or $9x = 36$; $x = 4$. The height is twice the width, or 8 feet.)

SUBTRACTION WITH REGROUPING

A great way to make use of some of the features built into the decimal system would be regrouping when attempting longform subtraction operations. When subtracting within a place value, sometimes the minuend is smaller than the subtrahend, **regrouping** enables you to 'borrow' a unit from a place value to the left in order to get a positive difference. For example, consider subtracting 189 from 525 with regrouping.

First, set up the subtraction problem in vertical form:

$$\begin{array}{r} 525 \\ -\ 189 \\ \hline \end{array}$$

Notice that the numbers in the ones and tens columns of 525 are smaller than the numbers in the ones and tens columns of 189. This means you will need to use regrouping to perform subtraction:

	5	2	5
−	1	8	9

To subtract 9 from 5 in the ones column you will need to borrow from the 2 in the tens columns:

	5	1	15
−	1	8	9
			6

Next, to subtract 8 from 1 in the tens column you will need to borrow from the 5 in the hundreds column:

	4	11	15
−	1	8	9
		3	6

Last, subtract the 1 from the 4 in the hundreds column:

	4	11	15
−	1	8	9
	3	3	6

Copyright © Mometrix Media. You have been licensed one copy of this document for personal use only. Any other reproduction or redistribution is strictly prohibited. All rights reserved.
This content is provided for test preparation purposes only and does not imply an endorsement by Mometrix of any particular political, scientific, or religious point of view.

Review Video: <u>Subtracting Large Numbers</u>
Visit mometrix.com/academy and enter code: 603350

ORDER OF OPERATIONS

The **order of operations** is a set of rules that dictates the order in which we must perform each operation in an expression so that we will evaluate it accurately. If we have an expression that includes multiple different operations, the order of operations tells us which operations to do first. The most common mnemonic for the order of operations is **PEMDAS**, or "Please Excuse My Dear Aunt Sally." PEMDAS stands for parentheses, exponents, multiplication, division, addition, and subtraction. It is important to understand that multiplication and division have equal precedence, as do addition and subtraction, so those pairs of operations are simply worked from left to right in order.

For example, evaluating the expression $5 + 20 \div 4 \times (2 + 3)^2 - 6$ using the correct order of operations would be done like this:

- **P:** Perform the operations inside the parentheses: $(2 + 3) = 5$
- **E:** Simplify the exponents: $(5)^2 = 5 \times 5 = 25$
  - The expression now looks like this: $5 + 20 \div 4 \times 25 - 6$
- **MD:** Perform multiplication and division from left to right: $20 \div 4 = 5$; then $5 \times 25 = 125$
  - The expression now looks like this: $5 + 125 - 6$
- **AS:** Perform addition and subtraction from left to right: $5 + 125 = 130$; then $130 - 6 = 124$

Review Video: <u>Order of Operations</u>
Visit mometrix.com/academy and enter code: 259675

The properties of exponents are as follows:

Property	Description
$a^1 = a$	Any number to the power of 1 is equal to itself
$1^n = 1$	The number 1 raised to any power is equal to 1
$a^0 = 1$	Any number raised to the power of 0 is equal to 1
$a^n \times a^m = a^{n+m}$	Add exponents to multiply powers of the same base number
$a^n \div a^m = a^{n-m}$	Subtract exponents to divide powers of the same base number
$(a^n)^m = a^{n \times m}$	When a power is raised to a power, the exponents are multiplied
$(a \times b)^n = a^n \times b^n$ $(a \div b)^n = a^n \div b^n$	Multiplication and division operations inside parentheses can be raised to a power. This is the same as each term being raised to that power.
$a^{-n} = \dfrac{1}{a^n}$	A negative exponent is the same as the reciprocal of a positive exponent

Copyright © Mometrix Media. You have been licensed one copy of this document for personal use only. Any other reproduction or redistribution is strictly prohibited. All rights reserved.
This content is provided for test preparation purposes only and does not imply an endorsement by Mometrix of any particular political, scientific, or religious point of view.

Note that exponents do not have to be integers. Fractional or decimal exponents follow all the rules above as well. Example: $5^{\frac{1}{4}} \times 5^{\frac{3}{4}} = 5^{\frac{1}{4}+\frac{3}{4}} = 5^1 = 5$.

Review Video: Properties of Exponents
Visit mometrix.com/academy and enter code: 532558

FACTORS AND GREATEST COMMON FACTOR

Factors are numbers that are multiplied together to obtain a **product**. For example, in the equation $2 \times 3 = 6$, the numbers 2 and 3 are factors. A **prime number** has only two factors (1 and itself), but other numbers can have many factors.

A **common factor** is a number that divides exactly into two or more other numbers. For example, the factors of 12 are 1, 2, 3, 4, 6, and 12, while the factors of 15 are 1, 3, 5, and 15. The common factors of 12 and 15 are 1 and 3.

A **prime factor** is also a prime number. Therefore, the prime factors of 12 are 2 and 3. For 15, the prime factors are 3 and 5.

The **greatest common factor (GCF)** is the largest number that is a factor of two or more numbers. For example, the factors of 15 are 1, 3, 5, and 15; the factors of 35 are 1, 5, 7, and 35. Therefore, the greatest common factor of 15 and 35 is 5.

Review Video: Factors
Visit mometrix.com/academy and enter code: 920086
Review Video: Prime Numbers and Factorization
Visit mometrix.com/academy and enter code: 760669
Review Video: Greatest Common Factor and Least Common Multiple
Visit mometrix.com/academy and enter code: 838699

MULTIPLES AND LEAST COMMON MULTIPLE

Often listed out in multiplication tables, **multiples** are integer increments of a given factor. In other words, dividing a multiple by the factor will result in an integer. For example, the multiples of 7 include: $1 \times 7 = 7$, $2 \times 7 = 14$, $3 \times 7 = 21$, $4 \times 7 = 28$, $5 \times 7 = 35$. Dividing 7, 14, 21, 28, or 35 by 7 will result in the integers 1, 2, 3, 4, and 5, respectively.

The least common multiple **(LCM)** is the smallest number that is a multiple of two or more numbers. For example, the multiples of 3 include 3, 6, 9, 12, 15, etc.; the multiples of 5 include 5, 10, 15, 20, etc. Therefore, the least common multiple of 3 and 5 is 15.

Review Video: Multiples
Visit mometrix.com/academy and enter code: 626738

Copyright © Mometrix Media. You have been licensed one copy of this document for personal use only. Any other reproduction or redistribution is strictly prohibited. All rights reserved. This content is provided for test preparation purposes only and does not imply an endorsement by Mometrix of any particular political, scientific, or religious point of view.

FRACTIONS

A **fraction** is a number that is expressed as one integer written above another integer, with a dividing line between them $\left(\frac{x}{y}\right)$. It represents the **quotient** of the two numbers "x divided by y." It can also be thought of as x out of y equal parts.

The top number of a fraction is called the **numerator**, and it represents the number of parts under consideration. The 1 in $\frac{1}{4}$ means that 1 part out of the whole is being considered in the calculation. The bottom number of a fraction is called the **denominator**, and it represents the total number of equal parts. The 4 in $\frac{1}{4}$ means that the whole consists of 4 equal parts. A fraction cannot have a denominator of zero; this is referred to as "*undefined*."

Fractions can be manipulated, without changing the value of the fraction, by multiplying or dividing (but not adding or subtracting) both the numerator and denominator by the same number. If you divide both numbers by a common factor, you are **reducing** or simplifying the fraction. Two fractions that have the same value but are expressed differently are known as **equivalent fractions**. For example, $\frac{2}{10}, \frac{3}{15}, \frac{4}{20},$ and $\frac{5}{25}$ are all equivalent fractions. They can also all be reduced or simplified to $\frac{1}{5}$.

When two fractions are manipulated so that they have the same denominator, this is known as finding a **common denominator**. The number chosen to be that common denominator should be the least common multiple of the two original denominators. Example: $\frac{3}{4}$ and $\frac{5}{6}$; the least common multiple of 4 and 6 is 12. Manipulating to achieve the common denominator: $\frac{3}{4} = \frac{9}{12}; \frac{5}{6} = \frac{10}{12}$.

> **Review Video: <u>Overview of Fractions</u>**
> Visit mometrix.com/academy and enter code: 262335

PROPER FRACTIONS AND MIXED NUMBERS

A fraction whose denominator is greater than its numerator is known as a **proper fraction**, while a fraction whose numerator is greater than its denominator is known as an **improper fraction**. Proper fractions have values *less than one* and improper fractions have values *greater than one*.

A **mixed number** is a number that contains both an integer and a fraction. Any improper fraction can be rewritten as a mixed number. Example: $\frac{8}{3} = \frac{6}{3} + \frac{2}{3} = 2 + \frac{2}{3} = 2\frac{2}{3}$. Similarly, any mixed number can be rewritten as an improper fraction. Example: $1\frac{3}{5} = 1 + \frac{3}{5} = \frac{5}{5} + \frac{3}{5} = \frac{8}{5}$.

> **Review Video: <u>Improper Fractions and Mixed Numbers</u>**
> Visit mometrix.com/academy and enter code: 211077

ADDING AND SUBTRACTING FRACTIONS

If two fractions have a common denominator, they can be added or subtracted simply by adding or subtracting the two numerators and retaining the same denominator. If the two fractions do not

Copyright © Mometrix Media. You have been licensed one copy of this document for personal use only. Any other reproduction or redistribution is strictly prohibited. All rights reserved.
This content is provided for test preparation purposes only and does not imply an endorsement by Mometrix of any particular political, scientific, or religious point of view.

already have the same denominator, one or both of them must be manipulated to achieve a common denominator before they can be added or subtracted. Example: $\frac{1}{2} + \frac{1}{4} = \frac{2}{4} + \frac{1}{4} = \frac{3}{4}$.

Review Video: Adding and Subtracting Fractions
Visit mometrix.com/academy and enter code: 378080

MULTIPLYING FRACTIONS

Two fractions can be multiplied by multiplying the two numerators to find the new numerator and the two denominators to find the new denominator. Example: $\frac{1}{3} \times \frac{2}{3} = \frac{1 \times 2}{3 \times 3} = \frac{2}{9}$.

DIVIDING FRACTIONS

Two fractions can be divided by flipping the numerator and denominator of the second fraction and then proceeding as though it were a multiplication problem. Example: $\frac{2}{3} \div \frac{3}{4} = \frac{2}{3} \times \frac{4}{3} = \frac{8}{9}$.

Review Video: Multiplying and Dividing Fractions
Visit mometrix.com/academy and enter code: 473632

MULTIPLYING A MIXED NUMBER BY A WHOLE NUMBER OR A DECIMAL

When multiplying a mixed number by something, it is usually best to convert it to an improper fraction first. Additionally, if the multiplicand is a decimal, it is most often simplest to convert it to a fraction. For instance, to multiply $4\frac{3}{8}$ by 3.5, begin by rewriting each quantity as a whole number plus a proper fraction. Remember, a mixed number is a fraction added to a whole number and a decimal is a representation of the sum of fractions, specifically tenths, hundredths, thousandths, and so on:

$$4\frac{3}{8} \times 3.5 = \left(4 + \frac{3}{8}\right) \times \left(3 + \frac{1}{2}\right)$$

Next, the quantities being added need to be expressed with the same denominator. This is achieved by multiplying and dividing the whole number by the denominator of the fraction. Recall that a whole number is equivalent to that number divided by 1:

$$= \left(\frac{4}{1} \times \frac{8}{8} + \frac{3}{8}\right) \times \left(\frac{3}{1} \times \frac{2}{2} + \frac{1}{2}\right)$$

When multiplying fractions, remember to multiply the numerators and denominators separately:

$$= \left(\frac{4 \times 8}{1 \times 8} + \frac{3}{8}\right) \times \left(\frac{3 \times 2}{1 \times 2} + \frac{1}{2}\right)$$
$$= \left(\frac{32}{8} + \frac{3}{8}\right) \times \left(\frac{6}{2} + \frac{1}{2}\right)$$

Now that the fractions have the same denominators, they can be added:

$$= \frac{35}{8} \times \frac{7}{2}$$

Copyright © Mometrix Media. You have been licensed one copy of this document for personal use only. Any other reproduction or redistribution is strictly prohibited. All rights reserved.
This content is provided for test preparation purposes only and does not imply an endorsement by Mometrix of any particular political, scientific, or religious point of view.

Finally, perform the last multiplication and then simplify:

$$= \frac{35 \times 7}{8 \times 2} = \frac{245}{16} = \frac{240}{16} + \frac{5}{16} = 15\frac{5}{16}$$

DECIMALS

Decimals are one way to represent parts of a whole. Using the place value system, each digit to the right of a decimal point denotes the number of units of a corresponding *negative* power of ten. For example, consider the decimal 0.24. We can use a model to represent the decimal. Since a dime is worth one-tenth of a dollar and a penny is worth one-hundredth of a dollar, one possible model to represent this fraction is to have 2 dimes representing the 2 in the tenths place and 4 pennies representing the 4 in the hundredths place:

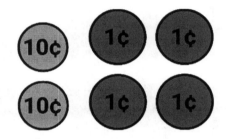

To write the decimal as a fraction, put the decimal in the numerator with 1 in the denominator. Multiply the numerator and denominator by tens until there are no more decimal places. Then simplify the fraction to lowest terms. For example, converting 0.24 to a fraction:

$$0.24 = \frac{0.24}{1} = \frac{0.24 \times 100}{1 \times 100} = \frac{24}{100} = \frac{6}{25}$$

Review Video: Decimals
Visit mometrix.com/academy and enter code: 837268

OPERATIONS WITH DECIMALS

ADDING AND SUBTRACTING DECIMALS

When adding and subtracting decimals, the decimal points must always be aligned. Adding decimals is just like adding regular whole numbers. Example: $4.5 + 2.0 = 6.5$.

If the problem-solver does not properly align the decimal points, an incorrect answer of 4.7 may result. An easy way to add decimals is to align all of the decimal points in a vertical column visually. This will allow you to see exactly where the decimal should be placed in the final answer. Begin adding from right to left. Add each column in turn, making sure to carry the number to the left if a column adds up to more than 9. The same rules apply to the subtraction of decimals.

Review Video: Adding and Subtracting Decimals
Visit mometrix.com/academy and enter code: 381101

MULTIPLYING DECIMALS

A simple multiplication problem has two components: a **multiplicand** and a **multiplier**. When multiplying decimals, work as though the numbers were whole rather than decimals. Once the final product is calculated, count the number of places to the right of the decimal in both the multiplicand and the multiplier. Then, count that number of places from the right of the product and place the decimal in that position.

Copyright © Mometrix Media. You have been licensed one copy of this document for personal use only. Any other reproduction or redistribution is strictly prohibited. All rights reserved. This content is provided for test preparation purposes only and does not imply an endorsement by Mometrix of any particular political, scientific, or religious point of view.

For example, 12.3×2.56 has a total of three places to the right of the respective decimals. Multiply 123×256 to get 31,488. Now, beginning on the right, count three places to the left and insert the decimal. The final product will be 31.488.

Review Video: How to Multiply Decimals
Visit mometrix.com/academy and enter code: 731574

DIVIDING DECIMALS

Every division problem has a **divisor** and a **dividend**. The dividend is the number that is being divided. In the problem $14 \div 7$, 14 is the dividend and 7 is the divisor. In a division problem with decimals, the divisor must be converted into a whole number. Begin by moving the decimal in the divisor to the right until a whole number is created. Next, move the decimal in the dividend the same number of spaces to the right. For example, 4.9 into 24.5 would become 49 into 245. The decimal was moved one space to the right to create a whole number in the divisor, and then the same was done for the dividend. Once the whole numbers are created, the problem is carried out normally: $245 \div 49 = 5$.

Review Video: How to Divide Decimals
Visit mometrix.com/academy and enter code: 560690
Review Video: Dividing Decimals by Whole Numbers
Visit mometrix.com/academy and enter code: 535669

PERCENTAGES

Percentages can be thought of as fractions that are based on a whole of 100; that is, one whole is equal to 100%. The word **percent** means "per hundred." Percentage problems are often presented in three main ways:

- Find what percentage of some number another number is.
  - Example: What percentage of 40 is 8?
- Find what number is some percentage of a given number.
  - Example: What number is 20% of 40?
- Find what number another number is a given percentage of.
  - Example: What number is 8 20% of?

There are three components in each of these cases: a **whole** (W), a **part** (P), and a **percentage** (%). These are related by the equation: $P = W \times \%$. This can easily be rearranged into other forms that may suit different questions better: $\% = \frac{P}{W}$ and $W = \frac{P}{\%}$. Percentage problems are often also word problems. As such, a large part of solving them is figuring out which quantities are what. For example, consider the following word problem:

In a school cafeteria, 7 students choose pizza, 9 choose hamburgers, and 4 choose tacos. What percentage of student choose tacos?

To find the whole, you must first add all of the parts: $7 + 9 + 4 = 20$. The percentage can then be found by dividing the part by the whole $\left(\% = \frac{P}{W}\right)$: $\frac{4}{20} = \frac{20}{100} = 20\%$.

Review Video: Computation with Percentages
Visit mometrix.com/academy and enter code: 693099

Copyright © Mometrix Media. You have been licensed one copy of this document for personal use only. Any other reproduction or redistribution is strictly prohibited. All rights reserved.
This content is provided for test preparation purposes only and does not imply an endorsement by Mometrix of any particular political, scientific, or religious point of view.

CONVERTING BETWEEN PERCENTAGES, FRACTIONS, AND DECIMALS

Converting decimals to percentages and percentages to decimals is as simple as moving the decimal point. To *convert from a decimal to a percentage*, move the decimal point **two places to the right**. To *convert from a percentage to a decimal*, move it **two places to the left**. It may be helpful to remember that the percentage number will always be larger than the equivalent decimal number. Example:

$$0.23 = 23\% \quad 5.34 = 534\% \quad 0.007 = 0.7\%$$
$$700\% = 7.00 \quad 86\% = 0.86 \quad 0.15\% = 0.0015$$

To convert a fraction to a decimal, simply divide the numerator by the denominator in the fraction. To convert a decimal to a fraction, put the decimal in the numerator with 1 in the denominator. Multiply the numerator and denominator by tens until there are no more decimal places. Then simplify the fraction to lowest terms. For example, converting 0.24 to a fraction:

$$0.24 = \frac{0.24}{1} = \frac{0.24 \times 100}{1 \times 100} = \frac{24}{100} = \frac{6}{25}$$

Fractions can be converted to a percentage by finding equivalent fractions with a denominator of 100. Example:

$$\frac{7}{10} = \frac{70}{100} = 70\% \quad \frac{1}{4} = \frac{25}{100} = 25\%$$

To convert a percentage to a fraction, divide the percentage number by 100 and reduce the fraction to its simplest possible terms. Example:

$$60\% = \frac{60}{100} = \frac{3}{5} \quad 96\% = \frac{96}{100} = \frac{24}{25}$$

> **Review Video: <u>Converting Fractions to Percentages and Decimals</u>**
> Visit mometrix.com/academy and enter code: 306233
>
> **Review Video: <u>Converting Percentages to Decimals and Fractions</u>**
> Visit mometrix.com/academy and enter code: 287297
>
> **Review Video: <u>Converting Decimals to Fractions and Percentages</u>**
> Visit mometrix.com/academy and enter code: 986765
>
> **Review Video: <u>Converting Decimals, Improper Fractions, and Mixed Numbers</u>**
> Visit mometrix.com/academy and enter code: 696924

Copyright © Mometrix Media. You have been licensed one copy of this document for personal use only. Any other reproduction or redistribution is strictly prohibited. All rights reserved. This content is provided for test preparation purposes only and does not imply an endorsement by Mometrix of any particular political, scientific, or religious point of view.

Algebraic Thinking

PROPORTIONS

A proportion is a relationship between two quantities that dictates how one changes when the other changes. A **direct proportion** describes a relationship in which a quantity increases by a set amount for every increase in the other quantity, or decreases by that same amount for every decrease in the other quantity. Example: Assuming a constant driving speed, the time required for a car trip increases as the distance of the trip increases. The distance to be traveled and the time required to travel are directly proportional.

An **inverse proportion** is a relationship in which an increase in one quantity is accompanied by a decrease in the other, or vice versa. Example: the time required for a car trip decreases as the speed increases and increases as the speed decreases, so the time required is inversely proportional to the speed of the car.

> **Review Video: Proportions**
> Visit mometrix.com/academy and enter code: 505355

RATIOS

A **ratio** is a comparison of two quantities in a particular order. Example: If there are 14 computers in a lab, and the class has 20 students, there is a student to computer ratio of 20 to 14, commonly written as 20: 14. Ratios are normally reduced to their smallest whole number representation, so 20: 14 would be reduced to 10: 7 by dividing both sides by 2.

> **Review Video: Ratios**
> Visit mometrix.com/academy and enter code: 996914

CONSTANT OF PROPORTIONALITY

When two quantities have a proportional relationship, there exists a **constant of proportionality** between the quantities. The product of this constant and one of the quantities is equal to the other quantity. For example, if one lemon costs $0.25, two lemons cost $0.50, and three lemons cost $0.75, there is a proportional relationship between the total cost of lemons and the number of lemons purchased. The constant of proportionality is the **unit price**, namely $0.25/lemon. Notice that the total price of lemons, t, can be found by multiplying the unit price of lemons, p, and the number of lemons, n: $t = pn$.

WORK/UNIT RATE

Unit rate expresses a quantity of one thing in terms of one unit of another. For example, if you travel 30 miles every two hours, a unit rate expresses this comparison in terms of one hour: in one hour you travel 15 miles, so your unit rate is 15 miles per hour. Other examples are how much one ounce of food costs (price per ounce) or figuring out how much one egg costs out of the dozen (price per 1 egg, instead of price per 12 eggs). The denominator of a unit rate is always 1. Unit rates are used to compare different situations to solve problems. For example, to make sure you get the best deal when deciding which kind of soda to buy, you can find the unit rate of each. If soda #1 costs $1.50 for a 1-liter bottle, and soda #2 costs $2.75 for a 2-liter bottle, it would be a better deal to buy soda #2, because its unit rate is only $1.375 per 1-liter, which is cheaper than soda #1. Unit rates can also help determine the length of time a given event will take. For example, if you can

Copyright © Mometrix Media. You have been licensed one copy of this document for personal use only. Any other reproduction or redistribution is strictly prohibited. All rights reserved.
This content is provided for test preparation purposes only and does not imply an endorsement by Mometrix of any particular political, scientific, or religious point of view.

paint 2 rooms in 4.5 hours, you can determine how long it will take you to paint 5 rooms by solving for the unit rate per room and then multiplying that by 5.

Review Video: Rates and Unit Rates
Visit mometrix.com/academy and enter code: 185363

TERMS AND COEFFICIENTS

Mathematical expressions consist of a combination of one or more values arranged in terms that are added together. As such, an expression could be just a single number, including zero. A **variable term** is the product of a real number, also called a **coefficient**, and one or more variables, each of which may be raised to an exponent. Expressions may also include numbers without a variable, called **constants** or **constant terms**. The expression $6s^2$, for example, is a single term where the coefficient is the real number 6 and the variable term is s^2. Note that if a term is written as simply a variable to some exponent, like t^2, then the coefficient is 1, because $t^2 = 1t^2$.

LINEAR EXPRESSIONS

A **single variable linear expression** is the sum of a single variable term, where the variable has no exponent, and a constant, which may be zero. For instance, the expression $2w + 7$ has $2w$ as the variable term and 7 as the constant term. It is important to realize that terms are separated by addition or subtraction. Since an expression is a sum of terms, expressions such as $5x - 3$ can be written as $5x + (-3)$ to emphasize that the constant term is negative. A real-world example of a single variable linear expression is the perimeter of a square, four times the side length, often expressed: $4s$.

In general, a **linear expression** is the sum of any number of variable terms so long as none of the variables have an exponent. For example, $3m + 8n - \frac{1}{4}p + 5.5q - 1$ is a linear expression, but $3y^3$ is not. In the same way, the expression for the perimeter of a general triangle, the sum of the side lengths $(a + b + c)$ is considered to be linear, but the expression for the area of a square, the side length squared (s^2) is not.

SLOPE

On a graph with two points, (x_1, y_1) and (x_2, y_2), the **slope** is found with the formula $m = \frac{y_2 - y_1}{x_2 - x_1}$; where $x_1 \neq x_2$ and m stands for slope. If the value of the slope is **positive**, the line has an *upward direction* from left to right. If the value of the slope is **negative**, the line has a *downward direction* from left to right. Consider the following example:

A new book goes on sale in bookstores and online stores. In the first month, 5,000 copies of the book are sold. Over time, the book continues to grow in popularity. The data for the number of copies sold is in the table below.

# of Months on Sale	1	2	3	4	5
# of Copies Sold (In Thousands)	5	10	15	20	25

So, the number of copies that are sold and the time that the book is on sale is a proportional relationship. In this example, an equation can be used to show the data: $y = 5x$, where x is the

Copyright © Mometrix Media. You have been licensed one copy of this document for personal use only. Any other reproduction or redistribution is strictly prohibited. All rights reserved.
This content is provided for test preparation purposes only and does not imply an endorsement by Mometrix of any particular political, scientific, or religious point of view.

number of months that the book is on sale. Also, y is the number of copies sold. So, the slope of the corresponding line is $\frac{\text{rise}}{\text{run}} = \frac{5}{1} = 5$.

Review Video: <u>Finding the Slope of a Line</u>
Visit mometrix.com/academy and enter code: 766664

LINEAR EQUATIONS

Equations that can be written as $ax + b = 0$, where $a \neq 0$, are referred to as **one variable linear equations**. A solution to such an equation is called a **root**. In the case where we have the equation $5x + 10 = 0$, if we solve for x we get a solution of $x = -2$. In other words, the root of the equation is –2. This is found by first subtracting 10 from both sides, which gives $5x = -10$. Next, simply divide both sides by the coefficient of the variable, in this case 5, to get $x = -2$. This can be checked by plugging –2 back into the original equation $(5)(-2) + 10 = -10 + 10 = 0$.

The **solution set** is the set of all solutions of an equation. In our example, the solution set would simply be –2. If there were more solutions (there usually are in multivariable equations) then they would also be included in the solution set. When an equation has no true solutions, it is referred to as an **empty set**. Equations with identical solution sets are **equivalent equations**. An **identity** is a term whose value or determinant is equal to 1.

Linear equations can be written many ways. Below is a list of some forms linear equations can take:

- **Standard Form**: $Ax + By = C$; the slope is $\frac{-A}{B}$ and the y-intercept is $\frac{C}{B}$
- **Slope Intercept Form**: $y = mx + b$, where m is the slope and b is the y-intercept
- **Point-Slope Form**: $y - y_1 = m(x - x_1)$, where m is the slope and (x_1, y_1) is a point on the line
- **Two-Point Form**: $\frac{y - y_1}{x - x_1} = \frac{y_2 - y_1}{x_2 - x_1}$, where (x_1, y_1) and (x_2, y_2) are two points on the given line
- **Intercept Form**: $\frac{x}{x_1} + \frac{y}{y_1} = 1$, where $(x_1, 0)$ is the point at which a line intersects the x-axis, and $(0, y_1)$ is the point at which the same line intersects the y-axis

Review Video: <u>Slope-Intercept and Point-Slope Forms</u>
Visit mometrix.com/academy and enter code: 113216

Review Video: <u>Linear Equations Basics</u>
Visit mometrix.com/academy and enter code: 793005

SOLVING ONE-VARIABLE LINEAR EQUATIONS

Multiply all terms by the lowest common denominator to eliminate any fractions. Look for addition or subtraction to undo so you can isolate the variable on one side of the equal sign. Divide both

Copyright © Mometrix Media. You have been licensed one copy of this document for personal use only. Any other reproduction or redistribution is strictly prohibited. All rights reserved.
This content is provided for test preparation purposes only and does not imply an endorsement by Mometrix of any particular political, scientific, or religious point of view.

sides by the coefficient of the variable. When you have a value for the variable, substitute this value into the original equation to make sure you have a true equation. Consider the following example:

Kim's savings are represented by the table below. Represent her savings, using an equation.

X (Months)	Y (Total Savings)
2	$1,300
5	$2,050
9	$3,050
11	$3,550
16	$4,800

The table shows a function with a constant rate of change, or slope, of 250. Given the points on the table, the slopes can be calculated as $\frac{(2,050-1300)}{(5-2)}$, $\frac{(3,050-2,050)}{(9-5)}$, $\frac{(3,550-3,050)}{(11-9)}$, and $\frac{(4,800-3,550)}{(16-11)}$, each of which equals 250. Thus, the table shows a constant rate of change, indicating a linear function. The slope-intercept form of a linear equation is written as $y = mx + b$, where m represents the slope and b represents the y-intercept. Substituting the slope into this form gives $y = 250x + b$. Substituting corresponding x- and y-values from any point into this equation will give the y-intercept, or b. Using the point, (2, 1,300), gives $1,300 = 250(2) + b$, which simplifies as $b = 800$. Thus, her savings may be represented by the equation, $y = 250x + 800$.

RULES FOR MANIPULATING EQUATIONS
LIKE TERMS

Like terms are terms in an equation that have the same variable, regardless of whether or not they also have the same coefficient. This includes terms that *lack* a variable; all constants (i.e., numbers without variables) are considered like terms. If the equation involves terms with a variable raised to different powers, the like terms are those that have the variable raised to the same power.

For example, consider the equation $x^2 + 3x + 2 = 2x^2 + x - 7 + 2x$. In this equation, 2 and –7 are like terms; they are both constants. $3x$, x, and $2x$ are like terms, they all include the variable x raised to the first power. x^2 and $2x^2$ are like terms, they both include the variable x, raised to the second power. $2x$ and $2x^2$ are not like terms; although they both involve the variable x, the variable is not raised to the same power in both terms. The fact that they have the same coefficient, 2, is not relevant.

> **Review Video: Rules for Manipulating Equations**
> Visit mometrix.com/academy and enter code: 838871

CARRYING OUT THE SAME OPERATION ON BOTH SIDES OF AN EQUATION

When solving an equation, the general procedure is to carry out a series of operations on both sides of an equation, choosing operations that will tend to simplify the equation when doing so. The reason why the same operation must be carried out on both sides of the equation is because that leaves the meaning of the equation unchanged, and yields a result that is equivalent to the original equation. This would not be the case if we carried out an operation on one side of an equation and not the other. Consider what an equation means: it is a statement that two values or expressions are equal. If we carry out the same operation on both sides of the equation—add 3 to both sides, for example—then the two sides of the equation are changed in the same way, and so remain equal. If

Copyright © Mometrix Media. You have been licensed one copy of this document for personal use only. Any other reproduction or redistribution is strictly prohibited. All rights reserved.
This content is provided for test preparation purposes only and does not imply an endorsement by Mometrix of any particular political, scientific, or religious point of view.

we do that to only one side of the equation—add 3 to one side but not the other—then that wouldn't be true; if we change one side of the equation but not the other then the two sides are no longer equal.

ADVANTAGE OF COMBINING LIKE TERMS

Combining like terms refers to adding or subtracting like terms—terms with the same variable—and therefore reducing sets of like terms to a single term. The main advantage of doing this is that it simplifies the equation. Often, combining like terms can be done as the first step in solving an equation, though it can also be done later, such as after distributing terms in a product.

For example, consider the equation $2(x + 3) + 3(2 + x + 3) = -4$. The 2 and the 3 in the second set of parentheses are like terms, and we can combine them, yielding $2(x + 3) + 3(x + 5) = -4$. Now we can carry out the multiplications implied by the parentheses, distributing the outer 2 and 3 accordingly: $2x + 6 + 3x + 15 = -4$. The $2x$ and the $3x$ are like terms, and we can add them together: $5x + 6 + 15 = -4$. Now, the constants 6, 15, and –4 are also like terms, and we can combine them as well: subtracting 6 and 15 from both sides of the equation, we get $5x = -4 - 6 - 15$, or $5x = -25$, which simplifies further to $x = -5$.

> **Review Video: Solving Equations by Combining Like Terms**
> Visit mometrix.com/academy and enter code: 668506

CANCELING TERMS ON OPPOSITE SIDES OF AN EQUATION

Two terms on opposite sides of an equation can be canceled if and only if they *exactly* match each other. They must have the same variable raised to the same power and the same coefficient. For example, in the equation $3x + 2x^2 + 6 = 2x^2 - 6$, $2x^2$ appears on both sides of the equation and can be canceled, leaving $3x + 6 = -6$. The 6 on each side of the equation *cannot* be canceled, because it is added on one side of the equation and subtracted on the other. While they cannot be canceled, however, the 6 and –6 are like terms and can be combined, yielding $3x = -12$, which simplifies further to $x = -4$.

It's also important to note that the terms to be canceled must be independent terms and cannot be part of a larger term. For example, consider the equation $2(x + 6) = 3(x + 4) + 1$. We cannot cancel the x's, because even though they match each other they are part of the larger terms $2(x + 6)$ and $3(x + 4)$. We must first distribute the 2 and 3, yielding $2x + 12 = 3x + 12 + 1$. Now we see that the terms with the x's do not match, but the 12s do, and can be canceled, leaving $2x = 3x + 1$, which simplifies to $x = -1$.

PROCESS FOR MANIPULATING EQUATIONS
ISOLATING VARIABLES

To **isolate a variable** means to manipulate the equation so that the variable appears by itself on one side of the equation, and does not appear at all on the other side. Generally, an equation or inequality is considered to be solved once the variable is isolated and the other side of the equation or inequality is simplified as much as possible. In the case of a two-variable equation or inequality, only one variable needs to be isolated; it will not usually be possible to simultaneously isolate both variables.

For a linear equation—an equation in which the variable only appears raised to the first power—isolating a variable can be done by first moving all the terms with the variable to one side of the equation and all other terms to the other side. (*Moving* a term really means adding the inverse of the term to both sides; when a term is *moved* to the other side of the equation its sign is flipped.)

Copyright © Mometrix Media. You have been licensed one copy of this document for personal use only. Any other reproduction or redistribution is strictly prohibited. All rights reserved. This content is provided for test preparation purposes only and does not imply an endorsement by Mometrix of any particular political, scientific, or religious point of view.

Then combine like terms on each side. Finally, divide both sides by the coefficient of the variable, if applicable. The steps need not necessarily be done in this order, but this order will always work.

> **Review Video: Solving One-Step Equations**
> Visit mometrix.com/academy and enter code: 777004

EQUATIONS WITH MORE THAN ONE SOLUTION

Some types of non-linear equations, such as equations involving squares of variables, may have more than one solution. For example, the equation $x^2 = 4$ has two solutions: 2 and –2. Equations with absolute values can also have multiple solutions: $|x| = 1$ has the solutions $x = 1$ and $x = -1$.

It is also possible for a linear equation to have more than one solution, but only if the equation is true regardless of the value of the variable. In this case, the equation is considered to have infinitely many solutions, because any possible value of the variable is a solution. We know a linear equation has infinitely many solutions if when we combine like terms the variables cancel, leaving a true statement. For example, consider the equation $2(3x + 5) = x + 5(x + 2)$. Distributing, we get $6x + 10 = x + 5x + 10$; combining like terms gives $6x + 10 = 6x + 10$, and the $6x$-terms cancel to leave $10 = 10$. This is clearly true, so the original equation is true for any value of x. We could also have canceled the 10s leaving $0 = 0$, but again this is clearly true—in general if both sides of the equation match exactly, it has infinitely many solutions.

EQUATIONS WITH NO SOLUTION

Some types of non-linear equations, such as equations involving squares of variables, may have no solution. For example, the equation $x^2 = -2$ has no solutions in the real numbers, because the square of any real number must be positive. Similarly, $|x| = -1$ has no solution, because the absolute value of a number is always positive.

It is also possible for an equation to have no solution even if does not involve any powers greater than one, absolute values, or other special functions. For example, the equation $2(x + 3) + x = 3x$ has no solution. We can see that if we try to solve it: first we distribute, leaving $2x + 6 + x = 3x$. But now if we try to combine all the terms with the variable, we find that they cancel: we have $3x$ on the left and $3x$ on the right, canceling to leave us with $6 = 0$. This is clearly false. In general, whenever the variable terms in an equation cancel leaving different constants on both sides, it means that the equation has no solution. (If we are left with the *same* constant on both sides, the equation has infinitely many solutions instead.)

FEATURES OF EQUATIONS THAT REQUIRE SPECIAL TREATMENT
LINEAR EQUATIONS

A linear equation is an equation in which variables only appear by themselves: not multiplied together, not with exponents other than one, and not inside absolute value signs or any other functions. For example, the equation $x + 1 - 3x = 5 - x$ is a linear equation; while x appears multiple times, it never appears with an exponent other than one, or inside any function. The two-variable equation $2x - 3y = 5 + 2x$ is also a linear equation. In contrast, the equation $x^2 - 5 = 3x$ is *not* a linear equation, because it involves the term x^2. $\sqrt{x} = 5$ is not a linear equation, because it involves a square root. $(x - 1)^2 = 4$ is not a linear equation because even though there's no exponent on the x directly, it appears as part of an expression that is squared. The two-variable equation $x + xy - y = 5$ is not a linear equation because it includes the term xy, where two variables are multiplied together.

185

Copyright © Mometrix Media. You have been licensed one copy of this document for personal use only. Any other reproduction or redistribution is strictly prohibited. All rights reserved. This content is provided for test preparation purposes only and does not imply an endorsement by Mometrix of any particular political, scientific, or religious point of view.

Linear equations can always be solved (or shown to have no solution) by combining like terms and performing simple operations on both sides of the equation. Some non-linear equations can be solved by similar methods, but others may require more advanced methods of solution, if they can be solved analytically at all.

SOLVING EQUATIONS INVOLVING ROOTS

In an equation involving roots, the first step is to isolate the term with the root, if possible, and then raise both sides of the equation to the appropriate power to eliminate it. Consider an example equation, $2\sqrt{x+1} - 1 = 3$. In this case, begin by adding 1 to both sides, yielding $2\sqrt{x+1} = 4$, and then dividing both sides by 2, yielding $\sqrt{x+1} = 2$. Now square both sides, yielding $x + 1 = 4$. Finally, subtracting 1 from both sides yields $x = 3$.

Squaring both sides of an equation may, however, yield a spurious solution—a solution to the squared equation that is *not* a solution of the original equation. It's therefore necessary to plug the solution back into the original equation to make sure it works. In this case, it does: $2\sqrt{3+1} - 1 = 2\sqrt{4} - 1 = 2(2) - 1 = 4 - 1 = 3$.

The same procedure applies for other roots as well. For example, given the equation $3 + \sqrt[3]{2x} = 5$, we can first subtract 3 from both sides, yielding $\sqrt[3]{2x} = 2$ and isolating the root. Raising both sides to the third power yields $2x = 2^3$; i.e., $2x = 8$. We can now divide both sides by 2 to get $x = 4$.

> **Review Video: Solving Equations Involving Roots**
> Visit mometrix.com/academy and enter code: 297670

SOLVING EQUATIONS WITH EXPONENTS

To solve an equation involving an exponent, the first step is to isolate the variable with the exponent. We can then take the appropriate root of both sides to eliminate the exponent. For instance, for the equation $2x^3 + 17 = 5x^3 - 7$, we can subtract $5x^3$ from both sides to get $-3x^3 + 17 = -7$, and then subtract 17 from both sides to get $-3x^3 = -24$. Finally, we can divide both sides by –3 to get $x^3 = 8$. Finally, we can take the cube root of both sides to get $x = \sqrt[3]{8} = 2$.

One important but often overlooked point is that equations with an exponent greater than 1 may have more than one answer. The solution to $x^2 = 9$ isn't simply $x = 3$; it's $x = \pm 3$ (that is, $x = 3$ or $x = -3$). For a slightly more complicated example, consider the equation $(x-1)^2 - 1 = 3$. Adding 1 to both sides yields $(x-1)^2 = 4$; taking the square root of both sides yields $x - 1 = 2$. We can then add 1 to both sides to get $x = 3$. However, there's a second solution. We also have the possibility that $x - 1 = -2$, in which case $x = -1$. Both $x = 3$ and $x = -1$ are valid solutions, as can be verified by substituting them both into the original equation.

> **Review Video: Solving Equations with Exponents**
> Visit mometrix.com/academy and enter code: 514557

SOLVING EQUATIONS WITH ABSOLUTE VALUES

When solving an equation with an absolute value, the first step is to isolate the absolute value term. We then consider two possibilities: when the expression inside the absolute value is positive or when it is negative. In the former case, the expression in the absolute value equals the expression on the other side of the equation; in the latter, it equals the additive inverse of that expression—the expression times negative one. We consider each case separately and finally check for spurious solutions.

Copyright © Mometrix Media. You have been licensed one copy of this document for personal use only. Any other reproduction or redistribution is strictly prohibited. All rights reserved.
This content is provided for test preparation purposes only and does not imply an endorsement by Mometrix of any particular political, scientific, or religious point of view.

For instance, consider solving $|2x - 1| + x = 5$ for x. We can first isolate the absolute value by moving the x to the other side: $|2x - 1| = -x + 5$. Now, we have two possibilities. First, that $2x - 1$ is positive, and hence $2x - 1 = -x + 5$. Rearranging and combining like terms yields $3x = 6$, and hence $x = 2$. The other possibility is that $2x - 1$ is negative, and hence $2x - 1 = -(-x + 5) = x - 5$. In this case, rearranging and combining like terms yields $x = -4$. Substituting $x = 2$ and $x = -4$ back into the original equation, we see that they are both valid solutions.

Note that the absolute value of a sum or difference applies to the sum or difference as a whole, not to the individual terms; in general, $|2x - 1|$ is not equal to $|2x + 1|$ or to $|2x| - 1$.

SPURIOUS SOLUTIONS

A **spurious solution** may arise when we square both sides of an equation as a step in solving it or under certain other operations on the equation. It is a solution to the squared or otherwise modified equation that is *not* a solution of the original equation. To identify a spurious solution, it's useful when you solve an equation involving roots or absolute values to plug the solution back into the original equation to make sure it's valid.

CHOOSING WHICH VARIABLE TO ISOLATE IN TWO-VARIABLE EQUATIONS

Similar to methods for a one-variable equation, solving a two-variable equation involves isolating a variable: manipulating the equation so that a variable appears by itself on one side of the equation, and not at all on the other side. However, in a two-variable equation, you will usually only be able to isolate one of the variables; the other variable may appear on the other side along with constant terms, or with exponents or other functions.

Often one variable will be much more easily isolated than the other, and therefore that's the variable you should choose. If one variable appears with various exponents, and the other is only raised to the first power, the latter variable is the one to isolate: given the equation $a^2 + 2b = a^3 + b + 3$, the b only appears to the first power, whereas a appears squared and cubed, so b is the variable that can be solved for: combining like terms and isolating the b on the left side of the equation, we get $b = a^3 - a^2 + 3$. If both variables are equally easy to isolate, then it's best to isolate the independent variable, if one is defined; if the two variables are x and y, the convention is that y is the independent variable.

FINDING AN UNKNOWN IN EQUIVALENT EXPRESSIONS

It is often necessary to apply information given about a rate or proportion to a new scenario. For example, if you know that Jedha can run a marathon (26.2 miles) in 3 hours, how long would it take her to run 10 miles at the same pace? Start by setting up equivalent expressions:

$$\frac{26.2 \text{ mi}}{3 \text{ hr}} = \frac{10 \text{ mi}}{x \text{ hr}}$$

Now, cross multiply and solve for x:

$$26.2x = 30$$
$$x = \frac{30}{26.2} = \frac{15}{13.1}$$
$$x \approx 1.15 \text{ hrs } or \text{ 1 hr 9 min}$$

Copyright © Mometrix Media. You have been licensed one copy of this document for personal use only. Any other reproduction or redistribution is strictly prohibited. All rights reserved. This content is provided for test preparation purposes only and does not imply an endorsement by Mometrix of any particular political, scientific, or religious point of view.

So, at this pace, Jedha could run 10 miles in about 1.15 hours or about 1 hour and 9 minutes.

Review Video: Cross Multiply Fractions
Visit mometrix.com/academy and enter code: 893904

GRAPHICAL SOLUTIONS TO EQUATIONS AND INEQUALITIES

When equations are shown graphically, they are usually shown on a **Cartesian coordinate plane**. The Cartesian coordinate plane consists of two number lines placed perpendicular to each other and intersecting at the zero point, also known as the origin. The horizontal number line is known as the x-axis, with positive values to the right of the origin, and negative values to the left of the origin. The vertical number line is known as the y-axis, with positive values above the origin, and negative values below the origin. Any point on the plane can be identified by an ordered pair in the form (x, y), called coordinates. The x-value of the coordinate is called the abscissa, and the y-value of the coordinate is called the ordinate. The two number lines divide the plane into **four quadrants**: I, II, III, and IV.

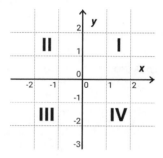

Note that in quadrant I $x > 0$ and $y > 0$, in quadrant II $x < 0$ and $y > 0$, in quadrant III $x < 0$ and $y < 0$, and in quadrant IV $x > 0$ and $y < 0$.

Recall that if the value of the slope of a line is positive, the line slopes upward from left to right. If the value of the slope is negative, the line slopes downward from left to right. If the y-coordinates are the same for two points on a line, the slope is 0 and the line is a **horizontal line**. If the x-coordinates are the same for two points on a line, there is no slope and the line is a **vertical line**. Two or more lines that have equivalent slopes are **parallel lines**. **Perpendicular lines** have slopes that are negative reciprocals of each other, such as $\frac{a}{b}$ and $\frac{-b}{a}$.

Review Video: Cartesian Coordinate Plane and Graphing
Visit mometrix.com/academy and enter code: 115173

GRAPHING EQUATIONS IN TWO VARIABLES

One way of graphing an equation in two variables is to plot enough points to get an idea for its shape and then draw the appropriate curve through those points. A point can be plotted by substituting in a value for one variable and solving for the other. If the equation is linear, we only need two points and can then draw a straight line between them.

For example, consider the equation $y = 2x - 1$. This is a linear equation—both variables only appear raised to the first power—so we only need two points. When $x = 0$, $y = 2(0) - 1 = -1$.

Copyright © Mometrix Media. You have been licensed one copy of this document for personal use only. Any other reproduction or redistribution is strictly prohibited. All rights reserved. This content is provided for test preparation purposes only and does not imply an endorsement by Mometrix of any particular political, scientific, or religious point of view.

When $x = 2, y = 2(2) - 1 = 3$. We can therefore choose the points $(0, -1)$ and $(2, 3)$, and draw a line between them:

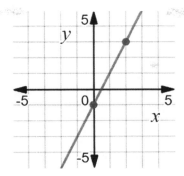

WORKING WITH INEQUALITIES

Commonly in algebra and other upper-level fields of math you find yourself working with mathematical expressions that do not equal each other. The statement comparing such expressions with symbols such as $<$ (less than) or $>$ (greater than) is called an *inequality*. An example of an inequality is $7x > 5$. To solve for x, simply divide both sides by 7 and the solution is shown to be $x > \frac{5}{7}$. Graphs of the solution set of inequalities are represented on a number line. Open circles are used to show that an expression approaches a number but is never quite equal to that number.

> **Review Video: Solving Multi-Step Inequalities**
> Visit mometrix.com/academy and enter code: 347842
>
> **Review Video: Solving Inequalities Using All 4 Basic Operations**
> Visit mometrix.com/academy and enter code: 401111

Conditional inequalities are those with certain values for the variable that will make the condition true and other values for the variable where the condition will be false. **Absolute inequalities** can have any real number as the value for the variable to make the condition true, while there is no real number value for the variable that will make the condition false. Solving inequalities is done by following the same rules for solving equations with the exception that when multiplying or dividing by a negative number the direction of the inequality sign must be flipped or reversed. **Double inequalities** are situations where two inequality statements apply to the same variable expression. Example: $-c < ax + b < c$.

> **Review Video: Conditional and Absolute Inequalities**
> Visit mometrix.com/academy and enter code: 980164

DETERMINING SOLUTIONS TO INEQUALITIES

To determine whether a coordinate is a solution of an inequality, you can substitute the values of the coordinate into the inequality, simplify, and check whether the resulting statement holds true. For instance, to determine whether $(-2,4)$ is a solution of the inequality $y \geq -2x + 3$, substitute the values into the inequality, $4 \geq -2(-2) + 3$. Simplify the right side of the inequality and the result is $4 \geq 7$, which is a false statement. Therefore, the coordinate is not a solution of the inequality. You can also use this method to determine which part of the graph of an inequality is

Copyright © Mometrix Media. You have been licensed one copy of this document for personal use only. Any other reproduction or redistribution is strictly prohibited. All rights reserved. This content is provided for test preparation purposes only and does not imply an endorsement by Mometrix of any particular political, scientific, or religious point of view.

shaded. The graph of $y \geq -2x + 3$ includes the solid line $y = -2x + 3$ and, since it excludes the point $(-2,4)$ to the left of the line, it is shaded to the right of the line.

Review Video: Graphing Linear Inequalities
Visit mometrix.com/academy and enter code: 439421

FLIPPING INEQUALITY SIGNS

When given an inequality, we can always turn the entire inequality around, swapping the two sides of the inequality and changing the inequality sign. For instance, $x + 2 > 2x - 3$ is equivalent to $2x - 3 < x + 2$. Aside from that, normally the inequality does not change if we carry out the same operation on both sides of the inequality. There is, however, one principal exception: if we *multiply* or *divide* both sides of the inequality by a *negative number*, the inequality is flipped. For example, if we take the inequality $-2x < 6$ and divide both sides by –2, the inequality flips and we are left with $x > -3$. This *only* applies to multiplication and division, and only with negative numbers. Multiplying or dividing both sides by a positive number, or adding or subtracting any number regardless of sign, does not flip the inequality. Another special case that flips the inequality sign is when reciprocals are used. For instance, $3 > 2$ but the relation of the reciprocals is $\frac{1}{2} < \frac{1}{3}$.

COMPOUND INEQUALITIES

A **compound inequality** is an equality that consists of two inequalities combined with *and* or *or*. The two components of a proper compound inequality must be of opposite type: that is, one must be greater than (or greater than or equal to), the other less than (or less than or equal to). For instance, "$x + 1 < 2$ or $x + 1 > 3$" is a compound inequality, as is "$2x \geq 4$ and $2x \leq 6$." An *and* inequality can be written more compactly by having one inequality on each side of the common part: "$2x \geq 1$ and $2x \leq 6$," can also be written as $1 \leq 2x \leq 6$.

In order for the compound inequality to be meaningful, the two parts of an *and* inequality must overlap; otherwise, no numbers satisfy the inequality. On the other hand, if the two parts of an *or* inequality overlap, then *all* numbers satisfy the inequality and as such the inequality is usually not meaningful.

Solving a compound inequality requires solving each part separately. For example, given the compound inequality "$x + 1 < 2$ or $x + 1 > 3$," the first inequality, $x + 1 < 2$, reduces to $x < 1$, and the second part, $x + 1 > 3$, reduces to $x > 2$, so the whole compound inequality can be written as "$x < 1$ or $x > 2$." Similarly, $1 \leq 2x \leq 6$ can be solved by dividing each term by 2, yielding $\frac{1}{2} \leq x \leq 3$.

Review Video: Compound Inequalities
Visit mometrix.com/academy and enter code: 786318

SOLVING INEQUALITIES INVOLVING ABSOLUTE VALUES

To solve an inequality involving an absolute value, first isolate the term with the absolute value. Then proceed to treat the two cases separately as with an absolute value equation, but flipping the inequality in the case where the expression in the absolute value is negative (since that essentially involves multiplying both sides by –1.) The two cases are then combined into a compound inequality; if the absolute value is on the greater side of the inequality, then it is an *or* compound inequality, if on the lesser side, then it's an *and*.

Consider the inequality $2 + |x - 1| \geq 3$. We can isolate the absolute value term by subtracting 2 from both sides: $|x - 1| \geq 1$. Now, we're left with the two cases $x - 1 \geq 1$ or $x - 1 \leq -1$: note that in the latter, negative case, the inequality is flipped. $x - 1 \geq 1$ reduces to $x \geq 2$, and $x - 1 \leq -1$

Copyright © Mometrix Media. You have been licensed one copy of this document for personal use only. Any other reproduction or redistribution is strictly prohibited. All rights reserved.
This content is provided for test preparation purposes only and does not imply an endorsement by Mometrix of any particular political, scientific, or religious point of view.

reduces to $x \leq 0$. Since in the inequality $|x - 1| \geq 1$ the absolute value is on the greater side, the two cases combine into an *or* compound inequality, so the final, solved inequality is "$x \leq 0$ or $x \geq 2$."

> **Review Video: <u>Solving Absolute Value Inequalities</u>**
> Visit mometrix.com/academy and enter code: 997008

SOLVING INEQUALITIES INVOLVING SQUARE ROOTS

Solving an inequality with a square root involves two parts. First, we solve the inequality as if it were an equation, isolating the square root and then squaring both sides of the equation. Second, we restrict the solution to the set of values of x for which the value inside the square root sign is non-negative.

For example, in the inequality, $\sqrt{x - 2} + 1 < 5$, we can isolate the square root by subtracting 1 from both sides, yielding $\sqrt{x - 2} < 4$. Squaring both sides of the inequality yields $x - 2 < 16$, so $x < 18$. Since we can't take the square root of a negative number, we also require the part inside the square root to be non-negative. In this case, that means $x - 2 \geq 0$. Adding 2 to both sides of the inequality yields $x \geq 2$. Our final answer is a compound inequality combining the two simple inequalities: $x \geq 2$ and $x < 18$, or $2 \leq x < 18$.

Note that we only get a compound inequality if the two simple inequalities are in opposite directions; otherwise, we take the one that is more restrictive.

The same technique can be used for other even roots, such as fourth roots. It is *not*, however, used for cube roots or other odd roots—negative numbers *do* have cube roots, so the condition that the quantity inside the root sign cannot be negative does not apply.

> **Review Video: <u>Solving Inequalities Involving Square Roots</u>**
> Visit mometrix.com/academy and enter code: 800288

SPECIAL CIRCUMSTANCES

Sometimes an inequality involving an absolute value or an even exponent is true for all values of x, and we don't need to do any further work to solve it. This is true if the inequality, once the absolute value or exponent term is isolated, says that term is greater than a negative number (or greater than or equal to zero). Since an absolute value or a number raised to an even exponent is *always* non-negative, this inequality is always true.

GRAPHICAL SOLUTIONS TO INEQUALITIES

GRAPHING SIMPLE INEQUALITIES

To graph a simple inequality, we first mark on the number line the value that signifies the end point of the inequality. If the inequality is strict (involves a less than or greater than), we use a hollow circle; if it is not strict (less than or equal to or greater than or equal to), we use a solid circle. We then fill in the part of the number line that satisfies the inequality: to the left of the marked point for less than (or less than or equal to), to the right for greater than (or greater than or equal to).

For example, we would graph the inequality $x < 5$ by putting a hollow circle at 5 and filling in the part of the line to the left:

Copyright © Mometrix Media. You have been licensed one copy of this document for personal use only. Any other reproduction or redistribution is strictly prohibited. All rights reserved. This content is provided for test preparation purposes only and does not imply an endorsement by Mometrix of any particular political, scientific, or religious point of view.

GRAPHING COMPOUND INEQUALITIES

To graph a compound inequality, we fill in both parts of the inequality for an *or* inequality, or the overlap between them for an *and* inequality. More specifically, we start by plotting the endpoints of each inequality on the number line. For an *or* inequality, we then fill in the appropriate side of the line for each inequality. Typically, the two component inequalities do not overlap, which means the shaded part is *outside* the two points. For an *and* inequality, we instead fill in the part of the line that meets both inequalities.

For the inequality "$x \leq -3$ or $x > 4$," we first put a solid circle at –3 and a hollow circle at 4. We then fill the parts of the line *outside* these circles:

GRAPHING INEQUALITIES INCLUDING ABSOLUTE VALUES

An inequality with an absolute value can be converted to a compound inequality. To graph the inequality, first convert it to a compound inequality, and then graph that normally. If the absolute value is on the greater side of the inequality, we end up with an *or* inequality; we plot the endpoints of the inequality on the number line and fill in the part of the line *outside* those points. If the absolute value is on the smaller side of the inequality, we end up with an *and* inequality; we plot the endpoints of the inequality on the number line and fill in the part of the line *between* those points.

For example, the inequality $|x + 1| \geq 4$ can be rewritten as $x \geq 3$ or $x \leq -5$. We place solid circles at the points 3 and –5 and fill in the part of the line *outside* them:

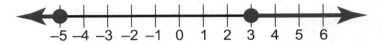

GRAPHING INEQUALITIES IN TWO VARIABLES

To graph an inequality in two variables, we first graph the border of the inequality. This means graphing the equation that we get if we replace the inequality sign with an equals sign. If the inequality is strict (> or <), we graph the border with a dashed or dotted line; if it is not strict ($\geq$ or $\leq$), we use a solid line. We can then test any point not on the border to see if it satisfies the inequality. If it does, we shade in that side of the border; if not, we shade in the other side. As an example, consider $y > 2x + 2$. To graph this inequality, we first graph the border, $y = 2x + 2$. Since it is a strict inequality, we use a dashed line. Then, we choose a test point. This can be any point not on the border; in this case, we will choose the origin, (0,0). (This makes the calculation easy and is generally a good choice unless the border passes through the origin.) Putting this into the original

Copyright © Mometrix Media. You have been licensed one copy of this document for personal use only. Any other reproduction or redistribution is strictly prohibited. All rights reserved.
This content is provided for test preparation purposes only and does not imply an endorsement by Mometrix of any particular political, scientific, or religious point of view.

inequality, we get $0 > 2(0) + 2$, i.e., $0 > 2$. This is *not* true, so we shade in the side of the border that does *not* include the point (0,0):

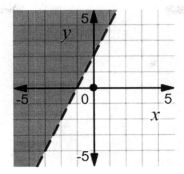

GRAPHING COMPOUND INEQUALITIES IN TWO VARIABLES

One way to graph a compound inequality in two variables is to first graph each of the component inequalities. For an *and* inequality, we then shade in only the parts where the two graphs overlap; for an *or* inequality, we shade in any region that pertains to either of the individual inequalities.

Consider the graph of "$y \geq x - 1$ and $y \leq -x$":

We first shade in the individual inequalities:

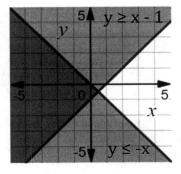

Now, since the compound inequality has an *and*, we only leave shaded the overlap—the part that pertains to *both* inequalities:

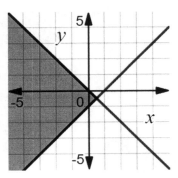

Copyright © Mometrix Media. You have been licensed one copy of this document for personal use only. Any other reproduction or redistribution is strictly prohibited. All rights reserved.
This content is provided for test preparation purposes only and does not imply an endorsement by Mometrix of any particular political, scientific, or religious point of view.

If instead the inequality had been "$y \geq x - 1$ or $y \leq -x$," our final graph would involve the *total* shaded area:

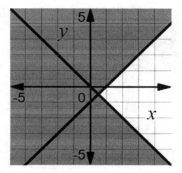

Review Video: Graphing Solutions to Inequalities
Visit mometrix.com/academy and enter code: 391281

SOLVING SYSTEMS OF EQUATIONS

A **system of equations** is a set of simultaneous equations that all use the same variables. A solution to a system of equations must be true for each equation in the system. **Consistent systems** are those with at least one solution. **Inconsistent systems** are systems of equations that have no solution.

Review Video: Solving Systems and Linear Equations
Visit mometrix.com/academy and enter code: 746745

SUBSTITUTION

To solve a system of linear equations by **substitution**, start with the easier equation and solve for one of the variables. Express this variable in terms of the other variable. Substitute this expression in the other equation and solve for the other variable. The solution should be expressed in the form (x, y). Substitute the values into both of the original equations to check your answer. Consider the following system of equations:

$$x + 6y = 15$$
$$3x - 12y = 18$$

Solving the first equation for x: $x = 15 - 6y$

Substitute this value in place of x in the second equation, and solve for y:

$$3(15 - 6y) - 12y = 18$$
$$45 - 18y - 12y = 18$$
$$30y = 27$$
$$y = \frac{27}{30} = \frac{9}{10} = 0.9$$

Copyright © Mometrix Media. You have been licensed one copy of this document for personal use only. Any other reproduction or redistribution is strictly prohibited. All rights reserved.
This content is provided for test preparation purposes only and does not imply an endorsement by Mometrix of any particular political, scientific, or religious point of view.

Plug this value for y back into the first equation to solve for x:

$$x = 15 - 6(0.9) = 15 - 5.4 = 9.6$$

Check both equations if you have time:

$$9.6 + 6(0.9) = 15 \qquad 3(9.6) - 12(0.9) = 18$$
$$9.6 + 5.4 = 15 \qquad 28.8 - 10.8 = 18$$
$$15 = 15 \qquad 18 = 18$$

Therefore, the solution is $(9.6, 0.9)$.

> **Review Video: The Substitution Method**
> Visit mometrix.com/academy and enter code: 565151

ELIMINATION

To solve a system of equations using **elimination**, begin by rewriting both equations in standard form $Ax + By = C$. Check to see if the coefficients of one pair of like variables add to zero. If not, multiply one or both of the equations by a non-zero number to make one set of like variables add to zero. Add the two equations to solve for one of the variables. Substitute this value into one of the original equations to solve for the other variable. Check your work by substituting into the other equation. Now, let's look at solving the following system using the elimination method:

$$5x + 6y = 4$$
$$x + 2y = 4$$

If we multiply the second equation by -3, we can eliminate the y-terms:

$$5x + 6y = 4$$
$$-3x - 6y = -12$$

Add the equations together and solve for x:

$$2x = -8$$
$$x = \frac{-8}{2} = -4$$

Plug the value for x back in to either of the original equations and solve for y:

$$-4 + 2y = 4$$
$$y = \frac{4 + 4}{2} = 4$$

Check both equations if you have time:

$$5(-4) + 6(4) = 4 \qquad -4 + 2(4) = 4$$
$$-20 + 24 = 4 \qquad -4 + 8 = 4$$
$$4 = 4 \qquad 4 = 4$$

Copyright © Mometrix Media. You have been licensed one copy of this document for personal use only. Any other reproduction or redistribution is strictly prohibited. All rights reserved.
This content is provided for test preparation purposes only and does not imply an endorsement by Mometrix of any particular political, scientific, or religious point of view.

Therefore, the solution is $(-4,4)$.

Review Video: The Elimination Method
Visit mometrix.com/academy and enter code: 449121

GRAPHICALLY

To solve a system of linear equations **graphically**, plot both equations on the same graph. The solution of the equations is the point where both lines cross. If the lines do not cross (are parallel), then there is **no solution**.

For example, consider the following system of equations:

$$y = 2x + 7$$
$$y = -x + 1$$

Since these equations are given in slope-intercept form, they are easy to graph; the y-intercepts of the lines are $(0,7)$ and $(0,1)$. The respective slopes are 2 and –1, thus the graphs look like this:

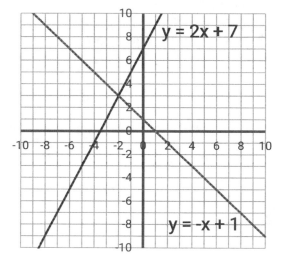

The two lines intersect at the point $(-2,3)$, thus this is the solution to the system of equations.

Solving a system graphically is generally only practical if both coordinates of the solution are integers; otherwise the intersection will lie between gridlines on the graph and the coordinates will be difficult or impossible to determine exactly. It also helps if, as in this example, the equations are in slope-intercept form or some other form that makes them easy to graph. Otherwise, another method of solution (by substitution or elimination) is likely to be more useful.

Review Video: Solving Systems by Graphing
Visit mometrix.com/academy and enter code: 634812

SOLVING SYSTEMS OF EQUATIONS USING THE TRACE FEATURE

Using the trace feature on a calculator requires that you rewrite each equation, isolating the y-variable on one side of the equal sign. Enter both equations in the graphing calculator and plot the graphs simultaneously. Use the trace cursor to find where the two lines cross. Use the zoom feature if necessary to obtain more accurate results. Always check your answer by substituting into the

Copyright © Mometrix Media. You have been licensed one copy of this document for personal use only. Any other reproduction or redistribution is strictly prohibited. All rights reserved.
This content is provided for test preparation purposes only and does not imply an endorsement by Mometrix of any particular political, scientific, or religious point of view.

original equations. The trace method is likely to be less accurate than other methods due to the resolution of graphing calculators but is a useful tool to provide an approximate answer.

SOLVING A SYSTEM OF EQUATIONS CONSISTING OF A LINEAR EQUATION AND A QUADRATIC EQUATION

ALGEBRAICALLY

Generally, the simplest way to solve a system of equations consisting of a linear equation and a quadratic equation algebraically is through the method of substitution. One possible strategy is to solve the linear equation for y and then substitute that expression into the quadratic equation. After expansion and combining like terms, this will result in a new quadratic equation for x, which, like all quadratic equations, may have zero, one, or two solutions. Plugging each solution for x back into one of the original equations will then produce the corresponding value of y.

For example, consider the following system of equations:

$$x + y = 1$$
$$y = (x + 3)^2 - 2$$

We can solve the linear equation for y to yield $y = -x + 1$. Substituting this expression into the quadratic equation produces $-x + 1 = (x + 3)^2 - 2$. We can simplify this equation:

$$-x + 1 = (x + 3)^2 - 2$$
$$-x + 1 = x^2 + 6x + 9 - 2$$
$$-x + 1 = x^2 + 6x + 7$$
$$0 = x^2 + 7x + 6$$

This quadratic equation can be factored as $(x + 1)(x + 6) = 0$. It therefore has two solutions: $x_1 = -1$ and $x_2 = -6$. Plugging each of these back into the original linear equation yields $y_1 = -x_1 + 1 = -(-1) + 1 = 2$ and $y_2 = -x_2 + 1 = -(-6) + 1 = 7$. Thus, this system of equations has two solutions, $(-1,2)$ and $(-6,7)$.

It may help to check your work by putting each x- and y-value back into the original equations and verifying that they do provide a solution.

GRAPHICALLY

To solve a system of equations consisting of a linear equation and a quadratic equation graphically, plot both equations on the same graph. The linear equation will, of course, produce a straight line, while the quadratic equation will produce a parabola. These two graphs will intersect at zero, one, or two points; each point of intersection is a solution of the system.

For example, consider the following system of equations:

$$y = -2x + 2$$
$$y = -2x^2 + 4x + 2$$

The linear equation describes a line with a y-intercept of $(0,2)$ and a slope of -2.

To graph the quadratic equation, we can first find the vertex of the parabola: the x-coordinate of the vertex is $h = -\frac{b}{2a} = -\frac{4}{2(-2)} = 1$, and the y-coordinate is $k = -2(1)^2 + 4(1) + 2 = 4$. Thus, the

Copyright © Mometrix Media. You have been licensed one copy of this document for personal use only. Any other reproduction or redistribution is strictly prohibited. All rights reserved. This content is provided for test preparation purposes only and does not imply an endorsement by Mometrix of any particular political, scientific, or religious point of view.

vertex lies at (1,4). To get a feel for the rest of the parabola, we can plug in a few more values of x to find more points; by putting in $x = 2$ and $x = 3$ in the quadratic equation, we find that the points (2,2) and (3, −4) lie on the parabola; by symmetry, so must (0, 2) and (−1, −4). We can now plot both equations:

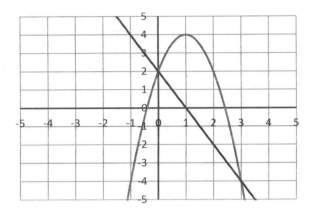

These two curves intersect at the points (0,2) and (3, −4), thus these are the solutions of the equation.

Review Video: Solving a System of Equations Consisting of a Linear Equation and Quadratic Equations
Visit mometrix.com/academy and enter code: 194870

CALCULATIONS USING POINTS

Sometimes you need to perform calculations using only points on a graph as input data. Using points, you can determine what the **midpoint** and **distance** are. If you know the equation for a line, you can calculate the distance between the line and the point.

To find the **midpoint** of two points (x_1, y_1) and (x_2, y_2), average the x-coordinates to get the x-coordinate of the midpoint, and average the y-coordinates to get the y-coordinate of the midpoint. The formula is: $\left(\frac{x_1+x_2}{2}, \frac{y_1+y_2}{2}\right)$.

The **distance** between two points is the same as the length of the hypotenuse of a right triangle with the two given points as endpoints, and the two sides of the right triangle parallel to the x-axis and y-axis, respectively. The length of the segment parallel to the x-axis is the difference between the x-coordinates of the two points. The length of the segment parallel to the y-axis is the difference between the y-coordinates of the two points. Use the Pythagorean theorem $a^2 + b^2 = c^2$ or $c = \sqrt{a^2 + b^2}$ to find the distance. The formula is $d = \sqrt{(x_2 - x_1)^2 + (y_2 - y_1)^2}$.

When a line is in the format $Ax + By + C = 0$, where A, B, and C are coefficients, you can use a point (x_1, y_1) not on the line and apply the formula $d = \frac{|Ax_1+By_1+C|}{\sqrt{A^2+B^2}}$ to find the distance between the line and the point (x_1, y_1).

Review Video: Calculations Using Points on a Graph
Visit mometrix.com/academy and enter code: 883228

Copyright © Mometrix Media. You have been licensed one copy of this document for personal use only. Any other reproduction or redistribution is strictly prohibited. All rights reserved.
This content is provided for test preparation purposes only and does not imply an endorsement by Mometrix of any particular political, scientific, or religious point of view.

MONOMIALS AND POLYNOMIALS

A **monomial** is a single constant, variable, or product of constants and variables, such as 7, x, $2x$, or x^3y. There will never be addition or subtraction symbols in a monomial. Like monomials have like variables, but they may have different coefficients. **Polynomials** are algebraic expressions that use addition and subtraction to combine two or more monomials. Two terms make a **binomial**, three terms make a **trinomial**, etc. The **degree of a monomial** is the sum of the exponents of the variables. The **degree of a polynomial** is the highest degree of any individual term.

> **Review Video: Polynomials**
> Visit mometrix.com/academy and enter code: 305005

SIMPLIFYING POLYNOMIALS

Simplifying polynomials requires combining like terms. The like terms in a polynomial expression are those that have the same variable raised to the same power. It is often helpful to connect the like terms with arrows or lines in order to separate them from the other monomials. Once you have determined the like terms, you can rearrange the polynomial by placing them together. Remember to include the sign that is in front of each term. Once the like terms are placed together, you can apply each operation and simplify. When adding and subtracting polynomials, only add and subtract the **coefficient**, or the number part; the variable and exponent stay the same.

> **Review Video: Adding and Subtracting Polynomials**
> Visit mometrix.com/academy and enter code: 124088

THE FOIL METHOD

In general, multiplying polynomials is done by multiplying each term in one polynomial by each term in the other and adding the results. In the specific case for multiplying binomials, there is a useful acronym, FOIL, that can help you make sure to cover each combination of terms. The **FOIL method** for $(Ax + By)(Cx + Dy)$ would be:

F	Multiply the *first* terms of each binomial	$(\overset{first}{\widetilde{Ax}} + By)(\overset{first}{\widetilde{Cx}} + Dy)$	ACx^2
O	Multiply the *outer* terms	$(\overset{outer}{\widetilde{Ax}} + By)(Cx + \overset{outer}{\widetilde{Dy}})$	$ADxy$
I	Multiply the *inner* terms	$(Ax + \overset{inner}{\widetilde{By}})(\overset{inner}{\widetilde{Cx}} + Dy)$	$BCxy$
L	Multiply the *last* terms of each binomial	$(Ax + \overset{last}{\widetilde{By}})(Cx + \overset{last}{\widetilde{Dy}})$	BDy^2

Then, add up the result of each and combine like terms: $ACx^2 + (AD + BC)xy + BDy^2$.

For example, using the FOIL method on binomials $(x + 2)$ and $(x - 3)$:

$$
\begin{aligned}
\text{First:} \quad & (\boxed{x} + 2)(\boxed{x} + (-3)) \quad \rightarrow \quad (x)(x) = x^2 \\
\text{Outer:} \quad & (\boxed{x} + 2)(x + \boxed{(-3)}) \quad \rightarrow \quad (x)(-3) = -3x \\
\text{Inner:} \quad & (x + \boxed{2})(\boxed{x} + (-3)) \quad \rightarrow \quad (2)(x) = 2x \\
\text{Last:} \quad & (x + \boxed{2})(x + \boxed{(-3)}) \quad \rightarrow \quad (2)(-3) = -6
\end{aligned}
$$

Copyright © Mometrix Media. You have been licensed one copy of this document for personal use only. Any other reproduction or redistribution is strictly prohibited. All rights reserved. This content is provided for test preparation purposes only and does not imply an endorsement by Mometrix of any particular political, scientific, or religious point of view.

This results in: $(x^2) + (-3x) + (2x) + (-6)$

Combine like terms: $x^2 + (-3 + 2)x + (-6) = x^2 - x - 6$

| Review Video: **Multiplying Terms Using the FOIL Method** |
| Visit mometrix.com/academy and enter code: 854792 |

DIVIDING POLYNOMIALS

Use long division to divide a polynomial by either a monomial or another polynomial of equal or lesser degree.

When **dividing by a monomial**, divide each term of the polynomial by the monomial.

When **dividing by a polynomial**, begin by arranging the terms of each polynomial in order of one variable. You may arrange in ascending or descending order, but be consistent with both polynomials. To get the first term of the quotient, divide the first term of the dividend by the first term of the divisor. Multiply the first term of the quotient by the entire divisor and subtract that product from the dividend. Repeat for the second and successive terms until you either get a remainder of zero or a remainder whose degree is less than the degree of the divisor. If the quotient has a remainder, write the answer as a mixed expression in the form:

$$\text{quotient} + \frac{\text{remainder}}{\text{divisor}}$$

For example, we can evaluate the following expression in the same way as long division:

$$\frac{x^3 - 3x^2 - 2x + 5}{x - 5}$$

$$
\begin{array}{r}
x^2 + 2x + 8 \\
x - 5 \overline{)\; x^3 - 3x^2 - 2x + 5} \\
-(x^3 - 5x^2) \\
\hline
2x^2 - 2x \\
-(2x^2 - 10x) \\
\hline
8x + 5 \\
-(8x - 40) \\
\hline
45
\end{array}
$$

$$\frac{x^3 - 3x^2 - 2x + 5}{x - 5} = x^2 + 2x + 8 + \frac{45}{x - 5}$$

When **factoring** a polynomial, first check for a common monomial factor, that is, look to see if each coefficient has a common factor or if each term has an x in it. If the factor is a trinomial but not a perfect trinomial square, look for a factorable form, such as one of these:

$$x^2 + (a + b)x + ab = (x + a)(x + b)$$
$$(ac)x^2 + (ad + bc)x + bd = (ax + b)(cx + d)$$

For factors with four terms, look for groups to factor. Once you have found the factors, write the original polynomial as the product of all the factors. Make sure all of the polynomial factors are

Copyright © Mometrix Media. You have been licensed one copy of this document for personal use only. Any other reproduction or redistribution is strictly prohibited. All rights reserved. This content is provided for test preparation purposes only and does not imply an endorsement by Mometrix of any particular political, scientific, or religious point of view.

prime. Monomial factors may be *prime* or *composite*. Check your work by multiplying the factors to make sure you get the original polynomial.

Below are patterns of some special products to remember to help make factoring easier:

- Perfect trinomial squares: $x^2 + 2xy + y^2 = (x+y)^2$ or $x^2 - 2xy + y^2 = (x-y)^2$
- Difference between two squares: $x^2 - y^2 = (x+y)(x-y)$
- Sum of two cubes: $x^3 + y^3 = (x+y)(x^2 - xy + y^2)$
   - Note: the second factor is *not* the same as a perfect trinomial square, so do not try to factor it further.
- Difference between two cubes: $x^3 - y^3 = (x-y)(x^2 + xy + y^2)$
   - Again, the second factor is *not* the same as a perfect trinomial square.
- Perfect cubes: $x^3 + 3x^2y + 3xy^2 + y^3 = (x+y)^3$ and $x^3 - 3x^2y + 3xy^2 - y^3 = (x-y)^3$

RATIONAL EXPRESSIONS

Rational expressions are fractions with polynomials in both the numerator and the denominator; the value of the polynomial in the denominator cannot be equal to zero. Be sure to keep track of values that make the denominator of the original expression zero as the final result inherits the same restrictions. For example, a denominator of $x - 3$ indicates that the expression is not defined when $x = 3$ and, as such, regardless of any operations done to the expression, it remains undefined there.

To **add or subtract** rational expressions, first find the common denominator, then rewrite each fraction as an equivalent fraction with the common denominator. Finally, add or subtract the numerators to get the numerator of the answer, and keep the common denominator as the denominator of the answer.

When **multiplying** rational expressions, factor each polynomial and cancel like factors (a factor which appears in both the numerator and the denominator). Then, multiply all remaining factors in the numerator to get the numerator of the product, and multiply the remaining factors in the denominator to get the denominator of the product. Remember: cancel entire factors, not individual terms.

To **divide** rational expressions, take the reciprocal of the divisor (the rational expression you are dividing by) and multiply by the dividend.

> **Review Video: Rational Expressions**
> Visit mometrix.com/academy and enter code: 415183

SIMPLIFYING RATIONAL EXPRESSIONS

To simplify a rational expression, factor the numerator and denominator completely. Factors that are the same and appear in the numerator and denominator have a ratio of 1. For example, look at the following expression:

$$\frac{x - 1}{1 - x^2}$$

Copyright © Mometrix Media. You have been licensed one copy of this document for personal use only. Any other reproduction or redistribution is strictly prohibited. All rights reserved. This content is provided for test preparation purposes only and does not imply an endorsement by Mometrix of any particular political, scientific, or religious point of view.

The denominator, $(1 - x^2)$, is a difference of squares. It can be factored as $(1 - x)(1 + x)$. The factor $1 - x$ and the numerator $x - 1$ are opposites and have a ratio of -1. Rewrite the numerator as $-1(1 - x)$. So, the rational expression can be simplified as follows:

$$\frac{x - 1}{1 - x^2} = \frac{-1(1 - x)}{(1 - x)(1 + x)} = \frac{-1}{1 + x}$$

Note that since the original expression is only defined for $x \neq \{-1, 1\}$, the simplified expression has the same restrictions.

> **Review Video: Reducing Rational Expressions**
> Visit mometrix.com/academy and enter code: 788868

SOLVING QUADRATIC EQUATIONS

Quadratic equations are a special set of trinomials of the form $y = ax^2 + bx + c$ that occur commonly in math and real-world applications. The **roots** of a quadratic equation are the solutions that satisfy the equation when $y = 0$; in other words, where the graph touches the x-axis. There are several ways to determine these solutions including using the quadratic formula, factoring, completing the square, and graphing the function.

> **Review Video: Quadratic Equations Overview**
> Visit mometrix.com/academy and enter code: 476276
>
> **Review Video: Solutions of a Quadratic Equation on a Graph**
> Visit mometrix.com/academy and enter code: 328231

QUADRATIC FORMULA

The **quadratic formula** is used to solve quadratic equations when other methods are more difficult. To use the quadratic formula to solve a quadratic equation, begin by rewriting the equation in standard form $ax^2 + bx + c = 0$, where a, b, and c are coefficients. Once you have identified the values of the coefficients, substitute those values into the quadratic formula

$$x = \frac{-b \pm \sqrt{b^2 - 4ac}}{2a}$$

Evaluate the equation and simplify the expression. Again, check each root by substituting into the original equation. In the quadratic formula, the portion of the formula under the radical ($b^2 - 4ac$) is called the **discriminant**. If the discriminant is zero, there is only one root: $-\frac{b}{2a}$. If the discriminant is positive, there are two different real roots. If the discriminant is negative, there are no real roots; you will instead find complex roots. Often these solutions don't make sense in context and are ignored.

> **Review Video: Using the Quadratic Formula**
> Visit mometrix.com/academy and enter code: 163102

FACTORING

To solve a quadratic equation by factoring, begin by rewriting the equation in standard form, $x^2 + bx + c = 0$. Remember that the goal of factoring is to find numbers f and g such that

Copyright © Mometrix Media. You have been licensed one copy of this document for personal use only. Any other reproduction or redistribution is strictly prohibited. All rights reserved. This content is provided for test preparation purposes only and does not imply an endorsement by Mometrix of any particular political, scientific, or religious point of view.

$(x + f)(x + g) = x^2 + (f + g)x + fg$, in other words $(f + g) = b$ and $fg = c$. This can be a really useful method when b and c are integers. Determine the factors of c and look for pairs that could sum to b.

For example, consider finding the roots of $x^2 + 6x - 16 = 0$. The factors of -16 include, -4 and 4, -8 and 2, -2 and 8, -1 and 16, and 1 and -16. The factors that sum to 6 are -2 and 8. Write these factors as the product of two binomials, $0 = (x - 2)(x + 8)$. Finally, since these binomials multiply together to equal zero, set them each equal to zero and solve each for x. This results in $x - 2 = 0$, which simplifies to $x = 2$ and $x + 8 = 0$, which simplifies to $x = -8$. Therefore, the roots of the equation are 2 and -8.

> **Review Video: Factoring Quadratic Equations**
> Visit mometrix.com/academy and enter code: 336566

COMPLETING THE SQUARE

One way to find the roots of a quadratic equation is to find a way to manipulate it such that it follows the form of a perfect square $(x^2 + 2px + p^2)$ by adding and subtracting a constant. This process is called **completing the square**. In other words, if you are given a quadratic that is not a perfect square, $x^2 + bx + c = 0$, you can find a constant d that could be added in to make it a perfect square:

$$x^2 + bx + c + (d - d) = 0; \ \{\text{Let } b = 2p \text{ and } c + d = p^2\}$$

then:

$$x^2 + 2px + p^2 - d = 0 \text{ and } d = \frac{b^2}{4} - c$$

Once you have completed the square you can find the roots of the resulting equation:

$$x^2 + 2px + p^2 - d = 0$$
$$(x + p)^2 = d$$
$$x + p = \pm\sqrt{d}$$
$$x = -p \pm \sqrt{d}$$

It is worth noting that substituting the original expressions into this solution gives the same result as the quadratic formula where $a = 1$:

$$x = -p \pm \sqrt{d} = -\frac{b}{2} \pm \sqrt{\frac{b^2}{4} - c} = -\frac{b}{2} \pm \frac{\sqrt{b^2 - 4c}}{2} = \frac{-b \pm \sqrt{b^2 - 4c}}{2}$$

Copyright © Mometrix Media. You have been licensed one copy of this document for personal use only. Any other reproduction or redistribution is strictly prohibited. All rights reserved.
This content is provided for test preparation purposes only and does not imply an endorsement by Mometrix of any particular political, scientific, or religious point of view.

Completing the square can be seen as arranging block representations of each of the terms to be as close to a square as possible and then filling in the gaps. For example, consider the quadratic expression $x^2 + 6x + 2$:

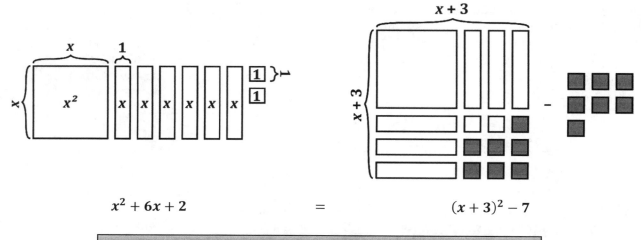

$$x^2 + 6x + 2 \qquad = \qquad (x+3)^2 - 7$$

Review Video: <u>Completing the Square</u>
Visit mometrix.com/academy and enter code: 982479

USING GIVEN ROOTS TO FIND QUADRATIC EQUATION

One way to find the roots of a quadratic equation is to factor the equation and use the **zero product property**, setting each factor of the equation equal to zero to find the corresponding root. We can use this technique in reverse to find an equation given its roots. Each root corresponds to a linear equation which in turn corresponds to a factor of the quadratic equation.

For example, we can find a quadratic equation whose roots are $x = 2$ and $x = -1$. The root $x = 2$ corresponds to the equation $x - 2 = 0$, and the root $x = -1$ corresponds to the equation $x + 1 = 0$.

These two equations correspond to the factors $(x - 2)$ and $(x + 1)$, from which we can derive the equation $(x - 2)(x + 1) = 0$, or $x^2 - x - 2 = 0$.

Any integer multiple of this entire equation will also yield the same roots, as the integer will simply cancel out when the equation is factored. For example, $2x^2 - 2x - 4 = 0$ factors as $2(x - 2)(x + 1) = 0$.

FUNCTION AND RELATION

When expressing functional relationships, the **variables** x and y are typically used. These values are often written as the **coordinates** (x, y). The x-value is the independent variable and the y-value is the dependent variable. A **relation** is a set of data in which there is not a unique y-value for each x-value in the dataset. This means that there can be two of the same x-values assigned to different y-values. A relation is simply a relationship between the x- and y-values in each coordinate but does not apply to the relationship between the values of x and y in the data set. A **function** is a relation where one quantity depends on the other. For example, the amount of money that you make depends on the number of hours that you work. In a function, each x-value in the data set has one unique y-value because the y-value depends on the x-value.

Copyright © Mometrix Media. You have been licensed one copy of this document for personal use only. Any other reproduction or redistribution is strictly prohibited. All rights reserved. This content is provided for test preparation purposes only and does not imply an endorsement by Mometrix of any particular political, scientific, or religious point of view.

FUNCTIONS

A function has exactly one value of **output variable** (dependent variable) for each value of the **input variable** (independent variable). The set of all values for the input variable (here assumed to be x) is the domain of the function, and the set of all corresponding values of the output variable (here assumed to be y) is the range of the function. When looking at a graph of an equation, the easiest way to determine if the equation is a function or not is to conduct the vertical line test. If a vertical line drawn through any value of x crosses the graph in more than one place, the equation is not a function.

DETERMINING A FUNCTION

You can determine whether an equation is a **function** by substituting different values into the equation for x. You can display and organize these numbers in a data table. A **data table** contains the values for x and y, which you can also list as coordinates. In order for a function to exist, the table cannot contain any repeating x-values that correspond with different y-values. If each x-coordinate has a unique y-coordinate, the table contains a function. However, there can be repeating y-values that correspond with different x-values. An example of this is when the function contains an exponent. Example: if $x^2 = y$, $2^2 = 4$, and $(-2)^2 = 4$.

> **Review Video: Definition of a Function**
> Visit mometrix.com/academy and enter code: 784611

FINDING THE DOMAIN AND RANGE OF A FUNCTION

The **domain** of a function $f(x)$ is the set of all input values for which the function is defined. The **range** of a function $f(x)$ is the set of all possible output values of the function—that is, of every possible value of $f(x)$, for any value of x in the function's domain. For a function expressed in a table, every input-output pair is given explicitly. To find the domain, we just list all the x-values and to find the range, we just list all the values of $f(x)$. Consider the following example:

x	–1	4	2	1	0	3	8	6
$f(x)$	3	0	3	–1	–1	2	4	6

In this case, the domain would be $\{-1, 4, 2, 1, 0, 3, 8, 6\}$ or, putting them in ascending order, $\{-1, 0, 1, 2, 3, 4, 6, 8\}$. (Putting the values in ascending order isn't strictly necessary, but generally makes the set easier to read.) The range would be $\{3, 0, 3, -1, -1, 2, 4, 6\}$. Note that some of these values appear more than once. This is entirely permissible for a function; while each value of x must be matched to a unique value of $f(x)$, the converse is not true. We don't need to list each value more than once, so eliminating duplicates, the range is $\{3, 0, -1, 2, 4, 6\}$, or, putting them in ascending order, $\{-1, 0, 2, 3, 4, 6\}$.

Note that by definition of a function, no input value can be matched to more than one output value. It is good to double-check to make sure that the data given follows this and is therefore actually a function.

> **Review Video: Domain and Range**
> Visit mometrix.com/academy and enter code: 778133
>
> **Review Video: Domain and Range of Quadratic Functions**
> Visit mometrix.com/academy and enter code: 331768

Copyright © Mometrix Media. You have been licensed one copy of this document for personal use only. Any other reproduction or redistribution is strictly prohibited. All rights reserved. This content is provided for test preparation purposes only and does not imply an endorsement by Mometrix of any particular political, scientific, or religious point of view.

WRITING A FUNCTION RULE USING A TABLE

If given a set of data, place the corresponding x- and y-values into a table and analyze the relationship between them. Consider what you can do to each x-value to obtain the corresponding y-value. Try adding or subtracting different numbers to and from x and then try multiplying or dividing different numbers to and from x. If none of these **operations** give you the y-value, try combining the operations. Once you find a rule that works for one pair, make sure to try it with each additional set of ordered pairs in the table. If the same operation or combination of operations satisfies each set of coordinates, then the table contains a function. The rule is then used to write the equation of the function in "$y = f(x)$" form.

DIRECT AND INVERSE VARIATIONS OF VARIABLES

Variables that vary directly are those that either both increase at the same rate or both decrease at the same rate. For example, in the functions $y = kx$ or $y = kx^n$, where k and n are positive, the value of y increases as the value of x increases and decreases as the value of x decreases.

Variables that vary inversely are those where one increases while the other decreases. For example, in the functions $y = \frac{k}{x}$ or $y = \frac{k}{x^n}$ where k and n are positive, the value of y increases as the value of x decreases and decreases as the value of x increases.

In both cases, k is the constant of variation.

PROPERTIES OF FUNCTIONS

There are many different ways to classify functions based on their structure or behavior. Important features of functions include:

- **End behavior**: the behavior of the function at extreme values ($f(x)$ as $x \to \pm\infty$)
- **y-intercept**: the value of the function at $f(0)$
- **Roots**: the values of x where the function equals zero ($f(x) = 0$)
- **Extrema**: minimum or maximum values of the function or where the function changes direction ($f(x) \geq k$ or $f(x) \leq k$)

CLASSIFICATION OF FUNCTIONS

An **invertible function** is defined as a function, $f(x)$, for which there is another function, $f^{-1}(x)$, such that $f^{-1}(f(x)) = x$. For example, if $f(x) = 3x - 2$ the inverse function, $f^{-1}(x)$, can be found:

$$x = 3(f^{-1}(x)) - 2$$
$$\frac{x + 2}{3} = f^{-1}(x)$$

$$f^{-1}(f(x)) = \frac{3x - 2 + 2}{3}$$
$$= \frac{3x}{3}$$
$$= x$$

Note that $f^{-1}(x)$ is a valid function over all values of x.

In a **one-to-one function**, each value of x has exactly one value for y on the coordinate plane (this is the definition of a function) and each value of y has exactly one value for x. While the vertical line test will determine if a graph is that of a function, the horizontal line test will determine if a function is a one-to-one function. If a horizontal line drawn at any value of y intersects the graph in more than one place, the graph is not that of a one-to-one function. Do not make the mistake of using the horizontal line test exclusively in determining if a graph is that of a one-to-one function. A one-to-

Copyright © Mometrix Media. You have been licensed one copy of this document for personal use only. Any other reproduction or redistribution is strictly prohibited. All rights reserved. This content is provided for test preparation purposes only and does not imply an endorsement by Mometrix of any particular political, scientific, or religious point of view.

one function must pass both the vertical line test and the horizontal line test. As such, one-to-one functions are invertible functions.

A **many-to-one function** is a function whereby the relation is a function, but the inverse of the function is not a function. In other words, each element in the domain is mapped to one and only one element in the range. However, one or more elements in the range may be mapped to the same element in the domain. A graph of a many-to-one function would pass the vertical line test, but not the horizontal line test. This is why many-to-one functions are not invertible.

A **monotone function** is a function whose graph either constantly increases or constantly decreases. Examples include the functions $f(x) = x$, $f(x) = -x$, or $f(x) = x^3$.

An **even function** has a graph that is symmetric with respect to the y-axis and satisfies the equation $f(x) = f(-x)$. Examples include the functions $f(x) = x^2$ and $f(x) = ax^n$, where a is any real number and n is a positive even integer.

An **odd function** has a graph that is symmetric with respect to the origin and satisfies the equation $f(x) = -f(-x)$. Examples include the functions $f(x) = x^3$ and $f(x) = ax^n$, where a is any real number and n is a positive odd integer.

> **Review Video: Even and Odd Functions**
> Visit mometrix.com/academy and enter code: 278985

Constant functions are given by the equation $f(x) = b$, where b is a real number. There is no independent variable present in the equation, so the function has a constant value for all x. The graph of a constant function is a horizontal line of slope 0 that is positioned b units from the x-axis. If b is positive, the line is above the x-axis; if b is negative, the line is below the x-axis.

Identity functions are identified by the equation $f(x) = x$, where every value of the function is equal to its corresponding value of x. The only zero is the point (0,0). The graph is a line with a slope of 1.

In **linear functions**, the value of the function changes in direct proportion to x. The rate of change, represented by the slope on its graph, is constant throughout. The standard form of a linear equation is $ax + cy = d$, where a, c, and d are real numbers. As a function, this equation is commonly in the form $y = mx + b$ or $f(x) = mx + b$ where $m = -\frac{a}{c}$ and $b = \frac{d}{c}$. This is known as the slope-intercept form, because the coefficients give the slope of the graphed function (m) and its y-intercept (b). Solve the equation $mx + b = 0$ for x to get $x = -\frac{b}{m}$, which is the only zero of the function. The domain and range are both the set of all real numbers.

> **Review Video: Linear Functions**
> Visit mometrix.com/academy and enter code: 699478

Algebraic functions are those that exclusively use polynomials and roots. These would include polynomial functions, rational functions, square root functions, and all combinations of these functions, such as polynomials as the radicand. These combinations may be joined by addition, subtraction, multiplication, or division, but may not include variables as exponents.

> **Review Video: Common Functions**
> Visit mometrix.com/academy and enter code: 629798

Copyright © Mometrix Media. You have been licensed one copy of this document for personal use only. Any other reproduction or redistribution is strictly prohibited. All rights reserved. This content is provided for test preparation purposes only and does not imply an endorsement by Mometrix of any particular political, scientific, or religious point of view.

ABSOLUTE VALUE FUNCTIONS

An **absolute value function** is in the format $f(x) = |ax + b|$. Like other functions, the domain is the set of all real numbers. However, because absolute value indicates positive numbers, the range is limited to positive real numbers. To find the zero of an absolute value function, set the portion inside the absolute value sign equal to zero and solve for x. An absolute value function is also known as a piecewise function because it must be solved in pieces—one for if the value inside the absolute value sign is positive, and one for if the value is negative. The function can be expressed as:

$$f(x) = \begin{cases} ax + b \text{ if } ax + b \geq 0 \\ -(ax + b) \text{ if } ax + b < 0 \end{cases}$$

This will allow for an accurate statement of the range. The graph of an example absolute value function, $f(x) = |2x - 1|$, is below:

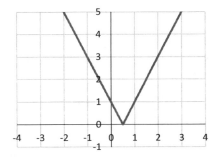

PIECEWISE FUNCTIONS

A **piecewise function** is a function that has different definitions on two or more different intervals. The following, for instance, is one example of a piecewise-defined function:

$$f(x) = \begin{cases} x^2, & x < 0 \\ x, & 0 \leq x \leq 2 \\ (x - 2)^2, & x > 2 \end{cases}$$

To graph this function, you would simply graph each part separately in the appropriate domain. The final graph would look like this:

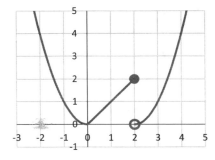

Note the filled and hollow dots at the discontinuity at $x = 2$. This is important to show which side of the graph that point corresponds to. Because $f(x) = x$ on the closed interval $0 \leq x \leq 2$, $f(2) = 2$. The point $(2, 2)$ is therefore marked with a filled circle, and the point $(2,0)$, which is the endpoint of

Copyright © Mometrix Media. You have been licensed one copy of this document for personal use only. Any other reproduction or redistribution is strictly prohibited. All rights reserved.
This content is provided for test preparation purposes only and does not imply an endorsement by Mometrix of any particular political, scientific, or religious point of view.

the rightmost $(x - 2)^2$ part of the graph but *not actually part of the function*, is marked with a hollow dot to indicate this.

Review Video: Piecewise Functions
Visit mometrix.com/academy and enter code: 707921

QUADRATIC FUNCTIONS

A **quadratic function** is a function in the form $y = ax^2 + bx + c$, where a does not equal 0. While a linear function forms a line, a quadratic function forms a **parabola**, which is a u-shaped figure that either opens upward or downward. A parabola that opens upward is said to be a **positive quadratic function,** and a parabola that opens downward is said to be a **negative quadratic function**. The shape of a parabola can differ, depending on the values of a, b, and c. All parabolas contain a **vertex**, which is the highest possible point, the **maximum**, or the lowest possible point, the **minimum**. This is the point where the graph begins moving in the opposite direction. A quadratic function can have zero, one, or two solutions, and therefore zero, one, or two x-intercepts. Recall that the x-intercepts are referred to as the zeros, or roots, of a function. A quadratic function will have only one y-intercept. Understanding the basic components of a quadratic function can give you an idea of the shape of its graph.

Example graph of a positive quadratic function, $x^2 + 2x - 3$:

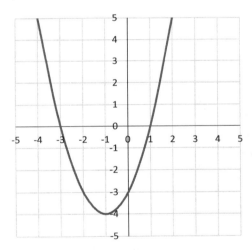

POLYNOMIAL FUNCTIONS

A **polynomial function** is a function with multiple terms and multiple powers of x, such as:

$$f(x) = a_n x^n + a_{n-1} x^{n-1} + a_{n-2} x^{n-2} + \cdots + a_1 x + a_0$$

where n is a non-negative integer that is the highest exponent in the polynomial and $a_n \neq 0$. The domain of a polynomial function is the set of all real numbers. If the greatest exponent in the polynomial is even, the polynomial is said to be of even degree and the range is the set of real numbers that satisfy the function. If the greatest exponent in the polynomial is odd, the polynomial is said to be odd and the range, like the domain, is the set of all real numbers.

RATIONAL FUNCTIONS

A **rational function** is a function that can be constructed as a ratio of two polynomial expressions: $f(x) = \frac{p(x)}{q(x)}$, where $p(x)$ and $q(x)$ are both polynomial expressions and $q(x) \neq 0$. The domain is the

Copyright © Mometrix Media. You have been licensed one copy of this document for personal use only. Any other reproduction or redistribution is strictly prohibited. All rights reserved.
This content is provided for test preparation purposes only and does not imply an endorsement by Mometrix of any particular political, scientific, or religious point of view.

set of all real numbers, except any values for which $q(x) = 0$. The range is the set of real numbers that satisfies the function when the domain is applied. When you graph a rational function, you will have vertical asymptotes wherever $q(x) = 0$. If the polynomial in the numerator is of lesser degree than the polynomial in the denominator, the x-axis will also be a horizontal asymptote. If the numerator and denominator have equal degrees, there will be a horizontal asymptote not on the x-axis. If the degree of the numerator is exactly one greater than the degree of the denominator, the graph will have an oblique, or diagonal, asymptote. The asymptote will be along the line $y = \frac{p_n}{q_{n-1}} x + \frac{p_{n-1}}{q_{n-1}}$, where p_n and q_{n-1} are the coefficients of the highest degree terms in their respective polynomials.

SQUARE ROOT FUNCTIONS

A **square root function** is a function that contains a radical and is in the format $f(x) = \sqrt{ax + b}$. The domain is the set of all real numbers that yields a positive radicand or a radicand equal to zero. Because square root values are assumed to be positive unless otherwise identified, the range is all real numbers from zero to infinity. To find the zero of a square root function, set the radicand equal to zero and solve for x. The graph of a square root function is always to the right of the zero and always above the x-axis.

Example graph of a square root function, $f(x) = \sqrt{2x + 1}$:

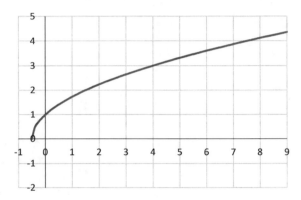

Geometry and Measurement

ROUNDING AND ESTIMATION

Rounding is reducing the digits in a number while still trying to keep the value similar. The result will be less accurate but in a simpler form and easier to use. Whole numbers can be rounded to the nearest ten, hundred, or thousand.

When you are asked to estimate the solution to a problem, you will need to provide only an approximate figure or **estimation** for your answer. In this situation, you will need to round each number in the calculation to the level indicated (nearest hundred, nearest thousand, etc.) or to a level that makes sense for the numbers involved. When estimating a sum **all numbers must be**

Copyright © Mometrix Media. You have been licensed one copy of this document for personal use only. Any other reproduction or redistribution is strictly prohibited. All rights reserved.
This content is provided for test preparation purposes only and does not imply an endorsement by Mometrix of any particular political, scientific, or religious point of view.

rounded to the same level. You cannot round one number to the nearest thousand while rounding another to the nearest hundred.

Review Video: <u>Rounding and Estimation</u>
Visit mometrix.com/academy and enter code: 126243

SCIENTIFIC NOTATION

Scientific notation is a way of writing large numbers in a shorter form. The form $a \times 10^n$ is used in scientific notation, where a is greater than or equal to 1 but less than 10, and n is the number of places the decimal must move to get from the original number to a. Example: The number 230,400,000 is cumbersome to write. To write the value in scientific notation, place a decimal point between the first and second numbers, and include all digits through the last non-zero digit ($a = 2.304$). To find the appropriate power of 10, count the number of places the decimal point had to move ($n = 8$). The number is positive if the decimal moved to the left, and negative if it moved to the right. We can then write 230,400,000 as 2.304×10^8. If we look instead at the number 0.00002304, we have the same value for a, but this time the decimal moved 5 places to the right ($n = -5$). Thus, 0.00002304 can be written as 2.304×10^{-5}. Using this notation makes it simple to compare very large or very small numbers. By comparing exponents, it is easy to see that 3.28×10^4 is smaller than 1.51×10^5, because 4 is less than 5.

Review Video: <u>Scientific Notation</u>
Visit mometrix.com/academy and enter code: 976454

PRECISION, ACCURACY, AND ERROR

Precision: How reliable and repeatable a measurement is. The more consistent the data is with repeated testing, the more precise it is. For example, hitting a target consistently in the same spot, which may or may not be the center of the target, is precision.

Accuracy: How close the data is to the correct data. For example, hitting a target consistently in the center area of the target, whether or not the hits are all in the same spot, is accuracy.

211

Copyright © Mometrix Media. You have been licensed one copy of this document for personal use only. Any other reproduction or redistribution is strictly prohibited. All rights reserved.
This content is provided for test preparation purposes only and does not imply an endorsement by Mometrix of any particular political, scientific, or religious point of view.

Note: it is possible for data to be precise without being accurate. If a scale is off balance, the data will be precise, but will not be accurate. For data to have precision and accuracy, it must be repeatable and correct.

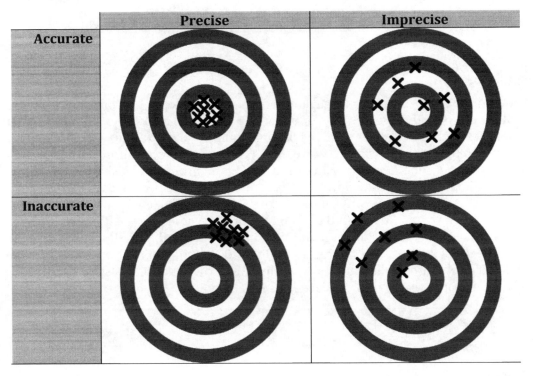

Approximate error: The amount of error in a physical measurement. Approximate error is often reported as the measurement, followed by the $\pm$ symbol and the amount of the approximate error.

Maximum possible error: Half the magnitude of the smallest unit used in the measurement. For example, if the unit of measurement is 1 centimeter, the maximum possible error is $\frac{1}{2}$ cm, written as ±0.5 cm following the measurement. It is important to apply significant figures in reporting maximum possible error. Do not make the answer appear more accurate than the least accurate of your measurements.

> **Review Video: Precision, Accuracy, and Error**
> Visit mometrix.com/academy and enter code: 520377

METRIC MEASUREMENT PREFIXES

Giga-	One billion	1 *giga*watt is one billion watts
Mega-	One million	1 *mega*hertz is one million hertz
Kilo-	One thousand	1 *kilo*gram is one thousand grams
Deci-	One-tenth	1 *deci*meter is one-tenth of a meter
Centi-	One-hundredth	1 *centi*meter is one-hundredth of a meter
Milli-	One-thousandth	1 *milli*liter is one-thousandth of a liter
Micro-	One-millionth	1 *micro*gram is one-millionth of a gram

Copyright © Mometrix Media. You have been licensed one copy of this document for personal use only. Any other reproduction or redistribution is strictly prohibited. All rights reserved.
This content is provided for test preparation purposes only and does not imply an endorsement by Mometrix of any particular political, scientific, or religious point of view.

Review Video: <u>Metric System Conversion - How the Metric System Works</u>

Visit mometrix.com/academy and enter code: 163709

MEASUREMENT CONVERSION

When converting between units, the goal is to maintain the same meaning but change the way it is displayed. In order to go from a larger unit to a smaller unit, multiply the number of the known amount by the equivalent amount. When going from a smaller unit to a larger unit, divide the number of the known amount by the equivalent amount.

For complicated conversions, it may be helpful to set up conversion fractions. In these fractions, one fraction is the **conversion factor**. The other fraction has the unknown amount in the numerator. So, the known value is placed in the denominator. Sometimes, the second fraction has the known value from the problem in the numerator and the unknown in the denominator. Multiply the two fractions to get the converted measurement. Note that since the numerator and the denominator of the factor are equivalent, the value of the fraction is 1. That is why we can say that the result in the new units is equal to the result in the old units even though they have different numbers.

It can often be necessary to chain known conversion factors together. As an example, consider converting 512 square inches to square meters. We know that there are 2.54 centimeters in an inch and 100 centimeters in a meter, and we know we will need to square each of these factors to achieve the conversion we are looking for.

$$\frac{512 \text{ in}^2}{1} \times \left(\frac{2.54 \text{ cm}}{1 \text{ in}}\right)^2 \times \left(\frac{1 \text{ m}}{100 \text{ cm}}\right)^2 = \frac{512 \text{ in}^2}{1} \times \left(\frac{6.4516 \text{ cm}^2}{1 \text{ in}^2}\right) \times \left(\frac{1 \text{ m}^2}{10,000 \text{ cm}^2}\right) = 0.330 \text{ m}^2$$

Review Video: <u>Measurement Conversions</u>

Visit mometrix.com/academy and enter code: 316703

COMMON UNITS AND EQUIVALENTS

METRIC EQUIVALENTS

1000 µg (microgram)	1 mg
1000 mg (milligram)	1 g
1000 g (gram)	1 kg
1000 kg (kilogram)	1 metric ton
1000 mL (milliliter)	1 L
1000 µm (micrometer)	1 mm
1000 mm (millimeter)	1 m
100 cm (centimeter)	1 m
1000 m (meter)	1 km

DISTANCE AND AREA MEASUREMENT

Unit	Abbreviation	US equivalent	Metric equivalent
Inch	in	1 inch	2.54 centimeters
Foot	ft	12 inches	0.305 meters
Yard	yd	3 feet	0.914 meters
Mile	mi	5280 feet	1.609 kilometers
Acre	ac	4840 square yards	0.405 hectares
Square Mile	sq. mi. or mi.^{2}	640 acres	2.590 square kilometers

Copyright © Mometrix Media. You have been licensed one copy of this document for personal use only. Any other reproduction or redistribution is strictly prohibited. All rights reserved.
This content is provided for test preparation purposes only and does not imply an endorsement by Mometrix of any particular political, scientific, or religious point of view.

CAPACITY MEASUREMENTS

Unit	Abbreviation	US equivalent	Metric equivalent
Fluid Ounce	fl oz	8 fluid drams	29.573 milliliters
Cup	c	8 fluid ounces	0.237 liter
Pint	pt.	16 fluid ounces	0.473 liter
Quart	qt.	2 pints	0.946 liter
Gallon	gal.	4 quarts	3.785 liters
Teaspoon	t or tsp.	1 fluid dram	5 milliliters
Tablespoon	T or tbsp.	4 fluid drams	15 or 16 milliliters
Cubic Centimeter	cc or cm^3	0.271 drams	1 milliliter

WEIGHT MEASUREMENTS

Unit	Abbreviation	US equivalent	Metric equivalent
Ounce	oz	16 drams	28.35 grams
Pound	lb	16 ounces	453.6 grams
Ton	tn.	2,000 pounds	907.2 kilograms

VOLUME AND WEIGHT MEASUREMENT CLARIFICATIONS

Always be careful when using ounces and fluid ounces. They are not equivalent.

$$1 \text{ pint} = 16 \text{ fluid ounces} \qquad 1 \text{ fluid ounce} \neq 1 \text{ ounce}$$
$$1 \text{ pound} = 16 \text{ ounces} \qquad 1 \text{ pint} \neq 1 \text{ pound}$$

Having one pint of something does not mean you have one pound of it. In the same way, just because something weighs one pound does not mean that its volume is one pint.

In the United States, the word "ton" by itself refers to a short ton or a net ton. Do not confuse this with a long ton (also called a gross ton) or a metric ton (also spelled *tonne*), which have different measurement equivalents.

$$1 \text{ US ton} = 2000 \text{ pounds} \qquad \neq \qquad 1 \text{ metric ton} = 1000 \text{ kilograms}$$

POINTS AND LINES

A **point** is a fixed location in space, has no size or dimensions, and is commonly represented by a dot. A **line** is a set of points that extends infinitely in two opposite directions. It has length, but no width or depth. A line can be defined by any two distinct points that it contains. A **line segment** is a portion of a line that has definite endpoints. A **ray** is a portion of a line that extends from a single point on that line in one direction along the line. It has a definite beginning, but no ending.

Point   Line   Segment   Ray

INTERACTIONS BETWEEN LINES

Intersecting lines are lines that have exactly one point in common. **Concurrent lines** are multiple lines that intersect at a single point. **Perpendicular lines** are lines that intersect at right angles. They are represented by the symbol ⊥. The shortest distance from a line to a point not on the line is a perpendicular segment from the point to the line. **Parallel lines** are lines in the same plane that

214

Copyright © Mometrix Media. You have been licensed one copy of this document for personal use only. Any other reproduction or redistribution is strictly prohibited. All rights reserved.
This content is provided for test preparation purposes only and does not imply an endorsement by Mometrix of any particular political, scientific, or religious point of view.

have no points in common and never meet. It is possible for lines to be in different planes, have no points in common, and never meet, but they are not parallel because they are in different planes.

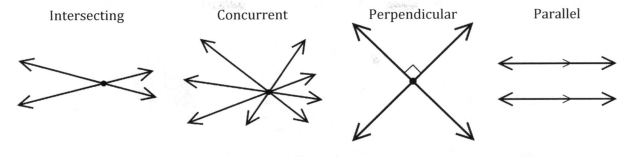

Intersecting   Concurrent   Perpendicular   Parallel

> **Review Video: <u>Parallel and Perpendicular Lines</u>**
> Visit mometrix.com/academy and enter code: 815923

A **transversal** is a line that intersects at least two other lines, which may or may not be parallel to one another. A transversal that intersects parallel lines is a common occurrence in geometry. A **bisector** is a line or line segment that divides another line segment into two equal lengths. A **perpendicular bisector** of a line segment is composed of points that are equidistant from the endpoints of the segment it is dividing.

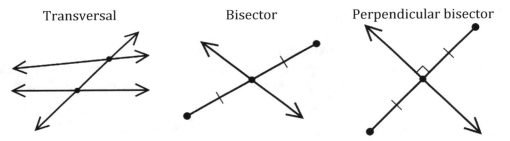

Transversal   Bisector   Perpendicular bisector

The **projection of a point on a line** is the point at which a perpendicular line drawn from the given point to the given line intersects the line. This is also the shortest distance from the given point to the line. The **projection of a segment on a line** is a segment whose endpoints are the points formed when perpendicular lines are drawn from the endpoints of the given segment to the given line. This is similar to the length a diagonal line appears to be when viewed from above.

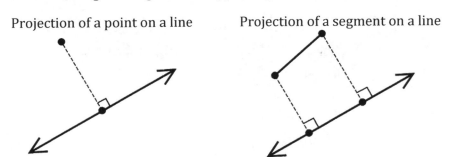

Projection of a point on a line   Projection of a segment on a line

PLANES

A **plane** is a two-dimensional flat surface defined by three non-collinear points. A plane extends an infinite distance in all directions in those two dimensions. It contains an infinite number of points, parallel lines and segments, intersecting lines and segments, as well as parallel or intersecting rays.

Copyright © Mometrix Media. You have been licensed one copy of this document for personal use only. Any other reproduction or redistribution is strictly prohibited. All rights reserved.
This content is provided for test preparation purposes only and does not imply an endorsement by Mometrix of any particular political, scientific, or religious point of view.

A plane will never contain a three-dimensional figure or skew lines, which are lines that don't intersect and are not parallel. Two given planes are either parallel or they intersect at a line. A plane may intersect a circular conic surface to form **conic sections**, such as a parabola, hyperbola, circle or ellipse.

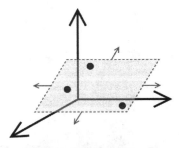

Review Video: Lines and Planes
Visit mometrix.com/academy and enter code: 554267

ANGLES AND VERTICES

An **angle** is formed when two lines or line segments meet at a common point. It may be a common starting point for a pair of segments or rays, or it may be the intersection of lines. Angles are represented by the symbol ∠.

The **vertex** is the point at which two segments or rays meet to form an angle. If the angle is formed by intersecting rays, lines, and/or line segments, the vertex is the point at which four angles are formed. The pairs of angles opposite one another are called vertical angles, and their measures are equal.

- An **acute** angle is an angle with a degree measure less than 90°.
- A **right** angle is an angle with a degree measure of exactly 90°.
- An **obtuse** angle is an angle with a degree measure greater than 90° but less than 180°.
- A **straight angle** is an angle with a degree measure of exactly 180°. This is also a semicircle.
- A **reflex angle** is an angle with a degree measure greater than 180° but less than 360°.

A **full angle** is an angle with a degree measure of exactly 360°. This is also a circle.

Review Video: Angles
Visit mometrix.com/academy and enter code: 264624

RELATIONSHIPS BETWEEN ANGLES

Two angles whose sum is exactly 90° are said to be **complementary**. The two angles may or may not be adjacent. In a right triangle, the two acute angles are complementary.

Two angles whose sum is exactly 180° are said to be **supplementary**. The two angles may or may not be adjacent. Two intersecting lines always form two pairs of supplementary angles. Adjacent supplementary angles will always form a straight line.

Copyright © Mometrix Media. You have been licensed one copy of this document for personal use only. Any other reproduction or redistribution is strictly prohibited. All rights reserved.
This content is provided for test preparation purposes only and does not imply an endorsement by Mometrix of any particular political, scientific, or religious point of view.

Two angles that have the same vertex and share a side are said to be **adjacent**. Vertical angles are not adjacent because they share a vertex but no common side.

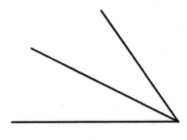 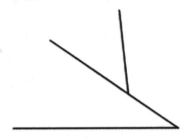

Adjacent   **Not adjacent**
Share vertex and side **Share part of a side, but not vertex**

When two parallel lines are cut by a transversal, the angles that are between the two parallel lines are **interior angles**. In the diagram below, angles 3, 4, 5, and 6 are interior angles.

When two parallel lines are cut by a transversal, the angles that are outside the parallel lines are **exterior angles**. In the diagram below, angles 1, 2, 7, and 8 are exterior angles.

When two parallel lines are cut by a transversal, the angles that are in the same position relative to the transversal and a parallel line are **corresponding angles**. The diagram below has four pairs of corresponding angles: angles 1 and 5, angles 2 and 6, angles 3 and 7, and angles 4 and 8. Corresponding angles formed by parallel lines are congruent.

When two parallel lines are cut by a transversal, the two interior angles that are on opposite sides of the transversal are called **alternate interior angles**. In the diagram below, there are two pairs of alternate interior angles: angles 3 and 6, and angles 4 and 5. Alternate interior angles formed by parallel lines are congruent.

When two parallel lines are cut by a transversal, the two exterior angles that are on opposite sides of the transversal are called **alternate exterior angles**.

In the diagram below, there are two pairs of alternate exterior angles: angles 1 and 8, and angles 2 and 7. Alternate exterior angles formed by parallel lines are congruent.

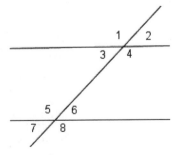

When two lines intersect, four angles are formed. The non-adjacent angles at this vertex are called vertical angles. Vertical angles are congruent. In the diagram, $\angle ABD \cong \angle CBE$ and $\angle ABC \cong \angle DBE$.

Copyright © Mometrix Media. You have been licensed one copy of this document for personal use only. Any other reproduction or redistribution is strictly prohibited. All rights reserved.
This content is provided for test preparation purposes only and does not imply an endorsement by Mometrix of any particular political, scientific, or religious point of view.

The other pairs of angles, ($\angle ABC$, $\angle CBE$) and ($\angle ABD$, $\angle DBE$), are supplementary, meaning the pairs sum to 180°.

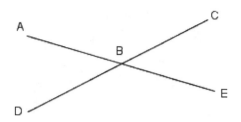

POLYGONS

A **polygon** is a closed, two-dimensional figure with three or more straight line segments called **sides**. The point at which two sides of a polygon intersect is called the **vertex**. In a polygon, the number of sides is always equal to the number of vertices. A polygon with all sides congruent and all angles equal is called a **regular polygon**. Common polygons are:

Triangle = 3 sides
Quadrilateral = 4 sides
Pentagon = 5 sides
Hexagon = 6 sides
Heptagon = 7 sides
Octagon = 8 sides
Nonagon = 9 sides
Decagon = 10 sides
Dodecagon = 12 sides

More generally, an n-gon is a polygon that has n angles and n sides.

Review Video: Intro to Polygons
Visit mometrix.com/academy and enter code: 271869

The sum of the interior angles of an n-sided polygon is $(n - 2) \times 180°$. For example, in a triangle $n = 3$. So the sum of the interior angles is $(3 - 2) \times 180° = 180°$. In a quadrilateral, $n = 4$, and the sum of the angles is $(4 - 2) \times 180° = 360°$.

Review Video: Sum of Interior Angles
Visit mometrix.com/academy and enter code: 984991

CONVEX AND CONCAVE POLYGONS

A **convex polygon** is a polygon whose diagonals all lie within the interior of the polygon. A **concave polygon** is a polygon with a least one diagonal that is outside the polygon. In the diagram below,

Copyright © Mometrix Media. You have been licensed one copy of this document for personal use only. Any other reproduction or redistribution is strictly prohibited. All rights reserved.
This content is provided for test preparation purposes only and does not imply an endorsement by Mometrix of any particular political, scientific, or religious point of view.

quadrilateral $ABCD$ is concave because diagonal $\overline{AC}$ lies outside the polygon and quadrilateral $EFGH$ is convex because both diagonals lie inside the polygon.

Concave

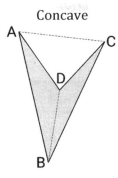

Convex

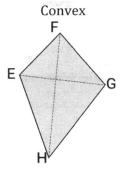

APOTHEM AND RADIUS

A line segment from the center of a polygon that is perpendicular to a side of the polygon is called the **apothem**. A line segment from the center of a polygon to a vertex of the polygon is called a **radius**. In a regular polygon, the apothem can be used to find the area of the polygon using the formula $A = \frac{1}{2}ap$, where a is the apothem, and p is the perimeter.

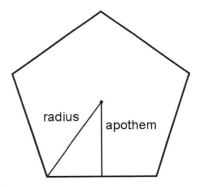

A **diagonal** is a line segment that joins two non-adjacent vertices of a polygon. The number of diagonals a polygon has can be found by using the formula:

$$\text{number of diagonals} = \frac{n(n-3)}{2}$$

Note that n is the number of sides in the polygon. This formula works for all polygons, not just regular polygons.

Copyright © Mometrix Media. You have been licensed one copy of this document for personal use only. Any other reproduction or redistribution is strictly prohibited. All rights reserved.
This content is provided for test preparation purposes only and does not imply an endorsement by Mometrix of any particular political, scientific, or religious point of view.

CONGRUENCE AND SIMILARITY

Congruent figures are geometric figures that have the same size and shape. All corresponding angles are equal, and all corresponding sides are equal. Congruence is indicated by the symbol ≅.

Congruent polygons

Similar figures are geometric figures that have the same shape, but do not necessarily have the same size. All corresponding angles are equal, and all corresponding sides are proportional, but they do not have to be equal. It is indicated by the symbol ~.

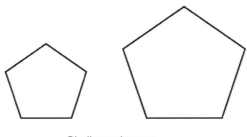

Similar polygons

Note that all congruent figures are also similar, but not all similar figures are congruent.

> **Review Video: <u>What is a Congruent Shape?</u>**
> Visit mometrix.com/academy and enter code: 492281

Copyright © Mometrix Media. You have been licensed one copy of this document for personal use only. Any other reproduction or redistribution is strictly prohibited. All rights reserved.
This content is provided for test preparation purposes only and does not imply an endorsement by Mometrix of any particular political, scientific, or religious point of view.

LINE OF SYMMETRY

A line that divides a figure or object into congruent parts is called a **line of symmetry**. An object may have no lines of symmetry, one line of symmetry, or multiple (i.e., more than one) lines of symmetry.

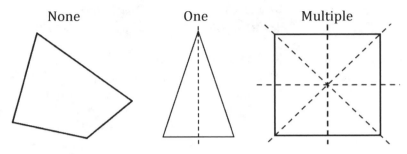

None   One   Multiple

> **Review Video: <u>Symmetry</u>**
> Visit mometrix.com/academy and enter code: 528106

TRIANGLES

A triangle is a three-sided figure with the sum of its interior angles being 180°. The **perimeter of any triangle** is found by summing the three side lengths; $P = a + b + c$. For an equilateral triangle, this is the same as $P = 3a$, where a is any side length, since all three sides are the same length.

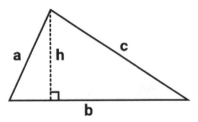

> **Review Video: <u>Proof that a Triangle is 180 Degrees</u>**
> Visit mometrix.com/academy and enter code: 687591
>
> **Review Video: <u>Area and Perimeter of a Triangle</u>**
> Visit mometrix.com/academy and enter code: 853779

The **area of any triangle** can be found by taking half the product of one side length referred to as the base, often given the variable b and the perpendicular distance from that side to the opposite vertex called the altitude or height and given the variable h. In equation form that is $A = \frac{1}{2}bh$.

Another formula that works for any triangle is $A = \sqrt{s(s-a)(s-b)(s-c)}$, where s is the semiperimeter: $\frac{a+b+c}{2}$, and a, b, and c are the lengths of the three sides. Special cases include

Copyright © Mometrix Media. You have been licensed one copy of this document for personal use only. Any other reproduction or redistribution is strictly prohibited. All rights reserved.
This content is provided for test preparation purposes only and does not imply an endorsement by Mometrix of any particular political, scientific, or religious point of view.

isosceles triangles, $A = \frac{1}{2}b\sqrt{a^2 - \frac{b^2}{4}}$, where b is the unique side and a is the length of one of the two congruent sides, and equilateral triangles, $A = \frac{\sqrt{3}}{4}a^2$, where a is the length of a side.

Review Video: Area of Any Triangle
Visit mometrix.com/academy and enter code: 138510

PARTS OF A TRIANGLE

An **altitude** of a triangle is a line segment drawn from one vertex perpendicular to the opposite side. In the diagram that follows, $\overline{BE}$, $\overline{AD}$, and $\overline{CF}$ are altitudes. The length of an altitude is also called the height of the triangle. The three altitudes in a triangle are always concurrent. The point of concurrency of the altitudes of a triangle, O, is called the **orthocenter**. Note that in an obtuse triangle, the orthocenter will be outside the triangle, and in a right triangle, the orthocenter is the vertex of the right angle.

A **median** of a triangle is a line segment drawn from one vertex to the midpoint of the opposite side. In the diagram that follows, $\overline{BH}$, $\overline{AG}$, and $\overline{CI}$ are medians. This is not the same as the altitude, except the altitude to the base of an isosceles triangle and all three altitudes of an equilateral triangle. The point of concurrency of the medians of a triangle, T, is called the **centroid**. This is the same point as the orthocenter only in an equilateral triangle. Unlike the orthocenter, the centroid is always inside the triangle. The centroid can also be considered the exact center of the triangle. Any shape triangle can be perfectly balanced on a tip placed at the centroid. The centroid is also the point that is two-thirds the distance from the vertex to the opposite side.

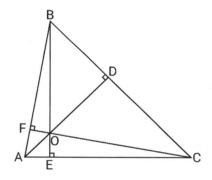 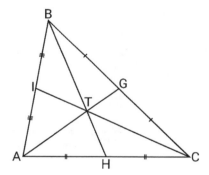

Review Video: Centroid, Incenter, Circumcenter, and Orthocenter
Visit mometrix.com/academy and enter code: 598260

CLASSIFICATIONS OF TRIANGLES

A **scalene triangle** is a triangle with no congruent sides. A scalene triangle will also have three angles of different measures. The angle with the largest measure is opposite the longest side, and the angle with the smallest measure is opposite the shortest side. An **acute triangle** is a triangle whose three angles are all less than 90°. If two of the angles are equal, the acute triangle is also an **isosceles triangle**. An isosceles triangle will also have two congruent angles opposite the two congruent sides. If the three angles are all equal, the acute triangle is also an **equilateral triangle**. An equilateral triangle will also have three congruent angles, each 60°. All equilateral triangles are

Copyright © Mometrix Media. You have been licensed one copy of this document for personal use only. Any other reproduction or redistribution is strictly prohibited. All rights reserved. This content is provided for test preparation purposes only and does not imply an endorsement by Mometrix of any particular political, scientific, or religious point of view.

also acute triangles. An **obtuse triangle** is a triangle with exactly one angle greater than 90°. The other two angles may or may not be equal. If the two remaining angles are equal, the obtuse triangle is also an isosceles triangle. A **right triangle** is a triangle with exactly one angle equal to 90°. All right triangles follow the Pythagorean theorem. A right triangle can never be acute or obtuse.

The table below illustrates how each descriptor places a different restriction on the triangle:

Angles / Sides	Acute: All angles < 90°	Obtuse: One angle > 90°	Right: One angle = 90°
Scalene: No equal side lengths	$90° > \angle a > \angle b > \angle c$ $x > y > z$	$\angle a > 90° > \angle b > \angle c$ $x > y > z$	$90° = \angle a > \angle b > \angle c$ $x > y > z$
Isosceles: Two equal side lengths	$90° > \angle a, \angle b, \text{or } \angle c$ $\angle b = \angle c, \quad y = z$	$\angle a > 90° > \angle b = \angle c$ $x > y = z$	$\angle a = 90°$ $\angle b = \angle c = 45°$ $x > y = z$
Equilateral: Three equal side lengths	$60° = \angle a = \angle b = \angle c$ $x = y = z$		

> **Review Video: Introduction to Types of Triangles**
> Visit mometrix.com/academy and enter code: 511711

GENERAL RULES FOR TRIANGLES

The **triangle inequality theorem** states that the sum of the measures of any two sides of a triangle is always greater than the measure of the third side. If the sum of the measures of two sides were equal to the third side, a triangle would be impossible because the two sides would lie flat across the third side and there would be no vertex. If the sum of the measures of two of the sides was less than the third side, a closed figure would be impossible because the two shortest sides would never meet. In other words, for a triangle with sides lengths A, B, and C: $A + B > C$, $B + C > A$, and $A + C > B$.

Copyright © Mometrix Media. You have been licensed one copy of this document for personal use only. Any other reproduction or redistribution is strictly prohibited. All rights reserved.
This content is provided for test preparation purposes only and does not imply an endorsement by Mometrix of any particular political, scientific, or religious point of view.

The sum of the measures of the interior angles of a triangle is always 180°. Therefore, a triangle can never have more than one angle greater than or equal to 90°.

In any triangle, the angles opposite congruent sides are congruent, and the sides opposite congruent angles are congruent. The largest angle is always opposite the longest side, and the smallest angle is always opposite the shortest side.

The line segment that joins the midpoints of any two sides of a triangle is always parallel to the third side and exactly half the length of the third side.

> **Review Video: General Rules (Triangle Inequality Theorem)**
> Visit mometrix.com/academy and enter code: 166488

SIMILARITY AND CONGRUENCE RULES

Similar triangles are triangles whose corresponding angles are equal and whose corresponding sides are proportional. Represented by AAA. Similar triangles whose corresponding sides are congruent are also congruent triangles.

Triangles can be shown to be **congruent** in 5 ways:

- **SSS**: Three sides of one triangle are congruent to the three corresponding sides of the second triangle.
- **SAS**: Two sides and the included angle (the angle formed by those two sides) of one triangle are congruent to the corresponding two sides and included angle of the second triangle.
- **ASA**: Two angles and the included side (the side that joins the two angles) of one triangle are congruent to the corresponding two angles and included side of the second triangle.
- **AAS**: Two angles and a non-included side of one triangle are congruent to the corresponding two angles and non-included side of the second triangle.
- **HL**: The hypotenuse and leg of one right triangle are congruent to the corresponding hypotenuse and leg of the second right triangle.

> **Review Video: Similar Triangles**
> Visit mometrix.com/academy and enter code: 398538

ROTATION

A **rotation** is a transformation that turns a figure around a point called the **center of rotation**, which can lie anywhere in the plane. If a line is drawn from a point on a figure to the center of rotation, and another line is drawn from the center to the rotated image of that point, the angle

Copyright © Mometrix Media. You have been licensed one copy of this document for personal use only. Any other reproduction or redistribution is strictly prohibited. All rights reserved.
This content is provided for test preparation purposes only and does not imply an endorsement by Mometrix of any particular political, scientific, or religious point of view.

between the two lines is the **angle of rotation**. The vertex of the angle of rotation is the center of rotation.

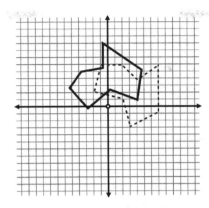

Review Video: <u>Rotation</u>
Visit mometrix.com/academy and enter code: 602600

TRANSLATION AND DILATION

A **translation** is a transformation which slides a figure from one position in the plane to another position in the plane. The original figure and the translated figure have the same size, shape, and orientation. A **dilation** is a transformation which proportionally stretches or shrinks a figure by a **scale factor**. The dilated image is the same shape and orientation as the original image but a different size. A polygon and its dilated image are similar.

Translation

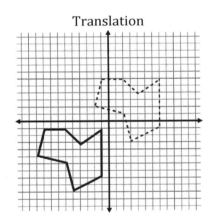

Dilation

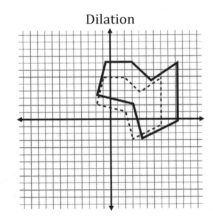

Review Video: <u>Translation</u>
Visit mometrix.com/academy and enter code: 718628

Review Video: <u>Dilation</u>
Visit mometrix.com/academy and enter code: 471630

A **reflection of a figure over a line** (a "flip") creates a congruent image that is the same distance from the line as the original figure but on the opposite side. The **line of reflection** is the perpendicular bisector of any line segment drawn from a point on the original figure to its reflected image (unless the point and its reflected image happen to be the same point, which happens when a figure is reflected over one of its own sides). A **reflection of a figure over a point** (an inversion) in two dimensions is the same as the rotation of the figure 180° about that point. The image of the

Copyright © Mometrix Media. You have been licensed one copy of this document for personal use only. Any other reproduction or redistribution is strictly prohibited. All rights reserved.
This content is provided for test preparation purposes only and does not imply an endorsement by Mometrix of any particular political, scientific, or religious point of view.

figure is congruent to the original figure. The **point of reflection** is the midpoint of a line segment which connects a point in the figure to its image (unless the point and its reflected image happen to be the same point, which happens when a figure is reflected in one of its own points).

Reflection of a figure over a line

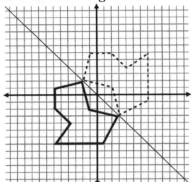

Reflection of a figure over a point

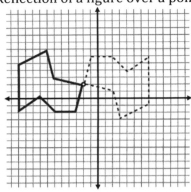

Review Video: Reflection
Visit mometrix.com/academy and enter code: 955068

PYTHAGOREAN THEOREM

The side of a triangle opposite the right angle is called the **hypotenuse**. The other two sides are called the legs. The Pythagorean theorem states a relationship among the legs and hypotenuse of a right triangle: $(a^2 + b^2 = c^2)$, where a and b are the lengths of the legs of a right triangle, and c is the length of the hypotenuse. Note that this formula will only work with right triangles.

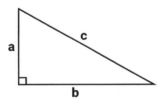

Review Video: Pythagorean Theorem
Visit mometrix.com/academy and enter code: 906576

Copyright © Mometrix Media. You have been licensed one copy of this document for personal use only. Any other reproduction or redistribution is strictly prohibited. All rights reserved.
This content is provided for test preparation purposes only and does not imply an endorsement by Mometrix of any particular political, scientific, or religious point of view.

TRIGONOMETRIC FORMULAS

In the diagram below, angle C is the right angle, and side c is the hypotenuse. Side a is the side opposite to angle A and side b is the side opposite to angle B. Using ratios of side lengths as a means to calculate the sine, cosine, and tangent of an acute angle only works for right triangles.

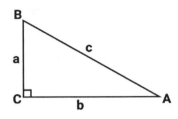

$$\sin A = \frac{\text{opposite side}}{\text{hypotenuse}} = \frac{a}{c} \qquad \csc A = \frac{1}{\sin A} = \frac{\text{hypotenuse}}{\text{opposite side}} = \frac{c}{a}$$

$$\cos A = \frac{\text{adjacent side}}{\text{hypotenuse}} = \frac{b}{c} \qquad \sec A = \frac{1}{\cos A} = \frac{\text{hypotenuse}}{\text{adjacent side}} = \frac{c}{b}$$

$$\tan A = \frac{\text{opposite side}}{\text{adjacent side}} = \frac{a}{b} \qquad \cot A = \frac{1}{\tan A} = \frac{\text{adjacent side}}{\text{opposite side}} = \frac{b}{a}$$

LAWS OF SINES AND COSINES

The **law of sines** states that $\frac{\sin A}{a} = \frac{\sin B}{b} = \frac{\sin C}{c}$, where A, B, and C are the angles of a triangle, and a, b, and c are the sides opposite their respective angles. This formula will work with all triangles, not just right triangles.

The **law of cosines** is given by the formula $c^2 = a^2 + b^2 - 2ab(\cos C)$, where a, b, and c are the sides of a triangle, and C is the angle opposite side c. This is a generalized form of the Pythagorean theorem that can be used on any triangle.

> **Review Video: <u>Law of Sines</u>**
> Visit mometrix.com/academy and enter code: 206844
>
> **Review Video: <u>Law of Cosines</u>**
> Visit mometrix.com/academy and enter code: 158911

QUADRILATERALS

A **quadrilateral** is a closed two-dimensional geometric figure that has four straight sides. The sum of the interior angles of any quadrilateral is 360°.

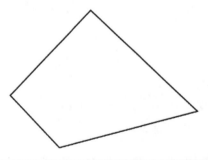

> **Review Video: <u>Diagonals of Parallelograms, Rectangles, and Rhombi</u>**
> Visit mometrix.com/academy and enter code: 320040

Copyright © Mometrix Media. You have been licensed one copy of this document for personal use only. Any other reproduction or redistribution is strictly prohibited. All rights reserved. This content is provided for test preparation purposes only and does not imply an endorsement by Mometrix of any particular political, scientific, or religious point of view.

KITE

A **kite** is a quadrilateral with two pairs of adjacent sides that are congruent. A result of this is perpendicular diagonals. A kite can be concave or convex and has one line of symmetry.

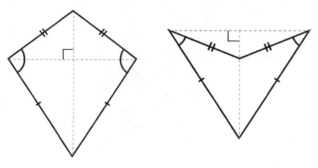

TRAPEZOID

Trapezoid: A trapezoid is defined as a quadrilateral that has at least one pair of parallel sides. There are no rules for the second pair of sides. So, there are no rules for the diagonals and no lines of symmetry for a trapezoid.

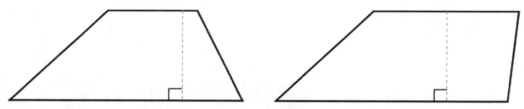

The **area of a trapezoid** is found by the formula $A = \frac{1}{2}h(b_1 + b_2)$, where h is the height (segment joining and perpendicular to the parallel bases), and b_1 and b_2 are the two parallel sides (bases). Do not use one of the other two sides as the height unless that side is also perpendicular to the parallel bases.

The **perimeter of a trapezoid** is found by the formula $P = a + b_1 + c + b_2$, where $a, b_1, c,$ and b_2 are the four sides of the trapezoid.

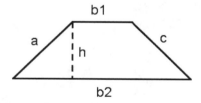

Review Video: Area and Perimeter of a Trapezoid
Visit mometrix.com/academy and enter code: 587523

Copyright © Mometrix Media. You have been licensed one copy of this document for personal use only. Any other reproduction or redistribution is strictly prohibited. All rights reserved. This content is provided for test preparation purposes only and does not imply an endorsement by Mometrix of any particular political, scientific, or religious point of view.

Isosceles trapezoid: A trapezoid with equal base angles. This gives rise to other properties including: the two nonparallel sides have the same length, the two non-base angles are also equal, and there is one line of symmetry through the midpoints of the parallel sides.

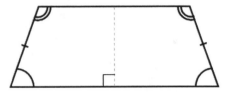

PARALLELOGRAM

A **parallelogram** is a quadrilateral that has two pairs of opposite parallel sides. As such it is a special type of trapezoid. The sides that are parallel are also congruent. The opposite interior angles are always congruent, and the consecutive interior angles are supplementary. The diagonals of a parallelogram divide each other. Each diagonal divides the parallelogram into two congruent triangles. A parallelogram has no line of symmetry, but does have 180-degree rotational symmetry about the midpoint.

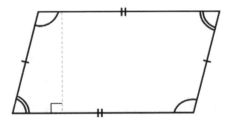

The **area of a parallelogram** is found by the formula $A = bh$, where b is the length of the base, and h is the height. Note that the base and height correspond to the length and width in a rectangle, so this formula would apply to rectangles as well. Do not confuse the height of a parallelogram with the length of the second side. The two are only the same measure in the case of a rectangle.

The **perimeter of a parallelogram** is found by the formula $P = 2a + 2b$ or $P = 2(a + b)$, where a and b are the lengths of the two sides.

> **Review Video: How to Find the Area and Perimeter of a Parallelogram**
> Visit mometrix.com/academy and enter code: 718313

RECTANGLE

A **rectangle** is a quadrilateral with four right angles. All rectangles are parallelograms and trapezoids, but not all parallelograms or trapezoids are rectangles. The diagonals of a rectangle are

Copyright © Mometrix Media. You have been licensed one copy of this document for personal use only. Any other reproduction or redistribution is strictly prohibited. All rights reserved.
This content is provided for test preparation purposes only and does not imply an endorsement by Mometrix of any particular political, scientific, or religious point of view.

congruent. Rectangles have two lines of symmetry (through each pair of opposing midpoints) and 180-degree rotational symmetry about the midpoint.

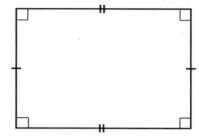

The **area of a rectangle** is found by the formula $A = lw$, where A is the area of the rectangle, l is the length (usually considered to be the longer side) and w is the width (usually considered to be the shorter side). The numbers for l and w are interchangeable.

The **perimeter of a rectangle** is found by the formula $P = 2l + 2w$ or $P = 2(l + w)$, where l is the length, and w is the width. It may be easier to add the length and width first and then double the result, as in the second formula.

RHOMBUS

A **rhombus** is a quadrilateral with four congruent sides. All rhombuses are parallelograms and kites; thus, they inherit all the properties of both types of quadrilaterals. The diagonals of a rhombus are perpendicular to each other. Rhombi have two lines of symmetry (along each of the diagonals) and 180° rotational symmetry. The **area of a rhombus** is half the product of the diagonals: $A = \frac{d_1 d_2}{2}$ and the perimeter of a rhombus is: $P = 2\sqrt{(d_1)^2 + (d_2)^2}$.

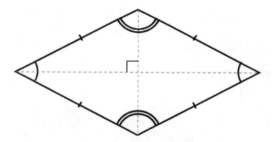

SQUARE

A **square** is a quadrilateral with four right angles and four congruent sides. Squares satisfy the criteria of all other types of quadrilaterals. The diagonals of a square are congruent and perpendicular to each other. Squares have four lines of symmetry (through each pair of opposing midpoints and along each of the diagonals) as well as 90° rotational symmetry about the midpoint.

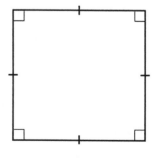

Copyright © Mometrix Media. You have been licensed one copy of this document for personal use only. Any other reproduction or redistribution is strictly prohibited. All rights reserved. This content is provided for test preparation purposes only and does not imply an endorsement by Mometrix of any particular political, scientific, or religious point of view.

The **area of a square** is found by using the formula $A = s^2$, where s is the length of one side. The **perimeter of a square** is found by using the formula $P = 4s$, where s is the length of one side. Because all four sides are equal in a square, it is faster to multiply the length of one side by 4 than to add the same number four times. You could use the formulas for rectangles and get the same answer.

> **Review Video: Area and Perimeter of Rectangles and Squares**
> Visit mometrix.com/academy and enter code: 428109

Copyright © Mometrix Media. You have been licensed one copy of this document for personal use only. Any other reproduction or redistribution is strictly prohibited. All rights reserved.
This content is provided for test preparation purposes only and does not imply an endorsement by Mometrix of any particular political, scientific, or religious point of view.

HIERARCHY OF QUADRILATERALS

The hierarchy of quadrilaterals is as follows:

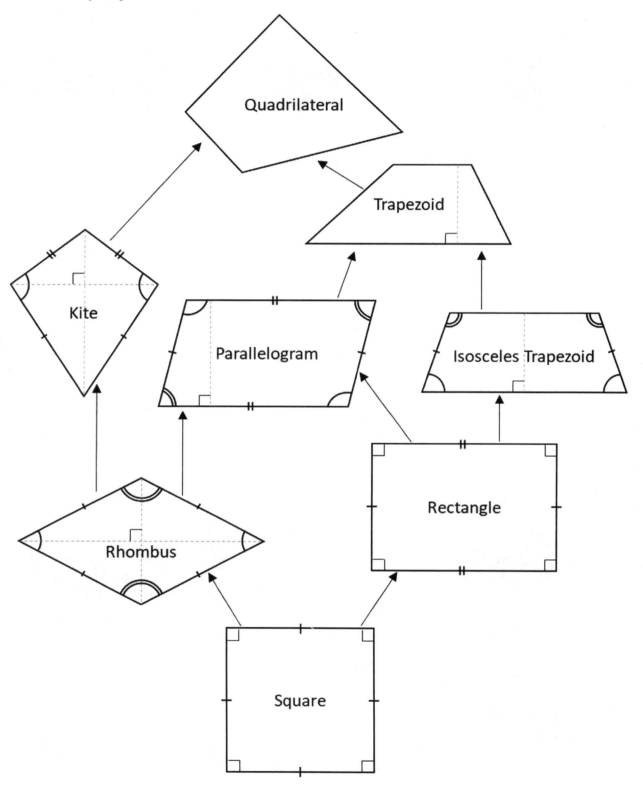

Copyright © Mometrix Media. You have been licensed one copy of this document for personal use only. Any other reproduction or redistribution is strictly prohibited. All rights reserved.
This content is provided for test preparation purposes only and does not imply an endorsement by Mometrix of any particular political, scientific, or religious point of view.

CIRCLES

The **center** of a circle is the single point from which every point on the circle is **equidistant**. The **radius** is a line segment that joins the center of the circle and any one point on the circle. All radii of a circle are equal. Circles that have the same center but not the same length of radii are **concentric**. The **diameter** is a line segment that passes through the center of the circle and has both endpoints on the circle. The length of the diameter is exactly twice the length of the radius. Point O in the diagram below is the center of the circle, segments $\overline{OX}$, $\overline{OY}$, and $\overline{OZ}$ are radii; and segment $\overline{XZ}$ is a diameter.

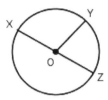

> **Review Video: Points of a Circle**
> Visit mometrix.com/academy and enter code: 420746
>
> **Review Video: The Diameter, Radius, and Circumference of Circles**
> Visit mometrix.com/academy and enter code: 448988

The **area of a circle** is found by the formula $A = \pi r^2$, where r is the length of the radius. If the diameter of the circle is given, remember to divide it in half to get the length of the radius before proceeding.

The **circumference** of a circle is found by the formula $C = 2\pi r$, where r is the radius. Again, remember to convert the diameter if you are given that measure rather than the radius.

> **Review Video: Area and Circumference of a Circle**
> Visit mometrix.com/academy and enter code: 243015

INSCRIBED AND CIRCUMSCRIBED FIGURES

These terms can both be used to describe a given arrangement of figures, depending on perspective. If each of the vertices of figure A lie on figure B, then it can be said that figure A is **inscribed** in figure B, but it can also be said that figure B is **circumscribed** about figure A. The

Copyright © Mometrix Media. You have been licensed one copy of this document for personal use only. Any other reproduction or redistribution is strictly prohibited. All rights reserved.
This content is provided for test preparation purposes only and does not imply an endorsement by Mometrix of any particular political, scientific, or religious point of view.

following table and examples help to illustrate the concept. Note that the figures cannot both be circles, as they would be completely overlapping and neither would be inscribed or circumscribed.

Given	Description	Equivalent Description	Figures
Each of the sides of a pentagon is tangent to a circle	The circle is inscribed in the pentagon	The pentagon is circumscribed about the circle	
Each of the vertices of a pentagon lie on a circle	The pentagon is inscribed in the circle	The circle is circumscribed about the pentagon	

ARCS

An **arc** is a portion of a circle. Specifically, an arc is the set of points between and including two points on a circle. An arc does not contain any points inside the circle. When a segment is drawn from the endpoints of an arc to the center of the circle, a sector is formed. A **minor arc** is an arc that has a measure less than 180°. A **major arc** is an arc that has a measure of at least 180°. Every minor arc has a corresponding major arc that can be found by subtracting the measure of the minor arc from 360°. A **semicircle** is an arc whose endpoints are the endpoints of the diameter of a circle. A semicircle is exactly half of a circle.

Arc length is the length of that portion of the circumference between two points on the circle. The formula for arc length is $s = \frac{\pi r \theta}{180°}$, where s is the arc length, r is the length of the radius, and θ is the angular measure of the arc in degrees, or $s = r\theta$, where θ is the angular measure of the arc in radians (2π radians = 360 degrees).

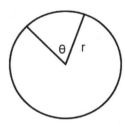

ANGLES OF CIRCLES

A **central angle** is an angle whose vertex is the center of a circle and whose legs intercept an arc of the circle. The measure of a central angle is equal to the measure of the minor arc it intercepts.

An **inscribed angle** is an angle whose vertex lies on a circle and whose legs contain chords of that circle. The portion of the circle intercepted by the legs of the angle is called the intercepted arc. The

Copyright © Mometrix Media. You have been licensed one copy of this document for personal use only. Any other reproduction or redistribution is strictly prohibited. All rights reserved.
This content is provided for test preparation purposes only and does not imply an endorsement by Mometrix of any particular political, scientific, or religious point of view.

measure of the intercepted arc is exactly twice the measure of the inscribed angle. In the following diagram, angle ABC is an inscribed angle. $\overset{\frown}{AC} = 2(\text{m}\angle ABC)$.

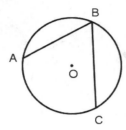

Any angle inscribed in a semicircle is a right angle. The intercepted arc is 180°, making the inscribed angle half that, or 90°. In the diagram below, angle ABC is inscribed in semicircle ABC, making angle ABC equal to 90°.

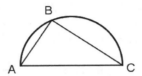

Review Video: <u>Arcs and Angles of Circles</u>
Visit mometrix.com/academy and enter code: 652838

SECANTS, CHORDS, AND TANGENTS

A **secant** is a line that intersects a circle in two points. The segment of a secant line that is contained within the circle is called a **chord**. Two secants may intersect inside the circle, on the circle, or outside the circle. When the two secants intersect on the circle, an inscribed angle is formed. When two secants intersect inside a circle, the measure of each of two vertical angles is equal to half the sum of the two intercepted arcs. Consider the following diagram where $\text{m}\angle AEB = \frac{1}{2}(\overset{\frown}{AB} + \overset{\frown}{CD})$ and $\text{m}\angle BEC = \frac{1}{2}(\overset{\frown}{BC} + \overset{\frown}{AD})$.

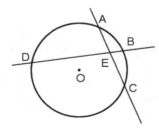

Copyright © Mometrix Media. You have been licensed one copy of this document for personal use only. Any other reproduction or redistribution is strictly prohibited. All rights reserved.
This content is provided for test preparation purposes only and does not imply an endorsement by Mometrix of any particular political, scientific, or religious point of view.

When two secants intersect outside a circle, the measure of the angle formed is equal to half the difference of the two arcs that lie between the two secants. In the diagram below, $m\angle AEB = \frac{1}{2}(\widehat{AB} - \widehat{CD})$.

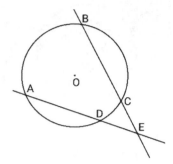

A **tangent** is a line in the same plane as a circle that touches the circle in exactly one point. The point at which a tangent touches a circle is called the **point of tangency**. While a line segment can be tangent to a circle as part of a line that is tangent, it is improper to say a tangent can be simply a line segment that touches the circle in exactly one point.

In the diagram below, $\overleftrightarrow{EB}$ is a secant and contains chord $\overline{EB}$, and $\overleftrightarrow{CD}$ is tangent to circle A. Notice that $\overline{FB}$ is not tangent to the circle. $\overline{FB}$ is a line segment that touches the circle in exactly one point, but if the segment were extended, it would touch the circle in a second point. In the diagram below, point B is the point of tangency.

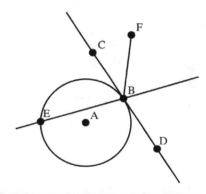

Review Video: <u>Secants, Chords, and Tangents</u>
Visit mometrix.com/academy and enter code: 258360

Review Video: <u>Tangent Lines of a Circle</u>
Visit mometrix.com/academy and enter code: 780167

Copyright © Mometrix Media. You have been licensed one copy of this document for personal use only. Any other reproduction or redistribution is strictly prohibited. All rights reserved.
This content is provided for test preparation purposes only and does not imply an endorsement by Mometrix of any particular political, scientific, or religious point of view.

SECTORS

A **sector** is the portion of a circle formed by two radii and their intercepted arc. While the arc length is exclusively the points that are also on the circumference of the circle, the sector is the entire area bounded by the arc and the two radii.

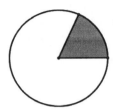

The **area of a sector** of a circle is found by the formula, $A = \frac{\theta r^2}{2}$, where A is the area, θ is the measure of the central angle in radians, and r is the radius. To find the area with the central angle in degrees, use the formula, $A = \frac{\theta \pi r^2}{360}$, where θ is the measure of the central angle and r is the radius.

SOLIDS

The **surface area of a solid object** is the area of all sides or exterior surfaces. For objects such as prisms and pyramids, a further distinction is made between base surface area (B) and lateral surface area (LA). For a prism, the total surface area (SA) is $SA = LA + 2B$. For a pyramid or cone, the total surface area is $SA = LA + B$.

The **surface area of a sphere** can be found by the formula $A = 4\pi r^2$, where r is the radius. The volume is given by the formula $V = \frac{4}{3}\pi r^3$, where r is the radius. Both quantities are generally given in terms of π.

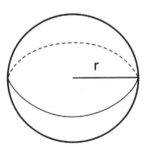

Review Video: <u>Volume and Surface Area of a Sphere</u>
Visit mometrix.com/academy and enter code: 786928

The **volume of any prism** is found by the formula $V = Bh$, where B is the area of the base, and h is the height (perpendicular distance between the bases). The surface area of any prism is the sum of

Copyright © Mometrix Media. You have been licensed one copy of this document for personal use only. Any other reproduction or redistribution is strictly prohibited. All rights reserved.
This content is provided for test preparation purposes only and does not imply an endorsement by Mometrix of any particular political, scientific, or religious point of view.

the areas of both bases and all sides. It can be calculated as $SA = 2B + Ph$, where P is the perimeter of the base.

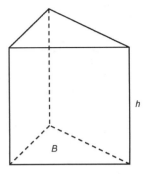

Review Video: Volume and Surface Area of a Prism
Visit mometrix.com/academy and enter code: 420158

For a **rectangular prism**, the volume can be found by the formula $V = lwh$, where V is the volume, l is the length, w is the width, and h is the height. The surface area can be calculated as $SA = 2lw + 2hl + 2wh$ or $SA = 2(lw + hl + wh)$.

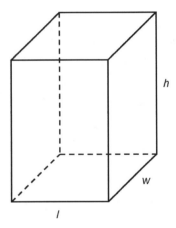

Review Video: Volume and Surface Area of a Rectangular Prism
Visit mometrix.com/academy and enter code: 282814

The **volume of a cube** can be found by the formula $V = s^3$, where s is the length of a side. The surface area of a cube is calculated as $SA = 6s^2$, where SA is the total surface area and s is the length of a side. These formulas are the same as the ones used for the volume and surface area of a rectangular prism, but simplified since all three quantities (length, width, and height) are the same.

Review Video: Volume and Surface Area of a Cube
Visit mometrix.com/academy and enter code: 664455

The **volume of a cylinder** can be calculated by the formula $V = \pi r^2 h$, where r is the radius, and h is the height. The surface area of a cylinder can be found by the formula $SA = 2\pi r^2 + 2\pi rh$. The

Copyright © Mometrix Media. You have been licensed one copy of this document for personal use only. Any other reproduction or redistribution is strictly prohibited. All rights reserved.
This content is provided for test preparation purposes only and does not imply an endorsement by Mometrix of any particular political, scientific, or religious point of view.

first term is the base area multiplied by two, and the second term is the perimeter of the base multiplied by the height.

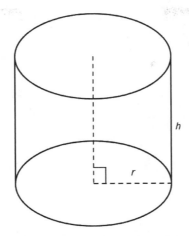

Review Video: Finding the Volume and Surface Area of a Right Circular Cylinder
Visit mometrix.com/academy and enter code: 226463

The **volume of a pyramid** is found by the formula $V = \frac{1}{3}Bh$, where B is the area of the base, and h is the height (perpendicular distance from the vertex to the base). Notice this formula is the same as $\frac{1}{3}$ times the volume of a prism. Like a prism, the base of a pyramid can be any shape.

Finding the **surface area of a pyramid** is not as simple as the other shapes we've looked at thus far. If the pyramid is a right pyramid, meaning the base is a regular polygon and the vertex is directly over the center of that polygon, the surface area can be calculated as $SA = B + \frac{1}{2}Ph_s$, where P is the perimeter of the base, and h_s is the slant height (distance from the vertex to the midpoint of one side of the base). If the pyramid is irregular, the area of each triangle side must be calculated individually and then summed, along with the base.

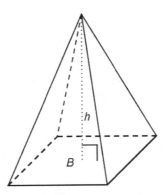

Review Video: Finding the Volume and Surface Area of a Pyramid
Visit mometrix.com/academy and enter code: 621932

239

Copyright © Mometrix Media. You have been licensed one copy of this document for personal use only. Any other reproduction or redistribution is strictly prohibited. All rights reserved.
This content is provided for test preparation purposes only and does not imply an endorsement by Mometrix of any particular political, scientific, or religious point of view.

The **volume of a cone** is found by the formula $V = \frac{1}{3}\pi r^2 h$, where r is the radius, and h is the height. Notice this is the same as $\frac{1}{3}$ times the volume of a cylinder. The surface area can be calculated as $SA = \pi r^2 + \pi r s$, where s is the slant height. The slant height can be calculated using the Pythagorean theorem to be $\sqrt{r^2 + h^2}$, so the surface area formula can also be written as $SA = \pi r^2 + \pi r \sqrt{r^2 + h^2}$.

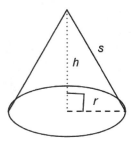

Review Video: Volume and Surface Area of a Right Circular Cone
Visit mometrix.com/academy and enter code: 573574

Data, Statistics, and Probability

PROBABILITY

Probability is the likelihood of a certain outcome occurring for a given event. An **event** is any situation that produces a result. It could be something as simple as flipping a coin or as complex as launching a rocket. Determining the probability of an outcome for an event can be equally simple or complex. As such, there are specific terms used in the study of probability that need to be understood:

- **Compound event**—an event that involves two or more independent events (rolling a pair of dice and taking the sum)
- **Desired outcome** (or success)—an outcome that meets a particular set of criteria (a roll of 1 or 2 if we are looking for numbers less than 3)
- **Independent events**—two or more events whose outcomes do not affect one another (two coins tossed at the same time)
- **Dependent events**—two or more events whose outcomes affect one another (two cards drawn consecutively from the same deck)
- **Certain outcome**—probability of outcome is 100% or 1
- **Impossible outcome**—probability of outcome is 0% or 0
- **Mutually exclusive outcomes**—two or more outcomes whose criteria cannot all be satisfied in a single event (a coin coming up heads and tails on the same toss)
- **Random variable**—refers to all possible outcomes of a single event which may be discrete or continuous.

Review Video: Intro to Probability
Visit mometrix.com/academy and enter code: 212374

Copyright © Mometrix Media. You have been licensed one copy of this document for personal use only. Any other reproduction or redistribution is strictly prohibited. All rights reserved.
This content is provided for test preparation purposes only and does not imply an endorsement by Mometrix of any particular political, scientific, or religious point of view.

SAMPLE SPACE

The total set of all possible results of a test or experiment is called a **sample space**, or sometimes a universal sample space. The sample space, represented by one of the variables S, Ω, or U (for universal sample space) has individual elements called outcomes. Other terms for outcome that may be used interchangeably include elementary outcome, simple event, or sample point. The number of outcomes in a given sample space could be infinite or finite, and some tests may yield multiple unique sample sets. For example, tests conducted by drawing playing cards from a standard deck would have one sample space of the card values, another sample space of the card suits, and a third sample space of suit-denomination combinations. For most tests, the sample spaces considered will be finite.

An **event**, represented by the variable E, is a portion of a sample space. It may be one outcome or a group of outcomes from the same sample space. If an event occurs, then the test or experiment will generate an outcome that satisfies the requirement of that event. For example, given a standard deck of 52 playing cards as the sample space, and defining the event as the collection of face cards, then the event will occur if the card drawn is a J, Q, or K. If any other card is drawn, the event is said to have not occurred.

For every sample space, each possible outcome has a specific likelihood, or probability, that it will occur. The probability measure, also called the **distribution**, is a function that assigns a real number probability, from zero to one, to each outcome. For a probability measure to be accurate, every outcome must have a real number probability measure that is greater than or equal to zero and less than or equal to one. Also, the probability measure of the sample space must equal one, and the probability measure of the union of multiple outcomes must equal the sum of the individual probability measures.

Probabilities of events are expressed as real numbers from zero to one. They give a numerical value to the chance that a particular event will occur. The probability of an event occurring is the sum of the probabilities of the individual elements of that event. For example, in a standard deck of 52 playing cards as the sample space and the collection of face cards as the event, the probability of drawing a specific face card is $\frac{1}{52} = 0.019$, but the probability of drawing any one of the twelve face cards is $12(0.019) = 0.228$. Note that rounding of numbers can generate different results. If you multiplied 12 by the fraction $\frac{1}{52}$ before converting to a decimal, you would get the answer $\frac{12}{52} = 0.231$.

THEORETICAL AND EXPERIMENTAL PROBABILITY

Theoretical probability can usually be determined without actually performing the event. The likelihood of an outcome occurring, or the probability of an outcome occurring, is given by the formula:

$$P(A) = \frac{\text{Number of acceptable outcomes}}{\text{Number of possible outcomes}}$$

Note that $P(A)$ is the probability of an outcome A occurring, and each outcome is just as likely to occur as any other outcome. If each outcome has the same probability of occurring as every other possible outcome, the outcomes are said to be equally likely to occur. The total number of acceptable outcomes must be less than or equal to the total number of possible outcomes. If the two are equal, then the outcome is certain to occur and the probability is 1. If the number of acceptable outcomes is zero, then the outcome is impossible and the probability is 0. For example, if there are

Copyright © Mometrix Media. You have been licensed one copy of this document for personal use only. Any other reproduction or redistribution is strictly prohibited. All rights reserved. This content is provided for test preparation purposes only and does not imply an endorsement by Mometrix of any particular political, scientific, or religious point of view.

20 marbles in a bag and 5 are red, then the theoretical probability of randomly selecting a red marble is 5 out of 20, $\left(\frac{5}{20} = \frac{1}{4}, 0.25, \text{ or } 25\%\right)$.

If the theoretical probability is unknown or too complicated to calculate, it can be estimated by an experimental probability. **Experimental probability**, also called empirical probability, is an estimate of the likelihood of a certain outcome based on repeated experiments or collected data. In other words, while theoretical probability is based on what *should* happen, experimental probability is based on what *has* happened. Experimental probability is calculated in the same way as theoretical probability, except that actual outcomes are used instead of possible outcomes. The more experiments performed or datapoints gathered, the better the estimate should be.

Theoretical and experimental probability do not always line up with one another. Theoretical probability says that out of 20 coin-tosses, 10 should be heads. However, if we were actually to toss 20 coins, we might record just 5 heads. This doesn't mean that our theoretical probability is incorrect; it just means that this particular experiment had results that were different from what was predicted. A practical application of empirical probability is the insurance industry. There are no set functions that define lifespan, health, or safety. Insurance companies look at factors from hundreds of thousands of individuals to find patterns that they then use to set the formulas for insurance premiums.

> **Review Video: Empirical Probability**
> Visit mometrix.com/academy and enter code: 513468

OBJECTIVE AND SUBJECTIVE PROBABILITY

Objective probability is based on mathematical formulas and documented evidence. Examples of objective probability include raffles or lottery drawings where there is a pre-determined number of possible outcomes and a predetermined number of outcomes that correspond to an event. Other cases of objective probability include probabilities of rolling dice, flipping coins, or drawing cards. Most gambling games are based on objective probability.

In contrast, **subjective probability** is based on personal or professional feelings and judgments. Often, there is a lot of guesswork following extensive research. Areas where subjective probability is applicable include sales trends and business expenses. Attractions set admission prices based on subjective probabilities of attendance based on varying admission rates in an effort to maximize their profit.

COMPLEMENT OF AN EVENT

Sometimes it may be easier to calculate the possibility of something not happening, or the **complement of an event**. Represented by the symbol $\bar{A}$, the complement of A is the probability that event A does not happen. When you know the probability of event A occurring, you can use the formula $P(\bar{A}) = 1 - P(A)$, where $P(\bar{A})$ is the probability of event A not occurring, and $P(A)$ is the probability of event A occurring.

ADDITION RULE

The **addition rule** for probability is used for finding the probability of a compound event. Use the formula $P(A \cup B) = P(A) + P(B) - P(A \cap B)$, where $P(A \cap B)$ is the probability of both events occurring to find the probability of a compound event. The probability of both events occurring at the same time must be subtracted to eliminate any overlap in the first two probabilities.

Copyright © Mometrix Media. You have been licensed one copy of this document for personal use only. Any other reproduction or redistribution is strictly prohibited. All rights reserved.
This content is provided for test preparation purposes only and does not imply an endorsement by Mometrix of any particular political, scientific, or religious point of view.

CONDITIONAL PROBABILITY

Given two events A and B, the **conditional probability** $P(A|B)$ is the probability that event A will occur, given that event B has occurred. The conditional probability cannot be calculated simply from $P(A)$ and $P(B)$; these probabilities alone do not give sufficient information to determine the conditional probability. It can, however, be determined if you are also given the probability of the intersection of events A and B, $P(A \cap B)$, the probability that events A and B both occur. Specifically, $P(A|B) = \frac{P(A \cap B)}{P(B)}$. For instance, suppose you have a jar containing two red marbles and two blue marbles, and you draw two marbles at random. Consider event A being the event that the first marble drawn is red, and event B being the event that the second marble drawn is blue. If we want to find the probability that B occurs given that A occurred, $P(B|A)$, then we can compute it using the fact that $P(A)$ is $\frac{1}{2}$, and $P(A \cap B)$ is $\frac{1}{3}$. (The latter may not be obvious, but may be determined by finding the product of $\frac{1}{2}$ and $\frac{2}{3}$). Therefore $P(B|A) = \frac{P(A \cap B)}{P(A)} = \frac{1/3}{1/2} = \frac{2}{3}$.

CONDITIONAL PROBABILITY IN EVERYDAY SITUATIONS

Conditional probability often arises in everyday situations in, for example, estimating the risk or benefit of certain activities. The conditional probability of having a heart attack given that you exercise daily may be smaller than the overall probability of having a heart attack. The conditional probability of having lung cancer given that you are a smoker is larger than the overall probability of having lung cancer. Note that changing the order of the conditional probability changes the meaning: the conditional probability of having lung cancer given that you are a smoker is a very different thing from the probability of being a smoker given that you have lung cancer. In an extreme case, suppose that a certain rare disease is caused only by eating a certain food, but even then, it is unlikely. Then the conditional probability of having that disease given that you eat the dangerous food is nonzero but low, but the conditional probability of having eaten that food given that you have the disease is 100%!

> **Review Video: Conditional Probability**
> Visit mometrix.com/academy and enter code: 397924

INDEPENDENCE

The conditional probability $P(A|B)$ is the probability that event A will occur given that event B occurs. If the two events are independent, we do not expect that whether or not event B occurs should have any effect on whether or not event A occurs. In other words, we expect $P(A|B) = P(A)$.

This can be proven using the usual equations for conditional probability and the joint probability of independent events. The conditional probability $P(A|B) = \frac{P(A \cap B)}{P(B)}$. If A and B are independent, then $P(A \cap B) = P(A)P(B)$. So $P(A|B) = \frac{P(A)P(B)}{P(B)} = P(A)$. By similar reasoning, if A and B are independent then $P(B|A) = P(B)$.

MULTIPLICATION RULE

The **multiplication rule** can be used to find the probability of two independent events occurring using the formula $P(A \cap B) = P(A) \times P(B)$, where $P(A \cap B)$ is the probability of two independent

Copyright © Mometrix Media. You have been licensed one copy of this document for personal use only. Any other reproduction or redistribution is strictly prohibited. All rights reserved. This content is provided for test preparation purposes only and does not imply an endorsement by Mometrix of any particular political, scientific, or religious point of view.

events occurring, $P(A)$ is the probability of the first event occurring, and $P(B)$ is the probability of the second event occurring.

The multiplication rule can also be used to find the probability of two dependent events occurring using the formula $P(A \cap B) = P(A) \times P(B|A)$, where $P(A \cap B)$ is the probability of two dependent events occurring and $P(B|A)$ is the probability of the second event occurring after the first event has already occurred.

Use a **combination of the multiplication** rule and the rule of complements to find the probability that at least one outcome of the element will occur. This is given by the general formula $P(\text{at least one event occurring}) = 1 - P(\text{no outcomes occurring})$. For example, to find the probability that at least one even number will show when a pair of dice is rolled, find the probability that two odd numbers will be rolled (no even numbers) and subtract from one. You can always use a tree diagram or make a chart to list the possible outcomes when the sample space is small, such as in the dice-rolling example, but in most cases it will be much faster to use the multiplication and complement formulas.

> **Review Video: Multiplication Rule**
> Visit mometrix.com/academy and enter code: 782598

UNION AND INTERSECTION OF TWO SETS OF OUTCOMES

If A and B are each a set of elements or outcomes from an experiment, then the **union** (symbol $\cup$) of the two sets is the set of elements found in set A or set B. For example, if $A = \{2, 3, 4\}$ and $B = \{3, 4, 5\}$, $A \cup B = \{2, 3, 4, 5\}$. Note that the outcomes 3 and 4 appear only once in the union. For statistical events, the union is equivalent to "or"; $P(A \cup B)$ is the same thing as $P(A \text{ or } B)$. The **intersection** (symbol $\cap$) of two sets is the set of outcomes common to both sets. For the above sets A and B, $A \cap B = \{3, 4\}$. For statistical events, the intersection is equivalent to "and"; $P(A \cap B)$ is the same thing as $P(A \text{ and } B)$. It is important to note that union and intersection operations commute. That is:

$$A \cup B = B \cup A \text{ and } A \cap B = B \cap A$$

PERMUTATIONS AND COMBINATIONS

When trying to calculate the probability of an event using the $\frac{\text{desired outcomes}}{\text{total outcomes}}$ formula, you may frequently find that there are too many outcomes to individually count them. **Permutation** and **combination formulas** offer a shortcut to counting outcomes. A permutation is an arrangement of a specific number of a set of objects in a specific order. The number of **permutations** of r items given a set of n items can be calculated as $_nP_r = \frac{n!}{(n-r)!}$. Combinations are similar to permutations, except there are no restrictions regarding the order of the elements. While ABC is considered a different permutation than BCA, ABC and BCA are considered the same combination. The number of **combinations** of r items given a set of n items can be calculated as $_nC_r = \frac{n!}{r!(n-r)!}$ or $_nC_r = \frac{_nP_r}{r!}$.

Suppose you want to calculate how many different 5-card hands can be drawn from a deck of 52 cards. This is a combination since the order of the cards in a hand does not matter. There are 52

Copyright © Mometrix Media. You have been licensed one copy of this document for personal use only. Any other reproduction or redistribution is strictly prohibited. All rights reserved.
This content is provided for test preparation purposes only and does not imply an endorsement by Mometrix of any particular political, scientific, or religious point of view.

cards available, and 5 to be selected. Thus, the number of different hands is $_{52}C_5 = \frac{52!}{5! \times 47!} =$ 2,598,960.

Review Video: Probability - Permutation and Combination
Visit mometrix.com/academy and enter code: 907664

TREE DIAGRAM

For a simple sample space, possible outcomes may be determined by using a **tree diagram** or an organized chart. In either case, you can easily draw or list out the possible outcomes. For example, to determine all the possible ways three objects can be ordered, you can draw a tree diagram:

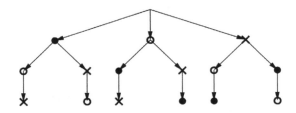

Review Video: Tree Diagrams
Visit mometrix.com/academy and enter code: 829158

You can also make a chart to list all the possibilities:

First object	Second object	Third object
●	X	O
●	O	X
O	●	X
O	X	●
X	●	O
X	O	●

Either way, you can easily see there are six possible ways the three objects can be ordered.

If two events have no outcomes in common, they are said to be **mutually exclusive**. For example, in a standard deck of 52 playing cards, the event of all card suits is mutually exclusive to the event of all card values. If two events have no bearing on each other so that one event occurring has no influence on the probability of another event occurring, the two events are said to be independent. For example, rolling a standard six-sided die multiple times does not change that probability that a particular number will be rolled from one roll to the next. If the outcome of one event does affect the probability of the second event, the two events are said to be dependent. For example, if cards are drawn from a deck, the probability of drawing an ace after an ace has been drawn is different than the probability of drawing an ace if no ace (or no other card, for that matter) has been drawn.

In probability, the **odds in favor of an event** are the number of times the event will occur compared to the number of times the event will not occur. To calculate the odds in favor of an event, use the formula $\frac{P(A)}{1-P(A)}$, where $P(A)$ is the probability that the event will occur. Many times,

Copyright © Mometrix Media. You have been licensed one copy of this document for personal use only. Any other reproduction or redistribution is strictly prohibited. All rights reserved.
This content is provided for test preparation purposes only and does not imply an endorsement by Mometrix of any particular political, scientific, or religious point of view.

odds in favor is given as a ratio in the form $\frac{a}{b}$ or $a:b$, where a is the probability of the event occurring and b is the complement of the event, the probability of the event not occurring. If the odds in favor are given as 2:5, that means that you can expect the event to occur two times for every 5 times that it does not occur. In other words, the probability that the event will occur is $\frac{2}{2+5} = \frac{2}{7}$.

In probability, the **odds against an event** are the number of times the event will not occur compared to the number of times the event will occur. To calculate the odds against an event, use the formula $\frac{1-P(A)}{P(A)}$, where $P(A)$ is the probability that the event will occur. Many times, odds against is given as a ratio in the form $\frac{b}{a}$ or $b:a$, where b is the probability the event will not occur (the complement of the event) and a is the probability the event will occur. If the odds against an event are given as 3:1, that means that you can expect the event to not occur 3 times for every one time it does occur. In other words, 3 out of every 4 trials will fail.

TWO-WAY FREQUENCY TABLES

If we have a two-way frequency table, it is generally a straightforward matter to read off the probabilities of any two events A and B, as well as the joint probability of both events occurring, $P(A \cap B)$. We can then find the conditional probability $P(A|B)$ by calculating $P(A|B) = \frac{P(A \cap B)}{P(B)}$. We could also check whether or not events are independent by verifying whether $P(A)P(B) = P(A \cap B)$.

For example, a certain store's recent T-shirt sales:

	Small	Medium	Large	Total
Blue	25	40	35	100
White	27	25	22	74
Black	8	23	15	46
Total	60	88	72	220

Suppose we want to find the conditional probability that a customer buys a black shirt (event A), given that the shirt he buys is size small (event B). From the table, the probability $P(B)$ that a customer buys a small shirt is $\frac{60}{220} = \frac{3}{11}$. The probability $P(A \cap B)$ that he buys a small, black shirt is $\frac{8}{220} = \frac{2}{55}$. The conditional probability $P(A|B)$ that he buys a black shirt, given that he buys a small shirt, is therefore $P(A|B) = \frac{2/55}{3/11} = \frac{2}{15}$.

Similarly, if we want to check whether the event a customer buys a blue shirt, A, is independent of the event that a customer buys a medium shirt, B. From the table, $P(A) = \frac{100}{220} = \frac{5}{11}$ and $P(B) = \frac{88}{220} = \frac{4}{10}$. Also, $P(A \cap B) = \frac{40}{220} = \frac{2}{11}$. Since $\left(\frac{5}{11}\right)\left(\frac{4}{10}\right) = \frac{20}{110} = \frac{2}{11}$, $P(A)P(B) = P(A \cap B)$ and these two events are indeed independent.

Copyright © Mometrix Media. You have been licensed one copy of this document for personal use only. Any other reproduction or redistribution is strictly prohibited. All rights reserved.
This content is provided for test preparation purposes only and does not imply an endorsement by Mometrix of any particular political, scientific, or religious point of view.

EXPECTED VALUE

Expected value is a method of determining the expected outcome in a random situation. It is a sum of the weighted probabilities of the possible outcomes. Multiply the probability of an event occurring by the weight assigned to that probability (such as the amount of money won or lost). A practical application of the expected value is to determine whether a game of chance is really fair. If the sum of the weighted probabilities is equal to zero, the game is generally considered fair because the player has a fair chance to at least break even. If the expected value is less than zero, then players are expected to lose more than they win. For example, a lottery drawing might allow the player to choose any three-digit number, 000–999. The probability of choosing the winning number is 1:1000. If it costs $1 to play, and a winning number receives $500, the expected value is $\left(-\$1 \times \frac{999}{1,000}\right) + \left(\$499 \times \frac{1}{1,000}\right) = -\$0.50$. You can expect to lose on average 50 cents for every dollar you spend.

> **Review Video: Expected Value**
> Visit mometrix.com/academy and enter code: 643554

EXPECTED VALUE AND SIMULATORS

A die roll simulator will show the results of n rolls of a die. The result of each die roll may be recorded. For example, suppose a die is rolled 100 times. All results may be recorded. The numbers of 1s, 2s, 3s, 4s, 5s, and 6s, may be counted. The experimental probability of rolling each number will equal the ratio of the frequency of the rolled number to the total number of rolls. As the number of rolls increases, or approaches infinity, the experimental probability will approach the theoretical probability of $\frac{1}{6}$. Thus, the expected value for the roll of a die is shown to be $\left(1 \times \frac{1}{6}\right) + \left(2 \times \frac{1}{6}\right) + \left(3 \times \frac{1}{6}\right) + \left(4 \times \frac{1}{6}\right) + \left(5 \times \frac{1}{6}\right) + \left(6 \times \frac{1}{6}\right)$, or 3.5.

STATISTICS

Statistics is the branch of mathematics that deals with collecting, recording, interpreting, illustrating, and analyzing large amounts of **data**. The following terms are often used in the discussion of data and **statistics**:

- **Data** – the collective name for pieces of information (singular is datum)
- **Quantitative data** – measurements (such as length, mass, and speed) that provide information about quantities in numbers
- **Qualitative data** – information (such as colors, scents, tastes, and shapes) that cannot be measured using numbers
- **Discrete data** – information that can be expressed only by a specific value, such as whole or half numbers. (e.g., since people can be counted only in whole numbers, a population count would be discrete data.)
- **Continuous data** – information (such as time and temperature) that can be expressed by any value within a given range
- **Primary data** – information that has been collected directly from a survey, investigation, or experiment, such as a questionnaire or the recording of daily temperatures. (Primary data that has not yet been organized or analyzed is called **raw data**.)
- **Secondary data** – information that has been collected, sorted, and processed by the researcher

Copyright © Mometrix Media. You have been licensed one copy of this document for personal use only. Any other reproduction or redistribution is strictly prohibited. All rights reserved.
This content is provided for test preparation purposes only and does not imply an endorsement by Mometrix of any particular political, scientific, or religious point of view.

- **Ordinal data** – information that can be placed in numerical order, such as age or weight
- **Nominal data** – information that *cannot* be placed in numerical order, such as names or places

DATA COLLECTION

POPULATION

In statistics, the **population** is the entire collection of people, plants, etc., that data can be collected from. For example, a study to determine how well students in local schools perform on a standardized test would have a population of all the students enrolled in those schools, although a study may include just a small sample of students from each school. A **parameter** is a numerical value that gives information about the population, such as the mean, median, mode, or standard deviation. Remember that the symbol for the mean of a population is μ and the symbol for the standard deviation of a population is σ.

SAMPLE

A **sample** is a portion of the entire population. Whereas a parameter helped describe the population, a **statistic** is a numerical value that gives information about the sample, such as mean, median, mode, or standard deviation. Keep in mind that the symbols for mean and standard deviation are different when they are referring to a sample rather than the entire population. For a sample, the symbol for mean is $\bar{x}$ and the symbol for standard deviation is s. The mean and standard deviation of a sample may or may not be identical to that of the entire population due to a sample only being a subset of the population. However, if the sample is random and large enough, statistically significant values can be attained. Samples are generally used when the population is too large to justify including every element or when acquiring data for the entire population is impossible.

INFERENTIAL STATISTICS

Inferential statistics is the branch of statistics that uses samples to make predictions about an entire population. This type of statistic is often seen in political polls, where a sample of the population is questioned about a particular topic or politician to gain an understanding of the attitudes of the entire population of the country. Often, exit polls are conducted on election days using this method. Inferential statistics can have a large margin of error if you do not have a valid sample.

SAMPLING DISTRIBUTION

Statistical values calculated from various samples of the same size make up the **sampling distribution**. For example, if several samples of identical size are randomly selected from a large population and then the mean of each sample is calculated, the distribution of values of the means would be a sampling distribution.

The **sampling distribution of the mean** is the distribution of the sample mean, $\bar{x}$, derived from random samples of a given size. It has three important characteristics. First, the mean of the sampling distribution of the mean is equal to the mean of the population that was sampled. Second, assuming the standard deviation is non-zero, the standard deviation of the sampling distribution of the mean equals the standard deviation of the sampled population divided by the square root of the sample size. This is sometimes called the standard error. Finally, as the sample size gets larger, the sampling distribution of the mean gets closer to a normal distribution via the central limit theorem.

Copyright © Mometrix Media. You have been licensed one copy of this document for personal use only. Any other reproduction or redistribution is strictly prohibited. All rights reserved. This content is provided for test preparation purposes only and does not imply an endorsement by Mometrix of any particular political, scientific, or religious point of view.

SURVEY STUDY

A **survey study** is a method of gathering information from a small group in an attempt to gain enough information to make accurate general assumptions about the population. Once a survey study is completed, the results are then put into a summary report.

Survey studies are generally in the format of surveys, interviews, or questionnaires as part of an effort to find opinions of a particular group or to find facts about a group.

It is important to note that the findings from a survey study are only as accurate as the sample chosen from the population.

CORRELATIONAL STUDIES

Correlational studies seek to determine how much one variable is affected by changes in a second variable. For example, correlational studies may look for a relationship between the amount of time a student spends studying for a test and the grade that student earned on the test or between student scores on college admissions tests and student grades in college.

It is important to note that correlational studies cannot show a cause and effect, but rather can show only that two variables are or are not potentially correlated.

EXPERIMENTAL STUDIES

Experimental studies take correlational studies one step farther, in that they attempt to prove or disprove a cause-and-effect relationship. These studies are performed by conducting a series of experiments to test the hypothesis. For a study to be scientifically accurate, it must have both an experimental group that receives the specified treatment and a control group that does not get the treatment. This is the type of study pharmaceutical companies do as part of drug trials for new medications. Experimental studies are only valid when the proper scientific method has been followed. In other words, the experiment must be well-planned and executed without bias in the testing process, all subjects must be selected at random, and the process of determining which subject is in which of the two groups must also be completely random.

OBSERVATIONAL STUDIES

Observational studies are the opposite of experimental studies. In observational studies, the tester cannot change or in any way control all of the variables in the test. For example, a study to determine which gender does better in math classes in school is strictly observational. You cannot change a person's gender, and you cannot change the subject being studied. The big downfall of observational studies is that you have no way of proving a cause-and-effect relationship because you cannot control outside influences. Events outside of school can influence a student's performance in school, and observational studies cannot take that into consideration.

RANDOM SAMPLES

For most studies, a **random sample** is necessary to produce valid results. Random samples should not have any particular influence to cause sampled subjects to behave one way or another. The goal is for the random sample to be a **representative sample**, or a sample whose characteristics give an accurate picture of the characteristics of the entire population. To accomplish this, you must make sure you have a proper **sample size**, or an appropriate number of elements in the sample.

BIASES

In statistical studies, biases must be avoided. **Bias** is an error that causes the study to favor one set of results over another. For example, if a survey to determine how the country views the president's

Copyright © Mometrix Media. You have been licensed one copy of this document for personal use only. Any other reproduction or redistribution is strictly prohibited. All rights reserved.
This content is provided for test preparation purposes only and does not imply an endorsement by Mometrix of any particular political, scientific, or religious point of view.

job performance only speaks to registered voters in the president's party, the results will be skewed because a disproportionately large number of responders would tend to show approval, while a disproportionately large number of people in the opposite party would tend to express disapproval. **Extraneous variables** are, as the name implies, outside influences that can affect the outcome of a study. They are not always avoidable but could trigger bias in the result.

DISPERSION

A **measure of dispersion** is a single value that helps to "interpret" the measure of central tendency by providing more information about how the data values in the set are distributed about the measure of central tendency. The measure of dispersion helps to eliminate or reduce the disadvantages of using the mean, median, or mode as a single measure of central tendency, and give a more accurate picture of the dataset as a whole. To have a measure of dispersion, you must know or calculate the range, standard deviation, or variance of the data set.

RANGE

The **range** of a set of data is the difference between the greatest and lowest values of the data in the set. To calculate the range, you must first make sure the units for all data values are the same, and then identify the greatest and lowest values. If there are multiple data values that are equal for the highest or lowest, just use one of the values in the formula. Write the answer with the same units as the data values you used to do the calculations.

> **Review Video: Statistical Range**
> Visit mometrix.com/academy and enter code: 778541

SAMPLE STANDARD DEVIATION

Standard deviation is a measure of dispersion that compares all the data values in the set to the mean of the set to give a more accurate picture. To find the **standard deviation of a sample**, use the formula

$$s = \sqrt{\frac{\sum_{i=1}^{n}(x_i - \bar{x})^2}{n-1}}$$

Note that s is the standard deviation of a sample, x_i represents the individual values in the data set, $\bar{x}$ is the mean of the data values in the set, and n is the number of data values in the set. The higher the value of the standard deviation is, the greater the variance of the data values from the mean. The units associated with the standard deviation are the same as the units of the data values.

> **Review Video: Standard Deviation**
> Visit mometrix.com/academy and enter code: 419469

SAMPLE VARIANCE

The **variance of a sample** is the square of the sample standard deviation (denoted s^2). While the mean of a set of data gives the average of the set and gives information about where a specific data value lies in relation to the average, the variance of the sample gives information about the degree to which the data values are spread out and tells you how close an individual value is to the average compared to the other values. The units associated with variance are the same as the units of the data values squared.

Copyright © Mometrix Media. You have been licensed one copy of this document for personal use only. Any other reproduction or redistribution is strictly prohibited. All rights reserved.
This content is provided for test preparation purposes only and does not imply an endorsement by Mometrix of any particular political, scientific, or religious point of view.

PERCENTILE

Percentiles and quartiles are other methods of describing data within a set. **Percentiles** tell what percentage of the data in the set fall below a specific point. For example, achievement test scores are often given in percentiles. A score at the 80th percentile is one which is equal to or higher than 80 percent of the scores in the set. In other words, 80 percent of the scores were lower than that score.

Quartiles are percentile groups that make up quarter sections of the data set. The first quartile is the 25th percentile. The second quartile is the 50th percentile; this is also the median of the dataset. The third quartile is the 75th percentile.

SKEWNESS

Skewness is a way to describe the symmetry or asymmetry of the distribution of values in a dataset. If the distribution of values is symmetrical, there is no skew. In general the closer the mean of a data set is to the median of the data set, the less skew there is. Generally, if the mean is to the right of the median, the data set is *positively skewed*, or right-skewed, and if the mean is to the left of the median, the data set is *negatively skewed*, or left-skewed. However, this rule of thumb is not infallible. When the data values are graphed on a curve, a set with no skew will be a perfect bell curve.

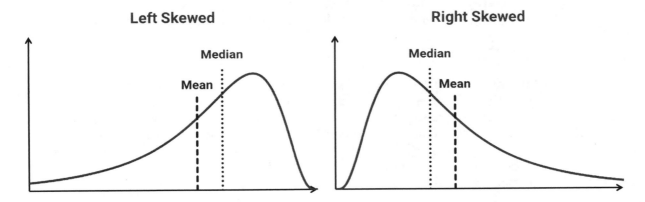

To estimate skew, use the formula:

$$\text{skew} = \frac{\sqrt{n(n-1)}}{n-2}\left(\frac{\frac{1}{n}\sum_{i=1}^{n}(x_i - \bar{x})^3}{\left(\frac{1}{n}\sum_{i=1}^{n}(x_i - \bar{x})^2\right)^{\frac{3}{2}}}\right)$$

Note that n is the datapoints in the set, x_i is the ith value in the set, and $\bar{x}$ is the mean of the set.

> **Review Video: Skew**
> Visit mometrix.com/academy and enter code: 661486

UNIMODAL VS. BIMODAL

If a distribution has a single peak, it would be considered **unimodal**. If it has two discernible peaks it would be considered **bimodal**. Bimodal distributions may be an indication that the set of data being considered is actually the combination of two sets of data with significant differences. A

Copyright © Mometrix Media. You have been licensed one copy of this document for personal use only. Any other reproduction or redistribution is strictly prohibited. All rights reserved.
This content is provided for test preparation purposes only and does not imply an endorsement by Mometrix of any particular political, scientific, or religious point of view.

uniform distribution is a distribution in which there is *no distinct peak or variation* in the data. No values or ranges are particularly more common than any other values or ranges.

OUTLIER

An outlier is an extremely high or extremely low value in the data set. It may be the result of measurement error, in which case, the outlier is not a valid member of the data set. However, it may also be a valid member of the distribution. Unless a measurement error is identified, the experimenter cannot know for certain if an outlier is or is not a member of the distribution. There are arbitrary methods that can be employed to designate an extreme value as an outlier. One method designates an outlier (or possible outlier) to be any value less than $Q_1 - 1.5(IQR)$ or any value greater than $Q_3 + 1.5(IQR)$.

DATA ANALYSIS

SIMPLE REGRESSION

In statistics, **simple regression** is using an equation to represent a relation between independent and dependent variables. The independent variable is also referred to as the explanatory variable or the predictor and is generally represented by the variable x in the equation. The dependent variable, usually represented by the variable y, is also referred to as the response variable. The equation may be any type of function – linear, quadratic, exponential, etc. The best way to handle this task is to use the regression feature of your graphing calculator. This will easily give you the curve of best fit and provide you with the coefficients and other information you need to derive an equation.

LINE OF BEST FIT

In a scatter plot, the **line of best fit** is the line that best shows the trends of the data. The line of best fit is given by the equation $\hat{y} = ax + b$, where a and b are the regression coefficients. The regression coefficient a is also the slope of the line of best fit, and b is also the y-coordinate of the point at which the line of best fit crosses the y-axis. Not every point on the scatter plot will be on the line of best fit. The differences between the y-values of the points in the scatter plot and the corresponding y-values according to the equation of the line of best fit are the residuals. The line of best fit is also called the least-squares regression line because it is also the line that has the lowest sum of the squares of the residuals.

CORRELATION COEFFICIENT

The **correlation coefficient** is the numerical value that indicates how strong the relationship is between the two variables of a linear regression equation. A correlation coefficient of –1 is a perfect negative correlation. A correlation coefficient of +1 is a perfect positive correlation. Correlation coefficients close to –1 or +1 are very strong correlations. A correlation coefficient equal to zero indicates there is no correlation between the two variables. This test is a good indicator of whether or not the equation for the line of best fit is accurate. The formula for the correlation coefficient is

$$r = \frac{\sum_{i=1}^{n}(x_i - \bar{x})(y_i - \bar{y})}{\sqrt{\sum_{i=1}^{n}(x_i - \bar{x})^2}\sqrt{\sum_{i=1}^{n}(y_i - \bar{y})^2}}$$

where r is the correlation coefficient, n is the number of data values in the set, (x_i, y_i) is a point in the set, and $\bar{x}$ and $\bar{y}$ are the means.

Copyright © Mometrix Media. You have been licensed one copy of this document for personal use only. Any other reproduction or redistribution is strictly prohibited. All rights reserved. This content is provided for test preparation purposes only and does not imply an endorsement by Mometrix of any particular political, scientific, or religious point of view.

Z-SCORE

A **z-score** is an indication of how many standard deviations a given value falls from the sample mean. To calculate a z-score, use the formula:

$$\frac{x - \bar{x}}{\sigma}$$

In this formula x is the data value, $\bar{x}$ is the mean of the sample data, and σ is the standard deviation of the population. If the z-score is positive, the data value lies above the mean. If the z-score is negative, the data value falls below the mean. These scores are useful in interpreting data such as standardized test scores, where every piece of data in the set has been counted, rather than just a small random sample. In cases where standard deviations are calculated from a random sample of the set, the z-scores will not be as accurate.

CENTRAL LIMIT THEOREM

According to the **central limit theorem**, regardless of what the original distribution of a sample is, the distribution of the means tends to get closer and closer to a normal distribution as the sample size gets larger and larger (this is necessary because the sample is becoming more all-encompassing of the elements of the population). As the sample size gets larger, the distribution of the sample mean will approach a normal distribution with a mean of the population mean and a variance of the population variance divided by the sample size.

MEASURES OF CENTRAL TENDENCY

A **measure of central tendency** is a statistical value that gives a reasonable estimate for the center of a group of data. There are several different ways of describing the measure of central tendency. Each one has a unique way it is calculated, and each one gives a slightly different perspective on the data set. Whenever you give a measure of central tendency, always make sure the units are the same. If the data has different units, such as hours, minutes, and seconds, convert all the data to the same unit, and use the same unit in the measure of central tendency. If no units are given in the data, do not give units for the measure of central tendency.

MEAN

The **statistical mean** of a group of data is the same as the arithmetic average of that group. To find the mean of a set of data, first convert each value to the same units, if necessary. Then find the sum of all the values, and count the total number of data values, making sure you take into consideration each individual value. If a value appears more than once, count it more than once. Divide the sum of the values by the total number of values and apply the units, if any. Note that the mean does not have to be one of the data values in the set, and may not divide evenly.

$$\text{mean} = \frac{\text{sum of the data values}}{\text{quantity of data values}}$$

For instance, the mean of the data set {88, 72, 61, 90, 97, 68, 88, 79, 86, 93, 97, 71, 80, 84, 89} would be the sum of the fifteen numbers divided by 15:

$$\frac{88 + 72 + 61 + 90 + 97 + 68 + 88 + 79 + 86 + 93 + 97 + 71 + 80 + 84 + 89}{15} = \frac{1242}{15}$$
$$= 82.8$$

Copyright © Mometrix Media. You have been licensed one copy of this document for personal use only. Any other reproduction or redistribution is strictly prohibited. All rights reserved. This content is provided for test preparation purposes only and does not imply an endorsement by Mometrix of any particular political, scientific, or religious point of view.

While the mean is relatively easy to calculate and averages are understood by most people, the mean can be very misleading if it is used as the sole measure of central tendency. If the data set has outliers (data values that are unusually high or unusually low compared to the rest of the data values), the mean can be very distorted, especially if the data set has a small number of values. If unusually high values are countered with unusually low values, the mean is not affected as much. For example, if five of twenty students in a class get a 100 on a test, but the other 15 students have an average of 60 on the same test, the class average would appear as 70. Whenever the mean is skewed by outliers, it is always a good idea to include the median as an alternate measure of central tendency.

A **weighted mean**, or weighted average, is a mean that uses "weighted" values. The formula is weighted mean $= \frac{w_1 x_1 + w_2 x_2 + w_3 x_3 \dots + w_n x_n}{w_1 + w_2 + w_3 + \dots + w_n}$. Weighted values, such as $w_1, w_2, w_3, \dots w_n$ are assigned to each member of the set $x_1, x_2, x_3, \dots x_n$. When calculating the weighted mean, make sure a weight value for each member of the set is used.

> **Review Video: All About Averages**
> Visit mometrix.com/academy and enter code: 176521

MEDIAN

The **statistical median** is the value in the middle of the set of data. To find the median, list all data values in order from smallest to largest or from largest to smallest. Any value that is repeated in the set must be listed the number of times it appears. If there are an odd number of data values, the median is the value in the middle of the list. If there is an even number of data values, the median is the arithmetic mean of the two middle values.

For example, the median of the data set {88, 72, 61, 90, 97, 68, 88, 79, 86, 93, 97, 71, 80, 84, 88} is 86 since the ordered set is {61, 68, 71, 72, 79, 80, 84, **86**, 88, 88, 88, 90, 93, 97, 97}.

The big disadvantage of using the median as a measure of central tendency is that is relies solely on a value's relative size as compared to the other values in the set. When the individual values in a set of data are evenly dispersed, the median can be an accurate tool. However, if there is a group of rather large values or a group of rather small values that are not offset by a different group of values, the information that can be inferred from the median may not be accurate because the distribution of values is skewed.

MODE

The **statistical mode** is the data value that occurs the greatest number of times in the data set. It is possible to have exactly one mode, more than one mode, or no mode. To find the mode of a set of data, arrange the data like you do to find the median (all values in order, listing all multiples of data values). Count the number of times each value appears in the data set. If all values appear an equal number of times, there is no mode. If one value appears more than any other value, that value is the mode. If two or more values appear the same number of times, but there are other values that appear fewer times and no values that appear more times, all of those values are the modes.

For example, the mode of the data set {**88**, 72, 61, 90, 97, 68, **88**, 79, 86, 93, 97, 71, 80, 84, **88**} is 88.

The main disadvantage of the mode is that the values of the other data in the set have no bearing on the mode. The mode may be the largest value, the smallest value, or a value anywhere in between in

Copyright © Mometrix Media. You have been licensed one copy of this document for personal use only. Any other reproduction or redistribution is strictly prohibited. All rights reserved.
This content is provided for test preparation purposes only and does not imply an endorsement by Mometrix of any particular political, scientific, or religious point of view.

the set. The mode only tells which value or values, if any, occurred the greatest number of times. It does not give any suggestions about the remaining values in the set.

> **Review Video: Mean, Median, and Mode**
> Visit mometrix.com/academy and enter code: 286207

FREQUENCY TABLES

Frequency tables show how frequently each unique value appears in a set. A **relative frequency table** is one that shows the proportions of each unique value compared to the entire set. Relative frequencies are given as percentages; however, the total percent for a relative frequency table will not necessarily equal 100 percent due to rounding. An example of a frequency table with relative frequencies is below.

Favorite Color	Frequency	Relative Frequency
Blue	4	13%
Red	7	22%
Green	3	9%
Purple	6	19%
Cyan	12	38%

> **Review Video: Data Interpretation of Graphs**
> Visit mometrix.com/academy and enter code: 200439

CIRCLE GRAPHS

Circle graphs, also known as *pie charts*, provide a visual depiction of the relationship of each type of data compared to the whole set of data. The circle graph is divided into sections by drawing radii to create central angles whose percentage of the circle is equal to the individual data's percentage of the whole set. Each 1% of data is equal to 3.6° in the circle graph. Therefore, data represented by a 90° section of the circle graph makes up 25% of the whole. When complete, a circle graph often looks like a pie cut into uneven wedges. The pie chart below shows the data from the frequency table referenced earlier where people were asked their favorite color.

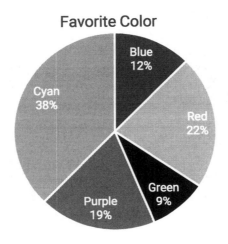

255

Copyright © Mometrix Media. You have been licensed one copy of this document for personal use only. Any other reproduction or redistribution is strictly prohibited. All rights reserved.
This content is provided for test preparation purposes only and does not imply an endorsement by Mometrix of any particular political, scientific, or religious point of view.

PICTOGRAPHS

A **pictograph** is a graph, generally in the horizontal orientation, that uses pictures or symbols to represent the data. Each pictograph must have a key that defines the picture or symbol and gives the quantity each picture or symbol represents. Pictures or symbols on a pictograph are not always shown as whole elements. In this case, the fraction of the picture or symbol shown represents the same fraction of the quantity a whole picture or symbol stands for. For example, a row with $3\frac{1}{2}$ ears of corn, where each ear of corn represents 100 stalks of corn in a field, would equal $3\frac{1}{2} \times 100 = 350$ stalks of corn in the field.

Review Video: Pictographs
Visit mometrix.com/academy and enter code: 147860

LINE GRAPHS

Line graphs have one or more lines of varying styles (solid or broken) to show the different values for a set of data. The individual data are represented as ordered pairs, much like on a Cartesian plane. In this case, the x- and y-axes are defined in terms of their units, such as dollars or time. The individual plotted points are joined by line segments to show whether the value of the data is increasing (line sloping upward), decreasing (line sloping downward), or staying the same (horizontal line). Multiple sets of data can be graphed on the same line graph to give an easy visual comparison. An example of this would be graphing achievement test scores for different groups of students over the same time period to see which group had the greatest increase or decrease in performance from year to year (as shown below).

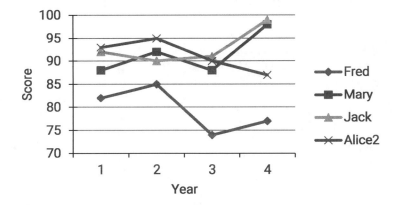

Review Video: How to Create a Line Graph
Visit mometrix.com/academy and enter code: 480147

LINE PLOTS

A **line plot**, also known as a *dot plot*, has plotted points that are not connected by line segments. In this graph, the horizontal axis lists the different possible values for the data, and the vertical axis lists the number of times the individual value occurs. A single dot is graphed for each value to show the number of times it occurs. This graph is more closely related to a bar graph than a line graph. Do not connect the dots in a line plot or it will misrepresent the data.

Review Video: Line Plot
Visit mometrix.com/academy and enter code: 754610

Copyright © Mometrix Media. You have been licensed one copy of this document for personal use only. Any other reproduction or redistribution is strictly prohibited. All rights reserved.
This content is provided for test preparation purposes only and does not imply an endorsement by Mometrix of any particular political, scientific, or religious point of view.

STEM AND LEAF PLOTS

A **stem and leaf plot** is useful for depicting groups of data that fall into a range of values. Each piece of data is separated into two parts: the first, or left, part is called the stem; the second, or right, part is called the leaf. Each stem is listed in a column from smallest to largest. Each leaf that has the common stem is listed in that stem's row from smallest to largest. For example, in a set of two-digit numbers, the digit in the tens place is the stem, and the digit in the ones place is the leaf. With a stem and leaf plot, you can easily see which subset of numbers (10s, 20s, 30s, etc.) is the largest. This information is also readily available by looking at a histogram, but a stem and leaf plot also allows you to look closer and see exactly which values fall in that range. Using a sample set of test scores (82, 88, 92, 93, 85, 90, 92, 95, 74, 88, 90, 91, 78, 87, 98, 99), we can assemble a stem and leaf plot like the one below.

Test Scores

7	4	8						
8	2	5	7	8	8			
9	0	0	1	2	2	3	5	8	9

Review Video: Stem and Leaf Plots
Visit mometrix.com/academy and enter code: 302339

BAR GRAPHS

A **bar graph** is one of the few graphs that can be drawn correctly in two different configurations – both horizontally and vertically. A bar graph is similar to a line plot in the way the data is organized on the graph. Both axes must have their categories defined for the graph to be useful. Rather than placing a single dot to mark the point of the data's value, a bar, or thick line, is drawn from zero to the exact value of the data, whether it is a number, percentage, or other numerical value. Longer bar lengths correspond to greater data values. To read a bar graph, read the labels for the axes to find the units being reported. Then, look where the bars end in relation to the scale given on the corresponding axis and determine the associated value.

The bar chart below represents the responses from our favorite-color survey.

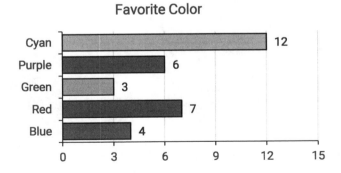

HISTOGRAMS

At first glance, a **histogram** looks like a vertical bar graph. The difference is that a bar graph has a separate bar for each piece of data and a histogram has one continuous bar for each *range* of data. For example, a histogram may have one bar for the range 0–9, one bar for 10–19, etc. While a bar graph has numerical values on one axis, a histogram has numerical values on both axes. Each range is of equal size, and they are ordered left to right from lowest to highest. The height of each column

Copyright © Mometrix Media. You have been licensed one copy of this document for personal use only. Any other reproduction or redistribution is strictly prohibited. All rights reserved.
This content is provided for test preparation purposes only and does not imply an endorsement by Mometrix of any particular political, scientific, or religious point of view.

on a histogram represents the number of data values within that range. Like a stem and leaf plot, a histogram makes it easy to glance at the graph and quickly determine which range has the greatest quantity of values. A simple example of a histogram is below.

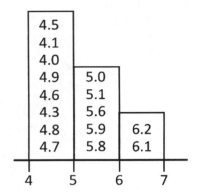

5-NUMBER SUMMARY

The **5-number summary** of a set of data gives a very informative picture of the set. The five numbers in the summary include the minimum value, maximum value, and the three quartiles. This information gives the reader the range and median of the set, as well as an indication of how the data is spread about the median.

BOX AND WHISKER PLOTS

A **box-and-whiskers plot** is a graphical representation of the 5-number summary. To draw a box-and-whiskers plot, plot the points of the 5-number summary on a number line. Draw a box whose ends are through the points for the first and third quartiles. Draw a vertical line in the box through the median to divide the box in half. Draw a line segment from the first quartile point to the minimum value, and from the third quartile point to the maximum value.

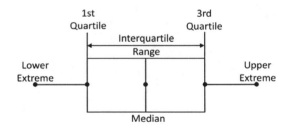

Review Video: Box and Whisker Plots
Visit mometrix.com/academy and enter code: 810817

EXAMPLE

Given the following data (32, 28, 29, 26, 35, 27, 30, 31, 27, 32), we first sort it into numerical order: 26, 27, 27, 28, 29, 30, 31, 32, 32, 35. We can then find the median. Since there are ten values, we take the average of the 5th and 6th values to get 29.5. We find the lower quartile by taking the median of the data smaller than the median. Since there are five values, we take the 3rd value, which is 27. We find the upper quartile by taking the median of the data larger than the overall median,

Copyright © Mometrix Media. You have been licensed one copy of this document for personal use only. Any other reproduction or redistribution is strictly prohibited. All rights reserved.
This content is provided for test preparation purposes only and does not imply an endorsement by Mometrix of any particular political, scientific, or religious point of view.

which is 32. Finally, we note our minimum and maximum, which are simply the smallest and largest values in the set: 26 and 35, respectively. Now we can create our box plot:

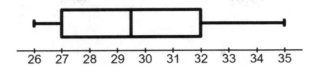

This plot is fairly "long" on the right whisker, showing one or more unusually high values (but not quite outliers). The other quartiles are similar in length, showing a fairly even distribution of data.

INTERQUARTILE RANGE

The **interquartile range, or IQR**, is the difference between the upper and lower quartiles. It measures how the data is dispersed: a high IQR means that the data is more spread out, while a low IQR means that the data is clustered more tightly around the median. To find the IQR, subtract the lower quartile value (Q_1) from the upper quartile value (Q_3).

EXAMPLE

To find the upper and lower quartiles, we first find the median and then take the median of all values above it and all values below it. In the following data set (16, 18, 13, 24, 16, 51, 32, 21, 27, 39), we first rearrange the values in numerical order: 13, 16, 16, 18, 21, 24, 27, 32, 39, 51. There are 10 values, so the median is the average of the 5th and 6th: $\frac{21+24}{2} = \frac{45}{2} = 22.5$. We do not actually need this value to find the upper and lower quartiles. We look at the set of numbers below the median: 13, 16, 16, 18, 21. There are five values, so the 3rd is the median (16), or the value of the lower quartile (Q_1). Then we look at the numbers above the median: 24, 27, 32, 39, 51. Again there are five values, so the 3rd is the median (32), or the value of the upper quartile (Q_3). We find the IQR by subtracting Q_1 from Q_3: $32 - 16 = 16$.

68-95-99.7 RULE

The **68–95–99.7 rule** describes how a normal distribution of data should appear when compared to the mean. This is also a description of a normal bell curve. According to this rule, 68 percent of the data values in a normally distributed set should fall within one standard deviation of the mean (34 percent above and 34 percent below the mean), 95 percent of the data values should fall within two standard deviations of the mean (47.5 percent above and 47.5 percent below the mean), and 99.7 percent of the data values should fall within three standard deviations of the mean, again, equally distributed on either side of the mean. This means that only 0.3 percent of all data values should fall more than three standard deviations from the mean. On the graph below, the normal

259

Copyright © Mometrix Media. You have been licensed one copy of this document for personal use only. Any other reproduction or redistribution is strictly prohibited. All rights reserved.
This content is provided for test preparation purposes only and does not imply an endorsement by Mometrix of any particular political, scientific, or religious point of view.

curve is centered on the *y*-axis. The *x*-axis labels are how many standard deviations away from the center you are. Therefore, it is easy to see how the 68-95-99.7 rule can apply.

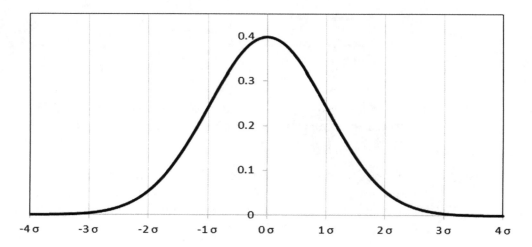

BIVARIATE DATA

Bivariate data is simply data from two different variables. (The prefix *bi-* means *two*.) In a *scatter plot*, each value in the set of data is plotted on a grid similar to a Cartesian plane, where each axis represents one of the two variables. By looking at the pattern formed by the points on the grid, you can often determine whether or not there is a relationship between the two variables, and what that relationship is, if it exists. The variables may be directly proportionate, inversely proportionate, or show no proportion at all. It may also be possible to determine if the data is linear, and if so, to find an equation to relate the two variables. The following scatter plot shows the relationship between preference for brand "A" and the age of the consumers surveyed.

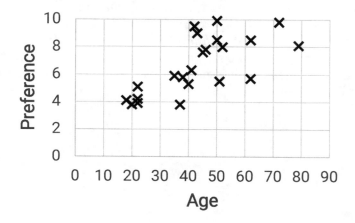

Copyright © Mometrix Media. You have been licensed one copy of this document for personal use only. Any other reproduction or redistribution is strictly prohibited. All rights reserved. This content is provided for test preparation purposes only and does not imply an endorsement by Mometrix of any particular political, scientific, or religious point of view.

SCATTER PLOTS

Scatter plots are also useful in determining the type of function represented by the data and finding the simple regression. Linear scatter plots may be positive or negative. Nonlinear scatter plots are generally exponential or quadratic. Below are some common types of scatter plots:

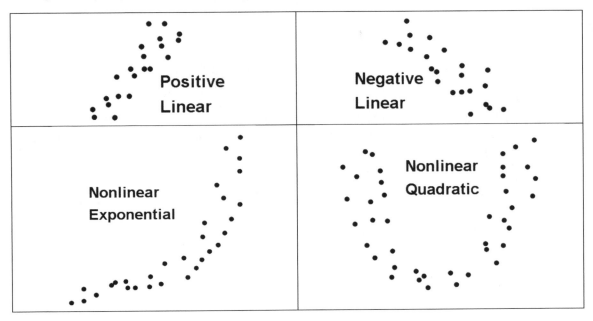

Review Video: **What is a Scatter Plot?**
Visit mometrix.com/academy and enter code: 596526

Copyright © Mometrix Media. You have been licensed one copy of this document for personal use only. Any other reproduction or redistribution is strictly prohibited. All rights reserved.
This content is provided for test preparation purposes only and does not imply an endorsement by Mometrix of any particular political, scientific, or religious point of view.

Social Studies

United States History

COLONIAL PERIOD (1607-1765)

The **colonial period** describes a time in which several European countries attempted to settle and colonize the Americas to expand their territories. The earliest attempts to colonize were by Spain and France, who conquered and settled much of what are now the southern and central parts of the United States of America. In the process of colonizing the Americas, many Native American groups were displaced or killed by disease and territorial expansion. The main focus of the colonial period in what is now the United States is often placed on the **thirteen English colonies**, which were located on the east coast. The primary reasons for the English colonization in the Americas were in response to England's policy of mercantilism and colonists' desire to be free from **religious persecution**. **Mercantilism** in England required the colonies to provide raw materials to England to continue to grow and support the mother country while also limiting trade with other nations. The other primary motivation for settlement included escape from persecution by the Church of England toward Catholic and other religious groups.

THE 13 COLONIES

The **thirteen colonies** were a group of English colonies that were overtly similar in their political and religious beliefs. The thirteen colonies were comprised of:

NEW ENGLAND COLONIES:

- New Hampshire
- Massachusetts
- Rhode Island
- Connecticut

CHESAPEAKE BAY COLONIES:

- Virginia
- Maryland

> **Review Video: The English Colony of Virginia**
> Visit mometrix.com/academy and enter code: 537399

MIDDLE COLONIES:

- New York
- Pennsylvania
- New Jersey
- Delaware

SOUTHERN COLONIES:

- North Carolina
- South Carolina
- Georgia

> **Review Video: Southern Colonies**
> Visit mometrix.com/academy and enter code: 703830

Copyright © Mometrix Media. You have been licensed one copy of this document for personal use only. Any other reproduction or redistribution is strictly prohibited. All rights reserved. This content is provided for test preparation purposes only and does not imply an endorsement by Mometrix of any particular political, scientific, or religious point of view.

FRENCH AND INDIAN WAR

The **French and Indian War** was essentially a war over territory between the English colonies and the French colonies. Rising competition between the English and French empires brought more British military support into the colonies, which created a stronger feeling of unity between the colonies and England than ever before. In 1763, the **Treaty of Paris** brought an end to the war, as France relinquished some of its Eastern territory to England, including the territory east of modern-day Louisiana all the way to the Great Lakes. In the aftermath of the war, **tensions** rose between the colonies and England because of unequal investment in the war. British taxpayers had supplied the majority of funding for the war, while the colonists were forced to fight in a war that served the monarchy's interests rather than their own interests. These tensions, along with continued British occupation, were the foundation for the coming revolution.

AMERICAN REVOLUTION (1765-1783)

THE INTOLERABLE ACTS

Following the French and Indian War, Britain increased taxes and continued to impose quartering on the colonies. The most famous of these included the Stamp Acts, the Tea Acts, and the Quartering Acts. The purpose of these laws was to force the colonies to be dependent on Britain, and to help restore the British economy following the wars of the previous years. These laws were known to the British as the **Coercive Acts**. In America, they were called the **Intolerable Acts,** due to the offensive nature of England's attempt to control and stifle the colonies. As tensions rose, members of the colonies began organizing rebellious protests, such as the Boston Tea Party, in response to particular tax laws that were passed. These inciting reasons and protests led up to the official start of the **American Revolution.**

IMPORTANT EVENTS AND GROUPS LEADING UP TO AMERICAN REVOLUTION

Over several years, various events and groups contributed to the rebellion that became a revolution:

- **Sons of Liberty** – This was the protest group headed by Samuel Adams that incited the Revolution.
- **Boston Massacre** – On March 5, 1770, British soldiers fired on a crowd and killed five people.
- **Committees of Correspondence** – These were set up throughout the colonies to transmit revolutionary ideas and create a unified response.
- **The Boston Tea Party** – On December 6, 1773, the Sons of Liberty, dressed as Mohawks, dumped tea into the harbor from a British ship to protest the tea tax. The harsh British response further aggravated the situation.
- **First Continental Congress** – This was held in 1774 to list grievances and develop a response, including boycotts. It was attended by all the colonies with the exception of Georgia.
- **The Shot Heard Round the World** – In April, 1775, English soldiers on their way to confiscate arms in Concord passed through Lexington, Massachusetts and met the colonial militia called the Minutemen. A fight ensued. In Concord, a larger group of Minutemen forced the British to retreat.

> **Review Video: The First and Second Continental Congress**
> Visit mometrix.com/academy and enter code: 835211

Copyright © Mometrix Media. You have been licensed one copy of this document for personal use only. Any other reproduction or redistribution is strictly prohibited. All rights reserved. This content is provided for test preparation purposes only and does not imply an endorsement by Mometrix of any particular political, scientific, or religious point of view.

ORIGINAL 13 COLONIES AND MAJOR TURNING POINTS OF THE REVOLUTION

The original **13 colonies** were: Connecticut, Delaware, Georgia, Maryland, Massachusetts, New Hampshire, New Jersey, New York, North Carolina, Pennsylvania, Rhode Island, South Carolina, and Virginia. Delaware was the first state to ratify the **constitution**.

The major turning points of the American Revolution were:

- The actions of the **Second Continental Congress** – This body established the Continental Army and chose George Washington as its commanding general. They allowed printing of money and created government offices.
- "**Common Sense**" – Published in 1776 by Thomas Paine, this pamphlet calling for independence was widely distributed.
- The **Declaration of Independence** – Written by Thomas Jefferson, it was ratified on July 4, 1776 by the Continental Congress assembled in Philadelphia.
- **Alliance with France** – Benjamin Franklin negotiated an agreement with France to fight with the Americans in 1778.
- **Treaty of Paris** – Signaled the official end of the war in 1782, granted independence to the colonies, and gave them generous territorial rights.

> **Review Video: Declaration of Independence**
> Visit mometrix.com/academy and enter code: 256838
>
> **Review Video: Colonization of the Americas**
> Visit mometrix.com/academy and enter code: 438412

FOUNDING OF A NATION

Each of the colonies overthrew the British representation within their own colonies and established their own state constitutions. The newly formed 13 states, with the guidance and primary authorship of Thomas Jefferson, unanimously adopted the **Declaration of Independence,** which officially separated the colonies from British rule. Shortly thereafter, the **Second Continental Congress**, made up of state representatives, met together to ratify the **Articles of Confederation**, which was the original constitution for the United States of America, outlining how sovereignty would be shared among the states in the new country. With the assistance of the French, the Americans were able to fend off a large scale naval and military invasion from the British and secure their revolution.

> **Review Video: Who are the Founding Fathers?**
> Visit mometrix.com/academy and enter code: 704562

CONFEDERATION PERIOD

The **Confederation Period** (1783-1788) was the period in U.S. history directly following the American Revolution. The Articles of Confederation held the states loosely, and the states were largely self-governing and did not have much political unity. In this format, the federal government was very weak, with no chief executive or judicial system. The weak federal government was bound to continue degrading in unity and would eventually fail if left without reform. In 1787, political leaders met to write a new constitution with more thoroughly written policies that would establish federal powers, while still sharing power with the state governments. This new constitution ended the confederation period and led the way into the Federalist Era.

Copyright © Mometrix Media. You have been licensed one copy of this document for personal use only. Any other reproduction or redistribution is strictly prohibited. All rights reserved. This content is provided for test preparation purposes only and does not imply an endorsement by Mometrix of any particular political, scientific, or religious point of view.

FEDERALIST ERA (1788-1801)

The 1787 convention that wrote the new **Constitution of the United States of America** established three government branches, the **legislative** (making laws) the **executive** (enforcing laws), and the **judicial** (interpreting and judging laws). Having three branches with separate powers helped to provide what is known as **checks and balances** in government, so that no one branch will have too much power. This was meant to maintain liberty and state powers, while giving the federal government enough power to effectively govern the new country. The new constitution also established voting practices on the individual and state level, including the controversial topic of slavery and voting practices for states that did not abolish slavery. At this point, some northern states had made slavery illegal, but the constitution of the time allowed for the states to determine their own laws on the matter. The Federalist Era placed more power in the hands of the federal government, but also established a place for political parties to advocate for the rights of the people.

BILL OF RIGHTS AND AMENDMENTS

Over the next few years, the need for revision to the constitution was made clear. In 1789, congress adopted several **amendments** to the constitution, mostly dealing with individual rights, such as the right to freedom of speech, the right to bear arms, and several others. The first ten amendments are called "**The Bill of Rights**." In the process of instituting these amendments, it was also laid out that any declarations (such as rights or laws) not specifically granted in the constitution or amendments to the constitution are reserved for the states or lower jurisdictions to establish.

JEFFERSONIAN ERA (1801-1817)

The **Jeffersonian Era** is defined by the influences of Thomas Jefferson and his political activism. In the Federalist Era, many of the political voices advocated for power going to those with wealth and property, rather than the equal rights of all people. Jefferson's political outlook was called **American Republicanism** (now the Democratic-Republican Party), which opposed aristocracy, elitism, and corruption in government. During Jefferson's presidency, he made significant strides toward a more inclusive voting system. He also managed to purchase Louisiana from France at an extremely reasonable price, thus roughly doubling the size of the United States at the time. From 1812-1815, a war ensued between the United Kingdom and the United States due to the British cutting off trade routes and fostering hostility between the Native Americans and the United States. The war concluded with no changes to boundaries, leading to the beginning of the **Era of Good Feelings**.

ERA OF GOOD FEELINGS AND THE JACKSONIAN ERA

The **Era of Good Feelings** (1817-1825) followed the Jeffersonian Era, and was marked by the collapse of the Federalist system. President James Monroe attempted to deter the partisan political system and prevent political parties from driving national politics. During the Era of Good Feelings, there was a **temporary sense of national security** and a **desire for unity** in America following the war of previous years. Following Monroe's presidency, votes were largely split between the two major parties of the time, the **Whigs** and the **Democrats**.

During the **Jacksonian Era** (1825-1849), **voting rights** were extended to most white men over 21 years old and revised other federal policies. The policy favored the idea of election by the "common man," which expanded voting rights, while continuing to deny rights to women, Native Americans and African Americans. This period also saw an increase in **expansionism**, encouraging territorial expansion to the west in the name of manifest destiny. During this period, issues of slavery were largely avoided at first, though they grew over the coming years, leading into the Civil War Era.

Copyright © Mometrix Media. You have been licensed one copy of this document for personal use only. Any other reproduction or redistribution is strictly prohibited. All rights reserved. This content is provided for test preparation purposes only and does not imply an endorsement by Mometrix of any particular political, scientific, or religious point of view.

Civil War Era (1850-1865)

The **Civil War Era** began with continued push from the northern states to expand democratic rights to Black people. The constitution of the time allowed for slavery to be a state's right to determine and enforce. Eleven states (with two to join later) determined to secede from the United States of America and become their own nation. In these eleven states, slavery was a major mode and means for the economy, and despite the overt ethical issues with slavery, these southern states were adamant about maintaining their way of life. The official Confederacy was formed in 1861 and continued until the end of the civil war in 1865.

Reconstruction Era (1865-1877)

Reconstruction and 13th, 14th, and 15th Amendments

Reconstruction was the period from 1865 to 1877, during which the South was under strict control of the U.S. government. In March, 1867, all state governments of the former Confederacy were terminated, and **military occupation** began. Military commanders called for constitutional conventions to reconstruct the state governments, to which delegates were to be elected by universal male suffrage. After a state government was in operation and the state had **ratified the 14th Amendment**, its representatives were admitted to Congress. Three constitutional amendments from 1865 to 1870, which tried to rectify the problems caused by slavery, became part of the Reconstruction effort. The **13th Amendment** declared slavery illegal. The **14th Amendment** made all persons born or naturalized in the country U.S. citizens, and forbade any state to interfere with their fundamental civil rights. The **15th Amendment** made it illegal to deny individuals the right to vote on the grounds of race. In his 1876 election campaign, President **Rutherford B. Hayes** promised to withdraw troops from the South, and did so in 1877.

Major Changes in Industry in the Late 1800s

Important events during this time of enormous business growth and large-scale exploitation of natural resources include:

- **Industrialization** – Like the rest of the world, the United States' entry into the Industrial Age was marked by many new inventions and the mechanization of factories.
- **Railroad expansion** – The Transcontinental Railroad was built from 1865 to 1969. Railroad tracks stretched over 35,000 miles in 1865, but that distance reached 240,000 miles by 1910. The raw materials and manufactured goods needed for the railroads kept mines and factories very busy.
- **Gold and silver mining** – Mines brought many prospectors to the West from 1850 to about 1875, but mining corporations soon took over.
- **Cattle ranching** – This was a large-scale enterprise beginning in the late 1860s, but by the 1880s open ranges were being fenced and plowed for farming and pastures. Millions of farmers moved into the high plains, establishing the "Bread Basket," which was the major wheat growing area of the country.

Gilded Age (1877-1895)

The **Gilded Age**, from the 1870s to 1890, was so named because of the enormous wealth and grossly opulent lifestyle enjoyed by a handful of powerful families. This was the time when huge mansions were built as summer "cottages" in Newport, Rhode Island, and great lodges were built in mountain areas for the pleasure of families such as the Vanderbilts, Ascots, and Rockefellers.

Control of the major industries was held largely by the following men:

Copyright © Mometrix Media. You have been licensed one copy of this document for personal use only. Any other reproduction or redistribution is strictly prohibited. All rights reserved.
This content is provided for test preparation purposes only and does not imply an endorsement by Mometrix of any particular political, scientific, or religious point of view.

- Jay Gould—railroads
- Andrew Carnegie—steel
- John D. Rockefeller Sr.—oil
- Philip Danforth Armour—meatpacking
- J. P. Morgan—banking
- John Jacob Astor—fur pelts
- Cornelius Vanderbilt—steamboat shipping

These men were were known as **Robber Barons** for their ruthless business practices and exploitation of workers. Of course, all of these heads of industry diversified and became involved in multiple business ventures. To curb cutthroat competition, particularly among the railroads, and to prohibit restrained trade, Congress created the **Interstate Commerce Commission** and the **Sherman Anti-Trust Act**. Neither of these, however, was enforced.

Review Video: The Gilded Age: An Overview
Visit mometrix.com/academy and enter code: 684770

Review Video: The Gilded Age: Chinese Immigration
Visit mometrix.com/academy and enter code: 624166

IMMIGRATION TRENDS IN LATE 1800S

The population of the United States doubled between 1860 and 1890, with the arrival of 10 million immigrants. Most lived in the north. Cities and their **slums** grew tremendously because of immigration and industrialization. While previous immigrants had come from Germany, Scandinavia, and Ireland, the 1880s saw a new wave of immigrants from Italy, Poland, Hungary, Bohemia, and Greece, as well as Jewish groups from central and eastern Europe, especially Russia. The Roman Catholic population grew from 1.6 million in 1850 to 12 million in 1900, a growth that ignited an anti-Catholic backlash from the anti-Catholic Know-Nothing Party of the 1880s and the Ku Klux Klan. Exploited immigrant workers started **labor protests** in the 1870s, and the **Knights of Labor** was formed in 1878, calling for sweeping social and economic reform. Its membership reached 700,000 by 1886. Eventually, this organization was replaced by the **American Federation of Labor**, headed by Samuel Gompers.

PROGRESSIVE ERA (1896–1916)

The **Progressive Era**, which was the time period from the 1890s to the 1920s, got its name from progressive, reform-minded political leaders who wanted to export a just and rational social order to the rest of the world while increasing trade with foreign markets. Consequently, the United States interfered in a dispute between Venezuela and Britain. America invoked the **Monroe Doctrine** and sided with Cuba in its struggle for independence from Spain. The latter resulted in the **Spanish-American Wars** in 1898 that ended with Cuba, Puerto Rico, the Philippines, and Guam becoming American protectorates at the same time the United States annexed Hawaii. In 1900, America declared an **Open Door policy** with China to support its independence and open markets. In 1903, Theodore Roosevelt helped Panama become independent of Colombia, and then secured the right to build the **Panama Canal**. Roosevelt also negotiated the peace treaty to end the Russo-Japanese War, which earned him the Nobel Peace prize. He then sent the American fleet on a world cruise to display his country's power.

Review Video: The Progressive Era
Visit mometrix.com/academy and enter code: 722394

Copyright © Mometrix Media. You have been licensed one copy of this document for personal use only. Any other reproduction or redistribution is strictly prohibited. All rights reserved. This content is provided for test preparation purposes only and does not imply an endorsement by Mometrix of any particular political, scientific, or religious point of view.

DOMESTIC ACCOMPLISHMENTS OF THE PROGRESSIVE ERA

To the Progressives, promoting law and order meant cleaning up city governments to make them honest and efficient, bringing more democracy and humanity to state governments, and establishing a core of social workers to improve slum housing, health, and education. Also during the **Progressive Era**, the national government strengthened or created the following regulatory agencies, services, and acts to oversee business enterprises:

- Passed in 1906, the **Hepburn A**ct reinforced the Interstate Commerce Commission. In 1902, Roosevelt used the Justice Department and lawsuits to try to break monopolies and enforce the **Sherman Anti-Trust Act**. The **Clayton Anti-Trust Act** was added in 1914.
- From 1898 to 1910, the **Forest Service** guided lumber companies in the conservation and more efficient use of woodland resources under the direction of Gifford Pinchot.
- In 1906, the **Pure Food and Drug Act** was passed to protect consumers from fraudulent labeling and adulteration of products.
- In 1913, the **Federal Reserve System** was established to supervise banking and commerce. In 1914, the **Fair Trade Commission** was established to ensure fair competition.

WORLD WAR I (1917–1919)

When World War I broke out in 1914, America declared **neutrality**. The huge demand for war goods by the Allies broke a seven-year industrial stagnation and gave American factories full-time work. The country's sympathies lay mostly with the Allies, and before long American business and banking were heavily invested in an Allied victory. In 1916, **Woodrow Wilson** campaigned on the slogan "He kept us out of war." However, when the British ship the *Lusitania* was torpedoed in 1915 by a German submarine and many Americans were killed, the United States broke its neutrality and directly entered the war. Eventually, when it was proven that Germany was trying to incite Mexico and Japan into attacking the United States, Wilson declared war in 1917, even though America was unprepared. Nonetheless, America quickly armed and transferred sufficient troops to Europe, bringing the **Allies** to victory in 1918.

> **Review Video: WWI Overview**
> Visit mometrix.com/academy and enter code: 659767

ROARING TWENTIES AND THE GREAT DEPRESSION

The **Roaring Twenties** (1920–1929) refers to the economically successful period of time following World War I. New technologies such as automobiles, new forms of media such as films, and new communication technology became widely available. In the wake of industrial growth and revolution, culture shifted toward more modern sentiments, and moved toward a more **practical** approach to life. New forms of art and music were born and thrived during this period, and during this timeframe civil rights were expanded to allow **women to vote**. In 1929, the stock market crashed and caused the end of the Roaring Twenties and the beginning of the **Great Depression**, which lasted from 1930 until 1941. The Great Depression was characterized by high unemployment rates and a slow-moving market with little profit to be made. Many banks failed during this time, and there was no governmental protection against bank failures. As a result, many depositors withdrew their money from banks to protect themselves, removing much of the money from the economy in an effect called economic contraction.

WORLD WAR II (1939–1945)

World War II began in 1939. As with World War I, the United States tried to stay out of World War II, even though the **Lend-Lease program** transferred munitions to Great Britain. However, on

Copyright © Mometrix Media. You have been licensed one copy of this document for personal use only. Any other reproduction or redistribution is strictly prohibited. All rights reserved.
This content is provided for test preparation purposes only and does not imply an endorsement by Mometrix of any particular political, scientific, or religious point of view.

December 7, 1941, Japan attacked **Pearl Harbor** in Hawaii. Since Japan was an ally of Germany, the United States declared war on all the Axis powers. Although there was fighting in both Europe and the Pacific, the decision was made to concentrate on defeating Hitler first. Since it did not have combat within its borders, the United States became the great manufacturer of goods and munitions for the war effort. Women went to work in the factories, while the men entered the military. All facets of American life were centered on the war effort, including rationing, metal collections, and buying war bonds. The benefit of this production was an **end to the economic depression**. The influx of American personnel and supplies eventually brought victory in Europe in April of 1945, and in Asia the following August.

> **Review Video: World War II**
> Visit mometrix.com/academy and enter code: 759402

MAJOR PROGRAMS AND EVENTS RESULTING FROM THE COLD WAR

After World War II, the Soviet Union kept control of Eastern Europe, including half of Germany. **Communism** spread around the world. Resulting fears led to:

- The **Truman Doctrine** (1947) – This was a policy designed to protect free peoples everywhere against oppression.
- The **Marshall Plan** (1948) – This devoted $12 billion to rebuild Western Europe and strengthen its defenses.
- The **Organization of American States** (1948) – This was established to bolster democratic relations in the Americas.
- The **Berlin Blockade** (1948-49) – The Soviets tried to starve out West Berlin, so the United States provided massive supply drops by air.
- The **North Atlantic Treaty Organization** (1949) – This was formed to militarily link the United States and western Europe so that an attack on one was an attack on both.
- The **Korean War** (1950-53) – This divided the country into the communist North and the democratic South.
- The **McCarthy era** (1950-54) – Senator Joseph McCarthy of Wisconsin held hearings on supposed Communist conspiracies that ruined innocent reputations and led to the blacklisting of suspected sympathizers in the government, Hollywood, and the media.

MAJOR EVENTS OF THE 1960S

The 1960s were a tumultuous time for the United States. Major events included:

- The **Cuban Missile Crisis** (1961) – This was a stand-off between the United States and the Soviet Union over a build-up of missiles in Cuba. Eventually, the Soviets stopped their shipments and a nuclear war was averted.
- The **assassinations** of President Kennedy (1963), Senator Robert Kennedy (1968), and Dr. Martin Luther King, Jr. (1968).
- The **Civil Rights Movement** – Protest marches were held across the nation to draw attention to the plight of Black citizens. From 1964 to 1968, race riots exploded in more than 100 cities.
- The **Vietnam War** (1964-73) – This resulted in a military draft. There was heavy involvement of American personnel and money. There were also protest demonstrations, particularly on college campuses. At Kent State, several students died after being shot by National Guardsmen.

Copyright © Mometrix Media. You have been licensed one copy of this document for personal use only. Any other reproduction or redistribution is strictly prohibited. All rights reserved. This content is provided for test preparation purposes only and does not imply an endorsement by Mometrix of any particular political, scientific, or religious point of view.

- **Major legislation** – Legislation passed during this decade included the Civil Rights Act, the Clean Air Act, and the Water Quality Act. This decade also saw the creation of the Peace Corps, Medicare, and the War on Poverty, in which billions were appropriated for education, urban redevelopment, and public housing.

PRESIDENTS AND VICE PRESIDENTS FROM 1972 TO 1974

In a two-year time span, the United States had two presidents and two vice presidents. This situation resulted first from the resignation of Vice President **Spiro T. Agnew** in October of 1973 because of alleged kickbacks. President **Richard M. Nixon** then appointed House Minority Leader **Gerald R. Ford** to be vice president. This was accomplished through Senate ratification, a process that had been devised after Harry Truman succeeded to the presidency upon the death of Franklin Roosevelt and went through nearly four years of his presidency without a vice president. Nixon resigned the presidency in August of 1974 because some Republican party members broke into Democratic headquarters at the **Watergate** building in Washington, DC, and the president participated in covering up the crime. Ford succeeded Nixon, and had to appoint another vice president. He chose **Nelson Rockefeller**, former governor of New York.

POST-WAR ERA AND THE CIVIL RIGHTS ERA

The **Post-War Era** (1945-1964) was a time of **economic recovery** and general growth in America. The wars of the past several decades inspired a more active foreign policy to deter such violent wars from occurring again. This largely focused on the Soviet Union and the expansion of Communism around the world. Several countries at this time participated in both a space race and an **arms race**, a rush to develop and accumulate more powerful weapons, particularly nuclear weapons, to become the world's strongest military power. The political differences and concerns over powerful armaments eventually led to the Cold War, Vietnam War, and Korean War. The 60s were also a major pivot-point for civil rights, leading into the **Civil Rights Era** (1965-1980). Due to the protesting and activism of several groups, including **Dr. Martin Luther King Jr**. and the **NAACP**, civil rights landmarks were made regarding racial equality, including laws dealing with **segregation**, **employment opportunity**, and **voting** rights.

REAGAN ERA (1981–1991)

The **Reagan Era** is an era largely describing the foreign policy of the United States during the 1980s and sometimes viewed as extending through the 1990s or early-2000s. During this period, conservative reforms worked to **increase military spending** while also **cutting taxes** and reducing or restricting the involvement of the national government. Ronald Reagan's financial policy revolved around the idea that if the government stepped back, the economy could grow, which would in turn help to reduce national debt.

1990S AND EARLY-2000S

The 1990s and early-2000s were characterized largely by new economic developments surrounding the availability of computers and the development of the internet, allowing new technology to drive the economy in new ways. The economy boomed in the late 1990s leading into the early 2000s. Amid all of the economic success, the United States faced attacks by terrorist groups such as al-Qaeda, which caused alarm and greater restriction to national security and border control. The most influential of these terror attacks was the September 11, 2001 airliner hijacking, where al-Qaeda members took over four airplanes and used them as weapons to crash into key governmental and trade buildings. These attacks triggered a focus of American attention on terrorist groups, and led to several wars in Afghanistan and Iraq.

Copyright © Mometrix Media. You have been licensed one copy of this document for personal use only. Any other reproduction or redistribution is strictly prohibited. All rights reserved.
This content is provided for test preparation purposes only and does not imply an endorsement by Mometrix of any particular political, scientific, or religious point of view.

2008 to Present

Following the economic success of the 1990s and 2000s, the housing industry collapsed, leading to what is known as the **Great Recession** in 2008. In 2008, President Barack Obama was elected as the country's first African-American president. The war on terror continued until 2011, when Obama announced the death of Osama bin Laden, the al-Qaeda leader of the time. Obama's primary focus during his presidency included large stimulus packages and reforms to health insurance programs, an attempt to make healthcare affordable and available to all Americans. In 2016, President Donald Trump took office. His campaigns centered around immigration laws and tax reforms. Other major trends within this time period include a new wave of social equality issues surrounding same-sex rights and racial tension issues within America.

Chapter Quiz

1. Which of the following Thirteen Colonies was NOT considered a Middle Colony?

a. New York
b. Pennsylvania
c. Delaware
d. Virginia

2. The French and Indian War was ended by the signing of which treaty?

a. The Treaty of London
b. The Treaty of Versailles
c. The Treaty of Paris
d. The Treaty of Gloucester

3. The Boston Massacre occurred on which of the following dates?

a. December 6, 1773
b. April 14, 1775
c. March 5, 1770
d. June 4, 1774

4. Who was the president of the United States during the Era of Good Feelings?

a. Thomas Jefferson
b. James Monroe
c. James Madison
d. George Washington

5. Which of the following "robber barons" was most well known for their meatpacking industry?

a. Philip Danforth Armour
b. Andrew Carnegie
c. J. P. Morgan
d. John Jacob Astor

Chapter Quiz Answer Key

1. D: The Thirteen Colonies were a group of English colonies that were overtly similar in their political and religious beliefs. The Thirteen Colonies were divided into four sub-colonies:

- New England Colonies: New Hampshire, Massachusetts, Rhode Island, Connecticut
- Chesapeake Bay Colonies: Virginia, Maryland

Copyright © Mometrix Media. You have been licensed one copy of this document for personal use only. Any other reproduction or redistribution is strictly prohibited. All rights reserved. This content is provided for test preparation purposes only and does not imply an endorsement by Mometrix of any particular political, scientific, or religious point of view.

- Middle Colonies: New York, Pennsylvania, New Jersey, Delaware
- Southern Colonies: North Carolina, South Carolina, Georgia

2. C: In 1763, the Treaty of Paris brought an end to the French and Indian War, as France relinquished some of its Eastern territory to England, including the territory east of modern-day Louisiana all the way to the Great Lakes.

3. C: Boston Massacre: On March 5, 1770, British soldiers fired on a crowd and killed five people.

4. B: The Era of Good Feelings lasted from 1817–1825. It followed the Jeffersonian Era and was marked by the collapse of the Federalist system. President James Monroe attempted to deter the partisan political system and prevent political parties from driving national politics. During the Era of Good Feelings, there was a temporary sense of national security and a desire for unity in America following the war of previous years.

5. A: The Gilded Age, from the 1870s to 1890, was so named because of the enormous wealth and grossly opulent lifestyle enjoyed by a handful of powerful families. This was the time when huge mansions were built as summer "cottages" in Newport, Rhode Island, and great lodges were built in mountain areas for the pleasure of families such as the Vanderbilts, Ascots, and Rockefellers.

Control of the major industries was held largely by the following men:

- Jay Gould controlled the railroads
- Andrew Carnegie controlled steel
- John D. Rockefeller, Sr. controlled oil
- Philip Danforth Armour controlled meatpacking
- J. P. Morgan controlled banking
- John Jacob Astor controlled fur trading
- Cornelius Vanderbilt controlled steamboat shipping

These men were were known as robber barons for their ruthless business practices and exploitation of workers. Of course, all of these heads of industry diversified and became involved in multiple business ventures. To curb cutthroat competition (particularly among the railroads) and to prohibit restrained trade, Congress created the Interstate Commerce Commission and the Sherman Anti-Trust Act. Neither of these, however, was enforced.

United States Government and Citizenship

PRINCIPLES OF THE CONSTITUTION

The six basic principles of the Constitution are:

1. **Popular Sovereignty** – The people establish government and give power to it; the government can function only with the consent of the people.
2. **Limited Government** – The Constitution specifies limits on government authority, and no official or entity is above the law.
3. **Separation of Powers** – Power is divided among three government branches: the legislative (Congress), the executive (President), and the judicial (federal courts).
4. **Checks and Balances** – This is a system that enforces the separation of powers and ensures that each branch has the authority and ability to restrain the powers of the other two branches, thus preventing tyranny.

Copyright © Mometrix Media. You have been licensed one copy of this document for personal use only. Any other reproduction or redistribution is strictly prohibited. All rights reserved.
This content is provided for test preparation purposes only and does not imply an endorsement by Mometrix of any particular political, scientific, or religious point of view.

5. **Judicial Review** – Judges in the federal courts ensure that no act of government is in violation of the Constitution. If an act is unconstitutional, the judicial branch has the power to nullify it.
6. **Federalism** – This is the division of power between the central government and local governments, which limits the power of the federal government and allows states to deal with local problems.

CLASSIC FORMS OF GOVERNMENT

Forms of government that have appeared throughout history include:

- **Feudalism** – This is based on the rule of local lords who are loyal to the king and control the lives and production of those who work on their land.
- **Classical republic** – This form is a representative democracy. Small groups of elected leaders represent the interests of the electorate.
- **Absolute monarchy** – A king or queen has complete control of the military and government.
- **Authoritarianism** – An individual or group has unlimited authority. There is no system in place to restrain the power of the government.
- **Dictatorship** – Those in power are not held responsible to the people.
- **Autocracy** – This is rule by one person (despot), not necessarily a monarch, who uses power tyrannically.
- **Oligarchy** – A small, usually self-appointed elite rules a region.
- **Liberal democracy** – This is a government based on the consent of the people that protects individual rights and freedoms from any intolerance by the majority.
- **Totalitarianism** – All facets of the citizens' lives are controlled by the government.

INFLUENCES OF PHILOSOPHERS ON POLITICAL STUDY

Ancient Greek philosophers **Aristotle** and **Plato** believed political science would lead to order in political matters, and that this scientifically organized order would create stable, just societies.

Thomas Aquinas adapted the ideas of Aristotle to a Christian perspective. His ideas stated that individuals have certain rights, but also certain duties, and that these rights and duties should determine the type and extent of government rule. In stating that laws should limit the role of government, he laid the groundwork for ideas that would eventually become modern constitutionalism.

Niccolò Machiavelli, author of *The Prince*, was a proponent of politics based solely on power.

PARLIAMENTARY AND DEMOCRATIC SYSTEMS OF GOVERNMENT

In a **parliamentary system**, government involves a legislature and a variety of political parties. The head of government, usually a Prime Minister, is typically the head of the dominant party. A head of state can be elected, or this position can be taken by a monarch, such as in Great Britain's constitutional monarchy system.

In a **democratic system** of government, the people elect their government representatives. The term democracy is a Greek term that means "for the rule of the people." There are two forms of democracy—direct and indirect. In a direct democracy, each issue or election is decided by a vote where each individual is counted separately. An indirect democracy employs a legislature that votes on issues that affect large number of people whom the legislative members represent.

Copyright © Mometrix Media. You have been licensed one copy of this document for personal use only. Any other reproduction or redistribution is strictly prohibited. All rights reserved. This content is provided for test preparation purposes only and does not imply an endorsement by Mometrix of any particular political, scientific, or religious point of view.

Democracy can exist as a Parliamentary system or a Presidential system. The US is a presidential, indirect democracy.

BILL OF RIGHTS

The **United States Bill of Rights** was based on principles established by the **Magna Carta** in 1215, the 1688 **English Bill of Rights**, and the 1776 **Virginia Bill of Rights**. In 1791, the federal government added 10 amendments to the United States Constitution that provided the following **protections**:

- Freedom of speech, religion, peaceful assembly, petition of the government, and petition of the press
- The right to keep and bear arms
- No quartering of soldiers on private property without the consent of the owner
- Regulations on government search and seizure
- Provisions concerning prosecution
- The right to a speedy, public trial and the calling of witnesses
- The right to trial by jury
- Freedom from excessive bail or cruel punishment
- These rights are not necessarily the only rights
- Powers not prohibited by the Constitution are reserved to the states

> **Review Video: Bill of Rights**
> Visit mometrix.com/academy and enter code: 585149

MAKING A FORMAL AMENDMENT TO THE CONSTITUTION

So far, there have been only **27 amendments** to the federal Constitution. There are four different ways to change the constitution: two methods for proposal and two methods for ratification:

1. An amendment is proposed by a two-thirds vote in each house of Congress and ratified by three-fourths of the state legislatures.
2. An amendment is proposed by a two-thirds vote in each house of Congress and ratified by three-fourths of the states in special conventions called for that purpose.
3. An amendment is proposed by a national convention that is called by Congress at the request of two-thirds of the state legislatures and ratified by three-fourths of the state legislatures.
4. An amendment is proposed by a national convention that is called by Congress at the request of two-thirds of the state legislatures and ratified by three-fourths of the states in special conventions called for that purpose.

DIVISION OF POWERS

The **division of powers** in the federal government system is as follows:

- **National** – This level can coin money, regulate interstate and foreign trade, raise and maintain armed forces, declare war, govern United States territories and admit new states, and conduct foreign relations.
- **Concurrent** – This level can levy and collect taxes, borrow money, establish courts, define crimes and set punishments, and claim private property for public use.
- **State** – This level can regulate trade and business within the state, establish public schools, pass license requirements for professionals, regulate alcoholic beverages, conduct elections, and establish local governments.

Copyright © Mometrix Media. You have been licensed one copy of this document for personal use only. Any other reproduction or redistribution is strictly prohibited. All rights reserved.
This content is provided for test preparation purposes only and does not imply an endorsement by Mometrix of any particular political, scientific, or religious point of view.

There are three types of **delegated powers** granted by the Constitution:

1. **Expressed or enumerated powers** – These are specifically spelled out in the Constitution.
2. **Implied** – These are not expressly stated, but are reasonably suggested by the expressed powers.
3. **Inherent** – These are powers not expressed by the Constitution but ones that national governments have historically possessed, such as granting diplomatic recognition.

Powers can also be classified as reserved or exclusive. **Reserved powers** are not granted to the national government, but not denied to the states. **Exclusive powers** are those reserved to the national government, including concurrent powers.

STAGES OF EXTENDING SUFFRAGE IN THE U.S.

Originally, the Constitution of 1789 provided the right to vote only to white male property owners. Through the years, suffrage was extended through the following five stages.

1. In the early 1800s, states began to eliminate **property ownership** and **tax payment qualifications**.
2. By 1810, there were no more **religious tests** for voting. In the late 1800s, the 15th Amendment protected citizens from being denied the right to vote because of **race or color**.
3. In 1920, the 19th Amendment prohibited the denial of the right to vote because of **gender**, and women were given the right to vote.
4. Passed in 1961 and ratified in 1964, the 23rd Amendment added the voters of the **District of Columbia** to the presidential electorate and eliminated the poll tax as a condition for voting in federal elections. The **Voting Rights Act of 1965** prohibited disenfranchisement through literacy tests and various other means of discrimination.
5. In 1971, the 26th Amendment set the minimum voting age at **18 years of age**.

MAJOR SUPREME COURT CASES

Out of the many Supreme Court rulings, several have had critical historical importance. These include:

- **Marbury v. Madison** (1803) – This ruling established judicial review as a power of the Supreme Court.
- **Dred Scott v. Sandford** (1857) – This decision upheld property rights over human rights in the case of a slave who had been transported to a free state by his master, but was still considered a slave.
- **Brown v. Board of Education** (1954) – The Court ruled that segregation was a violation of the Equal Protection Clause and that the "separate but equal" practice in education was unconstitutional. This decision overturned the 1896 Plessy v. Ferguson ruling that permitted segregation if facilities were equal.
- **Miranda v. Arizona** (1966) – This ruling compelled the reading of Miranda rights to those arrested for crimes the law. It ensured that confessions could not be illegally obtained and that citizen rights to fair trials and protection under the law would be upheld.

> **Review Video: Marbury v. Madison**
> Visit mometrix.com/academy and enter code: 573964
>
> **Review Video: What was the Dred Scott Decision?**
> Visit mometrix.com/academy and enter code: 364838

Copyright © Mometrix Media. You have been licensed one copy of this document for personal use only. Any other reproduction or redistribution is strictly prohibited. All rights reserved.
This content is provided for test preparation purposes only and does not imply an endorsement by Mometrix of any particular political, scientific, or religious point of view.

Famous Speeches in U.S. History that Defined Government Policy, Foreign Relations, and American Spirit

Among the best-known speeches and famous lines known to modern Americans are the following:

- The **Gettysburg Address** – Made by Abraham Lincoln on November 19, 1863, it dedicated the Gettysburg battleground's cemetery.
- The **Fourteen Points** – Made by Woodrow Wilson on January 18, 1918, this outlined Wilson's plans for peace and the League of Nations.
- **Address to Congress** – Made by Franklin Roosevelt on December 8, 1941, it declared war on Japan and described the attack on Pearl Harbor as "a day which will live in infamy."
- **Inaugural Address** – Made by John F. Kennedy on January 20, 1961, it contained the famous line: "Ask not what your country can do for you, ask what you can do for your country."
- **Berlin Address** – Made by John F. Kennedy on June 26, 1963, it contained the famous line "Ich bin ein Berliner," which expressed empathy for West Berliners in their conflict with the Soviet Union.
- "**I Have a Dream**" and "**I See the Promised Land**" – Made by Martin Luther King, Jr. on August 28, 1963 and April 3, 1968, respectively, these speeches were hallmarks of the Civil Rights Movement.
- **Brandenburg Gate speech** – Made by Ronald Reagan on June 12, 1987, this speech was about the Berlin Wall and the end of the Cold War. It contained the famous line "Tear down this wall."

Closed and Open Primaries in a Direct Primary System

The **direct primary system** is a means for members of a political party to participate in the selection of a candidate from their party to compete against the other party's candidate in a general election. A **closed primary** is a party nominating election in which only declared party members can vote. Party membership is usually established by registration. Currently, 26 states and the District of Columbia use this system. An **open primary** is a party nominating election in which any qualified voter can take part. The voter makes a public choice at the polling place about which primary to participate in, and the choice does not depend on any registration or previous choices. A **blanket primary**, which allowed voters to vote in the primaries of both parties, was used at various times by three states. The Supreme Court ruled against this practice in 2000.

Important Documents in United States History and Government

The following are among the greatest **American documents** because of their impact on foreign and domestic policy:

- Declaration of Independence (1776)
- The Articles of Confederation (1777)
- The Constitution (1787) and the Bill of Rights (1791)
- The Northwest Ordinance (1787)
- The Federalist Papers (1787-88)
- George Washington's Inaugural Address (1789) and Farewell Address (1796)
- The Alien and Sedition Act (1798)
- The Louisiana Purchase Treaty (1803)
- The Monroe Doctrine (1823); The Missouri Compromise (1830)
- The Compromise of 1850
- The Kansas-Nebraska Act (1854)

Copyright © Mometrix Media. You have been licensed one copy of this document for personal use only. Any other reproduction or redistribution is strictly prohibited. All rights reserved. This content is provided for test preparation purposes only and does not imply an endorsement by Mometrix of any particular political, scientific, or religious point of view.

- The Homestead Act (1862)
- The Emancipation Proclamation (1863)
- The agreement to purchase Alaska (1866)
- The Sherman Anti-Trust Act (1890)
- Theodore Roosevelt's Corollary to the Monroe Doctrine (1905)
- The Social Security Act (1935) and other acts of the New Deal in the 1930s; The Truman Doctrine (1947); The Marshall Plan (1948)
- The Civil Rights Act (1964)

FEDERAL TAXES

The four types of **federal taxes** are:

- **Income taxes on individuals** – This is a complex system because of demands for various exemptions and rates. Further, the schedule of rates can be lowered or raised according to economic conditions in order to stimulate or restrain economic activity. For example, a tax cut can provide an economic stimulus, while a tax increase can slow down the rate of inflation. Personal income tax generates about five times as much as corporate taxes. Rates are based on an individual's income, and range from 10 to 35 percent.
- **Income taxes on corporations** – The same complexity of exemptions and rates exists for corporations as individuals. Taxes can be raised or lowered according to the need to stimulate or restrain the economy.
- **Excise taxes** – These are taxes on specific goods such as tobacco, liquor, automobiles, gasoline, air travel, and luxury items, or on activities such as highway usage by trucks.
- **Customs duties** – These are taxes imposed on imported goods. They serve to regulate trade between the United States and other countries.

UNITED STATES CURRENCY SYSTEM

The Constitution of 1787 gave the United States Congress the central authority to **print or coin money** and to **regulate its value**. Before this time, states were permitted to maintain separate currencies. The currency system is based on a **modified gold standard**. There is an enormous store of gold to back up United States currency housed at Fort Knox, Kentucky. Paper money is actually **Federal Reserve notes** and coins. It is the job of the Bureau of Engraving and Printing in the Treasury Department to design plates, special types of paper, and other security measures for bills and bonds. This money is put into general circulation by the Treasury and Federal Reserve Banks, and is taken out of circulation when worn out. Coins are made at the Bureau of the Mint in Philadelphia, Denver, and San Francisco.

EMPLOYMENT ACT OF 1946

The **Employment Act of 1946** established the following entities to combat unemployment:

- The **Council of Economic Advisers** (CEA) – Composed of a chair and two other members appointed by the President and approved by the Senate, this council assists the President with the development and implementation of U.S. economic policy. The Council members and their staff, located in the Executive Office, are professionals in economics and statistics who forecast economic trends and provide analysis based on evidence-based research.
- The **Economic Report of the President** – This is presented every January by the President to Congress. Based on the work of the Council, the report recommends a program for maximizing employment, and may also recommend legislation.

Copyright © Mometrix Media. You have been licensed one copy of this document for personal use only. Any other reproduction or redistribution is strictly prohibited. All rights reserved.
This content is provided for test preparation purposes only and does not imply an endorsement by Mometrix of any particular political, scientific, or religious point of view.

- **Joint Economic Committee** (JEC) – This is a committee composed of 10 members of the House and 10 members of the Senate that makes a report early each year on its continuous study of the economy. Study is conducted through hearings and research, and the report is made in response to the president's recommendations.

QUALIFICATIONS OF A U.S. CITIZEN

Anyone born in the US, born abroad to a US citizen, or who has gone through a process of **naturalization** to become a citizen, is considered a **citizen** of the United States. It is possible to lose US citizenship as a result of conviction of certain crimes such as treason. Citizenship may also be lost if a citizen pledges an oath to another country or serves in the military of a country engaged in hostilities with the US. A US citizen can also choose to hold dual citizenship, work as an expatriate in another country without losing US citizenship, or even renounce citizenship if he or she so chooses.

RIGHTS, DUTIES, AND RESPONSIBILITIES GRANTED TO OR EXPECTED FROM US CITIZENS

Citizens are granted certain rights under the US government. The most important of these are defined in the **Bill of Rights**, and include freedom of speech, religion, assembly, and a variety of other rights the government is not allowed to remove.

Duties of a U.S. citizen include:

- Paying taxes
- Loyalty to the government, though the US does not prosecute those who criticize or seek to change the government
- Support and defend the Constitution
- Serve in the Armed Forces as required by law
- Obeying laws as set forth by the various levels of government.

Responsibilities of a U.S. citizen include:

- Voting in elections
- Respecting one another's rights and not infringing upon them
- Staying informed about various political and national issues
- Respecting one another's beliefs

CHAPTER QUIZ

1. An oligarchy is defined as which of the following?

- a. A king or queen has complete control of the military and government.
- b. An individual or group has unlimited authority. There is no system in place to restrain the power of the government.
- c. All facets of the citizens' lives are controlled by the government.
- d. A small, usually self-appointed elite rules a region.

2. The United States Bill of Rights was based on principles established by all of the following, EXCEPT?

- a. The Declaration of Independence
- b. Magna Carta
- c. English Bill of Rights
- d. Virginia Bill of Rights

Copyright © Mometrix Media. You have been licensed one copy of this document for personal use only. Any other reproduction or redistribution is strictly prohibited. All rights reserved.
This content is provided for test preparation purposes only and does not imply an endorsement by Mometrix of any particular political, scientific, or religious point of view.

3. How many amendments are in the Constitution of the United States?

    a. 29
    b. 27
    c. 25
    d. 24

CHAPTER QUIZ ANSWER KEY

1. D: There are many forms of government that have appeared throughout history.

- Feudalism: This is based on the rule of local lords who are loyal to the king and control the lives and production of those who work on their land.
- Classical republic: This form is a representative democracy. Small groups of elected leaders represent the interests of the electorate.
- Absolute monarchy: A king or queen has complete control of the military and government.
- Authoritarianism: An individual or group has unlimited authority. There is no system in place to restrain the power of the government.
- Dictatorship: Those in power are not held responsible to the people.
- Autocracy: This is rule by one person (despot), not necessarily a monarch, who uses power tyrannically.
- Oligarchy: A small, usually self-appointed elite rules a region.
- Liberal democracy: A government based on the consent of the people that protects individual rights and freedoms from any intolerance by the majority.
- Totalitarianism: All facets of the citizens' lives are controlled by the government.

2. A: The United States Bill of Rights was based on principles established by the Magna Carta in 1215, the 1688 English Bill of Rights, and the 1776 Virginia Bill of Rights. In 1791, the federal government added 10 amendments to the United States Constitution that provided the following protections:

- Freedom of speech, religion, peaceful assembly, petition of the government, and petition of the press
- The right to keep and bear arms
- No quartering of soldiers on private property without the consent of the owner
- Regulations on government search and seizure
- Provisions concerning prosecution
- The right to a speedy, public trial and the calling of witnesses
- The right to trial by jury
- Freedom from excessive bail or cruel punishment
- These rights are not necessarily the only rights
- Powers not prohibited by the Constitution are reserved to the states

3. B: To date, there are a total of 27 amendments to the Constitution of the United States.

REPRESENTATIVE DEMOCRACY

In a system of government characterized as a representative democracy, voters elect **representatives** to act in their interests. Typically, a representative is elected by and responsible to a specific subset of the total population of eligible voters; this subset of the electorate is referred to as a representative's constituency. A **representative democracy** may foster a more powerful legislature than other forms of government systems; to compensate for a strong legislature, most

Copyright © Mometrix Media. You have been licensed one copy of this document for personal use only. Any other reproduction or redistribution is strictly prohibited. All rights reserved. This content is provided for test preparation purposes only and does not imply an endorsement by Mometrix of any particular political, scientific, or religious point of view.

constitutions stipulate that measures must be taken to balance the powers within government, such as the creation of a separate judicial branch. Representative democracy became popular in post-industrial nations where increasing numbers of people expressed an interest in politics, but where technology and census counts remained incompatible with systems of direct democracy. Today, the majority of the world's population resides in representative democracies, including constitutional monarchies that possess a strong representative branch.

DEMOCRACY

Democracy, or rule by the people, is a form of government in which power is vested in the people and in which policy decisions are made by the majority in a decision-making process such as an election that is open to all or most citizens. Definitions of democracy have become more generalized and include aspects of society and political culture in democratic societies that do not necessarily represent a form of government. What defines a democracy varies, but some of the characteristics of a democracy could include the presence of a middle class, the presence of a civil society, a free market, political pluralism, universal suffrage, and specific rights and freedoms. In practice however, democracies do have limits on specific freedoms, which are justified as being necessary to maintain democracy and ensure democratic freedoms. For example, freedom of association is limited in democracies for individuals and groups that pose a threat to government or to society.

PRESIDENTIAL/CONGRESSIONAL SYSTEM

In a **presidential system**, also referred to as a **congressional system**, the legislative branch and the executive branches are elected separately from one another. The features of a presidential system include a *president* who serves as both the head of state and the head of the government, who has no formal relationship with the legislative branch, who is not a voting member, who cannot introduce bills, and who has a fixed term of office. *Elections* are held at scheduled times. The president's *cabinet* carries out the policies of the executive branch and the legislative branch.

POLITICAL PARTIES

A **political party** is an organization that advocates a particular ideology and seeks to gain power within government. The tendency of members of political parties to support their party's policies and interests relative to those of other parties is referred to as partisanship. Often, a political party is comprised of members whose positions, interests and perspectives on policies vary, despite having shared interests in the general ideology of the party. As such, many political parties will have divisions within them that have differing opinions on policy. Political parties are often placed on a political spectrum, with one end of the spectrum representing conservative, traditional values and policies and the other end of the spectrum representing radical, progressive value and policies.

TYPES OF PARTY SYSTEMS

There is a variety of **party systems**, including single-party systems, dominant-party systems, and dual-party systems. In a **single-party system**, only one political party may hold power. In this type of system, minor parties may be permitted, but they must accept the leadership of the dominant party. **Dominant-party systems** allow for multiple parties in opposition of one another, however the dominant party is the only party considered to have power. A **two-party system**, such as in the United States, is one in which there are two dominant political parties. In such a system, it is very difficult for any other parties to win an election. In most two-party systems, there is typically one right wing party and one left wing party.

DEMOCRATIC PARTY

The **Democratic Party** was founded in 1792. In the United States, it is one of the two dominant political parties, along with the Republican Party. The Democratic Party is to the left of the

Copyright © Mometrix Media. You have been licensed one copy of this document for personal use only. Any other reproduction or redistribution is strictly prohibited. All rights reserved.
This content is provided for test preparation purposes only and does not imply an endorsement by Mometrix of any particular political, scientific, or religious point of view.

Republican Party. The Democratic Party began as a conservative party in the mid-1800s, shifting to the left during the 1900s. There are many factions within the Democratic Party in the United States. The **Democratic National Committee (DNC)** is the official organization of the Democratic Party, and it develops and promotes the party's platform and coordinates fundraising and election strategies. There are Democratic committees in every U.S. state and most U.S. counties. The official symbol of the Democratic Party is the donkey.

REPUBLICAN PARTY

The **Republican Party** is often referred to as the **GOP**, which stands for *Grand Old Party*. The Republican Party is considered socially conservative and economically neoliberal relative to the Democratic Party. Like the Democratic Party, there are factions within the Republic Party that agree with the party's overall ideology, but disagree with the party's positions on specific issues. The official symbol of the Republican Party is the elephant. The **Republican National Committee (RNC)** is the official organization of the Republican Party, and it develops and promotes the party's platform and coordinates fundraising and election strategies. There are Republican committees in every U.S. state and most U.S. counties.

POLITICAL CAMPAIGNS

A **political campaign** is an organized attempt to influence the decisions of a particular group of people. Examples of campaigns could include elections or efforts to influence policy changes. One of the first steps in a campaign is to develop a **campaign message**. The message must then be delivered to the individuals and groups that the campaign is trying to reach and influence through a campaign plan. There are various ways for a campaign to communicate its message to the intended audience, including public media; paid media such as television, radio and newspaper ads, billboards and the internet; public events such as protests and rallies; meetings with speakers; mailings; canvassing; fliers; and websites. Through these efforts, the campaign attempts to attract additional support and, ultimately, to reach the goal of the campaign.

> **Review Video: Political Campaigns**
> Visit mometrix.com/academy and enter code: 838608

VOTING

Voting is a method of decision making that allows people to express their opinion or preference for a candidate or for a proposed resolution of an issue. In a democratic system, voting typically takes place as part of an **election**. An individual participates in the voting process by casting a vote, or a **ballot**; ballots are produced by states A *secret ballot* can be used at polls to protect voters' privacy. Individuals can also vote via *absentee ballot*. In some states voters can write-in a name to cast a vote for a candidate that is not on the ballot. Some states also use *straight ticket voting*, allowing the voter to vote for one party for all the elected positions on the ballot.

U.S. ELECTIONS

In the United States, **officials** are elected at the federal, state and local levels. The first two articles of the Constitution, as well as various amendments, establish how **federal elections** are to be held. The **President** is elected indirectly, by electors of an electoral college. Members of the electoral college nearly always vote along the lines of the popular vote of their respective states. Members of **Congress** are directly elected. At the state level, state law establishes most aspects of how elections are held. There are many elected offices at the state level, including a governor and state legislature. There are also elected offices at the local level.

Copyright © Mometrix Media. You have been licensed one copy of this document for personal use only. Any other reproduction or redistribution is strictly prohibited. All rights reserved. This content is provided for test preparation purposes only and does not imply an endorsement by Mometrix of any particular political, scientific, or religious point of view.

VOTER ELIGIBILITY

The United States Constitution establishes that individual people are permitted to **vote** in elections if they are citizens of the United States and are at least eighteen years old. The **fifteenth** and **nineteenth amendments** of the United States Constitution stipulate that the right to vote cannot be denied to any United States citizen based on race or sex, respectively. States regulate voter eligibility beyond the minimum qualifications stipulated by the United States Constitution. Depending on the regulations of individual states, individuals may be denied the right to vote if they are convicted criminals.

ADVANTAGES AND DISADVANTAGES TO TWO-PARTY SYSTEM

Advocates of the **two-party system** argue that its advantages are that they are stable because they enable policies and government to change slowly rather than rapidly due to the relative lack of influence from small parties representing unconventional ideologies. In addition, they seem to drive voters toward a middle ground and are less susceptible to revolutions, coups, or civil wars. Among the critiques of the two-party system is the claim that stability in and of itself is not necessarily desirable, as it often comes at the expense of democracy. Critics also argue that the two-party system promotes negative political campaigns, in which candidates and their respective parties only take positions on issues that will differentiate themselves from their opponents, rather than focusing on policy issues that are of significance to citizens. Another concern is that if one of the two major parties becomes weak, a dominant-party system may develop.

CAMPAIGN MESSAGE

Political campaigns consist of three main elements, which are the campaign message, the money that is necessary to run the campaign, and the "machine," or the capital that is necessary to run the campaign. A campaign message is a succinct statement expressing why voters should support the campaign and the individual or policy associated with that campaign. The message is one of the most significant aspects of a political campaign, and a considerable amount of time, money and effort is invested in devising a successful campaign message, as it will be repeated throughout the campaign and will be one of the most identifying factors of the campaign.

MODERN ELECTION CAMPAIGNS IN THE U.S.

Political campaigns in the U.S. have changed and continue to change as advances in technology permit varied campaign methods. Campaigns represent a civic practice, and today they are a high profit industry. The U.S. has an abundance of professional political consultants that employ highly sophisticated campaign management strategies and tools. The election process varies widely between the federal, state and local levels. Campaigns are typically controlled by individual candidates, rather than by the parties that they are associated with. Larger campaigns utilize a vast array of media to reach their targeted audiences, while smaller campaigns are typically limited to direct contact with voters, direct mailings and other forms of low-cost advertising to reach their audiences. In addition to fundraising and spending done by individual candidates, party committees and political action committees also raise money and spend it in ways that will advance the cause of the particular campaign they are associated with.

VOTER REGISTRATION

Individuals have the responsibility of **registering to vote**. Every state except North Dakota requires citizens to register to vote. In an effort to increase voter turnout, Congress passed the **National Voter Registration Act** in 1993. This Act is also known as "Motor Voter," because it required states to make the voter registration process easier by providing registration services through drivers' license registration centers, as well as through disability centers, schools, libraries, and mail-in

Copyright © Mometrix Media. You have been licensed one copy of this document for personal use only. Any other reproduction or redistribution is strictly prohibited. All rights reserved. This content is provided for test preparation purposes only and does not imply an endorsement by Mometrix of any particular political, scientific, or religious point of view.

registration. Some states are exempt because they permit same-day voter registration, which enables voters to register to vote on the day of the election.

PRESIDENTIAL ELECTIONS

The President of the United States is elected **indirectly**, by members of an **electoral college**. Members of the electoral college nearly always vote along the lines of the popular vote of their respective states. The winner of a presidential election is the candidate with at least 270 electoral college votes. It is possible for a candidate to win the electoral vote, and lose the popular vote. Incumbent Presidents and challengers typically prefer a balanced ticket, where the President and Vice President are elected together and generally balance one another with regard to geography, ideology, or experience working in government. The nominated Vice Presidential candidate is referred to as the President's *running mate*.

ELECTORAL COLLEGE

Electoral college votes are cast by state by a group of electors; each elector casts one electoral college vote. State law regulates how states cast their electoral college votes. In all states except Maine and Nebraska, the candidate winning the most votes receives all the state's electoral college votes. In Maine and Nebraska two electoral votes are awarded based on the winner of the statewide election, and the rest go to the highest vote-winner in each of the state's congressional districts. Critics of the electoral college argue that it is undemocratic because the President is elected indirectly as opposed to directly, and that it creates inequality between voters in different states because candidates focus attention on voters in swing states who could influence election results. Critics argue that the electoral college provides more representation for voters in small states than large states, where more voters are represented by a single electoral than in small states and discriminates against candidates that do not have support concentrated in a given state.

CONGRESSIONAL ELECTIONS

Congressional elections are every two years. Members of the **House of Representatives** are elected for a two year term and elections occur every two years on the first Tuesday after November 1st in even years. A Representative is elected from each of the 435 House districts in the U.S. House elections usually occur in the same year as Presidential elections. Members of the **Senate** are elected to six year terms; one-third of the Senate is elected every two years. Per the Seventeenth Amendment to the Constitution, which was passed in 1913, Senators are elected by the electorate of states. The country is divided into **Congressional districts**. Critics argue that this division eliminates voter choice, sometimes creating areas in which Congressional races are uncontested. Every ten years **redistricting** of Congressional districts occurs. However, redistricting is often partisan and therefore reduces the number of competitive districts. The division of voting districts resulting in an unfair advantage to one party in elections is known as gerrymandering. Gerrymandering has been criticized as being undemocratic.

STATE AND LOCAL ELECTIONS

State elections are regulated by state laws and constitutions. In keeping with the ideal of separation of powers, the legislature and the executive are elected separately at the state level, as they are at the federal level. In each state, a **Governor** and a **Lieutenant Governor** are elected. In some states, the Governor and Lieutenant Governor are elected on a joint ticket, while in other states they are elected separately from one another. In some states, executive positions such as Attorney General and Secretary of State are also elected offices. All members of state legislatures are elected, including state senators and state representatives. Depending on the state, members of the state supreme court and other members of the state judiciary may be chosen in elections. Local government can include the governments of counties and cities. At this level, nearly all government

Copyright © Mometrix Media. You have been licensed one copy of this document for personal use only. Any other reproduction or redistribution is strictly prohibited. All rights reserved. This content is provided for test preparation purposes only and does not imply an endorsement by Mometrix of any particular political, scientific, or religious point of view.

offices are filled through an election process. Elected local offices may include sheriffs, county school boards, and city mayors.

CAMPAIGN FINANCE AND INDEPENDENT EXPENDITURES

An individual or group is legally permitted to make unlimited **independent expenditures** in association with federal elections. An independent expenditure is an expenditure that is made to pay for a form of communication that supports the election or defeat of a candidate; the expenditure must be made independently from the candidate's own campaign. To be considered independent, the communication may not be made with the cooperation or consultation with, or at the request or suggestion of, any candidate, any committees or political party associated with the candidate, or any agent that acts on behalf of the candidate. There are no restrictions on the amount that anyone may spend on an independent expenditure, however, any individual making an independent expenditure must report it and disclose the source of the funds they used.

CAMPAIGN FINANCE AND ACTIVITIES OF POLITICAL PARTIES

Political parties participate in federal elections at the local, state and national levels. Most **party committees** must register with the **Federal Election Committee** and file reports disclosing federal campaign activities. While party committees may contribute funds directly to federal candidates, the amounts that they contribute are restricted by the campaign finance contribution limits. National and state party committees are permitted to make additional **coordinated expenditures**, within limits, to assist their nominees in general elections. However, national party committees are not permitted to make unlimited **independent expenditures**, also known as soft money, to support or oppose federal candidates. State and local party committees are also not permitted to use soft money for the purpose of supporting or opposing federal candidates, but they are allowed to spend soft money, up to a limit of $10,000 per source, on voter registration and on efforts aimed at increasing voter participation. All party committees are required to register themselves and file disclosure reports with the Federal Election Committee once their federal election activities exceed specified monetary limits.

PUBLIC OPINION

Public opinion represents the collective attitudes of individual members of the adult population in the United States of America. There are many varied forces that may influence public opinion. These forces include *public relations efforts* on the part of political campaigns and political parties. Another force affecting political opinion is the *political media* and the *mass media*. Public opinion is very important during elections, particularly Presidential elections, as it is an indicator of how candidates are perceived by the public and of how well candidates are doing during their election campaigns. Public opinion is often measured and evaluated using survey sampling.

MASS MEDIA AND PUBLIC OPINION

The **mass media** is critical in developing public opinion. In the short term people generally evaluate information they receive relative to their own beliefs; in the long term the media may have a considerable impact on people's beliefs. Due to the impact of the media on an individual's beliefs, some experts consider the effects of the media on an individual's independence and autonomy to be negative. Others view the impact of the media on individuals as a positive one, because the media provides information that expands worldviews and enriches lives, and fosters the development of opinions that are informed by many sources of information. A critical aspect of the relationship between the media and public opinion is who is in control of the knowledge and information that is disseminated through the media. Whoever controls the media can propagate their own agenda. The extent to which an individual interprets and evaluates information received through the media can influence behaviors such as voting patterns, consumer behavior, and social attitudes.

Copyright © Mometrix Media. You have been licensed one copy of this document for personal use only. Any other reproduction or redistribution is strictly prohibited. All rights reserved. This content is provided for test preparation purposes only and does not imply an endorsement by Mometrix of any particular political, scientific, or religious point of view.

CHAPTER QUIZ

1. Which state does NOT require a citizen to register to vote?

    a. North Dakota
    b. Alabama
    c. Florida
    d. Hawaii

2. What is the minimum number of electoral college votes needed to determine the winner of a presidential election?

    a. 210
    b. 230
    c. 250
    d. 270

CHAPTER QUIZ ANSWER KEY

1. A: Individuals have the responsibility of registering to vote. Every state except North Dakota requires citizens to register to vote. In an effort to increase voter turnout, Congress passed the National Voter Registration Act in 1993. This Act is also known as "Motor Voter" because it required states to make the voter registration process easier by providing registration services through drivers' license registration centers, as well as through disability centers, schools, libraries, and mail-in registration. Some states are exempt because they permit same-day voter registration, which enables voters to register to vote on the day of the election.

2. D: The President of the United States is elected indirectly by members of an electoral college. Members of the electoral college nearly always vote along the lines of the popular vote of their respective states. The winner of a presidential election is the candidate with at least 270 electoral college votes. It is possible for a candidate to win the electoral vote and lose the popular vote.

Geography, Anthropology, and Sociology

GEOGRAPHY

Geography involves learning about the world's primary **physical and cultural patterns** to help understand how the world functions as an interconnected and dynamic system. Combining information from different sources, geography teaches the basic patterns of climate, geology, vegetation, human settlement, migration, and commerce. Thus, geography is an **interdisciplinary** study of history, anthropology, and sociology. **History** incorporates geography in discussions of battle strategies, slavery (trade routes), ecological disasters (the Dust Bowl of the 1930s), and mass migrations. Geographic principles are useful when reading **literature** to help identify and visualize the setting, and also when studying **earth science**, **mathematics** (latitude, longitude, sun angle, and population statistics), and **fine arts** (song, art, and dance often reflect different cultures). Consequently, a good background in geography can help students succeed in other subjects as well.

THEMES OF GEOGRAPHY

The five themes of geography are:

- **Location** – This includes relative location (described in terms of surrounding geography such as a river, sea coast, or mountain) and absolute location (the specific point of latitude and longitude).

Copyright © Mometrix Media. You have been licensed one copy of this document for personal use only. Any other reproduction or redistribution is strictly prohibited. All rights reserved. This content is provided for test preparation purposes only and does not imply an endorsement by Mometrix of any particular political, scientific, or religious point of view.

- **Place** – This includes physical characteristics (deserts, plains, mountains, and waterways) and human characteristics (features created by humans, such as architecture, roads, religion, industries, and food and folk practices).
- **Human-environmental interaction** – This includes human adaptation to the environment (using an umbrella when it rains), human modification of the environment (building terraces to prevent soil erosion), and human dependence on the environment for food, water, and natural resources.
- **Movement** –Interaction through trade, migration, communications, political boundaries, ideas, and fashions.
- **Regions** – This includes formal regions (a city, state, country, or other geographical organization as defined by political boundaries), functional regions (defined by a common function or connection, such as a school district), and vernacular regions (informal divisions determined by perceptions or one's mental image, such as the "Far East").

> **Review Video: Regional Geography**
> Visit mometrix.com/academy and enter code: 350378

AREAS COVERED BY GEOGRAPHY

Geography is connected to many issues and provides answers to many everyday questions. Some of the areas covered by geography include:

- Geography investigates global climates, landforms, economies, political systems, human cultures, and migration patterns.
- Geography answers questions not only about where something is located, but also why it is there, how it got there, and how it is related to other things around it.
- Geography explains why people move to certain regions (climate, availability of natural resources, arable land, etc.).
- Geography explains world trade routes and modes of transportation.
- Geography identifies where various animals live and where various crops and forests grow.
- Geography identifies and locates populations that follow certain religions.
- Geography provides statistics on population numbers and growth, which aids in economic and infrastructure planning for cities and countries.

PHYSICAL AND CULTURAL GEOGRAPHY AND PHYSICAL AND POLITICAL LOCATIONS

- **Physical geography** is the study of climate, water, and land and their relationships with each other and humans. Physical geography locates and identifies the earth's surface features and explores how humans thrive in various locations according to crop and goods production.
- **Cultural geography** is the study of the influence of the environment on human behaviors as well as the effect of human activities such as farming, building settlements, and grazing livestock on the environment. Cultural geography also identifies and compares the features of different cultures and how they influence interactions with other cultures and the earth.
- **Physical location** refers to the placement of the hemispheres and the continents.
- **Political location** refers to the divisions within continents that designate various countries. These divisions are made with borders, which are set according to boundary lines arrived at by legal agreements.

Both physical and political locations can be precisely determined by geographical surveys and by latitude and longitude.

Copyright © Mometrix Media. You have been licensed one copy of this document for personal use only. Any other reproduction or redistribution is strictly prohibited. All rights reserved. This content is provided for test preparation purposes only and does not imply an endorsement by Mometrix of any particular political, scientific, or religious point of view.

SPATIAL ORGANIZATION

Spatial organization in geography refers to how things or people are grouped in a given space anywhere on earth. Spatial organization applies to the **placement of settlements**, whether hamlets, towns, or cities. These settlements are located to make the distribution of goods and services convenient. For example, in farm communities, people come to town to get groceries, to attend church and school, and to access medical services. It is more practical to provide these things to groups than to individuals. These settlements, historically, have been built close to water sources and agricultural areas. Lands that are topographically difficult, have few resources, or experience extreme temperatures do not have as many people as temperate zones and flat plains, where it is easier to live. Within settlements, a town or city will be organized into commercial and residential neighborhoods, with hospitals, fire stations, and shopping centers centrally located. All of these organizational considerations are spatial in nature.

IMPORTANT TERMS RELATED TO MAPS

The most important terms used when describing items on a map or globe are:

- **Latitude and longitude** – Latitude and longitude are the imaginary lines (horizontal and vertical, respectively) that divide the globe into a grid. Both are measured using the 360 degrees of a circle.
- **Coordinates** – These are the latitude and longitude measures for a place.
- **Absolute location** – This is the exact spot where coordinates meet. The grid system allows the location of every place on the planet to be identified.
- **Equator** – This is the line at 0° latitude that divides the earth into two equal halves called hemispheres.
- **Parallels** – This is another name for lines of latitude because they circle the earth in parallel lines that never meet.
- **Meridians** – This is another name for lines of longitude. The Prime Meridian is located at 0° longitude, and is the starting point for measuring distance (both east and west) around the globe. Meridians circle the earth and connect at the Poles.

> **Review Video: 5 Elements of any Map**
> Visit mometrix.com/academy and enter code: 437727

TYPES OF MAPS

- A **physical map** is one that shows natural features such as mountains, rivers, lakes, deserts, and plains. Color is used to designate the different features.
- A **topographic map** is a type of physical map that shows the relief and configuration of a landscape, such as hills, valleys, fields, forest, roads, and settlements. It includes natural and human-made features.
- A **topological map** is one on which lines are stretched or straightened for the sake of clarity, but retain their essential geometric relationship. This type of map is used, for example, to show the routes of a subway system.
- A **political map** uses lines for state, county, and country boundaries; points or dots for cities and towns; and various other symbols for features such as airports and roads.

Copyright © Mometrix Media. You have been licensed one copy of this document for personal use only. Any other reproduction or redistribution is strictly prohibited. All rights reserved.
This content is provided for test preparation purposes only and does not imply an endorsement by Mometrix of any particular political, scientific, or religious point of view.

MAP STYLES

There are three basic styles of maps:

- **Base maps** – Created from aerial and field surveys, base maps serve as the starting point for topographic and thematic maps.
- **Topographic maps** – These show the natural and human-made surface features of the earth, including mountain elevations, river courses, roads, names of lakes and towns, and county and state lines.
- **Thematic maps** – These use a base or topographic map as the foundation for showing data based on a theme, such as population density, wildlife distribution, hill-slope stability, economic trends, etc.

Scale is the size of a map expressed as a ratio of the actual size of the land (for example, 1 inch on a map represents 1 mile on land). In other words, it is the proportion between a distance on the map and its corresponding distance on earth. The scale determines the level of detail on a map. **Small-scale maps** depict larger areas, but include fewer details. **Large-scale maps** depict smaller areas, but include more details.

TIME ZONES

Time is linked to **longitude** in that a complete rotation of the Earth, or 360° of longitude, occurs every 24 hours. Each hour of time is therefore equivalent to 15° of longitude, or 4 minutes for each 1° turn. By the agreement of 27 nations at the 1884 International Meridian Conference, the time zone system consists of **24 time zones** corresponding to the 24 hours in a day. Although high noon technically occurs when the sun is directly above a meridian, calculating time that way would result in 360 different times for the 360 meridians. Using the 24-hour system, the time is the same for all locations in a 15° zone. The 1884 conference established the meridian passing through Greenwich, England, as the zero point, or **prime meridian**. The halfway point is found at the 180th meridian, a half day from Greenwich. It is called the **International Date Line**, and serves as the place where each day begins and ends on earth.

CARTOGRAPHY

Cartography is the art and science of **mapmaking**. Maps of local areas were drawn by the Egyptians as early as 1300 BC, and the Greeks began making maps of the known world in the 6th century BC. Cartography eventually grew into the field of geography. The first step in modern mapmaking is a **survey**. This involves designating a few key sites of known elevation as benchmarks to allow for measurement of other sites. **Aerial photography** is then used to chart the area by taking photos in sequence. Overlapping photos show the same area from different positions along the flight line. When paired and examined through a stereoscope, the cartographer gets a three-dimensional view that can be made into a **topographical map**. In addition, a field survey (on the ground) is made to determine municipal borders and place names. The second step is to compile the information and **computer-draft** a map based on the collected data. The map is then reproduced or printed.

GLOBE AND MAP PROJECTIONS

A **globe** is the only accurate representation of the earth's size, shape, distance, and direction since it, like the earth, is **spherical**. The flat surface of a map distorts these elements. To counter this problem, mapmakers use a variety of "**map projections**," a system for representing the earth's curvatures on a flat surface through the use of a grid that corresponds to lines of latitude and longitude. Some distortions are still inevitable, though, so mapmakers make choices based on the map scale, the size of the area to be mapped, and what they want the map to show. Some

288

Copyright © Mometrix Media. You have been licensed one copy of this document for personal use only. Any other reproduction or redistribution is strictly prohibited. All rights reserved. This content is provided for test preparation purposes only and does not imply an endorsement by Mometrix of any particular political, scientific, or religious point of view.

projections can represent a true shape or area, while others may be based on the equator and therefore become less accurate as they near the poles. In summary, all maps have some distortion in terms of the shape or size of features of the spherical earth.

TYPES OF MAP PROJECTIONS

There are three main types of map projections:

- **Conical** – This type of projection superimposes a cone over the sphere of the earth, with two reference parallels secant to the globe and intersecting it. There is no distortion along the standard parallels, but distortion increases further from the chosen parallels. A Bonne projection is an example of a conical projection, in which the areas are accurately represented but the meridians are not on a true scale.
- **Cylindrical** – This is any projection in which meridians are mapped using equally spaced vertical lines and circles of latitude (parallels) are mapped using horizontal lines. A Mercator's projection is a modified cylindrical projection that is helpful to navigators because it allows them to maintain a constant compass direction between two points. However, it exaggerates areas in high latitudes.
- **Azimuthal** – This is a stereographic projection onto a plane centered so that a straight line from the center to any other point represents the shortest distance. This distance can be measured to scale.

> **Review Video: Map Projections**
> Visit mometrix.com/academy and enter code: 327303

HEMISPHERES AND PARALLELS ON THE WORLD MAP

The definitions for these terms are as follows:

- **Northern Hemisphere** – This is the area above, or north, of the equator.
- **Southern Hemisphere** – This is the area below, or south, of the equator.
- **Western Hemisphere** – This is the area between the North and South Poles. It extends west from the Prime Meridian to the International Date Line.
- **Eastern Hemisphere** – This is the area between the North and South Poles. It extends east from the Prime Meridian to the International Date Line.
- **North and South Poles** – Latitude is measured in terms of the number of degrees north and south from the equator. The North Pole is located at 90°N latitude, while the South Pole is located at 90°S latitude.
- **Tropic of Cancer** – This is the parallel, or latitude, 23½° north of the equator.
- **Tropic of Capricorn** – This is the parallel, or latitude, 23½° south of the equator. The region between these two parallels is the tropics. The subtropics is the area located between 23½° and 40° north and south of the equator.
- **Arctic Circle** – This is the parallel, or latitude, 66½° north of the equator.
- **Antarctic Circle** – This is the parallel, or latitude, 66½° south of the equator.

> **Review Video: Geographical Features**
> Visit mometrix.com/academy and enter code: 773539

GPS

Global Positioning System (GPS) is a system of satellites that orbit the Earth and communicate with mobile devices to pinpoint the mobile device's position. This is accomplished by determining the distance between the mobile device and at least three satellites. A mobile device might calculate

Copyright © Mometrix Media. You have been licensed one copy of this document for personal use only. Any other reproduction or redistribution is strictly prohibited. All rights reserved.
This content is provided for test preparation purposes only and does not imply an endorsement by Mometrix of any particular political, scientific, or religious point of view.

a distance of 400 miles between it and the first satellite. The possible locations that are 400 miles from the first satellite and the mobile device will fall along a circle. The possible locations on Earth relative to the other two satellites will fall somewhere along different circles. The point on Earth at which these three circles intersect is the location of the mobile device. The process of determining position based on distance measurements from three satellites is called **trilateration**.

PHYSICAL AND CULTURAL FEATURES OF GEOGRAPHIC LOCATIONS AND COUNTRIES

PHYSICAL FEATURES

- **Vegetation zones, or biomes** – Forests, grasslands, deserts, and tundra are the four main types of vegetation zones.
- **Climate zones** – Tropical, dry, temperate, continental, and polar are the five different types of climate zones. Climate is the long-term average weather conditions of a place.

CULTURAL FEATURES

- **Population density** – This is the number of people living in each square mile or kilometer of a place. It is calculated by dividing population by area.
- **Religion** – This is the identification of the dominant religions of a place, whether Christianity, Hinduism, Judaism, Buddhism, Islam, Shinto, Taoism, or Confucianism. All of these originated in Asia.
- **Languages** – This is the identification of the dominant or official language of a place. There are 12 major language families. The Indo-European family (which includes English, Russian, German, French, and Spanish) is spoken over the widest geographic area, but Mandarin Chinese is spoken by the most people.

GEOMORPHOLOGY

The study of landforms is call **geomorphology** or physiography, a science that considers the relationships between *geological structures* and *surface landscape features*. It is also concerned with the processes that change these features, such as erosion, deposition, and plate tectonics. Biological factors can also affect landforms. Examples are when corals build a coral reef or when plants contribute to the development of a salt marsh or a sand dune. Rivers, coastlines, rock types, slope formation, ice, erosion, and weathering are all part of geomorphology. A **landform** is a landscape feature or geomorphological unit. These include hills, plateaus, mountains, deserts, deltas, canyons, mesas, marshes, swamps, and valleys. These units are categorized according to elevation, slope, orientation, stratification, rock exposure, and soil type. Landform elements include pits, peaks, channels, ridges, passes, pools, and plains. The highest order landforms are continents and oceans. Elementary landforms such as segments, facets, and relief units are the smallest homogenous divisions of a land surface at a given scale or resolution.

OCEANS, SEAS, LAKES, RIVERS, AND CANALS

- **Oceans** are the largest bodies of water on earth and cover nearly 71% of the earth's surface. There are five major oceans: Atlantic, Pacific (largest and deepest), Indian, Arctic, and Southern (surrounds Antarctica).
- **Seas** are smaller than oceans and are somewhat surrounded by land like a lake, but lakes are fresh water and seas are salt water. Seas include the Mediterranean, Baltic, Caspian, Caribbean, and Coral.
- **Lakes** are bodies of water in a depression on the earth's surface. Examples of lakes are the Great Lakes and Lake Victoria.

Copyright © Mometrix Media. You have been licensed one copy of this document for personal use only. Any other reproduction or redistribution is strictly prohibited. All rights reserved. This content is provided for test preparation purposes only and does not imply an endorsement by Mometrix of any particular political, scientific, or religious point of view.

- **Rivers** are a channeled flow of water that start out as a spring or stream formed by runoff from rain or snow. Rivers flow from higher to lower ground, and usually empty into a sea or ocean. Great rivers of the world include the Amazon, Nile, Rhine, Mississippi, Ganges, Mekong, and Yangtze.
- **Canals** are artificial waterways constructed by humans to connect two larger water bodies. Examples of canals are the Panama and the Suez.

MOUNTAINS, HILLS, FOOTHILLS, VALLEYS, PLATEAUS, AND MESAS

The definitions for these geographical features are as follows:

- **Mountains** are elevated landforms that rise fairly steeply from the earth's surface to a summit of at least 1,000-2,000 feet (definitions vary) above sea level.
- **Hills** are elevated landforms that rise 500-2,000 feet above sea level.
- **Foothills** are a low series of hills found between a plain and a mountain range.
- **Valleys** are a long depression located between hills or mountains. They are usually products of river erosion. Valleys can vary in terms of width and depth, ranging from a few feet to thousands of feet.
- **Plateaus** are elevated landforms that are fairly flat on top. They may be as high as 10,000 feet above sea level and are usually next to mountains.
- **Mesas** are flat areas of upland. Their name is derived from the Spanish word for table. They are smaller than plateaus and often found in arid or semi-arid areas.

FORMATION OF MOUNTAINS

Mountains are formed by the movement of geologic plates, which are rigid slabs of rocks beneath the earth's crust that float on a layer of partially molten rock in the earth's upper mantle. As the plates collide, they push up the crust to form mountains. This process is called **orogeny**. There are three basic forms of orogeny:

- If the collision of continental plates causes the crust to buckle and fold, a chain of **folded mountains**, such as the Appalachians, the Alps, or the Himalayas, is formed.
- If the collision of the plates causes a denser oceanic plate to go under a continental plate, a process called **subduction**; strong horizontal forces lift and fold the margin of the continent. A mountain range like the Andes is the result.
- If an oceanic plate is driven under another oceanic plate, **volcanic mountains** such as those in Japan and the Philippines are formed.

CORAL REEFS

Coral reefs are formed from millions of tiny, tube-shaped **polyps**, an animal life form encased in tough limestone skeletons. Once anchored to a rocky surface, polyps eat plankton and miniscule shellfish caught with poisonous tentacles near their mouth. Polyps use calcium carbonate absorbed from chemicals given off by algae to harden their body armor and cement themselves together in fantastic shapes of many colors. Polyps reproduce through eggs and larvae, but the reef grows by branching out shoots of polyps. There are three types of coral reefs:

- **Fringing reefs** – These surround, or "fringe," an island.
- **Barrier reefs** – Over the centuries, a fringe reef grows so large that the island sinks down from the weight, and the reef becomes a barrier around the island. Water trapped between the island and the reef is called a lagoon.
- **Atolls** – Eventually, the sinking island goes under, leaving the coral reef around the lagoon.

Copyright © Mometrix Media. You have been licensed one copy of this document for personal use only. Any other reproduction or redistribution is strictly prohibited. All rights reserved. This content is provided for test preparation purposes only and does not imply an endorsement by Mometrix of any particular political, scientific, or religious point of view.

PLAINS, DESERTS, DELTAS, AND BASINS

- **Plains** are extensive areas of low-lying, flat, or gently undulating land, and are usually lower than the landforms around them. Plains near the seacoast are called lowlands.
- **Deserts** are large, dry areas that receive less than 10 inches of rain per year. They are almost barren, containing only a few patches of vegetation.
- **Deltas** are accumulations of silt deposited at river mouths into the seabed. They are eventually converted into very fertile, stable ground by vegetation, becoming important crop-growing areas. Examples include the deltas of the Nile, Ganges, and Mississippi River.
- **Basins** come in various types. They may be low areas that catch water from rivers; large hollows that dip to a central point and are surrounded by higher ground, as in the Donets and Kuznetsk basins in Russia; or areas of inland drainage in a desert when the water can't reach the sea and flows into lakes or evaporates in salt flats as a result. An example is the Great Salt Lake in Utah.

MARSHES AND SWAMPS AND TUNDRA AND TAIGA

Marshes and swamps are both **wet lowlands**. The water can be fresh, brackish, or saline. Both host important ecological systems with unique wildlife. There are, however, some major differences. **Marshes** have no trees and are always wet because of frequent floods and poor drainage that leaves shallow water. Plants are mostly grasses, rushes, reeds, typhas, sedges, and herbs. **Swamps** have trees and dry periods. The water is very slow-moving, and is usually associated with adjacent rivers or lakes.

Both taiga and tundra regions have many plants and animals, but they have few humans or crops because of their harsh climates. **Taiga** has colder winters and hotter summers than tundra because of its distance from the Arctic Ocean. Taiga is the world's largest forest region, located just south of the tundra line. It contains huge mineral resources and fur-bearing animals. **Tundra** is a Russian word describing marshy plain in an area that has a very cold climate but receives little snow. The ground is usually frozen, but is quite spongy when it is not.

HUMID CONTINENTAL, PRAIRIE, SUBTROPICAL, AND MARINE CLIMATES

- A **humid continental climate** is one that has four seasons, including a cold winter and a hot summer, and sufficient rainfall for raising crops. Such climates can be found in the United States, Canada, and Russia. The best farmlands and mining areas are found in these countries.
- **Prairie climates**, or steppe regions, are found in the interiors of Asia and North America where there are dry flatlands (prairies that receive 10-20 inches of rain per year). These dry flatlands can be grasslands or deserts.
- **Subtropical climates** are very humid areas in the tropical areas of Japan, China, Australia, Africa, South America, and the United States. The moisture, carried by winds traveling over warm ocean currents, produces long summers and mild winters. It is possible to produce a continuous cycle of a variety of crops.
- A **marine climate** is one near or surrounded by water. Warm ocean winds bring moisture, mild temperatures year-round, and plentiful rain. These climates are found in Western Europe and parts of the United States, Canada, Chile, New Zealand, and Australia.

ADAPTATION TO ENVIRONMENTAL CONDITIONS

The environment influences the way people live. People **adapt** to **environmental conditions** in ways as simple as putting on warm clothing in a cold environment; finding means to cool their surroundings in an environment with high temperatures; building shelters from wind, rain, and temperature variations; and digging water wells if surface water is unavailable. More complex

Copyright © Mometrix Media. You have been licensed one copy of this document for personal use only. Any other reproduction or redistribution is strictly prohibited. All rights reserved. This content is provided for test preparation purposes only and does not imply an endorsement by Mometrix of any particular political, scientific, or religious point of view.

adaptations result from the physical diversity of the earth in terms of soil, climate, vegetation, and topography. Humans take advantage of opportunities and avoid or minimize limitations. Examples of environmental limitations are that rocky soils offer few opportunities for agriculture and rough terrain limits accessibility. Sometimes, **technology** allows humans to live in areas that were once uninhabitable or undesirable. For example, air conditioning allows people to live comfortably in hot climates; modern heating systems permit habitation in areas with extremely low temperatures, as is the case with research facilities in Antarctica; and airplanes have brought people to previously inaccessible places to establish settlements or industries.

NATURAL RESOURCES, RENEWABLE RESOURCES, NONRENEWABLE RESOURCES, AND COMMODITIES

Natural resources are things provided by nature that have commercial value to humans, such as minerals, energy, timber, fish, wildlife, and the landscape. **Renewable resources** are those that can be replenished, such as wind, solar radiation, tides, and water (with proper conservation and clean-up). Soil is renewable with proper conservation and management techniques, and timber can be replenished with replanting. Living resources such as fish and wildlife can replenish themselves if they are not over-harvested. **Nonrenewable resources** are those that cannot be replenished. These include fossil fuels such as oil and coal and metal ores. These cannot be replaced or reused once they have been burned, although some of their products can be recycled. **Commodities** are natural resources that have to be extracted and purified rather than created, such as mineral ores.

HARMFUL OR POTENTIALLY HARMFUL INTERACTION WITH ENVIRONMENT

Wherever humans have gone on the earth, they have made **changes** to their surroundings. Many are harmful or potentially harmful, depending on the extent of the alterations. Some of the changes and activities that can harm the **environment** include:

- Cutting into mountains by machine or blasting to build roads or construction sites
- Cutting down trees and clearing natural growth
- Building houses and cities
- Using grassland to graze herds
- Polluting water sources
- Polluting the ground with chemical and oil waste
- Wearing out fertile land and losing topsoil
- Placing communication lines cross country using poles and wires or underground cable
- Placing railway lines or paved roads cross country
- Building gas and oil pipelines cross country
- Draining wetlands
- Damming up or re-routing waterways
- Spraying fertilizers, pesticides, and defoliants
- Hunting animals to extinction or near extinction

CARRYING CAPACITY AND NATURAL HAZARDS

Carrying capacity is the maximum, sustained level of use of an environment can incur without sustaining significant environmental deterioration that would eventually lead to environmental destruction. Environments vary in terms of their carrying capacity, a concept humans need to learn to measure and respect before harm is done. Proper **assessment of environmental conditions** enables responsible decision making with respect to how much and in what ways the resources of a particular environment should be consumed. **Energy and water conservation** as well as recycling can extend an area's carrying capacity. In addition to carrying capacity limitations, the physical

Copyright © Mometrix Media. You have been licensed one copy of this document for personal use only. Any other reproduction or redistribution is strictly prohibited. All rights reserved.
This content is provided for test preparation purposes only and does not imply an endorsement by Mometrix of any particular political, scientific, or religious point of view.

environment can also have occasional extremes that are costly to humans. **Natural hazards** such as hurricanes, tornadoes, earthquakes, volcanoes, floods, tsunamis, and some forest fires and insect infestations are processes or events that are not caused by humans, but may have serious consequences for humans and the environment. These events are not preventable, and their precise timing, location, and magnitude are not predictable. However, some precautions can be taken to reduce the damage.

APPLYING GEOGRAPHY TO INTERPRETATION OF THE PAST

Space, environment, and chronology are three different points of view that can be used to study history. Events take place within **geographic contexts**. If the world is flat, then transportation choices are vastly different from those that would be made in a round world, for example. Invasions of Russia from the west have normally failed because of the harsh winter conditions, the vast distances that inhibit steady supply lines, and the number of rivers and marshes to be crossed, among other factors. Any invading or defending force anywhere must make choices based on consideration of space and environmental factors. For instance, lands may be too muddy or passages too narrow for certain equipment. Geography played a role in the building of the Panama Canal because the value of a shorter transportation route had to outweigh the costs of labor, disease, political negotiations, and equipment, not to mention a myriad of other effects from cutting a canal through an isthmus and changing a natural land structure as a result.

APPLYING GEOGRAPHY TO INTERPRETATION OF THE PRESENT AND PLANS FOR THE FUTURE

The decisions that individual people as well as nations make that may **affect the environment** have to be made with an understanding of spatial patterns and concepts, cultural and transportation connections, physical processes and patterns, ecosystems, and the impact, or "footprint," of people on the physical environment. Sample issues that fit into these considerations are recycling programs, loss of agricultural land to further urban expansion, air and water pollution, deforestation, and ease of transportation and communication. In each of these areas, present and future uses have to be balanced against possible harmful effects. For example, wind is a clean and readily available resource for electric power, but the access roads to and noise of wind turbines can make some areas unsuitable for livestock pasture. Voting citizens need to have an understanding of **geographical and environmental connections** to make responsible decisions.

CHAPTER QUIZ

1. How many time zones are there?
   a. 10
   b. 16
   c. 20
   d. 24

2. The Prime Meridian, or International Date Line, passes directly through which city?
   a. Rome, Italy
   b. Greenwich, England
   c. Oslo, Norway
   d. St. Petersburg, Russia

Copyright © Mometrix Media. You have been licensed one copy of this document for personal use only. Any other reproduction or redistribution is strictly prohibited. All rights reserved. This content is provided for test preparation purposes only and does not imply an endorsement by Mometrix of any particular political, scientific, or religious point of view.

3. Which of the following presents an accurate representation of Earth with no distortions?

    a. Globe
    b. Conical projection
    c. Cylindrical projection
    d. Azimuthal projection

4. A location with a parallel of 36 degrees south of the equator is in which region?

    a. Arctic circle
    b. Antarctic circle
    c. Tropics
    d. Subtropics

CHAPTER QUIZ ANSWER KEY

1. D: Time is linked to longitude in that a complete rotation of the Earth, or 360 degrees of longitude, occurs every 24 hours. Each hour of time is therefore equivalent to 15 degrees of longitude, or 4 minutes for each 1 degree turn. By the agreement of 27 nations at the 1884 International Meridian Conference, the time zone system consists of 24 time zones corresponding to the 24 hours in a day.

2. B: The 1884 conference established the meridian passing through Greenwich, England as the zero point, or prime meridian. The halfway point is found at the 180th meridian, a half day from Greenwich. It is called the International Date Line, and serves as the place where each day begins and ends on Earth.

3. A: A globe is the only accurate representation of the Earth's size, shape, distance, and direction because it, like the Earth, is spherical. The flat surface of a map distorts these elements. To counter this problem, mapmakers use a system for representing the Earth's curvatures on a flat surface through the use of a grid that corresponds to lines of latitude and longitude. These flat maps are called map projections. Distortions are inevitable even with the most sophisticated map projections, so mapmakers make choices based on the map scale, the size of the area to be mapped, and what they want the map to show.

4. C: Below are definitions for the following geography-related terms:

- Northern Hemisphere is the area above, or north, of the equator.
- Southern Hemisphere is the area below, or south, of the equator.
- Western Hemisphere is the area between the North and South Poles. It extends west from the Prime Meridian to the International Date Line.
- Eastern Hemisphere is the area between the North and South Poles. It extends east from the Prime Meridian to the International Date Line.
- North and South Poles are located at 90 degrees north latitude and 90 degrees south latitude, respectively. Latitude is measured in terms of the number of degrees north and south from the equator.
- Tropic of Cancer is the parallel, or latitude, 23.5 degrees north of the equator.
- Tropic of Capricorn is the parallel, or latitude, 23.5 degrees south of the equator. The region between these two parallels is the tropics. The subtropics is the area located between 23.5 degrees and 40 degrees north and south of the equator.
- Arctic Circle is the parallel, or latitude, 66.5 degrees north of the equator.
- Antarctic Circle is the parallel, or latitude, 66.5 degrees south of the equator.

Copyright © Mometrix Media. You have been licensed one copy of this document for personal use only. Any other reproduction or redistribution is strictly prohibited. All rights reserved. This content is provided for test preparation purposes only and does not imply an endorsement by Mometrix of any particular political, scientific, or religious point of view.

CULTURE

A **culture** is a comprehensive style of living that is developed in a society and maintained from generation to generation. Culture is manifested in a group's traditions, rituals, language, social norms, technology, and economic structures. Broadly speaking, culture is everything that is learned by a member of a particular society, though it may include things that an individual learns but which are never made explicit either in the individual's mind or in his or her social interactions. For this reason, many sociologists feel it is difficult to properly study one's own culture; they suggest that only the unclouded eyes of a foreign observer can perceive a society's most fundamental values.

SOCIOLOGY, PSYCHOLOGY, AND ANTHROPOLOGY

There are three branches of cultural studies known as psychology, sociology, and anthropology. Each of these categories deals with some form of studying humans and human behavior. **Anthropology** is the most material of the branches, as it deals with studying past and present ways of life for humans. It is an intersection between history, geography, technology, and art. Anthropology is the broadest of cultural studies and contains overlap with countless other disciplines. **Sociology** deals with social interaction and the cultures of human civilizations. Often, sociologists bring ethical, political, and historical matters into question. Sociology largely derives its viewpoints from principles of human interaction and external matters of life. **Psychology,** on the other hand, focuses mainly on the internal workings of the mind and the mental and biological processes involved in thinking.

MATERIAL CULTURE

A society's **material culture** is the set all of the physical objects that the people of that society have either created or to which they assign cultural meaning. Hence, material culture may include objects like books, jewelry, buildings, and furniture; but it may also include natural areas if those areas are assigned significance by the members of the society. As an example of this latter kind of material culture, a sociologist might point to the Native American society, in which the land itself held immense cultural value. Along with **verbal culture**, material culture makes up the sum total of what sociologists have at their disposal for study.

NONMATERIAL CULTURE

Nonmaterial culture is all of a society's customs, beliefs, political structures, languages, and ways of using material objects. In the United States, for instance, the emphasis placed on religious freedom and individual liberty might be considered an example of nonmaterial culture. The boundary between material and nonmaterial culture is never altogether clear; how, for instance, should one separate the American flag and what it stands for, namely the idea of freedom? **Values** and **norms**, as opposed to the physical things that are used to express values and norms, are what make up a society's nonmaterial culture. Typically, nonmaterial culture is more difficult to change than material culture, and its change is more difficult to observe.

VALUES

The **values** of a culture are its highest ideals. In the United States, for example, we would say that freedom and equality are two of our most important values. Values are usually very general concepts. They may be complementary, as for example the values of hard work and material success seem to go together. Values are quite fluid, and a major focus of sociology is observing how they change over time. Values may come into conflict with one another, which can create social conflict and disorganization. An example of this is the conflict in mid-twentieth-century America

Copyright © Mometrix Media. You have been licensed one copy of this document for personal use only. Any other reproduction or redistribution is strictly prohibited. All rights reserved. This content is provided for test preparation purposes only and does not imply an endorsement by Mometrix of any particular political, scientific, or religious point of view.

between the values of equal rights and segregation; ultimately, it was clear that only one of these values could remain.

SANCTIONS

In sociological terms, **sanctions** are any rewards or consequences given to an individual or group to pursue or renounce a certain course of behavior. Sanctions may be positive, as when a reward is promised for something done properly, or negative, as when a punishment is promised for something done improperly. Although the most common use of the word refers to *international economic pressures* (as in, for instance, the economic restrictions placed on Iraq during the 1990s), all societies place sanctions on their members in order to elicit approved behavior. People who uphold the values and norms of the society are rewarded with preferential treatment from their fellows, while those who transgress can be punished socially, economically, or legally.

NORMS

Norms are specific rules regulating behavior in a culture. Norms may or may not be directly codified in the law of a society, but they are intended to encourage behavior that promotes the society's values. Taking again the example of the United States, one might say that treating men and women equally is a social norm, insofar as equality between the sexes is a value aspired to by our culture. Norms, then, depend on values for their justification, and values depend on norms for their enactment. Norms may vary greatly from society to society, such that the same behavior may be approved or condemned depending on where it is performed. Most of the time, norms are so customary for the members of a society that they are performed automatically.

FORMAL NORMS AND INFORMAL NORMS

Norms may be considered formal or informal, depending on whether they are codified in the laws of the society in which they apply. **Formal norms** are written law; examples of formal norms include the prohibition of murder, the forced payment of taxes, and the sanctity of marriage. **Informal norms**, on the other hand, are unwritten codes of conduct. Examples of informal norms might include the prohibition of spitting in public or the encouragement of deference to women. Typically, a society formalizes the norms which are most important, and for which violators should be punished. Formal norms tend to be much more consistent among different societies than informal norms.

SOCIAL MARKERS, LAWS, AND FOLKWAYS

A **social marker** is any part of behavior that indicates the identity, character, or way of understanding of a particular group of people. Social markers can be laws, folkways, traditions, or other patterns of behavior. **Laws** are simply social norms that have been made explicit and are enforced by the government. There are plenty of norms, though, that are encoded in law but are also internalized-- the prohibition of murder, for instance. **Folkways** are social norms that have become habitual or traditional in a society. In the United States, we are accustomed to tipping a waiter or waitress for their service: that this is so ingrained in our daily life makes it an American folkway.

CULTURAL PLURALISM AND SUBCULTURE

Cultural pluralism exists when multiple distinct cultures exist within the same society after a process of accommodation. These self-contained cultures should not be confused with **subcultures**, which are smaller cultures within a large culture. Subcultures usually have a set of norms and values that are different from those held by the larger society of which they are a member. In the United States, we might consider punk rockers or hippies as subcultures, because

Copyright © Mometrix Media. You have been licensed one copy of this document for personal use only. Any other reproduction or redistribution is strictly prohibited. All rights reserved. This content is provided for test preparation purposes only and does not imply an endorsement by Mometrix of any particular political, scientific, or religious point of view.

they have different values than Americans on the whole, but do not really have a self-sustaining or separate society of their own.

COUNTERCULTURES

A **counterculture** is any group whose values and norms challenge and seek to alter the values and norms of the dominant culture in their society. Although the term when used today evokes memories of the 1960s youth rebellion in Western Europe and the United States, earlier countercultural movements include the Bohemians in nineteenth century France, or even the early Christians. Countercultures typically appear at a time when traditional norms and values are felt to no longer be appropriate or helpful in making sense of the world. As in the case of a social movement, a counterculture tends to have more and stronger adherents at the beginning of its life; once the counterculture's norms have been partially co-opted by the larger society, countercultures tend to lose steam.

DOMINANT CULTURE AND ETHNOCENTRISM

In any society, the **dominant culture** is the group whose norms, values, and behavior patterns are most widespread and influential on the rest of the society. Many nations, including the United States, have laws to restrain the dominant culture from extinguishing minority cultures. **Ethnocentrism** describes the tendency to view one's own cultural patterns as superior and to judge all others only as they relate to one's own. This philosophy has been at the root of some of humanity's worst atrocities, including the Holocaust, which was perpetrated by Germans who believed they must maintain the purity of their race, and colonial conquests, in which Western nations brutally imposed their customs on various indigenous peoples.

CHAPTER QUIZ

1. Which of the following is NOT considered one of the three main branches of cultural studies?

    a. Anthropology
    b. Sociology
    c. Psychology
    d. Archaeology

CHAPTER QUIZ ANSWER KEY

1. D: There are three branches of cultural studies: psychology, sociology, and anthropology. Each of these categories deals with some form of studying humans and human behavior. Anthropology is the most material of the branches, as it deals with studying past and present ways of life for humans. It is an intersection between history, geography, technology, and art. Anthropology is the broadest of cultural studies and contains overlap with countless other disciplines. Sociology deals with social interaction and the cultures of human civilizations. Often, sociologists bring ethical, political, and historical matters into question. Sociology largely derives its viewpoints from principles of human interaction and external matters of life. Psychology, on the other hand, focuses mainly on the internal workings of the mind and the mental and biological processes involved in thinking.

World History

PRE-HISTORICAL AND PRE-MODERN PERIODS

The earliest history of the human race is known as **pre-historical** due to the lack of record keeping. The earliest writing did not appear until the Sumerian civilization in Mesopotamia. In addition to

Copyright © Mometrix Media. You have been licensed one copy of this document for personal use only. Any other reproduction or redistribution is strictly prohibited. All rights reserved.
This content is provided for test preparation purposes only and does not imply an endorsement by Mometrix of any particular political, scientific, or religious point of view.

the overt lack of writing from early civilizations, historical records were much more localized than more modern historical records. Ancient history can be broken down many ways, but a common distinction is the **pre-modern period**, including early civilizations such as Egypt, Babylon, and the Greek and Roman Empires. These early civilizations saw invention of technologies such as wood and early metalwork and the domestication of animals. Early civilizations were heavily dependent on agriculture and usually needed access to rivers for a consistent water source. The pre-modern period is viewed as ending with the connection of mainland Europe and some of Africa and Asia by the Greek and Roman Empires. The growth of these empires during this period also saw the worldwide spread of religions such as Judaism and Christianity.

IMPORTANT CONTRIBUTIONS OF THE ANCIENT CIVILIZATIONS OF SUMER, EGYPT, AND INDUS VALLEY

These three ancient civilizations are distinguished by their unique contributions to the development of world civilization:

- **Sumer** used the first known writing system, which enabled the Sumerians to leave a sizeable written record of their myths and religion, advanced the development of the wheel and irrigation, and urbanized their culture.
- **Egypt** was united by the Nile River. Egyptians originally settled in villages on its banks, had a national religion that held their pharaohs as gods, had a central government that controlled civil and artistic affairs, and had writing and libraries.
- The **Indus Valley** was also called Harappan after the city of Harappa. This civilization started in the 3rd and 4th centuries BC and was widely dispersed over 400,000 square miles. It had a unified culture of luxury and refinement, no known national government, an advanced civic system, and prosperous trade routes.

> **Review Video: The Sumerians**
> Visit mometrix.com/academy and enter code: 939880
>
> **Review Video: Ancient Egypt**
> Visit mometrix.com/academy and enter code: 398041

COMMON TRAITS AND CULTURAL IDENTIFIERS OF THE EARLY EMPIRES OF MESOPOTAMIA, EGYPT, GREECE, AND ROME

These empires all had: a strong military; a centralized government; control and standardization of commerce, money, and taxes; a weight system; and an official language.

- **Mesopotamia** had a series of short-term empires that failed because of their oppression of subject peoples.
- **Egypt** also had a series of governments after extending its territory beyond the Nile area. Compared to Mesopotamia, these were more stable and long-lived because they blended different peoples to create a single national identity.
- **Greece** started as a group of city-states that were united by Alexander the Great and joined to create an empire that stretched from the Indus River to Egypt and the Mediterranean coast. Greece blended Greek values with those of the local cultures, which collectively became known as Hellenistic society.
- **Rome** was an Italian city-state that grew into an empire extending from the British Isles across Europe to the Middle East. It lasted for 1,000 years and became the foundation of the Western world's culture, language, and laws.

Copyright © Mometrix Media. You have been licensed one copy of this document for personal use only. Any other reproduction or redistribution is strictly prohibited. All rights reserved. This content is provided for test preparation purposes only and does not imply an endorsement by Mometrix of any particular political, scientific, or religious point of view.

Review Video: Ancient Greece
Visit mometrix.com/academy and enter code: 800829

CHARACTERISTICS OF CHINESE AND INDIAN EMPIRES

While the Chinese had the world's longest lasting and continuous empires, the Indians had more of a cohesive culture than an empire system. Their distinct characteristics are as follows:

- **China** – Since the end of the Warring States period in 221 BC, China has functioned as an empire. Although the dynasties changed several times, the basic governmental structure remained the same into the 20th century. The Chinese also have an extensive written record of their culture which heavily emphasizes history, philosophy, and a common religion.
- **India** – The subcontinent was seldom unified in terms of government until the British empire controlled the area in the 19th and 20th centuries. In terms of culture, India has had persistent institutions and religions that have loosely united the people, such as the caste system and guilds. These have regulated daily life more than any government.

MIDDLE AGES IN EUROPEAN HISTORY

The **Middle Ages**, or Medieval times, was a period that ran from approximately 500-1500 AD. The fall of the Greek and Roman civilizations marks the beginning of this period, allowing for the rise of new independent countries, largely relying on the feudal system of government, with kings who allotted power and territory to governors. During this time, the centers of European civilization moved from the Mediterranean countries to France, Germany, and England, where strong national governments were developing. Key events of this time include:

- **Roman Catholicism** was the cultural and religious center of medieval life, extending into politics and economics.
- **Knights**, with their systems of honor, combat, and chivalry, were loyal to their king.
- **Peasants**, or serfs, served a particular lord and his lands.
- Many **universities** were established that still function in modern times.
- The **Crusades**, the recurring wars between European Christians and Middle East Muslims, raged over the Holy Lands.
- Charles the Great, or **Charlemagne**, created an empire across France and Germany around 800 AD.
- The **Black Death plague** swept across Europe from 1347-1350, leaving between one third and one half of the population dead.

Review Video: The Middle Ages
Visit mometrix.com/academy and enter code: 413133

Review Video: Trade in the Middle Ages
Visit mometrix.com/academy and enter code: 650839

PROTESTANT REFORMATION

The dominance of the **Catholic Church** during the Middle Ages in Europe gave it immense power, which encouraged corrupt practices such as the selling of indulgences and clerical positions. The **Protestant Reformation** began as an attempt to reform the Catholic Church, but eventually led to separation from it. In 1517, Martin Luther posted his *Ninety-Five Theses* on the door of a church in Saxony, which criticized unethical practices, various doctrines, and the authority of the pope. Other reformers such as John Calvin and John Wesley soon followed, but disagreed among themselves and divided along doctrinal lines. Consequently, the Lutheran, Reformed, Calvinist, and Presbyterian

Copyright © Mometrix Media. You have been licensed one copy of this document for personal use only. Any other reproduction or redistribution is strictly prohibited. All rights reserved.
This content is provided for test preparation purposes only and does not imply an endorsement by Mometrix of any particular political, scientific, or religious point of view.

churches were founded, among others. In England, King Henry VIII was denied a divorce by the pope, so he broke away and established the **Anglican Church**. The Protestant reformation caused the Catholic Church to finally reform itself, but the Protestant movement continued, resulting in a proliferation of new denominations.

RENAISSANCE

Renaissance is the French word for rebirth, and is used to describe the renewal of interest in ancient Greek and Latin art, literature, and philosophy that occurred in Europe, especially Italy, from the 14th through the 16th centuries. Historically, it was also a time of great scientific inquiry, the rise of individualism, extensive geographical exploration, and the rise of secular values.

Notable figures of the Renaissance include:

- **Petrarch** – An Italian scholar, writer, and key figure in northern Italy, which is where the Renaissance started and where chief patrons came from the merchant class
- **Leonardo da Vinci** – Artist and inventor
- **Michelangelo** and **Raphael** – Artists
- **Desiderius Erasmus** – Applied historical scholarship to the New Testament and laid the seeds for the Protestant Reformation
- **Sir Thomas More** – A lawyer and author who wrote *Utopia*
- **Niccolò Machiavelli** – Author of *The Prince* and *Discourses*, which proposed a science of human nature and civil life
- **William Shakespeare** – A renowned playwright and poet

> **Review Video: Renaissance**
> Visit mometrix.com/academy and enter code: 123100

AGE OF DISCOVERY AND COLONIALISM

Throughout world history, there have been several waves of so-called **new imperialism**, in which established countries attempted to **colonize** territories that had not been explored by European nations. This was called the **Age of Discovery** largely because of the overseas exploration, "discovering" new lands, even though many of the explored lands were already populated. This colonialism was largely driven by the desire for increased wealth and resources, though many participants also sought after religious freedoms. Some of the earliest colonization attempts came from Spain and Portugal, who launched expeditions into Africa and Asia. These early colonial missions established the slave trade throughout Europe and for future colonial expansions. Later waves of colonialism included exploration of the **Americas** by Britain, France, and Spain. Other countries, such as China, Japan, and Russia, practiced imperialism in Asia. The process of colonizing many of these territories led to great injustices, such as the slave trade, and the horrific spread of disease and massacres of people groups such as the Aztecs in central Mexico and many Native American tribes in North America.

DECOLONIZATION

Following the powerful race for colonization throughout the world, many of the territories secured by European imperialism fought for their own **freedoms** and **independence**. Supporting these colonial missions was extremely costly and oftentimes, the colonials and the people from the ruling countries had very different priorities, which led to many disagreements. This was the case in the British colonies. Britain enacted many invasive and overcontrolling policies on the 13 established colonies. Tensions grew until the colonials revolted and declared their independence beginning the American Revolutionary War, which would solidify the United States of America as an independent

Copyright © Mometrix Media. You have been licensed one copy of this document for personal use only. Any other reproduction or redistribution is strictly prohibited. All rights reserved.
This content is provided for test preparation purposes only and does not imply an endorsement by Mometrix of any particular political, scientific, or religious point of view.

nation. Several other countries worldwide followed suit and eventually secured their own independence. Decolonization largely began in the Americas and ended as late as 1960 in many African countries.

WORLDWIDE ABOLITION OF SLAVERY

Slavery has been accepted in various forms throughout most of known history. Contemporary to the decolonization period, the issue of slavery started to gain attention as an ethical matter worldwide. The movement to end slavery worldwide is known as **abolitionism** and roughly began in the late 1700s, however, anti-slavery sentiment was a slow-moving cause. The profitability of the slave trade and the use of slaves as the primary workforce for much of agriculture and shipping was a huge deterrent to change. In America, slavery was largely left as a states' right until tensions grew, leading into the American Civil War. Slavery was abolished progressively throughout the world, though at varying rates. Eventually, the United Nations adopted a firm doctrine on slavery, known as the Universal Declaration of Human Rights in 1948, which abolished slavery internationally.

INDUSTRIAL REVOLUTION

The **Industrial Revolution** started in England with the construction of the first **cotton mill** in 1733. Other inventions and factories followed in rapid succession. The **steel industry** grew exponentially when manufacturers realized that cheap, abundant English coal could be used instead of wood for melting metals. The **steam engine**, which revolutionized transportation and work power, came next. Around 1830, a factory-based, **technological era** was ushered into the rest of Europe. Society changed from agrarian to urban. A need for cheap, unskilled labor resulted in the extensive employment and abuse of women and children, who worked up to 14 hours a day, six days a week in deplorable conditions. Expanding populations brought crowded, unsanitary conditions to the cities, and the factories created air and water pollution. Societies had to deal with these new situations by enacting **child labor laws** and creating **labor unions** to protect the safety of workers.

> **Review Video: The Industrial Revolution**
> Visit mometrix.com/academy and enter code: 372796

PARTICIPANTS OF WORLD WAR I AND WORLD WAR II

World War I, which began in 1914, was fought by the **Allies** including Britain, France, Russia, Greece, Italy, Romania, and Serbia. They fought against the **Central Powers** of Germany, Austria-Hungary, Bulgaria, and Turkey. In 1917, the United States joined the Allies, and Russia withdrew to pursue its own revolution. World War I ended in 1918.

World War II was truly a world war, with fighting occurring on nearly every continent. Germany occupied most of Europe and Northern Africa. It was opposed by the countries of the British Empire, free France and its colonies, Russia, and various national resistance forces. Japan, an **Axis** ally of Germany, had been forcefully expanding its territories in Korea, China, Indonesia, the Philippines, and the South Pacific for many years. When Japan attacked Pearl Harbor in 1941, the United States joined the **Allied** effort. Italy changed from the Axis to the Allied side mid-war after deposing its own dictator. The war ended in Europe in April 1945, and in Japan in August 1945.

IMPORTANCE OF CROSS-CULTURAL COMPARISONS IN WORLD HISTORY INSTRUCTION

It is important to make **cross-cultural comparisons** when studying world history so that the subject is **holistic** and not oriented to just Western civilization. Not only are the contributions of civilizations around the world important, but they are also interesting and more representative of the mix of cultures present in the United States. It is also critical to the understanding of world

Copyright © Mometrix Media. You have been licensed one copy of this document for personal use only. Any other reproduction or redistribution is strictly prohibited. All rights reserved.
This content is provided for test preparation purposes only and does not imply an endorsement by Mometrix of any particular political, scientific, or religious point of view.

relations to study the involvement of European countries and the United States in international commerce, colonization, and development. **Trade routes** from ancient times linked Africa, Asia, and Europe, resulting in exchanges and migrations of people, philosophies, and religions, as well as goods. While many civilizations in the Americas thrived, and some became very sophisticated, many were eventually overcome or even erased by **European expansion**. The historic isolation of China and the modern industrialization of Japan have had huge impacts on their relations with the rest of the world. The more students understand this history and its effects on the modern world, the better they will able to function in their own spheres.

CHAPTER QUIZ

1. How many theses did Martin Luther post to the door of a church in Saxony as one of the first major moments of the Protestant Reformation?

    a. 5
    b. 50
    c. 95
    d. 100

2. Which of the following countries was NOT part of the Central Powers in World War I?

    a. Germany
    b. Russia
    c. Hungary
    d. Bulgaria

CHAPTER QUIZ ANSWER KEY

1. C: The Protestant Reformation began as an attempt to reform the Catholic Church, but eventually led to separation from it. In 1517, Martin Luther posted his Ninety-five Theses on the door of a church in Saxony, which criticized unethical practices, various doctrines, and the authority of the pope. Other reformers such as John Calvin and John Wesley soon followed, but disagreed among themselves and divided along doctrinal lines. Consequently, the Lutheran, Reformed, Calvinist, and Presbyterian churches were founded, among others.

2. B: World War I, which began in 1914, was fought by the Allies including Britain, France, Russia, Greece, Italy, Romania, and Serbia. They fought against the Central Powers of Germany, Austria-Hungary, Bulgaria, and Turkey. In 1917, the United States joined the Allies, and Russia withdrew to pursue its own revolution. World War I ended in 1918.

Economics

EFFECTS ECONOMY CAN HAVE ON PURCHASING DECISIONS OF CONSUMERS

The **economy** plays an important role in how careful consumers are when using their resources. It also affects what they perceive as needs as opposed to what they perceive as wants. When the economy is doing well, unemployment figures are low, which means that people can easily attain their basic necessities. As a result, consumers are typically more willing to spend their financial resources. Consumers will also be more willing to spend their resources on products and services that are not necessary to their survival, but are instead products and services that they enjoy having and believe increase their quality of life. On the other hand, when the economy is in a slump, consumers are much more likely to cut back on their spending because they perceive a significantly higher risk of being unable to acquire basic necessities due to a lack of financial resources.

Copyright © Mometrix Media. You have been licensed one copy of this document for personal use only. Any other reproduction or redistribution is strictly prohibited. All rights reserved.
This content is provided for test preparation purposes only and does not imply an endorsement by Mometrix of any particular political, scientific, or religious point of view.

COMMON TERMINOLOGY IN ECONOMICS

- **Supply** is the amount of a product or service available to consumers.
- **Demand** is how much consumers are willing to pay for the product or service. These two facets of the market determine the price of goods and services. The higher the demand, the higher the price the supplier will charge; the lower the demand, the lower the price.
- **Scarcity** is a measure of supply. Demand is high when there is a scarcity, or low supply, of an item.
- **Choice** is related to scarcity and demand in that when an item in demand is scarce, consumers have to make difficult choices. They can pay more for an item, go without it, or go elsewhere for the item.
- **Money** is the cash or currency available for payment.
- **Resources** are the items one can barter in exchange for goods. Money is the cash reserves of a nation, while resources are the minerals, labor force, armaments, and other raw materials or assets a nation has available for trade.
- **Taxes** are legally required payments to the government for income, goods bought, or property owned. Taxes are categorized as direct or indirect.
- **Tariffs** are taxes specifically imposed on imports from another country.

EFFECTS OF ECONOMIC DOWNTURN OR RECESSION

When a **recession** happens, people at all levels of society feel the economic effects. For example:

- High **unemployment** results because businesses have to cut back to keep costs low, and may no longer have the work for the labor force they once did.
- **Mortgage rates** go up on variable-rate loans as banks try to increase their revenues, but the higher rates cause some people who cannot afford increased housing costs to sell or suffer foreclosure.
- **Credit** becomes less available as banks try to lessen their risk. This decreased lending affects business operations, home and auto loans, etc.
- **Stock market prices** drop, and the lower dividends paid to stockholders reduce their income. This is especially hard on retired people who rely on stock dividends.
- **Psychological depression and trauma** may occur in those who suffer bankruptcy, unemployment, or foreclosure during a depression.

ECONOMIC EFFECTS OF ABUNDANT NATURAL RESOURCES

The **positive economic aspects** of abundant natural resources are an increase in **revenue and new jobs** where those resources have not been previously accessed. For example, the growing demand for oil, gas, and minerals has led companies to venture into new regions.

The **negative economic aspects** of abundant natural resources are:

- **Environmental degradation**, if sufficient regulations are not in place to counter strip mining, deforestation, and contamination.
- **Corruption**, if sufficient regulations are not in place to counter bribery, political favoritism, and exploitation of workers as greedy companies try to maximize their profits.
- **Social tension**, if the resources are privately owned such that the rich become richer and the poor do not reap the benefits of their national resources. Class divisions become wider, resulting in social unrest.

Copyright © Mometrix Media. You have been licensed one copy of this document for personal use only. Any other reproduction or redistribution is strictly prohibited. All rights reserved. This content is provided for test preparation purposes only and does not imply an endorsement by Mometrix of any particular political, scientific, or religious point of view.

- **Dependence**, if income from the natural resources is not used to develop other industries as well. In this situation, the economy becomes dependent on one source, and faces potential crises if natural disasters or depletion take away that income source.

ECONOMICS AND KINDS OF ECONOMIES

Economics is the study of the buying choices that people make, the production of goods and services, and how our market system works. The two kinds of economies are command and market. In a **command economy**, the government controls what and how much is produced, the methods used for production, and the distribution of goods and services. In a **market economy**, producers make decisions about methods and distribution on their own. These choices are based on what will sell and bring a profit in the marketplace. In a market economy, consumers ultimately affect these decisions by choosing whether or not to buy certain goods and services. The United States has a market economy.

MARKET ECONOMY

The five characteristics of a **market economy** are:

- **Economic freedom** – There is freedom of choice with respect to jobs, salaries, production, and price.
- **Economic incentives** – A positive incentive is to make a profit. However, if the producer tries to make too high a profit, the consequences might be that no one will purchase the item at that price. A negative incentive would be a drop in profits, causing the producer to decrease or discontinue production. A boycott, which might cause the producer to change business practices or policies, is also a negative economic incentive.
- **Competition** – There is more than one producer for any given product. Consumers thereby have choices about what to buy, which are usually made based on quality and price. Competition is an incentive for a producer to make the best product at the best price. Otherwise, producers will lose business to the competition.
- **Private ownership** – Production and profits belong to an individual or to a private company, not to the government.
- **Limited government** – Government plays no role in the economic decisions of its individual citizens.

FACTORS OF PRODUCTION AND TYPES OF MARKETS THAT CREATE ECONOMIC FLOW

The factors of **production** are:

- **Land** – This includes not only actual land, but also forests, minerals, water, etc.
- **Labor** – This is the work force required to produce goods and services, including factors such as talent, skills, and physical labor.
- **Capital** – This is the cash and material equipment needed to produce goods and services, including buildings, property, tools, office equipment, roads, etc.
- **Entrepreneurship** – Persons with initiative can capitalize on the free market system by producing goods and services.

The two types of markets are factor and product markets. The **factor market** consists of the people who exchange their services for wages. The people are sellers and companies are buyers. The **product market** is the selling of products to the people who want to buy them. The people are the buyers and the companies are the sellers. This exchange creates a circular economic flow in which money goes from the producers to workers as wages, and then flows back to producers in the form of payment for products.

Copyright © Mometrix Media. You have been licensed one copy of this document for personal use only. Any other reproduction or redistribution is strictly prohibited. All rights reserved. This content is provided for test preparation purposes only and does not imply an endorsement by Mometrix of any particular political, scientific, or religious point of view.

ECONOMIC IMPACT OF TECHNOLOGY

At the start of the 21st century, the role of **information and communications technologies** (ICT) grew rapidly as the economy shifted to a knowledge-based one. Output is increasing in areas where ICT is used intensively, which are service areas and knowledge-intensive industries such as finance; insurance; real estate; business services; health care; environmental goods and services; and community, social, and personal services. Meanwhile, the economic share for manufacturers is declining in medium- and low-technology industries such as chemicals, food products, textiles, gas, water, electricity, construction, and transport and communication services. Industries that have traditionally been high-tech, such as aerospace, computers, electronics, and pharmaceuticals are remaining steady in terms of their economic share. Technology has become the strongest factor in determining **per capita income** for many countries. The ease of technology investments as compared to industries that involve factories and large labor forces has resulted in more foreign investments in countries that do not have natural resources to call upon.

CHAPTER QUIZ

1. Which of the following is NOT a characteristic of a market economy?

   a. Economic freedom
   b. Economic incentives
   c. Competition
   d. Public ownership

CHAPTER QUIZ ANSWER KEY

1. D: There are five characteristics of a market economy:

- Economic freedom: There is freedom of choice with respect to jobs, salaries, production, and price.

- Economic incentives: A positive incentive is to make a profit. However, if the producer tries to make too high a profit, the consequences might be that no one will purchase the item at that price. A negative incentive would be a drop in profits, causing the producer to decrease or discontinue production. A boycott, which might cause the producer to change business practices or policies, is also a negative economic incentive.

- Competition: There is more than one producer for any given product. Consumers thereby have choices about what to buy, which are usually made based on quality and price. Competition is an incentive for a producer to make the best product at the best price. Otherwise, producers will lose business to the competition.

- Private ownership: Production and profits belong to an individual or to a private company, not to the government.

- Limited government: Government plays no role in the economic decisions of its individual citizens.

Copyright © Mometrix Media. You have been licensed one copy of this document for personal use only. Any other reproduction or redistribution is strictly prohibited. All rights reserved.
This content is provided for test preparation purposes only and does not imply an endorsement by Mometrix of any particular political, scientific, or religious point of view.

Science

Earth Science

EARTH SYSTEM SCIENCE

The complex and interconnected dynamics of the continents, atmosphere, oceans, ice, and life forms are the subject of **earth system science**. These interconnected dynamics require an interdisciplinary approach that includes chemistry, physics, biology, mathematics, and applied sciences in order to study the Earth as an integrated system and determine (while considering human impact and interaction) the past, present, and future states of the earth. Scientific inquiry in this field includes exploration of:

- Extreme weather events as they pertain to a changing climate
- Earthquakes and volcanic eruptions as they pertain to tectonic shifts
- Losses in biodiversity in relation to the changes in the earth's ecosystems
- Causes and effects in the environment
- The sun's solar variability in relation to the earth's climate
- The atmosphere's increasing concentrations of carbon dioxide and aerosols
- Trends in the earth's systems in terms of changes and their consequences

TRADITIONAL EARTH SCIENCE DISCIPLINES

Modern science is approaching the study of the earth in an integrated fashion that sees the earth as an interconnected system that is impacted by humankind and, therefore, must include social dimensions. Traditionally, though, the following were the earth science disciplines:

- **Geology** – This is the study of the origin and structure of the earth and of the changes it has undergone and is in the process of undergoing. Geologists work from the crust inward.
- **Meteorology** – This is the study of the atmosphere, including atmospheric pressure, temperature, clouds, winds, precipitation, etc. It is also concerned with describing and explaining weather.
- **Oceanography** – This is the study of the oceans, which includes studying their extent and depth, the physics and chemistry of ocean waters, and the exploitation of their resources.
- **Ecology** – This is the study of living organisms in relation to their environment and to other living things. It is the study of the interrelations between the different components of the ecosystem.

GEOLOGICAL ERAS

Geologists divide the history of the earth into units of time called **eons**, which are divided into **eras**, then into **periods**, then into **epochs** and finally into **ages**. Dates are approximate of course, and there may be variations of a few million years. (Million years ago is abbreviated as Ma.) Some of the most commonly known time periods are:

- **Hadean Eon** – About 4.5 to 3.8 billion years ago
- **Archaean Eon** – 3.8 to 2.5 billion years ago
- **Proterozoic Eon** – 2.5 billion to 542 Ma
- **Phanerozoic Eon** – 542 Ma to the present
  - **Paleozoic Era** – 542 Ma to 251 Ma

Copyright © Mometrix Media. You have been licensed one copy of this document for personal use only. Any other reproduction or redistribution is strictly prohibited. All rights reserved. This content is provided for test preparation purposes only and does not imply an endorsement by Mometrix of any particular political, scientific, or religious point of view.

- ❖ **Cambrian Period** – 542 to 488 Ma
- ❖ **Ordovician Period** – 488 to 443 Ma
- ❖ **Silurian Period** – 443 to 416 Ma
- ❖ **Devonian Period** – 416 to 359 Ma
- ❖ **Carboniferous Period** – 359 to 290 Ma
- ❖ **Permian Period** – 290 to 252 Ma
- ○ **Mesozoic Era** – 252 to 65 Ma
  - ❖ **Triassic Period** – 252 to 200 Ma
  - ❖ **Jurassic Period** – 200 to 150 Ma
  - ❖ **Cretaceous Period** – 150 to 65 Ma
- ○ **Cenozoic Era** – 65 Ma to the present
  - ❖ **Paleogene Period** – 65 to 28 Ma
  - ❖ **Neogene Period** – 28 to 2 Ma
  - ❖ **Quaternary Period** – about 2 Ma to the present

DEVELOPMENT OF LIFE ON EARTH ACCORDING TO TIME PERIODS

The **evolution** of life on earth is believed to have occurred as follows:

- Igneous rocks formed. (Hadean Eon)
- The continents formed. (Archaean Eon)
- The first multi-cellular creatures such as hydras, jellyfish, and sponges appeared about 600 Ma.
- Flatworms, roundworms, and segmented worms appeared about 550 Ma.
- Moss, arthropods, octopus, and eels appeared. (Cambrian Period)
- Mushrooms, fungi, and other primitive plants appeared; sea animals began to use calcium to build bones and shells. (Ordovician Period)
- Fish with jaws appeared. (Silurian Period)
- Fish developed lungs and legs (frogs) and went on land; ferns appeared. (Devonian period)
- Reptiles developed the ability to lay eggs on land and pine trees appeared. (Carboniferous Period)
- Dinosaurs dominated the land during the Triassic and Jurassic Periods.
- Flying insects, birds, and the first flowering plants appeared; dinosaurs died out. (Cretaceous Period)
- Mammals evolved and dominated; grasses became widespread. (50 Ma)
- Hominids appeared more than 2 Ma.

HYDROSPHERE AND HYDROLOGIC CYCLE

The **hydrosphere** is anything on earth that is related to water, whether it is in the air, on land, or in a plant or animal system. A water molecule consists of only two atoms of hydrogen and one of oxygen, yet it is what makes life possible. Unlike the other planets, earth is able to sustain life because its temperature allows water to be in its liquid state most of the time. Water vapor and ice are of no use to living organisms. The **hydrologic cycle** is the journey water takes as it assumes different forms. Liquid surface water evaporates to form the gaseous state of a cloud, and then becomes liquid again in the form of rain. This process takes about 10 days if water becomes a cloud.

Copyright © Mometrix Media. You have been licensed one copy of this document for personal use only. Any other reproduction or redistribution is strictly prohibited. All rights reserved.
This content is provided for test preparation purposes only and does not imply an endorsement by Mometrix of any particular political, scientific, or religious point of view.

Water at the bottom of the ocean or in a glacier is not likely to change form, even over periods of thousands of years.

> **Review Video: Hydrologic Cycle**
> Visit mometrix.com/academy and enter code: 426578

AQUIFERS

An **aquifer** is an underground water reservoir formed from groundwater that has infiltrated from the surface by passing through the soil and permeable rock layers (the zone of aeration) to a zone of saturation where the rocks are impermeable. There are two types of aquifers. In one, the water is under pressure (**confined**) as the supply builds up between layers of impermeable rocks and has to move back towards the surface, resulting in a spring or artesian well. The second type of aquifer is called "**unconfined**" because it has room to expand and contract, and the water has to be pumped out. The highest level of the aquifer is called the water table. If water is pumped out of the aquifer such that the water table dips in a specific area, that area is called a cone of depression.

BIOSPHERE

Biosphere is the term used by physical geographers to describe the living world of trees, bugs, and animals. It refers to any place where life exists on earth, and is the intersection of the hydrosphere, the atmosphere, the land, and the energy that comes from space. The biosphere includes the upper areas of the atmosphere where birds and insects can travel, areas deep inside caves, and hydrothermal vents at the bottom of the ocean.

Factors that affect the biosphere include:

- The **distance and tilt** between the earth and the sun – This produces temperatures that are conducive to life and causes the seasons.
- **Climate, daily weather, and erosion** – These change the land and the organisms on and in it.
- Earthquakes, tornadoes, volcanoes, tsunamis, and other **natural phenomena** – These all change the land.
- **Chemical erosion** – This changes the composition of rocks and organic materials.
- **Biological erosion** – This is bacteria and single-celled organisms breaking down organic and inorganic materials.

ECOLOGICAL SYSTEM AND BIOME

An **ecological system**, or ecosystem, is the community of all the living organisms in a specific area interacting with non-living factors such as temperature, sunlight, atmospheric pressure, weather patterns, wind, types of nutrients, etc. An ecosystem's development depends on the energy that passes in and out of it. The boundaries of an ecosystem depend on the use of the term, whether it refers to an ecosystem under a rock or in a valley, pond, or ocean.

A **biome** is a general ecosystem type defined by the plants and animals that live there and the local climate patterns. Examples include tropical rainforests or savannas, deserts, grasslands, deciduous forests, tundra, woodlands, and ice caps. There can be more than one type of biome within a larger climate zone. The transition area between two biomes is an ecotone, which may have characteristics of both biomes.

Copyright © Mometrix Media. You have been licensed one copy of this document for personal use only. Any other reproduction or redistribution is strictly prohibited. All rights reserved. This content is provided for test preparation purposes only and does not imply an endorsement by Mometrix of any particular political, scientific, or religious point of view.

EROSION

Erosion is the process that breaks down matter, whether it is a rock that is broken into pebbles or mountains that are rained on until they become hills. Erosion always happens in a downhill direction. The erosion of land by weather or breaking waves is called **denudation**. **Mass wasting** is the movement of masses of dirt and rock from one place to another. This can occur in two ways: **mechanical** (such as breaking a rock with a hammer) or **chemical** (such as pouring acid on a rock to dissolve it). If the material changes color, it indicates that a break down was chemical in nature. Whatever is broken down must go somewhere, so erosion eventually builds something up. For example, an eroded mountain ends up in a river that carries the sediment towards the ocean, where it builds up and creates a wetland or delta at the mouth of the river.

CLIMATES

Scientists have determined the following different types of **climates**:

- Polar (ice caps)
- Polar (tundra)
- Subtropical (dry summer)
- Subtropical (dry winter)
- Subtropical (humid)
- Subtropical (marine west coast)
- Subtropical (Mediterranean)
- Subtropical (wet)
- Tropical (monsoon)
- Tropical (savannah/grasslands)
- Tropical (wet)

Several factors make up and affect climates. These include:

- Temperature
- Atmospheric pressure
- The number of clouds and the amount of dust or smog
- Humidity
- Winds

The moistest and warmest of all the climates is that of the tropical rainforest. It has daily convection thunderstorms caused by the surface daytime heat and the high humidity, which combine to form thunderclouds.

> **Review Video: Climates**
> Visit mometrix.com/academy and enter code: 991320

LAYERS OF THE EARTH

The earth has several distinct **layers**, each with its own properties:

- **Crust** – This is the outermost layer of the earth that is comprised of the continents and the ocean basins. It has a variable thickness (35-70 km in the continents and 5-10 km in the ocean basins) and is composed mostly of alumino-silicates.
- **Mantle** – This is about 2900 km thick, and is made up mostly of ferro-magnesium silicates. It is divided into an upper and lower mantle. Most of the internal heat of the earth is located in the mantle. Large convective cells circulate heat, and may cause plate tectonic movement.

Copyright © Mometrix Media. You have been licensed one copy of this document for personal use only. Any other reproduction or redistribution is strictly prohibited. All rights reserved.
This content is provided for test preparation purposes only and does not imply an endorsement by Mometrix of any particular political, scientific, or religious point of view.

- **Core** – This is separated into the liquid outer core and the solid inner core. The outer core is 2300 km thick (composed mostly of nickel-iron alloy), and the inner core (almost entirely iron) is 12 km thick. The earth's magnetic field is thought to be controlled by the liquid outer core.

COMPOSITION OF EARTH'S ATMOSPHERE

The earth's **atmosphere** is 79% nitrogen, 20% oxygen, and 1% other gases. The oxygen was originally produced almost entirely by algae-type plants. The atmosphere has four layers:

- **Troposphere** – This is the layer closest to the earth where all weather takes place. It is the region that contains rising and falling packets of air. Air pressure at sea level is 0.1 atmospheres, but the top of the troposphere is about 10% of that amount.
- **Stratosphere** – In this layer, air flow is mainly horizontal. The upper portion has a thin layer of concentrated ozone (a reactive form of oxygen) that is largely responsible for absorbing the sun's ultraviolet rays.
- **Mesosphere** – This is the coldest layer. Temperatures drop to -100°C at the top.
- **Thermosphere** – This is divided into the lower ionosphere and the higher exosphere. This layer is very thin and has many ionized atoms with a net electrical charge. The aurora and Van Allen Belts are here. This layer also absorbs the most energetic photons from the sun and reflects radio waves, enabling long distance radio communication.

> **Review Video: Earth's Atmosphere**
> Visit mometrix.com/academy and enter code: 417614

PALEONTOLOGY

Paleontology is the study of prehistoric plant and animal life through the analysis of **fossil remains**. These fossils reveal the ecologies of the past and the path of evolution for both extinct and living organisms. A historical science, paleontology seeks information about the identity, origin, environment, and evolution of past organisms and what they can reveal about the past of the earth as a whole. Paleontology explains causes as opposed to conducting experiments to observe effects. It is related to the fields of biology, geology, and archaeology, and is divided into several sub-disciplines concerned with the types of fossils studied, the process of fossilization, and the ecology and climate of the past. Paleontologists also help identify the composition of the earth's rock layers by the fossils that are found, thus identifying potential sites for oil, mineral, and water extraction.

DETERMINING THE ORDER IN WHICH GEOLOGIC EVENTS OCCURRED USING THE ROCK RECORD

The **Law of Superposition** logically assumes that the bottom layer of a series of sedimentary layers is the oldest, unless it has been overturned or older rock has been pushed over it. In addition, since **igneous intrusions** can cut through or flow above other rocks, these other rocks are older. For example, molten rock (lava) flows out over already present, older rocks. Another guideline for the rock record is that **rock layers** are older than the folds and faults in them because the rocks must exist before they can be folded or faulted. If a rock contains **atomic nuclei**, reference tables of the half-lives of commonly used radio isotopes can be used to match the decay rate of known substances to the nuclei in a rock, and thereby determine its age. Ages of rocks can also be determined from **contact metamorphism**, the re-crystallization of pre-existing rocks due to changes in physical and chemical conditions, such as heat, pressure, and chemically active fluids that might be present in lava or polluted waters.

Copyright © Mometrix Media. You have been licensed one copy of this document for personal use only. Any other reproduction or redistribution is strictly prohibited. All rights reserved.
This content is provided for test preparation purposes only and does not imply an endorsement by Mometrix of any particular political, scientific, or religious point of view.

MATCHING ROCKS AND GEOLOGIC EVENTS IN ONE PLACE WITH THOSE OF ANOTHER

Geologists physically follow rock layers from one location to another by a process called "walking the outcrop." Geologists walk along the outcropping to see where it goes and what the differences and similarities of the neighboring locations they cross are. Similar rock **types** or **patterns** of rock layers that are similar in terms of thickness, color, composition, and fossil remains tell geologists that two locations have a similar geologic history. Fossils are found all over the earth, but are from a relatively **small time period** in earth's history. Therefore, fossil evidence helps date a rock layer, regardless of where it occurs. **Volcanic ash** is a good time indicator since ash is deposited quickly over a widespread area. Matching the date of an eruption to the ash allows for a precise identification of time. Similarly, the **meteor impact** at the intersection of the Cretaceous and Tertiary Periods left a time marker. Wherever the meteor's iridium content is found, geologists are able to date rock layers.

SEQUENCING THE EARTH'S GEOLOGIC HISTORY FROM THE FOSSIL AND ROCK RECORD

Reference tables are used to match specimens and time periods. For example, the fossil record has been divided into time units of the earth's history. Rocks can therefore be dated by the fossils found with them. There are also reference tables for dating plate motions and mountain building events in geologic history. Since humans have been around for a relatively short period of time, **fossilized human remains** help to affix a date to a location. Some areas have missing **geologic layers** because of erosion or other factors, but reference tables specific to a region will list what is complete or missing. The theory of **uniformitarianism** assumes that geologic processes have been the same throughout history. Therefore, the way erosion or volcanic eruptions happen today is the same as the way these events happened millions of years ago because there is no reason for them to have changed. Therefore, knowledge about current events can be applied to the past to make judgments about events in the rock record.

REVEALING CHANGES IN EARTH'S HISTORY BY THE FOSSIL AND ROCK RECORDS

Fossils can show how animal and plant life have changed or remained the same over time. For example, fossils have provided evidence of the existence of dinosaurs even though they no longer roam the earth, and have also been used to prove that certain insects have been around for hundreds of millions of years. Fossils have been used to identify four basic eras: **Proterozoic**, the age of primitive life; **Paleozoic**, the age of fishes; **Mesozoic**, the age of dinosaurs; and **Cenozoic**, the age of mammals. Most ancient forms of life have disappeared, and there are reference tables that list when this occurred. Fossil records also show the evolution of certain life forms, such as the horse from the eohippus. However, the majority of changes do not involve evolution from simple to complex forms, but rather an increase in the variety of forms.

MOUNTAINS

A **mountain** is a portion of the earth that has been raised above its surroundings by volcanic action or tectonic plate movement. Mountains are made up of igneous, metamorphic, and sedimentary rocks, and most lie along active plate boundaries. There are two major mountain systems. The **Circum-Pacific** encircles the entire Pacific Ocean, from New Guinea up across Japan and the Aleutians and down to southern South America. The **Alpine-Himalaya** stretches from northern Africa across the Alps and to the Himalayas and Indonesia. **Orogeny** is the term for the process of natural mountain formation. Therefore, physical mountains are orogens. **Folded mountains** are created through the folding of rock layers when two crustal plates come together. The Alps and Himalayas are folded mountains. The latter was formed by the collision of India with Asia. **Fault-block mountains** are created from the tension forces of plate movements. These produce faults

312

Copyright © Mometrix Media. You have been licensed one copy of this document for personal use only. Any other reproduction or redistribution is strictly prohibited. All rights reserved.
This content is provided for test preparation purposes only and does not imply an endorsement by Mometrix of any particular political, scientific, or religious point of view.

that vertically displace one section to form a mountain. **Dome mountains** are created from magma pushing up through the earth's crust.

VOLCANOES AND VOLCANIC MOUNTAINS

Volcanoes are classified according to their activity level. An **active** volcano is in the process of erupting or building to an eruption; a dormant volcano has erupted before and may erupt again someday, but is not currently active; and an **extinct** volcano has died out volcanically and will not erupt ever again. Active volcanoes endanger plant and animal life, but lava and ash add enriching minerals to the soil. There are three types of volcanic mountains:

- **Shield volcanoes** are the largest volcanic mountains because of a repeated, viscous lava flow from small eruptions over a long period of time that cause the mountain to grow.
- **Cinder cone volcanoes**, or linear volcanoes, are small in size, but have massive explosions through linear shafts that spread cinders and ash around the vent. This results in a cone-shaped hill.
- **Composite volcanoes** get their name from the mix of lava and ash layers that build the mountain.

SUBDIVISIONS OF ROCK

The three major subdivisions of rock are:

- **Igneous** (magmatites) – This type is formed from the cooling of liquid magma. In the process, minerals crystallize and amalgamate. If solidification occurs deep in the earth (plutonic rock), the cooling process is slow. This allows for the formation of large crystals, giving rock a coarse-grained texture (granite). Quickly cooled magma has a glassy texture (obsidian).
- **Metamorphic** – Under conditions of high temperature and pressure within the earth's crust, rock material melts and changes structure, transitioning or metamorphosing into a new type of rock with different minerals. If the minerals appear in bands, the rock is foliated. Examples include marble (unfoliated) and slate (foliated).
- **Sedimentary** – This is the most common type of rock on earth. It is formed by sedimentation, compaction, and then cementation of many small particles of mineral, animal, or plant material. There are three types of sedimentary rocks: clastic, clay, and sand that came from disintegrated rocks; chemical (rock salt and gypsum), formed by evaporation of aqueous solutions; and biogenic (coal), formed from animal or plant remnants.

> **Review Video: Igneous, Sedimentary, and Metamorphic Rocks**
> Visit mometrix.com/academy and enter code: 689294

GLACIERS

Glaciers start high in the mountains, where snow and ice accumulate inside a cirque (a small semicircular depression). The snow becomes firmly packed into masses of coarse-grained ice that are slowly pulled down a slope by gravity. Glaciers grow with large amounts of snowfall and retreat (diminish) if warm weather melts more ice than can be replaced. Glaciers once covered large areas of both the northern and southern hemispheres with mile-thick ice that carved out valleys, fjords, and other land formations. They also moved plants, animals, and rocks from one area to another. There were two types of glaciers: **valley**, which produced U-shaped erosion and sharp-peaked mountains; and **continental**, which moved over and rounded mountain tops and ridges. These

Copyright © Mometrix Media. You have been licensed one copy of this document for personal use only. Any other reproduction or redistribution is strictly prohibited. All rights reserved. This content is provided for test preparation purposes only and does not imply an endorsement by Mometrix of any particular political, scientific, or religious point of view.

glaciers existed during the ice ages, the last of which occurred from 2.5 million years ago to 12,000 years ago.

CHAPTER QUIZ

1. Which of the following lists the units of time from least to most expansive?

a. Eon, era, epoch, age, period
b. Age, period, eon, epoch, era
c. Age, epoch, period, era, eon
d. Period, age, era, epoch, eon

2. What is the coldest layer of the atmosphere?

a. Troposphere
b. Stratosphere
c. Mesosphere
d. Thermosphere

3. Orogeny refers to which of the following?

a. The process of sedimentary layers developing over time.
b. The process of natural mountain formation.
c. The study of the formation of ecological systems.
d. The study of prehistoric plant and animal life through the analysis of fossil remains.

CHAPTER QUIZ ANSWER KEY

1. C: Geologists divide the history of the Earth into units of time called eons, which are divided into eras, then into periods, then into epochs, and finally into ages. Dates are approximate of course, and there may be variations of a few million years. ("Million years ago" is abbreviated as *Ma, myr, and mya*.)

2. C: The Earth's atmosphere is 79 percent nitrogen, 20 percent oxygen, and 1 percent other gases. The oxygen was originally produced almost entirely by algae-type plants. The atmosphere has four layers, described below.

- Troposphere: This is the layer closest to the Earth where all weather takes place. It is the region that contains rising and falling packets of air. Air pressure at sea level is 0.1 atmospheres, but the top of the troposphere is about 10 percent of that amount.
- Stratosphere: In this layer, air flow is mainly horizontal. The upper portion has a thin layer of concentrated ozone (a reactive form of oxygen) that is largely responsible for absorbing the sun's ultraviolet rays.
- Mesosphere: This is the coldest layer. Temperatures drop to -100 °C at the top.
- Thermosphere: This is divided into the lower ionosphere and the higher exosphere. This layer is very thin and has many ionized atoms with a net electrical charge. The aurora and Van Allen belts are here. This layer also absorbs the most energetic photons from the sun and reflects radio waves, enabling long-distance radio communication.

3. B: Orogeny is the term for the process of natural mountain formation. Therefore, physical mountains are orogens.

LAYERS ABOVE THE SURFACE OF EARTH

The **ozone layer**, although contained within the stratosphere, is determined by ozone (O_3) concentrations. It absorbs the majority of ultraviolet light from the Sun. The ionosphere is part of

Copyright © Mometrix Media. You have been licensed one copy of this document for personal use only. Any other reproduction or redistribution is strictly prohibited. All rights reserved.
This content is provided for test preparation purposes only and does not imply an endorsement by Mometrix of any particular political, scientific, or religious point of view.

both the exosphere and the thermosphere. It is characterized by the fact that it is a plasma, a partially ionized gas in which free electrons and positive ions are attracted to each other, but are too energetic to remain fixed as a molecule. It starts at about 50 km above Earth's surface and goes to 1,000 km. It affects radio wave transmission and auroras. The ionosphere pushes against the inner edge of the Earth's magnetosphere, which is the highly magnetized, non-spherical region around the Earth. The homosphere encompasses the troposphere, stratosphere, and mesosphere. Gases in the homosphere are considered well mixed. In the heterosphere, the distance that particles can move without colliding is large. As a result, gases are stratified according to their molecular weights. Heavier gases such as oxygen and nitrogen occur near the bottom of the heterosphere, while hydrogen, the lightest element, is found at the top.

Review Video: Earth's Atmosphere
Visit mometrix.com/academy and enter code: 417614

Tropospheric Circulation

Most weather takes place in the **troposphere**. Air circulates in the atmosphere by convection and in various types of "cells." Air near the equator is warmed by the Sun and rises. Cool air rushes under it, and the higher, warmer air flows toward Earth's poles. At the poles, it cools and descends to the surface. It is now under the hot air, and flows back to the equator. Air currents coupled with ocean currents move heat around the planet, creating winds, weather, and climate. Winds can change direction with the seasons. For example, in Southeast Asia and India, summer monsoons are caused by air being heated by the Sun. This air rises, draws moisture from the ocean, and causes daily rains. In winter, the air cools, sinks, pushes the moist air away, and creates dry weather.

Common Weather Phenomena and Equipment to Measure Them

Common **atmospheric conditions** that are frequently measured are temperature, precipitation, wind, and humidity. These weather conditions are often measured at permanently fixed **weather stations** so weather data can be collected and compared over time and by region. Measurements may also be taken by ships, buoys, and underwater instruments. Measurements may also be taken under special circumstances. The measurements taken include temperature, barometric pressure, humidity, wind speed, wind direction, and precipitation. Usually, the following instruments are used: A *thermometer* is used for measuring temperature; a *barometer* is used for measuring barometric/air pressure; a *hygrometer* is used for measuring humidity; an *anemometer* is used for measuring wind speed; a *weather vane* is used for measuring wind direction; and a *rain gauge* is used for measuring precipitation.

Weather, Climate, and Meteorology

Meteorology is the study of the atmosphere, particularly as it pertains to forecasting the weather and understanding its processes. **Weather** is the condition of the atmosphere at any given moment. Most weather occurs in the troposphere and includes changing events such as clouds, storms, and temperature, as well as more extreme events such as tornadoes, hurricanes, and blizzards. **Climate** refers to the average weather for a particular area over time, typically at least 30 years. Latitude is an indicator of climate. Changes in climate occur over long time periods.

Winds and Global Wind Belts

Winds are the result of air moving by convection. Masses of warm air rise, and cold air sweeps into their place. The warm air also moves, cools, and sinks. The term "prevailing wind" refers to the wind that usually blows in an area in a single direction. *Dominant winds* are the winds with the highest speeds. Belts or bands that run latitudinally and blow in a specific direction are associated with *convection cells. Hadley cells* are formed directly north and south of the equator. The *Farrell*

Copyright © Mometrix Media. You have been licensed one copy of this document for personal use only. Any other reproduction or redistribution is strictly prohibited. All rights reserved.
This content is provided for test preparation purposes only and does not imply an endorsement by Mometrix of any particular political, scientific, or religious point of view.

cells occur at about 30° to 60°. The jet stream runs between the Farrell cells and the polar cells. At the higher and lower latitudes, the direction is easterly. At mid latitudes, the direction is westerly. From the North Pole to the south, the surface winds are Polar High Easterlies, Subpolar Low Westerlies, Subtropical High or Horse Latitudes, North-East Trade winds, Equatorial Low or Doldrums, South-East Trades, Subtropical High or Horse Latitudes, Subpolar Low Easterlies, and Polar High.

> **Review Video: Where Does Wind Come From?**
> Visit mometrix.com/academy and enter code: 451712

RELATIVE HUMIDITY, ABSOLUTE HUMIDITY, AND DEW POINT TEMPERATURE

Humidity refers to water vapor contained in the air. The amount of moisture contained in air depends upon its temperature. The higher the air temperature, the more moisture it can hold. These higher levels of moisture are associated with higher humidity. **Absolute humidity** refers to the total amount of moisture air is capable of holding at a certain temperature. **Relative humidity** is the ratio of water vapor in the air compared to the amount the air is capable of holding at its current temperature. As temperature decreases, absolute humidity stays the same and relative humidity increases. A hygrometer is a device used to measure humidity. The **dew point** is the temperature at which water vapor condenses into water at a particular humidity.

PRECIPITATION

After clouds reach the dew point, **precipitation** occurs. Precipitation can take the form of a liquid or a solid. It is known by many names, including rain, snow, ice, dew, and frost. **Liquid** forms of precipitation include rain and drizzle. Rain or drizzle that freezes on contact is known as freezing rain or freezing drizzle. **Solid or frozen** forms of precipitation include snow, ice needles or diamond dust, sleet or ice pellets, hail, and graupel or snow pellets. Virga is a form of precipitation that evaporates before reaching the ground. It usually looks like sheets or shafts falling from a cloud. The amount of rainfall is measured with a rain gauge. Intensity can be measured according to how fast precipitation is falling or by how severely it limits visibility. Precipitation plays a major role in the water cycle since it is responsible for depositing much of the Earth's fresh water.

CLOUDS

Clouds form when air cools and warm air is forced to give up some of its water vapor because it can no longer hold it. This vapor condenses and forms tiny droplets of water or ice crystals called clouds. Particles, or aerosols, are needed for water vapor to form water droplets. These are called **condensation nuclei**. Clouds are created by surface heating, mountains and terrain, rising air masses, and weather fronts. Clouds precipitate, returning the water they contain to Earth. Clouds can also create atmospheric optics. They can scatter light, creating colorful phenomena such as rainbows, colorful sunsets, and the green flash phenomenon.

> **Review Video: Clouds**
> Visit mometrix.com/academy and enter code: 803166

HIGH, MIDDLE, AND LOW CLOUD TYPES

Most clouds can be classified according to the altitude of their base above Earth's surface. **High clouds** occur at altitudes between 5,000 and 13,000 meters. **Middle clouds** occur at altitudes between 2,000 and 7,000 meters. **Low clouds** occur from the Earth's surface to altitudes of 2,000 meters. Types of high clouds include cirrus (Ci), thin wispy mare's tails that consist of ice; cirrocumulus (Cc), small, pillow-like puffs that often appear in rows; and cirrostratus (Cs), thin, sheet-like clouds that often cover the entire sky. Types of middle clouds include altocumulus (Ac),

Copyright © Mometrix Media. You have been licensed one copy of this document for personal use only. Any other reproduction or redistribution is strictly prohibited. All rights reserved.
This content is provided for test preparation purposes only and does not imply an endorsement by Mometrix of any particular political, scientific, or religious point of view.

gray-white clouds that consist of liquid water; and altostratus (As), grayish or blue-gray clouds that span the sky. Types of low clouds include stratus (St), gray and fog-like clouds consisting of water droplets that take up the whole sky; stratocumulus (Sc), low-lying, lumpy gray clouds; and nimbostratus (Ns), dark gray clouds with uneven bases that indicate rain or snow. Two types of clouds, cumulus (Cu) and cumulonimbus (Cb), are capable of great vertical growth. They can start at a wide range of altitudes, from the Earth's surface to altitudes of 13,000 meters.

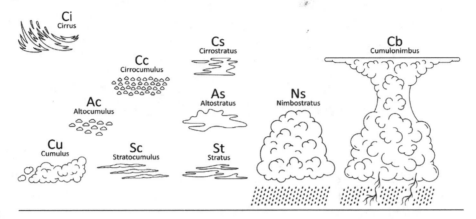

AIR MASSES

Air masses are large volumes of air in the troposphere of the Earth. They are categorized by their temperature and by the amount of water vapor they contain. *Arctic* and *Antarctic* air masses are cold, polar air masses are cool, and tropical and equatorial air masses are hot. Other types of air masses include *maritime* and *monsoon*, both of which are moist and unstable. There are also *continental* and *superior* air masses, which are dry. A **weather front** separates two masses of air of different densities. It is the principal cause of meteorological phenomena. Air masses are quickly and easily affected by the land they are above. They can have certain characteristics, and then develop new ones when they get blown over a different area.

WEATHER FRONTS AND WEATHER MAPS

A **weather front** is the area between two differing masses of air that affects weather. Frontal movements are influenced by the jet stream and other high winds. Movements are determined by the type of front. Cold fronts move up to twice as fast as warm ones. It is in the turbulent frontal area that commonplace and dramatic weather events take place. This area also creates temperature changes. Weather phenomena include rain, thunderstorms, high winds, tornadoes, cloudiness, clear skies, and hurricanes. Different fronts can be plotted on weather maps using a set of designated symbols. Surface weather maps can also include symbols representing clouds, rain, temperature, air pressure, and fair weather.

CHAPTER QUIZ

1. Air masses are large volumes of air in which layer of Earth's atmosphere?

    a. Magnetosphere
    b. Ionosphere
    c. Troposphere
    d. Stratosphere

CHAPTER QUIZ ANSWER KEY

1. C: Air masses are large volumes of air in the troposphere of the Earth. They are categorized by their temperature and by the amount of water vapor they contain. Arctic and Antarctic air masses

Copyright © Mometrix Media. You have been licensed one copy of this document for personal use only. Any other reproduction or redistribution is strictly prohibited. All rights reserved. This content is provided for test preparation purposes only and does not imply an endorsement by Mometrix of any particular political, scientific, or religious point of view.

are cold, polar air masses are cool, and tropical and equatorial air masses are hot. Other types of air masses include maritime and monsoon, both of which are moist and unstable. There are also continental and superior air masses, which are dry.

ASTRONOMY

Astronomy is the scientific study of celestial objects and their positions, movements, and structures. *Celestial* does not refer to the Earth by itself, but does include its movement through space. Other celestial objects include the Sun, the Moon, planets, satellites, asteroids, meteors, comets, stars, galaxies, the universe, and other space phenomena. The term astronomy has its roots in the Greek words "astro" and "nomos," which means "laws of the stars."

> **Review Video: Astronomy**
> Visit mometrix.com/academy and enter code: 640556

UNIVERSE

ORIGIN

The **universe** can be said to consist of everything and nothing. The universe contains all of space, matter, energy, and time. There are likely still phenomena that have yet to be discovered. The universe can also be thought of as nothing, since a vast portion of the known universe is empty space. It is believed that the universe is expanding. The *Big Bang theory*, which is widely accepted among astronomers, was developed to explain the origin of the universe. There are other theories regarding the origin of the universe, such as the *Steady-State theory* and the *Creationist theory*. The Big Bang theory states that all the matter in the universe was once in one place. This matter underwent a huge explosion that spread it into space. Galaxies formed from, this material and the universe is still expanding.

STRUCTURE

What can be seen of the universe is believed to be at least 93 billion light years across. To put this into perspective, the Milky Way galaxy is about 100,000 light years across. Our view of matter in the universe is that it forms into clumps which become stars, galaxies, clusters of galaxies, superclusters, and the Great Wall of galaxies. **Galaxies** consist of stars, some with planetary systems. Some estimates state that the universe is about 13 billion years old. It is not considered dense and is believed to consist of 73% dark energy, 23% cold dark matter, and 4% regular matter. Cosmology is the study of the universe. Interstellar medium (ISM) is the gas and dust in the interstellar space between a galaxy's stars.

GALAXIES

Galaxies consist of stars, stellar remnants, and dark matter. **Dwarf galaxies** contain as few as 10 million stars, while giant galaxies contain as many as 1 trillion stars. Galaxies are gravitationally bound, meaning that stars, star systems, other gases, and dust orbit the galaxy's center. The Earth exists in the **Milky Way galaxy** and the nearest galaxy to ours is the **Andromeda galaxy**. Galaxies can be classified by their visual shape into elliptical, spiral, irregular, and starburst galaxies. It is estimated that there are more than 100 billion galaxies in the universe ranging from 1,000 to 100,000 parsecs in diameter. Galaxies can be megaparsecs apart. Intergalactic space consists of a gas with an average density of less than one atom per cubic meter. Galaxies are organized into clusters which form superclusters. Dark matter may account for up to 90% of the mass of galaxies. Dark matter is still not well understood.

Copyright © Mometrix Media. You have been licensed one copy of this document for personal use only. Any other reproduction or redistribution is strictly prohibited. All rights reserved. This content is provided for test preparation purposes only and does not imply an endorsement by Mometrix of any particular political, scientific, or religious point of view.

PLANETS

In order of their distance from the sun (closest to furthest away), the **planets** are: Mercury, Venus, Earth, Mars, Jupiter, Saturn, Uranus, and Neptune (Pluto is now considered to be a dwarf planet). All the planets revolve around the sun, which is an average-sized star in the spiral Milky Way galaxy. They revolve in the same direction in nearly circular orbits. If the planets were viewed by looking down from the sun, they would rotate in a counter-clockwise direction. All the planets are in, or near, the same plane, called the ecliptic, and their axis of rotation is nearly perpendicular to the ecliptic. The only exception is Uranus, which is tipped on its side.

TERRESTRIAL PLANETS, JOVIAN PLANETS, AND MASS OF PLANETS

The **Terrestrial Planets** are: Mercury, Venus, Earth, and Mars. These are the four planets closest to the sun. They are called terrestrial because they all have a compact, rocky surface similar to the Earth's. Venus, Earth, and Mars have significant atmospheres, but Mercury has almost no atmosphere.

The **Jovian Planets** are: Jupiter (the largest planet), Saturn, Uranus, and Neptune. They are called Jovian (Jupiter-like) because of their huge sizes in relation to that of the Earth, and because they all have a gaseous nature like Jupiter. Although gas giants, some or all of the Jovian Planets may have small, solid cores.

The sun represents 99.85% of all the matter in our solar system. Combined, the planets make up only 0.135% of the mass of the solar system, with Jupiter having twice the mass of all the other planets combined. The remaining 0.015% of the mass comes from comets, planetary satellites, asteroids, meteoroids, and interplanetary medium.

DEFINITION OF PLANET

On August 24, 2006, the International Astronomical Union redefined the criteria a body must meet to be classified as a planet, stating that the following conditions must be met:

- "A planet orbits around a star and is neither a star nor a moon."
- "Its shape is spherical due to its gravity."
- "It has 'cleared' the space of its orbit."

A **dwarf planet** such as Pluto does not meet the third condition. Small solar system bodies such as asteroids and comets meet only the first condition.

SOLAR SYSTEM

The **solar system** developed about 4.6 billion years ago out of an enormous cloud of dust and gas circling around the sun. Four rocky planets orbit relatively close to the sun. Their inside orbits are separated from the outside orbits of the four, larger gaseous planets by an asteroid belt. Pluto, some comets, and several small objects circle in the Kuiper belt outside Neptune's orbit. The Oort cloud, composed of icy space objects, encloses the planetary system like a shell.

> **Review Video: Solar System**
> Visit mometrix.com/academy and enter code: 273231

EARTH'S MOON

Earth's **moon** is the closest celestial body to earth. Its proximity has allowed it to be studied since the invention of the telescope. As a result, its landforms have been named after astronomers, philosophers, and other scholars. Its surface has many craters created by asteroids since it has no

Copyright © Mometrix Media. You have been licensed one copy of this document for personal use only. Any other reproduction or redistribution is strictly prohibited. All rights reserved. This content is provided for test preparation purposes only and does not imply an endorsement by Mometrix of any particular political, scientific, or religious point of view.

protective atmosphere. These dark lowlands looked like seas to early astronomers, but there is virtually no water on the moon except possibly in its polar regions. These impact craters and depressions actually contain solidified lava flows. The bright highlands were thought to be continents, and were named terrae. The rocks of the moon have been pounded by asteroids so often that there is a layer of rubble and dust called the regolith. Also, because there is no protective atmosphere, temperatures on the moon vary widely, from 265°F to -255°F.

EARTH'S SUN AND OTHER STARS

A **star** begins as a cloud of hydrogen and some heavier elements drawn together by their own mass. This matter then begins to rotate. The core heats up to several million degrees Fahrenheit, which causes the hydrogen atoms to lose their shells and their nuclei to fuse. This releases enormous amounts of energy. The star then becomes stable during a stage called the **main sequence**. This is the stage our sun is in, and it will remain in this stage until its supply of hydrogen fuel runs out. Stars are not always alone like our sun, and may exist in pairs or groups. The hottest stars shine blue-white; medium-hot stars like our sun glow yellow; and cooler stars appear orange. The earth's sun is an **average star** in terms of mass, light production, and size. All stars, including our sun, have a **core** where fusion happens; a **photosphere** (surface) that produces sunspots (cool, dark areas); a red **chromosphere** that emits solar (bright) flares and shooting gases; and a **corona**, the transparent area only seen during an eclipse.

> **Review Video: The Sun**
> Visit mometrix.com/academy and enter code: 699233

COMETS, ASTEROIDS, AND METEOROIDS

Comets are celestial bodies composed of dust, rock, frozen gases, and ice. Invisible until they near the sun, comets emit volatile components in jets of gas and dust when exposed to the sun's heat. The **coma** is the comet's fog-like envelope that glows as it reflects sunlight and releases radiation. **Solar winds** blow a comet away from the sun and give it a tail of dust or electrically charged molecules. Each orbit of a comet causes it to lose matter until it breaks up or vaporizes into the sun.

Asteroids are irregularly-shaped boulders, usually less than 60 miles in diameter, that orbit the sun. Most are made of graphite; about 25% are silicates, or iron and nickel. Collisions or gravitational forces can cause them to fly off and possibly hit a planet.

Meteoroids are fragments of asteroids of various sizes. If they come through earth's atmosphere, they are called meteors or shooting stars. If they land on earth, they are called meteorites, and create craters on impact (the Barringer Crater in Arizona).

CHAPTER QUIZ

1. What is the nearest galaxy to the Milky Way?

    a. Cygnus A
    b. Virgo A
    c. Canis Major Dwarf Galaxy
    d. Andromeda Galaxy

2. Which of the following is NOT a Jovian planet?

    a. Venus
    b. Neptune
    c. Uranus
    d. Jupiter

Copyright © Mometrix Media. You have been licensed one copy of this document for personal use only. Any other reproduction or redistribution is strictly prohibited. All rights reserved. This content is provided for test preparation purposes only and does not imply an endorsement by Mometrix of any particular political, scientific, or religious point of view.

CHAPTER QUIZ ANSWER KEY

1. D: The Earth exists in the Milky Way galaxy, and the nearest galaxy to the Milky Way is the Andromeda galaxy. Galaxies can be classified by their visual shape into elliptical, spiral, irregular, and starburst galaxies. It is estimated that there are more than 100 billion galaxies in the universe, ranging from 1,000 to 100,000 parsecs in diameter. Galaxies can be megaparsecs apart. Intergalactic space consists of a gas with an average density of less than one atom per cubic meter. Galaxies are organized into clusters, and clusters form into superclusters. Dark matter may account for up to 90 percent of the mass of galaxies. Dark matter is still not well understood.

2. A: The Jovian planets are: Jupiter (the largest planet), Saturn, Uranus, and Neptune. They are called Jovian ("Jupiter-like") because of their huge sizes in relation to that of the Earth, and because they all have a gaseous nature like Jupiter. Although gas giants, some or all of the Jovian planets may have small, solid cores.

Life Science

SUBFIELDS OF BIOLOGY

There are a number of subfields of biology:

- **Zoology** – The study of animals
- **Botany** – The study of plants
- **Biophysics** – The application of the laws of physics to the processes of organisms and the application of the facts about living things to human processes and inventions
- **Biochemistry** – The study of the chemistry of living organisms, including diseases and the pharmaceutical drugs used to cure them
- **Cytology** – The study of cells
- **Histology** – The study of the tissues of plants and animals
- **Organology** – The study of tissues organized into organs
- **Physiology** – The study of the way organisms function, including metabolism, the exchange of matter and energy in nutrition, the senses, reproduction and development, and the work of the nervous system and brain
- **Genetics** – The study of heredity as it relates to the transmission of genes
- **Ethology** – The study of animal behavior
- **Ecology** – The study of the relationship of living organisms to their environments

CLASSIFICATION OF LIFE FORMS

All living creatures can be classified into one of three domains and then into one of six kingdoms:

- Domain Bacteria
  - **Kingdom Eubacteria**—single celled prokaryotes with little internal complexity, contains peptidoglycan. Members have just one chromosome, reproduce asexually, may have flagella, and are very simple in form.
- Domain Archaea
  - **Kingdom Archaebacteria**—single celled prokaryotes with little internal complexity, does not contain peptidoglycan. Members have just one chromosome, reproduce asexually, may have flagella, and are very simple in form.
- Domain Eukarya

Copyright © Mometrix Media. You have been licensed one copy of this document for personal use only. Any other reproduction or redistribution is strictly prohibited. All rights reserved. This content is provided for test preparation purposes only and does not imply an endorsement by Mometrix of any particular political, scientific, or religious point of view.

- Kingdom Protista—single celled eukaryotes with greater internal complexity than Bacteria or Archaea. They have a true nucleus surrounded by a membrane that separates it from the cytoplasm. Most are one-celled and have no complex tissues like plants.
- Kingdom Fungi—single celled or multicellular with considerable variation and complexity. Members have no chlorophyll, so they don't make their own food like plants. They reproduce using spores. Fungi are made up of filaments called hyphae that, in larger fungi, can interlace to form a tissue called mycelium.
- Kingdom Plantae—multicellular with great variation and complexity, rigid cell walls. This group consists of organisms that have chlorophyll and make their own food. Plants have differentiated tissues and reproduce either sexually or asexually.
- Kingdom Animalia—multicellular with much variation and complexity, cell membrane. This group consists of organisms that move around and have to feed on existing organic material.

> **Review Video: Kingdom Animalia**
> Visit mometrix.com/academy and enter code: 558413
>
> **Review Video: Kingdom Fungi**
> Visit mometrix.com/academy and enter code: 315081
>
> **Review Video: Kingdom Plantae**
> Visit mometrix.com/academy and enter code: 710084

CHARACTERISTICS OF INVERTEBRATES

Invertebrates are animals with no internal skeletons. They can be divided into three groups:

1. **Marine Invertebrates** – Members of this group live in oceans and seas. Marine invertebrates include sponges, corals, jellyfish, snails, clams, octopuses, squids, and crustaceans, none of which live on the surface.
2. **Freshwater Invertebrates** – Members of this group live in lakes and rivers. Freshwater invertebrates include worms on the bottom, microscopic crustaceans, and terrestrial insect larvae that live in the water column, but only where there is no strong current. Some live on the surface of the water.
3. **Terrestrial Invertebrates** – Members of this group live on dry ground. Terrestrial invertebrates include insects, mollusks (snails, slugs), arachnids, and myriapods (centipedes and millipedes). Terrestrial invertebrates breathe through a series of tubes that penetrate into the body (trachea) and deliver oxygen into tissues. Underground terrestrial invertebrates are generally light-colored with atrophied eyes and no cuticle to protect them from desiccation. They include worms that live underground and in caves and rock crevices. This group also includes insects such as ants that create colonies underground.

CHARACTERISTICS OF VERTEBRATE GROUPS

The **vertebrates**, animals with an internal skeleton, are divided into four groups:

1. **Fish** – This group is the most primitive, but is also the group from which all other groups evolved. Fish live in water, breathe with gills, are cold-blooded, have fins and scales, and are typically oviparous, which means they lay eggs. Fish typically have either cartilaginous skeletons (such as rays and sharks) or bony skeletons.

322

Copyright © Mometrix Media. You have been licensed one copy of this document for personal use only. Any other reproduction or redistribution is strictly prohibited. All rights reserved. This content is provided for test preparation purposes only and does not imply an endorsement by Mometrix of any particular political, scientific, or religious point of view.

2. **Amphibians** – The skin of animals in this group is delicate and permeable, so they need water to keep it moist. Amphibians are oviparous. The young start out in water with gills, but the adults use lungs.

3. **Reptiles and birds** – The skin of animals in this group has very hard, horn-like scales. Birds have exchanged scales for feathers. Reptiles and birds are oviparous, although birds care for their eggs and reptiles do not. Members have a cloaca, an excretory and reproductive cavity that opens to the outside. Reptiles are cold-blooded, but birds are warm-blooded.

4. **Mammals** – These are the most highly evolved vertebrates. Mammals have bodies covered with fur; are warm-blooded; are viviparous, meaning they give birth to live young which are fed with milk from female mammary glands; and are tetrapods (four-legged). Most live on the ground (except whales and dolphins) and a few fly (bats).

HUNTERS AND PREY ANIMALS

The interaction between **predators** and their **prey** is important to controlling the balance of an ecosystem. **Hunters** are **carnivorous** animals at the top of the ecological pyramid that eat other animals. Hunters tend to be territorial, leaving signs to warn others to stay out or risk a fight. Hunters are equipped to capture with claws, curved beaks, spurs, fangs, etc. They try to use a minimum amount of energy for each capture, so they prey upon the more vulnerable (the old, ill, or very young) when given a choice. Predators never kill more than they can eat. Some hunters have great speed, some stalk, and some hunt in groups. **Prey** animals are those that are captured by predators for food. They are usually **herbivores** further down the ecological pyramid. Prey animals have special characteristics to help them flee from predators. They may hide in nests or caves, become totally immobile to escape detection, have protective coloration or camouflage, have warning coloration to indicate being poisonous, or have shells or quills for protection.

LIFE PROCESSES THAT ALL LIVING THINGS HAVE IN COMMON

Living things share many **processes** that are necessary to survival, but the ways these processes and interactions occur are highly diverse. Processes include those related to:

- **Nutrition** – the process of obtaining, ingesting, and digesting foods; excreting unused or excess substances; and extracting energy from the foods to maintain structure.
- **Transport** (circulation) – the process of circulating essential materials such as nutrients, cells, hormones, and gases (oxygen and hydrogen) to the places they are needed by moving them through veins, arteries, and capillaries. Needed materials do not travel alone, but are "piggybacked" on transporting molecules.
- **Respiration** – the process of breathing, which is exchanging gases between the interior and exterior using gills, trachea (insects), or lungs.
- **Regulation** – the process of coordinating life activities through the nervous and endocrine systems.
- **Reproduction and growth** – the process of producing more of one's own kind and growing from birth to adulthood. The more highly evolved an animal is, the longer its growth time is.
- **Locomotion** (in animals) – the process of moving from place to place in the environment by using legs, flight, or body motions.

Copyright © Mometrix Media. You have been licensed one copy of this document for personal use only. Any other reproduction or redistribution is strictly prohibited. All rights reserved.
This content is provided for test preparation purposes only and does not imply an endorsement by Mometrix of any particular political, scientific, or religious point of view.

ORGANISMS THAT INTERFERE WITH CELL ACTIVITY

Viruses, bacteria, fungi, and other parasites may infect plants and animals and interfere with normal life functions, create imbalances, or disrupt the operations of cells.

- **Viruses** – These enter the body by inhalation (airborne) or through contact with contaminated food, water, or infected tissues. They affect the body by taking over the cell's protein synthesis mechanism to make more viruses. They kill the host cell and impact tissue and organ operations. Examples of viruses include measles, rabies, pneumonia, and AIDS.
- **Bacteria** – These enter the body through breaks in the skin or contaminated food or water, or by inhalation. They reproduce rapidly and produce toxins that kill healthy host tissues. Examples include diphtheria, bubonic plague, tuberculosis, and syphilis.
- **Fungi** – These feed on healthy tissues of the body by sending rootlike tendrils into the tissues to digest them extracellularly. Examples include athlete's foot and ringworm.
- **Parasites** – These enter the body through the skin, via insect bites, or through contaminated food or water. Examples include tapeworms, malaria, or typhus.

HYDROCARBONS AND CARBOHYDRATES

Carbon is an element found in all living things. Two types of carbon molecules that are essential to life are hydrocarbons and carbohydrates. **Hydrocarbons**, composed only of hydrogen and carbon, are the simplest organic molecules. The simplest of these is methane, which has one carbon atom and four hydrogen atoms. Methane is produced by the decomposition of animal or vegetable matter, and is part of petroleum and natural gas. **Carbohydrates** are compounds made of hydrogen, carbon, and oxygen. There are three types of these macromolecules (large molecules):

1. **Sugars** are soluble in water and, although they have less energy than fats, provide energy more quickly.
2. **Starches**, insoluble in water, are long chains of glucose that act as reserve substances. Potatoes and cereals are valuable foods because they are rich in starch. Animals retain glucose in their cells as glycogen, a special type of starch.
3. **Cellulose**, composed of glucose chains, makes up the cells and tissues of plants. It is one of the most common organic materials.

> **Review Video: Basics of Hydrocarbons**
> Visit mometrix.com/academy and enter code: 824749

LIPIDS, PROTEINS, AND NUCLEIC ACIDS

Besides hydrocarbons and carbohydrates, there are three other types of carbon molecules that are essential to life: lipids, proteins, and nucleic acids. **Lipids** are compounds that are insoluble or only partially soluble in water. There are three main types: fats, which act as an energy reserve for organisms; phospholipids, which are one of the essential components of cell membranes; and steroids such as cholesterol and estrogen, which are very important to metabolism. **Proteins** are complex substances that make up almost half the dry weight of animal bodies. These molecules contain hydrogen, carbon, oxygen, and other elements, chiefly nitrogen and sulfur. Proteins make up muscle fibers and, as enzymes, act as catalysts. **Nucleic acids** are large molecules (polymers) composed of a large number of simpler molecules (nucleotides). Each one has a sugar containing five carbons (pentose), a phosphorous compound (phosphate group), and a nitrogen compound (nitrogenated base). Nucleic acids facilitate perpetuation of the species because they carry genetic information as DNA and RNA.

Copyright © Mometrix Media. You have been licensed one copy of this document for personal use only. Any other reproduction or redistribution is strictly prohibited. All rights reserved. This content is provided for test preparation purposes only and does not imply an endorsement by Mometrix of any particular political, scientific, or religious point of view.

Cell

The **cell** is the basic organizational unit of all living things. Each piece within a cell has a function that helps organisms grow and survive. There are many different types of cells, but cells are unique to each type of organism. The one thing that all cells have in common is a **membrane**, which is comparable to a semi-permeable plastic bag. The membrane is composed of phospholipids. There are also some **transport holes**, which are proteins that help certain molecules and ions move in and out of the cell. The cell is filled with a fluid called **cytoplasm** or cytosol. Within the cell are a variety of **organelles**, groups of complex molecules that help a cell survive, each with its own unique membrane that has a different chemical makeup from the cell membrane. The larger the cell, the more organelles it will need to live.

> **Review Video: Difference Between Plant and Animal Cells**
> Visit mometrix.com/academy and enter code: 115568
>
> **Review Video: An Introduction to Cellular Biology**
> Visit mometrix.com/academy and enter code: 629967
>
> **Review Video: Cell Structure**
> Visit mometrix.com/academy and enter code: 591293

Nucleus and Mitochondria in Eukaryotic Cells

Eukaryotic cells have a nucleus, a big dark spot floating somewhere in the center that acts like the brain of the cell by controlling eating, movement, and reproduction. A **nuclear envelope** surrounds the nucleus and its contents, but allows RNA and proteins to pass through. **Chromatin**, made up of DNA, RNA, and nuclear proteins, is present in the nucleus. The nucleus also contains a nucleolus made of RNA and protein. **Mitochondria** are very small organelles that take in nutrients, break them down, and create energy for the cell through a process called cellular respiration. There might be thousands of mitochondria depending on the cell's purpose. A muscle cell needs more energy for movement than a cell that transmits nerve impulses, for example. Mitochondria have two membranes: a **cover** and the **inner cristae** that folds over many times to increase the surface work area. The fluid inside the mitochondria, the matrix, is filled with water and enzymes that take food molecules and combine them with oxygen so they can be digested.

> **Review Video: Mitochondria**
> Visit mometrix.com/academy and enter code: 444287
>
> **Review Video: Cellular Energy Production**
> Visit mometrix.com/academy and enter code: 743401
>
> **Review Video: Cell Functions**
> Visit mometrix.com/academy and enter code: 883787

Chloroplasts of Plant Cells

Chloroplasts, which make plants green, are the food producers of a plant cell. They differ from an animal cell's mitochondria, which break down sugars and nutrients. **Photosynthesis** occurs when the energy from the sun hits a chloroplast and the chlorophyll uses that energy to combine carbon dioxide and water to make sugars and oxygen. The nutrition and oxygen obtained from plants makes them the basis of all life on earth. A chloroplast has two membranes to contain and protect the inner parts. The **stroma** is an area inside the chloroplast where reactions occur and starches are created. A **thylakoid** has chlorophyll molecules on its surface, and a stack of thylakoids is called

Copyright © Mometrix Media. You have been licensed one copy of this document for personal use only. Any other reproduction or redistribution is strictly prohibited. All rights reserved.
This content is provided for test preparation purposes only and does not imply an endorsement by Mometrix of any particular political, scientific, or religious point of view.

a granum. The stacks of sacs are connected by **stromal lamellae**, which act like the skeleton of the chloroplast, keeping all the sacs a safe distance from each other and maximizing the efficiency of the organelle.

PASSIVE AND ACTIVE TRANSPORT

Passive transport within a cell does not require energy and work. For example, when there is a large concentration difference between the outside and the inside of a cell, the pressure of the greater concentration, not energy, will move molecules across the lipid bilayer into the cell. Another example of passive transport is osmosis, which is the movement of water across a membrane. Too much water in a cell can cause it to burst, so the cell moves ions in and out to help equalize the amount of water. **Active transport** is when a cell uses energy to move individual molecules across the cell membrane to maintain a proper balance. **Proteins** embedded in the lipid bilayer do most of the transport work. There are hundreds of different types of proteins because they are specific. For instance, a protein that moves glucose will not move calcium. The activity of these proteins can be stopped by inhibitors or poisons, which can destroy or plug up a protein.

> **Review Video: Passive Transport: Diffusion and Osmosis**
> Visit mometrix.com/academy and enter code: 642038

MITOTIC CELL REPLICATION

Mitosis is the duplication of a cell and all its parts, including the DNA, into two identical daughter cells. There are five phases in the life cycle of a cell:

1. **Prophase** – This is the process of duplicating everything in preparation for division.
2. **Metaphase** – The cell's different pieces align themselves for the split. The DNA lines up along a central axis and the centrioles send out specialized tubules that connect to the centromere. The centromere has two strands of a chromosome (condensed DNA) attached to it.
3. **Anaphase** – Half of the chromosomes go one way and half go another.
4. **Telophase** – When the chromosomes get to the side of the cell, the cell membrane closes in and splits the cell into two pieces. This results in two separate cells, each with half of the original DNA.
5. **Interphase** – This is the normal state of the cell, or the resting stage between divisions. During this stage, the cell duplicates nucleic acids in preparation for the next division.

> **Review Video: Mitosis**
> Visit mometrix.com/academy and enter code: 849894
>
> **Review Video: Cellular Division: Mitosis and Meiosis**
> Visit mometrix.com/academy and enter code: 109813

MICROBES

Microbes are the smallest, simplest, and most abundant organisms on earth. Their numbers are incalculable, and a microscope is required to see them. There is a huge variety of microbes, including bacteria, fungi, some algae, and protozoa. Microbes can be harmful or helpful.

Microbes can be **heterotrophic** (eat other things) or **autotrophic** (make food for themselves). They can be solitary or colonial, sexual or asexual. Examples include mold, a multi-cellular type of fungus, and yeasts, which are single-celled (but may live in colonies). A **mushroom** is a fungus that lives as a group of strands underground called hyphae that decompose leaves or bark on the

Copyright © Mometrix Media. You have been licensed one copy of this document for personal use only. Any other reproduction or redistribution is strictly prohibited. All rights reserved.
This content is provided for test preparation purposes only and does not imply an endorsement by Mometrix of any particular political, scientific, or religious point of view.

ground. When it reproduces, it develops a mushroom whose cap contains spores. **Mold** is a type of zygote fungi that reproduces with a stalk, but releases zygospores. **Good bacteria** can be those that help plants absorb the nitrogen needed for growth or help grazing animals break down the cellulose in plants. Some **bad bacteria** are killed by the penicillin developed from a fungus.

ROOTS, STEMS, AND LEAVES

Roots are structures designed to pull water and minerals from soil or water. In large plants such as trees, the roots usually go deep into the ground to not only reach the water, but also to support and stabilize the tree. There are some plant species that have roots above ground, and there are also plants called epiphytes that live in trees with their roots clinging to the branches. Some roots, like carrots and turnips, serve as food. Roots are classified as **primary** and **lateral** (like a trunk and branches). The **apical meristem** is the tip of a root or shoot that helps the plant increase in length. **Root hairs** are fuzzy root extensions that help with the absorption of water and nutrients. The majority of the plant above ground is made up of the stems (trunk and branches) and leaves. **Stems** transport food and water and act as support structures. **Leaves** are the site for photosynthesis, and are connected to the rest of the plant by a vascular system.

GYMNOSPERMS, CYCADS, AND CONIFERS

Gymnosperms are plants with vascular systems and seeds but no flowers (flowers are an evolutionary advancement). The function of the seed is to ensure offspring can be produced by the plant by providing a protective coating that lets the plant survive for long periods until it germinates. It also stores food for the new plant to use until it can make its own. Seeds can be spread over a wide area. **Cycads** are sturdy plants with big, waxy fronds that make them look like ferns or palms. They can survive in harsh conditions if there is warm weather. For reproduction, they have big cones located in the center of the plant. The female plant grows a fruit in the middle of the stem. **Conifers** are trees that thrive in northern latitudes and have cones. Examples of conifers are pine, cedar, redwood, and spruce. Conifers are evergreens because they have needles that take full advantage of the sun year-round. They are also very tall and strong because of the chemical substance xylem in their systems.

ANGIOSPERMS

Angiosperms are plants that have flowers. This is advantageous because the plant's seeds and pollen can be spread not only by gravity and wind, but also by insects and animals. Flowers are able to attract organisms that can help pollinate the plant and distribute seeds. Some flowering plants also produce fruit. When an animal eats the fruit, the plant seeds within will be spread far and wide in the animal's excrement. There are two kinds of angiosperm seeds: monocotyledons (monocots) and dicotyledons (dicots). A **cotyledon** is the seed leaf or food package for the developing plant. **Monocots** are simple flowering plants such as grasses, corn, palm trees, and lilies. They always have three petals on their flowers, and their leaves are long strands (like a palm frond). A **dicot** has seeds with two cotyledons, or two seed leaves of food. Most everyday flowers are dicots with four or five petals and extremely complex leaves with veins. Examples include roses, sunflowers, cacti, and cherry trees.

ARTHROPODS

Arthropods have a number of unique characteristics:

- They have an **exoskeleton** (outside instead of inside).
- They **molt**. As the arthropod grows, it must shed its old shell and grow a new one.
- They have several **legs**, which are jointed.

Copyright © Mometrix Media. You have been licensed one copy of this document for personal use only. Any other reproduction or redistribution is strictly prohibited. All rights reserved. This content is provided for test preparation purposes only and does not imply an endorsement by Mometrix of any particular political, scientific, or religious point of view.

- Their advanced **nervous systems** allow for hunting, moving around, finding a mate, and learning new behaviors for adaptation.
- They develop through **metamorphosis**. As arthropods develop, they change body shape. There are two types of metamorphosis:
  - *Complete* – The entire body shape changes. An example is butterflies, which change from worm-like larvae to insects with wings.
  - *Gradual* – The arthropod starts off small with no wings, and then molts and grows wings. Example: Grasshoppers.

Arthropods include spiders, crustaceans, and the enormous insect species (26 orders) called uniramians. Ranging from fleas to mosquitoes, beetles, dragonflies, aphids, bees, flies, and many more, uniramians have exoskeletons made of chitin, compound eyes, complex digestive systems, and usually six legs. This group is extremely diverse. Some can fly, some have toxins or antennae, and some can make wax, silk, or honey.

REPTILES

One group of vertebrates is the **reptile**. This group includes:

- **Crocodilia** – This is a group of reptiles that can grow quite large, and includes alligators and crocodiles. Normally found near the water in warmer climates, Crocodilia might be more closely related to birds than other reptiles.
- **Squamata** – This is the order of reptiles that includes snakes and lizards. Snakes are special because they have no legs and no ears. They feel vibrations, smell with their tongues, have specialized scales, and can unhinge their jaws to swallow prey that is larger than they are. Like snakes, lizards have scales, but they differ in that they have legs, can dig, can climb trees, and can grab things.
- **Chelonia** – This is the order of reptiles that includes turtles and tortoises. It is a special group because its members have shells. Different varieties live in forests, water, and deserts, or anywhere the climate is warm enough. They also live a long time, up to hundreds of years. Turtles are typically found near water and tortoises on land, even dry areas.

REPRODUCTION IN MAMMALS

When classified according to how they reproduce, there are three types of mammals:

1. **Monotremes** are rare mammals that lay eggs. These were the first mammals, and are more closely related to reptiles than other mammals. Examples include the duck-billed platypus and the spiny anteater.
2. **Marsupials** are special mammals. They give birth to live young, but the babies mature in pouches, where they are carried and can feed on milk. Many are found in Australia. The isolation of this island continent prevented placental mammals from taking hold. Examples of marsupials include kangaroos, possums, and koalas.
3. **Placental mammals** give birth from the females' placenta to live young. The young may be able to walk immediately, or they may need to be carried. They are still dependent on parental care for at least a short time. Placental mammals are the dominant form of mammals. Members of this group include cetaceans such as whales and dolphins, which are mammals that evolved but returned to the ocean.

RESPIRATORY SYSTEM

The **respiratory system** exchanges gases with the environment. Amphibians exchange gases through their moist skin, and fish use gills, but mammals, birds, and reptiles have lungs. The human

Copyright © Mometrix Media. You have been licensed one copy of this document for personal use only. Any other reproduction or redistribution is strictly prohibited. All rights reserved.
This content is provided for test preparation purposes only and does not imply an endorsement by Mometrix of any particular political, scientific, or religious point of view.

respiratory system is made up of the nose, mouth, pharynx, trachea, and two lungs. The purpose of the respiratory system is to bring oxygen into the body and expel carbon dioxide. The respiratory system can inhale viruses, bacteria, and dangerous chemicals, so it is vulnerable to toxins and diseases such as pneumonia, which causes the lungs to fill with fluid until they cannot take in enough oxygen to support the body. **Emphysema**, often caused by smoking tobacco, destroys the tissues in the lungs, which cannot be regenerated. The respiratory system interacts with the **digestive system** in that the mouth and pharynx are used to swallow food and drink, as well as to breathe. It interacts with the circulatory system in that it provides fresh oxygen through blood vessels that pass through the lungs. This oxygen is then carried by the circulatory system throughout the body.

> **Review Video: Respiratory System**
> Visit mometrix.com/academy and enter code: 783075

SKELETAL SYSTEM

The human body has an **endoskeleton**, meaning it is inside the body. It is made up of bones instead of the hard plate of exoskeletons or fluids in tubes, which comprise the hydrostatic system of the starfish. The purpose of the skeleton is to support the body, provide a framework to which the muscles and organs can connect, and protect the inner organs. The skull protects the all-important brain and the ribs protect the internal organs from impact. The skeletal system interacts with the muscular system to help the body move, and softer cartilage works with the calcified bone to allow smooth movement of the body. The skeletal system also interacts with the circulatory system in that the marrow inside the bones helps produce both white and red blood cells.

> **Review Video: Skeletal System**
> Visit mometrix.com/academy and enter code: 256447

NERVOUS SYSTEM

The **nervous system** is divided into two parts: the **central nervous system** (brain and spinal cord) and the **peripheral nervous system** (a network of billions of neurons of different types throughout the entire body). The neurons are connected end to end, and transmit electrical impulses to each other. **Efferent neurons** send impulses from the central system to the limbs and organs. **Afferent neurons** receive sensory information and transmit it back to the central system. The nervous system is concerned with **senses and action**. In other words, it senses something and then acts upon it. An example is a predator sensing prey and attacking it. The nervous system also automatically senses activity inside the body and reacts to stimuli. For example, the first bite of a meal sets the whole digestive system into motion. The nervous system **interacts** with every other system in the body because all the tissues and organs need instruction, even when individuals are not aware of any activity occurring. For instance, the endocrine system is constantly working to produce hormones or adrenaline as needed.

> **Review Video: The Nervous System**
> Visit mometrix.com/academy and enter code: 708428

GENETICS, GENES, AND CHROMOSOMES

Genetics is the science devoted to the study of how characteristics are transmitted from one generation to another. In the 1800s, Gregor Mendel discovered the three laws of heredity that explain how genetics works. Genes are the hereditary units of material that are transmitted from one generation to the next. They are capable of undergoing mutations, can be recombined with other genes, and can determine the nature of an organism, including its color, shape, and size.

Copyright © Mometrix Media. You have been licensed one copy of this document for personal use only. Any other reproduction or redistribution is strictly prohibited. All rights reserved. This content is provided for test preparation purposes only and does not imply an endorsement by Mometrix of any particular political, scientific, or religious point of view.

Genotype is the genetic makeup of an individual based on one or more characteristics, while phenotype is the external manifestation of the genotype. For example, genotype determines hair color genes, whereas phenotype is the actual color of the hair observed. **Chromosomes** are the structures inside the nucleus of a cell made up primarily of deoxyribonucleic acid (DNA) and proteins. The chromosomes carry the genes. The numbers vary according to the species, but they are always the same for each species. For example, the human has 46 chromosomes, and the water lily has 112.

> **Review Video: Gene & Alleles**
> Visit mometrix.com/academy and enter code: 363997
>
> **Review Video: Genetic vs. Environmental Traits**
> Visit mometrix.com/academy and enter code: 750684
>
> **Review Video: Chromosomes**
> Visit mometrix.com/academy and enter code: 132083

MENDEL'S CONTRIBUTIONS TO GENETICS

Johann Gregor Mendel is known as the father of **genetics**. Mendel was an Austrian monk who performed thousands of experiments involving the breeding of the common pea plant in the garden of his monastery. Mendel kept detailed records including seed color, pod color, seed type, flower color, and plant height for eight years and published his work in 1865. Unfortunately, his work was largely ignored until the early 1900s. Mendel's work showed that genes come in pairs and that dominant and recessive traits are inherited independently of each other. His work established the law of segregation, the law of independent assortment, and the law of dominance.

DARWIN'S CONTRIBUTIONS TO THE THEORY OF EVOLUTION

Charles Darwin's theory of evolution is the unifying concept in biology today. From 1831 to 1836, Darwin traveled as a naturalist on a five-year voyage on the *H.M.S. Beagle* around the tip of South America and to the Galápagos Islands. He studied finches, took copious amounts of meticulous notes, and collected thousands of plant and animal specimens. He collected 13 species of finches each with a unique bill for a distinct food source, which led him to believe, due to similarities between the finches, that the finches shared a common ancestor. The similarities and differences of fossils of extinct rodents and modern mammal fossils led him to believe that the mammals had changed over time. Darwin believed that these changes were the result of random genetic changes called mutations. He believed that mutations could be beneficial and eventually result in a different organism over time. In 1859, in his first book, *On the Origin of Species*, Darwin proposed that natural selection was the means by which adaptations would arise over time. He coined the term "natural selection" and said that it is the mechanism of evolution. Because variety exists among individuals of a species, he stated that those individuals must compete for the same limited resources. Some would die, and others would survive. According to Darwin, evolution is a slow, gradual process. In 1871, Darwin published his second book, *Descent of Man, and Selection in Relation to Sex*, in which he discussed the evolution of man.

> **Review Video: Darwin's Contributions to Theory of Evolution**
> Visit mometrix.com/academy and enter code: 898980

CONTRIBUTION TO GENETICS MADE BY ALFRED HERSHEY AND MARTHA CHASE

Alfred Hershey and Martha Chase did a series of experiments in 1952 known as the **Hershey-Chase experiments**. These experiments showed that deoxyribonucleic acid (DNA), not protein, is the

Copyright © Mometrix Media. You have been licensed one copy of this document for personal use only. Any other reproduction or redistribution is strictly prohibited. All rights reserved. This content is provided for test preparation purposes only and does not imply an endorsement by Mometrix of any particular political, scientific, or religious point of view.

genetic material that transfers information for inheritance. The Hershey-Chase experiments used a bacteriophage, a virus that infects bacteria, to infect the bacteria *Escherichia coli.* The bacteriophage T2 is basically a small piece of DNA enclosed in a protein coating. The DNA contains phosphorus, and the protein coating contains sulfur. In the first set of experiments, the T2 was marked with radioactive phosphorus-32. In the second set of experiments, the T2 was marked with radioactive sulfur-35. For both sets of experiments, after the *E. coli* was infected by the T2, the *E. coli* was isolated using a centrifuge. In the first set of experiments, the radioactive isotope (P-32) was found in the *E. coli*, showing that the genetic information was transferred by the DNA. In the second set of experiments, the radioactive isotope (S-35) was not found in the *E. coli*, showing that the genetic information was not transferred by the protein as was previously thought. Hershey and Chase conducted further experiments allowing the bacteria from the first set of experiments to reproduce, and the offspring was also found to contain the radioactive isotope (P-32) further confirming that the DNA transferred the genetic material.

CHAPTER QUIZ

1. Living organisms can be categorized into eight major classifications: domain, kingdom, phylum, class, order, family, genus, and species. How many kingdoms are there?

    a. Four
    b. Five
    c. Six
    d. Seven

2. What does it mean for an animal to be oviparous?

    a. It stands on four legs.
    b. It is cold-blooded.
    c. It is warm-blooded.
    d. It lays eggs.

3. A stack of thylakoids is known as which of the following?

    a. Granum
    b. Callosum
    c. Lamellae
    d. Chloroplast

4. Roots are classified as which of the following?

    a. Primary and secondary
    b. Medial and lateral
    c. Long or short
    d. Primary and lateral

CHAPTER QUIZ ANSWER KEY

1. C: All living creatures can be classified into one of three domains and then into one of six kingdoms: Eubacteria, Archaebacteria, Protista, Fungi, Plantae, and Animalia.

2. D: Fish live in water, breathe with gills, are cold-blooded, have fins and scales, and are typically oviparous, which means they lay eggs.

3. A: A chloroplast has two membranes to contain and protect the inner parts. The stroma is an area inside the chloroplast where reactions occur and starches are created. A thylakoid has chlorophyll molecules on its surface, and a stack of thylakoids is called a granum. The stacks of sacs are

Copyright © Mometrix Media. You have been licensed one copy of this document for personal use only. Any other reproduction or redistribution is strictly prohibited. All rights reserved. This content is provided for test preparation purposes only and does not imply an endorsement by Mometrix of any particular political, scientific, or religious point of view.

connected by stromal lamellae, which act like the skeleton of the chloroplast, keeping all the sacs a safe distance from each other and maximizing the efficiency of the organelle.

4. D: Roots are structures designed to pull water and minerals from soil or water. In large plants such as trees, the roots usually go deep into the ground to not only reach the water, but also to support and stabilize the tree. There are some plant species that have roots above ground, and there are also plants called epiphytes that live in trees with their roots clinging to the branches. Some roots, like carrots and turnips, serve as food. Roots are classified as primary and lateral (like a trunk and branches).

AUTOTROPHS, PRODUCERS, HERBIVORES, CARNIVORES, OMNIVORES, AND DECOMPOSERS

Energy flows in one direction: from the sun, through photosynthetic organisms such as green plants (producers) and algae (autotrophs), and then to herbivores, carnivores, and decomposers. **Autotrophs** are organisms capable of producing their own food. The organic molecules they produce are food for all other organisms (heterotrophs). **Producers** are green plants that manufacture food by photosynthesis. **Herbivores** are animals that eat only plants (deer, rabbits, etc.). Since they are the first animals to receive the energy captured by producers, herbivores are called primary consumers. **Carnivores**, or secondary consumers, are animals that eat the bodies of other animals for food. Predators (wolves, lions, etc.) kill other animals, while scavengers consume animals that are already dead from predation or natural causes (buzzards). **Omnivores** are animals that eat both plants and other animals (humans). **Decomposers** include saprophytic fungi and bacteria that break down the complex structures of the bodies of living things into simpler forms that can be used by other living things. This recycling process releases energy from organic molecules.

ABIOTIC FACTORS AND BIOTIC FACTORS

Abiotic factors are the physical and chemical factors in the environment that are nonliving but upon which the growth and survival of living organisms depends. These factors can determine the types of plants and animals that will establish themselves and thrive in a particular area. Abiotic factors include:

- Light intensity available for photosynthesis
- Temperature range
- Available moisture
- Type of rock substratum
- Type of minerals
- Type of atmospheric gases
- Relative acidity (pH) of the system

Biotic factors are the living components of the environment that affect, directly or indirectly, the ecology of an area, possibly limiting the type and number of resident species. The relationships of predator/prey, producer/consumer, and parasite/host can define a community. Biotic factors include:

- Population levels of each species
- The food requirements of each species
- The interactions between species
- The wastes produced

Copyright © Mometrix Media. You have been licensed one copy of this document for personal use only. Any other reproduction or redistribution is strictly prohibited. All rights reserved.
This content is provided for test preparation purposes only and does not imply an endorsement by Mometrix of any particular political, scientific, or religious point of view.

HOW PLANTS MANUFACTURE FOOD

Plants are the only organisms capable of transforming **inorganic material** from the environment into **organic matter** by using water and solar energy. This transformation is made possible by chloroplasts, flat structures inside plant cells. **Chloroplasts**, located primarily in leaves, contain chlorophyll (the pigment capable of absorbing light and storing it in chemical compounds), DNA, ribosomes, and numerous enzymes. Chloroplasts are surrounded by a membrane. The leaves of plants are the main producers of oxygen, which helps purify the air. The **chlorophyll** in chloroplasts is responsible for the light, or luminous, phase of photosynthesis. The energy it absorbs breaks down water absorbed through the roots into hydrogen and oxygen to form ATP molecules that store energy. In the dark phase, when the plant has no light, the energy molecules are used to attach carbon dioxide to water and form glucose, a sugar.

PRODUCERS, CONSUMERS, AND DECOMPOSERS

The **food chain**, or food web, is a series of events that happens when one organism consumes another to survive. Every organism is involved in dozens of connections with others, so what happens to one affects the environment of the others. In the food chain, there are three main categories:

- **Producers** – Plants and vegetables are at the beginning of the food chain because they take energy from the sun and make food for themselves through photosynthesis. They are food sources for other organisms.
- **Consumers** – There are three levels of consumers: the organisms that eat plants (primary consumers, or herbivores); the organisms that eat the primary consumers (secondary consumers, or carnivores); and, in some ecosystems, the organisms that eat both plants and animals (tertiary consumers, or omnivores).
- **Decomposers** – These are the organisms that eat dead things or waste matter and return the nutrients to the soil, thus returning essential molecules to the producers and completing the cycle.

> **Review Video: Food Webs**
> Visit mometrix.com/academy and enter code: 853254

SYSTEM OF CLASSIFICATION FOR LIVING ORGANISMS

The main characteristic by which living organisms are classified is the degree to which they are **related**, not the degree to which they resemble each other. The science of classification is called **taxonomy**. This classification is challenging since the division lines between groups is not always clear. Some animals have characteristics of two separate groups. The current system of taxonomy involves placing an organism into a **domain** (Bacteria, Archaea, and Eukarya), and then into a **kingdom** (Eubacteria, Archaeabacteria, Protista, Fungi, Plantae, and Animalia). The kingdoms are divided into phyla, then classes, then orders, then families, and finally genuses and species. For example, the family cat is in the domain of eukaryotes, the kingdom of animals, the phylum of chordates, the class of mammals, the order of carnivores, the family of felidae, and the genus of felis. All species of living beings can be identified with Latin scientific names that are assigned by the worldwide binomial system. The genus name comes first, and is followed by the name of the species. The family cat is *felis domesticus*.

> **Review Video: Biological Classification Systems**
> Visit mometrix.com/academy and enter code: 736052

Copyright © Mometrix Media. You have been licensed one copy of this document for personal use only. Any other reproduction or redistribution is strictly prohibited. All rights reserved. This content is provided for test preparation purposes only and does not imply an endorsement by Mometrix of any particular political, scientific, or religious point of view.

PROPERTIES THAT CONTRIBUTE TO EARTH'S LIFE-SUSTAINING SYSTEM

Life on earth is dependent on:

- All three states of **water** – gas (water vapor), liquid, and solid (ice)
- A variety of forms of **carbon**, the basis of life (carbon-based units)
- In the atmosphere, carbon dioxide, in the forms of methane and black carbon soot, produces the **greenhouse effect** that provides a habitable atmosphere.
- The earth's **atmosphere and electromagnetic field**, which shield the surface from harmful radiation and allow useful radiation to go through.
- The **earth's relationship to the sun and the moon**, which creates the four seasons and the cycles of plant and animal life.
- The combination of **water, carbon, and nutrients** that provides sustenance for life and regulates the climate system in a habitable temperature range with non-toxic air.

CHAPTER QUIZ

1. Which of the following is NOT an abiotic factor that directly or indirectly affects an environment?

  a. Available moisture
  b. Light intensity
  c. Relative acidity
  d. The wastes produced

CHAPTER QUIZ ANSWER KEY

1. D: Abiotic factors are the physical and chemical factors in the environment that are nonliving but upon which the growth and survival of living organisms depends. These factors can determine the types of plants and animals that will establish themselves and thrive in a particular area. Abiotic factors include:

- Light intensity available for photosynthesis
- Temperature range
- Available moisture
- Type of rock substratum
- Type of minerals
- Type of atmospheric gases
- Relative acidity (pH) of the system

Biotic factors are the living components of the environment that directly or indirectly affect the ecology of an area, possibly limiting the type and number of resident species. The relationships of predator and prey, producer and consumer, and parasite and host can define a community. Biotic factors include:

- Population levels of each species
- The food requirements of each species
- The interactions between species
- The wastes produced

Copyright © Mometrix Media. You have been licensed one copy of this document for personal use only. Any other reproduction or redistribution is strictly prohibited. All rights reserved. This content is provided for test preparation purposes only and does not imply an endorsement by Mometrix of any particular political, scientific, or religious point of view.

Physical Science

LAWS OF THERMODYNAMICS

The **laws of thermodynamics** are generalized principles dealing with energy and heat.

- The **zeroth law** of thermodynamics states that two objects in thermodynamic equilibrium with a third object are also in equilibrium with each other. Being in thermodynamic equilibrium basically means that different objects are at the same temperature.
- The **first law** deals with conservation of energy. It states that neither mass nor energy can be destroyed; only converted from one form to another.
- The **second law** states that the entropy (the amount of energy in a system that is no longer available for work or the amount of disorder in a system) of an isolated system can only increase. The second law also states that heat is not transferred from a lower-temperature system to a higher-temperature one unless additional work is done.
- The **third law** of thermodynamics states that as temperature approaches absolute zero, entropy approaches a constant minimum. It also states that a system cannot be cooled to absolute zero.

> **Review Video: Laws of Thermodynamics**
> Visit mometrix.com/academy and enter code: 253607

HEAT AND TEMPERATURE

Heat is energy transfer (other than direct work) from one body or system to another due to thermal contact. Everything tends to become less organized and less orderly over time (**entropy**). In all energy transfers, therefore, the overall result is that the energy is spread out uniformly. This transfer of heat energy from hotter to cooler objects is accomplished by conduction, radiation, or convection. **Temperature** is a measurement of an object's stored heat energy. More specifically, temperature is the average kinetic energy of an object's particles. When the temperature of an object increases and its atoms move faster, kinetic energy also increases. Temperature is not energy since it changes and is not conserved. Thermometers are used to measure temperature.

MASS, WEIGHT, VOLUME, DENSITY, AND SPECIFIC GRAVITY

Mass — Mass is a measure of the amount of substance in an object.

Weight — Weight is a measure of the gravitational pull of Earth on an object.

Volume — Volume is a measure of the amount of space occupied. There are many formulas to determine volume. For example, the volume of a cube is the length of one side cubed (a^3) and the volume of a rectangular prism is length times width times height ($l \times w \times h$). The volume of an irregular shape can be determined by how much water it displaces.

Copyright © Mometrix Media. You have been licensed one copy of this document for personal use only. Any other reproduction or redistribution is strictly prohibited. All rights reserved.
This content is provided for test preparation purposes only and does not imply an endorsement by Mometrix of any particular political, scientific, or religious point of view.

Density — Density is a measure of the amount of mass per unit volume. The formula to find density is mass divided by volume (D = m/V). It is expressed in terms of mass per cubic unit (e.g., grams per cubic centimeter $\frac{g}{cm^3}$).

Specific gravity — This is a measure of the ratio of a substance's density compared to the density of water.

| Review Video: **Mass, Weight, Volume, Density, and Specific Gravity** |
| Visit mometrix.com/academy and enter code: 920570 |

THERMAL CONTACT

Thermal contact refers to energy transferred to a body by a means other than work. A system in thermal contact with another can exchange energy with it through the process of heat transfer. Thermal contact does not necessarily involve direct physical contact. **Heat** is energy that can be transferred from one body or system to another without work being done. Everything tends to become less organized and less useful over time (entropy). In all energy transfers, therefore, the overall result is that the heat is spread out so that objects are in thermodynamic equilibrium and the heat can no longer be transferred without additional work.

MODELS FOR FLOW OF ELECTRIC CHARGE

Models that can be used to explain the **flow of electric current, potential, and circuits** include water, gravity, and roller coasters. For example, just as a mass can have a potential for energy based on its location, so can a charge within an electrical field. Just as a force is required to move an object uphill, a force is also required to move a charge from a low to high potential. Another example is water. Water does not flow when it is level. If it is lifted to a point and then placed on a downward path, it will flow. A roller coaster car requires work to be performed to transport it to a point where it has potential energy (the top of a hill). Once there, gravity provides the force for it to flow (move) downward. If either path is broken, the flow or movement stops or is not completed.

ATOMIC STRUCTURES

MAGNETIC FIELDS

The motions of subatomic structures (nuclei and electrons) produce a **magnetic field**. It is the direction of the spin and orbit that indicates the direction of the field. The strength of a magnetic field is known as the **magnetic moment**. As electrons spin and orbit a nucleus, they produce a magnetic field. Pairs of electrons that spin and orbit in opposite directions cancel each other out, creating a net magnetic field of zero. Materials that have an unpaired electron are magnetic. Those with a weak attractive force are referred to as paramagnetic materials, while ferromagnetic materials have a strong attractive force. A diamagnetic material has electrons that are paired and, therefore, does not typically have a magnetic moment. There are, however, some diamagnetic materials that have a weak magnetic field.

ELECTRIC CHARGES

The attractive force between the electrons and the nucleus is called the **electric force**. A positive (+) charge or a negative (−) charge creates a field of sorts in the empty space around it, which is known as an **electric field**. The direction of a positive charge is away from the electric field and the direction of a negative charge is towards it. An electron within the force of the field is pulled towards a positive charge because an electron has a negative charge. A particle with a positive charge is pushed away, or repelled, by another positive charge. Like charges repel each other and

Copyright © Mometrix Media. You have been licensed one copy of this document for personal use only. Any other reproduction or redistribution is strictly prohibited. All rights reserved. This content is provided for test preparation purposes only and does not imply an endorsement by Mometrix of any particular political, scientific, or religious point of view.

opposite charges attract. Lines of force show the paths of charges. The **electric force** between two objects is directly proportional to the product of the charge magnitudes and inversely proportional to the square of the distance between the two objects. **Electric charge** is measured with the unit Coulomb (C). It is the amount of charge moved in one second by a steady current of one ampere (1C = 1A × 1s).

Review Video: Electric Charge
Visit mometrix.com/academy and enter code: 323587

ELECTRIC CURRENT MOVEMENT THROUGH CIRCUITS

Electric current is the sustained flow of electrons that are part of an electric charge moving along a path in a circuit. This differs from a static electric charge, which is a constant non-moving charge rather than a continuous flow. The **rate of flow of electric charge** is expressed using the ampere (amp or A) and can be measured using an ammeter. A current of 1 ampere means that 1 coulomb of charge passes through a given area every second. Electric charges typically only move from areas of high electric potential to areas of low electric potential. To get charges to flow into a high potential area, you must connect it to an area of higher potential by introducing a battery or other voltage source.

SIMPLE CIRCUITS

Movement of electric charge along a path between areas of high electric potential and low electric potential, with a resistor or load device between them, is the definition of a **simple circuit**. It is a closed conducting path between the high and low potential points, such as the positive and negative terminals on a battery. One example of a circuit is the flow from one terminal of a car battery to the other. The electrolyte solution of water and sulfuric acid provides work in chemical form to start the flow. A frequently used classroom example of circuits involves using a D cell (1.5 V) battery, a small light bulb, and a piece of copper wire to create a circuit to light the bulb.

Review Video: Resistance of Electric Currents
Visit mometrix.com/academy and enter code: 668423

MAGNETS

A **magnet** is a piece of metal, such as iron, steel, or magnetite (lodestone) that can affect another substance within its **field of force** that has like characteristics. Magnets can either attract or repel other substances. Magnets have two **poles**: north and south. Like poles repel and opposite poles (pairs of north and south) attract. The magnetic field is a set of invisible lines representing the paths of attraction and repulsion. Magnetism can occur naturally, or ferromagnetic materials can be magnetized. Certain matter that is magnetized can retain its magnetic properties indefinitely and become a permanent magnet. Other matter can lose its magnetic properties. For example, an iron nail can be temporarily magnetized by stroking it repeatedly in the same direction using one pole of another magnet. Once magnetized, it can attract or repel other magnetically inclined materials, such as paper clips. Dropping the nail repeatedly will cause it to lose its charge.

Review Video: Magnets
Visit mometrix.com/academy and enter code: 570803

MAGNETIC FIELDS, CURRENT, AND MAGNETIC DOMAINS

A **magnetic field** can be formed not only by a magnetic material, but also by electric current flowing through a wire. When a coiled wire is attached to the two ends of a battery, for example, an electromagnet can be formed by inserting a ferromagnetic material such as an iron bar within the

Copyright © Mometrix Media. You have been licensed one copy of this document for personal use only. Any other reproduction or redistribution is strictly prohibited. All rights reserved.
This content is provided for test preparation purposes only and does not imply an endorsement by Mometrix of any particular political, scientific, or religious point of view.

coil. When electric current flows through the wire, the bar becomes a magnet. If there is no current, the magnetism is lost. A **magnetic domain** occurs when the magnetic fields of atoms are grouped and aligned. These groups form what can be thought of as miniature magnets within a material. This is what happens when an object like an iron nail is temporarily magnetized. Prior to magnetization, the organization of atoms and their various polarities are somewhat random with respect to where the north and south poles are pointing. After magnetization, a significant percentage of the poles are lined up in one direction, which is what causes the magnetic force exerted by the material.

MOTION AND DISPLACEMENT

Motion is a change in the location of an object and is the result of an unbalanced net force acting on the object. Understanding motion requires an understanding of three basic quantities: displacement, velocity, and acceleration.

When something moves from one place to another, it has undergone **displacement**. Displacement along a straight line is a very simple example of a vector quantity. If an object travels from position $x = -5$ cm to $x = 5$ cm, it has undergone a displacement of 10 cm. If it traverses the same path in the opposite direction, its displacement is -10 cm. A vector that spans the object's displacement in the direction of travel is known as a displacement vector.

> **Review Video: Displacement in Physics**
> Visit mometrix.com/academy and enter code: 236197

GRAVITATIONAL FORCE

Gravitational force is a universal force that causes every object to exert a force on every other object. The gravitational force between two objects can be described by the formula, $F = Gm_1m_2 /r^2$, where m_1 and m_2 are the masses of two objects, r is the distance between them, and G is the gravitational constant, $G = 6.672 \times 10^{-11}$ N m^2/kg^2. In order for this force to have a noticeable effect, one or both of the objects must be extremely large, so the equation is generally only used in problems involving planetary bodies. For problems involving objects on the earth being affected by earth's gravitational pull, the force of gravity is simply calculated as $F = mg$, where g is 9.81 m/s^2 toward the ground.

> **Review Video: What is Acceleration Due to Gravity?**
> Visit mometrix.com/academy and enter code: 938774

NEWTON'S FIRST TWO LAWS OF MOTION
NEWTON'S FIRST LAW

An object at rest or in motion will remain at rest or in motion unless acted upon by an external force.

This phenomenon is commonly referred to as **inertia**, the tendency of a body to remain in its present state of motion. In order for the body's state of motion to change, it must be acted on by an unbalanced force.

> **Review Video: Newton's First Law of Motion**
> Visit mometrix.com/academy and enter code: 590367

Copyright © Mometrix Media. You have been licensed one copy of this document for personal use only. Any other reproduction or redistribution is strictly prohibited. All rights reserved.
This content is provided for test preparation purposes only and does not imply an endorsement by Mometrix of any particular political, scientific, or religious point of view.

NEWTON'S SECOND LAW

An object's acceleration is **directly proportional** to the net force acting on the object and **inversely proportional** to the object's mass.

This law is generally written in equation form $F = ma$, where F is the net force acting on a body, m is the mass of the body, and a is its acceleration. Note that since the mass is always a positive quantity, the acceleration is always in the same direction as the force.

> **Review Video: Newton's Second Law of Motion**
> Visit mometrix.com/academy and enter code: 737975

SIMPLE MACHINES

Simple machines include the inclined plane, lever, wheel and axle, and pulley. These simple machines have no internal source of energy. More **complex or compound machines** can be formed from them. Simple machines provide a force known as a mechanical advantage and make it easier to accomplish a task. The **inclined plane** enables a force less than the object's weight to be used to push an object to a greater height. A **lever** enables a multiplication of force. The wheel and axle allows for movement with less resistance. Single or double **pulleys** allow for easier direction of force. The wedge and screw are forms of the inclined plane. A **wedge** turns a smaller force working over a greater distance into a larger force. The **screw** is similar to an incline that is wrapped around a shaft.

> **Review Video: Simple Machines**
> Visit mometrix.com/academy and enter code: 950789
>
> **Review Video: Simple Machines – Wheel and Axle**
> Visit mometrix.com/academy and enter code: 574045

FRICTION

Friction is a force that arises as a **resistance to motion** where two surfaces are in contact. The maximum magnitude of the frictional force (f) can be calculated as $f = F_c \mu$, where F_c is the contact force between the two objects and μ is a coefficient of friction based on the surfaces' material composition. Two types of friction are static and kinetic. To illustrate these concepts, imagine a book resting on a table. The force of its weight (W) is equal and opposite to the force of the table on the book, or the normal force (N). If we exert a small force (F) on the book, attempting to push it to one side, a frictional force (f) would arise, equal and opposite to our force. At this point, it is a **static frictional force** because the book is not moving. If we increase our force on the book, we will eventually cause it to move. At this point, the frictional force opposing us will be a **kinetic frictional force**. Generally, the kinetic frictional force is lower than static frictional force (because

Copyright © Mometrix Media. You have been licensed one copy of this document for personal use only. Any other reproduction or redistribution is strictly prohibited. All rights reserved.
This content is provided for test preparation purposes only and does not imply an endorsement by Mometrix of any particular political, scientific, or religious point of view.

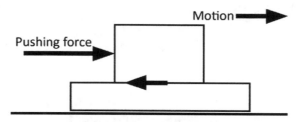

the frictional coefficient for static friction is larger), which means that the amount of force needed to maintain the movement of the book will be less than what was needed to start it moving.

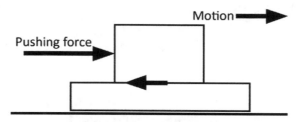

Review Video: Friction
Visit mometrix.com/academy and enter code: 716782

Review Video: Push and Pull Forces
Visit mometrix.com/academy and enter code: 104731

SOUND

Sound is a pressure disturbance that moves through a medium in the form of mechanical waves, which transfer energy from one particle to the next. Sound requires a medium to travel through, such as air, water, or other matter since it is the vibrations that transfer energy to adjacent particles, not the actual movement of particles over a great distance. Sound is transferred through the movement of atomic particles, which can be atoms or molecules. Waves of sound energy move outward in all directions from the source. Sound waves consist of compressions (particles are forced together) and rarefactions (particles move farther apart and their density decreases). A wavelength consists of one compression and one rarefaction. Different sounds have different wavelengths. Sound is a form of kinetic energy.

Review Video: Sound
Visit mometrix.com/academy and enter code: 562378

PITCH, LOUDNESS, SOUND INTENSITY, TIMBRE, AND OSCILLATION

Pitch — Pitch is the quality of sound determined by frequency. For example, a musical note can be tuned to a specific frequency. A, for instance, has a frequency of 440 Hz, which is a higher frequency than middle C. Humans can detect frequencies between about 20 Hz to 20,000 Hz.

Loudness — Loudness is a human's perception of sound intensity.

Sound intensity — Sound intensity is measured as the sound power per unit area and can be expressed in decibels.

Timbre — This is a human's perception of the type or quality of sound.

Oscillation — This is a measurement, usually of time, against a basic value, equilibrium, or rest point.

DOPPLER EFFECT

The **Doppler effect** refers to the effect the relative motion of the source of the wave and the location of the observer has on waves. The Doppler effect is easily observable in sound waves. What a person hears when a train approaches or a car honking its horn passes by are examples of the Doppler effect. The pitch of the sound is different not because the *emitted frequency* has changed, but because the *received frequency* has changed. The frequency is higher (as is the pitch) as the train

Copyright © Mometrix Media. You have been licensed one copy of this document for personal use only. Any other reproduction or redistribution is strictly prohibited. All rights reserved. This content is provided for test preparation purposes only and does not imply an endorsement by Mometrix of any particular political, scientific, or religious point of view.

approaches, the same as emitted just as it passes, and lower as the train moves away. This is because the wavelength changes. The Doppler effect can occur when an observer is stationary, and can also occur when two trains approach and pass each other. **Electromagnetic waves** are also affected in this manner. The motion of the medium can also affect the wave. For waves that do not travel in a medium, such as light waves, it is the difference in velocity that determines the outcome.

WAVES

Waves have energy and can transfer energy when they interact with matter. Although waves transfer energy, they do not transport matter. They are a disturbance of matter that transfers energy from one particle to an adjacent particle. There are many types of waves, including sound, seismic, water, light, micro, and radio waves. The two basic categories of waves are mechanical and electromagnetic. **Mechanical waves** are those that transmit energy through matter. **Electromagnetic waves** can transmit energy through a vacuum. A **transverse wave** provides a good illustration of the features of a wave, which include crests, troughs, amplitude, and wavelength.

ELECTROMAGNETIC SPECTRUM

The electromagnetic spectrum is defined by frequency (f) and wavelength (λ). Frequency is typically measured in hertz and wavelength is usually measured in meters. Because light travels at a fairly constant speed, frequency is inversely proportional to wavelength, a relationship expressed by the formula $f = c/\lambda$, where c is the speed of light (about 3.0×10^8 m/s). Frequency multiplied by wavelength equals the speed of the wave; for electromagnetic waves, this is the speed of light, with some variance for the medium in which it is traveling. Electromagnetic waves include (from largest to smallest wavelength) radio waves, microwaves, infrared radiation (radiant heat), visible light, ultraviolet radiation, x-rays, and gamma rays. The energy of electromagnetic waves is carried in packets that have a magnitude inversely proportional to the wavelength. Radio waves have a range of wavelengths, from about 10^{-3} to 10^5 meters, while their frequencies range from 10^3 to about 10^{11} Hz.

> **Review Video: Electromagnetic Spectrum**
> Visit mometrix.com/academy and enter code: 771761

VISIBLE LIGHT

Light is the portion of the electromagnetic spectrum that is visible because of its ability to stimulate the retina. It is absorbed and emitted by electrons, atoms, and molecules that move from one energy level to another. **Visible light** interacts with matter through molecular electron excitation (which occurs in the human retina) and through plasma oscillations (which occur in metals). Visible light is between ultraviolet and infrared light on the spectrum. The wavelengths of visible light cover a range from 380 nm (violet) to 760 nm (red). Different wavelengths correspond to different colors.

> **Review Video: What is Light?**
> Visit mometrix.com/academy and enter code: 900556

REFLECTION AND REFRACTION

Reflection is the rebound of a light wave from a surface back toward the medium from where it came. A light wave that hits a reflecting surface at a 90-degree angle retraces its original path back to its source. Striking the surface at any other angle results in reflection of the wave at an angle in the opposite direction. Reflectance is the amount of light a material reflects; metals have high reflectance. The smoother a surface, the higher its reflectance. **Refraction** is the change in the

Copyright © Mometrix Media. You have been licensed one copy of this document for personal use only. Any other reproduction or redistribution is strictly prohibited. All rights reserved. This content is provided for test preparation purposes only and does not imply an endorsement by Mometrix of any particular political, scientific, or religious point of view.

direction of a light wave when it passes through a transparent medium with a different optical density from the one in which the wave had been traveling. This results in a change in the wave's velocity. The ratio of the sine of the angle of the incoming ray to the sine of the angle of refraction is equal to the ratio of the speed of light in the original medium to the speed of light in the refracting medium.

$$\frac{\sin \theta_{in}}{\sin \theta_{ref}} = \frac{v_{in}}{v_{ref}}$$

Review Video: Reflection, Transmission, and Absorption of Light
Visit mometrix.com/academy and enter code: 109410

CHAPTER QUIZ

1. Which law of thermodynamics states that the entropy of an isolated system can only increase?

 a. Zeroth
 b. First
 c. Second
 d. Third

2. Energy transferred to a body by a means other than work refers to which of the following?

 a. Entropy
 b. Thermal contact
 c. Enthalpy
 d. Diffusion

3. A human's perception of the type or quality of sound is known as:

 a. Pitch.
 b. Timbre.
 c. Sound intensity.
 d. Oscillation.

CHAPTER QUIZ ANSWER KEY

1. C: The laws of thermodynamics are generalized principles dealing with energy and heat.

- The zeroth law of thermodynamics states that two objects in thermodynamic equilibrium with a third object are also in equilibrium with each other. Being in thermodynamic equilibrium basically means that different objects are at the same temperature.
- The first law deals with conservation of energy. It states that neither mass nor energy can be destroyed, only converted from one form to another.
- The second law states that the entropy (the amount of disorder in a system or the amount of energy in a system that is no longer available for work) of an isolated system can only increase. The second law also states that heat is not transferred from a lower-temperature system to a higher-temperature one unless additional work is done.
- The third law of thermodynamics states that, as temperature approaches absolute zero, entropy approaches a constant minimum. It also states that a system cannot be cooled to absolute zero.

Copyright © Mometrix Media. You have been licensed one copy of this document for personal use only. Any other reproduction or redistribution is strictly prohibited. All rights reserved. This content is provided for test preparation purposes only and does not imply an endorsement by Mometrix of any particular political, scientific, or religious point of view.

2. B: Thermal contact refers to energy transferred to a body by a means other than work. A system in thermal contact with another can exchange energy with it through the process of heat transfer.

3. B: Below are the definitions for pitch, loudness, sound intensity, timbre, and oscillation:

- Pitch is the quality of sound determined by frequency. For example, a musical note can be tuned to a specific frequency. The musical note *A*, for instance, has a frequency of 440 Hz, which is a higher frequency than middle *C*. Humans can detect frequencies between about 20 Hz and 20,000 Hz.
- Loudness is a human's perception of sound intensity.
- Sound intensity is measured as the sound power per unit area and can be expressed in decibels.
- Timbre is a human's perception of the type or quality of sound.
- Oscillation is a measurement, usually of time, against a basic value, equilibrium, or rest point.

PAST ATOMIC MODELS AND THEORIES

There have been many revisions to theories regarding the structure of **atoms** and their **particles**. Part of the challenge in developing an understanding of matter is that atoms and their particles are too small to be seen. It is believed that the first conceptualization of the atom was developed by **Democritus** in 400 B.C. Some of the more notable models are the solid sphere or billiard ball model postulated by John Dalton, the plum pudding or raisin bun model by J.J. Thomson, the planetary or nuclear model by Ernest Rutherford, the Bohr or orbit model by Niels Bohr, and the electron cloud or quantum mechanical model by Louis de Broglie and Erwin Schrodinger. Rutherford directed the alpha scattering experiment that discounted the plum pudding model. The shortcoming of the Bohr model was the belief that electrons orbited in fixed rather than changing ecliptic orbits.

> **Review Video: Atomic Models**
> Visit mometrix.com/academy and enter code: 434851

MODELS OF ATOMS

Atoms are extremely small. A hydrogen atom is about 5×10^{-8} mm in diameter. According to some estimates, five trillion hydrogen atoms could fit on the head of a pin. **Atomic radius** refers to the average distance between the nucleus and the outermost electron. Models of atoms that include the proton, nucleus, and electrons typically show the electrons very close to the nucleus and revolving around it, similar to how the Earth orbits the sun. However, another model relates the Earth as the nucleus and its atmosphere as electrons, which is the basis of the term "**electron cloud**." Another description is that electrons swarm around the nucleus. It should be noted that these atomic models are not to scale. A more accurate representation would be a nucleus with a diameter of about 2 cm in a stadium. The electrons would be in the bleachers. This model is similar to the not-to-scale solar system model. In reference to the periodic table, atomic radius increases as energy levels are added and decreases as more protons are added (because they pull the electrons closer to the nucleus). Essentially, atomic radius increases toward the left and toward the bottom of the periodic table (i.e., Francium (Fr) has the largest atomic radius while Helium (He) has the smallest).

STRUCTURE OF ATOMS

All matter consists of **atoms**. Atoms consist of a nucleus and electrons. The **nucleus** consists of protons and neutrons. The properties of these are measurable; they have mass and an electrical charge. The nucleus is positively charged due to the presence of protons. **Electrons** are negatively charged and orbit the nucleus. The nucleus has considerably more mass than the surrounding

343

Copyright © Mometrix Media. You have been licensed one copy of this document for personal use only. Any other reproduction or redistribution is strictly prohibited. All rights reserved. This content is provided for test preparation purposes only and does not imply an endorsement by Mometrix of any particular political, scientific, or religious point of view.

electrons. Atoms can bond together to make **molecules**. Atoms that have an equal number of protons and electrons are electrically neutral. If the number of protons and electrons in an atom is not equal, the atom has a positive or negative charge and is an ion.

ATOMIC NUMBER, NEUTRONS, NUCLEON, AND ELEMENT

- **Atomic number** (proton number) — The atomic number of an element refers to the number of protons in the nucleus of an atom. It is a unique identifier. It can be represented as Z. Atoms with a neutral charge have an atomic number that is equal to the number of electrons.
- **Neutrons** — Neutrons are the uncharged atomic particles contained within the nucleus. The number of neutrons in a nucleus can be represented as "N."
- **Nucleon** — This refers collectively to both neutrons and protons.
- **Element** — An element is matter with one particular type of atom. It can be identified by its atomic number or the number of protons in its nucleus. There are approximately 117 elements currently known, 94 of which occur naturally on Earth. Elements from the periodic table include hydrogen, carbon, iron, helium, mercury, and oxygen.

MOLECULES

Electrons in an atom can orbit different levels around the nucleus. They can absorb or release energy, which can change the location of their orbit or even allow them to break free from the atom. The outermost layer is the **valence layer**, which contains the valence electrons. The valence layer tends to have or share eight electrons. **Molecules** are formed by a chemical bond between atoms, a bond that occurs at the valence level. Two basic types of bonds are covalent and ionic. A **covalent bond** is formed when atoms share electrons. An **ionic bond** is formed when an atom transfers an electron to another atom. A cation or positive ion is formed when an atom loses one or more electrons. An anion or negative ion is formed when an atom gains one or more electrons. A **hydrogen bond** is a weak bond between a hydrogen atom of one molecule and an electronegative atom (such as nitrogen, oxygen, or fluorine) of another molecule. The **Van der Waals force** is a weak force between molecules. This type of force is much weaker than actual chemical bonds between atoms.

> **Review Video: Molecules**
> Visit mometrix.com/academy and enter code: 349910
>
> **Review Video: Anion, Cation, and Octet Rule**
> Visit mometrix.com/academy and enter code: 303525
>
> **Review Video: What is an Ionic Bond?**
> Visit mometrix.com/academy and enter code: 116546

INTERACTION OF ATOMS TO FORM COMPOUNDS

Atoms interact by **transferring** or sharing the electrons furthest from the nucleus. Known as the outer or **valence electrons**, they are responsible for the chemical properties of an element. **Bonds** between atoms are created when electrons are paired up by being transferred or shared. If electrons are transferred from one atom to another, the bond is ionic. If electrons are shared, the bond is covalent. Atoms of the same element may bond together to form molecules or crystalline solids. When two or more different types of atoms bind together chemically, a compound is made. The physical properties of compounds reflect the nature of the interactions among their molecules. These interactions are determined by the structure of the molecule, including the atoms they consist of and the distances and angles between them.

Copyright © Mometrix Media. You have been licensed one copy of this document for personal use only. Any other reproduction or redistribution is strictly prohibited. All rights reserved.
This content is provided for test preparation purposes only and does not imply an endorsement by Mometrix of any particular political, scientific, or religious point of view.

MATTER

Matter refers to substances that have mass and occupy space (or volume). The traditional definition of matter describes it as having three states: solid, liquid, and gas. These different states are caused by differences in the distances and angles between molecules or atoms, which result in differences in the energy that binds them. **Solid** structures are rigid or nearly rigid and have strong bonds. Molecules or atoms of **liquids** move around and have weak bonds, although they are not weak enough to readily break. Molecules or atoms of **gases** move almost independently of each other, are typically far apart, and do not form bonds. The current definition of matter describes it as having four states. The fourth is **plasma**, which is an ionized gas that has some electrons that are described as free because they are not bound to an atom or molecule.

> **Review Video: States of Matter**
> Visit mometrix.com/academy and enter code: 742449

MOST ABUNDANT ELEMENTS IN THE UNIVERSE AND ON EARTH

Aside from dark energy and dark matter, which are thought to account for all but four percent of the universe, the two most abundant elements in the universe are **hydrogen** (H) and **helium** (He). After hydrogen and helium, the most abundant elements are oxygen, neon, nitrogen, carbon, silicon, and magnesium. The most abundant isotopes in the solar system are hydrogen-1 and helium-4. Measurements of the masses of elements in the Earth's crust indicate that oxygen (O), silicon (Si), and aluminum (Al) are the most abundant on Earth. Hydrogen in its plasma state is the most abundant chemical element in stars in their main sequences but is relatively rare on planet Earth.

ENERGY TRANSFORMATIONS

The following are some examples of energy transformations:

- **Electric to mechanical**: Ceiling fan
- **Chemical to heat**: A familiar example of a chemical to heat energy transformation is the internal combustion engine, which transforms the chemical energy (a type of potential energy) of gas and oxygen into heat. This heat is transformed into propulsive energy, which is kinetic. Lighting a match and burning coal are also examples of chemical to heat energy transformations.
- **Chemical to light**: Phosphorescence and luminescence (which allow objects to glow in the dark) occur because energy is absorbed by a substance (charged) and light is re-emitted comparatively slowly. This process is different from the one involved with glow sticks. They glow due to chemiluminescence, in which an excited state is created by a chemical reaction and transferred to another molecule.
- **Heat to electricity**: Examples include thermoelectric, geothermal, and ocean thermal.
- **Nuclear to heat**: Examples include nuclear reactors and power plants.
- **Mechanical to sound**: Playing a violin or almost any instrument
- **Sound to electric**: Microphone
- **Light to electric**: Solar panels
- **Electric to light**: Light bulbs

RELATIONSHIP BETWEEN CONSERVATION OF MATTER AND ATOMIC THEORY

Atomic theory is concerned with the characteristics and properties of atoms that make up matter. It deals with matter on a *microscopic level* as opposed to a *macroscopic level*. Atomic theory, for instance, discusses the kinetic motion of atoms in order to explain the properties of macroscopic quantities of matter. John Dalton (1766-1844) is credited with making many contributions to the

Copyright © Mometrix Media. You have been licensed one copy of this document for personal use only. Any other reproduction or redistribution is strictly prohibited. All rights reserved. This content is provided for test preparation purposes only and does not imply an endorsement by Mometrix of any particular political, scientific, or religious point of view.

field of atomic theory that are still considered valid. This includes the notion that all matter consists of atoms and that atoms are indestructible. In other words, atoms can be neither created nor destroyed. This is also the theory behind the conservation of matter, which explains why chemical reactions do not result in any detectable gains or losses in matter. This holds true for chemical reactions and smaller-scale processes. When dealing with large amounts of energy, however, atoms can be destroyed by nuclear reactions. This can happen in particle colliders or atom smashers.

> **Review Video: John Dalton**
> Visit mometrix.com/academy and enter code: 565627

DIFFERENCE BETWEEN ATOMS AND MOLECULES

Elements from the periodic table such as hydrogen, carbon, iron, helium, mercury, and oxygen are **atoms**. Atoms combine to form molecules. For example, two atoms of hydrogen (H) and one atom of oxygen (O) combine to form one molecule of water (H_2O).

CHEMICAL AND PHYSICAL PROPERTIES

Matter has both physical and chemical properties. **Physical properties** can be seen or observed without changing the identity or composition of matter. For example, the mass, volume, and density of a substance can be determined without permanently changing the sample. Other physical properties include color, boiling point, freezing point, solubility, odor, hardness, electrical conductivity, thermal conductivity, ductility, and malleability. **Chemical properties** cannot be measured without changing the identity or composition of matter. Chemical properties describe how a substance reacts or changes to form a new substance. Examples of chemical properties include flammability, corrosivity, oxidation states, enthalpy of formation, and reactivity with other chemicals.

CHEMICAL AND PHYSICAL CHANGES

Physical changes do not produce new substances. The atoms or molecules may be rearranged, but no new substances are formed. Phase changes or changes of state such as melting, freezing, and sublimation are physical changes. For example, physical changes include the melting of ice, the boiling of water, sugar dissolving into water, and the crushing of a piece of chalk into a fine powder. **Chemical changes** involve a chemical reaction and do produce new substances. When iron rusts, iron oxide is formed, indicating a chemical change. Other examples of chemical changes include baking a cake, burning wood, digesting a cracker, and mixing an acid and a base.

PHYSICAL AND CHEMICAL PROPERTIES AND CHANGES

Both physical changes and chemical reactions are everyday occurrences. **Physical changes** do not result in different substances. For example, when water becomes ice it has undergone a physical change, but not a chemical change. It has changed its form, but not its composition. It is still H_2O. **Chemical properties** are concerned with the constituent particles that make up the physicality of a substance. Chemical properties are apparent when **chemical changes** occur. The chemical properties of a substance are influenced by its electron configuration, which is determined in part by the number of protons in the nucleus (the atomic number). Carbon, for example, has 6 protons and 6 electrons. It is an element's outermost valence electrons that mainly determine its chemical properties. Chemical reactions may release or consume energy.

> **Review Video: Chemical and Physical Properties of Matter**
> Visit mometrix.com/academy and enter code: 717349

Copyright © Mometrix Media. You have been licensed one copy of this document for personal use only. Any other reproduction or redistribution is strictly prohibited. All rights reserved. This content is provided for test preparation purposes only and does not imply an endorsement by Mometrix of any particular political, scientific, or religious point of view.

ELEMENTS, COMPOUNDS, SOLUTIONS, AND MIXTURES

- **Elements** — These are substances that consist of only one type of atom.
- **Compounds** — These are substances containing two or more elements. Compounds are formed by chemical reactions and frequently have different properties than the original elements. Compounds are decomposed by a chemical reaction rather than separated by a physical one.
- **Solutions** — These are homogeneous mixtures composed of two or more substances that have become one.
- **Mixtures** — Mixtures contain two or more substances that are combined but have not reacted chemically with each other. Mixtures can be separated using physical methods, while compounds cannot.

HEAT, ENERGY, WORK, AND THERMAL ENERGY

- **Heat** — Heat is the transfer of energy from a body or system as a result of thermal contact. Heat consists of random motion and the vibration of atoms, molecules, and ions. The higher the temperature is, the greater the atomic or molecular motion will be.
- **Energy** — Energy is the capacity to do work.
- **Work** — Work is the quantity of energy transferred by one system to another due to changes in a system that is the result of external forces, or macroscopic variables. Another way to put this is that work is the amount of energy that must be transferred to overcome a force. Lifting an object in the air is an example of work. The opposing force that must be overcome is gravity. Work is measured in joules (J). The rate at which work is performed is known as power.
- **Thermal energy** — Thermal energy is the energy present in a system due to temperature.

TYPES OF ENERGY

Some discussions of energy consider only two types of energy: **kinetic energy** (the energy of motion) and **potential energy** (which depends on relative position or orientation). There are, however, other types of energy. **Electromagnetic waves**, for example, are a type of energy contained by a field. Another type of potential energy is electrical energy, which is the energy it takes to pull apart positive and negative electrical charges. **Chemical energy** refers to the manner in which atoms form into molecules, and this energy can be released or absorbed when molecules regroup. **Solar energy** comes in the form of visible light and non-visible light, such as infrared and ultraviolet rays. **Sound energy** refers to the energy in sound waves.

> **Review Video: Potential and Kinetic Energy**
> Visit mometrix.com/academy and enter code: 491502

CHEMICAL REACTIONS

Chemical reactions measured in human time can take place quickly or slowly. They can take fractions of a second or billions of years. The rates of chemical reactions are determined by how frequently reacting atoms and molecules interact. Rates are also influenced by the temperature and various properties (such as shape) of the reacting materials. **Catalysts** accelerate chemical reactions, while inhibitors decrease reaction rates. Some types of reactions release energy in the form of heat and light. Some types of reactions involve the transfer of either electrons or hydrogen ions between reacting ions, molecules, or atoms. In other reactions, chemical bonds are broken down by heat or light to form reactive radicals with electrons that will readily form new bonds.

Copyright © Mometrix Media. You have been licensed one copy of this document for personal use only. Any other reproduction or redistribution is strictly prohibited. All rights reserved. This content is provided for test preparation purposes only and does not imply an endorsement by Mometrix of any particular political, scientific, or religious point of view.

Processes such as the formation of ozone and greenhouse gases in the atmosphere and the burning and processing of fossil fuels are controlled by radical reactions.

> **Review Video: Understanding Chemical Reactions**
> Visit mometrix.com/academy and enter code: 579876
>
> **Review Video: Catalysts**
> Visit mometrix.com/academy and enter code: 288189

READING CHEMICAL EQUATIONS

Chemical equations describe chemical reactions. The reactants are on the left side before the arrow. The products are on the right side after the arrow. The arrow is the mark that points to the reaction or change. The coefficient is the number before the element. This gives the ratio of reactants to products in terms of moles.

The equation for making water from hydrogen and oxygen is $2H_{2(g)} + O_{2(g)} \rightarrow 2H_2O_{(l)}$. The number 2 before hydrogen and water is the coefficient. This means that there are 2 moles of hydrogen and 2 of water. There is 1 mole of oxygen. This does not need to have the number 1 before the symbol for the element. For additional information, the following subscripts are often included to indicate the state of the substance: (g) stands for gas, (l) stands for liquid, (s) stands for solid, and (aq) stands for aqueous. Aqueous means the substance is dissolved in water. Charges are shown by superscript for individual ions, not for ionic compounds. Polyatomic ions are separated by parentheses. This is done so the kind of ion will not be confused with the number of ions.

> **Review Video: What is the Process of a Reaction?**
> Visit mometrix.com/academy and enter code: 808039

BALANCING EQUATIONS

An **unbalanced equation** is one that does not follow the **law of conservation of mass**, which states that matter can only be changed, not created or destroyed. If an equation is unbalanced, the numbers of atoms indicated by the stoichiometric coefficients on each side of the arrow will not be equal. Start by writing the formulas for each species in the reaction. Count the atoms on each side and determine if the number is equal. Coefficients must be whole numbers. Fractional amounts, such as half a molecule, are not possible. Equations can be balanced by adjusting the coefficients of each part of the equation to the smallest possible whole number coefficient. $H_2 + O_2 \rightarrow H_2O$ is an example of an unbalanced equation. The balanced equation is $2H_2 + O_2 \rightarrow 2H_2O$, which indicates that it takes two moles of hydrogen and one of oxygen to produce two moles of water.

> **Review Video: How Do You Balance Chemical Equations?**
> Visit mometrix.com/academy and enter code: 341228

PERIODIC TABLE

The **periodic table** groups elements with similar chemical properties together. The grouping of elements is based on **atomic structure**. It shows periodic trends of physical and chemical properties and identifies families of elements with similar properties. It is a common model for organizing and understanding elements. In the periodic table, each element has its own cell that includes varying amounts of information presented in symbol form about the properties of the element. Cells in the table are arranged in **rows** (periods) and **columns** (groups or families). At minimum, a cell includes the symbol for the element and its atomic number. The cell for hydrogen,

Copyright © Mometrix Media. You have been licensed one copy of this document for personal use only. Any other reproduction or redistribution is strictly prohibited. All rights reserved.
This content is provided for test preparation purposes only and does not imply an endorsement by Mometrix of any particular political, scientific, or religious point of view.

for example, which appears first in the upper left corner, includes an "H" and a "1" above the letter. Elements are ordered by atomic number, left to right, top to bottom.

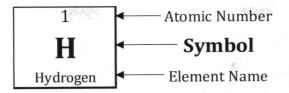

Review Video: Periodic Table
Visit mometrix.com/academy and enter code: 154828

SOLUTIONS

A **solution** is a homogeneous mixture. A **mixture** is two or more different substances that are mixed together, but not combined chemically. Homogeneous mixtures are those that are uniform in their composition. Solutions consist of a solute (the substance that is dissolved) and a solvent (the substance that does the dissolving). An example is sugar water. The solvent is the water and the solute is the sugar. The intermolecular attraction between the solvent and the solute is called solvation. **Hydration** refers to solutions in which water is the solvent. Solutions are formed when the forces between the molecules of the solute and the solvent are as strong as the forces holding the solute together. An example is that salt (NaCl) dissolves in water to create a solution. The Na^+ and the Cl^- ions in salt interact with the molecules of water and vice versa to overcome the intramolecular forces of the solute.

Review Video: Solutions
Visit mometrix.com/academy and enter code: 995937

Review Video: Volume Percent of a Solution
Visit mometrix.com/academy and enter code: 400152

MIXTURES, SUSPENSIONS, COLLOIDS, EMULSIONS, AND FOAMS

A **mixture** is a combination of two or more substances that are not bonded. **Suspensions** are mixtures of heterogeneous materials. Particles in suspensions are usually larger than those found in true solutions. Dirt mixed vigorously with water is an example of a suspension. The dirt is temporarily suspended in water, but the two separate once the mixing is ceased. A mixture of large (1 nm to 500 nm) particles is called a **colloidal suspension**. The particles are termed dispersants and the dispersing medium is similar to the solvent in a solution. Sol refers to a liquid or a solid that also has solids dispersed through it, such as milk or gelatin. An aerosol spray is a colloid suspension of gas and the solid or liquid being dispersed. An **emulsion** refers to a liquid or a solid that has small droplets of another liquid dispersed through it. A **foam** is a liquid that has gas dispersed through it.

pH

The **potential of hydrogen** (pH) is a measurement of the concentration of hydrogen ions in a substance in terms of the number of moles of H^+ per liter of solution. All substances fall between 0 and 14 on the pH scale. A lower pH indicates a higher H^+ concentration, while a higher pH indicates a lower H^+ concentration. Pure water has a neutral pH, which is 7. Anything with a pH lower than water (0-7) is considered acidic. Anything with a pH higher than water (7-14) is a base. Drain cleaner, soap, baking soda, ammonia, egg whites, and sea water are common bases. Urine, stomach acid, citric acid, vinegar, hydrochloric acid, and battery acid are acids. A pH indicator is a substance

Copyright © Mometrix Media. You have been licensed one copy of this document for personal use only. Any other reproduction or redistribution is strictly prohibited. All rights reserved. This content is provided for test preparation purposes only and does not imply an endorsement by Mometrix of any particular political, scientific, or religious point of view.

that acts as a detector of hydrogen or hydronium ions. It is halochromic, meaning it changes color to indicate that hydrogen or hydronium ions have been detected.

Review Video: Overview of pH Levels
Visit mometrix.com/academy and enter code: 187395

PROPERTIES OF ACIDS

When they are dissolved in aqueous solutions, some properties of **acids** are that they conduct electricity, change blue litmus paper to red, have a sour taste, react with bases to neutralize them, and react with active metals to free hydrogen. A **weak acid** is one that does not donate all of its protons or disassociate completely. **Strong acids** include hydrochloric, hydriodic, hydrobromic, perchloric, nitric, and sulfuric. They ionize completely. **Superacids** are those that are stronger than 100 percent sulfuric acid. They include fluoroantimonic, magic, and perchloric acids. Acids can be used in pickling, a process used to remove rust and corrosion from metals. They are also used as catalysts in the processing of minerals and the production of salts and fertilizers. Phosphoric acid (H_3PO_4) is added to sodas and other acids are added to foods as preservatives or to add taste.

Review Video: Properties of Acids and Bases
Visit mometrix.com/academy and enter code: 645283

PROPERTIES OF BASES

When they are dissolved in aqueous solutions, some properties of **bases** are that they conduct electricity, change red litmus paper to blue, feel slippery, and react with acids to neutralize their properties. A **weak base** is one that does not completely ionize in an aqueous solution, and usually has a low pH. **Strong bases** can free protons in very weak acids. Examples of strong bases are hydroxide compounds such as potassium, barium, and lithium hydroxides. Most are in the first and second groups of the periodic table. A **superbase** is extremely strong compared to sodium hydroxide and cannot be kept in an aqueous solution. Superbases are organized into organic, organometallic, and inorganic classes. Bases are used as insoluble catalysts in heterogeneous reactions and as catalysts in hydrogenation.

PROPERTIES OF SALTS

Some properties of **salts** are that they are formed from acid base reactions, are ionic compounds consisting of metallic and nonmetallic ions, dissociate in water, and are comprised of tightly bonded ions. Some common salts are sodium chloride ($NaCl$), sodium bisulfate ($NaHSO_4$), potassium dichromate ($K_2Cr_2O_7$), and calcium chloride ($CaCl_2$). Calcium chloride is used as a drying agent, and may be used to absorb moisture when freezing mixtures. Potassium nitrate (KNO_3) is used to make fertilizer and in the manufacturing of explosives. Sodium nitrate ($NaNO_3$) is also used in the making of fertilizer. Baking soda [sodium bicarbonate ($NaHCO_3$)] is a salt, as are Epsom salts [magnesium sulfate ($MgSO_4$)]. Salt and water can react to form a base and an acid. This is called a **hydrolysis reaction**.

UNIQUE PROPERTIES OF WATER

The important properties of water (H_2O) are high polarity, hydrogen bonding, cohesiveness, adhesiveness, high specific heat, high latent heat, and high heat of vaporization. Water is vital to life as we know it. The reason is that water is one of the main parts of many living things.

Water is a liquid at room temperature. The high specific heat of water means that it does not easily break its hydrogen bonds. Also, it resists heat and motion. This is why it has a high boiling point and high vaporization point.

Copyright © Mometrix Media. You have been licensed one copy of this document for personal use only. Any other reproduction or redistribution is strictly prohibited. All rights reserved. This content is provided for test preparation purposes only and does not imply an endorsement by Mometrix of any particular political, scientific, or religious point of view.

Most substances are denser in their solid forms. However, water is different because its solid-state floats in its liquid state. Water is cohesive. This means that it is drawn to itself. It is also adhesive. This means that it draws in other molecules. If water will attach to another substance, the substance is said to be hydrophilic. Because of its cohesive and adhesive properties, water makes a good solvent. Substances with polar ions and molecules easily dissolve in water.

KINETIC THEORY OF GASES

The **kinetic theory of gases** assumes that gas molecules are small compared to the distances between them and that they are in constant random motion. The attractive and repulsive forces between gas molecules are negligible. Their kinetic energy does not change with time as long as the temperature remains the same. The higher the temperature is, the greater the motion will be. As the temperature of a gas increases, so does the kinetic energy of the molecules. In other words, gas will occupy a greater volume as the temperature is increased and a lesser volume as the temperature is decreased. In addition, the same amount of gas will occupy a greater volume as the temperature increases, but pressure remains constant. At any given temperature, gas molecules have the same average kinetic energy. The **ideal gas law** is derived from the kinetic theory of gases.

> **Review Video: Ideal Gas vs. Real Gas**
> Visit mometrix.com/academy and enter code: 619477

ORGANIC COMPOUNDS

Two of the main characteristics of **organic compounds** are that they **include carbon** and are formed by **covalent bonds**. Carbon can form long chains, double and triple bonds, and rings. While inorganic compounds tend to have high melting points, organic compounds tend to melt at temperatures below 300° C. They also tend to boil, sublimate, and decompose below this temperature. Unlike inorganic compounds, they are not very water-soluble. Organic molecules are organized into functional groups based on their specific atoms, which helps determine how they will react chemically. A few groups are alkanes, nitro, alkenes, sulfides, amines, and carbolic acids. The hydroxyl group (−OH) consists of alcohols. These molecules are polar, which increases their solubility. By some estimates, there are more than 16 million organic compounds.

> **Review Video: Organic Compounds**
> Visit mometrix.com/academy and enter code: 264922

HYDROGEN BONDS

Hydrogen bonds are weaker than covalent and ionic bonds and refer to the type of attraction in an electronegative atom such as oxygen, fluorine, or nitrogen. Hydrogen bonds can form within a single molecule or between molecules. A water molecule is **polar**, meaning it is partially positively charged on one end (the hydrogen end) and partially negatively charged on the other (the oxygen end). This is because the hydrogen atoms are arranged around the oxygen atom in a close tetrahedron. Hydrogen is **oxidized** (its number of electrons is reduced) when it bonds with oxygen to form water. Hydrogen bonds tend not only to be weak but also short-lived. They also tend to be numerous. Hydrogen bonds give water many of its important properties, including its high specific heat and high heat of vaporization, its solvent qualities, its adhesiveness and cohesiveness, its hydrophobic qualities, and its ability to float in its solid form. Hydrogen bonds are also an important component of proteins, nucleic acids, and DNA.

INORGANIC COMPOUNDS

The main trait of **inorganic compounds** is that they lack carbon. Inorganic compounds include mineral salts, alloys, non-metallic compounds such as phosphate, and metal complexes. A metal

Copyright © Mometrix Media. You have been licensed one copy of this document for personal use only. Any other reproduction or redistribution is strictly prohibited. All rights reserved. This content is provided for test preparation purposes only and does not imply an endorsement by Mometrix of any particular political, scientific, or religious point of view.

complex has a central atom (or ion) bonded to surrounding ligands (molecules or anions). The ligands sacrifice the donor atoms (in the form of at least one pair of electrons) to the central atom. Many inorganic compounds are ionic, meaning they form ionic bonds rather than share electrons. They may have high melting points because of this. They may also be colorful, but this is not an absolute identifier of an inorganic compound. Salts, which are inorganic compounds, are an example of inorganic bonding of cations and anions. Some examples of salts are magnesium chloride ($MgCl_2$) and sodium oxide (Na_2O). Oxides, carbonates, sulfates, and halides are classes of inorganic compounds. They are typically poor conductors, are very water soluble, and crystallize easily. Minerals and silicates are also inorganic compounds.

Chapter Quiz

1. Which of the following are thought to be the two most abundant elements in the universe?

    a. Hydrogen and carbon
    b. Helium and hydrogen
    c. Carbon and oxygen
    d. Hydrogen and oxygen

2. Which of the following is NOT a superacid?

    a. Hydrochloric
    b. Magic
    c. Fluoroantimonic
    d. Perchloric

3. What is the chemical name of $NaNO_3$?

    a. Potassium nitroxide
    b. Sodium pentothal
    c. Sodium nitrate
    d. Sodium chloride

4. Which of the following is NOT a characteristic of an organic compound?

    a. Typically have a melting point above 300 °C
    b. Usually not very water-soluble
    c. Includes carbon as a major component
    d. Formed by covalent bonds

Chapter Quiz Answer Key

1. B: Aside from dark energy and dark matter, which are thought to account for all but four percent of the universe, the two most abundant elements in the universe are hydrogen (H) and helium (He). After hydrogen and helium, the most abundant elements are oxygen, neon, nitrogen, carbon, silicon, and magnesium.

2. A: A weak acid is one that does not donate all of its protons or disassociate completely. Strong acids include hydrochloric, hydriodic, hydrobromic, perchloric, nitric, and sulfuric. They ionize completely. Superacids are those that are stronger than 100 percent sulfuric acid. They include fluoroantimonic, magic, and perchloric acids. Acids can be used in pickling, a process used to remove rust and corrosion from metals.

3. C: Some common salts are sodium chloride (NaCl), sodium bisulfate ($NaHSO_4$), potassium dichromate ($K_2Cr_2O_7$), and calcium chloride ($CaCl_2$). Calcium chloride is used as a drying agent, and may be used to absorb moisture when freezing mixtures. Potassium nitrate (KNO_3) is used to make

Copyright © Mometrix Media. You have been licensed one copy of this document for personal use only. Any other reproduction or redistribution is strictly prohibited. All rights reserved.
This content is provided for test preparation purposes only and does not imply an endorsement by Mometrix of any particular political, scientific, or religious point of view.

fertilizer and in the manufacturing of explosives. Sodium nitrate ($NaNO_3$) is also used in the making of fertilizer. Sodium bicarbonate ($NaHCO_3$, better known as baking soda) is a salt, as is magnesium sulfate ($MgSO_4$, better known as Epsom salts). Salt and water can react to form a base and an acid.

4. A: Two of the main characteristics of organic compounds are that they include carbon and are formed by covalent bonds. Carbon can form long chains, double and triple bonds, and rings. While inorganic compounds tend to have high melting points, organic compounds tend to melt at temperatures below 300 °C. They also tend to boil, sublimate, and decompose below this temperature. Unlike inorganic compounds, they are not very water-soluble. Organic molecules are organized into functional groups based on their specific atoms, which helps determine how they will react chemically.

Scientific Inquiry and Impact

COMPONENTS OF SCIENTIFIC EXPERIMENTATION

- A **hypothesis** is a tentative supposition about a phenomenon (or a fact or set of facts) made in order to examine and test its logical or empirical consequences through investigation or methodological experimentation.
- A **theory** is a scientifically proven, general principle offered to explain phenomena. A theory is derived from a hypothesis and verified by experimentation and research.
- A **scientific law** is a generally accepted conclusion about a body of observations to which no exceptions have been found. Scientific laws explain things, but do not describe them.
- A **control** is a normal, unchanged situation used for comparison against experimental data.
- **Constants** are factors in an experiment that remain the same.
- **Independent variables** are factors, traits, or conditions that are changed in an experiment. A good experiment has only one independent variable so that the scientist can track one thing at a time. The independent variable changes from experiment to experiment.
- **Dependent variables** are changes that result from variations in the independent variable.

SCIENCE AS A SERIES OF PROCESSES

Science is not just the steps of experimentation. While the process of posing a question, forming a hypothesis, testing the hypothesis, recording data, and drawing a conclusion is at the heart of **scientific inquiry**, there are other processes that are important as well. Once the scientist has completed the testing of a hypothesis and possibly come up with a theory, the scientist should then go through the process of getting feedback from colleagues, publishing an article about the work in a peer-reviewed journal, or otherwise reporting the results to the scientific community, replicating the experiment for verification of results (by the original scientist or others), and developing new questions. Science is not just a means of satisfying curiosity, but is also a process for developing technology, addressing social issues, building knowledge, and solving everyday problems.

DRAWING CONCLUSIONS AFTER EXPERIMENTS

Conclusions are based on data analysis and background research. The scientist has to take a hard look at the results of an experiment and check the accuracy of the data to draw preliminary conclusions. These should be compared to the background research to find out if the preliminary conclusion can be supported by previous research experiments. If the results do not support the hypothesis, or if they are contrary to what the background research predicted, then further research is needed. The focus should be on finding a reason for the different results. Finally, the scientist provides a discussion of findings that includes a summary of the results of the experiment, a statement as to whether the hypothesis was proven or disproven, a statement of the relationship

Copyright © Mometrix Media. You have been licensed one copy of this document for personal use only. Any other reproduction or redistribution is strictly prohibited. All rights reserved.
This content is provided for test preparation purposes only and does not imply an endorsement by Mometrix of any particular political, scientific, or religious point of view.

between the independent and dependent variable, a summary and evaluation of the procedures of the experiment (including comments about successes and effectiveness), and suggestions for changes/modifications in procedures for further studies.

STEPS OF THE SCIENTIFIC METHOD

The steps of the **scientific method** are as follows:

1. The scientific method begins with, and absolutely depends upon, the **observation** of objective, unbiased data. Any prejudice or bias in the observed data nullifies its validity. Thus the basic input from the observations must be rigorously screened to ensure objectivity.
2. The development of a **theory or hypothesis** based on objective data is the next step in the scientific method. These theories or hypotheses pose logical expectations that the experiment may yield.
3. Construction of a rigorous and valid **experimental method** designed to test the theories is the next phase of the scientific method. This experimental method must be carefully constructed to give objective, unbiased conclusions based on the hypotheses posited.
4. Careful and statistically correct **analysis and evaluation** of the experimental results make up the next stage.
5. **Modification and replication** of the experiment must then follow to provide a statistically accurate demonstration of the validity of the hypothesis. Equivalent results must be shown from a number of repetitions of the experiment.

> **Review Video: The Scientific Method**
> Visit mometrix.com/academy and enter code: 191386

STEPS OF THE SCIENTIFIC INQUIRY

Scientific inquiry is the impetus and catalyst for all scientific research and experimentation. It grows from questions about the observed world and gives us a template with which to apply the scientific method. Steps in scientific inquiry include the following principles:

- Determination of the content and scope of the questions to be investigated is the first step. These may range from simple to extremely complex questions to be explored by scientists.
- The design, strategy, and method of the inquiry are then carefully considered, and a model for the inquiry is constructed.
- The formulation of theories and models based on the careful observation of objective, unbiased data then follows. This formulation is derived from the scope of the scientific inquiry and the questions to be investigated.
- Analysis of possible alternative conclusions drawn from the models and results of experimentation follows.
- Postulating a theory or constructing a scientific statement based on conclusions is the next logical step.
- Defending the scientific statement against alternative hypotheses is a critical function of scientific inquiry.
- Defense of the theory or conclusion against critical analysis is the final step in the process.

SCIENCE

Science is a method of acquiring and obtaining knowledge. It is the process of gaining reliable information about the real world, including the explanation of phenomena. It is the development of a body of knowledge about observable phenomena, using the best capabilities humans have at their

Copyright © Mometrix Media. You have been licensed one copy of this document for personal use only. Any other reproduction or redistribution is strictly prohibited. All rights reserved. This content is provided for test preparation purposes only and does not imply an endorsement by Mometrix of any particular political, scientific, or religious point of view.

disposal. The process of organizing and classifying knowledge, through objective observation and evaluation, is a major goal of science. Science can be considered *reliable*, but it is not *infallible*. The limits of human knowledge are constantly growing, often making yesterday's science obsolete and simplistic. Science is thus never fixed; it is always subject to change as new information is gained and synthesized with existing knowledge. Ultimately, science is the sum total of knowledge in any period of time, based on the current abilities of man to understand the world of phenomena, verifiable by observable data.

LIMITATIONS OF SCIENCE

There are clear **limits** on what science can explain. The demand for objectivity both strengthens knowledge we gain from scientific experiments and limits what we can explore. Beyond the realm of scientific inquiry are such questions as "Why does anything exist?" or "What is the meaning of life?" These are subjective questions that do not lend themselves easily to scientific inquiry. These questions, and others like them, come from within, and their conclusions, not validated by science, shape the very fabric of a society. They attempt to give meaning to what may be viewed as chaos.

Periodically, science will impact these **subjective conclusions** with new evidence. For example, the theory of evolution is regarded as blasphemy by many religious fundamentalists. These conflicts may cause great upheavals in society, leaving many to wonder how science and religious belief can be reconciled. Ultimately, observation of the external world must stand as the true test of science.

HYPOTHETICO-DEDUCTIVE PROCESS

The **hypothetico-deductive process** states that to have an idea and then formulate a hypothesis are essentially creative processes, driven by eons of human experience. Statements about reality are the logical conclusions of observed experience. Such creative propositions are the basis for scientific inquiry. Empirical evidence must then validate these hypotheses. Creative inspiration and scientific validation are interdependent aspects of scientific inquiry. New observations often are the catalyst for creative new theories. Science thus proceeds through creative thinking and scientific validation. There are criticisms of the hypothetico-deductive process: The problem of deduction points out that the original hypothesis may be proved wrong in the future, thus invalidating all subsequent conclusions. The problem of induction, building a theory from generalizations, is that any generalization may be proved wrong by future objective observations. The hypothetico-deductive process, and its problems, is a fascinating subject to philosophers of science.

HYPOTHESIS

It is important to form a **hypothesis** in order to make a tentative explanation that accounts for an unbiased observation. To be scientific, the hypothesis must be testable through experimentation. Careful construction of the experiment provides that predictions derived from the hypothesis are valid. The hypothesis must be formulated in a manner designed to provide a framework for evaluating the results of an experiment. In many scientific experiments, a hypothesis is posited in negative terms because scientists may accept logically plausible ideas until they are proven false. It is more difficult to prove that a hypothesis is true because its validity must be proven in all possible situations under endless variable conditions. Scientists tend to construct hypotheses for testing by creating experiments that might prove them false. If they succeed in proving it false, the hypothesis must be modified or discarded.

Copyright © Mometrix Media. You have been licensed one copy of this document for personal use only. Any other reproduction or redistribution is strictly prohibited. All rights reserved. This content is provided for test preparation purposes only and does not imply an endorsement by Mometrix of any particular political, scientific, or religious point of view.

BASIC SCIENCE AND APPLIED SCIENCE

Basic science and applied science share many attributes but are generally motivated by different influences:

- **Basic science** is spurred on by scientific inquiry, the human need to explain the observed physical world. It may have no specific goal, but is mankind's response to questions that arise from human curiosity and interest. It is usually an attempt to explain the laws of nature by using the scientific method.
- **Applied science** has a specific practical goal or application: It is designed to solve a problem. Industry and government are institutions that use applied science regularly.

Thus, basic and applied science share many qualities, including scientific inquiry and the scientific method. The goals of each can be very different. It should be pointed out that basic science very often provides results that have uses in applied science.

BENEFITS OF BASIC SCIENCE

Although **basic science** may have no stated goal or target, it provides many benefits to society:

- Basic science contributes greatly to human understanding and culture, enriching society in many ways.
- Basic science has been responsible for major breakthroughs that have great social and economic impact.
- Basic science provides derivative solutions that can be used in applied science. For example, basic science was critical to the development of the space program, from which countless valuable applications have been derived.
- Basic science contributes to education and research across the broad spectrum of society.

MEASURING, ORGANIZING, AND CLASSIFYING DATA

Measuring data is a crucial part of the scientific process. Measurements are most useful if they are quantified—expressed in numbers. Measuring is the process of determining variables such as time, space, and temperature of objects and processes in precise numbers. The metric system is the universal standard of measurement in science. Data must be **organized** in a practical, useful manner to be valuable. Scientists use graphs, charts, tables, and other organizational tools to make data more useful. Data must then be **classified**—grouped into organizational schemes for easy access and use. These schemes attempt to organize the maximum amount of useful data in a format that scientists can use. Although these steps may be less glamorous than other areas of science, they are essential.

> **Review Video: <u>Understanding Charts and Tables</u>**
> Visit mometrix.com/academy and enter code: 882112

Copyright © Mometrix Media. You have been licensed one copy of this document for personal use only. Any other reproduction or redistribution is strictly prohibited. All rights reserved.
This content is provided for test preparation purposes only and does not imply an endorsement by Mometrix of any particular political, scientific, or religious point of view.

SCIENTIFIC LAWS

Scientific principles must meet a high standard to be classified as laws; scientific laws are identified as follows:

- **Scientific laws** must be true, not just probable. A highly probable principle may still be proven false.
- Laws are statements of patterns found in nature.
- Laws may have a universal form but be stated conditionally. For example, the statement "All living human beings breathe," may be restated "If a thing is a living human being it must breathe."
- Laws refer to a general, not a particular, class.
- Laws have purely qualitative predicates.
- Laws must have a formal language of expression to be fully understood. Such a language does not exist now.
- Laws may be probabilistic. For example, a law may state "Eight percent of all dogs are terriers."

COMMON CRITICISMS OF THE DEDUCTIVE MODEL

The **deductive model** of the scientific method has the following criticisms:

- The deductive model fails to make logical distinctions among explanations, predictions, and descriptions of things to be explained.
- The deductive model is restrictive: It excludes most scientific examples.
- The deductive model is too inclusive: It admits data that cannot be explained.
- The deductive model requires an account of cause, law, and probability, which are basically unsound.
- The deductive model leaves out the elements of context, judgment, and understanding.

PREDICTION

These are the two widely accepted definitions of **scientific prediction**:

1. In the language of science, prediction is stating in advance the outcome from testing a theory or hypothesis in a controlled experiment. Based on objective observation of data, scientists move from observation of facts to a general explanation, or hypothesis, which must be confirmed by testing through experimentation.
2. Another definition of prediction favored by scientific philosophers is the ability of a hypothesis to lead to deductions of scientific statements that could not be anticipated when the hypothesis was posited. In this sense, prediction means what the scientist can verify from what he or she has deduced from the hypothesis.

LABORATORY SAFETY

The following basic rules should be supplemented by standards appropriate to individual laboratories:

- Hazardous areas must be identified and warnings posted regarding risks.
- A hazard containment plan must be in effect and readily available.
- Safe control of airflow must be maintained at all times.
- Safe work practices must be taught to all who work in the lab.
- Proper maintenance of laboratory equipment must be enforced.
- Safe storage of hazardous material must be implemented.

357

Copyright © Mometrix Media. You have been licensed one copy of this document for personal use only. Any other reproduction or redistribution is strictly prohibited. All rights reserved.
This content is provided for test preparation purposes only and does not imply an endorsement by Mometrix of any particular political, scientific, or religious point of view.

- Procedures for safe disposal of hazardous wastes must be followed at all times.
- An updated emergency procedure manual must be available.
- A complete emergency first aid kit should be accessible at all times.
- Regular education on the basics of lab safety should be implemented.

VERIFICATION AND CONFIRMATION OF DATA IN VALID SCIENCE

A critical distinction should be made between confirmation and verification of scientific data. **Verification** establishes once and for all the truth of the statement. **Confirmation** is the testing of claims to see how true they are. For a claim to be testable, an experiment must be devised to ensure the validity of the results. A claim can only be confirmed when we know the conditions for verification. A claim confirmation is always relative to the testing procedures. Test results must always be objective and observable. Actually, no factual claim can ever be verified because there is always the possibility of new evidence appearing that proves the claim false. A scientific law must also be confirmed by making predictions based on unbiased, observable data.

SCIENTIFIC MEASUREMENT AND UNIT SYSTEMS

The basis of quantitative measurement is the **unit system**. In order to properly describe how large, how heavy, or how hot something is, it is necessary to have some reference unit. The most commonly used unit system in the world is the **SI**, short for the Systeme International d'Unites, although the English system is still in popular use in the United States. In SI, there are base units and derived units. Derived units may be stated as some combination of the base units. The SI base units for length, mass, time, temperature, and electric current are meter (m), kilogram (kg), second (s), kelvin (K), and ampere (A), respectively. Some common derived units are newtons (kg m/s^2) and pascals (kg/(m s^2)). Most SI units can be scaled up or down by adding a prefix. To alter a unit by 10^3, 10^6, or 10^9, add a prefix of kilo (k), mega (M), or giga (G). For instance, a kilometer (km) is 10^3 meters. To change the unit by a factor of 10^{-3}, 10^{-6}, or 10^{-9}, add a prefix of milli (m), micro (μ), or nano (n). For instance, a microsecond (μs) is 10^{-6} seconds. It is important to note that the SI base unit kilogram has already employed a prefix to scale up the smaller unit, gram (g). *Order of magnitude* is a concept that deals with the comparison between two values. If one value differs from the other by a factor of 10^n, it may be said that it differs by n orders of magnitude. Other SI base units include the mole and the candela. Some lesser used prefixes include: hecto (h), 10^2; deca (da), 10^1; deci (d), 10^{-1}; and centi (c), 10^{-2}.

DATA COLLECTION AND ANALYSIS

In order to take **data measurements** from their experimental setups, scientists will often use measurement devices wired to a computer running data-acquisition software. This allows them to take numerous readings per second if necessary. Once the data is collected, it will often be organized using a spreadsheet, such as Microsoft Excel. This multipurpose program contains several options for displaying the data in graphs or charts, as well as tools for performing statistical analyses or linear regressions. Linear regression is a technique used to determine whether gathered data fits a particular trend or equation. It attempts to fit a common line or curve equation to the data set. A very important concept to understand when taking data is that of **significant figures**. Significant figures, or significant digits, indicate how precisely a quantity is known. Each non-zero digit is always significant. A zero is significant if either: 1) it is to the right of both a non-zero digit and the decimal point; or 2) it is between two other significant digits. For instance, 1.0230 has five significant figures while 0.0230 has only three because the trailing zero is the only zero to the right of both a non-zero and the decimal. When multiplying (or dividing), the product (quotient) has as many significant figures as the factor (dividend or divisor) with the fewest. When adding (or

Copyright © Mometrix Media. You have been licensed one copy of this document for personal use only. Any other reproduction or redistribution is strictly prohibited. All rights reserved. This content is provided for test preparation purposes only and does not imply an endorsement by Mometrix of any particular political, scientific, or religious point of view.

subtracting), the sum (difference) should be rounded to the highest final decimal place of the involved terms. For example, $3.4 + 56.78 = 60.18$ rounded to three significant figures is 60.2.

INTERPRETATION AND DRAWING OF CONCLUSIONS FROM DATA PRESENTED IN TABLES, CHARTS, AND GRAPHS

One of the reasons data are so often plotted on graphs is that this format makes it much easier to see **trends** and draw **conclusions**. For instance, on a simple position vs. time graph, the slope of the curve indicates the object's velocity at each point in time. If the curve becomes level, this means the object is not moving. In a simple velocity vs. time graph, the slope of the curve indicates the object's acceleration at each point in time. Additionally, the area contained under the curve indicates the total distance traveled. For instance, if the object is traveling at a constant 5 m/s for 10 s, the velocity vs. time graph will be a straight line at $y = 5$ between $x = 0$ and $x = 10$. The area under this curve is $(5 \text{ m/s})(10 \text{ s}) = 50$ m. Thus, the object traveled 50 meters. Nearly any type of quantity may be graphed, so it is important to always check the axis labels to ensure that you know what the graph represents and what units are being used.

DATA ERRORS AND ERROR ANALYSIS

No measurements are ever 100% accurate. There is always some amount of **error** regardless of how careful the observer or how good the equipment. The important thing for the scientist to know is how much error is present in a given measurement. Two commonly misunderstood terms regarding error are accuracy and precision. **Accuracy** is a measure of how close a measurement is to the true value. **Precision** is a measure of how close repeated measurements are to one another. Error is usually quantified using a confidence interval and an uncertainty value. For instance, if the quantity is measured as 100 ± 2 on a 95% confidence interval, this means that there is a 95% chance that the actual value falls between 98 and 102. When looking for the uncertainty in a derived quantity such as density, the errors in the constituent quantities, mass and volume in this case, are propagated to the derived quantity. The percent uncertainty in the density, U_ρ/ρ, can be found by the equation:

$$\frac{U_\rho}{\rho} = \sqrt{\left(\frac{U_m}{m}\right)^2 + \left(\frac{U_V}{V}\right)^2}$$

CHAPTER QUIZ

1. What makes a hypothesis scientific?
   a. Stated in negative terms
   b. Logical consistency based on prior knowledge
   c. Testable through experimentation
   d. Original in its conception

2. Which of the following is NOT true concerning scientific laws?
   a. Laws refer to a particular class, not a general one.
   b. Laws are statements of patterns found in nature.
   c. Laws may be probabilistic.
   d. Laws have purely qualitative predicates.

Copyright © Mometrix Media. You have been licensed one copy of this document for personal use only. Any other reproduction or redistribution is strictly prohibited. All rights reserved. This content is provided for test preparation purposes only and does not imply an endorsement by Mometrix of any particular political, scientific, or religious point of view.

3. Which of the following correctly describes the prefix *hecto-*?

    a. 10^{-2}
    b. 10^{-1}
    c. 10^1
    d. 10^2

CHAPTER QUIZ ANSWER KEY

1. C: It is important to form a hypothesis in order to make a tentative explanation that accounts for an unbiased observation. To be scientific, the hypothesis must be testable through experimentation. Careful construction of the experiment provides that predictions derived from the hypothesis are valid. The hypothesis must be formulated in a manner designed to provide a framework for evaluating the results of an experiment. In many scientific experiments, a hypothesis is posited in negative terms because scientists may accept logically plausible ideas until they are proven false. It is more difficult to prove that a hypothesis is true because its validity must be proven in all possible situations under endless variable conditions. Scientists tend to construct hypotheses for testing by creating experiments that might prove them false. If they succeed in proving it false, the hypothesis must be modified or discarded.

2. A: Scientific principles must meet a high standard to be classified as laws. Scientific laws are identified as follows:

- Scientific laws must be true, not just probable. A highly probable principle may still be proven false.
- Laws are statements of patterns found in nature.
- Laws may have a universal form, but they should be stated conditionally. For example, the statement, "All living human beings breathe," may be restated as, "If a thing is a living human being it must breathe."
- Laws refer to a general class, not a particular one.
- Laws have purely qualitative predicates.
- Laws must have a formal language of expression to be fully understood. Such a language does not exist now.
- Laws may be probabilistic. For example, a law may state, "Eight percent of all dogs are terriers."

3. D: Order of magnitude is a concept that deals with the comparison between two values. If one value differs from the other by a factor of 10^n, it may be said that it differs by *n* orders of magnitude. Other SI base units include the mole and the candela. Some lesser used prefixes include *hecto-* (h), 10^2; *deca-* (da), 10^1; *deci-* (d), 10^{-1}; and *centi-* (c), 10^{-2}.

DEBATE OVER SCIENCE AND ETHICS

Debates over issues paramount to **science and ethics** are rarely resolved unambiguously. Ethical conclusions should be based on reason, logic, and accepted principles that represent a consensus of current thinking on a question. Education and debate are important in clarifying issues and allowing intelligent participation in a democratic process. Deciding issues of science and society usually requires an examination of individual cases. Generalizations in these areas tend to lead to extreme positions that exclude mainstream opinions. There are no blanket solutions to most problems involving science, technology, and societal ethics.

Copyright © Mometrix Media. You have been licensed one copy of this document for personal use only. Any other reproduction or redistribution is strictly prohibited. All rights reserved.
This content is provided for test preparation purposes only and does not imply an endorsement by Mometrix of any particular political, scientific, or religious point of view.

MAJOR EFFECTS OF IMPROVEMENTS IN SCIENTIFIC AND TECHNOLOGICAL KNOWLEDGE ON HUMAN AND OTHER LIFE

Since the Industrial Revolution, **technological improvements** to agricultural production have made agriculture productive on an industrial scale, while advances in medical knowledge have brought about the cures for many diseases. People in many parts of the world live longer and enjoy a higher standard of living than ever before. However, this progress does not come without a price. The effects on the **environment** of industrialization are almost exclusively negative. Monoculture farming practices resulting from industrialization mean that farming no longer exists as a closed ecosystem; the chemical fertilizers that create record crop yields have changed the nutrient environment, and the waste products of industrial agriculture pollute the water rather than fertilizing the soil. Increased travel creates dangerous carbon dioxide emissions and depletes the earth's limited store of fossil fuels. Water pollution means limited access to potable water, and deforestation has begun to change the makeup of ecosystems and cause the extinction of many species. Through the increased contact made available by improved technology, however, humans are also collaborating on solutions to these new problems.

> **Review Video: Industrialization**
> Visit mometrix.com/academy and enter code: 893924

MAJOR ENERGY ISSUES

Since the Industrial Revolution, **energy** for industrialized human needs has come from fossil fuels, particularly coal and petroleum, but increased use means that this source of fuel is quickly being depleted, in addition to causing pollution. The search for **alternative, safe sources** of energy for an increasingly industrialized world population is therefore increasingly important to scientists. An ideal source of energy would be efficient, renewable, and sustainable. Various sources of alternative energy have been proposed, including wind, water, solar, nuclear, geothermal, and biomass, but thus far none have been made practically available on a large scale. Some, such as wind and water, blight the landscape, while the conversion methods for other sources, such as solar and biomass, are still relatively inefficient. The scientific community is still unclear on the best way to harness the power of photosynthesis and biomass for energy needs in a way that would allow a large-scale energy industry to use it. Scientists remain at work studying the long-term solutions to an increasingly urgent problem for humanity.

CONTROVERSIES SURROUNDING USE OF NUCLEAR POWER

Nuclear fission power, while sustainable, has a host of attendant controversial problems. Among them is the incredibly dangerous transportation and long-term storage of its radioactive waste products, for which there is still no safe long-term solution. The effects on those environments and creatures that come in contact with nuclear waste are still largely unknown. In addition, nuclear materials can be used in weaponry, and accidents at nuclear power plants like the one at Chernobyl can be devastating for thousands of years. Scientists continue their study of the process of **nuclear fusion**, hoping that if humans can learn to harness the energy produced by smashing atoms rather than splitting them, the attendant problems of nuclear waste storage will be minimized.

> **Review Video: Nuclear Fusion**
> Visit mometrix.com/academy and enter code: 381782

EFFECTS OF INCREASED PRODUCTION OF CONSUMER GOODS AFTER INDUSTRIAL REVOLUTION

Electric-based, industrial production of **manufactured goods** has led to an increase in the standard of living for many, especially those in the industrialized world. Consumer goods are produced more

Copyright © Mometrix Media. You have been licensed one copy of this document for personal use only. Any other reproduction or redistribution is strictly prohibited. All rights reserved. This content is provided for test preparation purposes only and does not imply an endorsement by Mometrix of any particular political, scientific, or religious point of view.

cheaply than ever before, since the means of production is not as dependent on the physical abilities of human beings. Scientific advancements have led to a huge number of new synthetic materials from which goods can be made, including plastics and nylon. However, this increased production damages the **environment**. Waste products are now created of which humans can make no use, a new phenomenon. Trash created from these new products is buried in landfills, where it has no access to the air, water, and sunlight that are a necessary part of biodegradation; trash made from some synthetic materials does not biodegrade at all. While some waste products can be recycled, many byproducts of industrial manufacturing are hazardous, with no safe way to dispose of them. The long-term sustainability of the environment as a result of massively increased consumer production is an issue of increasing urgency for scientists.

ISSUES CONCERNING MANAGEMENT OF RENEWABLE RESOURCES

Natural resources can be divided into two types, renewable and non-renewable. **Renewable resources** include plants and animals, along with water, air, and soil. A pre-industrial earth was a self-sustaining system, maintaining a natural balance among plants, animals, and non-living elements in which waste products from one natural process were the fuel for another. Modern humans have intervened in this process in a way that upsets the natural balance of life. Humans have introduced non-native species from one part of the world to another, resulting in the devastation of local populations. Industrial-scale buildings can create disasters for local ecosystems, ruining habitats for animal populations. Humans remove an increasing amount of the world's resources for industrial use, too quickly for nature to recover from easily. Renewable resources must be carefully managed to maintain a balanced ecosystem; over-harvesting of forests or over-hunting of animal populations can be devastating. Pollution of the air and water with chemical pollutants has far-reaching effects on the ecosystems of the earth, including the depletion of the ozone layer that protects life on earth from ultraviolet rays. The removal of forests, which produce the earth's oxygen, further depletes the ozone layer.

ISSUES CONCERNING MANAGEMENT OF NON-RENEWABLE RESOURCES

Non-renewable resources include minerals, which are created naturally over millions of years. The industrialized world extracts minerals for fuel as well as for use in electronic equipment and medicine. Increased human extraction of non-renewable resources has endangered their availability, and over-mining has created other ecological problems, including runoff and water pollution. The use of fossil fuels for energy and transportation causes air pollution and is unsustainable. Fossil fuels cannot be replaced once depleted, and they are being depleted at an increasing rate. The need to find a sustainable alternative to the use of non-renewable fossil fuels is imperative.

> **Review Video: <u>Renewable and Nonrenewable Resources</u>**
> Visit mometrix.com/academy and enter code: 840194

RECENT APPLICATIONS OF SCIENCE AND TECHNOLOGY TO HEALTH CARE, THE ENVIRONMENT, AGRICULTURE, AND INFORMATION TECHNOLOGY

Scientific and technological developments have led to the widespread availability of **technologies** heretofore unheard of, including cellular phones, satellite-based applications, and a worldwide network of connected computers. Some notable recent applications include:

- **Health care**: Antibiotics, genetic screening for diseases, the sequencing of the human genome. Issues include problems with health care distribution on an increasingly industrialized planet.

Copyright © Mometrix Media. You have been licensed one copy of this document for personal use only. Any other reproduction or redistribution is strictly prohibited. All rights reserved. This content is provided for test preparation purposes only and does not imply an endorsement by Mometrix of any particular political, scientific, or religious point of view.

- **The environment**: Computerized models of climate change and pollution monitoring. Issues include increased pollution of the water, air, and soil, and the over-harvesting of natural resources with mechanized equipment.
- **Agriculture**: Genetic improvements in agricultural practices, including increased output on the same amount of arable land. Issues include unknown environmental effects of hybrid species, cross-pollination with organic species, and pollution caused by synthetic chemical fertilizers.
- **Information technology**: New Internet-based industries, increased worldwide collaboration, and access to information. Issues include the depletion of natural resources for electronics production.

SOCIAL IMPACTS OF RECENT DEVELOPMENTS IN SCIENCE AND TECHNOLOGY

Recent **developments in science and technology** have had both positive and negative effects on human society. The issue of sustainable growth is an increasingly important one, as humans realize that the resources they use are not unlimited. Genetic research into diseases, stem cell research, and cloning technology have created great controversies as they have been introduced, and an increasing number of people reject the morality of scientific practices like animal testing in the pursuit of scientific advancement. In addition, an increasingly technology-based world has produced a new social inequality based on access to computers and Internet technology. These issues are beginning to be debated at all levels of human government, from city councils to the United Nations. Does science provide the authoritative answer to all human problems, or do ethics carry weight in scientific debates as well? Ultimately, humans must weigh the competing needs of facilitating scientific pursuits and maintaining an ethical society as they face new technological questions.

HUMAN IMPACTS ON ECOSYSTEMS

Human impacts on ecosystems take many forms and have many causes. They include widespread disruptions and specific niche disturbances. Humans practice many forms of environmental manipulation that affect plants and animals in many biomes and ecosystems. Many human practices involve the consumption of natural resources for food and energy production, the changing of the environment to produce food and energy, and the intrusion on ecosystems to provide shelter. These general behaviors include a multitude of specific behaviors, including the use and overuse of pesticides, the encroachment upon habitat, over hunting and over fishing, the introduction of plant and animal species into non-native ecosystems, not recycling, and the introduction of hazardous wastes and chemical byproducts into the environment. These behaviors have led to a number of consequences, such as acid rain, ozone depletion, deforestation, urbanization, accelerated species loss, genetic abnormalities, endocrine disruption in populations, and harm to individual animals.

GREENHOUSE EFFECT

The **greenhouse effect** refers to the naturally occurring and necessary process of **greenhouse gasses**, ozone, carbon dioxide, water vapor, and methane, trapping infrared radiation that is reflected toward the atmosphere. This is actually beneficial in that warm air is trapped. Without the greenhouse effect, it is estimated that the temperature on Earth would be 30 degrees less on average. The problem lies in human activity generating more greenhouse gases than are necessary. Excess greenhouse gases cause more infrared radiation to become trapped, which increases the temperature at the Earth's surface. The practices that increase the amount of greenhouse gases are the burning of natural gas and oil, farming practices that result in the release of methane and nitrous oxide, factory operations that produce gases, and deforestation practices that decrease the amount of oxygen available to offset greenhouse gases. Population growth also increases the volume of gases released.

Copyright © Mometrix Media. You have been licensed one copy of this document for personal use only. Any other reproduction or redistribution is strictly prohibited. All rights reserved. This content is provided for test preparation purposes only and does not imply an endorsement by Mometrix of any particular political, scientific, or religious point of view.

IMPACT

Rising temperatures may lead to an increase in sea levels as polar ice melts, lower amounts of available fresh water as coastal areas flood, and species extinction as habitats change. They'll also cause increases in certain diseases and a decreased standard of living for humans. Less fresh water and losses of habitat for humans and other species can also lead to decreased agricultural production and food supply shortages. Increased desertification leads to habitat loss for humans and certain other species. Decreases in animal populations from losses of habitat and increased hunting by other species can lead to extinction. Increases in severe weather, such as huge sustained snowstorms, may also occur at unlikely latitudes. Even though global warming results in weather that is drier and warmer overall, it still gets cold enough to snow. There may be more moisture in the atmosphere due to evaporation. **Global warming** may cause the permanent loss of glaciers and permafrost. There might also be increases in air pollution and acid rain.

IMPACT OF SCIENCE AND TECHNOLOGY ON ENVIRONMENT AND HUMAN AFFAIRS

Since the industrial revolution, science and technology have had a profound impact on **human affairs**. There has been a rapid increase in the number of discoveries in many fields. Many major and minor discoveries have led to a great improvement in the quality of life of many people. This includes longer life spans because of better nutrition, increased access to medical care, and a decrease in workplace health hazards. Not all problems, such as health hazards and poor nutrition, have been solved, and many still exist in one form or another. For example, even though there are means to recycle, not every business does so because of economic factors. These advances, while improving the lives of many humans, have also taken their toll on the environment. A possible solution may arise when the carrying capacity for humans on Earth is reached. The population will decline, and solutions will have to be found. Otherwise, an immediate halt or decrease in the human behaviors that are causing environmental damage will need to happen.

PURPOSE OF STUDYING INTERACTIONS AMONG HUMANS, NATURAL HAZARDS, AND THE ENVIRONMENT

In science class, students will learn that the **human population** on earth can be affected by various factors from both their natural environments and from the technologies they use in their daily lives. These factors can be positive or negative, so students need to learn how to prepare for, respond to, and evaluate the consequences of environmental occurrences over a long period of time. Natural disasters are a negative experience, but so are human-made disasters such as pollution and deforestation. Students need to understand that science is involved in the interactions between the human population, natural hazards, and the environment. They should know that the aim of science is to make these interactions **balanced and positive**. Science is a discipline that can help find ways to increase safety during and remediate destruction after natural disasters. Science can also advance technology and transportation in an environmentally safe manner, prevent and cure diseases, and remediate the effects of pollution and resource depletion.

SUBJECTS COVERED IN PERSONAL HEALTH PORTION OF SCIENCE CLASS

Among the personal and social perspectives of science are the issues of **personal and public health care**. In this area, students learn such things as:

- The importance of regular **exercise** to the maintenance and improvement of health
- The need for **risk assessment** and educated decisions to prevent injuries and illnesses because of the potential for accidents and the existence of hazards
- The risk of illness and the social and psychological factors associated with the use of **tobacco products**

Copyright © Mometrix Media. You have been licensed one copy of this document for personal use only. Any other reproduction or redistribution is strictly prohibited. All rights reserved. This content is provided for test preparation purposes only and does not imply an endorsement by Mometrix of any particular political, scientific, or religious point of view.

- The dangers of abusing **alcohol and other drug substances**, including addiction and damage to body functions
- The energy and nutrition values of various **foods**, their role in growth and development, and the requirements of the body according to variable factors
- The complexities of **human sexuality** and the dangers of sexually transmitted infections
- The relationship between **environmental and human health**, and the need to monitor soil, water, and air standards

RISK AND BENEFIT ANALYSIS AS STUDIED IN PERSONAL AND SOCIAL PERSPECTIVES OF SCIENCE

Risk analysis considers the type of hazard and estimates the number of people who might be exposed and the number likely to suffer consequences. The results are used to determine options for reducing or eliminating risks. For example, the Center for Disease Control must analyze the risk of a certain new virus strain causing a pandemic, how many people and what age groups need to be vaccinated first, and what precautions can be taken to guard against the spread of the disease. **Risk and benefit analysis** involves having students consider the dangers of natural (major storms), chemical (pollution), biological (pollen and bacteria), social (occupational safety and transportation), and personal (smoking, dieting, and drugs) hazards. Students then use a systematic approach to think critically about these hazards, apply probability estimates to the risks, and compare them to estimated and perceived personal and social benefits.

INTERACTIONS OF SCIENCE AND TECHNOLOGY WITH SOCIETY

The interactions of science and technology with society include:

- **Scientific knowledge** and the procedures used by scientists influence the way many people think about themselves, others, and the environment.
- **Technology** influences society through its products and processes. It influences quality of life and the ways people act and interact. Technological changes are often accompanied by social, political, and economic changes. Science and technology contribute enormously to economic growth and productivity. The introduction of the cell phone into society is a perfect example of technology influencing society, quality of life, human interaction, and the economy.
- **Societal challenges** often inspire questions for scientific research, and social priorities often influence research priorities through the availability of research funding.

Science and technology have been advanced through the contributions of many different people in a variety of cultures during different time periods in history. Scientists and engineers work in colleges, businesses and industries, research institutes, and government agencies, touching many lives in a variety of settings.

CHAPTER QUIZ
1. Which of the following is NOT a renewable resource?
    a. Water
    b. Minerals
    c. Soil
    d. Air

Copyright © Mometrix Media. You have been licensed one copy of this document for personal use only. Any other reproduction or redistribution is strictly prohibited. All rights reserved. This content is provided for test preparation purposes only and does not imply an endorsement by Mometrix of any particular political, scientific, or religious point of view.

2. Which of the following is NOT a greenhouse gas?

    a. Nitrogen
    b. Carbon dioxide
    c. Methane
    d. Ozone

CHAPTER QUIZ ANSWER KEY

1. B: Natural resources can be divided into two types: renewable and non-renewable. Renewable resources include plants, animals, water, air, and soil.

2. A: The greenhouse effect refers to the naturally occurring and necessary process of greenhouse gases—ozone, carbon dioxide, water vapor, and methane—trapping infrared radiation that is reflected toward the atmosphere. This is actually beneficial in that warm air is trapped. Without the greenhouse effect, it is estimated that the temperature on Earth would be 30 degrees Celsius less on average. The problem lies in human activity generating more greenhouse gases than are necessary.

Copyright © Mometrix Media. You have been licensed one copy of this document for personal use only. Any other reproduction or redistribution is strictly prohibited. All rights reserved.
This content is provided for test preparation purposes only and does not imply an endorsement by Mometrix of any particular political, scientific, or religious point of view.

Praxis Practice Test #1

Reading and Language Arts

1. The pairs of words *sea* and *see*, *fair* and *fare*, are called:
- a. Homophones
- b. Antonyms
- c. Homographs
- d. Twin words

2. In preparation for writing a paper, a class has been instructed to skim a number of online and print documents. The students are being asked to:
- a. Read the documents several times, skimming to a deeper level of understanding each time.
- b. Read the documents quickly, looking for those that offer the most basic, general information.
- c. Read the documents quickly, looking for key words in order to gather the basic premise of each.
- d. Read the documents carefully, looking for those that offer the most in-depth information.

3. Which of the following is the best definition of information literacy?
- a. It is the set of skills required for reading and comprehending different information.
- b. It is the cognitive skill set necessary to amass a comprehensive base of knowledge.
- c. It is the skill set required for the finding, retrieval, analysis, and use of information.
- d. It is the set of skills necessary for effectively communicating information to others.

4. Which of the following choices describes the best introduction to a unit on oral traditions from around the world?
- a. Introducing games that practice new sight words, encoding words based on phonics rules, and answering short comprehension questions.
- b. Setting up video-conferencing with a school in Asia so that students can communicate with children from other countries.
- c. Inviting a guest speaker from a nearby Native American group to demonstrate oral storytelling to the class.
- d. Creating a slide show presentation about various types of oral cultures and traditions and characteristics of each.

5. A syllable must contain:
- a. A vowel
- b. A consonant
- c. Both a vowel and a consonant
- d. A meaning

Copyright © Mometrix Media. You have been licensed one copy of this document for personal use only. Any other reproduction or redistribution is strictly prohibited. All rights reserved. This content is provided for test preparation purposes only and does not imply an endorsement by Mometrix of any particular political, scientific, or religious point of view.

6. A class is reading a 14-line poem in iambic pentameter. There are three stanzas of four lines each, and a two-line couplet at the end. Words at the end of each line rhyme with another word in the same stanza. The class is reading a:

    a. Sonnet
    b. Villanelle
    c. Sestina
    d. Limerick

7. According to MLA guidelines for writing research papers, which of the following is correct regarding citations of Web sources if you cannot immediately see the name of a source's author?

    a. Assume the author is not named, as this is a common occurrence online.
    b. Do not name an agency or corporation as the author if it is the sponsor of the source.
    c. Author names are often on websites, but sometimes they are hard to find.
    d. It is not permissible to cite the book or article title in lieu of an author's name.

8. A student says, "We learned that knowledge and understanding of language is important." This is an example of an error in which of these?

    a. Phonology
    b. Semantics
    c. Syntax
    d. Pragmatics

9. The purpose of corrective feedback is:

    a. To provide students with methods for explaining to the teacher or classmates what a passage was about
    b. To correct an error in reading a student has made, specifically clarifying where and how the error was made so that the student can avoid similar errors in the future
    c. To provide a mental framework that will help the student correctly organize new information
    d. To remind students that error is essential in order to truly understand and that it is not something to be ashamed of

10. A third grader knows he needs to write from left to right and from top to bottom on the page. He knows what sounds are associated with specific letters. He can recognize individual letters and can hear word families. He correctly identifies prefixes, suffixes, and homonyms, and his reading comprehension is very good. However, when he is asked to write, he becomes very upset. He has trouble holding a pencil, his letters are very primitively executed, and his written work is not legible. He most likely has:

    a. Dysgraphia
    b. Dyslexia
    c. Dyspraxia
    d. Nonverbal learning disorder

Copyright © Mometrix Media. You have been licensed one copy of this document for personal use only. Any other reproduction or redistribution is strictly prohibited. All rights reserved.
This content is provided for test preparation purposes only and does not imply an endorsement by Mometrix of any particular political, scientific, or religious point of view.

11. Which statement is correct regarding the relationship of your audience profile to the decisions you make in completing a writing assignment?

    a. How much time you spend on research is unrelated to your audience.
    b. Your audience does not influence how much information you include.
    c. The writing style, tone, and wording you use depend on your audience.
    d. How you organize information depends on structure, not on audience.

12. A classroom teacher observes that a new ELL student consistently omits the /h/ sound in words. Of these, what is the first factor the teacher should consider?

    a. The student may have an articulation disorder.
    b. The student may be a native Spanish speaker.
    c. The student may need a hearing assessment.
    d. The student may have a respiratory problem.

13. _Phone, they, church._ The underlined letters in these words are examples of:

    a. Consonant blend
    b. Consonant shift
    c. Continental shift
    d. Consonant digraph

14. Examples of onomatopoeia are:

    a. Sink, drink, mink, link
    b. Their, there, they're
    c. Drip, chirp, splash, giggle
    d. Think, in, thin, ink

15. Which of the following exercises would be the most appropriate tool for helping students evaluate the effectiveness of their own spoken messages?

    a. Discuss written and oral assignments in class before completing them. Once the assignments are completed, the teacher meets individually with each student to discuss the content and effectiveness of each student's work.
    b. Instruct students to present oral reports in class, which are then "graded" by classmates. A score of 1-10 is assigned based on students' perception of the reports' clarity. The students' average scores determine the effectiveness of each report.
    c. Ask each student to prepare an oral report and a content quiz that highlights the report's main idea. The student then uses classmates' scores on the reviews to determine the report's effectiveness.
    d. Put students into groups of three. Two students complete a role-playing assignment based on prompts provided by the teacher. The third student gives constructive feedback on how the other two can refine and clarify their speech.

16. When teaching students relationships between sounds and letters and between letters and words, what practices should teachers best follow?

    a. Use a variety of instructional techniques, but including only the auditory and visual modes.
    b. Incorporate multisensory modalities within a variety of instructional strategies and materials.
    c. Always adhere to the same exact instructional method and materials to ensure consistency.
    d. Introduce similar-looking letters and similar-sounding phonemes together for discrimination.

Copyright © Mometrix Media. You have been licensed one copy of this document for personal use only. Any other reproduction or redistribution is strictly prohibited. All rights reserved.
This content is provided for test preparation purposes only and does not imply an endorsement by Mometrix of any particular political, scientific, or religious point of view.

17. Which is greater, the number of English phonemes or the number of letters in the alphabet?

    a. The number of letters in the alphabet, because they can be combined to create phonemes.

    b. The number of phonemes. A phoneme is the smallest measure of language sound.

    c. They are identical; each letter "owns" a correspondent sound.

    d. Neither. Phonemes and alphabet letters are completely unrelated.

18. An understanding of the meanings of prefixes and suffixes such as *dis, mis, un, re, able,* and *ment* are important for:

    a. Reading comprehension

    b. Word recognition

    c. Vocabulary building

    d. Reading fluency

19. When considering strategies for writing assignments, it helps to know the cognitive (or learning) objective(s) your teacher is aiming to meet with an assignment. If the assignment asks you to "describe," "explain," "summarize," "restate," "classify," or "review" some material you read, what is the cognitive objective?

    a. Knowledge recall

    b. Application

    c. Comprehension

    d. Evaluation

20. Among the following, which is NOT a common academic standard for kindergarten students in decoding and identifying words?

    a. Showing knowledge that letter sequences correspond to phoneme sequences

    b. Understanding that word sounds and meanings change along with word letters

    c. Decoding monosyllabic words using initial and final consonant and vowel sounds

    d. Matching letters to consonant sounds; reading simple, monosyllabic sight words

21. Which of the following choices will be most important when designing a reading activity or lesson for students?

    a. Selecting a text

    b. Determining the number of students participating

    c. Analyzing the point in the school year at which the lesson is given

    d. Determining a purpose for instruction

Copyright © Mometrix Media. You have been licensed one copy of this document for personal use only. Any other reproduction or redistribution is strictly prohibited. All rights reserved. This content is provided for test preparation purposes only and does not imply an endorsement by Mometrix of any particular political, scientific, or religious point of view.

22. Silent reading fluency can best be assessed by:

a. Having the student retell or summarize the material to determine how much was understood.

b. Giving a written test that covers plot, theme, character development, sequence of events, rising action, climax, falling action, and outcome. A student must test at a 95% accuracy rate to be considered fluent at silent reading.

c. Giving a three-minute Test of Silent Contextual Reading Fluency four times a year. The student is presented with text in which spaces between words and all punctuation have been removed. The student must divide one word from another with slash marks, as in the example: The/little/sailboat/bobbed/so/far/in/the/distance/it/looked/like/a/toy. The more words a student accurately separates, the higher her silent reading fluency score.

d. Silent reading fluency cannot be assessed. It is a private act between the reader and the text and does not invite critique.

23. Which of the following strategies would not be helpful in building the word-identification skills of emergent readers?

a. Allowing for invented spelling in written assignments or in-class work.

b. Reinforcing phonemic awareness while reading aloud.

c. Using dictionaries to look up unfamiliar words.

d. Studying and reviewing commonly used sight words at the students' ability level.

24. According to the Texas Essential Knowledge and Skills (TEKS) for English Language Arts and Reading, which of the following are students in grades 1-3 expected to do?

a. Regularly read materials at the independent level, i.e., text containing one in 10 or fewer difficult words

b. Select text to read independently using author knowledge, difficulty estimation, and personal interest

c. Regularly read materials at the instructional level (i.e., text containing 1 in 20 or fewer difficult words)

d. Read aloud from unfamiliar texts fluently (i.e., with accuracy, phrasing, expression, and punctuation)

25. A student is able to apply strategies to comprehend the meanings of unfamiliar words; can supply definitions for words with several meanings such as *crucial, criticism,* and *witness*; and is able to reflect on her background knowledge in order to decipher a word's meaning. These features of effective reading belong to which category?

a. Word recognition

b. Vocabulary

c. Content

d. Comprehension

26. Which of the following was the author of *The Pilgrim's Progress?*

a. John Bunyan

b. William Congreve

c. Daniel Defoe

d. Samuel Butler

Copyright © Mometrix Media. You have been licensed one copy of this document for personal use only. Any other reproduction or redistribution is strictly prohibited. All rights reserved.
This content is provided for test preparation purposes only and does not imply an endorsement by Mometrix of any particular political, scientific, or religious point of view.

27. Which of the following gives an example of a fallacy of inconsistency?

   a. "There are exceptions to all general statements."
   b. "Please pass me; my parents will be upset if I fail."
   c. "He is guilty: there is no evidence he is innocent."
   d. "Have you stopped cheating on your assignments?"

28. Which statement accurately reflects a principle regarding self-questioning techniques for increasing student reading comprehension?

   a. Asking only what kinds of "expert questions" fit the text's subject matter
   b. Asking only those questions that the text raises for the individual student
   c. Asking how each text portion relates to chapter main ideas is unnecessary
   d. Asking how the text information fits with what the student already knows

29. A student encounters a multisyllabic word. She's not sure if she's seen it before. What should she do first? What should she do next?

   a. Locate familiar word parts, then locate the consonants
   b. Locate the consonants, then locate the vowels
   c. Locate the vowels, then locate familiar word parts
   d. Look it up in the dictionary, then write down the meaning

30. In the model known in reading instruction as the Three Cueing Systems, which of these relate most to how sounds are used to communicate meaning?

   a. Syntactic cues
   b. Semantic cues
   c. Phonological cues
   d. Pragmatic cues

31. Which choice does NOT describe a common outcome of reading or writing?

   a. Communication of ideas
   b. Character development
   c. Enjoyment
   d. Language acquisition

32. Of the following examples, which one is NOT an open-ended question?

   a. "When does the climax of this story occur?"
   b. "Is this expression a simile or a metaphor?"
   c. "How are similes and metaphors different?"
   d. "What are some reasons we have poetry?"

33. *Bi, re,* and *un* are:

   a. Suffixes, appearing at the beginning of base words to change their meaning
   b. Suffixes, appearing at the end of base words to enhance their meaning
   c. Prefixes, appearing at the beginning of base words to emphasize their meaning
   d. Prefixes, appearing at the beginning of base words to change their meanings

Copyright © Mometrix Media. You have been licensed one copy of this document for personal use only. Any other reproduction or redistribution is strictly prohibited. All rights reserved.
This content is provided for test preparation purposes only and does not imply an endorsement by Mometrix of any particular political, scientific, or religious point of view.

34. Some experts maintain that teaching reading comprehension entails not just the application of skills, but the process of actively constructing meaning. They describe this process as *interactive, strategic,* and *adaptable.* Which of the following best defines the *interactive* aspect of this process?

    a.   The process involves the text, the reader, and the context in which reading occurs.
    b.   The process involves readers' using a variety of strategies in constructing meaning.
    c.   The process involves readers' changing their strategies to read different text types.
    d.   The process involves changing strategies according to different reasons for reading.

35. Mr. Harris divides his 3rd-grade English class into two sections each day. Approximately 60% of the class period is spent on phonics and sight word practice, and 40% is spent on learning comprehension strategies. Which statement is most true regarding Mr. Harris' approach?

    a.   This approach neglects several important components of language instruction.
    b.   This approach will bore the students and possibly create negative feelings about English class.
    c.   This approach will provide the best balance of reading instruction for this age group.
    d.   This approach could be improved by spending equal amounts of time on each component, as they are equally important.

36. After only two or three months into 1st grade, a new substitute teacher gives grades in the 80s to a student who had been receiving 100s from the regular teacher before the teacher had to take emergency leave. The substitute deducts points when the student occasionally reverses a letter or number, or misspells words like *biscuit, butterfly,* and *swallowed.* Which of the following most accurately describes this scenario?

    a.   The regular teacher should not have given 100s; the substitute grades errors more thoroughly.
    b.   The student should be evaluated for possible dyslexia because she reverses letters and numbers.
    c.   The student's writing is developmentally appropriate; the substitute's grading is inappropriate.
    d.   The student's occasional reversals are not important, but the misspellings need interventions.

37. Collaborative Strategic Reading (CSR) is a teaching technique that depends on two teaching practices. These practices are:

    a.   Cooperative learning and reading comprehension
    b.   Cooperative reading and metacognition
    c.   Reading comprehension and metacognition
    d.   Cooperative learning and metacognition

38. Which of the following is the most accurate characterization of dialects?

    a.   They are non-standard versions of any language.
    b.   They are often seen as less socially acceptable.
    c.   They include linguistic features that are incorrect.
    d.   They indicate poor/incomplete language learning.

Copyright © Mometrix Media. You have been licensed one copy of this document for personal use only. Any other reproduction or redistribution is strictly prohibited. All rights reserved.
This content is provided for test preparation purposes only and does not imply an endorsement by Mometrix of any particular political, scientific, or religious point of view.

39. Which of the following choices would be the least effective example of an integrated curriculum that includes language arts instruction?

a. Ms. Smith, a language teacher, confers with Mr. Langston, a history and social studies teacher. Ms. Smith shows Mr. Langston how to model previewing and predicting skills before he introduces a new unit or assignment so that the students build their comprehension skills while reading for information.

b. A science teacher recognizes that the students are having difficulty retaining information from their science textbooks when test time arrives. She creates a study guide with leading questions designed to help jog the students' memory about important concepts before the test.

c. Ms. Shannon, an art teacher, plans a field trip to see the latest exhibit featuring a symbolic artist. A language teacher at her school joins the students at the museum to lead a discussion about the function of symbols and their meanings, as well as different methods of interpreting shared symbols in a society.

d. A 1st-grade teacher uses children's books that introduce mathematical skills. For example, she reads a book weekly that tells a story about children preparing for a picnic, adding and subtracting items they need for the trip along the way. She encourages the children to solve the math questions along with her during the story.

40. A teacher has a student in her class who is not very motivated to write because he finds it difficult. She observes he has a highly visual learning style, does not like reading books but loves graphic novels, and has considerable artistic drawing talent and interest. Which of the following instructional strategies would best address his individual needs, strengths, and interests?

a. Giving him audio recordings to accompany and guide his writing homework
b. Letting him complete all assignments by drawing pictures instead of writing
c. Having him draw the pictures and write accompanying text in graphic novels
d. Providing and assigning him to view animated videos on the topic of writing

41. A reading teacher feels that some of his strategies aren't effective. He has asked a specialist to observe him and make suggestions as to how he can improve. The reading specialist should suggest that first:

a. The teacher should set up a video camera and record several sessions with different students for the specialist to review. The presence of an observer changes the outcome; if the specialist is in the room, it will negatively affect the students' ability to read.

b. The teacher should reflect on his strategies himself. Which seem to work? Which don't? Can the teacher figure out why? It is always best to encourage teachers to find their own solutions so that they can handle future issues themselves.

c. They should meet to discuss areas the teacher is most concerned about and decide on the teacher's goals.

d. The specialist should arrive unannounced to observe the teacher interacting with students. This will prevent the teacher from unconsciously over-preparing.

42. Which of the following is an example of a portmanteau?

a. Fax
b. Brunch
c. Babysitter
d. Saxophone

Copyright © Mometrix Media. You have been licensed one copy of this document for personal use only. Any other reproduction or redistribution is strictly prohibited. All rights reserved.
This content is provided for test preparation purposes only and does not imply an endorsement by Mometrix of any particular political, scientific, or religious point of view.

43. Amelia has been having trouble in her 1st-grade class for several months. When her teacher, Mrs. Gant, calls Amelia for one-on-one reading practice, Amelia avoids her and protests that she is working on something else at the time. Amelia knows all her letter-sounds when she sees them individually. However, she still cannot consistently decode simple words. Amelia often seems "lost" when her teacher gives her instructions or explains an activity to the group. She usually needs to ask several times for directions to be repeated and oftentimes does not understand what is being asked of her. Amelia sometimes misbehaves in class, hiding during lesson time or arguing with other students during group activities. Which answer choice describes the best sort of classroom modifications for Amelia, given her difficulties?

    a.   A multi-sensory literacy approach using tactile, kinesthetic, visual and auditory techniques in combination with systematic instruction.
    b.   Modified lessons that teach concepts without the use of reading skills.
    c.   Extra practice in reading on a daily basis.
    d.   Creating engaging activities that will capture Amelia's interest in reading and introducing texts that will motivate her to complete lessons.

44. To measure children's emergent literacy development, an early childhood teacher informally evaluates their performance and behaviors during daily classroom activities. This is an example of what kind of assessment?

    a.   Formative assessment
    b.   Summative assessment
    c.   Both (a) and (b)
    d.   Neither (a) nor (b)

45. Round-robin reading refers to the practice of allowing children to take turns reading portions of a text aloud to the rest of the group during class. Which of the following statements is <u>least</u> true about this practice?

    a.   Students have the chance to practice reading aloud with this strategy.
    b.   This practice is ineffective in its use of time, leaving students who are not reading aloud to become bored or daydream.
    c.   Round-robin reading lacks the creativity or engaging qualities that will interest students in building literacy skills.
    d.   This practice helps students feel comfortable with reading aloud due to continuous practice and encouragement from the teacher and peers.

46. Which of the basic elements of the writing process should be completed before the first draft is written?

    a.   Prewriting
    b.   Revising
    c.   Conferencing
    d.   Editing

47. The words *chow*, *whoosh*, and *stalk* all contain:

    a.   Blends
    b.   Digraphs
    c.   Trigraphs
    d.   Monoliths

Copyright © Mometrix Media. You have been licensed one copy of this document for personal use only. Any other reproduction or redistribution is strictly prohibited. All rights reserved.
This content is provided for test preparation purposes only and does not imply an endorsement by Mometrix of any particular political, scientific, or religious point of view.

48. Research indicates that developing oral language proficiency in emergent readers is important because:

  a. Proficiency with oral language enhances students' phonemic awareness and increases vocabulary.
  b. The more verbally expressive emergent readers are, the more confident they become. Such students will embrace both Academic and Independent reading levels.
  c. It encourages curiosity about others. With strong oral language skills, students begin to question the world around them. The more they ask, the richer their background knowledge.
  d. It demonstrates to students that their ideas are important and worth sharing.

49. Arthur writes a paper. One classmate identifies ideas and words that resonated with her when she read it. Another describes how reading the paper changed his thinking. A third asks Arthur some questions about what he meant by certain statements in the paper. A fourth suggests a portion of the paper that needs more supporting information. This description is most typical of which of the following?

  a. Portfolio assessment
  b. Holistic scoring
  c. Scoring rubric
  d. Peer review

50. Which text should a teacher choose in order to practice the skills of previewing and reviewing information?

  a. A poem
  b. A chapter from the students' science class textbook
  c. A library book of each student's own choosing
  d. A short story from language arts class

51. "Language load" refers to:

  a. The basic vocabulary words a first grader has committed to memory.
  b. The number of unrecognizable words an English language learner encounters when reading a passage or listening to a teacher.
  c. The damage that carrying a pile of heavy books could cause to a child's physique.
  d. The number of different languages a person has mastered

Copyright © Mometrix Media. You have been licensed one copy of this document for personal use only. Any other reproduction or redistribution is strictly prohibited. All rights reserved.
This content is provided for test preparation purposes only and does not imply an endorsement by Mometrix of any particular political, scientific, or religious point of view.

52. The first-grade teacher wants her class to understand that stories have a certain order. She reads them a story, then orally reviews how each event that happened in the story caused the next event to happen. To reinforce the lesson, the teacher should:

a. Give each child a piece of drawing paper that has been folded in half and then in half again, creating four boxes, along with a piece that has not been folded. The teacher should then ask the students to draw a cartoon about the story. Each of the first four boxes will show the events in order. The second page is to show how the story ends.

b. Give each child a piece of drawing paper and ask the students to draw the most important scene.

c. Give each child a piece of drawing paper and ask the students to draw the story's beginning on the front of the page and ending on the back.

d. Give each child a piece of drawing paper that has been folded in half and then in half again, creating four boxes, along with a piece that has not been folded. The teacher should then ask the students to draw a cartoon about anything they want. She reminds them to put their story cartoons in proper order.

53. Which of the following typically combines signal phrases and parenthetical references for documenting sources in literature?

a. An MLA list of the works cited
b. MLA in-text citations in a paper
c. Adding MLA information notes
d. All APA citations

54. Following instruction time, Ms. Pitman provides each student with a small sign that can be hung around the waist or neck. Ten children in her class receive signs displaying a single weekly vocabulary word. Five students get signs with the following: *dis-*, *re-*, *pre-*, *un-*, and *mis-*. The remaining students have signs with the following: *-ing*, *-ed*, *-s*, *-less*, and *-ful*. What is the best choice for a follow-up class activity based on this information?

a. The students are arranged into groups to demonstrate tangibly that certain parts of the English language have fixed functions.

b. Each student must use his or her sign to brainstorm a list of possible words that include those letters.

c. Each time a bell is rung, students must find a new partner with whom he or she can combine signs to make a new word.

d. Ask each student to explain what his or her sign means and how it functions in the English language.

55. At the beginning of each month, Mr. Yi has Jade read a page or two from a book she hasn't seen before. He notes the total number of words in the section and the number of times she leaves out or misreads a word. If Jade reads the passage with less than 3% error, Mr. Yi is satisfied that Jade is:

a. Reading with full comprehension
b. Probably bored and should try a more difficult book
c. Reading at her independent reading level
d. Comfortable with the syntactical meaning

Copyright © Mometrix Media. You have been licensed one copy of this document for personal use only. Any other reproduction or redistribution is strictly prohibited. All rights reserved. This content is provided for test preparation purposes only and does not imply an endorsement by Mometrix of any particular political, scientific, or religious point of view.

56. Which assessment will determine a student's ability to identify initial, medial, blended, final, segmented, and manipulated "units"?

   a. Phonological awareness assessment
   b. High-frequency word assessment
   c. Reading fluency assessment
   d. Comprehension quick-check

57. When you have a writing assignment, which of the following is true about your audience?

   a. You need not identify the audience because it is the teacher who gave the assignment.
   b. You should consider how your readers are likely to use what you write.
   c. You should know your writing purpose more than a reader's purposes.
   d. You are overthinking to wonder about readers' likely attitude/reaction.

58. Which of the following is correct regarding phonological awareness in kindergarteners?

   a. Children with delayed language development have benefited from phonological awareness training.
   b. Researchers into instruction in phonological awareness advise against using SLPs and their methods.
   c. Phonological awareness in kindergarteners requires changing phonemes in words to change meaning.
   d. Phonological awareness instruction for kindergarteners involves only the individual phoneme level.

59. Sight words are:

   a. Common words with irregular spelling
   b. Words that can easily be found on educational websites
   c. Any word that can be seen, including text words, words on signs, brochures, banners, and so forth
   d. There is no such thing; because oral language is learned before written language, all words are ultimately based on sound. The correct term is sound words and includes all words necessary to decode a particular text.

60. A second-grade teacher wants to help her students enrich their vocabulary. She's noticed that their writing journals are filled with serviceable but unexciting verbs such as "said" and "went," and general rather than specific nouns. The most effective lesson would involve:

   a. Suggesting students use a thesaurus to replace common words with more unusual words
   b. Suggesting students add an adjective to each noun
   c. Brainstorming a list of verbs that mean ways of talking or ways of going, then adding them to the word wall along with some nouns that specify common topics
   d. Suggesting students look up the meanings of boring words and consider another way to express them

Copyright © Mometrix Media. You have been licensed one copy of this document for personal use only. Any other reproduction or redistribution is strictly prohibited. All rights reserved.
This content is provided for test preparation purposes only and does not imply an endorsement by Mometrix of any particular political, scientific, or religious point of view.

61. Which of the following students may need extra instruction and evaluation with respect to oral language skills?

    a. Rosa: whose first language is Spanish. Rosa speaks with a distinct accent and can be difficult to understand when speaking about a new or unfamiliar topic.

    b. Greer: who avoids oral assignments when possible. He avoids speaking up in class and only responds when called upon.

    c. Ashley: who often has trouble answering questions in class. Her responses are often off-topic. She also struggles with oral presentations, seeming to present a string of unrelated facts.

    d. Brett: who frequently becomes loud and disruptive whenever group work is assigned. He often becomes involved in heated discussions with classmates when discussing ideas.

62. Which of the following factors affects ELL students' English-language literacy development?

    a. A Chinese student's L1 is not written alphabetically like English is.

    b. A Spanish student's L1 is more phonetically regular than English is.

    c. Neither one of these has any effects on L2 literacy development.

    d. Both factors affect L2 literacy development but in different ways.

63. The term "common words" means:

    a. One-syllable words with fewer than three letters. Some examples are *it*, *an*, *a*, *I*, *go*, *to*, and *in*. They are the first words an emergent writer learns.

    b. One-syllable words with fewer than five letters. Some examples include *sing*, *goes*, *sit*, *rock*, *walk*, and *took*.

    c. Words that are ordinary or unexceptional; because they tend to flatten a piece of writing, they should be avoided.

    d. Familiar, frequently used words that do not need to be taught beyond primary grades.

64. Which choice is NOT a cueing system used to understand unfamiliar words?

    a. Syntactic

    b. Semantic

    c. Graphophonic

    d. Auditory

65. Which of the following is most accurate regarding writing style?

    a. The kind of diction you use does not affect style.

    b. You add style later to give your writing personality.

    c. Style is unrelated to your control of your content.

    d. Your purpose for writing guides your writing style.

66. What statement is most accurate regarding the context(s) wherein students develop literacy?

    a. Students develop literacy by reading, writing, listening, and speaking.

    b. Students develop literacy by reading, writing, and listening to speech.

    c. Students develop literacy by reading and writing only.

    d. Students develop literacy only by reading.

Copyright © Mometrix Media. You have been licensed one copy of this document for personal use only. Any other reproduction or redistribution is strictly prohibited. All rights reserved.
This content is provided for test preparation purposes only and does not imply an endorsement by Mometrix of any particular political, scientific, or religious point of view.

67. The most effective strategy for decoding sight words is:

a. Segmenting sight words into syllables. Beginning readers are understandably nervous when encountering a long word that isn't familiar. Blocking off all but a single syllable at a time renders a word manageable and allows the reader a sense of control over the act of reading.

b. Word families. By grouping the sight word with similar words, patterns emerge.

c. A phonemic approach. When students understand the connection between individual words and their sounds, they will be able to sound out any sight word they encounter.

d. None; sight words cannot be decoded. Readers must learn to recognize these as whole words on sight.

68. Editing involves:

a. Correcting surface features such as sentence fragments, spelling, and punctuation

b. Fine-tuning the underlying structure of the piece to make the theme stand out

c. Reconsidering ideas, adding or subtracting information, and changing the underlying structure

d. Adding illustrations, charts, and other useful addenda

69. A teacher wants to work on her students' listening comprehension in addition to their reading comprehension since she understands that the skills are interrelated. She has a series of short stories that she thinks the students will enjoy. Which of the following would be the best supplement to typical written comprehension exercises?

a. Preview the content and then read the stories aloud to the students. Assess listening comprehension through verbal and written questions.

b. Ask the students to choose one story each to read aloud to a small group. Encourage the students to discuss what they have learned afterward.

c. Assign each student a story to read and require them to write a report on it. Each student should then present his or her report based on what he or she has learned to the class.

d. Have the students read stories aloud to the class, and create mock tests based upon the main ideas which they identify.

70. Which of the following MOST accurately summarizes the relationship between reading fluency and reading comprehension?

a. As students develop greater reading comprehension, their reading fluency also improves.

b. When students develop greater reading fluency, their reading comprehension improves.

c. The relationship between reading fluency and reading comprehension is a reciprocal one.

d. Reading fluency and reading comprehension are two separate, mainly unrelated skill sets.

71. Phonological awareness activities are:

a. Oral

b. Visual

c. Tactile

d. Semantically based

72. William Shakespeare wrote during which historical and literary period?

a. Medieval

b. Renaissance

c. Restoration

d. Enlightenment

Copyright © Mometrix Media. You have been licensed one copy of this document for personal use only. Any other reproduction or redistribution is strictly prohibited. All rights reserved.
This content is provided for test preparation purposes only and does not imply an endorsement by Mometrix of any particular political, scientific, or religious point of view.

73. Of the following sentences, which one appeals to emotion?
a. It is dangerous to use a cell phone while driving because you steer one-handed.
b. Statistics of greater accident risk show cell phone use while driving is dangerous.
c. It is really stupid to use a cell phone when you drive because it is so dangerous.
d. Many state laws ban cell phone use when driving due to data on more accidents.

74. To determine the subject matter of a section within a text chapter, what should the teacher tell the student to do?
a. Read the section heading
b. Read the chapter glossary
c. Read the index in the text
d. Read through the section

75. A class is reading *The Heart Is a Lonely Hunter*. The teacher asks students to write a short paper explaining the story's resolution. She is asking them to locate and discuss the story's:
a. Outcome
b. Highest or most dramatic moment
c. Plot
d. Lowest point

76. In the word-recognition model of the Three Cueing Systems used in teaching reading, which of the following is most associated with the meanings of words?
a. Using pragmatic cues
b. The phonological system
c. The syntactic system
d. The semantic system

77. Abi, a fifth-grader, is reading aloud to his teacher during one-on-one reading time. His teacher uses this time to evaluate ongoing fluency and comprehension skills. Following today's reading, Abi's teacher determines that he needs practice with words that begin with digraphs. Which of the following sets of words would most likely be part of this assignment?
a. Chicken, Shells, That
b. Were, Frame, Click
c. Sponge, Think, Blank
d. Packed, Blistered, Smoothed

78. To support student vocabulary development, which of the following most accurately describes the instructional materials teachers should use?
a. Teachers should only use literature and expository texts to support student vocabulary development.
b. Teachers should use newspapers, magazines, etc., in addition to literature and expository textbooks.
c. Teachers should use trade books, content-specific texts, and technology for vocabulary development.
d. Teachers should use a broad variety of instructional materials, including all of the above and others.

Copyright © Mometrix Media. You have been licensed one copy of this document for personal use only. Any other reproduction or redistribution is strictly prohibited. All rights reserved.
This content is provided for test preparation purposes only and does not imply an endorsement by Mometrix of any particular political, scientific, or religious point of view.

79. A fifth-grader has prepared a report on reptiles, which is something he knows a great deal about. He rereads his report and decides to make a number of changes. He moves a sentence from the top to the last paragraph. He crosses out several words and replaces them with more specific words. He circles key information and draws an arrow to show another place the information could logically be placed. He is engaged in:

   a. Editing
   b. Revising
   c. First editing, then revising
   d. Reviewing

80. When students are taught to use effective reading comprehension strategies, they not only achieve deeper understanding, they also learn to think about how they think when reading. This is known as which of the following?

   a. Schemata
   b. Scaffolding
   c. Metacognition
   d. Metamorphosis

Copyright © Mometrix Media. You have been licensed one copy of this document for personal use only. Any other reproduction or redistribution is strictly prohibited. All rights reserved. This content is provided for test preparation purposes only and does not imply an endorsement by Mometrix of any particular political, scientific, or religious point of view.

Mathematics

1. Determine the number of diagonals of a dodecagon.

   a. 12
   b. 24
   c. 54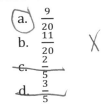
   d. 108

2. A dress is marked down by 20% and placed on a clearance rack, on which is posted a sign reading, "Take an extra 25% off already reduced merchandise." What fraction of the original price is the final sale price of the dress?

   a. $\frac{9}{20}$
   b. $\frac{11}{20}$
   c. $\frac{2}{5}$
   d. $\frac{3}{5}$

3. Aaron goes on a run every morning down the straight country road that he lives on. The graph below shows Aaron's distance from home at times throughout his morning run. Which of the following statements is (are) true?

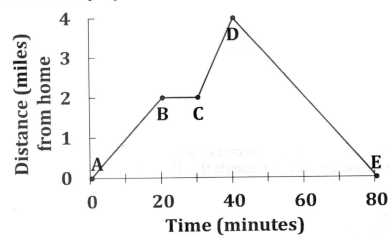

   I. Aaron's average running speed was 6 mph.
   II. Aaron's running speed from A to B was the same as from D to E.
   III. Aaron ran a total distance of four miles.

   a. I only
   b. II only
   c. I and II
   d. I, II, and III

Copyright © Mometrix Media. You have been licensed one copy of this document for personal use only. Any other reproduction or redistribution is strictly prohibited. All rights reserved. This content is provided for test preparation purposes only and does not imply an endorsement by Mometrix of any particular political, scientific, or religious point of view.

16. **Which of the following transformations has been applied to △ABC?**

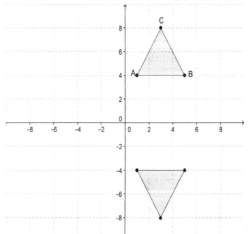

    a. Translation
    b. Rotation of 90 degrees
    (c.) Reflection
    d. Dilation

17. **Kayla rolls a die and tosses a coin. What is the probability she gets an even number and heads?**

    a. $\frac{1}{6}$
    b. $\frac{1}{4}$
    (c.) $\frac{1}{3}$
    d. 1

18. **Mrs. Miller is teaching a unit on numbers and operations with her sixth-grade class. At the beginning of class, she asks the students to work in groups to sketch a Venn diagram to classify whole numbers, integers, and rational numbers on a white board. Which of the following types of assessments has the teacher used?**

    a. Summative assessment
    b. Formative assessment
    c. Formal assessment
    (d.) Informal assessment

19. **Which of the following learning goals is most appropriate for a fourth-grade unit on geometry and measurement?**

    a. The students will be able to use a protractor to determine the approximate measures of angles in degrees to the nearest whole number.
    b. The students will be able to describe the process for graphing ordered pairs of numbers in the first quadrant of the coordinate plane.
    c. The students will be able to determine the volume of a rectangular prism with whole number side lengths in problems related to the number of layers times the number of unit cubes in the area of the base.
    d. The students will be able to classify two-dimensional figures in a hierarchy of sets and subsets using graphic organizers based on their attributes and properties.

Copyright © Mometrix Media. You have been licensed one copy of this document for personal use only. Any other reproduction or redistribution is strictly prohibited. All rights reserved.
This content is provided for test preparation purposes only and does not imply an endorsement by Mometrix of any particular political, scientific, or religious point of view.

20. **Sophia is at the market buying fruit for her family of four. Kiwifruit is only sold in packages of three. If Sophia would like each family member to have the same number of kiwifruits, which of the following approaches can Sophia use to determine the fewest number of kiwifruits she should buy?**

    a. Sophia needs to determine the greatest common multiple of 3 and 4.
    b. Sophia needs to determine the least common multiple of 3 and 4.
    c. Sophia needs to determine the least common divisor of 3 and 4.
    d. Sophia needs to determine the greatest common divisor of 3 and 4.

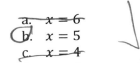

21. **A 6th grade math teacher is introducing the concept of positive and negative numbers to a group of students. Which of the following models would be the most effective when introducing this concept?**

    a. Fraction strips
    b. Venn diagrams
    c. Shaded regions
    d. Number lines

22. **Which of the following problems demonstrates the associative property of multiplication?**

    a. $2(3 + 4) = 2(3) + 2(4)$
    b. $(3 \times 6) \times 2 = (4 \times 3) \times 3$
    c. $(2 \times 3) \times 4 = 2 \times (3 \times 4)$
    d. $6 \times 4 = 4 \times 6$

23. **Which of the following is the correct solution for x in the following system of equations?**

$$x - 1 = y$$
$$y + 3 = 7$$

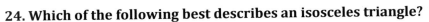

    a. $x = 6$
    b. $x = 5$
    c. $x = 4$
    d. $x = 8$

24. **Which of the following best describes an isosceles triangle?**

    a. A triangle with no sides of equal measurement and one obtuse angle
    b. A triangle with three sides of equal measurement
    c. A triangle with two sides of equal measurement and at least two acute angles
    d. A triangle with one right angle and two non-congruent acute angles

25. **Mr. Amad draws a line with a slope of $-\frac{2}{3}$ on the white board through three points. Which of the sets could possibly be these three points?**

    a. $(-6, -2), (-7, -4), (-8, -6)$
    b. $(-4, 7), (-8, 13), (-6, 10)$
    c. $(-3, -1), (-6, 1), (0, -3)$
    d. $(-2, -3), (-1, -3), (0, -3)$

Copyright © Mometrix Media. You have been licensed one copy of this document for personal use only. Any other reproduction or redistribution is strictly prohibited. All rights reserved. This content is provided for test preparation purposes only and does not imply an endorsement by Mometrix of any particular political, scientific, or religious point of view.

26. Given this stem and leaf plot, what are the mean and median?

Stem	Leaf
1	6 8
2	0 1
3	4
4	5 9

  a.   Mean = 28 and median = 20
  b.   Mean = 29 and median = 20
  c.   Mean = 29 and median = 21
  d.   Mean = 28 and median = 21

27. The 6th grade teachers at Washington Elementary School are doing a collaborative unit on cherry trees. Miss Wilson's math classes are making histograms summarizing the heights of black cherry trees located at a local fruit orchard. How many of the trees at this local orchard are 73 feet tall?

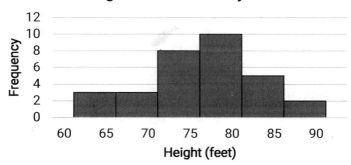

Heights of Black Cherry Trees

  a.   8
  b.   That information cannot be obtained from this graph
  c.   9
  d.   17

28. Elementary teachers in one school surveyed their students and discovered that 15% of their students have iPhones. Which of the following correctly states 15% in fraction, decimal, and ratio equivalents?

  a. $\frac{3}{20}$, 0.15, 3 : 20
  b. $\frac{3}{25}$, 0.15, 3 : 25
  c. $\frac{15}{10}$, 1.5%, 15 : 10
  d. $\frac{2}{1}$, 1.5%, 2 : 1

Copyright © Mometrix Media. You have been licensed one copy of this document for personal use only. Any other reproduction or redistribution is strictly prohibited. All rights reserved.
This content is provided for test preparation purposes only and does not imply an endorsement by Mometrix of any particular political, scientific, or religious point of view.

29. Mrs. Vories, a fifth-grade teacher, asks her class to use compatible numbers to help her determine approximately how many chicken nuggets she needs to buy for a school-wide party. The school has 589 students and each student will be served nine nuggets. Which student correctly applied the concept of compatible numbers?

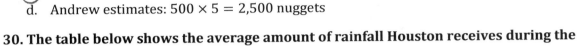

    a.   Madison estimates: $500 \times 10 = 5{,}000$ nuggets
    b.   Audrey estimates: $600 \times 5 = 3{,}000$ nuggets
    c.   Ian estimates: $600 \times 10 = 6{,}000$ nuggets
    d.   Andrew estimates: $500 \times 5 = 2{,}500$ nuggets

30. The table below shows the average amount of rainfall Houston receives during the summer and autumn months.

Month	Amount of Rainfall (in inches)
June	5.35
July	3.18
August	3.83
September	4.33
October	4.5
November	4.19

What percentage of rainfall received during this timeframe is received during the month of October?

    a.   13.5%
    b.   15.1%
    c.   16.9%
    d.   17.7%

31. A can has a radius of 1.5 inches and a height of 3 inches. Which of the following best represents the volume of the can?

    a. 17.2 in^3
    b. 19.4 in^3
    c. 21.2 in^3
    d. 23.4 in^3

Copyright © Mometrix Media. You have been licensed one copy of this document for personal use only. Any other reproduction or redistribution is strictly prohibited. All rights reserved. This content is provided for test preparation purposes only and does not imply an endorsement by Mometrix of any particular political, scientific, or religious point of view.

32. What is the approximate area of the shaded region between the circle and the square in the figure shown below? Use 3.14 for π.

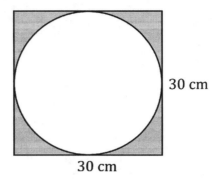

30 cm

30 cm

a. 177 cm^2
b. 181 cm^2
c. 187 cm^2
d. 193 cm^2

33. What is the perimeter of the trapezoid graphed below?

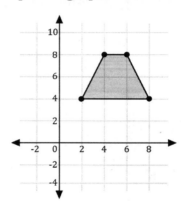

a. $4 + \sqrt{10}$
b. $8 + 4\sqrt{5}$
c. $4 + 2\sqrt{5}$
d. $8 + 2\sqrt{22}$

Copyright © Mometrix Media. You have been licensed one copy of this document for personal use only. Any other reproduction or redistribution is strictly prohibited. All rights reserved. This content is provided for test preparation purposes only and does not imply an endorsement by Mometrix of any particular political, scientific, or religious point of view.

34. What is the slope of the leg marked x in the triangle graphed below?

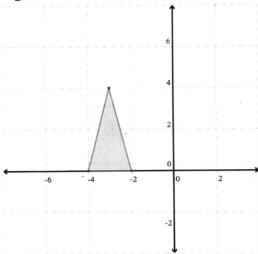

   a. 2
   (b.) 3.5
   c. 4
   d. 4.5

35. $A = \{5, 9, 2, 3, -1, 8\}$ and $B = \{2, 0, 4, 5, 6, 8\}$. What is $A \cap B$?
   (a.) $\{5, 2, 8\}$
   b. $\{-1, 0, 2, 3, 4, 5, 6, 8, 9\}$
   c. $\emptyset$
   d. $\{5, 8\}$

36. In a pack of 20 jelly beans, there are two licorice- and four cinnamon-flavored jelly beans. What is the probability of choosing a licorice jelly bean followed by a cinnamon jelly bean?
   a. $\frac{2}{5}$
   b. $\frac{8}{20}$
   c. $\frac{2}{95}$
   d. $\frac{1}{50}$

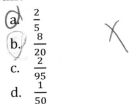

37. Amy saves \$450 every 3 months. How much does she save after 3 years?
   a. \$4,800
   b. \$5,200
   (c.) \$5,400
   d. \$5,800

Copyright © Mometrix Media. You have been licensed one copy of this document for personal use only. Any other reproduction or redistribution is strictly prohibited. All rights reserved. This content is provided for test preparation purposes only and does not imply an endorsement by Mometrix of any particular political, scientific, or religious point of view.

38. The ratio of employee wages and benefits to all other operational costs of a business is 2:3. If a business's total operating expenses are $130,000 per month, how much money does the company spend on employee wages and benefits?

   a. $43,333.33
   b. $86,666.67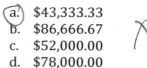
   c. $52,000.00
   d. $78,000.00

39. Given that x is a prime number and the greatest common factor of x and y is greater than 1, compare the two quantities.

   Quantity A   Quantity B
   y the least common multiple of x and y

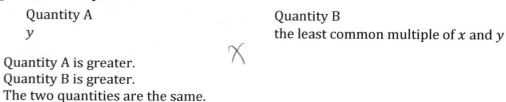

   a. Quantity A is greater.
   b. Quantity B is greater.
   c. The two quantities are the same.
   d. The relationship cannot be determined from the given information.

40. If 1 inch on a map represents 60 feet, how many yards apart are two points if the distance between the points on the map is 10 inches?

   a. 1,800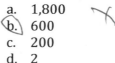
   b. 600
   c. 200
   d. 2

41. The vertices of a polygon are $(2, 3)$, $(8, 1)$, $(6, -5)$, and $(0, -3)$. Which of the following describes the polygon most specifically?

   a. Parallelogram
   b. Rhombus
   c. Rectangle
   d. Square

Copyright © Mometrix Media. You have been licensed one copy of this document for personal use only. Any other reproduction or redistribution is strictly prohibited. All rights reserved. This content is provided for test preparation purposes only and does not imply an endorsement by Mometrix of any particular political, scientific, or religious point of view.

42. **Which of these tables properly displays the measures of central tendency that can be used for nominal, interval, and ordinal data?**

a.

	Mean	Median	Mode
Nominal			X
Interval	X	X	X
Ordinal		X	X

b.

	Mean	Median	Mode
Nominal			X
Interval	X	X	X
Ordinal	X	X	X

c.

	Mean	Median	Mode
Nominal	X	X	X
Interval	X	X	X
Ordinal	X	X	X

d.

	Mean	Median	Mode
Nominal			X
Interval	X	X	
Ordinal	X	X	X

43. **Eli rolls a die and tosses a coin. What is the probability he gets a prime number or tails?**

a. $\frac{1}{4}$

b. $\frac{1}{3}$

c. $\frac{1}{2}$

d. $\frac{3}{4}$

Copyright © Mometrix Media. You have been licensed one copy of this document for personal use only. Any other reproduction or redistribution is strictly prohibited. All rights reserved.
This content is provided for test preparation purposes only and does not imply an endorsement by Mometrix of any particular political, scientific, or religious point of view.

Refer to the following for question 44:

The box-and-whisker plot displays student test scores by class period.

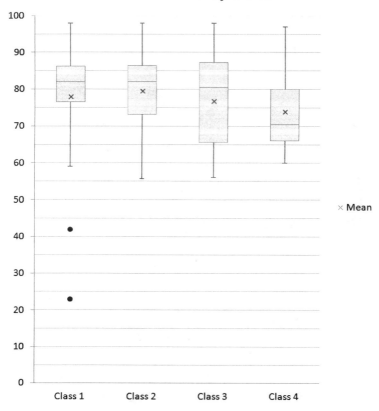

44. Which of the following statements is true of the data?

a. The mean better reflects student performance in class 1 than the median.

b. The mean test score for class 1 and 2 is the same.

c. The median test score for class 1 and 2 is the same.

d. The median test score is above the mean for class 4.

394

Copyright © Mometrix Media. You have been licensed one copy of this document for personal use only. Any other reproduction or redistribution is strictly prohibited. All rights reserved. This content is provided for test preparation purposes only and does not imply an endorsement by Mometrix of any particular political, scientific, or religious point of view.

45. A random sample of 90 students at an elementary school were asked these three questions:

Do you like carrots?
Do you like broccoli?
Do you like cauliflower?

The results of the survey are shown below. If these data are representative of the population of students at the school, which of these is most probable?

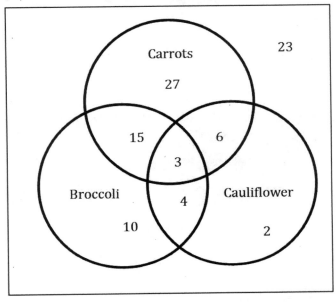

a. A student chosen at random likes broccoli.
b. If a student chosen at random likes carrots, they will also like at least one other vegetable.
c. If a student chosen at random likes cauliflower and broccoli, they will also like carrots.
d. A student chosen at random does not like carrots, broccoli, or cauliflower.

46. Robert buys a car for $24,210. The price of the car has been marked down by 10%. What was the original price of the car?

a. $25,900
b. $26,300
c. $26,900
d. $27,300

47. Which of the following formulas may be used to represent the sequence 8, 13, 18, 23, 28, ...?

a. $a_n = 5n + 3; n \in \mathbb{N}$
b. $a_n = n + 5; n \in \mathbb{N}$
c. $a_n = n + 8; n \in \mathbb{N}$
d. $a_n = 5n + 8; n \in \mathbb{N}$

Copyright © Mometrix Media. You have been licensed one copy of this document for personal use only. Any other reproduction or redistribution is strictly prohibited. All rights reserved.
This content is provided for test preparation purposes only and does not imply an endorsement by Mometrix of any particular political, scientific, or religious point of view.

48. Elijah pays a $30 park entrance fee plus $4 for every ticket purchased. Which of the following equations represents the cost?

   a. $y = 30x + 4$
   b. $y = 34x$
   c. $y = 4x + 30$
   d. $y = 34x + 30$

49. Hannah spends at least $16 on 4 packages of coffee. Which of the following inequalities represents the possible costs?

   a. $16 \geq 4p$
   b. $16 < 4p$
   c. $16 > 4p$
   d. $16 \leq 4p$

50. A cylindrical carrot stick is sliced with a knife. Which of the following shapes is NOT a possible cross-section?

   a.   Circle
   b.   Rectangle
   c.   Ellipse
   d.   Triangle

Copyright © Mometrix Media. You have been licensed one copy of this document for personal use only. Any other reproduction or redistribution is strictly prohibited. All rights reserved. This content is provided for test preparation purposes only and does not imply an endorsement by Mometrix of any particular political, scientific, or religious point of view.

Social Studies

1. Which of the following statements is NOT true regarding English expansionism in the 16th century?

    a. England's defeat of the Spanish Armada in 1588 brought a decisive end to their war with Spain.

    b. King Henry VIII's desire to divorce Catherine of Aragon strengthened English expansionism.

    c. Queen Elizabeth's support for the Protestant Reformation strengthened English expansionism.

    d. Sir Francis Drake and other English sea captains plundered the goods that the Spaniards took from indigenous peoples.

2. During the decolonization of the Cold War years, which of the following events occurred chronologically latest?

    a. The Eastern Bloc and Satellite states became independent from the Soviet Union.

    b. Canada became totally independent from British Parliament via the Canada Act.

    c. The Bahamas, in the Caribbean, became independent from the United Kingdom.

    d. The Algerian War ended, and Algeria became independent from France.

3. Who negotiates treaties?

    a. The President

    b. The House of Representatives

    c. Ambassadors

    d. The Senate

4. How long can members of the Federal Judiciary serve?

    a. Four years

    b. Eight years

    c. For life

    d. Six years

5. Guaranteed rights enumerated in the Declaration of Independence, possessed by all people, are referred to as:

    a. Universal rights

    b. Unalienable rights

    c. Voting rights

    d. Peoples' rights

6. Which of the following statements is NOT true about the Gilded Age in America?

    a. The Gilded Age was the era of the "robber barons" in the business world.

    b. The Gilded Age got its name from the excesses of the wealthy upper class.

    c. The Gilded Age had philanthropy Carnegie called the "Gospel of Wealth".

    d. The Gilded Age is a term whose origins have not been identified clearly.

7. Which of the following exemplifies the multiplier effect of large cities?

    a. The presence of specialized equipment for an industry attracts even more business.

    b. The large population lowers the price of goods.

    c. Public transportation means more people can commute to work.

    d. A local newspaper can afford to give away the Sunday edition.

Copyright © Mometrix Media. You have been licensed one copy of this document for personal use only. Any other reproduction or redistribution is strictly prohibited. All rights reserved. This content is provided for test preparation purposes only and does not imply an endorsement by Mometrix of any particular political, scientific, or religious point of view.

8. Criminal cases are tried under:

I. State law
II. Federal law
III. Civil court

a. I and III
b. II only
c. I only
d. I and II

9. Which of the following is NOT a true statement regarding the Louisiana Purchase?

a. Jefferson sent a delegation to Paris to endeavor to purchase only the city of New Orleans from Napoleon.
b. Napoleon, anticipating U.S. intrusions into Louisiana, offered to sell the U.S. the entire Louisiana territory.
c. The American delegation accepted Napoleon's offer, though they were only authorized to buy New Orleans.
d. The Louisiana Purchase, once it was completed, increased the territory of the U.S. by 50% overnight.

10. The idea that the purpose of the American colonies was to provide Great Britain with raw materials and a market for its goods is an expression of:

a. Free trade
b. Most favored nation status
c. Mercantilism
d. Laissez-faire capitalism

11. During the early Medieval period in Europe, before the 5th century, where were the main centers of literacy found?

a. They were in the homes of the wealthy.
b. They were in the churches and monasteries.
c. They were in the local artisan and craft guilds.
d. There were no centers of literacy.

12. How must inferior courts interpret the law?

a. According to the Supreme Court's interpretation
b. According to the Constitution
c. However they choose
d. According to the political climate

13. Which entity in American government is the closest to direct democracy?

a. The Electoral College
b. The House of Representatives
c. Committees within the Senate
d. The Supreme Court

Copyright © Mometrix Media. You have been licensed one copy of this document for personal use only. Any other reproduction or redistribution is strictly prohibited. All rights reserved.
This content is provided for test preparation purposes only and does not imply an endorsement by Mometrix of any particular political, scientific, or religious point of view.

14. Power divided between local and central branches of government is a definition of what term?

    a. Bicameralism
    b. Checks and balances
    c. Legislative oversight
    d. Federalism

15. Virginian _____ advocated a stronger central government and was influential at the Constitutional Convention.

    a. Benjamin Franklin
    b. James Madison
    c. George Mason
    d. Robert Yates

16. Which of the following will result if two nations use the theory of comparative advantage when making decisions of which goods to produce and trade?

    a. Each nation will make all of their own goods.
    b. Both nations will specialize in the production of the same specific goods.
    c. Each nation will specialize in the production of different specific goods.
    d. Neither nation will trade with one another.

17. The presidential veto of legislation passed by Congress illustrates which principal in American government?

    a. Checks and balances
    b. Federal regulation
    c. Freedom of speech
    d. Separation of church and state

18. A filibuster is used to delay a bill. Where can a filibuster take place?

    a. The House of Representatives
    b. The Senate
    c. Committees
    d. The Supreme Court

19. To be President of the United States, one must meet these three requirements:

    a. The President must be college educated, at least 30 years old, and a natural citizen.
    b. The President must be a natural citizen, have lived in the US for 14 years, and have a college education.
    c. The President must be a natural citizen, be at least 35 years old, and have lived in the US for 14 years.
    d. The President must be at least 30 years old, be a natural citizen, and have lived in the US for 14 years.

20. Which of the following is most likely to benefit from inflation?

    a. A bond investor who owns fixed-rate bonds
    b. A retired widow with no income other than fixed Social Security payments
    c. A person who has taken out a fixed-rate loan
    d. A local bank who has loaned money out at fixed rate

Copyright © Mometrix Media. You have been licensed one copy of this document for personal use only. Any other reproduction or redistribution is strictly prohibited. All rights reserved.
This content is provided for test preparation purposes only and does not imply an endorsement by Mometrix of any particular political, scientific, or religious point of view.

21. After the Civil War, urban populations increased. This growth was likely due to:
    a.   An increased reliance on agriculture
    b.   The Industrial Revolution
    c.   Prohibition
    d.   Slavery persisting in some areas

22. As a form of government, what does oligarchy mean?
    a.   Rule by one
    b.   Rule by a few
    c.   Rule by law
    d.   Rule by many

23. The Trail of Tears was:
    a.   The forced removal of British soldiers after the American Revolution
    b.   The forced evacuation of Cherokee peoples into Oklahoma
    c.   The forced evacuation of freed slaves from the South after the Civil War
    d.   The tears of Betsy Ross while she sewed the first American flag

24. What is the main reason that tropical regions near the Equator tend to experience relatively constant year-round temperatures?
    a.   They are usually located near the ocean.
    b.   The angle at which sunlight hits them remains relatively constant throughout the year.
    c.   They are located along the "Ring of Fire."
    d.   They do not have seasons.

25. Which of the following is NOT correct regarding assumptions of mercantilism?
    a.   The money and the wealth of a nation are identical properties.
    b.   In order to prosper, a nation should try to increase its imports.
    c.   In order to prosper, a nation should try to increase its exports.
    d.   Economic protectionism by national governments is advisable.

26. Which scientist first proposed the heliocentric universe instead of a geocentric one?
    a.   Galileo
    b.   Ptolemy
    c.   Copernicus
    d.   Isaac Newton

27. Congressional elections are held every _____ years.
    a.   Four
    b.   Two
    c.   Six
    d.   Three

28. All else being equal, which of the following locations is likely to have the coolest climate?
    a.   A city located at 6,000 feet above sea level
    b.   A city located at 500 feet above sea level
    c.   A city that receives less than 10 inches of precipitation per year
    d.   A city that receives more than 50 inches of precipitation per year

Copyright © Mometrix Media. You have been licensed one copy of this document for personal use only. Any other reproduction or redistribution is strictly prohibited. All rights reserved.
This content is provided for test preparation purposes only and does not imply an endorsement by Mometrix of any particular political, scientific, or religious point of view.

29. **Which Italian Renaissance figure was best known as a political philosopher?**
   a. Dante Alighieri
   b. Leonardo Da Vinci
   c. Francesco Petrarca
   d. Niccolò Machiavelli

30. **Which of the following empires still existed following the armistice ending World War I?**
   a. The Austro-Hungarian Empire
   b. The Ottoman Empire
   c. The German Empire
   d. The British Empire

31. **What is the main difference between a primary election and a caucus?**
   a. A primary election is privately run by political parties, and a caucus is held by local governments.
   b. Caucuses are always held on the same day, but the dates of state primaries vary.
   c. A caucus is privately run by political parties, and a primary is an indirect election run by state and local governments.
   d. Primary elections are all held on the same date, but the dates of caucuses vary.

32. **How are members of the Federal Judiciary chosen?**
   a. They are elected by voters.
   b. They are appointed by the president and confirmed by the House of Representatives.
   c. They are chosen by a committee.
   d. They are appointed by the president and confirmed by the Senate.

33. **Which of the following conquistadores unwittingly gave smallpox to the indigenous peoples and destroyed the Aztec empire in Mexico?**
   a. Vasco Núñez de Balboa
   b. Juan Ponce de León
   c. Hernán Cortés
   d. Álvar Núñez Cabeza de Vaca

34. **Which of the following statements is false regarding the Puritans?**
   a. In terms of their theology, the Puritans were considered Calvinists.
   b. Many Puritans agreed with radical views that criticized the Swiss Calvinists.
   c. Many of those identified as Calvinists opposed the Puritans.
   d. The Restoration and the Uniformity Act reunified the Puritan movement and the Church of England.

35. **Of the following economists, who advocated government intervention to prevent and remedy recessions and depressions?**
   a. Adam Smith
   b. John Maynard Keynes
   c. Friedrich Hayek
   d. Milton Friedman

Copyright © Mometrix Media. You have been licensed one copy of this document for personal use only. Any other reproduction or redistribution is strictly prohibited. All rights reserved.
This content is provided for test preparation purposes only and does not imply an endorsement by Mometrix of any particular political, scientific, or religious point of view.

36. The Supreme Court has nine members. How is this number determined?

a. It is outlined in the Constitution.
b. Congress determines the number.
c. The President determines the number.
d. The Court decides on the number.

37. The first amendment guarantees all below except:

a. Freedom of assembly
b. The right to bear arms
c. Freedom of the press
d. The right to speak freely

38. Which of the following is NOT one of the demographic variables?

a. Fertility
b. Diversity
c. Mortality
d. Migration

39. John Maynard Keynes advocated what?

a. Supply-side economics
b. Demand-side economics
c. Laissez faire economics
d. The Laffer Curve

40. The bubonic plague spread through Europe in which of the following ways?

a. It spread along rivers and through contaminated drinking water.
b. It was carried by birds that migrated south during the winter.
c. It spread along trade routes, carried by infected animals and people on ships.
d. It was carried by travelers on religious pilgrimages.

41. Which of the following was NOT an immediate effect of rapid urban growth in the 1800s?

a. Poor sanitation conditions in the cities
b. Epidemics of diseases in the cities
c. Inadequate police and fire protection
d. Widespread urban political corruption

42. Which of the following is the best example of a factor resulting from Europe's Commercial Revolution that contributed to the 1700s' Industrial Revolution?

a. The rediscovery of concrete
b. New advances in making iron
c. The steam engine's invention
d. Increases in population growth

43. A group that grew in numbers as a result of the Industrial Revolution was:

a. Small farmers.
b. Unskilled workers.
c. Skilled craftsmen.
d. The rural population.

Copyright © Mometrix Media. You have been licensed one copy of this document for personal use only. Any other reproduction or redistribution is strictly prohibited. All rights reserved. This content is provided for test preparation purposes only and does not imply an endorsement by Mometrix of any particular political, scientific, or religious point of view.

44. The primary expense for most state and local governments is:
   a. Emergency medical services
   b. Transportation services
   c. Police and fire departments
   d. Education

45. Of the following, which person or group was NOT instrumental in advancement of civil rights and desegregation during the 1940s and 1950s?
   a. The President
   b. The Supreme Court
   c. The Congress
   d. The NAACP

46. Which of the following is true of social changes and the Industrial Revolution in Europe in the 18th and early 19th centuries?
   a. They gave rise to a new middle-class
   b. They improved working conditions
   c. They were the result of urbanization
   d. They were caused by the labor unions

47. Which Supreme Court case enforced the civil rights of citizens to not incriminate themselves?
   a. Marbury v. Madison
   b. Miranda v. Arizona
   c. Youngstown Sheet and Tube Company v. Sawyer
   d. United States v. Carolene Products Company

48. Which of the following are true of the demand curve?
   I. It is normally downward sloping
   II. It is normally upward sloping
   III. It is influenced by the law of diminishing marginal unity
   IV. It is unaffected by the law of diminishing marginal unity

   a. I and III only
   b. I and IV only
   c. II and III only
   d. II and IV only

49. Which of the following was the reason the economy of colonial New England focused mainly on manufacture and trade?
   a. The soil and climate conditions in New England were not conducive to year-round farming.
   b. The New England colonists were primarily merchants from England and Scotland.
   c. Slavery did not exist in the northern colonies.
   d. The New England colonists wanted to achieve economic dominance over the Middle Atlantic colonies.

Copyright © Mometrix Media. You have been licensed one copy of this document for personal use only. Any other reproduction or redistribution is strictly prohibited. All rights reserved. This content is provided for test preparation purposes only and does not imply an endorsement by Mometrix of any particular political, scientific, or religious point of view.

50. Which of the following world religions believes in many gods and goddesses?

a. Confucianism
b. Hinduism
c. Sikhism
d. Islam

51. The president serves as commander-in-chief. What are the president's two limitations in that role?

a. The president cannot declare war or oversee military regulations.
b. The president cannot enforce blockades or declare war.
c. The president cannot enforce quarantines or oversee military regulations.
d. The president cannot enforce blockades or quarantines.

52. When the prices farmers receive for their crops decline in a developing country, this typically results in which of the following?

a. Increased urbanization
b. Increased college enrollment
c. Declining literacy rates
d. Higher prices for those crops in developed countries

53. Which of the following is NOT true about the Crusades?

a. Their purpose was for European rulers to retake the Middle East from Muslims.
b. The Crusades succeeded at European kings' goal of reclaiming the "holy land."
c. The Crusades accelerated the already incipient decline of the Byzantine Empire.
d. Egypt saw a return as a major Middle Eastern power as a result of the Crusades.

54. Every citizen 18 years of age and older has the constitutional right to vote. What do states govern in the voting process?

a. The registration for and timing of federal elections
b. The administration and timing of federal elections
c. The registration for and administration of federal elections
d. The registration for federal elections only

55. Who may write a bill?

a. Anyone
b. A member of the House
c. A Senator
d. Any member of Congress

56. Social dialects typically emerge when

a. a particular group is isolated from the rest of society due to class, race, age, or gender differences.
b. a group of new immigrants is assimilated into society.
c. two social groups that share a common language become geographically isolated.
d. specialized jargons develop in certain industries and academic disciplines.

Copyright © Mometrix Media. You have been licensed one copy of this document for personal use only. Any other reproduction or redistribution is strictly prohibited. All rights reserved.
This content is provided for test preparation purposes only and does not imply an endorsement by Mometrix of any particular political, scientific, or religious point of view.

57. On which type of map are different countries represented in different colors, with no two adjacent countries sharing a color?

    a.   Physical map
    b.   Political map
    c.   Climate map
    d.   Contour map

58. What would you expect to happen to marginal product as the number of inputs used is increased?

    a.   It will consistently increase
    b.   It will consistently decrease
    c.   It will decrease, stay constant, then increase
    d.   It will increase, stay constant, then decrease
    e.   It will stay the same

59. Which of the following statements correctly describes totemism?

    a.   It is a Native American practice in which a totem pole is worshipped.
    b.   It is the Chinese practice of asking ancestors for guidance in daily life.
    c.   It is associated with the East Asian concept of filial piety.
    d.   It characterizes clans in which members believe they are all descendants of a common ancestor, often an animal.

60. A caste system is BEST described as

    a.   a primarily social phenomenon that has no economic consequences.
    b.   a system that discriminates mainly based on race, but permits upward social mobility.
    c.   a system wherein individuals' social, economic, and political destinies are determined at birth by group membership.
    d.   equivalent to the modern-day class system.

Copyright © Mometrix Media. You have been licensed one copy of this document for personal use only. Any other reproduction or redistribution is strictly prohibited. All rights reserved.
This content is provided for test preparation purposes only and does not imply an endorsement by Mometrix of any particular political, scientific, or religious point of view.

Science

1. Scientists often form hypotheses based on particular observations. Which of the following is NOT true of a good hypothesis?

    a. A good hypothesis is complex.
    b. A good hypothesis is testable.
    c. A good hypothesis is logical.
    d. A good hypothesis predicts future events.

2. What will happen to light waves as they hit a convex lens?

    a. They will be refracted and converge.
    b. They will be refracted and diverge.
    c. They will be reflected and converge.
    d. They will be reflected and diverge.

3. Which of the following animal structures is NOT paired to its correct function?

    a. Muscle System – controls movement through three types of muscle tissue
    b. Nervous System – controls sensory responses by carrying impulses away from and toward the cell body
    c. Digestive System – breaks down food for absorption into the blood stream where it is delivered to cells for respiration
    d. Circulatory System – exchanges gases with the environment by delivering oxygen to the bloodstream and releasing carbon dioxide

4. What type of change occurs when a liquid transitions to a gas?

    a. A phase change
    b. A chemical change
    c. Sublimation
    d. Condensation

5. After a science laboratory exercise, some solutions remain unused and are left over. What should be done with these solutions?

    a. Dispose of the solutions according to local disposal procedures.
    b. Empty the solutions into the sink and rinse with warm water and soap.
    c. Ensure the solutions are secured in closed containers and throw away.
    d. Store the solutions in a secured, dry place for later use.

6. If an atom has a neutral charge, what must be true of the atom?

    a. The nucleus contains only neutrons and no protons.
    b. The atomic mass is equal to the number of neutrons.
    c. The atomic number is equal to the number of neutrons.
    d. The atomic number is equal to the number of electrons.

7. Which of the following words is NOT connected to the process of mountain building?

    a. Folding
    b. Faulting
    c. Transform
    d. Convergent

Copyright © Mometrix Media. You have been licensed one copy of this document for personal use only. Any other reproduction or redistribution is strictly prohibited. All rights reserved.
This content is provided for test preparation purposes only and does not imply an endorsement by Mometrix of any particular political, scientific, or religious point of view.

8. What laboratory practice can increase the accuracy of a measurement?

    a. Repeating the measurement several times
    b. Calibrating the equipment each time you use it
    c. Using metric measuring devices
    d. Reading the laboratory instructions before the lab

9. Elements on the periodic table are arranged into groups and periods and ordered according to all of the following EXCEPT:

    a. Atomic number
    b. Refractive index
    c. Reactivity
    d. Number of protons

10. A gas is held in a closed container and held at constant temperature. What is the effect of increasing the volume of the container by 3 times?

    a. The pressure is tripled.
    b. The pressure increases by one-third.
    c. The pressure decreases to one-third.
    d. The pressure remains constant.

11. Which of the following terms describes an intrusion of magma injected between two layers of sedimentary rock, forcing the overlying strata upward to create a dome-like form?

    a. Sill
    b. Dike
    c. Laccolith
    d. Caldera

12. Which of the following is needed for an experiment to be considered successful?

    a. A reasonable hypothesis
    b. A well-written lab report
    c. Data that others can reproduce
    d. Computer-aided statistical analysis

13. Which of the following statements about heat transfer is NOT true?

    a. As the energy of a system changes, its thermal energy must change or work must be done.
    b. Heat transfer from a warmer object to a cooler object can occur spontaneously.
    c. Heat transfer can never occur from a cooler object to a warmer object.
    d. If two objects reach the same temperature, energy is no longer available for work.

14. A man accidentally drops his wallet in a swimming pool. He can see his wallet at the bottom of the pool. He jumps in to retrieve it, but the wallet is not where it appeared to be. What is the reason for the optical illusion?

    a. The reflection of sunlight off of the water disrupted his view
    b. Light is refracted as it enters the water changing the wallet's apparent location
    c. The current at the bottom of the pool caused the wallet to move
    d. The heat from the Sun has impaired the man's vision

Copyright © Mometrix Media. You have been licensed one copy of this document for personal use only. Any other reproduction or redistribution is strictly prohibited. All rights reserved. This content is provided for test preparation purposes only and does not imply an endorsement by Mometrix of any particular political, scientific, or religious point of view.

15. The precision of a number of data points refers to:

a. How accurate the data is
b. How many errors the data contains
c. How close the data points are to the mean of the data
d. How close the actual data is to the predicted result

16. The most recently formed parts of the Earth's crust can be found at:

a. Subduction zones
b. Compressional boundaries
c. Extensional boundaries
d. Mid-ocean ridges

17. Which type of nuclear process features atomic nuclei splitting apart to form smaller nuclei?

a. Fission
b. Fusion
c. Decay
d. Ionization

18. How does adding a solute to a liquid solvent affect the vapor pressure of the liquid?

a. The vapor pressure increases by an amount proportional to the amount of solute.
b. The vapor pressure increases by an amount proportional to the amount of solvent.
c. The vapor pressure decreases by an amount proportional to the amount of solute.
d. The amount of solute present in a liquid solvent does not have any effect on vapor pressure.

19. What drives weather systems to move west to east in the mid-latitudes?

a. The prevailing westerlies
b. The prevailing easterlies
c. The trade winds
d. The doldrums

20. How are organisms, such as snakes, cacti, and coyotes, able to survive in harsh desert conditions?

a. Over thousands of years, these organisms have developed adaptations to survive in arid climates.
b. These organisms migrate out of the desert during the summer months, only living in the desert for a portion of the year.
c. Snakes, cacti, and coyotes work together to find sources of food and water.
d. Snakes, cacti, and coyotes are all aquatic species that live in ponds and rivers during the hot day.

21. In which of the following scenarios is work NOT applied to the object?

a. Mario moves a book from the floor to the top shelf.
b. A book drops off the shelf and falls to the floor.
c. Mario pushes a box of books across the room.
d. Mario balances a book on his head.

Copyright © Mometrix Media. You have been licensed one copy of this document for personal use only. Any other reproduction or redistribution is strictly prohibited. All rights reserved.
This content is provided for test preparation purposes only and does not imply an endorsement by Mometrix of any particular political, scientific, or religious point of view.

22. Which of the following would not be used as evidence for evolution?

   a. Fossil record
   b. DNA sequences
   c. Anatomical structures
   d. Reproductive habits

23. Which of the following is considered a non-renewable resource?

   a. Glass
   b. Wood
   c. Cattle
   d. Soil

24. The stream of charged particles that escape the Sun's gravitational pull is best described by which of the following terms?

   a. Solar wind
   b. Solar flare
   c. Solar radiation
   d. Sunspots

25. According to Ohm's Law, how are voltage and current related in an electrical circuit?

   a. Voltage and current are inversely proportional to one another.
   b. Voltage and current are directly proportional to one another.
   c. Voltage acts to oppose the current along an electrical circuit.
   d. Voltage acts to decrease the current along an electrical circuit.

26. Where are the reproductive organs of a plant?

   a. Style
   b. Stigma
   c. Flowers
   d. Sepals

27. What is the scientific definition of work?

   a. The amount of energy used to accomplish a job
   b. The force used to move a mass over a distance
   c. The amount of energy used per unit of time
   d. Energy stored in an object due to its position

28. Which of the following are formed when the plasma membrane surrounds a particle outside of the cell?

   a. Golgi bodies
   b. Rough endoplasmic reticulum
   c. Secretory vesicles
   d. Endocytic vesicles

29. What causes the motion of glaciers?

   a. Gravity
   b. Erosion
   c. Wind
   d. Temperature change

Copyright © Mometrix Media. You have been licensed one copy of this document for personal use only. Any other reproduction or redistribution is strictly prohibited. All rights reserved.
This content is provided for test preparation purposes only and does not imply an endorsement by Mometrix of any particular political, scientific, or religious point of view.

30. What term is used to describe two waves that are out of phase as they come together to produce a new wave?

    a. Incomplete interference
    b. Distorted interference
    c. Constructive interference
    d. Destructive interference

31. What part of a plant system responds to stimuli by releasing water via transpiration, except during adverse conditions like a drought when it closes up to prevent the plant from dehydration?

    a. Pith
    b. Stomata
    c. Guard cells
    d. Sepals

32. The electrolysis of water is an example of which of the following?

    a. An adiabatic process
    b. A chemical change
    c. A synthesis reaction
    d. Reverse osmosis

33. When using a light microscope, how is the total magnification determined?

    a. By multiplying the ocular lens power by the objective being used
    b. By looking at the objective you are using only
    c. By looking at the ocular lens power only
    d. By multiplying the objective you are using by two

34. Why do balloons filled with helium float while balloons filled with air do not float?

    a. Balloons filled with air are larger than balloons filled with helium, which makes them heavier preventing them from floating.
    b. Helium is less dense than air, which allows balloons filled with helium to float.
    c. Helium balloons travel on higher air currents and balloons filled with air travel on lower air currents.
    d. Air causes balloons to generate static electricity so the balloon will be attracted to the ground.

35. Which of the following sources of fresh water is unavailable for human use?

    a. Rivers
    b. Estuaries
    c. Aquifers
    d. Glaciers

Copyright © Mometrix Media. You have been licensed one copy of this document for personal use only. Any other reproduction or redistribution is strictly prohibited. All rights reserved. This content is provided for test preparation purposes only and does not imply an endorsement by Mometrix of any particular political, scientific, or religious point of view.

36. When heat is removed from water during condensation, which of the following are formed.

    a. Atoms
    b. Covalent bonds
    c. Intermolecular bonds
    d. Ionic bonds

37. The amount of potential energy an object has depends on all of the following except its

    a. Mass
    b. Height above ground
    c. Gravitational attraction
    d. Temperature

38. Which statement accurately describes a state of matter?

    a. Solids take the shape of their container
    b. Gases maintain a fixed shape
    c. Liquids will expand to fill the volume of a container
    d. Gases expand to fill an entire space

39. Which of the following situations would result in the generation of new crust?

    a. Two crustal plates converge.
    b. Two crustal plates move apart.
    c. Two crustal plates slide past one another.
    d. A crustal plate is pushed down into the mantle.

40. What is the purpose of conducting an experiment?

    a. To test a hypothesis
    b. To collect data
    c. To identify a control state
    d. To choose variables

41. A long nail is heated at one end. After a few seconds, the other end of the nail becomes equally hot. What type of heat transfer does this represent?

    a. Radiation
    b. Conduction
    c. Convection
    d. Entropy

42. Which of the following would increase the reaction rate of a chemical reaction?

    a. Low kinetic energy
    b. Low temperature
    c. High concentration of reactants
    d. High activation energy

43. Which of the following is an example of a trace fossil?

    a. A mouse jaw
    b. A footprint
    c. A shark tooth
    d. A cast of a skull

Copyright © Mometrix Media. You have been licensed one copy of this document for personal use only. Any other reproduction or redistribution is strictly prohibited. All rights reserved.
This content is provided for test preparation purposes only and does not imply an endorsement by Mometrix of any particular political, scientific, or religious point of view.

44. When two tectonic plates are moving laterally in opposing directions, this is called a(n):
   a. Transform boundary
   b. Compressional boundary
   c. Oppositional boundary
   d. Lateral boundary

45. If an atom's outer shell is filled, what must be true?
   a. It reacts with other atoms through chemical reactions.
   b. It exchanges electrons to form bonds with other atoms.
   c. It has 32 electrons in its outer shell.
   d. It is a stable atom.

46. What type of substance is least likely to be soluble in water?
   a. Ionic
   b. Polar
   c. Hydrophilic
   d. Non-polar

47. Which of the following describes the physical or non-biological part of the carbon cycle?
   a. Phytoplankton use carbon dioxide and other nutrients to produce carbohydrates and oxygen.
   b. Cold water dissolves atmospheric carbon dioxide, stores it, and releases it back out to the atmosphere as needed.
   c. Carbon dioxide is dissolved in sea water and is broken up to free carbon for use by marine life.
   d. Warm, surface water dissolves carbon dioxide where it is converted to nitrogen and phosphorus for use by marine life.

48. In a food chain, where does energy go after the secondary consumer dies?
   a. Back to the Sun
   b. To the producers
   c. Into the air, becoming wind
   d. To decomposers

49. When you walk barefoot on a hot sidewalk, what process is primarily responsible for heat transfer from the sidewalk to your foot?
   a. Conduction
   b. Convection
   c. Radiation
   d. None of the above.

50. Where is the type of RNA that carries and positions amino acids for further assembly located in the cell?
   a. Cytoplasm
   b. Nucleus
   c. Ribosome
   d. Mitochondria

Copyright © Mometrix Media. You have been licensed one copy of this document for personal use only. Any other reproduction or redistribution is strictly prohibited. All rights reserved.
This content is provided for test preparation purposes only and does not imply an endorsement by Mometrix of any particular political, scientific, or religious point of view.

51. Which is an example of convection as a method of heat transfer?

    a. A person warming his hands by placing them on an electric blanket
    b. A person warming his hands by placing them near the sides of a light bulb
    c. A person warming his hands by washing with hot water
    d. A person warming his hands by rubbing them together

52. When an animal takes in more energy that it uses over an extended time, the extra chemical energy is stored as:

    a. Fat
    b. Starch
    c. Protein
    d. Enzymes

53. Which of the following statements correctly compares rocks and minerals?

    a. Minerals may contain traces of organic compounds, while rocks do not.
    b. Rocks are classified by their formation and the minerals they contain, while minerals are classified by their chemical composition and physical properties.
    c. Both rocks and minerals can be polymorphs.
    d. Both rocks and minerals may contain mineraloids.

54. Which of the following options is a serious direct impact of climate change?

    a. Soil erosion
    b. Deforestation
    c. Water pollution
    d. Increase in average sea level

55. Which of the following is a source of nonrenewable energy?

    a. Solar power
    b. Wind power
    c. Wood
    d. Coal

Copyright © Mometrix Media. You have been licensed one copy of this document for personal use only. Any other reproduction or redistribution is strictly prohibited. All rights reserved.
This content is provided for test preparation purposes only and does not imply an endorsement by Mometrix of any particular political, scientific, or religious point of view.

Answer Key and Explanations

Reading and Language Arts

1. A: Homophones. Homophones are a type of homonym that sound alike but are spelled differently and have different meanings. Other examples are *two*, *to*, and *too* and *their*, *they're*, and *there*.

2. C: The students have been instructed to read the documents quickly, looking for key words in order to gather the basic premise of each. Skimming allows a reader to quickly gain a broad understanding of a piece of writing in order to determine if a more thorough reading is warranted. Skimming allows students who are researching a topic on the internet or in print to consider a substantial body of information in order to select only that of particular relevance.

3. C: According to the Association of College and Research Libraries, information literacy is the set of skills that an individual must have for finding, retrieving, analyzing, and using information. It is required not just for reading and understanding information (A). Information literacy does not mean learning and retaining a lot of information (B), or only sharing it with others (D), but rather knowing how to find information one does not already have and how to evaluate that information critically for its quality and apply it judiciously to meet one's purposes.

4. C: Oral language is a vital aspect of any language arts instruction. Often, the first concepts of language are transmitted via oral and auditory processes. The first Americans also possessed a rich oral culture in which stories and histories were passed down through generations via storytelling. Inviting a guest speaker who is part of this culture helps students understand more about cultures in their world, as well as the value of oral language and storytelling. This introduction gives students a relevant personal experience with which to connect what they will be learning in class.

5. A: A syllable is a minimal sound unit arranged around a vowel. For example, *academic* has four syllables: *a/ca/dem/ic.* It is possible for a syllable to be a single vowel, as in the above example. It is not possible for a syllable to be a single consonant.

6. A: There are three primary types of sonnets. The Shakespearean sonnet is specifically what these students are reading. A Spenserian sonnet is also composed of three four-line stanzas followed by a two-line couplet; however, the rhymes are not contained within each stanza but spill from one stanza to the next (*abab bcbc cdcd ee).* A Petrarchan sonnet divides into an eight-line stanza and a six-line stanza.

7. C: On the internet, it often occurs that the name of the author of an article or book is actually provided but is not obviously visible at first glance. Web sources frequently include the author's name, but on another page of the same site, such as the website's home page, or in a tiny font at the very end of the web page, rather than in a more conspicuous location. In such cases, students doing online research may have to search more thoroughly than usual to find the author's name. Therefore, they should not immediately assume the author is not named (A). Also, many web sources are sponsored by government agencies or private corporations and do not give individual author names. In these cases, the research paper *should* cite the agency or corporation name as author (B). Finally, it is much more common for online sources to omit an author's name than it is in print sources. In these cases, it is both permitted and advised by the MLA to cite the article or book title instead (D).

Copyright © Mometrix Media. You have been licensed one copy of this document for personal use only. Any other reproduction or redistribution is strictly prohibited. All rights reserved. This content is provided for test preparation purposes only and does not imply an endorsement by Mometrix of any particular political, scientific, or religious point of view.

8. C: The example has an error in subject-verb agreement, which is a component of syntax (sentence structure and word order). Phonology (A) involves recognition and production of speech sounds and phonemes, including differentiation, segmentation, and blending. Semantics (B) involves the meanings of words. Pragmatics (D) involves the social use of language to communicate and meet one's needs.

9. B: A reading teacher offers corrective feedback to a student in order to explain why a particular error in reading is, in fact, an error. Corrective feedback is specific; it locates where and how the student went astray so that similar errors can be avoided in future reading.

10. A: Individuals with dysgraphia have difficulty with the physical act of writing. They find holding and manipulating a pencil problematic. Their letters are primitively formed, and their handwriting is illegible.

11. C: The kind of audience for whom you are writing, as well as your purpose for writing, will determine what style, tone, and wording you choose. Knowing who your audience is will enable you to select writing strategies, a style and tone, and specific word choices that will be most understandable and appealing to your readers. Knowing the type of audience will also dictate how much time to spend on research (A). Some readers will expect more supporting evidence while others will be bored or overwhelmed by it. Similarly, you will want to include more or less information depending on who will be reading what you write (B). And while the structure of your piece does inform how you organize your information, you should also vary your organization according to who will read it (D).

12. B: In the Spanish language, the letter h is typically silent. Because the student is an ELL and the USA has many people—both immigrants and those born here—whose first and/or only language is Spanish, this is the first factor to consider among the choices. An articulation disorder (A) is possible, but the teacher should not assume this first with an ELL student. (An SLP evaluation can determine the difference.) While a hearing assessment (C) is always a good idea, if /h/ omission were due to hearing loss the student would likely omit or distort other unvoiced fricatives like /f/, /s/, /ʃ/, and /θ/. If the student had a breathing problem (D), other symptoms would occur in addition to not articulating /h/.

13. D: Consonant digraph. A consonant digraph is a group of consonants in which all letters represent a single sound.

14. C: *Drip, chirp, splash, giggle.* Onomatopoeia refers to words that sound like what they represent.

15. C: Each answer can be an effective tool in teaching students to build oral language skills. The question makes clear that the objective is to help students evaluate their own oral language skills, which will assist them in both spoken and written assignments. The only answer choice that involves the students evaluating their own message is choice C. When the students prepare a review/quiz based upon important information, they will be more able to speak specifically to that information. When classmates complete the review, each student can identify any patterns in the questions' answers that give clues as to how well those main ideas were communicated. In this way, the student can evaluate how effective the oral presentation was, without relying on classmates or the teacher.

16. B: Teachers should apply a variety of instructional techniques to enable students with different strengths, needs, and learning styles to understand sound-letter and letter-word relationships, but they should not restrict the instructional modalities to auditory and visual (A) simply because sounds are auditory and letters are visual. Multisensory modalities (B) are more effective because

Copyright © Mometrix Media. You have been licensed one copy of this document for personal use only. Any other reproduction or redistribution is strictly prohibited. All rights reserved. This content is provided for test preparation purposes only and does not imply an endorsement by Mometrix of any particular political, scientific, or religious point of view.

different students use different senses to learn; redundancy is necessary for learning; and input to multiple senses affords a more multidimensional learning experience, promoting comprehension and retention. While some aspects of this instruction should be consistent (e.g., starting with high-frequency letters and with phonemes children can produce more easily), sticking to only one method and set of materials (C) prevents using variety to reach all students. Visually similar letters and auditorily similar phonemes should *not* be introduced together (D) before students can discriminate among them; teachers should begin with more obvious differences.

17. B: A phoneme is the smallest measure of language sound. English language phonemes, about 40 in number, are composed of individual letters as well as letter combinations. A number of letters have more than one associated sound. For example, "c" can be pronounced as a hard "c" (cake) or a soft "c" (Cynthia). Vowels in particular have a number of possible pronunciations.

18. A: Prefixes and suffixes are important for reading comprehension because they change the meanings of the root word to which they are attached. A student who understands that *un* means "not" will be able to decipher the meanings of words such as *unwanted, unhappy,* or *unreasonable.*

19. C: The verbs quoted all refer to interpreting information in your own words. This task targets the cognitive objective of comprehension. Tasks targeting the cognitive objective of knowledge recall would ask you to name, label, list, define, repeat, memorize, order, or arrange the information. Tasks targeting the cognitive objective of application would ask you to calculate, solve, practice, operate, sketch, use, prepare, illustrate, or apply the material. Tasks targeting the cognitive objective of evaluation would ask you to judge, appraise, evaluate, conclude, predict, score, or compare the information.

20. C: Decoding monosyllabic words by referring to the initial and final consonant, short vowel, and long vowel sounds represented by their letters is a common academic standard for 1st-grade students. Typical academic standards for kindergarten students include demonstrating knowledge of letter-sound correspondences; understanding the alphabetic principle; matching letters to their corresponding consonant (and short vowel) sounds; and reading simple, monosyllabic sight words, i.e., high-frequency words.

21. D: It is impossible to include every text desired into the language curriculum—there are simply too many good books, stories, poems, speeches, and media available. Teachers must first think about what skills their students need to acquire, as well as what skills they have already mastered. In designing activities for class, a good teacher will start first with the purpose for instruction. For example, purposes of reading can include: reading for information, reading for enjoyment, understanding a message, identifying main or supporting ideas, or developing an appreciation for artistic expression/perception. Once the purpose or intended learning outcome has been identified, the teacher will have a much better idea of which texts, strategies, and activities will support that purpose.

22. C: Silent reading fluency can be monitored over time by giving the Test of Silent Contextual Reading Fluency (TSCRF) four times a year. A similar assessment tool is the Test of Silent Word Reading Fluency (TOSWRF), in which words of increasing complexity are given as a single, undifferentiated, and unpunctuated strand. As with the TSCRF, three minutes are given for the student to separate each word from the next. *Itwillcannotschoolbecomeagendaconsistentphilosophysuperfluous* is an example of such a strand.

23. A: Emergent readers are those who are not yet reading fluently (with appropriate speed and accuracy). Choice B refers to the practice of reviewing relationships between letters and sounds,

Copyright © Mometrix Media. You have been licensed one copy of this document for personal use only. Any other reproduction or redistribution is strictly prohibited. All rights reserved.
This content is provided for test preparation purposes only and does not imply an endorsement by Mometrix of any particular political, scientific, or religious point of view.

which is vital to building reading skills. Choice C would help students build vocabulary retention by requiring them to find unfamiliar words in the dictionary. This practice causes the student to analyze and retain spelling of unfamiliar words, as well as reinforces dictionary/reference skills. Choice D addresses the fact that many words in the English language are irregularly spelled and cannot be decoded with conventional phonetic instruction. While invented spelling described in Choice A may be permitted in emergent readers, this practice is not likely to build specific reading skills.

24. B: The TEKS for ELA and Reading expect 1st- to 3rd-graders to read materials regularly that are at the independent level, which they define as text where approximately one in 20 words or fewer are difficult for the student—not one in 10. Students are also expected to select text to read independently, informed by their knowledge of authors, text genres and types; their estimation of text difficulty levels; and their personal interest. They should also read text regularly that is at the instructional level, which they define as including no more than one in 10 words the reader finds difficult—not one in 20. Finally, TEKS expects students to read aloud fluently from familiar texts, not unfamiliar ones.

25. B: Strategizing in order to understand the meaning of a word, knowing multiple meanings of a single word, and applying background knowledge to glean a word's meaning are all ways in which an effective reader enhances vocabulary. Other skills include an awareness of word parts and word origins, the ability to apply word meanings in a variety of content areas, and a delight in learning the meanings of unfamiliar words.

26. A: John Bunyan (1628-1688) was the author of *The Pilgrim's Progress*, a religious allegory, among many other works. William Congreve (1670-1729) wrote *The Way of the World*, originally a play not successful on the theater stage, but subsequently highly regarded as a literary exemplar of the comedy of manners. Daniel Defoe (circa 1660-1731) is known for *Robinson Crusoe* and other adventure novels, and *The Apparition of Mrs. Veal*, a ghost story later found to be factually based. Samuel Butler (1612-1680), one of the Augustan poets, wrote the burlesque poem *Hudibras*.

27. A: A fallacy of inconsistency exists in a statement that contradicts itself or defeats itself. Saying there are exceptions to all general statements is itself a general statement; therefore, according to the content, this statement must also have an exception, implying there are NOT exceptions to all general statements. Choice B is an example of a fallacy of irrelevance: passing or failing is determined by course performance, so asking to pass because parents will be upset if one fails is an irrelevant reason for appealing to a teacher for a passing grade. Choice C is an example of a fallacy of insufficiency: a statement is made with insufficient evidence to support it. A lack of evidence of innocence is not enough to prove one is guilty because there could also be an equal lack of evidence of guilt. Choice D is an example of a fallacy of inappropriate presumption: asking someone if he or she has stopped cheating presumes that he or she has cheated in the past. The person being asked this question cannot answer either "yes" or "no" without confirming that he or she has indeed been cheating. If the person being asked has not been cheating, then the person asking the question is making a false assumption.

28. D: When students ask themselves how the information in a text they are reading fits with what they already know, they are relating the text to their own prior knowledge, which increases their reading comprehension. Students should not only ask themselves what kinds of "expert questions" fit the subject matter of the text (A)—e.g., classification, physical, and chemical properties are typical question topics in science; genre, character, plot, and theme are typical of literature questions; sequence, cause-and-effect, and comparison-contrast questions are typical of history— but also what questions the material brings up for them personally (B). It is necessary and

Copyright © Mometrix Media. You have been licensed one copy of this document for personal use only. Any other reproduction or redistribution is strictly prohibited. All rights reserved. This content is provided for test preparation purposes only and does not imply an endorsement by Mometrix of any particular political, scientific, or religious point of view.

important for students to ask themselves continually how each text portion relates to its chapter's main ideas (C) as they read to optimize their reading comprehension and retention.

29. C: She should locate the vowels, then locate familiar word parts. Syllables are organized around vowels. In order to determine the syllables, this student should begin by locating the vowels. It's possible to have a syllable that is a single vowel (*a/gain*). It isn't possible to have a syllable that is a single consonant. Once the word has been broken into its component syllables the reader is able to study the syllables to find ones that are familiar and might give her a clue as to the word's meaning, such as certain prefixes or suffixes.

30. C: Phonological cues are based on the speech sounds in words and their alphabetic representations in print. Readers can identify words by knowing sound-to-letter correspondences. Syntactic cues (A) are based on how words are arranged and ordered to create meaningful phrases, clauses and sentences. Semantic cues (B) are based on the meanings of morphemes and words and how they combine to create additional meanings. Pragmatic cues (D) are based on the readers' purposes for reading and their understanding of how textual structures function in the texts that they read.

31. B: Character development is not a common function of reading and writing; it is a skill set for a specific type of writing. Reading can achieve a variety of purposes. Initially, students learn to read as a form of language acquisition. This process also enables them to learn about various concepts through written texts, both inside and outside of school. Individuals will write and read to share thoughts, stories, and ideas with others. As language develops, many individuals will view reading as a common form of entertainment or enjoyment, regardless of the text's perceived instructional value or content.

32. B: This is an example of a closed question because the student can only answer "simile" or "metaphor" without needing to elaborate unless asked to explain the answer. In contrast, choice C is an open-ended question because the student must both define simile and metaphor and explain the difference between them. Choice A is an open-ended literature question because the student cannot answer with yes, no, or some other single word or short phrase; he or she has to describe the action or events in a story that represent its climax, which requires understanding story structure, story elements, knowing the definition of a story's climax, reading the story, and understanding it. Choice D is a very open-ended question, as students have considerable latitude in giving the reasons each of them perceives for having poetry.

33. D: Suffixes appear at the end of words. Prefixes are attached to the beginning of words to change their meanings. *Un+happy, bi+monthly,* and *re+examine* are prefixes that, by definition, change the meanings of the words to which they are attached.

34. A: The process of actively constructing meaning from reading is interactive, in that it involves the text itself, the person reading it, and the setting in which the reading is done: the reader interacts with the text, and the text interacts with the reader by affecting him or her; the context of reading interacts with the text and the reader by affecting them both; and the reader interacts with the reading context as well as with the text. Choice B is a better definition of the *strategic* aspect of the process. Choices C and D are better definitions of the *adaptable* aspect of the process.

35. A: In order to achieve a balanced language program, a teacher must spend time on many different skills that have been mentioned in previous questions and answers. Language skills cannot be reduced to the process of reading (fluency plus comprehension). Students develop their language skills over a long period of time, and they do so across multiple domains. Students' ability

Copyright © Mometrix Media. You have been licensed one copy of this document for personal use only. Any other reproduction or redistribution is strictly prohibited. All rights reserved.
This content is provided for test preparation purposes only and does not imply an endorsement by Mometrix of any particular political, scientific, or religious point of view.

to listen and speak, write, view, respond, synthesize information, and read for a variety of purposes all must be included in daily instruction. By practicing only fluency and comprehension, students will not fully understand the various functions of language skills and may even lack an appreciation for them.

36. C: It is normal for students to reverse letters and numbers occasionally not only in 1st grade but through the end of 2nd grade. Thus, they do not indicate possible dyslexia (B) at this age. The words cited are above 1st-grade spelling level, particularly so early in the school year, so misspelling them is normal, should not be marked incorrect, and does not require intervention (D). Also, teachers should not deduct points for misspelling in written compositions unless the misspelled words are included in weekly class spelling lists. First-graders are frequently in transitional phases of writing when phonetic spelling is not only common but desirable. The student's writing is developmentally appropriate; the substitute's grading is inappropriate. Hence choice A is incorrect.

37. A: Cooperative learning occurs when a group of students at various levels of reading ability have goals in common. Reading comprehension is achieved through reading both orally and silently, developing vocabulary, a reader's ability to predict what will occur in a piece of writing, a reader's ability to summarize the main points in a piece of writing, and a reader's ability to reflect on the text's meaning and connect that meaning to another text or personal experience.

38. B: As linguists have long pointed out, dialects are NOT non-standard versions of a language (A). In linguistics, dialects are *differing* varieties of any language, but these may be vernacular (nonstandard) OR standard versions of a language. They are often considered less socially acceptable, especially in educational, occupational, and professional settings, than whichever standard version is most accepted. The linguistic features of dialects are not incorrect (C), but simply different. Their use does not indicate poor or incomplete language learning (D).

39. B: Integrated curriculum is vital to student growth and to fostering a love of learning. In reality, all subject areas are related, and a good teacher will find ways to highlight the connection of concepts across the curriculum. In choice B, the science teacher provides a way to help students study for a test. However, she would probably be better advised to work with the students on comprehension and retention before test time arrives. She could use a variety of previewing and reviewing skills, as well as creative ways to bring the information to life during class discussions and activities. This teacher might also benefit from discussing the situation with a language arts teacher to get ideas on how to build skills in reading for information, main ideas, and supporting concepts.

40. C: Because this student loves reading graphic novels and has both talent and enjoyment in drawing, having him create his own graphic novels is a good way to motivate him to write by using his visual style, ability, and interest to access writing activity. Giving audio recordings (A) to a highly visual student is not as appropriate to his strengths and interests. Letting him substitute drawing pictures for all writing assignments (B) would address his strengths and interests but not his needs for learning to write. Having him watch animated videos about writing (D) would suit his visual learning style but would not give him the actual writing practice he needs.

41. C: They should meet to discuss areas the teacher is most concerned about and decide on the teacher's goals. In order to best achieve goals, those goals must be understood and established.

42. B: The word *brunch* is a blend of *breakfast* and *lunch*. Blends of two or more words are known as portmanteau words. (*Portmanteau* is a French word meaning a suitcase.) "Fax" (A) is an example of clipping, or shortening a word, from its original "facsimile." "Babysitter" (C) is an example of

Copyright © Mometrix Media. You have been licensed one copy of this document for personal use only. Any other reproduction or redistribution is strictly prohibited. All rights reserved. This content is provided for test preparation purposes only and does not imply an endorsement by Mometrix of any particular political, scientific, or religious point of view.

compounding, or combining two or more words into one. "Saxophone" (D) is an example of proper noun transfer: A Belgian family that built musical instruments had the last name of Sax, and this wind instrument was named after them. These represent some of the ways that new words have entered—and still do enter—the English language.

43. A: Most traditional methods teach reading via aural and visual techniques. However, students with auditory processing problems or dyslexia will not learn to read effectively with these methods, no matter how much practice is provided. Therefore, most students with this type of difficulty will benefit from a multi-sensory technique in which they can make use of all their senses. Combined with systematic instruction and a great deal of practice, the multi-sensory technique is very effective in building reading and processing skills in students with this kind of lifelong learning difference.

44. A: This is an example of formative assessment, which can be formal or informal but is more often informal; it is conducted during instruction to inform teachers of student progress and enable them to adjust instruction if it is not effective enough; this is done on an ongoing basis. Summative assessment (B) is typically formal; it is conducted after instruction to measure final results for grading, promotion, accountability, etc. and inform changes to future instruction, but does not enable adjusting the current instruction. Therefore, it is not an example of choices C or D.

45. D: Round-robin reading is a common practice in language arts classes and has been for many years. In this process, students take turns reading aloud for their peers. Other students are asked to follow along silently in their texts while a peer is reading. This strategy does provide a way for students to read texts in class and include as many students as possible, which is often the intended outcome. However, this process often creates a boring atmosphere, since only one student at a time is actively engaged. While that student is reading, other students may become distracted by their own thoughts, other school work, or off-task interaction with each other. All of these issues subvert the intended outcome of the process. There is rarely enough time for each student to practice reading aloud to build students' reading fluency or comprehension in significant ways.

46. A: Prewriting must occur before drafting. Conferencing refers to collaborating with others so they may critique the draft or offer suggestions to improve it. Revising and editing both refer to changes a writer makes to a draft to improve it. Since choices B, C, and D are meant to help a writer improve a draft, they cannot be completed before the first draft is written.

47. B: The term "blend" is commonly used to refer to a grapheme consisting of two sounds, such as the /fl/ in *flip*. In this word, the /f/ and /l/ sounds are distinctly audible. However, the words from the question prompt contain phoneme combinations in which a completely new sound is formed. The /ch/ sound is similar to neither the /c/ nor /h/. This type of combination is called a "digraph," which is a kind of blended sound.

48. A: Proficiency with oral language enhances students' phonemic awareness and increases vocabulary. Understanding that words are scripted with specific letters representing specific sounds is essential to decoding a text. Students cannot effectively learn to read without the ability to decode. An enhanced vocabulary supports the act of reading; the larger an emergent reader's vocabulary, the more quickly he will learn to read. He will be able to decode more words, which he can organize into word families and use to decode unfamiliar words.

49. D: This description is most typical of the process of peer review. Classmates read Arthur's paper and then they identify values in it, describe it, ask questions about it, and suggest points for revision. These are types of helpful feedback identified by experts on writing and collaborative

Copyright © Mometrix Media. You have been licensed one copy of this document for personal use only. Any other reproduction or redistribution is strictly prohibited. All rights reserved.
This content is provided for test preparation purposes only and does not imply an endorsement by Mometrix of any particular political, scientific, or religious point of view.

writing. The other choices, however, are not typically collaborative. For a portfolio assessment (A), the teacher collects finished work products from a student over time, eventually assembling a portfolio of work. This affords a more authentic assessment using richer, more multidimensional, and more visual and tactile products for assessment instead of using only standardized test scores for assessment. Holistic scoring (B) is a method of scoring a piece of writing for overall quality (evaluating general elements such as focus, organization, support, and conventions) rather than being overly concerned with any individual aspect of writing. A scoring rubric (C) is a guide that gives examples of the levels of typical characteristics in a piece of writing that correspond to each available score (for example, scores from 1-5).

50. B: Previewing and reviewing are skills that assist in learning detailed or large amounts of information. Using these concepts, students learn skills such as skimming and outlining to get an idea of what the text is about before actually reading it. After reading, the students learn to review the information they learned and compare it to their initial previews. This method is particularly helpful when individuals are reading in order to learn new information, as they would be when reading their science texts.

51. B: Language load is the number of unrecognizable words an English language learner encounters when reading a passage or listening to a teacher. Language load is one of the barriers English language learners face. To lighten this load, a teacher can rephrase, eliminate unnecessary words, divide complex sentences into smaller units, and teach essential vocabulary before the student begins the lesson.

52. A: The teacher should give each child a piece of drawing paper that has been folded in half and then in half again, creating four boxes, along with a piece that has not been folded. The teacher should then ask the students to draw a cartoon about the story. Each of the first four boxes will show the events in order. The second page is to show how the story ends. When a child is able to visually see the way a familiar story has unfolded, that child can find causal or thematic connections in the action that increases her comprehension of the story overall. Asking the class to draw a single picture or to draw the beginning and end doesn't sufficiently demonstrate the importance of order to meaning. While some first-graders may be able to create their own cartoon stories that demonstrate a logical series of events, many first-graders are not yet ready to organize thought into a linear progression.

53. B: The MLA (Modern Language Association) system for documenting literary sources defines in-line citations in a paper as combining signal phrases, which usually include the author's name and introduce information from a source via a fact, summary, paraphrase, or quotation; parenthetical references following the material cited, frequently at the end of the sentence; and, except for web sources that are unpaginated, page number(s). MLA defines a list of works cited (A) as an alphabetized list found at the end of a research paper that gives the information sources referenced in the paper, including each source's publication information, quotations, summaries, and paraphrases. Guidelines for preparing the list of works cited are provided in the *MLA Handbook*. MLA information notes (C) are an optional addition to the MLA parenthetical documentation system. These notes can be used to add important material without interrupting the paper's flow, and/or to supply comments about sources or make references to multiple sources. They may be endnotes or footnotes. Because only one of the answers is correct, Option D is not possible.

54. C: One-half of the class receives signs showing vocabulary words, which are probably used as root words. The remaining students are split into two general groups: those with prefixes on their signs and those with suffixes. The best approach is to get the students moving, listening, and talking

Copyright © Mometrix Media. You have been licensed one copy of this document for personal use only. Any other reproduction or redistribution is strictly prohibited. All rights reserved. This content is provided for test preparation purposes only and does not imply an endorsement by Mometrix of any particular political, scientific, or religious point of view.

in order to solidify their understanding of how roots, suffixes, and prefixes work together to make new meanings out of various root words. This approach also allows the students to participate in a game in a group context, making the activity more fun and engaging.

55. C: When reading independently, students are at the correct level if they read with at least 97% accuracy.

56. A: The words in this question prompt are most often used to refer to *sounds* made while reading. Initial/onset, medial, and final sounds are decoded in the beginning, middle, and end of words. When a teacher needs to assess an emergent or struggling reader's ability to differentiate between sounds in words, he or she may use a phonological awareness assessment. This tool will provide the teacher with information about the student's current ability to decode or encode words.

57. B: For any writing assignment, you should first target an audience, perform an audience analysis, and develop an audience profile to determine what you should include in and omit from your writing. Even though the assigning teacher may be the only one to read your writing, you should not assume he or she is your main audience (A) because the teacher may expect you to write for other readers. In addition to first knowing your purpose for writing before beginning, you should also consider what purpose your writing will meet for your readers (C) and how they are likely to use it. Considering your audience's attitude toward what you will write and their likely reactions is also important to shaping your writing and is NOT overthinking (D).

58. A: Multiple research studies have found that teaching phonological awareness skills to kindergarteners with delayed language development has enhanced their language development. Researchers also recommend involving speech-language pathologists (SLPs) and their instructional methods as effective in teaching phonological awareness skills (B). Phonological awareness involves being able to recognize and change phonemes (speech sounds) without any reference to meanings (C) of words, syllables, or morphological units. Researchers and others instructing kindergarteners in phonological awareness skills have provided training at both the individual phoneme level (identifying and differentiating phonemes, matching initial and final phonemes, deleting phonemes, blending phonemes, etc.) and above (D) the phoneme level (syllable, word, and rhyme awareness).

59. A: Sight words occur in many types of writing; they are high-frequency words. Sight words are also words with irregular spelling. Some examples of sight words include *talk, some,* and *the.* Fluent readers need to recognize these words visually.

60. C: The most effective lesson would be brainstorming a list of verbs that mean ways of talking or ways of going, then adding them to the word wall along with some nouns that specify common topics. Second graders aren't developmentally ready for a thesaurus; most will believe that any words in a particular list are interchangeable. For example, a student who wrote *my little sister walks like a baby* might find the verbs *strut, sidle,* and *amble* in the thesaurus. None of these verbs would be an appropriate substitution. Supplementing a noun with an adjective often results in flat writing: *There's a tree in my yard* might become *There's a nice tree in my big yard.* Adjectives such as *pretty, fun, cute, funny,* and so forth don't add much in terms of meaning, but they are the adjectives younger writers reach for first. A more specific noun is both more meaningful and more interesting. *There's a weeping willow in my yard* is evocative.

61. C: Oral language skills can be distinguished from specific speech characteristics exhibited by some children. Many students like Rosa, whose first language is not English, will speak with an accent and may be less clear when speaking about a topic that is unfamiliar. In fact, even those who

Copyright © Mometrix Media. You have been licensed one copy of this document for personal use only. Any other reproduction or redistribution is strictly prohibited. All rights reserved. This content is provided for test preparation purposes only and does not imply an endorsement by Mometrix of any particular political, scientific, or religious point of view.

are not English Language Learners may exhibit difficulty speaking on new topics. Greer may avoid oral assignments or speaking in class for a number of reasons, such as self-consciousness. This student could be helped by evaluating oral language skills in a one-on-one environment or by introducing peer scaffolding to help reduce anxiety. Brett's demeanor in group assignments may also be due to social characteristics rather than oral skills; it would be important to evaluate his skills in various contexts. Ashley, however, shows marked problems communicating orally both in class discussion and in prepared assignments. She would benefit from specific instruction related to presenting ideas orally.

62. D: The concept in question is known as language transfer, also known as L1 interference, in which language features from the first language affects the acquisition of a second language. This is particularly noteworthy in language features that exist in one language, but not in the other. For instance, in English, plural nouns are usually marked by adding -s to the end of the word, whereas Chinese does not make use of a plural indicator. This grammatical feature, therefore, is commonly difficult to accurately acquire. Regarding the options in the question, the Chinese written language is ideographic rather than alphabetic (A)—that is, its written symbols represent concepts visually rather than being letters representing speech sounds. Also, the fact that Spanish is much more phonetically regular than English (B) (i.e., many more words are pronounced the same way as they are spelled than in English) contributes different effects to ELL students' English-language literacy development. Therefore, choice C is incorrect.

63. D: Familiar, frequently used words that do not need to be taught beyond primary grades. Common or basic words are the first tier of three-tier words. These words are widely used across the spoken and written spectrum. Some examples are *walk, go, wish, the, look, happy,* and *always.* This essential vocabulary is taught early in a reader's instruction, and beyond that it need not be taught.

64. D: There are various cueing systems that readers can use to help them understand how to read or comprehend unfamiliar words. Semantic cueing helps with understanding word meaning; the reader uses the meaning of the words around an unfamiliar word to understand what that word means. Syntactical cueing can also be called "grammatical cueing," in which a reader uses the syntax of a sentence to understand more about an unfamiliar word. Graphophonic cueing is most useful in decoding, or breaking words down into smaller components.

65. D: Knowing your purpose for writing means knowing what you want to achieve with the content of your writing, and knowing this will determine your writing style. Your choice of words and how formal or informal your writing is—your diction—does affect your style (A). Diction and tone should be consistent in your writing style and should reflect vocabulary and writing patterns that suit your writing purpose best. Style is not added later to give writing personality (B). It develops from your purpose for writing, or what you want to accomplish with your writing. Style is directly related to your control of the content (C) of your writing.

66. A: Students develop literacy within multiple contexts by learning to listen to, speak, read, and write language. Therefore, it is inaccurate to say that only reading, writing, and listening (B) are activities for developing literacy. Literacy development is not confined to reading and writing (C) as some non-educators may believe. Some may even have the mistaken impression that reading is the only activity important for literacy development (D). However, literacy develops through all activities using language.

67. D: None; sight words cannot be decoded. Readers must learn to recognize these as whole words on sight. Sight words have irregular spelling. Segmenting them into syllables or using a phonemic

Copyright © Mometrix Media. You have been licensed one copy of this document for personal use only. Any other reproduction or redistribution is strictly prohibited. All rights reserved.
This content is provided for test preparation purposes only and does not imply an endorsement by Mometrix of any particular political, scientific, or religious point of view.

approach are ineffective strategies to aid a reader in recognizing a sight word because these approaches depend on rules a sight word doesn't follow. Word families group words that share common patterns of consonants and vowels. The spelling of those words is, therefore, regular because they follow a predictable pattern. Sight words are irregular, do not follow a predictable pattern, and must be instantaneously recognized for writing fluency. No decoding is useful.

68. A: Editing is the final step in the writing process and involves correcting surface features such as sentence fragments, spelling, and punctuation. The writer has already decided the ideas or events are in proper order, have been sufficiently described, and are clear. Now the writer turns his or her attention to surface features, "scrubbing" errors in spelling, punctuation, and syntax from the writing.

69. A: In choice A, the teacher guides previewing of information to show students how to put themselves in the right frame of mind to listen carefully for meaning. Students are then able to listen in a guided way based upon the previewing. By varying the type of comprehension assessment, the teacher will get a better understanding of what the students learned. Choice B is a good exercise but does not provide for direct instruction by the teacher or a particularly skilled student. In Choice C, students are focusing more on reading comprehension than listening since they must read the story to themselves and then write a report. There is then no way to gauge what they have learned. Choice D would be useful but does not include teacher-guided previewing, which is very helpful in building comprehension.

70. C: Researchers and educators have found that reading fluency and reading comprehension have a reciprocal relationship: the more fluently a student can read, the more able the student's brain is to process the meaning of text. For example, developing automaticity of word identification enhances comprehension. Conversely, the better a student can understand the text, the more fluently she or he can read it. Therefore, while choices A and B are both true, each represents only half of the relationship whereas choice C indicates the relationship's mutual nature. Choice D is incorrect as reading fluency and reading comprehension are interrelated components in deriving meaning from text and not separate.

71. A: Phonological awareness refers to an understanding of the sounds a word makes. While phonological awareness leads to fluent reading skills, activities designed to develop an awareness of word sounds are, by definition, oral.

72. B: Shakespeare (1564-1616) wrote during the Renaissance. The Medieval (A) era (also known as the Middle Ages) was earlier, ending before the 16th century (circa 1485), and included authors like Geoffrey Chaucer, Dante Alighieri, the Pearl Poet (author of *Sir Gawain and the Green Knight*), and Sir Thomas Malory. The Restoration (C) period followed the Renaissance, circa 1660-1700, and included authors like John Dryden, who wrote poetry, satire, and criticism. The Enlightenment (D) occurred from 1700-1785 and included the authors Jonathan Swift, Alexander Pope, Dr. Samuel Johnson, and James Boswell.

73. C: This sentence appeals to the reader's emotions by stating simply that it is dangerous and "really stupid" to use a cell phone while driving; it does not provide any evidence or logic to support the statement. Choice A offers a logical, common-sense argument in that steering one-handed makes driving more dangerous. Choice B refers to statistics of greater accident risk to support the statement that cell phone use while driving is dangerous. Such supporting evidence is an appeal to logic. Choice D cites the fact that many state laws ban cell phone use while driving to support the idea that it is dangerous and also refers to data on more accidents from doing so. These pieces of supporting evidence also appeal to logic rather than emotion.

Copyright © Mometrix Media. You have been licensed one copy of this document for personal use only. Any other reproduction or redistribution is strictly prohibited. All rights reserved. This content is provided for test preparation purposes only and does not imply an endorsement by Mometrix of any particular political, scientific, or religious point of view.

74. A: Students need to know why and how to use text features to inform their reading. Reading headings above sections within chapters (A) help students determine the main subject matter of each section. Reading the glossary for a chapter (B) gives students definitions of terms used in the chapter. Reading the index in a text (C) is a way to locate page numbers of references to subjects or authors in the text. Whether they will be reading the entire section or not, students need not read through the whole thing (D) only to determine its subject matter when its heading will typically indicate this. Headings inform students of topics in advance if they will be reading the section; if they are doing research or choosing what to read, headings can help them decide.

75. A: Story action can be analyzed in terms of rising action, story climax, falling action, and resolution. Rising action consists of those events that occur before and lead up to the story's most dramatic moment, or climax. The climax occurs toward the end of the book, but rarely, if ever, right at the end. Following the climax, the consequences of that dramatic moment are termed "falling action." The story reaches resolution with the outcome of the falling action.

76. D: *Semantics* refers to the meanings of words and language. The semantic system in the Three Cueing Systems model is the set of cues (including words, phrases, sentences, discourse, and complete text) that readers can use to recognize words based on meanings. Pragmatic cues (A) are based on reader purposes for reading and reader understanding of text structure. The phonological system (B) consists of cues related to the phonemic (or sound) structure of language. The syntactic system (C) consists of cues related to the sentence structure and word order of language.

77. A: It is important to evaluate specific reading skills, such as phonemic awareness, in a variety of contexts. Reading aloud with Abi allowed his teacher to notice that he consistently misread words beginning with digraphs. Digraphs are sounds in which two distinct letters, when combined, produce a single third sound (e.g., when *s* and *h* produce the *-sh* sound). Blends are words in which two letters produce a third sound which is a combination of both sounds put together (e.g., *b* and *l* combined to make *b*). The only set of words consisting only of digraphs is choice A.

78. D: Teachers should use a broad variety of instructional materials to support student vocabulary development, including not only literature and expository texts (A) but also newspapers, magazines (B), trade books, content-specific texts, technology (C), and other sources of vocabulary words to provide students with the richest and most authentic array of contexts possible for the greatest quantity and quality of exposure to and learning of vocabulary.

79. B: Revision (literally, *re+vision*) is the act of "seeing again." When revising, writers examine what they have written in order to improve the meaning of the work. Fine-tuning word choices, moving information to another location, and adding or deleting words are all acts of revision.

80. C: Thinking about thinking, or understanding our own cognitive processes, is known as metacognition. Explicitly teaching effective reading comprehension strategies does more than deepen student understanding of reading: it also promotes the higher-order, abstract cognitive skill of metacognition. Schemata (A) (plural, singular *schema*) is Piaget's term for mental constructs we form to understand the world. Piaget said we either assimilate new information into an existing schema or alter an existing schema to accommodate the new knowledge. Reading instruction experts may refer to experience or background knowledge as schemata because students undergo this cognitive process when they fit what they read to their existing knowledge/experience. Scaffolding (B), a term coined by Jerome Bruner, means the temporary support given to students as needed while they learn and is gradually reduced as they become more independent. Reading instruction experts may also describe students' connections of text to prior experience as scaffolding. Metamorphosis (D) is a term meaning a transformation.

Copyright © Mometrix Media. You have been licensed one copy of this document for personal use only. Any other reproduction or redistribution is strictly prohibited. All rights reserved. This content is provided for test preparation purposes only and does not imply an endorsement by Mometrix of any particular political, scientific, or religious point of view.

Mathematics

1. C: One strategy is to consider a progression of polygons with fewer sides and look for a pattern in the number of the polygons' diagonals.

Polygon	Sides	Diagonals	Additional Diagonals
	3	0	-
	4	2	2
	5	5	3
	6	9	4

A quadrilateral has two more diagonals than a triangle, a pentagon has three more diagonals than a quadrilateral, and a hexagon has four more diagonals than a pentagon. Continue this pattern to find that a dodecagon has 54 diagonals.

2. D: When the dress is marked down by 20%, the cost of the dress is 80% of its original price; thus, the reduced price of the dress can be written as $\frac{80}{100}x$, or $\frac{4}{5}x$, where x is the original price. When discounted an extra 25%, the dress costs 75% of the reduced price, or $\frac{75}{100}\left(\frac{4}{5}x\right)$, or $\frac{3}{4}\left(\frac{4}{5}x\right)$, which simplifies to $\frac{3}{5}x$. So, the final price of the dress is three-fifths of the original price.

3. C: Aaron ran four miles from home and then back again, so he ran a total of eight miles. Therefore, statement III is false. Statements I and II, however, are both true. Since Aaron ran eight miles in eighty minutes, he ran an average of one mile every ten minutes, or six miles per hour; he ran two miles from point A to B in 20 minutes and four miles from D to E in 40 minutes, so his running speed between both sets of points was the same.

4. D: Since a and b are even integers, each can be expressed as the product of 2 and an integer. So, if we write $a = 2x$ and $b = 2y$, $3(2x)^2 + 9(2y)^3 = c$.

$$3(4x^2) + 9(8y^3) = c$$
$$12x^2 + 72y^3 = c$$
$$12(x^2 + 6y^3) = c$$

Since c is the product of 12 and some other integer, 12 must be a factor of c. Incidentally, the numbers 2, 3, and 6 must also be factors of c since each is also a factor of 12.

Copyright © Mometrix Media. You have been licensed one copy of this document for personal use only. Any other reproduction or redistribution is strictly prohibited. All rights reserved. This content is provided for test preparation purposes only and does not imply an endorsement by Mometrix of any particular political, scientific, or religious point of view.

5. B: Notice that choice C cannot be correct since $x \neq 1$. ($x = 1$ results in a zero in the denominator.)

$$\frac{x-2}{x-1} = \frac{x-1}{x+1} + \frac{2}{x-1}$$
$$\frac{x-4}{x-1} = \frac{x-1}{x+1}$$
$$(x+1)(x-4) = (x-1)(x-1)$$
$$x^2 - 3x - 4 = x^2 - 2x + 1$$
$$-5 = x$$

6. B: A cube has six square faces. The arrangement of these faces in a two-dimensional figure is a net of a cube if the figure can be folded to form a cube. If this is folded, the bottom square in the second column will overlap the fourth square in the top row, so the figure does not represent a net of a cube. The other figures represent three of the eleven possible nets of a cube.

7. D: The point $(5, -5)$ lies on the line segment that has a slope of -2 and passes through $(3, -1)$. If $(5, -5)$ is one of the endpoints of the line segment, then the other would be $(1,3)$.

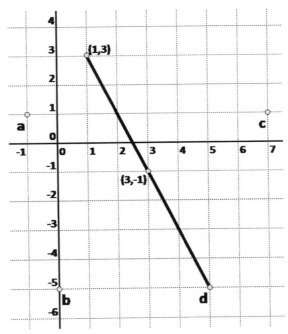

8. D: The Pythagorean theorem may be used to find the diagonal distance from the top of his head to the base of the shadow. The following equation may be written and solved for c: $5.8^2 + 6.2^2 = c^2$. Thus, $c \approx 8.5$. The distance is approximately 8.5 ft.

9. C: When rolling two dice, there is only one way to roll a sum of 2 (rolling a 1 on each die) and 12 (rolling 6 on each die). In contrast, there are two ways to obtain a sum of 3 (rolling a 2 and 1 or a 1 and 2) and 11 (rolling a 5 and 6 or a 6 and 5), three ways to obtain a sum of 4 (1 and 3; 2 and 2; 3 and 1) or 10 (4 and 6; 5 and 5; 6 and 4), and so on. Since the probability of obtaining each sum is inconsistent, this is not a random selection.

10. C: A number that is divisible by 6 is divisible by 2 and 3. For example, the number 12 is divisible by 2 and 3, so it is also divisible by 6. A number ending in 6, a number with the last two digits

Copyright © Mometrix Media. You have been licensed one copy of this document for personal use only. Any other reproduction or redistribution is strictly prohibited. All rights reserved.
This content is provided for test preparation purposes only and does not imply an endorsement by Mometrix of any particular political, scientific, or religious point of view.

divisible by 6 and a number with the last digit divisible by 2 or 3 is not necessarily divisible by 6; for example, 16 and 166 are not divisible by 6. Therefore, the correct choice is C.

11. C. The original price may be modeled by the equation:

$$(x - 0.45x) + 0.0875(x - 0.45x) = \$39.95$$

This simplifies to $0.598125x = \$39.95$. Dividing each side of the equation by the coefficient of x gives $x \approx \$66.79$.

12. C: An inversely proportional relationship is written in the form $y = \frac{k}{x}$, thus the equation $y = \frac{3}{x}$ shows that y is inversely proportional to x.

13. C: Using the points $(-3,1)$ and $(1, -11)$, the slope may be written as $m = \frac{-11-1}{1-(-3)}$ or $m = -3$. Substituting the slope of -3 and the x- and y-values from the point $(-3,1)$, into the slope-intercept form of an equation gives $1 = -3(-3) + b$, which simplifies to $1 = 9 + b$. Subtracting 9 from both sides of the equation gives $b = -8$. Thus, the linear equation that includes the data in the table is $y = -3x - 8$.

14. A: The inequality will be less than or equal to, since he may spend $100 or less on his purchase.

15. C: The surface area of a sphere may be calculated using the formula $SA = 4\pi r^2$. Substituting 9 for r gives $SA = 4\pi(9)^2$, which simplifies to $SA \approx 1,017.36$. So the surface area of the ball is approximately 1,017.36 square inches. There are twelve inches in a foot, so there are $12^2 = 144$ square inches in a square foot. In order to convert this measurement to square feet, the following proportion may be written and solved for x: $\frac{1}{144} = \frac{x}{1,017.36}$. So $x \approx 7.07$. He needs approximately 7.07 square feet of wrapping paper.

16. C: The original triangle was reflected across the x-axis. When reflecting across the x-axis, the x-values of each point remain the same, but the y-values of the points will be opposites.

$$(1,4) \to (1,-4) \quad (5,4) \to (5,-4) \quad (3,8) \to (3,-8)$$

17. B: The probability may be written as $P(E \text{ and } H) = P(E) \times P(H)$. Substituting the probability of each event gives $(E \text{ and } H) = \frac{1}{2} \times \frac{1}{2}$, which simplifies to $\frac{1}{4}$.

18. B: This is a formative assessment because she is assessing students while she is still teaching the unit. Summative assessments are given at the end of the unit. Formal assessments are usually quizzes or tests. Informal assessments include asking individual students questions. Therefore, the correct choice is B.

19. A: Choice A is correct because standards for fourth grade state that students will be able to use a protractor to determine the approximate measures of angles in degrees to the nearest whole number. Choices B, C, and D are stated in the standards for fifth grade.

20. B: Sophia needs to find multiples of 3 (3, 6, 9, 12, 15, ...) and multiples of 4 (4, 8, 12, 16, ...) and find the least common multiple between them, which is 12. The greatest common divisor of 3 and 4 is 1. The least common divisor between two numbers is always 1. The greatest common multiple can never be determined. Therefore, the correct choice is B.

Copyright © Mometrix Media. You have been licensed one copy of this document for personal use only. Any other reproduction or redistribution is strictly prohibited. All rights reserved. This content is provided for test preparation purposes only and does not imply an endorsement by Mometrix of any particular political, scientific, or religious point of view.

21. D: Number lines can help students understand the concepts of positive and negative numbers. Fraction strips are most commonly used with fractions. Venn diagrams are commonly used when comparing groups. Shaded regions are commonly used with fractions or percentages.

22. C: The associative property of multiplication states that when three or more numbers are multiplied, the product is the same regardless of the way in which the numbers are grouped. Choice C shows that the product of 2, 3, and 4 is the same with two different groupings of the factors. Choice A demonstrates the distributive property. Choice B shows grouping, but the factors are different. Choice D demonstrates the commutative property of multiplication. Therefore, the correct choice is C.

23. B: The equation $y + 3 = 7$ is solved by subtracting 3 from both sides to yield $y = 4$.

Substituting $y = 4$ into $x - 1 = y$ yields $x - 1 = 4$. Adding 1 to both sides of this equation yields $x = 5$.

24. C: Triangles can be classified as scalene, isosceles, or equilateral. Scalene triangles have no equal side measurements and no equal angle measurements. Isosceles triangles have two sides of equal measurement and two angles of equal measurement. Equilateral triangles have three sides of equal measurement and three angles of equal measurement. A right triangle is isosceles only if its two acute angles are congruent.

25. C: The slope of a line can be found from any two points by the formula $slope = \frac{y_2 - y_1}{x_2 - x_1}$. A sketch of $(-3, -1)$, $(-6, 1)$, $(0, -3)$ reveals a line with a negative slope. Substituting the last two points into the formula yields $slope = \frac{-3 - 1}{0 - (-6)}$ which reduces to $\frac{-4}{6}$ or $\frac{-2}{3}$.

26. C: The mean is the average of the data and can be found by dividing the sum of the data by the number of data: $\frac{16 + 18 + 20 + 21 + 34 + 45 + 49}{7} = 29$. The median is the middle data point when the data are ranked numerically. The median is 21.

27. B: The histogram only shows that there are eight trees between 70 and 75 feet tall. It does not show the individual heights of the trees. That information cannot be obtained from this graph.

28. A: To convert a percentage to a fraction, remove the percent sign and place the number over 100. That means 15% can be written as $\frac{15}{100}$, which reduces to $\frac{3}{20}$. To convert a percentage to a decimal, remove the percent sign and move the decimal two places to the left. To convert a percentage to a ratio, first write the percentage as a fraction, and then rewrite the fraction as a ratio.

29. C: The number 589 can be estimated to be 600. The number 9 can be estimated to be 10. The number of chicken nuggets is approximately 600×10, which is 6,000 nuggets. Therefore, the correct choice is C.

30. D: The total rainfall is 25.38 inches. Thus, the ratio $\frac{4.5}{25.38}$ represents the percentage of rainfall received during October. $\frac{4.5}{25.38} \approx 0.177$ or 17.7%.

31. C: The volume of a cylinder may be calculated using the formula $V = \pi r^2 h$, where r represents the radius and h represents the height. Substituting 1.5 for r and 3 for h gives $V = \pi (1.5)^2 (3)$, which simplifies to $V \approx 21.2$.

Copyright © Mometrix Media. You have been licensed one copy of this document for personal use only. Any other reproduction or redistribution is strictly prohibited. All rights reserved. This content is provided for test preparation purposes only and does not imply an endorsement by Mometrix of any particular political, scientific, or religious point of view.

32. D: The area of the square is $A = s^2 = (30 \text{ cm})^2 = 900 \text{ cm}^2$. The area of the circle is $A = \pi r^2 = \pi(15 \text{ cm})^2 \approx 707 \text{ cm}^2$. The area of the shaded region is equal to the difference of the area of the square and the area of the circle, or $900 \text{ cm}^2 - 707 \text{ cm}^2$, which equals 193 cm^2.

33. B: The perimeter is equal to the sum of the lengths of the two bases, 2 and 6 units, and the diagonal distances of the other two sides. Using the distance formula, each side length may be represented as $d = \sqrt{20} = 2\sqrt{5}$. Thus, the sum of the two sides is equal to $2\sqrt{20}$, or $4\sqrt{5}$. The whole perimeter is equal to $8 + 4\sqrt{5}$.

34. C: The slope may be written as $m = \frac{4-0}{-3-(-4)}$, which simplifies to $m = 4$.

35. A: $A \cap B$ means "A intersect B," or the elements that are common to both sets. "A intersect B" represents "A and B," that is, an element is in the intersection of A and B if it is in A *and* it is in B. The elements 2, 5, and 8 are common to both sets.

36. C: To find the probability of an event, divide the number of favorable outcomes by the total number of outcomes. When there are two events in which the first depends on the second, multiply the first ratio by the second ratio. In the first part of the problem, the probability of choosing a licorice jelly bean is two out of twenty possible outcomes, or $\frac{2}{20}$. Then, because one jelly bean has already been chosen, there are four cinnamon beans out of a total of 19, or $\frac{4}{19}$. By multiplying the two ratios and dividing by a common denominator, one arrives at the final probability of $\frac{2}{95}$.

37. C: There are 36 months in 3 years. The following proportion may be written: $\frac{450}{3} = \frac{x}{36}$. Cross multiplying gives you the equation $3x = 16{,}200$, which can be solved for x. Dividing both sides of the equation by 3 gives $x = 5{,}400$.

38. C: When you have a ratio, you can find the fraction that each part of the ratio is of the whole by putting it over the sum of the parts. In other words, since the ratio of wages and benefits to other costs is 2: 3, the amount of money spent on wages and benefits is $\frac{2}{2+3} = \frac{2}{5}$ of total expenditures.

$$\frac{2}{5} \times \$130{,}000 = \$52{,}000$$

39. C: If x is a prime number and the greatest common factor of x and y is greater than 1, the greatest common factor of x and y must be x. The least common multiple of two numbers is equal to the product of those numbers divided by their greatest common factor. So, the least common multiple of x and y is $\frac{xy}{x} = y$. Therefore, the two quantities are the same.

40. C: Start by setting up a proportion to solve by cross multiplication: $\frac{1 \text{ inch}}{60 \text{ feet}} = \frac{10 \text{ inches}}{x \text{ feet}}$. When the numbers are cross multiplied, you get $x = 600$ feet. Now we need to convert 600 feet to yards. There are 3 feet in 1 yard, so divide 600 by 3 to find the number of yards between the two points: $600 \div 3 = 200$ yards.

41. D: Since all of the answer choices are parallelograms, determine whether the parallelogram is also a rhombus, a rectangle, or both. One way to do this is by examining the parallelogram's diagonals. If the parallelogram's diagonals are perpendicular, then the parallelogram is a rhombus. If the parallelogram's diagonals are congruent, then the parallelogram is a rectangle. If a

Copyright © Mometrix Media. You have been licensed one copy of this document for personal use only. Any other reproduction or redistribution is strictly prohibited. All rights reserved. This content is provided for test preparation purposes only and does not imply an endorsement by Mometrix of any particular political, scientific, or religious point of view.

parallelogram is both a rhombus and a rectangle, then it is a square. A plot of the quadrilateral would be:

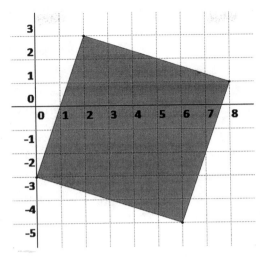

To determine whether the diagonals are perpendicular, find the slopes of the diagonals of the quadrilateral:

Diagonal 1
$$\frac{-5-3}{6-2} = \frac{-8}{4} = -2$$

Diagonal 2
$$\frac{-1-3}{0-8} = \frac{-4}{-8} = \frac{1}{2}$$

The diagonals have opposite inverse slopes and are therefore perpendicular. Thus, the parallelogram is a rhombus. To determine whether the diagonals are congruent, find the lengths of the diagonals of the quadrilateral:

Diagonal 1
$$\sqrt{(6-2)^2 + (-5-3)^2} = \sqrt{(4)^2 + (-8)^2}$$
$$= \sqrt{16 + 64}$$
$$= \sqrt{80}$$

Diagonal 2
$$\sqrt{(0-8)^2 + (-3-1)^2} = \sqrt{(-8)^2 + (-4)^2}$$
$$= \sqrt{64 + 16}$$
$$= \sqrt{80}$$

The diagonals are congruent, so the parallelogram is a rectangle. Since the polygon is a rhombus and a rectangle, it is also a square.

42. A: Nominal data are data that are collected which have no intrinsic quantity or order. For instance, a survey might ask the respondent to identify his or her gender. While it is possible to compare the relative frequency of each response (for example, "most of the respondents are women"), it is not possible to calculate the mean, which requires data to be numeric, or median, which requires data to be ordered. Interval data are both numeric and ordered, so mean and median can be determined, as can the mode, the interval within which there are the most data. Ordinal data has an inherent order, but there is not a set interval between two points. For example, a survey might ask the respondents whether they were very dissatisfied, dissatisfied, neutral, satisfied, or very satisfied with the customer service received. Since the data are not numeric, the mean cannot be calculated, but since ordering the data is possible, the median has context.

Copyright © Mometrix Media. You have been licensed one copy of this document for personal use only. Any other reproduction or redistribution is strictly prohibited. All rights reserved.
This content is provided for test preparation purposes only and does not imply an endorsement by Mometrix of any particular political, scientific, or religious point of view.

43. D: Since they are not mutually exclusive events, the probability may be written as $P(P \text{ or } T) = P(P) + P(T) - P(P \text{ and } T)$. Because the events are independent, $P(P \text{ and } T) = P(P) \times P(T)$. Substituting the probability of each event gives $(P \text{ or } T) = \frac{1}{2} + \frac{1}{2} - \left(\frac{1}{2} \times \frac{1}{2}\right) = \frac{3}{4}$.

44. C: The line through the center of the box represents the median. The median test score for classes 1 and 2 is 82.

Note that for class 1, the median is a better representation of the data than the mean. There are two outliers (points which lie outside of two standard deviations from the mean) which bring down the average test score. In cases such as this, the mean is not the best measure of central tendency.

45. B: Determine the probability of each option (if b = likes broccoli, c = likes carrots, and f = likes cauliflower).

For choice A, this is the total number of students in the broccoli circle of the Venn diagram divided by the total number of students surveyed:

$$P(b) = \frac{10 + 4 + 3 + 15}{90} = \frac{32}{90} \approx 35.6\%$$

For choice B, this is the total number of students in the carrots circle and also in at least one other circle divided by the total number in the carrots circle:

$$P(b \cup f | c) = \frac{15 + 3 + 6}{15 + 3 + 6 + 27} = \frac{24}{51} \approx 47.1\%$$

For choice C, this is the number of students in the intersection of all three circles divided by the total number in the overlap of the broccoli and cauliflower circles:

$$P(c | b \cap f) = \frac{3}{3 + 4} = \frac{3}{7} \approx 42.9\%$$

For choice D, this is the number of students outside of all the circles divided by the total number of students surveyed:

$$P([c \cup b \cup f]') = \frac{23}{90} \approx 25.6\%$$

46. C: The original price may be represented by the equation $24{,}210 = x - 0.10x$ or $24{,}210 = 0.9x$. Dividing both sides of the equation by 0.9 gives $x = 26{,}900$.

47. A: The sum of 3 and the product of each term number and 5 equals the term value. For example, for term number 4, the value is equal to $5(4) + 3$, or 23.

48. C: The slope is equal to 4, since each ticket costs $4. The y-intercept is represented by the constant fee of $30. Substituting 4 for m and 30 for b into the equation $y = mx + b$ gives $y = 4x + 30$.

49. D: Since she spends at least $16, the relation of the number of packages of coffee to the minimum cost may be written as $4p \geq 16$. Alternatively, the inequality may be written as $16 \leq 4p$.

Copyright © Mometrix Media. You have been licensed one copy of this document for personal use only. Any other reproduction or redistribution is strictly prohibited. All rights reserved.
This content is provided for test preparation purposes only and does not imply an endorsement by Mometrix of any particular political, scientific, or religious point of view.

50. D: The cross-section of a cylinder will never be a triangle.

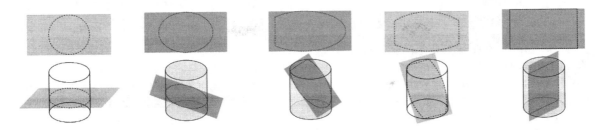

Social Studies

1. A: It is not true that England's defeat of the Spanish Armada in 1588 ended their war with Spain. It did establish England's naval dominance and strengthened England's future colonization of the New World, but the actual war between England and Spain did not end until 1604. It is true that Henry VIII's desire to divorce Catherine of Aragon strengthened English expansionism. Catherine was Spanish, and Henry split from the Catholic Church because it prohibited divorce. Henry's rejection of his Spanish wife and his subsequent support of the Protestant movement angered King Philip II of Spain and destroyed the formerly close ties between the two countries. When Elizabeth became Queen of England, she supported the Reformation as a Protestant, which also contributed to English colonization. Sir Francis Drake, one of the best-known English sea captains during this time period, would attack and plunder Spanish ships that had plundered Native Americans, adding to the enmity between Spain and England. Queen Elizabeth invested in Drake's voyages and gave him her support in claiming territories for England.

2. A: The latest occurring decolonization event was the Eastern Bloc and Soviet Satellite states of Armenia, Azerbaijan, Estonia, Georgia, Kazakhstan, Kyrgyzstan, Latvia, Lithuania, Moldova, Russia, Tajikistan, Turkmenistan, Ukraine, and Uzbekistan, which all became independent from the Soviet Union in 1991. (Note: This was the last decolonization of the Cold War years, as the end of the Soviet Union marked the end of the Cold War.) Canada completed its independence from British Parliament via the Canada Act in 1982. In the Caribbean, the Bahamas gained independence from the United Kingdom in 1973. Algeria won its independence from France when the Algerian War of Independence, begun in 1954, ended in 1962.

3. A: The president has the authority to negotiate and sign treaties. A two-thirds vote of the Senate, however, is needed to ratify a treaty for it to be upheld.

4. C: Article III judges are appointed for life and can retire at 65. They can only be removed from their posts by impeachment in the House and conviction in the Senate. Having judges serve life terms is meant to allow them to serve without being governed by the changing opinions of the public.

5. B: "...endowed by their Creator with certain unalienable Rights," is excerpted from the Declaration of Independence. These rights are unable to be taken away from individuals, referring to the colonists' rights that Great Britain could not oppress.

6. D: It is not true that the Gilded Age is a term whose origins have not been identified clearly. In 1873, Mark Twain and Charles Dudley Warner co-authored a book entitled *The Gilded Age: A Tale of Today*. Twain and Warner first coined this term to describe the extravagance and excesses of America's wealthy upper class, who became richer than ever due to industrialization. Furthermore, the Gilded Age was the era of the "robber barons" such as John D. Rockefeller, Cornelius Vanderbilt,

Copyright © Mometrix Media. You have been licensed one copy of this document for personal use only. Any other reproduction or redistribution is strictly prohibited. All rights reserved.
This content is provided for test preparation purposes only and does not imply an endorsement by Mometrix of any particular political, scientific, or religious point of view.

J.P. Morgan, and others. Because they accumulated enormous wealth through extremely aggressive and occasionally unethical monetary manipulations, critics dubbed them "robber barons" because they seemed to be elite lords of robbery. While these business tycoons grasped huge fortunes, some of them—such as Andrew Carnegie and Andrew Mellon—were also philanthropists, using their wealth to support and further worthy causes such as literacy, education, health care, charities, and the arts. They donated millions of dollars to fund social improvements. Carnegie himself dubbed this large philanthropic movement the "Gospel of Wealth." Another characteristic of the Gilded Age was the Beaux Arts architectural style, a neo-Renaissance style modeled after the great architectural designs of the European Renaissance. The Panic of 1893 ended the Gilded Age and began a severe four-year economic depression. The Progressive Era followed these events.

7. A: One example of the multiplier effect of large cities would be if the presence of specialized equipment for an industry attracted even more business. Large cities tend to grow even larger for a number of reasons: they have more skilled workers, they have greater concentrations of specialized equipment, and they have already-functioning markets. These factors all make it easier for a business to begin operations in a large city than elsewhere. Thus, the populations and economic productivity of large cities tend to grow quickly. Some governments have sought to mitigate this trend by clustering groups of similar industries in smaller cities.

8. D: Criminal cases are tried under both state law and federal law. The nature of the crime determines whether it is tried in state court or federal court.

9. D: The Louisiana Purchase actually increased the U.S.'s territory by 100% overnight, not 50%. The Louisiana territory doubled the size of the nation. It is true that Jefferson initially sent a delegation to Paris to see if Napoleon would agree to sell only New Orleans to the United States. It is also true that Napoleon, who expected America to encroach on Louisiana, decided to avoid this by offering to sell the entire territory to the U.S. It is likewise true that America only had authority to buy New Orleans. Nevertheless, the delegation accepted Napoleon's offer of all of Louisiana. Due to his belief in strict interpretation of the Constitution, Jefferson did require approval from Congress to make the purchase. When his advisors characterized the purchase as being within his purview based on the presidential power to make treaties, Congress agreed.

10. C: Mercantilism is the economic theory that nations advance the goal of accumulating capital by maintaining a balance of trade such that the value of exports exceeds that of imports. Great Britain maintained colonies to provide an inexpensive source of raw materials while creating markets for the goods manufactured in England. Under free trade, governments refrain from hindering the international exchange of goods and services. Nations that are granted most favored nation status are assured of enjoying equal advantages in international trade. A laissez-faire capitalist economy would theoretically be completely free of government regulation.

11. B: During the early Medieval period (or Middle Ages), Europe was characterized by widespread illiteracy, ignorance, and superstition once the unifying influence of the Roman Empire was lost. Few universities, like the university at Constantinople founded in 2 AD and those at Athens, Antioch, and Alexandria around the same time, existed then. Before the 5th and 6th centuries C.E., any education was conducted at cathedral or monastery schools or privately in the homes of wealthy families, which cannot be considered "main centers of literacy." More religious schools were created through Charlemagne's reforms in the 9th century, and early forms of universities began developing in the 11th and 12th centuries.

12. A: The Supreme Court interprets law and the Constitution. The inferior courts are bound to uphold the law as the Supreme Court interprets and rules on it.

Copyright © Mometrix Media. You have been licensed one copy of this document for personal use only. Any other reproduction or redistribution is strictly prohibited. All rights reserved. This content is provided for test preparation purposes only and does not imply an endorsement by Mometrix of any particular political, scientific, or religious point of view.

13. B: Direct democracy is a system in which all members of a population vote directly on the issue at hand. A representative democracy refers to a system in which representatives vote on behalf of the population. The House of Representatives, the Senate, and the Electoral College are all representative democracies. The House of Representatives gives weight to population, whereas the Senate and the Electoral College do not. Members of the House of Representatives are elected in proportion to the population of each state. Representation by senators is not based on population and is therefore skewed in electoral weight. The Electoral College can and has contradicted the popular vote in the Presidential election.

14. D: Federalists who helped frame the Constitution believed the central government needed to be stronger than what was established under the Articles of Confederation. Anti-federalists were against this and feared a strong federal government. A system of checks and balances was established to prevent the central government from taking too much power.

15. B: James Madison was a close friend of Thomas Jefferson and supported a stronger central government. George Mason and Robert Yates were both against expanding federal authority over the states. Benjamin Franklin was a proponent of a strong federal government, but he was from Massachusetts.

16. C: When a nation follows the theory of comparative advantage, it specializes in producing the goods and services it can make at a lower opportunity cost and then engages in trade to obtain other goods.

17. A: Presidents may veto legislation passed by both houses of Congress, and in turn Congress can override a presidential veto with a 2/3 majority. These governmental practices are a further manifestation that each branch of government is watched by the other branches and, when necessary, can undo a decision it deems ill-advised or unconstitutional.

18. B: The House has strict rules that limit debate. A filibuster can only occur in the Senate where senators can speak on topics other than the bill at hand and introduce amendments. A filibuster can be ended by a supermajority vote of 60 senators.

19. C: The President must be a natural citizen, be at least 35 years old, and have lived in the US for 14 years. There is no education requirement for becoming President. Truman did not have a college education, but most Presidents have had college degrees.

20. C: A person who has taken out a fixed-rate loan can benefit from inflation by paying back the loan with dollars that are less valuable than they were when the loan was taken out. In the other examples, inflation harms the individual or entity.

21. B: Growth of industry was concentrated in urban areas, which cyclically drew laborers into cities, growing the population of cities and increasing efficiency and quality in industry.

22. B: Oligarchy is defined as the rule by few. An example is aristocracy, which in ancient Greece, was government by an elite group of citizens as opposed to a monarchy. In later times, it meant government by the class of aristocrats, a privileged group, as opposed to democracy. The rule of one is called autocracy. Examples include monarchy, dictatorship, and many others. The rule by law is called a republic. Some examples are constitutional republics, parliamentary republics, and federal republics. The rule by many could apply to democracy, which governs according to the people's votes or to the collective leadership form of socialism, where no one individual has too much power.

Copyright © Mometrix Media. You have been licensed one copy of this document for personal use only. Any other reproduction or redistribution is strictly prohibited. All rights reserved. This content is provided for test preparation purposes only and does not imply an endorsement by Mometrix of any particular political, scientific, or religious point of view.

23. B: The Trail of Tears was the forcible removal of Native American tribes from their homes in the Southeastern US to Oklahoma. The name came due to the high number of Native Americans who died on the journey.

24. B: Tropical regions near the Equator tend to experience relatively constant temperatures year-round because the angle at which sunlight hits them remains relatively constant throughout the year. In regions that are farther north or south, the angle at which sunlight hits them changes much more drastically due to the changing angle of the Earth's axis relative to the Sun. This results in greater variations in the length of daylight and in temperatures. Tropical regions do have seasons (usually a "wet" season and a "dry" season), but temperature fluctuations are less pronounced than those in regions farther from the Equator.

25. B: In order to prosper, a nation should not try to increase its imports. Mercantilism is an economic theory including the idea that prosperity comes from a positive balance of international trade. For any one nation to prosper, that nation should increase its exports but decrease its imports. Exporting more to other countries while importing less from them will give a country a positive trade balance. This theory assumes that money and wealth are identical assets of a nation. In addition, this theory also assumes that the volume of global trade is an unchangeable quantity. Mercantilism dictates that a nation's government should apply a policy of economic protectionism by stimulating more exports and suppressing imports. Some ways to accomplish this task have included granting subsidies for exports and imposing tariffs on imports. Mercantilism can be regarded as essentially the opposite of the free trade policies that have been encouraged in more recent years.

26. C: Copernicus's *De Revolutionibus Orbium Coelestium (On the Revolutions of the Heavenly Spheres)* was published in 1543, almost simultaneously with his death. He was the first to contradict the then-accepted belief that the Earth was the center of the universe and the Sun and other bodies moved around it. This geocentric model was associated with Ptolemy and hence called the Ptolemaic system. Galileo Galilei published Siderius Nuncius (Starry Messenger) in 1610. In it, he revealed his observations, made through his improvements to the telescope, which corroborated Copernicus's theory. Sir Isaac Newton (1642–1727) built the first usable reflecting telescope and erased any lingering doubts about a heliocentric universe by describing universal gravitation and showing its congruence with Kepler's laws of planetary motion.

27. B: Members of the House are elected for two-year terms. Senators serve six-year terms, but the elections are staggered so roughly one-third of the Senate is elected every two years.

28. A: A city located at 6,000 feet above sea level is likely to have a cooler climate, all other things being equal. Since air is less dense at higher altitudes, it holds heat less effectively, and temperatures tend to be lower as a result. Precipitation is not as strong an indicator of temperature. Some areas that receive moderate or large amounts of precipitation are cooler (temperate and continental climates), while some areas that receive lots of precipitation, like the tropics, are warmer.

29. D: Niccolò Machiavelli, perhaps best known for his book The Prince, was an Italian Renaissance political philosopher noted for writing more realistic representations and rational interpretations of politics. In The Prince, he popularized the political concept of "the ends justify the means." Dante Alighieri was a great poet famous for his Commedia (additionally labeled Divina by contemporary poet and author Boccaccio, who wrote the Decameron and other works) or Divine Comedy, a trilogy consisting of Inferno, Purgatorio, and Paradiso (Hell, Purgatory, and Heaven). Dante's work helped

Copyright © Mometrix Media. You have been licensed one copy of this document for personal use only. Any other reproduction or redistribution is strictly prohibited. All rights reserved. This content is provided for test preparation purposes only and does not imply an endorsement by Mometrix of any particular political, scientific, or religious point of view.

propel the transition from the Medieval period to the Renaissance. Francesco Petrarca, known in English as Petrarch, was famous for his lyrical poetry, particularly sonnets.

30. D: Only the British Empire existed following the armistice ending WWI. The Austro-Hungarian Empire, the Ottoman Empire, and the German Empire were all among the Central powers that lost the war. As empires capitulated, armistices and peace treaties were signed and the map of Europe was redrawn as territories formerly occupied by Central powers were partitioned. For example, the former Austro-Hungarian Empire was partitioned into Austria, Hungary, Czechoslovakia, Yugoslavia, Transylvania, and Romania. The Treaty of Lausanne (1923) gave Turkey both independence and recognition as successor to the former Ottoman Empire after Turkey refused the earlier Treaty of Sèvres (1920), and Mustafa Kemal Ataturk led the Turkish Independence War. Greece, Bulgaria, and other former Ottoman possessions became independent. The Lausanne Treaty defined the boundaries of these countries as well as the boundaries of Iraq, Syria, Cyprus, Sudan, and Egypt.

31. C: Political parties organize their caucus as a private event while an official primary is an indirect election administered by state and local governments. Voters may award delegates to candidates for the national conventions, depending on state laws.

32. D: According to Article III of the Constitution, Justices of the Supreme Court, judges of the courts of appeals and district courts, and judges of the Court of International Trade are appointed by the president with the confirmation of the Senate. The judicial branch of the government is the only one not elected by the people.

33. C: Hernán Cortés conquered the Mexican Aztecs in 1519. He had several advantages over the indigenous peoples, including horses, armor for his soldiers, and guns. In addition, Cortés' troops unknowingly transmitted smallpox to the Aztecs, which devastated their population as they had no immunity to this foreign illness. Vasco Núñez de Balboa was the first European explorer to view the Pacific Ocean when he crossed the Isthmus of Panama in 1513. Juan Ponce de León visited and claimed Florida in Spain's name in 1513. Álvar Núñez Cabeza de Vaca was one of only four men out of 400 to return from an expedition led by Pánfilo de Narváez in 1528 and was responsible for spreading the story of the Seven Cities of Cibola (the "cities of gold").

34. D: Because the Puritans took on a Reformed theology, they were in this sense Calvinists. However, many Puritans endorsed radical views that criticized such Calvinists as John (Jean) Calvin and Huldrych (Ulrich) Zwingli in Switzerland. Not only were Puritans critical of Calvinists despite their mutual Reformed approaches, reciprocally many Calvinists were opposed to the Puritans as well. The Puritan movement changed less in American colonies than in England during the 1660s. Following the Restoration (1660) and the Uniformity Act (1662) in England, nearly all of the Puritan clergy objected and left the Church of England, thereby creating a dramatic change in the movement in that country. Nevertheless, in America, the Puritans who had emigrated from England continued their original Puritan traditions for a longer time, as they had neither the same Anglican Church as in England nor the legislation restoring earlier church status against which the English Puritans had reacted.

35. B: Keynesian economics is based on the notion that governments can effectively stimulate economic growth through taxation, adjustment of interest rates, and the funding of public projects. His economic philosophy contrasts sharply with the free-market philosophies of Smith, Hayek, and Friedman.

Copyright © Mometrix Media. You have been licensed one copy of this document for personal use only. Any other reproduction or redistribution is strictly prohibited. All rights reserved. This content is provided for test preparation purposes only and does not imply an endorsement by Mometrix of any particular political, scientific, or religious point of view.

36. B: Congress has the authority to shape the judicial branch. The Supreme Court once operated with only six members. Nine has been the standard number since 1869.

37. B: The first amendment to the Constitution states, "Congress shall make no law respecting an establishment of religion, or prohibiting the free exercise thereof; or abridging the freedom of speech or of the press; or the right of the people peaceably to assemble, and to petition the Government for a redress of grievances." The right to bear arms is guaranteed by the second amendment: "A well-regulated Militia, being necessary to the security of a free State, the right of the people to keep and bear Arms, shall not be infringed."

38. B: Diversity is not one of the demographic variables. Demographers, or those who study population, rely on fertility, mortality, and migration to determine the number of people in a region. The general equation is *Total Population = Original Population + Births – Deaths + Immigration – Emigration*. The natural increase, on the other hand, is calculated only with the number of births and deaths. The diversity of a population may be relevant to subsequent research performed by the demographer, but it is not considered one of the essential three demographic variables.

39. B: John Maynard Keynes argued that government could help revitalize a recessionary economy by increasing government spending and therefore increasing aggregate demand. This is known as demand-side economics.

40. C: The bubonic plague spread along trade routes, carried by infected animals and people on ships. After reaching Cyprus in 1347, the epidemic followed trade routes to infect the populations of Italy and France. Then, also through trade routes, it traveled north to Germany, England, and eventually Scandinavia and Russia in 1351.

41. D: Political corruption was not an immediate effect of the rapid urban growth during this time. The accelerated growth of cities in America did soon result in services being unable to keep up with that growth. The results of this included deficiencies in clean water delivery and garbage collection, causing poor sanitation. That poor sanitation led to outbreaks of cholera and typhus, as well as typhoid fever epidemics. Police and fire fighting services could not keep up with the population increases, and were often inadequate. With people moving to the cities at such a fast rate, there were also deficits in housing and public transportation.

42. D: Increases in population growth supplied additional labor forces, helping to enable the Industrial Revolution. These increases were due to the prosperity brought through Europe's Commercial Revolution, which preceded the Industrial Revolution. The rediscovery of concrete, new advances in iron making, and the invention of the steam engine are all examples of developments that occurred during the Industrial Revolution.

43. B: As production shifted to factories, a large number of unskilled workers were needed to operate the machinery that was beginning to put many skilled craftsmen out of work. As farms grew larger and increasingly mechanized, the number of people who owned their own farm began to decrease. The rural population declined as people flocked to the cities in search of employment.

44. D: Free public education has been a U.S. tradition since the 18th century. State constitutions govern the educational issues of each state, although federal, state, and local governments all work together on educational issues.

45. C: The person or group NOT instrumental in advancing civil rights and desegregation immediately after WWII was Congress. As African American soldiers came home from the war, racial discord increased. President Harry Truman appointed a Presidential Committee on Civil

Copyright © Mometrix Media. You have been licensed one copy of this document for personal use only. Any other reproduction or redistribution is strictly prohibited. All rights reserved. This content is provided for test preparation purposes only and does not imply an endorsement by Mometrix of any particular political, scientific, or religious point of view.

Rights in 1946. This committee published a report recommending that segregation and lynching be outlawed by the federal government. However, Congress ignored this report and took no action. Truman then used his presidential powers to enforce desegregation of the military and policies of "fair employment" in federal civil service jobs. The National Association for the Advancement of Colored People (NAACP) brought lawsuits against racist and discriminatory practices, and in resolving these suits, the Supreme Court further eroded segregation. For example, the Supreme Court ruled that primaries allowing only whites would be illegal, and it ended the segregation of interstate bus lines. The landmark civil rights laws were not passed by Congress until the 1960s.

46. A: The Industrial Revolution did create a new working class composed of professionals like doctors and lawyers, industrialists, and businessmen. Formerly, Europe was dominated by royalty and landed gentry over the poor working class. Industrialization allowed many ordinary people to start and run businesses. It did NOT, however, improve working conditions in the 18th and early 19th centuries, but the opposite occurred: Big factories with machines made conditions more dangerous, and child labor caused many deaths, injuries, illnesses, and so on. Women and children were only banned from working in mines in the mid-19th century; housing and work conditions only improved in the late 19th century. Urbanization was the result of industrialization and not vice versa: Mechanization allowed factory construction, and people moved to cities for jobs. Labor unions developed out of the Industrial Revolution, not vice versa, to establish and defend factory workers' rights.

47. B: The Supreme Court ruled that statements made in interrogation are not admissible unless the defendant is informed of the right to an attorney and waives that right. The case of Miranda v. Arizona was consolidated with Westover v. United States, Vignera v. New York, and California v. Stewart.

48. A: As people have more and more of something, they value it less and less. This is the law of diminishing marginal utility, and it is what causes the downward slope of the demand curve.

49. A: Agriculture was not a viable economic model for New Englanders. Although the colonists were mainly from England and Scotland, few were merchants before arriving in the colonies. Slavery existed in the north, although it was less important to the economy than it was in the agricultural south. New England colonists were not actively competing with their neighbors to the immediate south.

50. B: Followers of Hinduism, an indigenous religion of India, believes in one Supreme Reality (Brahman), manifested in many different gods and goddesses that oversee different aspects of life. Confucianism, a Chinese religion, does not address whether there are many gods or one. Followers of Sikhism, an Indian religion originating in Punjab, believe in a single god, Om or Ik Om Kar. Islam, founded by Muhammad in Saudi Arabia, purports a single god, Allah.

51. A: The president of the United States serves as commander-in-chief, but the writers of the Constitution, who feared how authority was used by monarchs, limited the president's power in this role. The president cannot declare war or oversee military regulations, although presidents have traditionally authorized the use of force without war being declared.

52. A: When the prices farmers receive for their crops decline in a developing country, this typically results in increased urbanization. When crop prices decline, farmers can no longer make a living from their land. As a result, they often choose to migrate to cities in search of low-wage employment in the manufacturing or service sectors.

Copyright © Mometrix Media. You have been licensed one copy of this document for personal use only. Any other reproduction or redistribution is strictly prohibited. All rights reserved. This content is provided for test preparation purposes only and does not imply an endorsement by Mometrix of any particular political, scientific, or religious point of view.

53. B: It is not true that the Crusades succeeded at Christians' reclaiming the "holy land" (the Middle East) from Muslims. Despite their number (nine not counting the Northern Crusades) and longevity (1095-1291 not counting later similar campaigns), the Crusades never accomplished this purpose. While they did not take back the Middle East, the Crusades did succeed in exacerbating the decline of the Byzantine Empire, which lost more and more territory to the Ottoman Turks during this period. In addition, the Crusades resulted in Egypt's rise once again to become a major power of the Middle East as it had been in the past.

54. C: Nebraska does not require voter registration, but all other states do and have their own process. State and local officials administer federal elections, and though each state has its own method for holding elections, federal elections are always held at the same time.

55. A: Anyone may write a bill, but only a member of Congress can introduce a bill. The President often suggests bills. Bills can change drastically throughout the review process.

56. A: Social dialects typically emerge when a particular group is isolated from the rest of society due to class, race, age, or gender differences. Dialects are language variants, and those that result from geographic isolation are called regional dialects. Assimilation of immigrants includes language acquisition, and thus would not typically produce a new dialect. Jargon is simply the development of a specialized vocabulary, and although it may be unintelligible to outsiders, this is the result of a vocabulary gap, not dialect differences.

57. B: On a political map, countries are represented in different colors, and countries that share a border are not given the same color. This is so that the borders between countries will be distinct. Political maps are used to illustrate those aspects of a country that have been determined by people: the capital, the provincial and national borders, and the large cities. Political maps sometimes include major physical features like rivers and mountains, but they are not intended to display all such information. On a physical, climate, or contour map, however, the borders between nations are more incidental. Colors are used on these maps to represent physical features, areas with similar climate, etc. It is possible that colors will overrun the borders and be shared by adjacent countries.

58. D: According to the Law of Diminishing Marginal Returns, marginal product will initially increase as the units of an input are increased, but then the curve will flatten out and eventually the marginal product will begin to decrease.

59. D: Totemism characterizes clans in which members believe they are all descendants of a common ancestor, often an animal. This belief characterized societies around the world, although it is most commonly associated with Native Americans.

60. C: A caste system is a system wherein individuals' social, economic, and political destinies are determined by group membership within the caste. Systems fitting this description have been in place throughout the world and directly impact each individual's economic destiny by circumscribing upward economic and social mobility regardless of ability. Class and caste are distinct in the sense that class is assigned based upon an individual's life path, while caste membership is assigned at birth and is essentially immutable. Also, caste systems have well-defined functions for each group, whereas class distinctions are based solely on wealth (as opposed to social function).

Copyright © Mometrix Media. You have been licensed one copy of this document for personal use only. Any other reproduction or redistribution is strictly prohibited. All rights reserved. This content is provided for test preparation purposes only and does not imply an endorsement by Mometrix of any particular political, scientific, or religious point of view.

Science

1. A: A good hypothesis is testable and logical, and can be used to predict future events. A good hypothesis is also simple, not complex.

2. A: When light waves hit a convex lens, they are refracted and converge. A convex lens curves or bulges with the middle being thicker and the edges thinner. A magnifying glass is an example. Light rays are refracted by different amounts as they pass through the lens. After light rays pass through, they converge at a point called the focus. An object viewed with a magnifying glass looks bigger because the lens bends the rays inward. Choice B would indicate a concave lens as it would cause the light to be refracted and diverge. Light is not reflected in this case, so neither choice C nor D would be applicable.

3. D: The circulatory system and gas exchange with the environment is not paired correctly. It is the respiratory system that exchanges gases with the environment by delivering oxygen to the bloodstream and releasing carbon dioxide. The circulatory system transports nutrients, gases, hormones, and blood to and away from cells. The muscle system controls movement through three types of muscle tissue. The nervous system controls sensory responses by carrying impulses away from and toward the cell body. The digestive system breaks down food for absorption into the bloodstream where it is delivered to cells for respiration.

4. A: The addition of energy causes a phase change. Phase changes are physical changes, not chemical changes. While sublimation is an example of a phase change, it occurs when a solid turns directly into a gas without passing through the liquid state. Condensation, another phase change, occurs when a gas turns to liquid.

5. A: Dispose of the solutions according to local disposal procedures. Solutions and compounds used in labs may be hazardous according to state and local regulatory agencies and should be treated with such precaution. Emptying the solutions into the sink and rinsing with warm water and soap does not take into account the hazards associated with a specific solution in terms of vapors or interactions with water, soap, and waste piping systems. Ensuring the solutions are secured in closed containers and throwing them away may allow toxic chemicals into landfills and subsequently into freshwater systems. Storing the solutions in a secured, dry place for later use is incorrect, as chemicals should not be reused due to the possibility of contamination.

6. D: An atom has a neutral charge if its atomic number is equal to its number of electrons. The atomic number (Z) of an element refers to the number of protons in the nucleus. If an atom has fewer or more electrons than its atomic number, then it will be positively or negatively charged, respectively. Cations are positively charged ions; anions are negatively charged ones.

7. C: Transform is not connected to the process of mountain building. Orogeny, or mountain building, occurs at the Earth's lithosphere or crust. Folding, or deformation, is a process that occurs to make mountains where two portions of the lithosphere collide. One is subducted and the other is pushed upward forming a mountain. This action produces various types of folding. Faulting can be characterized by a brittle deformation where the rock breaks abruptly (compared with folding). Faulting and fault types are associated with earthquakes and relatively rapid deformation. Convergent is a more general term used to describe plates interacting.

8. A: Repeating a measurement several times can increase the accuracy of the measurement. Calibrating the equipment (B) will increase the precision of the measurement. None of the other choices are useful strategies to increase the accuracy of a measurement.

Copyright © Mometrix Media. You have been licensed one copy of this document for personal use only. Any other reproduction or redistribution is strictly prohibited. All rights reserved. This content is provided for test preparation purposes only and does not imply an endorsement by Mometrix of any particular political, scientific, or religious point of view.

9. B: The refractive index is an optical property which is not related to the organization of the periodic table. Elements on the periodic table are arranged into periods, or rows, according to atomic number, which is the number of protons in the nucleus. The periodic table illustrates the recurrence of properties. Each column, or group, contains elements that share similar properties, such as reactivity.

10. C: The pressure decreases to one-third. A gas in a closed container at constant temperature will decrease in pressure to one-third when the volume of the container is tripled. The ideal gas law is $PV = nRT$ where P is pressure, V is volume, n is the moles of the gas, R is the gas constant, and T is temperature. Dividing by volume gives the following expression for pressure:

$$P = \frac{nRT}{V}$$

Boyle's Law indicates that pressure and volume are inversely proportional. The pressure cannot be increased because that would imply that pressure and volume are directly proportional.

11. C: A laccolith is formed when an intrusion of magma injected between two layers of sedimentary rock forces the overlying strata upward to create a dome-like form. Eventually, the magma cools, the sedimentary rock wears away and the formation is exposed. Sills and dikes are both examples of sheet intrusions, where magma has inserted itself into other rock. Sills are horizontal and dikes are vertical. A caldera is a crater-like feature that was formed from the collapse of a volcano after erupting.

12. C: For an experiment to be considered successful, it must yield data that others can reproduce. A reasonable hypothesis (A) may be considered part of a well-designed experiment. A well-written lab report (B) and computer-aided statistical analysis (D) may be considered part of an experiment that is reported on by individuals with expertise.

13. C: Heat transfer can never occur from a cooler object to a warmer object. While the second law of thermodynamics implies that heat never spontaneously transfers from a cooler object to a warmer object, it is possible for heat to be transferred to a warmer object, given the proper input of work to the system. This is the principle by which a refrigerator operates. Work is done to the system to transfer heat from the objects inside the refrigerator to the air surrounding the refrigerator. All other answer choices are true.

14. B: Light travels faster in air than it can in water. Water molecules are closer together than air particles are, which causes the light to slow down and bend as it enters the water. The bending of light is called refraction and creates the illusion of the wallet being next to where it actually is.

15. C: The closer the data points are to each other, the more precise the data. This does not mean the data is accurate, but that the results are very reproducible.

16. D: The most recently formed parts of the Earth's crust can be found at mid-ocean ridges. New crust forms here when magma erupts from these ridges and pushes pre-existing crust horizontally towards the continental plates. Such ridges include the Mid-Atlantic Ridge and the East Pacific Rise.

17. A: Fission is a nuclear process where atomic nuclei split apart to form smaller nuclei. Nuclear fission can release large amounts of energy, emit gamma rays, and form daughter products. It is used in nuclear power plants and bombs. Choice B, fusion, refers to a nuclear process whereby atomic nuclei join to form a heavier nucleus, such as with stars. This can release or absorb energy depending upon the original elements. Choice C, decay, refers to an atomic nucleus spontaneously

Copyright © Mometrix Media. You have been licensed one copy of this document for personal use only. Any other reproduction or redistribution is strictly prohibited. All rights reserved. This content is provided for test preparation purposes only and does not imply an endorsement by Mometrix of any particular political, scientific, or religious point of view.

losing energy and emitting ionizing particles and radiation. Choice D, ionization, refers to a process by which atoms obtain a positive or negative charge because the number of electrons does not equal that of protons.

18. C: The vapor pressure decreases by an amount proportional to the amount of solute. Raoult's law states that the vapor pressure of a solution containing a non-volatile solute is equal to the vapor pressure of the volatile solvent multiplied by its mole fraction, which is basically the proportion of the solution that is made up by solvent. In a liquid, some of the surface particles have higher than average energy and can break away to become a gas, or evaporate. The pressure of this gas right above the surface of the liquid is called the vapor pressure. Increasing the amount of solute in a liquid decreases the number of solvent particles at the surface. Because of this, fewer solvent molecules are able to escape, thus lowering the vapor pressure.

19. A: The prevailing westerlies drive weather systems to move west to east in the mid-latitudes. The direction refers to that which the wind is coming from. The polar easterlies that travel from the northeast occur between 90-60 degrees north latitude. The ones from the southeast are between 90-60 degrees south latitude. The trade winds refer to those occurring near the equator in the tropics moving east. The doldrums are also in the tropics, but refer to an area of low-pressure where frequently the winds are light and unpredictable.

20. A: Many organisms, especially organisms that live in harsh conditions such as deserts or frozen icy areas, have developed specific adaptations that allow them to survive. For example, cacti are able to expand to store large amounts of water, coyotes absorb some water from their food, and snakes can escape the heat by hiding within rocks.

21. D: Mario balances a book on his head. In this example, work is not applied to the book because the book is not moving. One definition of work is a force acting on an object to cause displacement. In this case, the book was not displaced by the force applied to it. Mario's head applied a vertical force to the book to keep it in the same position.

22. D: Reproductive habits would not be considered evidence for evolution. Usually, how a species reproduces does not support nor add to the body of evidence for the theory of evolution. Reproductive habits might exemplify how any given organism can adapt to changes in its environment as a way to survive. This does not necessarily show evolution. Fossil record is evidence for evolution as it shows evolutionary change of organisms over time. DNA sequences show that organisms that are related evolutionarily also have related gene sequences. Anatomical structures such as having an internal bony structure provide evidence of descent from a common ancestor.

23. A: Glass is manufactured and can be recycled, but is considered a non-renewable resource. Wood is considered a renewable resource because with proper management, an equilibrium can be reached between harvesting trees and planting new ones. Cattle are managed in herds and a balance can be achieved between those consumed and those born. Soil is the result of long-term erosion and includes organic matter and minerals needed by plants. Soil found naturally in the environment is renewed. Crops can be rotated to help maintain a healthy soil composition for farming.

24. A: The stream of charged particles that escape the Sun's gravitational pull is called solar wind. Solar wind is comprised primarily of protons and electrons, and these particles are deflected away from the Earth by its magnetic field. When stray particles do manage to enter the atmosphere, they

Copyright © Mometrix Media. You have been licensed one copy of this document for personal use only. Any other reproduction or redistribution is strictly prohibited. All rights reserved.
This content is provided for test preparation purposes only and does not imply an endorsement by Mometrix of any particular political, scientific, or religious point of view.

cause the aurorae (Northern and Southern Lights) and geomagnetic storms that can affect power grids.

25. B: Ohm's Law states that voltage and current in an electrical circuit are directly proportional to one another. Ohm's Law can be expressed as $V = IR$, where V is voltage, I is current and R is resistance. Voltage is also known as electrical potential difference and is the force that moves electrons through a circuit. For a given amount of resistance, an increase in voltage will result in an increase in current. Resistance and current are inversely proportional to each other. For a given voltage, an increase in resistance will result in a decrease in current.

26. C: Flowers are the reproductive organs of a plant. Flowering plants reproduce by sexual reproduction where the gametes join to form seeds. Pollen is sperm. Pollinators help transfer the sperm to the ovule, the egg. The style is the part of the female reproduction system that transports the sperm between the stigma and the ovary, which are all parts of the pistil. The stigma is the sticky tip of the style on which the pollen lands. Sepals are usually small leaves between or underneath the petals and are not as obvious or as large and colorful as the petals.

27. B: Work is defined as the force used to move a mass over a distance. The amount of energy used to accomplish a job is a non-scientific definition of work. The amount of energy used per unit of time is the definition of power. Energy stored in an object due to its position is the definition of potential energy.

28. D: Endocytosis is a process by which cells absorb larger molecules or even tiny organisms, such as bacteria, that would not be able to pass through the plasma membrane. Endocytic vesicles containing molecules from the extracellular environment often undergo further processing once they enter the cell.

29. A: Glaciers move because they are incredibly heavy, and the force of gravity slowly pulls them lower. Erosion is a result rather than a cause of glacier movement. Although large glaciers may only move a few inches a year or may not move at all, some valley glaciers in Europe move as much as 600 feet annually. The result is a rounded valley and a trail of rock and soil debris known as a moraine. The Great Lakes in the United States were formed by the passage of glaciers long ago.

30. D: Destructive interference describes two waves that are out of phase as they come together to produce a new wave. Out of phase refers to the crest of one and the trough of another arriving together. Interference, when used to discuss wave phenomenon, is the interaction of two or more waves passing the same point, which could be either destructive or constructive. Incomplete interference and distorted interference are not real terms. Constructive interference refers to wave interference that results in higher peaks than the waves singularly because the waves arrive in phase with one another (the crests arrive together).

31. B: A stoma (plural: stomata) is the part of a plant system that responds to stimuli by releasing water via transpiration. It can also close during adverse conditions like a drought to prevent the plant from dehydration. Stomata closure can also be triggered by the presence of bacteria. Pith refers to the central, spongy part of the stem in vascular plants. Guard cells flank stomata and regulate the opening. Sepals are modified leaves that protect the flower bud before it opens.

32. B: The electrolysis of water is a chemical change that transforms water into hydrogen and oxygen gases. Synthesis reactions are those that combine reactants to form a product, which is the opposite of what happens when electrolyzing water. Reverse osmosis is a technique often used to purify water by forcing impure water through a semipermeable membrane using a pressure differential.

Copyright © Mometrix Media. You have been licensed one copy of this document for personal use only. Any other reproduction or redistribution is strictly prohibited. All rights reserved. This content is provided for test preparation purposes only and does not imply an endorsement by Mometrix of any particular political, scientific, or religious point of view.

33. A: When using a light microscope, total magnification is determined by multiplying the ocular lens power times the objective being used. The ocular lens refers to the eyepiece, which has one magnification strength, typically 10x. The objective lens also has a magnification strength, often 4x, 10x, 40x, or 100x. Using a 10x eyepiece with the 4x objective lens will give a magnification strength of 40x. Using a 10x eyepiece with the 100x objective lens will give a magnification strength of 1,000x. The shorter lens is the lesser magnification; the longer lens is the greater magnification.

34. B: The air we breathe is composed of many types of molecules, and is quite heavy compared to helium. The reason helium balloons float is because helium is less dense than the surrounding air. Objects that are less dense will float in objects that are more dense, as a helium balloon does when surrounded by air.

35. D: Glaciers and ice caps are fresh water unavailable for human use as they are frozen. The hydrologic cycle refers to all the water on planet Earth. Some water is in forms that humans do not tend to use, such as oceans (too salty and expensive to desalinate) and glaciers. Water suitable for drinking can be found as surface water and in ground water, which is obtained through wells. Rivers, estuaries, and aquifers are all examples of surface water that are available to humans.

36. C: A physical change occurs when water condenses. The only thing formed during condensation is new intermolecular bonds. Therefore, no new covalent bonds form (B). The only time new atoms form is during a nuclear reaction (A). The water molecule is not ionizing, so no new ionic bonds form (D).

37. D: The amount of potential energy an object has depends on mass, height above ground and gravitational attraction, but not temperature. The formula for potential energy is PE = mgh, or potential energy equals mass times gravity times height. Answers A, B, and C are all valid answers as they are all contained in the formula for potential energy. Potential energy is the amount of energy stored in a system particularly because of its position.

38. D: The molecules that make up gases are far apart and move about very quickly. Because they have a weak attraction to each other, they expand to take up as much space as possible.

39. B: When two crustal plates move apart, magma welling up could result in the formation of new crust. This has been shown to be occurring on the ocean floor where places of the crust are weaker. The crust spreads apart at these trenches, pushing outward and erupting at the ridges. When two crustal plates converge, sublimation occurs as one plate runs under another pushing it up. Two crustal plates sliding past one another is an example of a transform fault, which does not create new crust. A crustal plate being pushed down into the mantle does not form new crust but perhaps recycles the old one.

40. A: The purpose of conducting an experiment is to test a hypothesis. Collecting data (B), identifying a control state (C), and choosing variables (D) are steps in conducting an experiment designed to test a hypothesis.

41. B: A long nail or other type of metal, substance, or matter that is heated at one end and then the other end becomes equally hot is an example of conduction. Conduction is energy transfer by neighboring molecules from an area of hotter temperature to cooler temperature. Answer A, radiation, or thermal radiation, refers to heat being transferred through empty space by electromagnetic radiation. An example is sunlight heating the earth. Answer C, convection, refers to heat being transferred by molecules moving from one location in the substance to another creating a heat current, usually in a gas or a liquid. Answer D, entropy, relates to the second law of

Copyright © Mometrix Media. You have been licensed one copy of this document for personal use only. Any other reproduction or redistribution is strictly prohibited. All rights reserved.
This content is provided for test preparation purposes only and does not imply an endorsement by Mometrix of any particular political, scientific, or religious point of view.

thermodynamics and refers to how much heat or energy is no longer available to do work in a system. It can also be stated as the amount of disorder in a system.

42. C: A higher concentration could increase the reaction rate of a chemical reaction. The rate of reaction is affected by concentration, pressure, and temperature. A higher concentration would allow for more potential collisions that set off the reaction. Low kinetic energy would lead to a lower rate of reaction, as does a lower temperature (usually). The term activation energy refers to the specific threshold that must be overcome for a reaction to occur. If the activation energy is lowered, for example, by a catalyst or enzyme, then the reaction can occur quicker. This rules out high activation energy.

43. B: A trace fossil shows evidence of existence but is not an organism itself. A trace fossil can be contrasted with a body fossil, which has been formed from an organism. Other examples of trace fossils include eggs, nests, burrows, borings, and coprolites (fossilized feces). A mouse jaw and a shark tooth are examples of body fossils. A cast of a skull is a replica and neither a body nor a trace fossil.

44. A: When two tectonic plates are moving laterally in opposing directions, this is called a transform boundary. When there is friction at transform boundaries and pressure builds up, it can result in shallow earthquakes (usually at a depth of less than 25 meters). California's San Andreas Fault is an example of a transform boundary.

45. D: It is a stable atom. If an atom's outer shell is filled, it is a stable atom. The outer shell refers to one of many energy levels, or shells, that electrons occupy around a nucleus. An atom whose outer shell is not filled wants to become stable by filling the outer shell. It fills its outer shell by forming bonds. The atom can do this by gaining electrons or losing electrons in ionic compounds, or if the atom is a part of a molecule, by sharing electrons. If an atom has a full outer shell, such as the noble gases, it does not readily react with other atoms and does not exchange electrons to form bonds. These atoms are known as inert. Therefore, Choices A and B cannot be true. Choice C, it has 32 electrons in its outer shell, is not necessarily true because not all elements have the fourth shell that can hold 32 electrons. Some have fewer shells that hold fewer electrons.

46. D: A non-polar substance is least likely to be soluble in water. A rule of thumb for a substance's solubility is that like dissolves like. Polarity is affected by the types of bonds between atoms and the bonds are affected by the types of atoms. An unequal sharing of electrons leads to polar bonding and polar substances. Water is polar and can dissolve many other polar substances. Hydrophilic molecules are polar and this word means "water-loving". Water also dissolves many ionic substances since they are composed of charged ions and can interact with the polar water molecules. Many organic compounds are non-polar and do not dissolve well in water.

47. B: Cold water dissolves atmospheric carbon dioxide, stores it, and releases it back out to the atmosphere as needed. This describes the physical or non-biological part of the carbon cycle. The carbon and nutrient cycles of the ocean are processed in part by the deep currents, mixing, and upwelling that occurs. Carbon dioxide (CO_2) from the atmosphere is dissolved into the ocean at the higher latitudes and distributed to the denser deep water. When upwelling occurs, CO_2 is brought back to the surface and emitted into the tropical air.

48. D: After a secondary consumer dies, such as a wolf, its body is partially consumed by decomposers, such as bacteria and fungi. Bacteria and fungi live in soil and digest body tissues of dead organisms, converting them into basic nutrients that plants need to grow. Therefore, after secondary consumers die, their energy is consumed by decomposers, who make nutrients available

Copyright © Mometrix Media. You have been licensed one copy of this document for personal use only. Any other reproduction or redistribution is strictly prohibited. All rights reserved. This content is provided for test preparation purposes only and does not imply an endorsement by Mometrix of any particular political, scientific, or religious point of view.

in the soil for producers to use. *Do not confuse nutrients in the soil with energy that producers get from the Sun to make their own food.*

49. A: Heat between objects in contact with each other is transferred by conduction, choice A. Convection is transfer by currents within a body of fluid, and radiation is the transfer of heat between objects *not* in contact, through light rays emitted by the hotter object and absorbed by the cooler one.

50. A: The type of RNA described by the question is transfer RNA (tRNA). The tRNA is found in the cytoplasm and carries and positions amino acids at the ribosome for protein synthesis. There are two other types of RNA. Messenger RNA (mRNA) contains the coding for the amino acid sequence in the protein. The mRNA is first made in the nucleus before traveling through the cytoplasm to a ribosome. Ribosomal RNA (rRNA) is the RNA that is found in the ribosome along with proteins, which allows the mRNA and tRNA to bind for protein synthesis. All three types of RNA originate in the nucleus where they are transcribed from DNA. Mitochondria are organelles that harbor mitochondrial DNA (mtDNA).

51. C: Methods of heat transfer include conduction, convection, and radiation. With convection, heat is transferred by moving currents in fluids such as air or water. When a person washes his hands with hot water, heat is transmitted to his hands by means of convection. With conduction, heat is transferred by direct contact such as when someone touches an electric blanket. In radiation, heat is transferred by electromagnetic waves such as when someone places his hands near the sides of a light bulb. When a person warms his hands by rubbing them together, heat is generated by friction.

52. A: Long term energy storage in animals takes the form of fat. Animals also store energy as glycogen, and plants store energy as starch, but these substances are for shorter-term use. Fats are a good storage form for chemical energy because fatty acids bond to glycerol in a condensation reaction to form fats (triglycerides). This reaction, which releases water, allows for the compacting of high-energy fatty acids in a concentrated form.

53. B: It is true that rocks are classified by their formation and the minerals they contain, while minerals are classified by their chemical composition and physical properties. Choice A is incorrect because rocks may contain traces of organic compounds. Choices C and D are incorrect because only minerals can be polymorphs and only rocks contain mineraloids.

54. D: Of these options, the only real direct impact of climate change is the rising sea level. This is due to the melting glaciers and ice sheets. Also, the oceans expand slightly as they get warmer.

55. D: Sources of renewable energy include geothermal power, solar energy, and wind power. Sources of nonrenewable energy include nuclear power, natural gas, and fossil fuels like coal, natural gas, and crude oil.

Copyright © Mometrix Media. You have been licensed one copy of this document for personal use only. Any other reproduction or redistribution is strictly prohibited. All rights reserved.
This content is provided for test preparation purposes only and does not imply an endorsement by Mometrix of any particular political, scientific, or religious point of view.

Praxis Practice Tests #2 and #3

To take these additional Praxis practice tests, visit our bonus page:
mometrix.com/bonus948/priieems5001

Copyright © Mometrix Media. You have been licensed one copy of this document for personal use only. Any other reproduction or redistribution is strictly prohibited. All rights reserved.
This content is provided for test preparation purposes only and does not imply an endorsement by Mometrix of any particular political, scientific, or religious point of view.

How to Overcome Test Anxiety

Just the thought of taking a test is enough to make most people a little nervous. A test is an important event that can have a long-term impact on your future, so it's important to take it seriously and it's natural to feel anxious about performing well. But just because anxiety is normal, that doesn't mean that it's helpful in test taking, or that you should simply accept it as part of your life. Anxiety can have a variety of effects. These effects can be mild, like making you feel slightly nervous, or severe, like blocking your ability to focus or remember even a simple detail.

If you experience test anxiety—whether severe or mild—it's important to know how to beat it. To discover this, first you need to understand what causes test anxiety.

Causes of Test Anxiety

While we often think of anxiety as an uncontrollable emotional state, it can actually be caused by simple, practical things. One of the most common causes of test anxiety is that a person does not feel adequately prepared for their test. This feeling can be the result of many different issues such as poor study habits or lack of organization, but the most common culprit is time management. Starting to study too late, failing to organize your study time to cover all of the material, or being distracted while you study will mean that you're not well prepared for the test. This may lead to cramming the night before, which will cause you to be physically and mentally exhausted for the test. Poor time management also contributes to feelings of stress, fear, and hopelessness as you realize you are not well prepared but don't know what to do about it.

Other times, test anxiety is not related to your preparation for the test but comes from unresolved fear. This may be a past failure on a test, or poor performance on tests in general. It may come from comparing yourself to others who seem to be performing better or from the stress of living up to expectations. Anxiety may be driven by fears of the future—how failure on this test would affect your educational and career goals. These fears are often completely irrational, but they can still negatively impact your test performance.

Elements of Test Anxiety

As mentioned earlier, test anxiety is considered to be an emotional state, but it has physical and mental components as well. Sometimes you may not even realize that you are suffering from test anxiety until you notice the physical symptoms. These can include trembling hands, rapid heartbeat, sweating, nausea, and tense muscles. Extreme anxiety may lead to fainting or vomiting. Obviously, any of these symptoms can have a negative impact on testing. It is important to recognize them as soon as they begin to occur so that you can address the problem before it damages your performance.

The mental components of test anxiety include trouble focusing and inability to remember learned information. During a test, your mind is on high alert, which can help you recall information and stay focused for an extended period of time. However, anxiety interferes with your mind's natural processes, causing you to blank out, even on the questions you know well. The strain of testing during anxiety makes it difficult to stay focused, especially on a test that may take several hours. Extreme anxiety can take a huge mental toll, making it difficult not only to recall test information but even to understand the test questions or pull your thoughts together.

Copyright © Mometrix Media. You have been licensed one copy of this document for personal use only. Any other reproduction or redistribution is strictly prohibited. All rights reserved. This content is provided for test preparation purposes only and does not imply an endorsement by Mometrix of any particular political, scientific, or religious point of view.

Effects of Test Anxiety

Test anxiety is like a disease—if left untreated, it will get progressively worse. Anxiety leads to poor performance, and this reinforces the feelings of fear and failure, which in turn lead to poor performances on subsequent tests. It can grow from a mild nervousness to a crippling condition. If allowed to progress, test anxiety can have a big impact on your schooling, and consequently on your future.

Test anxiety can spread to other parts of your life. Anxiety on tests can become anxiety in any stressful situation, and blanking on a test can turn into panicking in a job situation. But fortunately, you don't have to let anxiety rule your testing and determine your grades. There are a number of relatively simple steps you can take to move past anxiety and function normally on a test and in the rest of life.

Physical Steps for Beating Test Anxiety

While test anxiety is a serious problem, the good news is that it can be overcome. It doesn't have to control your ability to think and remember information. While it may take time, you can begin taking steps today to beat anxiety.

Just as your first hint that you may be struggling with anxiety comes from the physical symptoms, the first step to treating it is also physical. Rest is crucial for having a clear, strong mind. If you are tired, it is much easier to give in to anxiety. But if you establish good sleep habits, your body and mind will be ready to perform optimally, without the strain of exhaustion. Additionally, sleeping well helps you to retain information better, so you're more likely to recall the answers when you see the test questions.

Getting good sleep means more than going to bed on time. It's important to allow your brain time to relax. Take study breaks from time to time so it doesn't get overworked, and don't study right before bed. Take time to rest your mind before trying to rest your body, or you may find it difficult to fall asleep.

Along with sleep, other aspects of physical health are important in preparing for a test. Good nutrition is vital for good brain function. Sugary foods and drinks may give a burst of energy but this burst is followed by a crash, both physically and emotionally. Instead, fuel your body with protein and vitamin-rich foods.

Also, drink plenty of water. Dehydration can lead to headaches and exhaustion, especially if your brain is already under stress from the rigors of the test. Particularly if your test is a long one, drink water during the breaks. And if possible, take an energy-boosting snack to eat between sections.

Along with sleep and diet, a third important part of physical health is exercise. Maintaining a steady workout schedule is helpful, but even taking 5-minute study breaks to walk can help get your blood pumping faster and clear your head. Exercise also releases endorphins, which contribute to a positive feeling and can help combat test anxiety.

When you nurture your physical health, you are also contributing to your mental health. If your body is healthy, your mind is much more likely to be healthy as well. So take time to rest, nourish your body with healthy food and water, and get moving as much as possible. Taking these physical steps will make you stronger and more able to take the mental steps necessary to overcome test anxiety.

Copyright © Mometrix Media. You have been licensed one copy of this document for personal use only. Any other reproduction or redistribution is strictly prohibited. All rights reserved. This content is provided for test preparation purposes only and does not imply an endorsement by Mometrix of any particular political, scientific, or religious point of view.

Mental Steps for Beating Test Anxiety

Working on the mental side of test anxiety can be more challenging, but as with the physical side, there are clear steps you can take to overcome it. As mentioned earlier, test anxiety often stems from lack of preparation, so the obvious solution is to prepare for the test. Effective studying may be the most important weapon you have for beating test anxiety, but you can and should employ several other mental tools to combat fear.

First, boost your confidence by reminding yourself of past success—tests or projects that you aced. If you're putting as much effort into preparing for this test as you did for those, there's no reason you should expect to fail here. Work hard to prepare; then trust your preparation.

Second, surround yourself with encouraging people. It can be helpful to find a study group, but be sure that the people you're around will encourage a positive attitude. If you spend time with others who are anxious or cynical, this will only contribute to your own anxiety. Look for others who are motivated to study hard from a desire to succeed, not from a fear of failure.

Third, reward yourself. A test is physically and mentally tiring, even without anxiety, and it can be helpful to have something to look forward to. Plan an activity following the test, regardless of the outcome, such as going to a movie or getting ice cream.

When you are taking the test, if you find yourself beginning to feel anxious, remind yourself that you know the material. Visualize successfully completing the test. Then take a few deep, relaxing breaths and return to it. Work through the questions carefully but with confidence, knowing that you are capable of succeeding.

Developing a healthy mental approach to test taking will also aid in other areas of life. Test anxiety affects more than just the actual test—it can be damaging to your mental health and even contribute to depression. It's important to beat test anxiety before it becomes a problem for more than testing.

Study Strategy

Being prepared for the test is necessary to combat anxiety, but what does being prepared look like? You may study for hours on end and still not feel prepared. What you need is a strategy for test prep. The next few pages outline our recommended steps to help you plan out and conquer the challenge of preparation.

STEP 1: SCOPE OUT THE TEST

Learn everything you can about the format (multiple choice, essay, etc.) and what will be on the test. Gather any study materials, course outlines, or sample exams that may be available. Not only will this help you to prepare, but knowing what to expect can help to alleviate test anxiety.

STEP 2: MAP OUT THE MATERIAL

Look through the textbook or study guide and make note of how many chapters or sections it has. Then divide these over the time you have. For example, if a book has 15 chapters and you have five days to study, you need to cover three chapters each day. Even better, if you have the time, leave an extra day at the end for overall review after you have gone through the material in depth.

If time is limited, you may need to prioritize the material. Look through it and make note of which sections you think you already have a good grasp on, and which need review. While you are studying, skim quickly through the familiar sections and take more time on the challenging parts.

Copyright © Mometrix Media. You have been licensed one copy of this document for personal use only. Any other reproduction or redistribution is strictly prohibited. All rights reserved. This content is provided for test preparation purposes only and does not imply an endorsement by Mometrix of any particular political, scientific, or religious point of view.

Write out your plan so you don't get lost as you go. Having a written plan also helps you feel more in control of the study, so anxiety is less likely to arise from feeling overwhelmed at the amount to cover.

STEP 3: GATHER YOUR TOOLS

Decide what study method works best for you. Do you prefer to highlight in the book as you study and then go back over the highlighted portions? Or do you type out notes of the important information? Or is it helpful to make flashcards that you can carry with you? Assemble the pens, index cards, highlighters, post-it notes, and any other materials you may need so you won't be distracted by getting up to find things while you study.

If you're having a hard time retaining the information or organizing your notes, experiment with different methods. For example, try color-coding by subject with colored pens, highlighters, or post-it notes. If you learn better by hearing, try recording yourself reading your notes so you can listen while in the car, working out, or simply sitting at your desk. Ask a friend to quiz you from your flashcards, or try teaching someone the material to solidify it in your mind.

STEP 4: CREATE YOUR ENVIRONMENT

It's important to avoid distractions while you study. This includes both the obvious distractions like visitors and the subtle distractions like an uncomfortable chair (or a too-comfortable couch that makes you want to fall asleep). Set up the best study environment possible: good lighting and a comfortable work area. If background music helps you focus, you may want to turn it on, but otherwise keep the room quiet. If you are using a computer to take notes, be sure you don't have any other windows open, especially applications like social media, games, or anything else that could distract you. Silence your phone and turn off notifications. Be sure to keep water close by so you stay hydrated while you study (but avoid unhealthy drinks and snacks).

Also, take into account the best time of day to study. Are you freshest first thing in the morning? Try to set aside some time then to work through the material. Is your mind clearer in the afternoon or evening? Schedule your study session then. Another method is to study at the same time of day that you will take the test, so that your brain gets used to working on the material at that time and will be ready to focus at test time.

STEP 5: STUDY!

Once you have done all the study preparation, it's time to settle into the actual studying. Sit down, take a few moments to settle your mind so you can focus, and begin to follow your study plan. Don't give in to distractions or let yourself procrastinate. This is your time to prepare so you'll be ready to fearlessly approach the test. Make the most of the time and stay focused.

Of course, you don't want to burn out. If you study too long you may find that you're not retaining the information very well. Take regular study breaks. For example, taking five minutes out of every hour to walk briskly, breathing deeply and swinging your arms, can help your mind stay fresh.

As you get to the end of each chapter or section, it's a good idea to do a quick review. Remind yourself of what you learned and work on any difficult parts. When you feel that you've mastered the material, move on to the next part. At the end of your study session, briefly skim through your notes again.

But while review is helpful, cramming last minute is NOT. If at all possible, work ahead so that you won't need to fit all your study into the last day. Cramming overloads your brain with more information than it can process and retain, and your tired mind may struggle to recall even

Copyright © Mometrix Media. You have been licensed one copy of this document for personal use only. Any other reproduction or redistribution is strictly prohibited. All rights reserved.
This content is provided for test preparation purposes only and does not imply an endorsement by Mometrix of any particular political, scientific, or religious point of view.

previously learned information when it is overwhelmed with last-minute study. Also, the urgent nature of cramming and the stress placed on your brain contribute to anxiety. You'll be more likely to go to the test feeling unprepared and having trouble thinking clearly.

So don't cram, and don't stay up late before the test, even just to review your notes at a leisurely pace. Your brain needs rest more than it needs to go over the information again. In fact, plan to finish your studies by noon or early afternoon the day before the test. Give your brain the rest of the day to relax or focus on other things, and get a good night's sleep. Then you will be fresh for the test and better able to recall what you've studied.

STEP 6: TAKE A PRACTICE TEST

Many courses offer sample tests, either online or in the study materials. This is an excellent resource to check whether you have mastered the material, as well as to prepare for the test format and environment.

Check the test format ahead of time: the number of questions, the type (multiple choice, free response, etc.), and the time limit. Then create a plan for working through them. For example, if you have 30 minutes to take a 60-question test, your limit is 30 seconds per question. Spend less time on the questions you know well so that you can take more time on the difficult ones.

If you have time to take several practice tests, take the first one open book, with no time limit. Work through the questions at your own pace and make sure you fully understand them. Gradually work up to taking a test under test conditions: sit at a desk with all study materials put away and set a timer. Pace yourself to make sure you finish the test with time to spare and go back to check your answers if you have time.

After each test, check your answers. On the questions you missed, be sure you understand why you missed them. Did you misread the question (tests can use tricky wording)? Did you forget the information? Or was it something you hadn't learned? Go back and study any shaky areas that the practice tests reveal.

Taking these tests not only helps with your grade, but also aids in combating test anxiety. If you're already used to the test conditions, you're less likely to worry about it, and working through tests until you're scoring well gives you a confidence boost. Go through the practice tests until you feel comfortable, and then you can go into the test knowing that you're ready for it.

Test Tips

On test day, you should be confident, knowing that you've prepared well and are ready to answer the questions. But aside from preparation, there are several test day strategies you can employ to maximize your performance.

First, as stated before, get a good night's sleep the night before the test (and for several nights before that, if possible). Go into the test with a fresh, alert mind rather than staying up late to study.

Try not to change too much about your normal routine on the day of the test. It's important to eat a nutritious breakfast, but if you normally don't eat breakfast at all, consider eating just a protein bar. If you're a coffee drinker, go ahead and have your normal coffee. Just make sure you time it so that the caffeine doesn't wear off right in the middle of your test. Avoid sugary beverages, and drink enough water to stay hydrated but not so much that you need a restroom break 10 minutes into the

Copyright © Mometrix Media. You have been licensed one copy of this document for personal use only. Any other reproduction or redistribution is strictly prohibited. All rights reserved.
This content is provided for test preparation purposes only and does not imply an endorsement by Mometrix of any particular political, scientific, or religious point of view.

test. If your test isn't first thing in the morning, consider going for a walk or doing a light workout before the test to get your blood flowing.

Allow yourself enough time to get ready, and leave for the test with plenty of time to spare so you won't have the anxiety of scrambling to arrive in time. Another reason to be early is to select a good seat. It's helpful to sit away from doors and windows, which can be distracting. Find a good seat, get out your supplies, and settle your mind before the test begins.

When the test begins, start by going over the instructions carefully, even if you already know what to expect. Make sure you avoid any careless mistakes by following the directions.

Then begin working through the questions, pacing yourself as you've practiced. If you're not sure on an answer, don't spend too much time on it, and don't let it shake your confidence. Either skip it and come back later, or eliminate as many wrong answers as possible and guess among the remaining ones. Don't dwell on these questions as you continue—put them out of your mind and focus on what lies ahead.

Be sure to read all of the answer choices, even if you're sure the first one is the right answer. Sometimes you'll find a better one if you keep reading. But don't second-guess yourself if you do immediately know the answer. Your gut instinct is usually right. Don't let test anxiety rob you of the information you know.

If you have time at the end of the test (and if the test format allows), go back and review your answers. Be cautious about changing any, since your first instinct tends to be correct, but make sure you didn't misread any of the questions or accidentally mark the wrong answer choice. Look over any you skipped and make an educated guess.

At the end, leave the test feeling confident. You've done your best, so don't waste time worrying about your performance or wishing you could change anything. Instead, celebrate the successful completion of this test. And finally, use this test to learn how to deal with anxiety even better next time.

> **Review Video: Test Anxiety**
> Visit mometrix.com/academy and enter code: 100340

Important Qualification

Not all anxiety is created equal. If your test anxiety is causing major issues in your life beyond the classroom or testing center, or if you are experiencing troubling physical symptoms related to your anxiety, it may be a sign of a serious physiological or psychological condition. If this sounds like your situation, we strongly encourage you to seek professional help.

Copyright © Mometrix Media. You have been licensed one copy of this document for personal use only. Any other reproduction or redistribution is strictly prohibited. All rights reserved. This content is provided for test preparation purposes only and does not imply an endorsement by Mometrix of any particular political, scientific, or religious point of view.

How to Overcome Your Fear of Math

Not again. You're sitting in math class, look down at your test, and immediately start to panic. Your stomach is in knots, your heart is racing, and you break out in a cold sweat. You're staring at the paper, but everything looks like it's written in a foreign language. Even though you studied, you're blanking out on how to begin solving these problems.

Does this sound familiar? If so, then you're not alone! You may be like millions of other people who experience math anxiety. Anxiety about performing well in math is a common experience for students of all ages. In this article, we'll discuss what math anxiety is, common misconceptions about learning math, and tips and strategies for overcoming math anxiety.

What Is Math Anxiety?

Psychologist Mark H. Ashcraft explains math anxiety as a feeling of tension, apprehension, or fear that interferes with math performance. Having math anxiety negatively impacts people's beliefs about themselves and what they can achieve. It hinders achievement within the math classroom and affects the successful application of mathematics in the real world.

SYMPTOMS AND SIGNS OF MATH ANXIETY

To overcome math anxiety, you must recognize its symptoms. Becoming aware of the signs of math anxiety is the first step in addressing and resolving these fears.

NEGATIVE SELF-TALK

If you have math anxiety, you've most likely said at least one of these statements to yourself:

- "I hate math."
- "I'm not good at math."
- "I'm not a math person."

The way we speak to ourselves and think about ourselves matters. Our thoughts become our words, our words become our actions, and our actions become our habits. Thinking negatively about math creates a self-fulfilling prophecy. In other words, if you take an idea as a fact, then it will come true because your behaviors will align to match it.

AVOIDANCE

Some people who are fearful or anxious about math will tend to avoid it altogether. Avoidance can manifest in the following ways:

- Lack of engagement with math content
- Not completing homework and other assignments
- Not asking for help when needed
- Skipping class
- Avoiding math-related courses and activities

Avoidance is one of the most harmful impacts of math anxiety. If you steer clear of math at all costs, then you can't set yourself up for the success you deserve.

Copyright © Mometrix Media. You have been licensed one copy of this document for personal use only. Any other reproduction or redistribution is strictly prohibited. All rights reserved. This content is provided for test preparation purposes only and does not imply an endorsement by Mometrix of any particular political, scientific, or religious point of view.

LACK OF MOTIVATION

Students with math anxiety may experience a lack of motivation. They may struggle to find the incentive to get engaged with what they view as a frightening subject. These students are often overwhelmed, making it difficult for them to complete or even start math assignments.

PROCRASTINATION

Another symptom of math anxiety is procrastination. Students may voluntarily delay or postpone their classwork and assignments, even if they know there will be a negative consequence for doing so. Additionally, they may choose to wait until the last minute to start projects and homework, even when they know they need more time to put forth their best effort.

PHYSIOLOGICAL REACTIONS

Many people with a fear of math experience physiological side effects. These may include an increase in heart rate, sweatiness, shakiness, nausea, and irregular breathing. These symptoms make it difficult to focus on the math content, causing the student even more stress and fear.

STRONG EMOTIONAL RESPONSES

Math anxiety also affects people on an emotional level. Responding to math content with strong emotions such as panic, anger, or despair can be a sign of math anxiety.

LOW TEST SCORES AND PERFORMANCE

Low achievement can be both a symptom and a cause of math anxiety. When someone does not take the steps needed to perform well on tests and assessments, they are less likely to pass. The more they perform poorly, the more they accept this poor performance as a fact that can't be changed.

FEELING ALONE

People who experience math anxiety feel like they are the only ones struggling, even if the math they are working on is challenging to many people. Feeling isolated in what they perceive as failure can trigger tension or nervousness.

FEELING OF PERMANENCY

Math anxiety can feel very permanent. You may assume that you are naturally bad at math and always will be. Viewing math as a natural ability rather than a skill that can be learned causes people to believe that nothing will help them improve. They take their current math abilities as fact and assume that they can't be changed. As a result, they give up, stop trying to improve, and avoid engaging with math altogether.

LACK OF CONFIDENCE

People with low self-confidence in math tend to feel awkward and incompetent when asked to solve a math problem. They don't feel comfortable taking chances or risks when problem-solving because they second-guess themselves and assume they are incorrect. They don't trust in their ability to learn the content and solve problems correctly.

PANIC

A general sense of unexplained panic is also a sign of math anxiety. You may feel a sudden sense of fear that triggers physical reactions, even when there is no apparent reason for such a response.

Copyright © Mometrix Media. You have been licensed one copy of this document for personal use only. Any other reproduction or redistribution is strictly prohibited. All rights reserved. This content is provided for test preparation purposes only and does not imply an endorsement by Mometrix of any particular political, scientific, or religious point of view.

CAUSES OF MATH ANXIETY

Math anxiety can start at a young age and may have one or more underlying causes. Common causes of math anxiety include the following:

THE ATTITUDE OF PARENTS OR GUARDIANS

Parents often put pressure on their children to perform well in school. Although their intentions are usually good, this pressure can lead to anxiety, especially if the student is struggling with a subject or class.

Perhaps your parents or others in your life hold negative predispositions about math based on their own experiences. For instance, if your mother once claimed she was not good at math, then you might have incorrectly interpreted this as a predisposed trait that was passed down to you.

TEACHER INFLUENCE

Students often pick up on their teachers' attitudes about the content being taught. If a teacher is happy and excited about math, students are more likely to mirror these emotions. However, if a teacher lacks enthusiasm or genuine interest, then students are more inclined to disengage.

Teachers have a responsibility to cultivate a welcoming classroom culture that is accepting of mistakes. When teachers blame students for not understanding a concept, they create a hostile classroom environment where mistakes are not tolerated. This tension increases student stress and anxiety, creating conditions that are not conducive to inquiry and learning. Instead, when teachers normalize mistakes as a natural part of the problem-solving process, they give their students the freedom to explore and grapple with the math content. In such an environment, students feel comfortable taking chances because they are not afraid of being wrong.

Students need teachers that can help when they're having problems understanding difficult concepts. In doing so, educators may need to change how they teach the content. Since different people have unique learning styles, it's the job of the teacher to adapt to the needs of each student. Additionally, teachers should encourage students to explore alternate problem-solving strategies, even if it's not the preferred method of the educator.

FEAR OF BEING WRONG

Embarrassing situations can be traumatic, especially for young children and adolescents. These experiences can stay with people through their adult lives. Those with math anxiety may experience a fear of being wrong, especially in front of a group of peers. This fear can be paralyzing, interfering with the student's concentration and ability to focus on the problem at hand.

TIMED ASSESSMENTS

Timed assessments can help improve math fluency, but they often create unnecessary pressure for students to complete an unrealistic number of problems within a specified timeframe. Many studies have shown that timed assessments often result in increased levels of anxiety, reducing a student's overall competence and ability to problem-solve.

Copyright © Mometrix Media. You have been licensed one copy of this document for personal use only. Any other reproduction or redistribution is strictly prohibited. All rights reserved.
This content is provided for test preparation purposes only and does not imply an endorsement by Mometrix of any particular political, scientific, or religious point of view.

Debunking Math Myths

There are lots of myths about math that are related to the causes and development of math-related anxiety. Although these myths have been proven to be false, many people take them as fact. Let's go over a few of the most common myths about learning math.

MYTH: MEN ARE BETTER AT MATH THAN WOMEN

Math has a reputation for being a male-dominant subject, but this doesn't mean that men are inherently better at math than women. Many famous mathematical discoveries have been made by women. Katherine Johnson, Dame Mary Lucy Cartwright, and Marjorie Lee Brown are just a few of the many famous women mathematicians. Expecting to be good or bad at math because of your gender sets you up for stress and confusion. Math is a skill that can be learned, just like cooking or riding a bike.

MYTH: THERE IS ONLY ONE GOOD WAY TO SOLVE MATH PROBLEMS

There are many ways to get the correct answer when it comes to math. No two people have the same brain, so everyone takes a slightly different approach to problem-solving. Moreover, there isn't one way of problem-solving that's superior to another. Your way of working through a problem might differ from someone else's, and that is okay. Math can be a highly individualized process, so the best method for you should be the one that makes you feel the most comfortable and makes the most sense to you.

MYTH: MATH REQUIRES A GOOD MEMORY

For many years, mathematics was taught through memorization. However, learning in such a way hinders the development of critical thinking and conceptual understanding. These skill sets are much more valuable than basic memorization. For instance, you might be great at memorizing mathematical formulas, but if you don't understand what they mean, then you can't apply them to different scenarios in the real world. When a student is working from memory, they are limited in the strategies available to them to problem-solve. In other words, they assume there is only one correct way to do the math, which is the method they memorized. Having a variety of problem-solving options can help students figure out which method works best for them. Additionally, it provides students with a better understanding of how and why certain mathematical strategies work. While memorization can be helpful in some instances, it is not an absolute requirement for mathematicians.

MYTH: MATH IS NOT CREATIVE

Math requires imagination and intuition. Contrary to popular belief, it is a highly creative field. Mathematical creativity can help in developing new ways to think about and solve problems. Many people incorrectly assume that all things are either creative or analytical. However, this black-and-white view is limiting because the field of mathematics involves both creativity and logic.

MYTH: MATH ISN'T SUPPOSED TO BE FUN

Whoever told you that math isn't supposed to be fun is a liar. There are tons of math-based activities and games that foster friendly competition and engagement. Math is often best learned through play, and lots of mobile apps and computer games exemplify this.

Additionally, math can be an exceptionally collaborative and social experience. Studying or working through problems with a friend often makes the process a lot more fun. The excitement and satisfaction of solving a difficult problem with others is quite rewarding. Math can be fun if you look for ways to make it more collaborative and enjoyable.

Copyright © Mometrix Media. You have been licensed one copy of this document for personal use only. Any other reproduction or redistribution is strictly prohibited. All rights reserved. This content is provided for test preparation purposes only and does not imply an endorsement by Mometrix of any particular political, scientific, or religious point of view.

Myth: Not Everyone Is Capable of Learning Math

There's no such thing as a "math person." Although many people think that you're either good at math or you're not, this is simply not true. Everyone is capable of learning and applying mathematics. However, not everyone learns the same way. Since each person has a different learning style, the trick is to find the strategies and learning tools that work best for you. Some people learn best through hands-on experiences, and others find success through the use of visual aids. Others are auditory learners and learn best by hearing and listening. When people are overwhelmed or feel that math is too hard, it's often because they haven't found the learning strategy that works best for them.

Myth: Good Mathematicians Work Quickly and Never Make Mistakes

There is no prize for finishing first in math. It's not a race, and speed isn't a measure of your ability. Good mathematicians take their time to ensure their work is accurate. As you gain more experience and practice, you will naturally become faster and more confident.

Additionally, everyone makes mistakes, including good mathematicians. Mistakes are a normal part of the problem-solving process, and they're not a bad thing. The important thing is that we take the time to learn from our mistakes, understand where our misconceptions are, and move forward.

Myth: You Don't Need Math in the Real World

Our day-to-day lives are so infused with mathematical concepts that we often don't even realize when we're using math in the real world. In fact, most people tend to underestimate how much we do math in our everyday lives. It's involved in an enormous variety of daily activities such as shopping, baking, finances, and gardening, as well as in many careers, including architecture, nursing, design, and sales.

Tips and Strategies for Overcoming Math Anxiety

If your anxiety is getting in the way of your level of mathematical engagement, then there are lots of steps you can take. Check out the strategies below to start building confidence in math today.

Focus on Understanding, Not Memorization

Don't drive yourself crazy trying to memorize every single formula or mathematical process. Instead, shift your attention to understanding concepts. Those who prioritize memorization over conceptual understanding tend to have lower achievement levels in math. Students who memorize may be able to complete some math, but they don't understand the process well enough to apply it to different situations. Memorization comes with time and practice, but it won't help alleviate math anxiety. On the other hand, conceptual understanding will give you the building blocks of knowledge you need to build up your confidence.

Copyright © Mometrix Media. You have been licensed one copy of this document for personal use only. Any other reproduction or redistribution is strictly prohibited. All rights reserved.
This content is provided for test preparation purposes only and does not imply an endorsement by Mometrix of any particular political, scientific, or religious point of view.

REPLACE NEGATIVE SELF-TALK WITH POSITIVE SELF-TALK

Start to notice how you think about yourself. Whenever you catch yourself thinking something negative, try replacing that thought with a positive affirmation. Instead of continuing the negative thought, pause to reframe the situation. For ideas on how to get started, take a look at the table below:

Instead of thinking...	Try thinking...
"I can't do this math." "I'm not a math person."	"I'm up for the challenge, and I'm training my brain in math."
"This problem is too hard."	"This problem is hard, so this might take some time and effort. I know I can do this."
"I give up."	"What strategies can help me solve this problem?"
"I made a mistake, so I'm not good at this."	"Everyone makes mistakes. Mistakes help me to grow and understand."
"I'll never be smart enough."	"I can figure this out, and I am smart enough."

PRACTICE MINDFULNESS

Practicing mindfulness and focusing on your breathing can help alleviate some of the physical symptoms of math anxiety. By taking deep breaths, you can remind your nervous system that you are not in immediate danger. Doing so will reduce your heart rate and help with any irregular breathing or shakiness. Taking the edge off of the physiological effects of anxiety will clear your mind, allowing your brain to focus its energy on problem-solving.

DO SOME MATH EVERY DAY

Think about learning math as if you were learning a foreign language. If you don't use it, you lose it. If you don't practice your math skills regularly, you'll have a harder time achieving comprehension and fluency. Set some amount of time aside each day, even if it's just for a few minutes, to practice. It might take some discipline to build a habit around this, but doing so will help increase your mathematical self-assurance.

USE ALL OF YOUR RESOURCES

Everyone has a different learning style, and there are plenty of resources out there to support all learners. When you get stuck on a math problem, think about the tools you have access to, and use them when applicable. Such resources may include flashcards, graphic organizers, study guides, interactive notebooks, and peer study groups. All of these are great tools to accommodate your individual learning style. Finding the tools and resources that work for your learning style will give you the confidence you need to succeed.

REALIZE THAT YOU AREN'T ALONE

Remind yourself that lots of other people struggle with math anxiety, including teachers, nurses, and even successful mathematicians. You aren't the only one who panics when faced with a new or challenging problem. It's probably much more common than you think. Realizing that you aren't alone in your experience can help put some distance between yourself and the emotions you feel about math. It also helps to normalize the anxiety and shift your perspective.

Copyright © Mometrix Media. You have been licensed one copy of this document for personal use only. Any other reproduction or redistribution is strictly prohibited. All rights reserved. This content is provided for test preparation purposes only and does not imply an endorsement by Mometrix of any particular political, scientific, or religious point of view.

ASK QUESTIONS

If there's a concept you don't understand and you've tried everything you can, then it's okay to ask for help! You can always ask your teacher or professor for help. If you're not learning math in a traditional classroom, you may want to join a study group, work with a tutor, or talk to your friends. More often than not, you aren't the only one of your peers who needs clarity on a mathematical concept. Seeking understanding is a great way to increase self-confidence in math.

REMEMBER THAT THERE'S MORE THAN ONE WAY TO SOLVE A PROBLEM

Since everyone learns differently, it's best to focus on understanding a math problem with an approach that makes sense to you. If the way it's being taught is confusing to you, don't give up. Instead, work to understand the problem using a different technique. There's almost always more than one problem-solving method when it comes to math. Don't get stressed if one of them doesn't make sense to you. Instead, shift your focus to what does make sense. Chances are high that you know more than you think you do.

VISUALIZATION

Visualization is the process of creating images in your mind's eye. Picture yourself as a successful, confident mathematician. Think about how you would feel and how you would behave. What would your work area look like? How would you organize your belongings? The more you focus on something, the more likely you are to achieve it. Visualizing teaches your brain that you can achieve whatever it is that you want. Thinking about success in mathematics will lead to acting like a successful mathematician. This, in turn, leads to actual success.

FOCUS ON THE EASIEST PROBLEMS FIRST

To increase your confidence when working on a math test or assignment, try solving the easiest problems first. Doing so will remind you that you are successful in math and that you do have what it takes. This process will increase your belief in yourself, giving you the confidence you need to tackle more complex problems.

FIND A SUPPORT GROUP

A study buddy, tutor, or peer group can go a long way in decreasing math-related anxiety. Such support systems offer lots of benefits, including a safe place to ask questions, additional practice with mathematical concepts, and an understanding of other problem-solving explanations that may work better for you. Equipping yourself with a support group is one of the fastest ways to eliminate math anxiety.

REWARD YOURSELF FOR WORKING HARD

Recognize the amount of effort you're putting in to overcome your math anxiety. It's not an easy task, so you deserve acknowledgement. Surround yourself with people who will provide you with the positive reinforcement you deserve.

Remember, You Can Do This!

Conquering a fear of math can be challenging, but there are lots of strategies that can help you out. Your own beliefs about your mathematical capabilities can limit your potential. Working toward a growth mindset can have a tremendous impact on decreasing math-related anxiety and building confidence. By knowing the symptoms of math anxiety and recognizing common misconceptions about learning math, you can develop a plan to address your fear of math. Utilizing the strategies discussed can help you overcome this anxiety and build the confidence you need to succeed.

Copyright © Mometrix Media. You have been licensed one copy of this document for personal use only. Any other reproduction or redistribution is strictly prohibited. All rights reserved.
This content is provided for test preparation purposes only and does not imply an endorsement by Mometrix of any particular political, scientific, or religious point of view.

Tell Us Your Story

We at Mometrix would like to extend our heartfelt thanks to you for letting us be a part of your journey. It is an honor to serve people from all walks of life, people like you, who are committed to building the best future they can for themselves.

We know that each person's situation is unique. But we also know that, whether you are a young student or a mother of four, you care about working to make your own life and the lives of those around you better.

That's why we want to hear your story.

We want to know why you're taking this test. We want to know about the trials you've gone through to get here. And we want to know about the successes you've experienced after taking and passing your test.

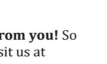

In addition to your story, which can be an inspiration both to us and to others, we value your feedback. We want to know both what you loved about our book and what you think we can improve on.

The team at Mometrix would be absolutely thrilled to hear from you! So please, send us an email at tellusyourstory@mometrix.com or visit us at mometrix.com/tellusyourstory.php and let's stay in touch.

Copyright © Mometrix Media. You have been licensed one copy of this document for personal use only. Any other reproduction or redistribution is strictly prohibited. All rights reserved.
This content is provided for test preparation purposes only and does not imply an endorsement by Mometrix of any particular political, scientific, or religious point of view.

Additional Bonus Material

Due to our efforts to try to keep this book to a manageable length, we've created a link that will give you access to all of your additional bonus material:

mometrix.com/bonus948/priieems5001

Copyright © Mometrix Media. You have been licensed one copy of this document for personal use only. Any other reproduction or redistribution is strictly prohibited. All rights reserved. This content is provided for test preparation purposes only and does not imply an endorsement by Mometrix of any particular political, scientific, or religious point of view.